Handbook of Market Research

Christian Homburg • Martin Klarmann •
Arnd Vomberg
Editors

Handbook of Market Research

Volume 1

With 211 Figures and 130 Tables

Editors
Christian Homburg
Department of Business-to-Business
Marketing, Sales, and Pricing
University of Mannheim
Mannheim, Germany

Martin Klarmann
Department of Marketing & Sales Research
Group
Karlsruhe Institute of Technology (KIT)
Karlsruhe, Germany

Arnd Vomberg
Marketing & Sales Department
University of Mannheim
Mannheim, Germany

ISBN 978-3-319-57411-0   ISBN 978-3-319-57413-4 (eBook)
ISBN 978-3-319-57412-7 (print and electronic bundle)
https://doi.org/10.1007/978-3-319-57413-4

© Springer Nature Switzerland AG 2022
This work is subject to copyright. All rights are reserved by the Publisher, whether the whole or part of the
material is concerned, specifically the rights of translation, reprinting, reuse of illustrations, recitation,
broadcasting, reproduction on microfilms or in any other physical way, and transmission or information
storage and retrieval, electronic adaptation, computer software, or by similar or dissimilar methodology
now known or hereafter developed.
The use of general descriptive names, registered names, trademarks, service marks, etc. in this publication
does not imply, even in the absence of a specific statement, that such names are exempt from the relevant
protective laws and regulations and therefore free for general use.
The publisher, the authors, and the editors are safe to assume that the advice and information in this book
are believed to be true and accurate at the date of publication. Neither the publisher nor the authors or the
editors give a warranty, expressed or implied, with respect to the material contained herein or for any errors
or omissions that may have been made. The publisher remains neutral with regard to jurisdictional claims
in published maps and institutional affiliations.

This Springer imprint is published by the registered company Springer Nature Switzerland AG.
The registered company address is: Gewerbestrasse 11, 6330 Cham, Switzerland

Preface

Already in 2015, the *Wall Street Journal* claimed that companies sit on a treasure trove of market data. They have an ever-increasing amount of data at their disposal. However, it is not only about access to data. Companies need to develop strong empirical and analytical skills to turn their data into a competitive advantage. Traditional market research firms and hundreds of new startup companies specializing in "Data Science" and analytics support companies in building and maintaining customer relationships, developing strategies to increase customer satisfaction, improving sales strategies, personalizing the marketing mix, and automating marketing processes in real time. The *Handbook of Market Research* seeks to provide material for both, firms specialized in data analysis and firms hiring those firms. On the one hand, it seeks to provide in-depth coverage of established and new marketing research methods. On the other hand, by giving examples throughout, it aims to be as accessible as possible.

The *Handbook of Market Research* helps readers apply advanced market research methods in their projects and provides them with a valuable overview of various analytical techniques. It targets three groups: graduate students, scholars, and data science practitioners. Graduate students obtain an introduction to diverse market research topics. Scholars can use the handbook as a reference, supporting their research and teaching. Practitioners receive a state-of-the-art overview of scientific practices.

What is special about the *Handbook of Market Research*?

- Chapters in this handbook are not purely technical but also offer an intuitive account of the discussed methodologies.
- Many chapters provide data and software code to replicate the analyses. Readers can find such supplementary material on the handbook's online site (https://link. springer.com/referencework/10.1007/978-3-319-05542-8).
- Nearly all chapters in this handbook have gone through a friendly review process. The friendly reviewers helped to improve all chapters of this handbook further.
- We publish the handbook dynamically. Novel chapters will appear continuously on the handbook's online site. Moreover, authors have the opportunity to update existing chapters online to respond to emerging trends and new methods.

The handbook has three parts: Data, Methods, and Applications. The Data part supports readers in collecting and handling different types of data. The Method part outlines how readers can analyze structured and unstructured data. The Application part equips readers with knowledge on how they can use data analytics in specific contexts.

Our special thanks go to the authors of the chapters for their willingness to share their knowledge and experience with the readers. Furthermore, we would like to take this opportunity to thank the friendly reviewers who have helped further to increase the high quality of the individual contributions. We want to thank Dr. Prashanth Mahagaonkar, Veronika Mang, and Barbara Wolf from Springer Verlag for their excellent cooperation.

Mannheim, Germany	Christian Homburg
Karlsruhe, Germany	Martin Klarmann
Germany	Arnd Vomberg
November 2021	

List of Reviewers

Last Name	First Name	Title	Description	Institution
Artz	Martin	Prof. Dr.	Professor for Management Accounting and Control	University of Münster
Atalay	Selin	Prof. Dr.	Professor of Marketing	Frankfurt School of Finance and Management
Becker	Jan-Michael	Dr.	Associate Professor at the Marketing Department	BI Norwegian Business School
Bhattacharya	Abhimanyu	Ph.D.	Assistant Professor at the Marketing Department	University of Alabama, Tuscaloosa
Bruno	Hernán	Prof. Dr.	Professor of Marketing and Digital Environment	University of Cologne
Colicev	Anatoli	Ph.D.	Assistant Professor at the Marketing Department	Bocconi University
De Vries	Thom	Dr.	Assistant Professor at the Faculty of Economics and Business	University of Groningen
Dehmamy	Keyvan	Dr.	Post-Doctoral Researcher at the Marketing Department	Goethe University Frankfurt
Delre	Sebastiano	Dr.	Associate Professor at the Marketing, Sales and Communication Department	Montpellier Business School
Dew	Ryan	Ph.D.	Assistant Professor at the Marketing Department	Wharton School of the University of Pennsylvania
Dinner	Isaac	Ph.D.	Director of Econometric Modeling	Indeed
Draganska	Michaela	Ph.D.	Associate Professor at the Marketing Department	Drexel University
Entrop	Oliver	Prof. Dr.	Professor of Finance and Banking, Chair of Finance and Banking	University of Passau

(continued)

Last Name	First Name	Title	Description	Institution
Fuchs	Christoph	Prof. Dr.	Professor of Marketing and Chair of Marketing	University of Vienna
Fürst	Andreas	Prof. Dr.	Chair of Business Administration (Marketing)	Friedrich-Alexander-Universität Erlangen-Nürnberg
Gensler	Sonja	Prof. Dr.	Extraordinary Professor at the Chair for Value-Based Marketing	University of Münster
Gijsenberg	Maarten J.	Prof. Dr.	Full Professor at the Marketing Department	University of Groningen
Groening	Christopher	Ph.D.	Associate Professor at the Marketing Department	Kent State University
Haans	Hans	Dr.	Marketing Department, Director Econasium	Tilburg University
Hahn	Carsten	Prof. Dr.	Professor für Innovation und Entrepreneurship	Karlsruhe University of Applied Sciences
Hartmann	Jochen	Dr.	Post-doctoral Researcher at the Chair Marketing and Branding	University of Hamburg
Hattula	Stefan	Dr.	Market analyst	Robert Bosch GmbH
Henseler	Jörg	Prof. Dr.	Chair of Product-Market Relations	University of Twente
Hohenberg	Sebastian	Dr.	Assistant Professor at the Marketing Department	University of Texas at Austin
Junc	Vanessa	Dr.	Senior CRM Analyst	Douglas GmbH
Kamleitner	Bernadette	Prof. Dr.	Marketing Department	WU Vienna
Klarmann	Martin	Prof. Dr.	Professor of Marketing	Karlsruhe Institute of Technology
Klein	Kristina	Prof. Dr.	Professor of Marketing	University of Bremen
Landwehr	Jan	Prof. Dr.	Professor of Marketing and Chair for Product Management and Marketing Communications	Goethe University Frankfurt
Lanz	Andreas	Dr.	Assistant Professor at the Marketing Department	HEC Paris
Lemmens	Aurélie	Dr.	Associate Professor of Marketing	Rotterdam School of Management, Erasmus University
Ludwig	Stephan	Dr.	Associate Professor at the Department of Management and Marketing	University of Melbourne
Mayer	Stefan	Prof. Dr.	Assistant Professor of Marketing Analytics	University of Tübingen
Miller	Klaus	Dr.	Assistant Professor at the Marketing Department	HEC Paris

(continued)

Last Name	First Name	Title	Description	Institution
Mooi	Erik	Dr.	Associate Professor at the Department of Management and Marketing	University of Melbourne
Nitzan	Irit	Dr.	Assistant Professor of Marketing	Coller School of Management
Osinga	Ernst Christiaan	Ph.D.	Associate Professor of Marketing	Singapore Management University
Otter	Thomas	Prof. Dr.	Professor of Marketing	Goethe University Frankfurt
Papies	Dominik	Prof. Dr.	Professor of Marketing	University of Tübingen
Roelen-Blasberg	Tobias		Co-Founder	MARA
Sarstedt	Marko	Prof. Dr.	Chair of Marketing	Otto von Guericke University Magdeburg
Schlereth	Christian	Prof. Dr.	Chair of Digital Marketing	WHU – Otto Beisheim School of Management
Schulze	Christian	Prof. Dr.	Associate Professor of Marketing	Frankfurt School of Finance and Management
Sichtmann	Christina	Prof. Dr.	Research Associate for the Chair of International Marketing	University of Vienna
Stahl	Florian	Prof. Dr.	Professor of Marketing at the Department of Business Administration	University of Mannheim
Totzek	Dirk	Prof. Dr.	Chair of Marketing and Services	University of Passau
Van Heerde	Harald	Ph.D.	S.H.A.R.P. Research Professor of Marketing	University of South Wales
Vomberg	Arnd	Prof. Dr.	Professor of Marketing	University of Mannheim
Weeth	Alexander	Dr.	Engagement Manager	McKinsey & Company
Weijters	Bert	Ph.D.	Associate Professor in the Department of Work, Organization and Society	Ghent University
Wentzel	Daniel	Prof. Dr.	Chair of Marketing	RWTH Aachen University
Yildirim	Gokham	Dr.	Associate Professor of Marketing	Imperial College London

Contents

Volume 1

Part I Data **1**

Experiments in Market Research 3
Torsten Bornemann and Stefan Hattula

Field Experiments 37
Veronica Valli, Florian Stahl, and Elea McDonnell Feit

**Crafting Survey Research: A Systematic Process for Conducting
Survey Research** 67
Arnd Vomberg and Martin Klarmann

Challenges in Conducting International Market Research 121
Andreas Engelen, Monika Engelen, and C. Samuel Craig

Fusion Modeling 147
Elea McDonnell Feit and Eric T. Bradlow

**Dealing with Endogeneity: A Nontechnical Guide for Marketing
Researchers** 181
P. Ebbes, D. Papies, and H. J. van Heerde

Part II Methods **219**

Cluster Analysis in Marketing Research 221
Thomas Reutterer and Daniel Dan

Finite Mixture Models 251
Sonja Gensler

Analysis of Variance 265
Jan R. Landwehr

Regression Analysis 299
Bernd Skiera, Jochen Reiner, and Sönke Albers

Logistic Regression and Discriminant Analysis 329
Sebastian Tillmanns and Manfred Krafft

Multilevel Modeling 369
Till Haumann, Roland Kassemeier, and Jan Wieseke

Panel Data Analysis: A Non-technical Introduction for Marketing Researchers 411
Arnd Vomberg and Simone Wies

Applied Time-Series Analysis in Marketing 469
Wanxin Wang and Gokhan Yildirim

Modeling Marketing Dynamics Using Vector Autoregressive (VAR) Models 515
Shuba Srinivasan

Volume 2

Structural Equation Modeling 549
Hans Baumgartner and Bert Weijters

Partial Least Squares Structural Equation Modeling 587
Marko Sarstedt, Christian M. Ringle, and Joseph F. Hair

Automated Text Analysis 633
Ashlee Humphreys

Image Analytics in Marketing 665
Daria Dzyabura, Siham El Kihal, and Renana Peres

Social Network Analysis 693
Hans Risselada and Jeroen van den Ochtend

Bayesian Models 719
Thomas Otter

Choice-Based Conjoint Analysis 781
Felix Eggers, Henrik Sattler, Thorsten Teichert, and Franziska Völckner

Exploiting Data from Field Experiments 821
Martin Artz and Hannes Doering

Mediation Analysis in Experimental Research 857
Nicole Koschate-Fischer and Elisabeth Schwille

Part III Applications **907**

Measuring Customer Satisfaction and Customer Loyalty 909
Sebastian Hohenberg and Wayne Taylor

Contents

xiii

Market Segmentation 939
Tobias Schlager and Markus Christen

Willingness to Pay 969
Wiebke Klingemann, Ju-Young Kim, and Kai Dominik Füller

Modeling Customer Lifetime Value, Retention, and Churn 1001
Herbert Castéran, Lars Meyer-Waarden, and Werner Reinartz

**Assessing the Financial Impact of Brand Equity with Short
Time-Series Data** 1035
Natalie Mizik and Eugene Pavlov

Measuring Sales Promotion Effectiveness 1055
Karen Gedenk

Return on Media Models 1073
Dominique M. Hanssens

Index 1097

About the Editors

Prof. Christian Homburg holds the Chair of Business-to-Business Marketing, Sales and Pricing at the University of Mannheim. He is also Distinguished Professorial Fellow of the University of Manchester (UK) and Director of the Institute for Market-Oriented Management (IMU) at the University of Mannheim. He specializes in market-oriented management, customer relationship management, and sales management. Professor Homburg has published numerous books and articles at the national and international levels and has thus established a research portfolio that places him as one of the leading German management professors and most productive scholars in the marketing discipline. In 2019 and 2020, WirtschaftsWoche honored Professor Homburg for his Lifetime Achievement as the leading management professor in Germany, Austria, and Switzerland.

He is currently a member of the editorial boards of five scientific journals in the United States and Europe. Since April 2011, he works as the first German area editor for the *Journal of Marketing*. Professor Homburg received several awards for his scientific research from the American Marketing Association, the world's leading scientific association in the area of marketing, and is the first European university professor to be honored as an AMA Fellow for his lifetime achievement in marketing research. In 2021, Professor Homburg ranked fourth in the American Marketing Association's global ranking, which is based on the number of publications in the most important marketing journals.

Prior to his academic career, Professor Homburg was Director of marketing, controlling, and strategic planning in an industrial company that operates globally.

In addition to his academic position, he is Chairman of the scientific advisory committee of Homburg & Partner, an international management consultancy.

Prof. Martin Klarmann is Professor of Marketing at the Karlsruhe Institute of Technology (KIT), Germany. Professor Klarmann's research is centered around three core themes: marketing using new technologies, marketing methods, and B2B sales management. His research has been published in several leading journals of the field, including the *Journal of Marketing*, the *Journal of Marketing Research*, the *Journal of the Academy of Marketing Science*, and the *International Journal of Research in Marketing*. Professor Klarmann has received several awards for his research, including an overall best paper award at the American Marketing Association's Winter Educators' Conference.

Prof. Arnd Vomberg is Professor of Digital Marketing and Marketing Transformation at the University of Mannheim, Germany. Professor Vomberg has also been an Associate Professor (with tenure) at the Marketing Department of the University of Groningen, The Netherlands. Professor Vomberg's research focuses on digital marketing and marketing transformation. He studies omnichannel strategies, online pricing, marketing automation, agile transformation, marketing technology, and marketing's impact on employees. His research has been published in several leading journals of the field, including *Journal of Marketing*, *Journal of Marketing Research*, *Strategic Management Journal*, *Journal of the Academy of Marketing Science*, and *International Journal of Research in Marketing*. Professor Vomberg has received several awards for his research, including the Ralph Alexander Best Dissertation Award from the Academy of Management.

Contributors

Sönke Albers Kuehne Logistics University, Hamburg, Germany

Martin Artz School of Business and Economics, University of Münster, Münster, Germany

Hans Baumgartner Smeal College of Business, The Pennsylvania State University, State College, PA, USA

Torsten Bornemann Department of Marketing, Goethe University Frankfurt, Frankfurt, Germany

Eric T. Bradlow The Wharton School, University of Pennsylvania, Philadelphia, PA, USA

Herbert Castéran Humanis Institute, EM Strasbourg Business School, Strasbourg, France

Markus Christen Faculty of Business and Economics (HEC) University of Lausanne, Lausanne, Switzerland

Daniel Dan Department of New Media, Modul University Vienna, Vienna, Austria

Hannes Doering School of Business and Economics, University of Münster, Münster, Germany

Daria Dzyabura New Economic School and Moscow School of Management SKOLKOVO, Moscow, Russia

P. Ebbes HEC Paris, Jouy-en-Josas, France

Felix Eggers University of Groningen, Groningen, The Netherlands

Siham El Kihal Frankfurt School of Finance and Management, Frankfurt, Germany

Andreas Engelen TU Dortmund University, Dortmund, Germany

Monika Engelen TH Köln, Cologne University of Applied Science, Köln, Germany

Elea McDonnell Feit LeBow College of Business, Drexel University, Philadelphia, PA, USA

Kai Dominik Füller Karlsruhe Institute of Technology, Institute for Information Systems and Marketing – Services Marketing, Karlsruhe, Germany

Karen Gedenk University of Hamburg, Hamburg, Germany

Sonja Gensler Marketing Center Münster – Institute for Value-based Marketing, University of Münster, Münster, Germany

Joseph F. Hair University of South Alabama, Mobile, AL, USA

Dominique M. Hanssens UCLA Anderson School of Management, Los Angeles, CA, USA

Stefan Hattula Department of Marketing, Goethe University Frankfurt, Frankfurt, Germany

Till Haumann South Westphalia University of Applied Sciences, Soest, Germany

Sebastian Hohenberg McCombs School of Business, The University of Texas, Austin, TX, USA

Ashlee Humphreys Integrated Marketing Communications, Medill School of Journalism, Media, and Integrated Marketing Communications, Northwestern University, Evanston, IL, USA

Roland Kassemeier Marketing Group, Warwick Business School, University of Warwick, Coventry, UK

Ju-Young Kim Goethe University Frankfurt, Department of Marketing, Frankfurt, Germany

Martin Klarmann Department of Marketing & Sales Research Group, Karlsruhe Institute of Technology (KIT), Karlsruhe, Germany

Wiebke Klingemann Karlsruhe Institute of Technology, Institute for Information Systems and Marketing – Services Marketing, Karlsruhe, Germany

Nicole Koschate-Fischer University of Erlangen-Nuremberg, Nuremberg, Germany

Manfred Krafft Institute of Marketing, Westfälische Wilhelms-Universität Münster, Muenster, Germany

Jan R. Landwehr Marketing Department, Goethe University Frankfurt, Frankfurt, Germany

Lars Meyer-Waarden School of Management, CRM CNRS University Toulouse 1 Capitole, IAE Toulouse, Toulouse, France

Natalie Mizik Foster School of Business, University of Washington, Seattle, WA, USA

Thomas Otter Goethe University Frankfurt am Main, Frankfurt am Main, Germany

D. Papies School of Business and Economics, University of Tübingen, Tübingen, Germany

Eugene Pavlov Foster School of Business, University of Washington, Seattle, WA, USA

Renana Peres School of Business Administration, Hebrew University of Jerusalem, Jerusalem, Israel

Werner Reinartz University of Cologne, Köln, Germany

Jochen Reiner Goethe University Frankfurt, Frankfurt, Germany

Thomas Reutterer Department of Marketing, WU Vienna University of Economics and Business, Vienna, Austria

Christian M. Ringle Hamburg University of Technology (TUHH), Hamburg, Germany
Faculty of Business and Law, University of Newcastle, Callaghan, NSW, Australia

Hans Risselada University of Groningen, Groningen, The Netherlands

C. Samuel Craig New York University, Stern School of Business, New York, NY, USA

Marko Sarstedt Otto-von-Guericke University, Magdeburg, Germany
Faculty of Business and Law, University of Newcastle, Callaghan, NSW, Australia

Henrik Sattler University of Hamburg, Hamburg, Germany

Tobias Schlager Faculty of Business and Economics (HEC) University of Lausanne, Lausanne, Switzerland

Elisabeth Schwille University of Erlangen-Nuremberg, Nuremberg, Germany

Bernd Skiera Goethe University Frankfurt, Frankfurt, Germany

Shuba Srinivasan Boston University Questrom School of Business, Boston, MA, USA

Florian Stahl University of Mannheim, Mannheim, Germany

Wayne Taylor Cox School of Business, Southern Methodist University, Dallas, TX, USA

Thorsten Teichert University of Hamburg, Hamburg, Germany

Sebastian Tillmanns Westfälische Wilhelms-Universität Münster, Muenster, Germany

Veronica Valli University of Mannheim, Mannheim, Germany

Franziska Völckner Department of Marketing and Brand Management, University of Cologne, Köln, Germany

Jeroen van den Ochtend University of Zürich, Zürich, Switzerland

H. J. van Heerde School of Communication, Journalism and Marketing, Massey University, Auckland, New Zealand

Arnd Vomberg Marketing Department, University of Groningen, Groningen, The Netherlands

Wanxin Wang Imperial College Business School, Imperial College London, London, UK

Bert Weijters Faculty of Psychology and Educational Sciences, Department of Work, Organization and Society, Ghent University, Ghent, Belgium

Simone Wies Goethe University Frankfurt, Frankfurt, Germany

Jan Wieseke Sales Management Department, University of Bochum, Bochum, Germany

Gokhan Yildirim Imperial College Business School, Imperial College London, London, UK

Part I
Data

Experiments in Market Research

Torsten Bornemann and Stefan Hattula

Contents

Introduction	4
Experimentation and Causality	5
Experimental Design	6
Definition of the Research Question	7
Determination and Operationalization of the Sources of Variation	7
Definition and Operationalization of the Measured Response-Variables	14
Decision About the Environmental Setting	17
Determination of the Experimental Units and Assignment to Treatments	21
Preliminary Testing	27
Exemplary Experimental Study	28
Ethical Issues in Experimental Research	31
Conclusion	32
References	33

Abstract

The question of how a certain activity (e.g., the intensity of communication activities during the launch of a new product) influences important outcomes (e.g., sales, preferences) is one of the key questions in applied (as well as academic) research in marketing. While such questions may be answered based on observed values of activities and the respective outcomes using survey and/or archival data, it is often not possible to claim that the particular activity has actually caused the observed changes in the outcomes. To demonstrate cause-effect relationships, experiments take a different route. Instead of observing activities, experimentation involves the systematic variation of an independent variable (factor) and the observation of the outcome only. The goal of this chapter

---

T. Bornemann (✉) · S. Hattula
Department of Marketing, Goethe University Frankfurt, Frankfurt, Germany
e-mail: torsten.bornemann@wiwi.uni-frankfurt.de; stefan.hattula@wiwi.uni-frankfurt.de

© Springer Nature Switzerland AG 2022
C. Homburg et al. (eds), *Handbook of Market Research*,
https://doi.org/10.1007/978-3-319-57413-4_2

is to discuss the parameters relevant to the proper execution of experimental studies. Among others, this involves decisions regarding the number of factors to be manipulated, the measurement of the outcome variable, the environment in which to conduct the experiment, and the recruitment of participants.

Keywords

Experimental design · Laboratory experiment · Data collection · Cause-effect relationship · Manipulation · Experimental units

---

Introduction

Former US-president Obama's election campaign in 2008 made him the president with more total votes than any other US-president before him. One of the challenges of Obama's team members – among them former Google manager Dan Siroker and the social psychologist Todd Rogers – was to increase the chance that a visitor of the campaign's website would provide her or his e-mail address to become a donor or volunteer. For instance, would visitors be more likely to sign-up when the respective button asked them to "Learn More," "Join Us Now," or "Sign Up Now"? And which accompanying picture of Obama would be more suitable? In order to identify the website design that would generate the highest sign-up rates, visitors were randomly exposed to different button/image combinations and the respective sign-up rates were tracked. Ultimately, the best performing combination was chosen for the campaign – and this most effective design led to 140 percent more donors than the least performing combination (Nisbett 2015).

This is actually an example of a type of experiment that is as effective as it is simple, often referred to as A/B testing. A/B testing is particularly common in online environments and heralded by companies such as Google and Amazon. In A/B testing, a fraction of users is exposed to a modified version of an existing website and their behavior is then compared to that of visitors of the standard website. If the modifications lead to superior results (e.g., conversion rates), they are adopted (Christian 2012). Later in this chapter, we will refer to such designs as between-subjects designs with one factor being manipulated at different levels.

The question of how a certain activity (e.g., the intensity of communication activities during the launch of a new product) influences important outcomes (e.g., sales, preferences) is one of the key questions in applied (as well as academic) research in marketing. While such questions may be answered based on *observed* values of activities and the respective outcomes using survey and/or archival data, it is often not possible to claim that the particular activity has actually *caused* the observed changes in the outcomes. For instance, the higher levels of communication intensity may have been made possible by the initial market success of the product, or some unobserved factor may have influenced both communication intensity and sales (see also chapter ▶ "Dealing with Endogeneity: A Nontechnical Guide for Marketing Researchers" by Papies, Ebbes, and van Heerde in this volume). To demonstrate cause-effect relationships, experiments take a different route. Instead of observing activities, experimentation involves the systematic *variation* of activities (factors) and the observation of the outcome only.

The goal of this chapter is to discuss the parameters relevant to the proper execution of experimental studies. Among others, this involves decisions regarding the number of factors to be manipulated, the measurement of the outcome variable, the environment in which to conduct the experiment, and the recruitment of participants. For information on statistical techniques to analyze the resulting experimental data, the reader may refer to chapter ▶ "Analysis of Variance" by Landwehr in this volume or to one of the various works on the statistics of experimental design (e.g., Maxwell and Delaney 2004).

Experimentation and Causality

Experiments aim at probing cause-effect relationships. Referring to the example from the introductory section of this chapter, a question that Obama's team might have asked was "What happens to conversion rates if we change the label caption from 'Learn More' to 'Join Us Now'?" Thus, the goal was to examine how an independent variable (the cause; here: label caption) influences a dependent variable (the effect; here conversion rate). The conditions required to actually demonstrate that a certain cause creates a certain effect has been subject to substantial philosophical debate, but generally accepted requirements are that (1) the cause temporally precedes the effect, that (2) variations in the cause are related to variations in the effect, and that (3) rival explanations for variations in the effect can be ruled out (Shadish et al. 2002).

The characteristics of experiments are in line with these considerations (Thye 2014). The requirement of temporal order is ensured because we first actively manipulate a presumed cause (such as the label caption), thereby exposing participants to different possible realizations of the cause, and then observe the effect (i.e., what happens to the dependent variable). Also, we can directly assess how far variations in the cause are associated to variations in the effect (since we can directly track differences in conversion rates). Finally, experiments rely on random assignment of participants to the different treatments (e.g., each website visitor has the same probability of being exposed to either the "Learn More" or the "Join Us Now" label) to ensure that the different groups are equally composed in terms of factors that may have an influence on the dependent variable (e.g., physical factors such as gender, weight, age, or personality factors such as preferences, values). Simply speaking, randomization mathematically equates the groups on any known and unknown factors, which is why measured differences in the dependent variable between groups can be ascribed to the manipulated cause. Experimental settings where randomization is not possible due to practical or ethical concerns are referred to as *quasi-experimental designs*. In such settings, approaches such as propensity score matching may be used to account for factors that may differ between participants in the experimental groups (e.g., Stuart and Rubin 2007).

Experimental Design

Experimental design refers to the process of planning an experimental study that meets the objectives specified at the outset. A concise planning ensures appropriate data quality and quantity to answer the underlying research question with the required precision (Meyvis and Van Osselaer 2018). In the following, we discuss the steps involved in designing an experiment (see Fig. 1) and subsequently illustrate this process with an example.

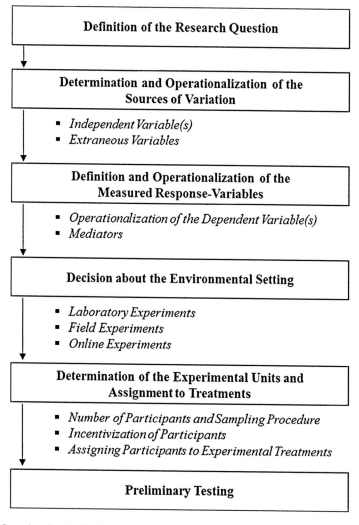

Fig. 1 Steps involved in the design of an experiment

Definition of the Research Question

The actual planning of a study starts with a precise formulation of the research problem(s) and, resulting from that, a clear definition of the objectives of the experiment. The problem statement typically lists the essential issues that will be tested in the experiment (Dean et al. 2017). It should be formulated as specific as possible to reduce complexity while at the same time avoiding so-called Type III errors, which refer to the problem of leaving out important factors from the experimental design and/or choosing insufficient measures of process performance. This also includes the determination of the response variable(s) and the population to be studied. For instance, a problem statement could ask which price promotion causes more sales – a 10% off or a 10€ off coupon.

The objectives of the experiment then determine the questions to be addressed (Morales et al. 2017). Typically, experimenters also propose answers to the questions being investigated by formulating hypotheses. This includes a null hypothesis suggesting no difference between the experimental treatments and an alternative hypothesis that argues for such a difference. For instance, the null hypothesis in the example above would suggest that the 10% off coupon and the 10€ off coupon show the same results, while the alternative hypothesis claims differences in resulting sales. As an important remark, experimenters should be careful to not formulate untestable hypotheses – i.e., those that cannot be easily interpreted, are unethical, or even empirically untestable. For instance, oftentimes it is more feasible to divide a very extensive hypothesized claim into several subhypotheses.

Determination and Operationalization of the Sources of Variation

In line with the idea of experimentation to systematically vary an independent variable and then observe changes in a dependent variable of interest, the second step in designing an experimental study entails an identification of the sources of variation. Sources of variation comprise the manipulated independent variable(s), whose effect on the outcome variable(s) is of primary interest, and extraneous variables, which may challenge the inference of causality and thus lead to wrong interpretations of the results.

Independent Variable(s)

In experimental research, the manipulated independent variable is referred to as a factor. The experimenter manipulates the factor by creating different levels of it. Thus, participants of the experiment are randomly assigned to different levels of a factor or, in other words, they are "treated" with different values of the factor, which is why the different factor levels are also referred to as treatments. In most instances, one level of a factor serves as a control in which no experimental treatment is administered. This control group makes it possible to determine whether the independent variable had any effect on the dependent variable. Central decisions in this step of the experimental design process thus involve the determination of the number of factors to be varied and their respective levels (which emanate from the research question) as well as the operationalization of the different treatments.

Factors and their levels. Single-factor designs are the most basic form of comparative studies, where one independent variable (factor) is manipulated at multiple, qualitatively distinct levels (the treatments). The idea of such a design is to study the causal main effect of one independent variable on one or multiple dependent variable(s). Single factor designs are often used to get an initial feeling of how a treatment works. For instance, experimenters may want to test the impact of ambient scent (cool vs. warm) on ad preference and product purchase intention. To determine whether scenting the environment has any effect at all on the dependent variables, a control group may be included where participants also indicate their ad preference and product purchase intention, but without being exposed to any scent. The result thus is a single-factor design involving three levels of ambient scent: cool [e.g., peppermint] vs. warm [e.g., cinnamon] vs. control [no scent] (Madzharov et al. 2015).

In contrast, multifactor designs systematically vary the levels of two or more independent variables (i.e., treatment factors) (Collins et al. 2009). These factors are crossed such that combinations of the respective levels are formed. The classic case of a multifactor design is the $2 \times 2 = 4$ experimental conditions case. It describes the combination of two independent variables, which are manipulated at two distinctive levels each. Such multifactor designs enable an examination of interactions between factors. For instance, the previously described effect of ambient scent (cool vs. warm) on product purchase intention may depend on the salesperson's behavior (rude vs. polite) (Madzharov et al. 2015). Such a multifactor design where all combinations of the respective levels are formed is referred to as a full factorial design.

Despite the advantages of multifactor designs, one should consider that an increasing number of independent variables may result in a large number of experimental conditions and thus an increased complexity of the experimental design (Koschate-Fischer and Schandelmeier 2014). For instance, the interpretation of interactions between two (two-way interactions) or three (three-way interactions) variables seems plausible. However, the more combinations of variables exist, the less meaningful are their interpretations. Some of those combinations may even be nonsensical, logistically impractical, or otherwise undesirable (Collins et al. 2009). Therefore, to make settings with a large number of variables feasible, reduced/fractional factorial designs are commonly applied (Cox 1992).

Fractional factorial designs describe designs where only a fraction of a full factorial experiment is used. Common is the so-called half fractional factorial design, where only half of the experimental treatments are used. For instance, experimenters may investigate a design with three factors and two levels each. This would involve $2^3 = 8$ experimental runs in a full factorial design. In Table 1, we illustrate this case for three factors (A, B, and C) that are each varied at two levels (high and low). The small letters denote treatment combinations, while capital letters refer to factors and effects. "I" denotes the identity column that only contains "+" signs (any other column multiplied by itself yields this column), while (1) describes the combination

Table 1 Example of a fractional design

Treatment combination	Identity column	Factor			Two-factor interaction			Three-factor interaction
	I	A	B	C	AB	AC	BC	ABC
(1)	+	−	−	−	+	+	+	−
a	+	+	−	−	−	−	+	+
b	+	−	+	−	−	+	−	+
ab	+	+	+	−	+	−	−	−
c	+	−	−	+	+	−	−	+
ac	+	+	−	+	−	+	−	−
bc	+	−	+	+	−	−	+	−
abc	+	+	+	+	+	+	+	+

of treatments where all factors are at their low levels. Moreover, a small letter in the treatment combination symbol indicates that the respective factor is at its high level; if the factor does not appear, it is at its low level (e.g., the treatment combination symbol ac indicates that factors A and C are at their high level, while factor B is at its low level). The "+" and "−" signs in the respective factor columns indicate that the factor is at its high or low level. Signs for the interaction columns are the result of taking the product of the signs of the involved factor columns.

If we were now restricted in our resources and only able to run four experimental conditions, we would have to resort to a fractional factorial design, which in this case would be written as 2^{3-1}. The central question is which four out of the eight conditions to choose. A first step is to select an interaction that can be neglected. Typically, experimenters choose to sacrifice the highest order interaction for this purpose since it is the most difficult to interpret interaction. In our case, we select ABC as the highest order interaction. Hence, ABC is used to generate the fraction of conditions to be tested. In order to identify those conditions, we select the conditions from those rows where the ABC column indicates a "+". So in our case, the four conditions to be run are a, b, c, and abc (see the shaded rows in Table 1).

Subsequently, we can determine which effects are aliases (i.e., are confounded). In our case of three factors, we would take the symbols for the highest order interaction (ABC) and attach them to every effect. Whenever the same factor appears twice in such a combination, it is erased – what remains is the alias of the original effect. For instance, if we take effect A, we have A(ABC). When we delete the A's, we are left with BC. That means the main effect of factor A is confounded with the BC interaction, or in other words, the BC interaction and factor A are aliases. In the current example, also B and AC as well as C and AB are aliases (for more details, see Montgomery 2009).

The specific number of levels that are manipulated for each factor is an important decision on its own. For instance, previous research indicates that attribute importance measures can be sensitive to the number of levels. The more levels exist for a particular attribute, the more attention and thus subjective importance is given to this attribute (Verlegh et al. 2002).

Decisions about the number of levels are easy if the independent variables are nominal-scaled (Koschate-Fischer and Schandelmeier 2014). They result directly from the research question. However, if the underlying scale is metric or quasi-metric, more than two levels might be necessary. This especially holds for research questions where nonmonotonic or nonlinear relationships between the independent variable and the dependent variable are likely (Cox 1992). For instance, previous research has examined the relationship between repeated advertising exposure and consumers' affective response in experimental designs with four levels (zero, low, medium, high) of the advertising repetition manipulation (Nordhielm 2002). Results suggest an inverted U-shaped relationship, where consumers' affective judgment was most positive for the moderate frequency of advertising exposure.

However, an increasing number of factor levels not only increases the experimental sensitivity, but also the number of treatments. Therefore, more than three levels may only be considered in single-factor designs in order to identify the most promising levels for further investigation. In multiple-factor designs, each individual variable should be limited to two or three manipulated levels each (Eriksson et al. 2008). If more than three levels are considered in multiple-factor designs, a fractional design may be advisable. As mentioned earlier, those designs consider not all possible treatments but only investigate logically useful ones to keep the complexity at a manageable and interpretable level (Cox 1992).

Operationalization of the treatments. A key challenge when translating a theoretically defined independent variable of interest into an operational treatment to be administered to participants is that the respective treatment might not incorporate all characteristics of the variable of interest (underrepresentation) or that it might contain content that is not part of the theoretical variable (thereby creating a confound). A number of aspects can lead to such mismatches (Shadish et al. 2002). For instance, a design that compares a treatment group with a control group may fail to detect an effect of the treatment on the dependent variable simply because the treatment is implemented at a too low level. Thus, in most instances, it is advisable to manipulate the independent variable at several levels. Appropriate and realistic levels of the independent variable can be identified based on a pretest (see section "Preliminary Testing").

The manipulation of the independent variable is often implemented within stimulus material containing text (a scenario in which the study is embedded, the instructions to the participants, and measures assessing the dependent variable), pictures, and sometimes video material. Rashotte et al. (2005) describe the creation of this material as "creating an alternate reality that volunteer participants will inhabit for a time" (p. 153). The design of such stimulus material requires great care, and it is indispensable to conduct preliminary tests before the experiment to ensure that participants interpret the material as intended. Generally, material and instructions should be as standardized as possible, avoiding complexity and ambiguity in the language used. A predetermined script conveys all necessary information to the participants and avoids any distractions. As a rule of thumb, all crucial instructions are repeated three times using slightly different wording to ensure reception of the information (Kuipers and Hysom 2014).

To assess whether the manipulation has worked successfully (and not created a confound) and how far participants have really attended to the information containing the manipulation of the independent variable (Oppenheimer et al. 2009), most (academic) research includes manipulation checks in the experimental material (Kuipers and Hysom 2014; Perdue and Summers 1986). Three aspects should be considered when designing a manipulation check in experiments.

First, the experimenter should be able to show that the manipulation indeed changes the theoretical variable that it was intended to alter (Perdue and Summers 1986). To check whether the manipulation meets this criterion, one has to find good indicators that assess the respective theoretical construct (Koschate-Fischer and Schandelmeier 2014). This is a rather easy task if the manipulated variable pertains to a simple construct such as price level. If the researcher has manipulated the price level (e.g., low/medium/high) of a given product to examine how different prices affect purchase intention, a simple single-item scale may serve as a manipulation check by asking participants whether they perceived the price as low vs. high. For a successful manipulation, significant differences in the single-item measure should be observed between the different treatment groups.

Second, experimenters should also detect and account for satisficing behavior of participants (Oppenheimer et al. 2009). Satisficing means that participants might wish to minimize cognitive effort in survey responses and therefore often do not properly read texts, questions, or instructions in the respective studies. Reception of such information, however, is necessary to produce useful data, which is why satisficing behavior can cause noise and reduce experimental power. This particularly holds for scenario-based experimental designs, where textual descriptions are used to create realistic experimental environments. To detect satisficing behavior, instructional manipulation checks have been developed (Oppenheimer et al. 2009). These are directly embedded in the experimental material and consist of questions that are similar to other questions in length and response format. If participants follow these instructions, experimenters get confirmation that texts, questions, and instructions have been read carefully and participants have spent the cognitive effort necessary to understand the experimental material. Figure 2 provides an example of such an instructional manipulation check. Here, participants are instructed to ignore the private transportation usage question but to proceed with the survey by directly clicking the continue button.

Third, experimenters have to decide about the point of time in the experiment when the manipulation check has to be answered. This also includes the question where to place the items that check the effectiveness of the manipulation – whether they appear before or after the measurement of the dependent variable (Perdue and Summers 1986). In this respect, it has long been argued that the items should be placed after measurement of the dependent variable in order to avoid demand effects (Wetzel 1977). However, this approach has been criticized since answering the dependent variable before might bias the subsequent manipulation check (particularly in self-report measures of the manipulation check). Moreover, the effect of the manipulation might weaken substantially over time (Kuipers and Hysom 2014; Perdue and Summers 1986). Placing the manipulation check before the assessment

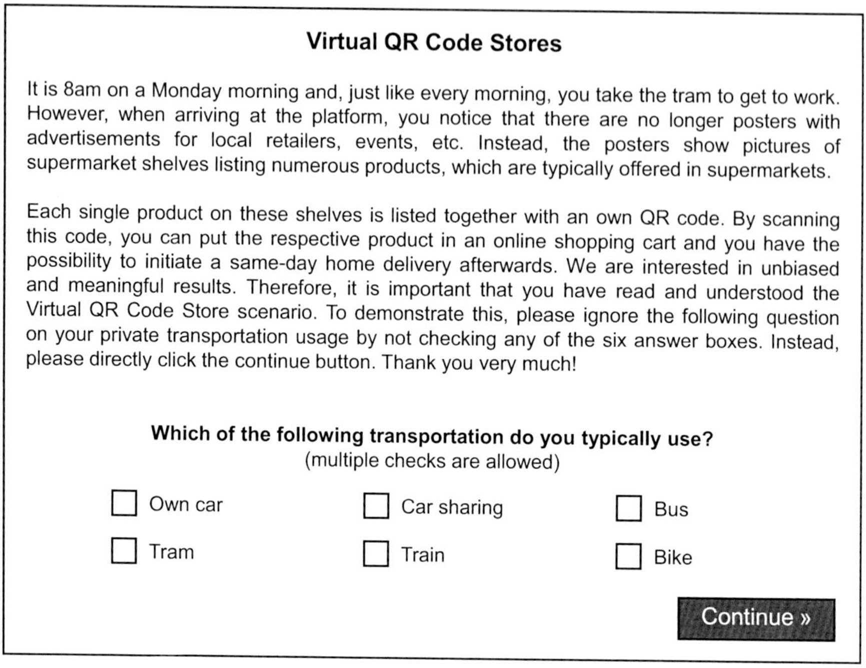

Virtual QR Code Stores

It is 8am on a Monday morning and, just like every morning, you take the tram to get to work. However, when arriving at the platform, you notice that there are no longer posters with advertisements for local retailers, events, etc. Instead, the posters show pictures of supermarket shelves listing numerous products, which are typically offered in supermarkets.

Each single product on these shelves is listed together with an own QR code. By scanning this code, you can put the respective product in an online shopping cart and you have the possibility to initiate a same-day home delivery afterwards. We are interested in unbiased and meaningful results. Therefore, it is important that you have read and understood the Virtual QR Code Store scenario. To demonstrate this, please ignore the following question on your private transportation usage by not checking any of the six answer boxes. Instead, please directly click the continue button. Thank you very much!

Which of the following transportation do you typically use?
(multiple checks are allowed)

☐ Own car   ☐ Car sharing   ☐ Bus

☐ Tram   ☐ Train   ☐ Bike

Continue »

Fig. 2 Example of instructional manipulation check

of the dependent variable, however, may cause interference with the effect of the manipulation or may even be interpreted as a necessary condition for the observed effect (Trafimow and Rice 2009).

Given these issues, researchers today call for careful evaluation of whether the benefits of a manipulation check truly outweigh the costs (Sawyer et al. 1995; Trafimow and Rice 2009). Many situations exist where manipulation checks add only little informational value to theory testing. This includes variables that are isomorphic with their operationalization such as black and white vs. colored pictures in advertising (Sawyer et al. 1995). Moreover, manipulation checks are not necessarily required in situations where well-known manipulations of variables are used and therefore confidence in the manipulation is backed by existing literature, or where the manipulations have been extensively pretested (see section "Preliminary Testing"). Verifying the appropriateness of a manipulation in the course of a pretest separately from the main experiment may therefore be advisable to circumvent the previously discussed problems associated with the placement of the manipulation check items.

Besides employing manipulation checks, also the use of more than one operationalization of a given theoretical variable may reduce the threat of false inferences. While it is relatively easy to use multiple measures to assess an outcome variable (e.g., different multi-item scales to capture variables such as attitude or preference), employing different manipulations for the independent variable is more challenging since it increases the required sample size. For instance, by manipulating psychological distance based on both temporal and social aspects, Bornemann and Homburg (2011) show that psychological distance differently impacts price perception depending on the respective operationalization of psychological distance.

Extraneous Variables

Different types of extraneous variables may challenge the inference of causality in experimental research. Most problematic are so-called confounding variables, which describe variables that are related to two variables of interest (i.e., factor and observed response variable) and thus may explain their relationship (Harris et al. 2006). A confounding variable may vary with the levels of the manipulated variable and at the same time be associated with the dependent variable. As a consequence, the observed causal relationship between the independent and the outcome variable can be the result of the confounding variable's impact.

Generally, randomization should solve the issues resulting from confounding effects by equally distributing both known and unknown confounding variables between experimental conditions. However, in some situations, randomization may be hard to apply (e.g., in quasi-experimental designs) or ineffective to achieve constant terms between experimental conditions (e.g., due to small sample sizes). Moreover, some manipulations may naturally cause more than just the intended effects. For instance, one may create different levels of crowding in stores to manipulate the extent of potential social contacts. Such contacts should be valued by older consumers as they constitute a compensation for the age-related loss of companionship (Myers and Lumbers 2008). However, there is also evidence that crowding increases perceived stress in a shopping environment, which may prevent older consumers from shopping at all (Albrecht et al. 2017). As such, not necessarily the level of social contact but instead the perceived stress may relate to older consumers' affective and behavioral states. To overcome the issues arising from confounding effects, researchers may include confound checks in experimental designs to show that the manipulation does not change related but different constructs (Perdue and Summers 1986). Similar to a manipulation checks, this involves the administration of indicators that assess the respective theoretical constructs (Sawyer et al. 1995).

The timing of measurement of confounding variables depends on their potential interrelationships with the manipulated independent variable, the manipulation check, and the outcome variable (Koschate-Fischer and Schandelmeier 2014). If the extraneous variable is affected by the manipulation (check), it should be measured after provision of the treatments to the participants (the manipulation check). The same order holds true if effects of the dependent variable on the confounding variables are likely.

In addition to confounding variables, so-called suppressor variables may affect the magnitude of the relationship between the independent and the dependent variable (Cohen et al. 2003). Suppressor variables are correlated with the independent variable but not with the outcome and therefore add irrelevant variance, which may hide or suppress the real relationship between the latter two variables. As a consequence, the relationship may actually become stronger or weaker or even change sign. When including these suppressor variables into the respective analysis, the unwanted variance is removed from the relationship of interest. For instance, we would like to know whether differences in knowledge of history exist between younger and older people and administer a test to both groups that has to be completed within an indicated time limit. We may expect that older people know more about history than younger people but find that younger people have answered more of the test's questions. A possible explanation for this finding may be that older people are simply slower readers. Slow reading has prevented them from answering all questions but is otherwise not associated with knowledge of history. In this case, reading speed constitutes a suppressor variable we want to control for in our analysis to obtain the true relationship between age and knowledge of history.

Definition and Operationalization of the Measured Response-Variables

Similar to the operationalization of the treatments, also the dependent variable of interest has to be translated into an operational measure. Moreover, additional variables may have to be assessed, particularly to reveal processes underlying a cause-effect relationship or to rule out alternative explanations.

Operationalization of the Dependent Variable(s)

Using interviews and surveys, experimenters mostly refer to self-report measures to capture participants' response to experimental manipulations (Morales et al. 2017). This approach involves asking respondents (multiple) direct questions about, for instance, their feelings, attitudes, or behavioral intentions. These questions typically come in the form of rating scales or fixed-choice questions. Rating scales capture how strong participants agree or disagree with the statements and can reveal the degree of response. In contrast, fixed-choice questions force respondents to make a fixed-choice answer such as "yes" or "no," or "buy" or "not buy."

Sometimes, researchers are interested in aspects they cannot operationalize due to restrictions they face when conducting an experimental study. For instance, marketing researchers may be interested in factors influencing brand choice, but are not able to actually measure real choice behavior and therefore resort to scales assessing brand attitude as a proxy. Unfortunately, the link between attitudes and actual behavior is not really stable and highly contingent on a number of factors. For instance, attitudes are better able to predict behavior when they are formed based on actual experience with an object and often retrieved from memory (Glasman and Albarracín 2006). This implies that particularly in case of new products, researchers should refrain from using attitude measures if the theoretical interest lies in behavioral consequences.

An additional aspect that poses challenges to the measurement of outcome variables is the demand effect described in the section "Assigning Participants to Experimental Treatments." In a within-subject design, where scores of an outcome variable are obtained repeatedly from the same participant, carryover-effects may occur or participants may guess the goal of the study and – consciously or not – act accordingly when providing scores for scale items that aim to assess the outcome variable. For instance, a huge stream of literature examines consequences of various treatments on participants' emotions (in a marketing context, this could be the impact of different advertisements on emotional reactions). While a first challenge in this context is the theoretical definition of emotions, how to measure them, particularly in within-subject designs, is even more difficult. Emotional reactions may manifest in various ways, such as facial action, vocal changes, cardiac responses, or subjective experiences. Particularly the latter are most often assessed based on self-report scales. In such cases, the standard deviations across the different measurement points may be compared to assess whether participants simply transfer a prior judgment to a subsequent assessment (stereotypic responding; Larsen and Fredrickson 1999).

Various outcome variables – including emotional reactions – can also be assessed without the need for participants' self-reports, thus circumventing this issue. In many marketing-related research questions, the degree to which participants attend to particular information depending on the structure of that information is of interest (for instance in the context of designing advertisements). In such cases, eye-tracking may be used to examine participants' attention to particular pieces of information. Also emotional reactions may be assessed continuously throughout the whole experiment based on physiological recording devices or via recording and coding participants' facial reactions during the experiment (Larsen and Fredrickson 1999). Since emotional reactions have been shown to systematically manifest in changes of facial muscles, several software solutions have been developed (e.g., IntraFace by Carnegie Mellon University's Human Sensing Laboratory) that code the recorded material into specific emotional reactions. More recent developments also show that mouse cursor movements may be used to index participants' emotional reactions (Hibbeln et al. 2017), providing an unobtrusive way to assess emotional reactions in online experiments.

Mediators

Assumptions on causal relationships in experiments should have a clear theoretical rationale, which is why researchers are increasingly interested in revealing the psychological processes underlying those relationships (Spencer et al. 2005). In other words, they search for variables that causally transmit the effects of the manipulated variable to the dependent variable – so-called mediators (Bullock et al. 2010). For instance, following the theory of cognitive dissonance, researchers postulate that the experience of incongruent information (e.g., positive impression of a brand and negative experience with one of its products) may cause an aversive arousal in individuals' minds, which in turn can initiate changes in their attitudes (Festinger 1957). In this case, the aversive arousal is the mediator of the incongruent information-attitude relationship. Such mediators can be particularly relevant for studies where no main effect of the independent variable on the dependent variable is found in initial studies. Often, researchers abandon their project at these stages in the assumption that there is no effect at all. However, multiple psychological processes may simultaneously mediate a relationship, but with opposite signs, thereby causing the nonsignificant main effect (Zhao et al. 2010). For instance, advertising may (1) increase the consideration set of consumers, which in turn increases price sensitivity. On the other hand, it may (2) increase perceived differences in utility among competing products, which negatively affects price sensitivity (Mitra and Lynch 1995).

To operationalize the mediator variable, three approaches exist. First, most experiments use a so-called *measurement-of-mediation* design, where the proposed mediator/s is/are measured using survey item scales (Spencer et al. 2005). Then, regression-based causal mediation analyses are applied (e.g., Zhao et al. 2010). This approach, however, has been criticized for several limitations (see Spencer et al. 2005 for further discussion), of which the causal inference of the mediator-dependent variable relationship is the most decisive (Pirlott and MacKinnon 2016). Randomly assigning participants to levels of the manipulated independent variable and measuring both the mediator and outcome variables enables interpretation of the independent variable-mediator and the independent variable-outcome relationships. However, it is not possible to decipher whether the mediator causes the outcome, the outcome causes the mediator, or unmeasured confounding variables cause both the mediator and the outcome variable. To overcome the limitations of this approach and thus make strong inferences about the causal chain of events, researchers suggest manipulating not only the independent variable but also the mediator. In this respect, the experimental-causal-chain and moderation-of-process designs are the most used design approaches (Spencer et al. 2005). In *experimental-causal-chain* designs, two experiments are conducted. In the first experiment, participants are randomly assigned to the levels of the independent variable while the mediator and the outcome variables are measured. This allows for an unambiguous interpretation of the effect of the independent variable on the mediator and outcome variables, respectively. In a second experiment, the causal effect of the mediator variable on the dependent variable is tested. Here, participants are randomly assigned to levels of the manipulated mediator variable and the outcome variable is measured. The respective levels are defined based on the changes of the mediator variable caused by the independent variable in the first experiment. In contrast, in *moderation-of-process* designs, the independent and the mediator variables are simultaneously manipulated in a two-factor experimental design. These manipulations allow for inferences about the causal effects of both the independent variable and the mediator variable on the measured outcome variable. Moreover, a manipulation check that measures the mediator variable is applied, which is why also the effect of the independent variable on the mediator variable can be tested.

However, experimental-causal-chain and moderation-of-process designs have some drawbacks as well. Some psychological processes such as personal commitment are not easy to manipulate. Moreover, the manipulation of the mediator must be the same as the measured variable before, which constitutes a serious limitation of this approach. For instance, Postmes et al. (2001) failed to show a successful manipulation of group norms when measuring this variable. Also, the additional manipulation of the mediator variable requires larger sample sizes.

Given the issues involved in the three designs, Spencer et al. (2005) make some suggestions regarding when to use which approach based on how easy it is to measure the proposed processes and how easy those processes are to manipulate. Specifically, the experimental-causal-chain design is the simplest and most straightforward approach if the mediator can be both measured and manipulated. If one has the resources, a series of studies conducting all three approaches would be the best option. In situations where the mediator can easily be manipulated but measuring it is difficult, the moderation-of-process design is recommended. The most prevalent approach in existing research – the measurement-of-mediation design – may be used if the manipulation of the mediator is difficult, but the mediator can be measured.

Decision About the Environmental Setting

Having identified and operationalized the sources of variation and response variables, experimenters need to decide about the environmental setting that best fits the defined requirements. Oftentimes, the environment of an experiment is chosen based on convenience aspects such as saving cost and time, or ease of application (Li et al. 2015). However, the experimental environment affects the controllability of the manipulation by the researcher as well as the participants' behavior. It is human nature to pay attention not only to the manipulated stimuli but also to the experiment's environment (Harrison and List 2003). Individuals employ learned strategies and heuristics to cope with those influences, which is why insights from isolated snapshots in controlled settings can provide misleading insights of "true" behavior. Against this background, the next subsections provide a deeper understanding of three prevalent environmental settings of experiments (laboratory, field, and online).

Laboratory Experiments

Laboratory experiments describe experimental designs in controlled environmental settings. They have been almost neglected until the late 1940s, but have since become an integral part of today's marketing research. For instance, between 2000 and 2007 alone, more than 1200 laboratory experiments have been published in the four leading marketing journals (Baum and Spann 2011). This prevalence in academia may result from the special merits of laboratory experiments. Employing artificial environments, experimenters can eliminate many of the confounding influences (e.g., noise level, architectural design) that may otherwise affect the results of experiments (Falk and Heckman 2009; Harrison and List 2003). Therefore, a higher internal validity – referring to the extent to which an experimental manipulation is truly responsible for variations in the dependent variable (Shadish et al. 2002) – is assigned to laboratory experiments compared to other environmental settings. Moreover, experiments in controlled environments enable randomized allocation of participants to conditions, counterbalancing, and the use of standardized instructions, which facilitates later replication (Aaker et al. 2011).

However, there is an intense discussion on whether the findings from laboratory experiments are realistic and "right" for theory testing. Researchers criticizing controlled environmental conditions as being unrealistic argue that the context in which participants' decisions are embedded (and the associated level of scrutiny) and the way they are selected to participate influence their behavior (List 2011). For instance, there is empirical evidence that participants in laboratory environments might make assumptions about the experimenter's objectives and adjust their behavior to align with these expectations (Benz and Meier 2008). To ensure that none of the participants is aware of the true purpose of the study, researchers increasingly administer suspicion probes in their experimental material (e.g., Hattula et al. 2015). Moreover, in natural environments, individuals may adapt their behavior in ways that can hardly be captured in a laboratory environment (Levitt and List 2007). For instance, individuals can simply stop shopping and leave the particular store. Consequently, the results from the laboratory may not be generalizable to real markets and thus limit the external validity of the respective findings.

External validity denotes how far a causal relationship that has been uncovered in an experimental study can be generalized beyond the context of the experiment in terms of people, places, treatments, and outcomes (Shadish et al. 2002). An important prerequisite for external validity is that the experiment's participants represent the true population of interest and that the experimental setting is perceived as realistic as possible. For instance, experimentation is often used to identify effective designs and layouts of advertisements. In such studies, participants are frequently exposed to variations of the focal advertisement only (in terms of pictures included, font sizes, etc.), whereas in real life, consumers normally are exposed to a sequence of advertisements for different brands and products (e.g., when watching TV-commercials or reading a magazine or newspaper). Thus, the attention participants pay to an isolated advertisement in an experimental study may be different from the attention they would pay for it in real life situations.

The extent of a laboratory experiment's external validity therefore depends on its design and execution in the specific context. "The external validity of an experiment cannot be evaluated either a priori or a posteriori (e.g., on the basis of sampling practices or realism) in the absence of a fairly deep understanding of the structural determinants of the behavior under study" (Lynch 1982, p. 238). In this respect, Koschate-Fischer and Schandelmeier (2014) discuss three aspects that influence the generalizability of findings generated from laboratory experiments. First, the naturalness of a laboratory setting strongly depends on the operationalization of the independent and dependent variable(s). For instance, the levels of the manipulation of the independent variable should be different enough to represent meaningful categories (Zikmund and Babin 2006). Second, not the mundane realism (i.e., physically resembling the real world) of an experiment is important, but the experimental realism matters (Berkowitz and Donnerstein 1982). That is, experiments should be designed such that participants are caught up in the procedures and forget that they are part of an experiment – they should perceive the research setting as natural. Finally, laboratory experiments should be conducted in different contexts to provide valid results. For instance, the threats to external validity can be varied in multiple experiments to examine their relevance (Falk and Heckman 2009) and thus to enhance the generalizability of the findings.

Field Experiments

Field experiments represent a conjunction of experimentation and fieldwork – they describe experimental designs conducted in mostly natural environmental settings (see also chapter ▶ "Field Experiments" by Valli, Stahl, and Feit in this volume). Literature in marketing has recently seen an increase in research using field experiments: more than 60% of all field experiments published in the leading marketing journals over the last 20 years were published in the most recent 5 years (Simester 2017). Following Harrison and List (2004), three types of field experiments can be differentiated (see Fig. 3). *Artefactual* field experiments are similar to laboratory experiments except for one feature – they involve a nonstandard pool of participants. Instead of recruiting students, participants of the experiment are drawn from the real market (List 2011). Thus, the respective research more closely features the real world actors of interest. Compared to artefactual field experiments, *framed* field experiments additionally consider a realistic task to avoid confounding effects that result from a laboratory setting. That is, the experiment is framed "in the field context of the commodity, task, stakes, or information set of the subjects" (List 2011, p. 5). Finally, *natural* field experiments are similar to framed field experiments, but here, participants naturally undertake the tasks and therefore are not aware of participating in an experiment. This combination of realism and randomization helps avoiding that participants adjust their behavior to align with assumed expectations of the experimenter (Benz and Meier 2008). Natural field experiments therefore maximize the generalizability and thus the external validity of experimental findings. They simulate as closely as possible the conditions under which a causal process occurs (List 2011).

However, the uncontrolled and frequently complex environmental settings in field experiments have been argued to limit the internal validity of those experiments (Aaker et al. 2011). Since confounding environmental characteristics are not held constant, establishing cause-effect relationships is difficult. Therefore, "an ideal field experiment not only increases external validity, but does so in a manner in which

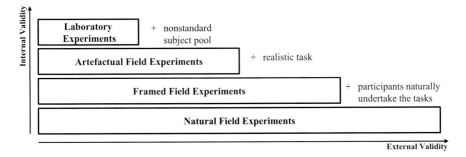

Fig. 3 Overview of laboratory and field experiments

little internal validity is foregone" (Harrison and List 2003, p. 37). To achieve this, several prerequisites have to be met. First, the treatment variable must be exogenous (Remler and Van Ryzin 2010). In other words, the dependent variable should not determine the manipulation of the independent variable. Second, the characteristics of the treatment and the control group must be truly comparable. For instance, finding comparable locations for both groups is crucial (Trafimow et al. 2016). Matching techniques can be applied, where locations are evaluated based on variables that might differentiate them. Finally, experimenters should capture as many control variables as possible to account for potential confounding effects (Arnold 2008).

At this point, one might expect a recommendation regarding whether to use laboratory or field experiments in market research. There is a lively debate on this question. Some researchers favor laboratory experiments due to their high internal validity, whereas others value the external validity of field experiments. "The obvious solution is to conduct experiments both ways: with and without naturally occurring field referents and context" (Harrison and List 2004, p. 1050). Combining the results from laboratory and field experiments can help understanding the mechanisms of behavior observed in the real market (Falk and Heckman 2009). For instance, differences in the findings between both settings indicate the need to study the environment in more detail in order to understand real world behavior of market actors.

Online Experiments

The third environmental setting is Internet based – the respective experimental design is mostly referred to as online experiments. Due to technological advancements and cost and distribution advantages (see Koschate-Fischer and Schandelmeier 2014 and Reips 2002 for further advantages), online experiments have become a standard instrument in today's market research. Descriptions of this experimental setting highlight the possibility of an interaction of participants with the experimenter or other participants via the Internet (Morton and Williams 2010). This interaction is direct, but virtually mediated through the internet. Due to the fact that participants of online experiments remain in their natural environment, some researchers suggest that online experiments pertain to the category of field experiments (Koschate-Fischer and Schandelmeier 2014). This categorization may hold for settings where online marketing phenomena such as e-commerce strategies are studied and the use of a computer thus describes the natural environment of the participants. However, online experiments are also applied to study offline phenomena and to validate and/or extend results from field and laboratory studies (Reips 2002). In this latter case, scenario techniques ask participants to imagine offline situations, which is why they do not act in their situation-specific natural environment anymore. Depending on the actual context and execution, online experiments may therefore share more common properties with either field or laboratory settings (Morton and Williams 2010).

Given the use of online experiments to study offline behavior, the question arises as to whether data obtained online and offline provide equivalent results.

Researchers arguing against this equivalence highlight confounding factors that may affect individual behavior. Online respondents cannot scan, preview, review, skip, or change items, which is why they may experience a different level of self-generated validity (Feldman and Lynch Jr. 1988). Moreover, results may be different in a more public offline setting, where aspects such as social pressure are present that could influence individual shopping behavior (Bearden and Etzel 1982). Recent research, in contrast, indicates equivalence of online and offline data and demonstrates acceptable levels of accuracy, completeness, and response quality in some settings (Hauser and Schwarz 2016). Moreover, due to their broad coverage, online experiments provide good generalizability of findings to the population (Horswill and Coster 2001) and to a good number of settings and situations (Laugwitz 2001).

Nonetheless, careful evaluation of the applicability of online experiments for the individual research question and context is necessary. Online experiments are less suited for studies that require high levels of attention to the study material and instructions and that ask for a high motivation (Goodman et al. 2013). Also, participants in online settings seem to mentally process the material differently in that they pay more attention to minor aspects of instructions (Hauser and Schwarz 2016). Similarly, it is difficult to reliably assess factual answers such as competencies, since participants of online studies can simply search for answers in the internet (Goodman et al. 2013).

Determination of the Experimental Units and Assignment to Treatments

The next step in the process of designing an experimental study involves the determination of the experimental units and the rule by which the experimental units are assigned to the different treatments. Experimental units describe the entities upon which the relationships of interest are tested, i.e., which are subjected to the respective treatments. In marketing research, the experimental units are typically human participants (e.g., customers, managers). The high percentage of student samples in existing experimental research studying market phenomena has sparked a lively discussion on their qualification as experimental units (Koschate-Fischer and Schandelmeier 2014). Critics highlight that students are not representative for the decision-making of "real" customers because they are better educated and represent less mature personalities (Sears 1986). Moreover, they constitute a very homogeneous group with little variation in factors such as age or income, which makes the study of personal characteristics more difficult. Even more critical is the use of student samples to address business problems such as the selection of employees in organizational settings. Such issues are generally addressed by managers whose qualifications and job experience is key to make the respective decisions (Hakel et al. 1970). Advocates of student samples, however, argue that only little research exists that finds generalizable significant differences in the decision-making of students and "real" customers or managers, respectively. Such differences only exist if the above-mentioned characteristics such as age or job experience truly influence the independent variable's effect on the dependent variable. This, however, is not very often the case for the phenomena studied in experimental research (Lynch 1982). The homogeneity in individual characteristics can even be beneficial to experiments because it reduces many confounding effects (see section "Extraneous Variables"). The conclusion from this discussion is that a careful evaluation of the suitability of students before conducting an experiment is required.

In the following, we will elaborate on the number of participants required and how to sample them, the question of whether and how to incentivize these participants, and finally how to assign participants to the different treatments.

Number of Participants and Sampling Procedure

One of the most frequently asked questions of students and practitioners in empirical projects is "How many participants do I need?" (Evans and Rooney 2013, p. 134). There is no universal answer to this question because different aspects have to be considered in determining this number. First, the required sample size depends on the specific experimental research design. A large number of treatments require a larger sample size especially in designs where each participant is exposed to only one of the multiple treatments (see section "Assigning Participants to Experimental Treatments"). In this respect, simple heuristics have been introduced suggesting to use approximately 30 participants for each experimental condition (Sawyer and Ball 1981). Usability professionals even argue that just 5 participants could be enough in qualitative experiments. They should reveal about 80% of all usability problems that exist in a product (Nielsen 2000). However, the number of participants should not be determined without considering the experimental setting itself. For instance, at least 39 users are required in eye-tracking studies to get stable heatmaps (Nielsen 2012).

More sophisticated approaches consider anticipated or previously observed effect sizes to calculate the statistical power and based on that estimate appropriate sample sizes (Fritz et al. 2012). The idea is that nonsignificant effects of independent variables in experiments are not necessarily the result of a missing relationship with the dependent variable but of low statistical power – a phenomenon called the dilemma of the nonrejected null hypothesis or simply Type II error. Significant effects may be found with quite small samples when the relationship between the manipulated variable and the dependent variable is strong and control is tight – that is, the effect size is large (Evans and Rooney 2013). However, small effect sizes require larger samples to achieve statistical significance. Experimenters make assumptions about the effect size by relying on previous research or on the smallest effect that would be meaningful. As an orientation, Cohen (1988) defines standardized effect sizes for common statistical tests. For instance, while for independent sample t-tests, he defines 0.20, 0.50, and 0.80 as small, medium, and large effect sizes, respectively, 0.10, 0.25, and 0.40 are the respective values for one-way ANOVAs. With respect to statistical power, a commonly suggested Type II error is 0.20, which indicates a power need of 0.80 (Ellis 2010). The sample size can then be estimated for a small, medium, or large anticipated effect size, considering the specified statistical power and significance level following Cohen's (1988) procedure. As an example, assuming a statistical power of 0.80 and a significance level of

0.05, the required total number of participants for an independent sample t-test (ANOVA with four group means) would be 786 (1096), 128 (180), and 52 (76) participants for a small, medium, and large effect size, respectively.

To obtain a pool of participants that constitutes a representative part of the total population of interest, two categories of sampling approaches can be applied: probability or nonprobability sampling (Evans and Rooney 2013). Probability sampling approaches subsume techniques where the likelihood of the selection of participants from a population is specified. The most prominent probability approach is *simple random sampling*. It assumes that all individuals of a population are included in the sample with the same probability. In an ideal case, all members of a population would be included in a list and then randomly picked until the desired sample size is reached. In contrast, *proportional random sampling* considers subgroups of the initial population, which are built first based on criteria such as age, gender, or income. Then, individuals are randomly selected from the respective subgroups. This technique is particularly useful when subgroups of the population such as women or older individuals represent the target segment. The third probability approach is *systematic random sampling*. Here, experimenters choose the first subject of a population and then every nth further subject is considered until the desired number of participants is reached. Finally, *multistage random sampling* combines at least two of the previously introduced approaches.

Nonprobability sampling approaches do not specify the likelihood of selecting an individual from the population, but select participants on the basis of accessibility or personal judgment (Evans and Rooney 2013). The most often used form of this sampling approach is *convenience sampling* (also known as haphazard or accidental sampling), where participants are selected based on simple recruitment. A common example in experimental research projects is the recruitment of students. Experimenters walk around the campus and ask them to participate in the respective experiment. This is convenient because it saves time and incentivizing students is less costly compared to other groups of a population.

Another nonprobability sampling approach is *volunteer sampling*. This technique describes the selection of participants from a group of volunteers and is used when it is difficult and unethical to randomly assign participants to the levels of a manipulation. This applies, for instance, to studies examining the effectiveness of pharmaceutical products. In an online context, opt-in panels are a popular volunteer sampling technique. People sign in or put their name on a mailing list to participate in experimental studies. Representatives of such opt-in panels are Amazon's Mechanical Turk (MTurk), CrowdFlower (CF), and Prolific Academic (ProA) (Peer et al. 2017). Particularly MTurk is increasingly drawing attention from practitioners and academics alike. It allows experimenters rapid data collection at low cost (ca. 10 cents per participant) and around the clock (Goodman et al. 2013). However, significant concerns exist regarding the use of MTurk in behavioral research. For instance, participants may pay less attention to instructions than traditional subject pools do because individuals are more likely to engage in distractions such as cell phone usage (Hauser and Schwarz 2016). Moreover, participants of MTurk may have different attitudes about money and time due to the low compensation (Goodman et al. 2013). Those issues may cause a serious bias in the respective data. Given these concerns, several studies examined data generated by MTurk participants. The results are mixed in that some studies provide evidence for a higher risk-aversion and lower attention of MTurk participants in case of longer surveys (Goodman et al. 2013). Other research, however, demonstrated high accuracy and validity as well as a good replicability in behavioral outcomes (Buhrmester et al. 2011). This discussion indicates the need for a careful assessment of the suitability of MTurk participants for the underlying research question. Experimenters are recommended to "use screening procedures to measure participants' attention levels and take into account that MTurk participants may vary from non-MTurk participants on social and financial traits" (Goodman et al. 2013, p. 222).

Finally, *quota sampling* describes a nonprobability sampling approach similar to convenience sampling, with one exception: participants with particular characteristics are selected until their proportion in the sample is large enough. For instance, this technique may be used if equal numbers of men and women are required.

Incentivization of Participants

The question what motivates individuals to participate in experiments is as old as experimental research itself. Besides altruistic (e.g., social obligations) and study-related (e.g., interesting topic) reasons, particularly egoistic motives have been shown to increase the willingness to contribute (Singer and Couper 2008). That is, individuals strive for a personal benefit when participating in experimental studies, which is why experimenters usually offer monetary and/or nonmonetary incentives (e.g., awarding of credit points or chance to win in a lottery drawing; Koschate-Fischer and Schandelmeier 2014). Such incentives have been shown to stimulate participation in experimental studies, especially when commitment to the task is low (Hansen 1980) and/or other motives are absent (Singer and Couper 2008).

Some aspects should be considered in this context. First, incentivization may not just impact the motivation of individuals to participate but also their performance in the experiment. An economic view holds that money generally lets individuals work harder, more persistently, and more effectively on a task, which improves the quality of the data received (Smith and Walker 1993). An increase in performance, however, has mostly been documented for mundane tasks such as memory or recall tasks, where financial incentives induce persistent diligence (Camerer and Hogarth 1999). In contrast, no effects on performance have been observed for more complex tasks. Even more problematic is that financial incentives may even decrease response quality – particularly in experimental settings where open-ended questions are asked. Here, the answers of incentivized participants were shorter and of lower quality compared to nonincentivized settings where participants contributed out of intrinsic motivation (Hansen 1980). Similarly, incentivization can produce inferior data quality in settings where incentives raise self-consciousness or may cause overreaction to feedback (Camerer 2011).

Second, one should consider that monetary and nonmonetary incentives are not equally attractive to potential participants. Generally, monetary incentives have been shown to be more effective to stimulate the willingness to participate in experiments

(Singer and Couper 2008). The amount of money offered, however, is not necessarily decisive for participation because participants see the monetary compensation more as a symbolic act (a thank you) than as a true income (Koschate-Fischer and Schandelmeier 2014). This is why participants may continue participation in future research for even less than the current payment (Singer and Couper 2008). The amount should be appropriate for the task to be solved, which means that it should compensate for the physical and psychological risks involved. Nonmonetary incentives such as lotteries are attractive to individuals if there is a realistic chance of winning (Koschate-Fischer and Schandelmeier 2014). Often, students are offered course credits as a compensation for their participation. This may be effective, but students may feel they have no other choice than participating to improve their grades. Meaningful extra credit options can reduce this coerciveness issue (Kalkoff et al. 2014). Similarly, the educational value of an experiment can be attractive to students. That is, they are more likely to participate in an experiment if they perceive that participation provides a valuable learning experience.

Finally, experimenters should be aware that response rates differ between incentives paid in advance (e.g., with the initial mailing) and those promised for the survey return (Singer et al. 1999). While both can be effective to increase response rates, prepaid incentives are more stimulating. This particularly holds for monetary incentives, where increases in response rates of more than 19% (compared to no incentivization) have been observed (Singer et al. 1999). In contrast, gifts as incentives accounted for increases of up to 8% only. With respect to promised incentives, charitable donations have been argued to be more effective to reduce costs and nonresponse bias than monetary incentives if the respective amount of money spent is low (Robertson and Bellenger 1978). This reasoning, however, could not be supported in an online context, where the monetary interest outweighed altruistic motives – particularly for longer studies (Deutskens et al. 2004).

Assigning Participants to Experimental Treatments

A fundamental issue pertaining to the design of experiments relates to the assignment of the experimental units (participants) to the different treatments. In a within-subject design, each participant of the experiment is (successively) exposed to multiple treatments, leading to multiple observations of the dependent variable from the same person. Thus, estimates of the causal effects of the treatments are obtained by measuring how the dependent variable changes with the successive exposure of the individual to the different treatments. In a between-subjects design, in contrast, each participant is (randomly) assigned to only one treatment combination, leading to one observation of the dependent variable per person. Hence, estimates of causal effects of the treatments are obtained by comparing the measure of the dependent variable between individuals of the different treatment groups.

Both approaches have their merits and weaknesses, and the application of one or another should be decided very carefully based on a number of factors. Consider, for instance, that the goal is to examine how far individuals infer quality from price. The hypothesis is that they indicate higher levels of perceived quality for the same type of product at a higher price as compared to a lower price. Examining this question in a within-subject design would imply exposing the same individual repeatedly to the product stimulus at varying price levels. In a between-subjects design, it would imply the randomized assignment of individuals to either the high price condition or the low price condition and the respective measurement of perceived quality. Meta-analytical findings have repeatedly shown that in within-subject designs, the observed relationship between the product's price level and perceived quality is significantly stronger than in between-subjects designs (Völckner and Hofmann 2007). To provide guidance on the choice of design, we will subsequently elaborate on the statistical, theoretical, and psychological issues that may lead to differences between the two design options. It should also be noted that the designs can be combined into mixed designs – where one factor is manipulated between-subjects and another factor is manipulated within-subject – to profit from the advantages of both (Maxwell and Delaney 2004).

From a statistical viewpoint, within-subject designs result in data for two or more treatments per participant, whereas between-subjects designs yield data for only one treatment per participant. Moreover, each participant serves as his own control group when comparing the treatment effects in within-subject designs. Thus, internal validity does not depend on random assignment as in between-subjects designs since individual differences of the participants are removed from the error term. As a consequence, the number of participants needed to reach a certain level of statistical power is generally lower for within-subject designs as compared to between-subjects designs (Maxwell and Delaney 2004). Within-subject designs therefore are often employed in contexts where the costs per participant are relatively high and/or accessibility to the required infrastructure is limited. For instance, experimental studies that require functional magnetic resonance imaging (fMRI) mostly employ within-subject designs.

Also theoretical considerations may guide the choice of design. If the real-world phenomenon that is examined in an experimental setting can be described as *whether* at all to make a particular decision, a between-subjects design may be appropriate. A choice about *which* decision to make, however, is more akin to a within-subject design (Charness et al. 2012). Thus, the question is which design exhibits higher external validity in that it comes closer to the phenomenon as it unfolds in reality. For instance, a between-subjects design does not provide participants with a clear anchor or reference point. Going back to the price-perceived quality example, the phenomenon to be studied may be consumers' search behavior in a store, where the consumer is being exposed to different prices for products of the same category, and hence reference price effects are likely to occur. Alternatively, the researcher may be interested in the effect of a single advertisement where only one price cue is present (Völckner and Hofmann 2007). Whereas a within-subject design may provide higher external validity in the former scenario, the latter scenario may better map onto a between-subjects design. The results of the meta-analysis described above thus may suggest that price-quality inferences are less likely if no clear reference point exists.

The heaviest critique on within-subject designs is due to psychological issues inherent in this design (Greenwald 1976). A first phenomenon that can be observed in some contexts is that participants simply become better in a task the more often they *practice* it. For instance, if the phenomenon to be studied involves the performance at a motor skill task (dependent variable) when being exposed to different types of distracting stimuli (treatment), participants in a within-subject design may become better in the task with every successive measurement simply due to practice of the task independent of the distracting stimuli. Such practice may confound the effect of the distraction treatment on task performance and thus threaten internal validity. A second phenomenon is the so-called *demand effect*: compared to a between-subjects design, participants in a within-subject design are more likely to guess the true purpose of the study and act in line with the inferred hypotheses. The more treatments a single participant is exposed to, the more likely is it that demand effects result (Greenwald 1976). For instance, successively exposing a participant to similar product stimuli with only price information being varied and asking this participant to indicate her or his quality perception of the product may indeed trigger thoughts on the purpose of the study. Finally, *carryover effects* may occur in a sense that the effect of a certain treatment persists over time and influences the subsequent measurement of the effect of another treatment. Such an effect may be observed if the effects of different drugs with unknown action times are examined in a within-subject design (Greenwald 1976; Maxwell and Delaney 2004). Moreover, individuals may use their evaluation of a prior treatment and transfer this prior judgment to a subsequent treatment if the prior judgment is accessible in memory and perceived as relevant and useful also in the new context (Lynch et al. 1988). This effect may occur when participants do not perceive that there is a substantial difference (e.g., new information) in subsequent treatments (Bornemann and Homburg 2011).

To counter some of these psychological issues, the order of the treatments in a within-subject design may be counterbalanced by randomly assigning participants to groups of equal size and presenting treatments to each group in a different order (e.g., with two treatments A and B, group 1 may first be given treatment A followed by B, while the reverse treatment order is administered to group 2). Maxwell and Delaney (2004) refer to such designs as *crossover designs*. To examine whether any effects caused by the order of the treatments exist, the factor "group" is included as a between-subjects factor in an analysis of variance. Nonsignificance of this "group" factor indicates that no order effects exist.

Preliminary Testing

As a final step in the design of an experimental study and before conducting the actual experiment, investigators have to conduct preliminary testing to ensure the adequacy of manipulations and measures (Perdue and Summers 1986). Weak experimental designs may make results unusable/uninterpretable and thus costly for researchers. This is especially the case for rather new research settings (Reynolds et al. 1993). Therefore, one should be able to modify potential shortcomings in advance and thus at a stage where corrections are less costly. Preliminary tests also make manipulation and confounding checks less necessary in the main experiment

(Perdue and Summers 1986). The only cases where skipping those preliminary analyses is acceptable relate to settings with very small target populations where at least some individuals of the preliminary test may equal those of the main experiment and to settings where the additional tests would adversely affect the main experiment (Reynolds et al. 1993).

Two types of preliminary testing may be considered. First, *pretesting* ensures the validity of aspects of the experiment such as instructions, tasks, and instruments. Participants of such pretests are instructed to evaluate these aspects in isolation, independent of the rest of the experimental design. Importantly, manipulation and confounding checks should be implemented in pretests to assess whether the manipulation adequately reflects the theoretical assumptions (Kuipers and Hysom 2014; Perdue and Summers 1986). Besides employing scale items, interviews with the participants or other qualitative techniques such as verbal protocols of scenarios or instructions can provide useful information on the credibility of the stimuli used. Moreover, pretesting can reveal issues related to missing response categories and the difficulty to answer particular questions (Reynolds et al. 1993).

In *pilot tests*, the second preliminary testing, the full experiment is provided to participants in situations comparable to those of the main experiment (Kuipers and Hysom 2014). Such pilot tests offer additional value to the experimenter since they provide information beyond individual parts of the experiment, including the measure of the dependent variable. Pilot testing can reveal whether there is enough variability in this measure. If this is not the case, the measure can be altered. Moreover, experimenters get information on readability and understandability of the instructions (e.g., logical flow), time required for completion, and the look of the design (Kuipers and Hysom 2014; Reynolds et al. 1993).

A general requirement for pre- and pilot testing is that participants should have the same characteristics as those targeted with the main experiment (Reynolds et al. 1993). This ensures that the adjustments made fit the requirements of this audience. Moreover, the same procedures and experimental instruments as in the main study are required to receive valid feedback for potential adjustments. Both the target population and the design of the instrument determine the sample size required for the preliminary analyses. The more subgroups of the total population to be considered and the more complex the experimental design (e.g., the more treatments), the more individuals are required. Usually, this sample size is rather small (5–10 to 50–100 participants; Reynolds et al. 1993). Finally, the feedback of participants should be captured directly after exposure to avoid any feedback bias that may result from later retrieval from memory (Perdue and Summers 1986).

Exemplary Experimental Study

We now illustrate the steps involved in the design of experiments with a real experiment that we conducted as part of a published research project (Albrecht et al. 2016). The project investigated the relevance of the interaction environment for customer response to interactional service experiences and required the manipulation of two factors: the service experience and an environmental trigger.

Definition of Research Question. The starting point for this study was the observation that, in daily practice, buying behavior is affected by frontline employees' emotions as observed by the customer. However, little was known about how this relationship is influenced by the purchase environment – typically an important information source for customers to evaluate store experiences. Specifically, we intended to test our hypothesis that the presence of cues/triggers in the respective store environment that help explaining a given frontline employee's emotional display towards the customer may influence customer reactions. We expected that the impact of the presence of the environmental trigger would differently affect the customer response to positive versus negative emotions shown by the employee. Moreover, we were interested in the underlying psychological processes.

Determination and Operationalization of the Sources of Variation. Considering the *independent variables*, the experiment's objectives suggested two factors of interest: the emotional display of a frontline employee and the presence of a trigger in the store environment that may provide an explanation for the employee's emotion. The first factor, emotional display of the frontline employee, was varied at two levels: negative versus positive. The second factor, emotion trigger, also consisted of two levels: a control condition and a treatment condition, where an observable environmental trigger existed. In the control condition, no such emotion trigger was provided. We hence applied a full factorial design.

With respect to the *operationalization of the treatments,* a key challenge of our online experiment dealing with an offline phenomenon was to create a realistic purchase situation. To achieve that, we employed a scenario role-play-based approach and produced videotapes, one for each of the four treatments. Particularly, we hired a professional cinematographer and actor to create stimulus material in a local hardware store simulating a typical customer-employee interaction. The actor was instructed either to express the negative emotion of unfriendliness or to show the positive emotional display condition of smile. The customer was not shown explicitly but the camera represented the "eyes" of the customer such that each participant could put him/herself into the customer's shoes. In the emotion trigger condition, before the service interaction, the participant could hear the employee's phone ringing, see how the employee answered the call, and see and hear his reaction to the colleague on the phone. This reaction was either positive or negative in line with the emotional display manipulation. No such phone call trigger was provided in the control condition.

We applied *manipulation checks* to ensure that the service interaction scenario was perceived as realistic and that the manipulations worked as intended. In this respect, appropriate single/multi-item scales had already been validated in previous research. Therefore, we included those items as self-report measures in our study. These checks were administered after the assessment of the dependent variables to avoid any interference with the effect of the manipulation. Moreover, previous research suggested potential *extraneous factors* that we accounted for by assessing them as covariates: participants' susceptibility to catching emotions, preencounter mood, and age.

Definition and Operationalization of the Measured Response-Variables. With respect to the response variables, we assessed participants' purchase intention as a reaction to the employee's emotion. The examined process explanations comprised the perceived authenticity of the employee's emotional display and the perceived sympathy for this behavior. We decided to capture both the *dependent* and *mediator variables* with well-established self-report measures. We screened existing literature and identified multi-item scales that already worked well to capture purchase intention, perceived authenticity, and perceived sympathy. Participants rated the items on disagree-agree rating scales.

Decision about the Environmental Setting. We conducted the experiment online; hence, participants viewed the stimulus material on a computer monitor. We used the online setting because of cost advantages and the suitability of the stimulus material (the role-play video) for this type of environment. Alternatively, a laboratory setting would have been adequate as well.

Determination of the Experimental Units and Assignment to Treatments. The objective of the research project implies (adult) *customers* as the relevant experimental unit. We purposely did not refer to a student sample because of the above-mentioned homogeneity restrictions. We applied simple heuristics and set a minimum of 30 participants for each experimental condition. We recruited participants by posting the link to the study in relevant online communities and web forums with audiences from different social class, gender, and age categories. As such, we employed convenience sampling because we did not specify the likelihood of selecting an individual from the population, but selected participants based on accessibility in these online channels. In the end, we received 138 usable responses.

Participants were not paid an *incentive* but took part voluntarily. They were instructed to turn on the sound of their computer to be able to follow the videos. Moreover, we informed participants about the general purpose and procedure of the research and their right to decline participation or withdraw from the study. We told participants that they take part in a study on customer service. The experiment's objectives did not require deception – that is, we did not disguise any relevant information throughout the experimental study.

Given its multiple advantages and its easy application in online experiments, we applied randomization of the participants to the experimental conditions. Moreover, we chose a between-subjects design, where each participant was (randomly) assigned to only one of the four treatment combinations (negative/positive emotional display × provision/nonprovision of the emotion trigger). We did so for theoretical considerations of realism. Typically, customers are confronted with a single employee showing either a positive or negative emotional display. Also, the trigger either exists or not, such that a mixed or within-subject design was not suited.

Preliminary Testing. We used different pretests to ensure the validity of our experimental manipulations. First, we provided the four videotapes to five doctoral students to ensure that participants had enough time to recognize all content of the videos. Second, we pretested the effectiveness of the manipulations and asked 246 persons to watch the videos and answer a few questions. Specifically, they were asked to rate the perceived unfriendliness and smiling of the frontline employee.

Finally, we provided the emotion trigger (cell phone call) sequence of the video to a university seminar class. Students watched the video sequence and wrote down their thoughts on what the talk was about and what the colleague on the phone had said to the frontline employee. We did so to ensure that the manipulation of the emotion trigger was perceived as "implicitly visible" to participants. All pretests confirmed the validity of our experimental manipulations.

Ethical Issues in Experimental Research

All research involving humans has to meet generally accepted ethical criteria to ensure the welfare of study participants and to protect them from physical and psychological harm. Building among others on regulatory requirements, the American Psychological Association (APA), for instance, has released the *Ethical Principles of Psychologists and Code of Conduct* (APA 2002) to provide guidance to researchers. The following aspects are part of the guidelines for research:

- *Institutional Approval*: Many organizations, particularly in the academic field, have created institutional review boards (IRBs) to protect the human dignity and welfare of participants of research projects. The IRB reviews research proposals submitted by researchers according to their conformance with ethical standards. Many academic journals now ask for such approval for submitted manuscripts.
- *Informed Consent*: Investigators are required to inform participants about the general purpose and procedure of the research and their right to decline participation or withdraw from the study.
- *Deception*: Investigators should generally refrain from deceiving participants unless the scientific value of the research is significant and the study cannot be realized without any deception. If unavoidable, such deception must not relate to aspects that may cause physical pain or severe emotional distress. After completion of the study, investigators are required to explain to participants the aspects involving deception and permit participants to withdraw their data.
- *Debriefing*: Investigators provide participants with the opportunity to obtain information about the results, conclusion, and purpose of the research and they correct potential misperceptions that participants may have.

While these aspects are relevant to all kinds of research involving humans, particularly issues related to deception are specific to experimental research since deception is sometimes used to ensure a high level of experimental control and to reduce the impact of extraneous factors.

Deception refers to the provision of false information or to withholding information to mislead participants into believing something that is not true (Hegtvedt 2014). Deception is distinct from the common practice to not fully inform participants about the hypotheses beforehand (e.g., through providing only partial information about the research question) to avoid demand effects (Hertwig and Ortmann 2008). An example of a rather serious form of deception is the provision of false feedback to participants regarding their performance in a task they have completed, particularly if such feedback may affect their self-confidence in general (Hegtvedt 2014; Kuipers and Hysom 2014).

The controversy on the legitimacy of the use of deception has been quite intense, providing a long list of negative consequences of deception, such as embarrassment and a loss of self-esteem of participants at the individual level and resulting suspicion and negative attitudes towards research in general. This view is particularly prevalent among economists, who more or less generally reject deception. They also argue that if participants expect or are aware of deception, their behavior may no longer be shaped by the circumstances of the study (e.g., monetary rewards) but by psychological reactions to suspected manipulations (Hertwig and Ortmann 2008). Sieber (1992) argues that deception may be justifiable if (1) there is no other means to achieve stimulus control, if (2) responses to low-frequency events are studied, if (3) absolutely no risk of harm is associated with the deception, and if (4) the information would otherwise be unobtainable because of participants' anxiety or defensiveness. Pascual-Leone et al. (2010) offer a checklist that investigators may use to assess whether deception can be justified in a given context. As a general recommendation, investigators should employ such aids to determine whether there is really no way to avoid deception. If deception is used, it is important to conduct proper debriefing of participants to unravel the deceptive practice (Kuipers and Hysom 2014).

Conclusion

This chapter described the relevant steps involved when planning and executing experimental research in marketing. While experimentation is a central type of data collection in academic research in marketing, its use in corporate practice is still comparatively limited. Instead, companies nowadays embrace the blessings of big data analytics. However, the tremendous amount of historical data that companies create and collect poses challenges regarding the required data analysis skills, and not every company can afford to permanently employ the respective specialists. Experimentation, on the other hand, is technically relatively easy to implement and requires managers to directly focus on the causes and effects of interest instead of mining data that *might* provide useful insights. Specifically, the "test-and-learn" approach inherent in experimentation, where certain activities are directed towards one group of customers and other or no activities at all are directed to a control group, enables managers to develop a more direct feeling for relevant cause-effect relationships. The ease of implementation to a large extent depends on how easy the relevant outcomes can be assessed, which is why e-commerce and online business in general is at the forefront of corporate use of experimentation (remember the example of A/B testing from the introductory section). But also other businesses may easily implement and profit from experimentation (Anderson and Simester 2011). We hope that this chapter provides the necessary insights to accomplish such an endeavor.

References

Aaker, D. A., Kumar, V., Day, G. S., & Leone, R. P. (2011). *Marketing research*. Hoboken: Wiley.

Albrecht, C.-M., Hattula, S., Bornemann, T., & Hoyer, W. D. (2016). Customer response to interactional service experience: The role of interaction environment. *Journal of Service Management, 27*(5), 704–729.

Albrecht, C.-M., Hattula, S., & Lehmann, D. R. (2017). The relationship between consumer shopping stress and purchase abandonment in task-oriented and recreation-oriented consumers. *Journal of the Academy of Marketing Science, 45*(5), 720–740.

Anderson, E. T., & Simester, D. (2011). A step-by-step guide to smart business experiments. *Harvard Business Review, 89*(3), 98–105.

APA. (2002). Ethical principles of psychologists and code of conduct. *American Psychologist, 57*(12), 1060–1073.

Arnold, V. (2008). *Advances in accounting behavioral research*. Bradford: Emerald Group Publishing.

Baum, D., & Spann, M. (2011). Experimentelle Forschung im Marketing: Entwicklung und zukünftige Chancen. *Marketing – Zeitschrift für Forschung und Praxis, 33*(3), 179–191.

Bearden, W. O., & Etzel, M. (1982). Reference group influence on product and brand decisions. *Journal of Consumer Research, 9*(April), 183–194.

Benz, M., & Meier, S. (2008). Do people behave in experiments as in the field?—Evidence from donations. *Experimental Economics, 11*(3), 268–281.

Berkowitz, L., & Donnerstein, E. (1982). External validity is more than skin deep: Some answers to criticisms of laboratory experiments. *American Psychologist, 37*(3), 245–257.

Bornemann, T., & Homburg, C. (2011). Psychological distance and the dual role of price. *Journal of Consumer Research, 38*(3), 490–504.

Buhrmester, M., Kwang, T., & Gosling, S. D. (2011). Amazon's mechanical Turk: A new source of inexpensive, yet high-quality, data? *Perspectives on Psychological Science, 6*(1), 3–5.

Bullock, J. G., Green, D. P., & Ha, S. E. (2010). Yes, but what's the mechanism? (don't expect an easy answer). *Journal of Personality and Social Psychology, 98*(4), 550–558.

Camerer, C. F. (2011). *The promise and success of lab-field generalizability in experimental economics: A critical reply to levitt and list*. Available at SSRN 1977749.

Camerer, C. F., & Hogarth, R. M. (1999). The effects of financial incentives in experiments: A review and capital-labor-production framework. *Journal of Risk and Uncertainty, 19*(1), 7–42.

Charness, G., Gneezy, U., & Kuhn, M. A. (2012). Experimental methods: Between-subject and within-subject design. *Journal of Economic Behavior & Organization, 81*(1), 1–8.

Christian, B. (2012). The a/b test: Inside the technology that's changing the rules of business. http://www.wired.com/business/2012/04/ff_abtesting. Accessed 15 Mar 2018.

Cohen, J. (1988). *Statistical power analysis for the behavioral sciences*. Hillsdale: Lawrence Erlbaum Associates.

Cohen, J., Cohen, P., West, S. G., & Aiken, L. S. (2003). *Applied multiple regression/correlation analysis for the behavioral sciences*. Hillsdale: Lawrence Erlbaum Associates.

Collins, L. M., Dziak, J. J., & Li, R. (2009). Design of experiments with multiple independent variables: A resource management perspective on complete and reduced factorial designs. *Psychological Methods, 14*(3), 202–224.

Cox, D. R. (1992). *Planning of experiments*. Hoboken: Wiley.

Dean, A., Voss, D., & Draguljić, D. (2017). *Design and analysis of experiments*. Cham: Springer.

Deutskens, E., de Ruyter, K., Wetzels, M., & Oosterveld, P. (2004). Response rate and response quality of internet-based surveys: An experimental study. *Marketing Letters, 15*(1), 21–36.

Ellis, P. D. (2010). *The essential guide to effect sizes: Statistical power, meta-analysis, and the interpretation of research results*. Cambridge: Cambridge University Press.

Eriksson, L., Johansson, E., Kettaneh-Wold, N., Wikström, C., & Wold, S. (2008). *Design of experiments: Principles and applications*. Stockholm: Umetrics AB, Umeå Learnways AB.

Evans, A. N., & Rooney, B. J. (2013). *Methods in psychological research*. Los Angeles: Sage.

Falk, A., & Heckman, J. J. (2009). Lab experiments are a major source of knowledge in the social sciences. *Science, 326*(5952), 535–538.

Feldman, J. M., & Lynch, J. G., Jr. (1988). Self-generated validity and other effects of measurement on belief, attitude, intention and behavior. *Journal of Applied Psychology, 73*(3), 421–435.

Festinger, L. A. (1957). *Theory of cognitive dissonance*. Stanford: Stanford University Press.

Fritz, C. O., Morris, P. E., & Richler, J. J. (2012). Effect size estimates: Current use, calculations, and interpretation. *Journal of Experimental Psychology: General, 141*(1), 2–18.

Glasman, L. R., & Albarracín, D. (2006). Forming attitudes that predict future behavior: A meta-analysis of the attitude-behavior relation. *Psychological Bulletin, 132*(5), 778–822.

Goodman, J. K., Cryder, C. E., & Cheema, A. (2013). Data collection in a flat world: The strengths and weaknesses of mechanical turk samples. *Journal of Behavioral Decision Making, 26*(3), 213–224.

Greenwald, A. G. (1976). Within-subjects designs: To use or not to use? *Psychological Bulletin, 83*(2), 314–320.

Hakel, M. D., Ohnesorge, J. P., & Dunnette, M. D. (1970). Interviewer evaluations of job applicants' resumes as a function of the qualifications of the immediately preceding applicants: An examination of contrast effects. *Journal of Applied Psychology, 54*(1, Pt.1), 27–30.

Hansen, R. A. (1980). A self-perception interpretation of the effect of monetary and nonmonetary incentives on mail survey respondent behavior. *Journal of Marketing Research, 17*(1), 77–83.

Harris, A. D., McGregor, J. C., Perencevich, E. N., Furuno, J. P., Zhu, J., Peterson, D. E., & Finkelstein, J. (2006). The use and interpretation of quasi-experimental studies in medical informatics. *Journal of the American Medical Informatics Association, 13*(1), 16–23.

Harrison, G. W., & List, J. A. (2003). *What constitutes a field experiment in economics? Working paper*. Columbia: Department of Economics, University of South Carolina http://faculty.haas.berkeley.edu/hoteck/PAPERS/field.pdf. Accessed 15 Mar 2018.

Harrison, G. W., & List, J. A. (2004). Field experiments. *Journal of Economic Literature, 42*(4), 1009–1055.

Hattula, J. D., Herzog, W., Dahl, D. W., & Reinecke, S. (2015). Managerial empathy facilitates egocentric predictions of consumer preferences. *Journal of Marketing Research, 52*(2), 235–252.

Hauser, D. J., & Schwarz, N. (2016). Attentive turkers: MTurk participants perform better on online attention checks than do subject pool participants. *Behavior Research Methods, 48*(1), 400–407.

Hegtvedt, K. A. (2014). Ethics and experiments. In M. Webster Jr. & J. Sell (Eds.), *Laboratory experiments in the social sciences* (pp. 23–51). Amsterdam/Heidelberg: Elsevier.

Hertwig, R., & Ortmann, A. (2008). Deception in experiments: Revisiting the arguments in its defense. *Ethics and Behavior, 18*(1), 59–92.

Hibbeln, M., Jenkins, J. L., Schneider, C., Valacich, J. S., & Weinmann, M. (2017). Inferring negative emotion from mouse cursor movements. *MIS Quarterly, 41*(1), 1–21.

Horswill, M. S., & Coster, M. E. (2001). User-controlled photographic animations, photograph-based questions, and questionnaires: Three internet-based instruments for measuring drivers' risk-taking behavior. *Behavior Research Methods, Instruments, & Computers, 33*(1), 46–58.

Kalkoff, W., Youngreen, R., Nath, L., & Lovaglia, M. J. (2014). Human participants in laboratory experiments in the social sciences. In M. Webster Jr. & J. Sell (Eds.), *Laboratory experiments in the social sciences* (pp. 127–144). Amsterdam/Heidelberg: Elsevier.

Koschate-Fischer, N., & Schandelmeier, S. (2014). A guideline for designing experimental studies in marketing research and a critical discussion of selected problem areas. *Journal of Business Economics, 84*(6), 793–826.

Kuipers, K. J., & Hysom, S. J. (2014). Common problems and solutions in experiments. In M. Webster Jr. & J. Sell (Eds.), *Laboratory experiments in the social sciences* (pp. 127–144). Amsterdam/Heidelberg: Elsevier.

Larsen, R. J., & Fredrickson, B. L. (1999). Measurement issues in emotion research. In D. Kahneman, E. Diener, & N. Schwarz (Eds.), *Well-being: Foundations of hedonic psychology* (pp. 40–60). New York: Russell Sage.

Laugwitz, B. (2001). *A web-experiment on colour harmony principles applied to computer user interface design*. Lengerich: Pabst Science.

Levitt, S. D., & List, J. A. (2007). Viewpoint: On the generalizability of lab behaviour to the field. *Canadian Journal of Economics, 40*(2), 347–370.

Li, J. Q., Rusmevichientong, P., Simester, D., Tsitsiklis, J. N., & Zoumpoulis, S. I. (2015). The value of field experiments. *Management Science, 61*(7), 1722–1740.

List, J. A. (2011). Why economists should conduct field experiments and 14 tips for pulling one off. *The Journal of Economic Perspectives, 25*(3), 3–15.

Lynch, J. G. (1982). On the external validity of experiments in consumer research. *Journal of Consumer Research, 9*(3), 225–239.

Lynch, J. G., Marmorstein, H., & Weigold, M. F. (1988). Choices from sets including remembered brands: Use of recalled attributes and prior overall evaluations. *Journal of Consumer Research, 15*(2), 169–184.

Madzharov, A. V., Block, L. G., & Morrin, M. (2015). The cool scent of power: Effects of ambient scent on consumer preferences and choice behavior. *Journal of Marketing, 79*(1), 83–96.

Maxwell, S. E., & Delaney, H. D. (2004). *Designing experiments and analyzing data: A model comparison perspective*. Mahwah: Lawrence Erlbaum Associates.

Meyvis, T., & Van Osselaer, S. M. J. (2018). Increasing the power of your study by increasing the effect size. *Journal of Consumer Research, 44*(5), 1157–1173.

Mitra, A., & Lynch, J. G. (1995). Toward a reconciliation of market power and information theories of advertising effects on price elasticity. *Journal of Consumer Research, 21*(4), 644–659.

Montgomery, D. C. (2009). *Design and analysis of experiments*. New York: Wiley.

Morales, A. C., Amir, O., & Lee, L. (2017). Keeping it real in experimental research—Understanding when, where, and how to enhance realism and measure consumer behavior. *Journal of Consumer Research, 44*(2), 465–476.

Morton, R. B., & Williams, K. C. (2010). *Experimental political science and the study of causality: From nature to the lab*. New York: Cambridge University Press.

Myers, H., & Lumbers, M. (2008). Understanding older shoppers: A phenomenological investigation. *Journal of Consumer Marketing, 25*(5), 294–301.

Nielsen, J. (2000). Why you only need to test with 5 users. https://www.nngroup.com/articles/why-you-only-need-to-test-with-5-users. Accessed 15 Mar 2018.

Nielsen, J. (2012). How many test users in a usability study. https://www.nngroup.com/articles/how-many-test-users. Accessed 15 Mar 2018.

Nisbett, R. E. (2015). *Mindware: Tools for smart thinking*. New York: Farrar, Straus and Giroux.

Nordhielm, C. L. (2002). The influence of level of processing on advertising repetition effects. *Journal of Consumer Research, 29*(3), 371–382.

Oppenheimer, D. M., Meyvis, T., & Davidenko, N. (2009). Instructional manipulation checks: Detecting satisficing to increase statistical power. *Journal of Experimental Social Psychology, 45*(4), 867–872.

Pascual-Leone, A., Singh, T., & Scoboria, A. (2010). Using deception ethically: Practical research guidelines for researchers and reviewers. *Canadian Psychology, 51*(4), 241–248.

Peer, E., Brandimarte, L., Samat, S., & Acquisti, A. (2017). Beyond the Turk: Alternative platforms for crowdsourcing behavioral research. *Journal of Experimental Social Psychology, 70*, 153–163.

Perdue, B. C., & Summers, J. O. (1986). Checking the success of manipulations in marketing experiments. *Journal of Marketing Research, 23*(4), 317–326.

Pirlott, A. G., & MacKinnon, D. P. (2016). Design approaches to experimental mediation. *Journal of Experimental Social Psychology, 66*(September), 29–38.

Postmes, T., Spears, R., & Cihangir, S. (2001). Quality of decision making and group norms. *Journal of Personality and Social Psychology, 80*(6), 918–930.

Rashotte, L. S., Webster, M., & Whitmeyer, J. M. (2005). Pretesting experimental instructions. *Sociological Methodology, 35*(1), 151–175.

Reips, U.-D. (2002). Standards for internet-based experimenting. *Experimental Psychology, 49*(4), 243–256.

Remler, D. K., & Van Ryzin, G. G. (2010). *Research methods in practice: Strategies for description and causation*. Thousand Oaks: Sage.

Reynolds, N., Diamantopoulos, A., & Schlegelmilch, B. (1993). Pretesting in questionnaire design: A review of the literature and suggestions for further research. *Journal of the Market Research Society, 35*(2), 171–183.

Robertson, D. H., & Bellenger, D. N. (1978). A new method of increasing mail survey responses: Contributions to charity. *Journal of Marketing Research, 15*(4), 632–633.

Sawyer, A. G., & Ball, A. D. (1981). Statistical power and effect size in marketing research. *Journal of Marketing Research, 18*(3), 275–290.

Sawyer, A. G., Lynch, J. G., & Brinberg, D. L. (1995). A bayesian analysis of the information value of manipulation and confounding checks in theory tests. *Journal of Consumer Research, 21*(4), 581–595.

Sears, D. O. (1986). College sophomores in the laboratory: Influences of a narrow data base on social psychology's view of human nature. *Journal of Personality and Social Psychology, 51*(3), 515–530.

Shadish, W. R., Cook, T. D., & Campbell, D. T. (2002). *Experimental and quasi-experimental designs for generalized causal inference*. Boston: Houghton Mifflin.

Sieber, J. E. (1992). *Planning ethically responsible research: A guide for students and internal review boards*. Newbury Park: Sage.

Simester, D. (2017). Field experiments in marketing. In E. Duflo & A. Banerjee (Eds.), *Handbook of economic field experiments* Amsterdam: North-Holland (pp. 465–497).

Singer, E., & Couper, M. P. (2008). Do incentives exert undue influence on survey participation? Experimental evidence. *Journal of Empirical Research on Human Research Ethics, 3*(3), 49–56.

Singer, E., Van Hoewyk, J., Gebler, N., & McGonagle, K. (1999). The effect of incentives on response rates in interviewer-mediated surveys. *Journal of Official Statistics, 15*(2), 217–230.

Smith, V. L., & Walker, J. M. (1993). Rewards, experience and decision cost in first price auctions. *Economic Inquiry, 31*(2), 237–244.

Spencer, S. J., Zanna, M. P., & Fong, G. T. (2005). Establishing a causal chain: Why experiments are often more effective than mediational analyses in examining psychological processes. *Journal of Personality and Social Psychology, 89*(6), 845–851.

Stuart, E. A., & Rubin, D. B. (2007). Best practices in quasi-experimental designs: Matching methods for causal inference. In J. Osborne (Ed.), *Best practices in quantitative methods* (pp. 155–176). New York. Thousand Oaks, CA: Sage.

Thye, S. R. (2014). Logical and philosophical foundations of experimental research in the social sciences. In M. Webster Jr. & J. Sell (Eds.), *Laboratory experiments in the social sciences* (pp. 53–82). Amsterdam/Heidelberg: Elsevier.

Trafimow, D., Leonhardt, J. M., Niculescu, M., & Payne, C. (2016). A method for evaluating and selecting field experiment locations. *Marketing Letters, 7*(3), 437–447.

Trafimow, D., & Rice, S. (2009). What if social scientists had reviewed great scientific works of the past? *Perspectives on Psychological Science, 4*(1), 65–78.

Verlegh, P. W. J., Schifferstein, H. N. J., & Wittink, D. R. (2002). Range and number-of-levels effects in derived and stated measures of attribute importance. *Marketing Letters, 13*(1), 41–52.

Völckner, F., & Hofmann, J. (2007). The price-perceived quality relationship: A meta-analytic review and assessment of its determinants. *Marketing Letters, 18*(3), 181–196.

Wetzel, C. G. (1977). Manipulation checks: A reply to kidd. *Representative Research in Social Psychology, 8*(2), 88–93.

Zhao, X., Lynch, J. G., Jr., & Chen, Q. (2010). Reconsidering baron and kenny: Myths and truths about mediation analysis. *Journal of Consumer Research, 37*(2), 197–206.

Zikmund, W., & Babin, B. (2006). *Exploring marketing research*. Mason: Thomson South-Western.

Field Experiments

Veronica Valli, Florian Stahl, and Elea McDonnell Feit

Contents

Introduction	38
Motivation	38
Defining a Field Experiment	40
Experimentation: Causal Inference and Generalizability	44
Estimating the Causal Effect of a Treatment	44
Generalizability of Findings and External Validity	50
Sample Size	51
Experimental Design and Multivariate Experiments	53
Examples of Field Experiments	57
Case Studies	57
Conclusions	62
Cross-References	63
References	63

Abstract

Digitalization of value chains and company processes offers new opportunities to measure and control a firm's activities and to make a business more efficient by better understanding markets, competitors, and consumers' behaviors. Among other methodologies, field experiments conducted in online and offline environments are rapidly changing the way companies make business decisions. Simple A/B tests as well as more complex multivariate experiments are increasingly employed by managers to inform their marketing decisions.

V. Valli (✉) · F. Stahl
University of Mannheim, Mannheim, Germany
e-mail: veronica.valli@bwl.uni-mannheim.de; florian.stahl@bwl.uni-mannheim.de

E. M. Feit
LeBow College of Business, Drexel University, Philadelphia, PA, USA
e-mail: efeit@drexel.edu

© Springer Nature Switzerland AG 2022
C. Homburg et al. (eds), *Handbook of Market Research*,
https://doi.org/10.1007/978-3-319-57413-4_3

This chapter explains why field experiments are a reliable way to reveal and to prove that a business action results in a desired outcome and provides guidelines on how to perform such experiments step by step covering issues such as randomization, sample selection, and data analysis. Various practical issues in the design of field experiments are covered with the main focus on causal inference and internal and external validity. We conclude the chapter with a practical case study as well as a brief literature review on recent published articles employing field experiments as a data collection method, providing the reader with a list of examples to consider and to refer to when conducting and designing a field experiment.

Keywords

Field experiment · A/B test · Randomized experiment · Online experiment · Digital experiment · Business optimization · Causal inference · Experimental design · Internal validity · External validity

Introduction

In God we trust, all others must bring data (Edward W. Deming[1]).

Motivation

Digitalization of value chains and company processes offers new opportunities to measure and control a firm's activities and to make a business more efficient by better understanding markets, competitors, and consumers' behaviors. Among others, the advent of two main sets of methodologies is changing the way organizations do business in the current digital age:

1. *Big Data Analytics*: data mining, machine learning, and other statistical techniques allow practitioners to handle and analyze huge sets of data with a reasonable effort.
2. *Business Field Experiments*: studies conducted outside of the lab by means of easy-to-use software allow managers to reliably answer causality questions at reasonable costs. At the same time, field experiments have become a primary method for investigating scientific phenomena and that is why this chapter considers field experiments aimed at testing theories, of the same importance as those aimed at testing tactical business strategies.

---

[1]Edward W. Deming was an eminent engineer, statistician, professor, and management consultant for more than half a century. His work on statistical process control and other strategies for data-driven decision making continues to be relevent today.

With the primary objective of informing marketing decisions, the fundamental value of market research is the collection, analysis, and interpretation of market-related information (Homburg et al. 2013). Depending on the objective, the research design can be exploratory, descriptive, or causal (Aaker et al. 2011). In particular, the *causal design* is the best approach to identify cause-effect relationships between variables based on preformulated hypotheses (Homburg 2015). Especially for practitioners, answers to the question "does A cause B?" are essential to derive managerial implications (Iacobucci and Churchill 2010), and, in such a context, an experiment is the most suitable and most popular method to establish causality (Crook et al. 2009; Homburg et al. 2013). For example, consider a marketer wishing to know the impact that a 20% discount will have on the proportion of customers making a purchase during a holiday sale. In such a case, comparing sales between a group of customers who were randomly chosen to be offered the discount and another group who was randomly assigned to not receive the offer will give a direct estimate of the incremental sales lift of the discount. For this reason, market researchers and other practitioners are increasingly making use of experiments in the field. Similarly academics have turned to field experiments, when once there was little experimentation outside of the lab. Field experiments are not only applied to inform almost every type of marketing decision (promotions, communications, visual designs, pricing, optimization of digital services, etc.) but also in disparate areas including business organization, product development, health care, human resource management, politics, and so on. As software tools and expertise grow, there are more and more A/B testing case studies showing that the practice of testing is becoming increasingly popular with small- and medium-sized businesses as well as with larger ones (see "A/B Testing Case Studies" on Optimizely.com for many examples of online field experiments or Applied Predictive Technologies Case Studies on www.pre dictivetechnologies.com for examples of offline field experiments).

The first field experiments in business practice date back to the first half of the 1900s when experiments revolutionized agriculture and created massive gains in farm productivity. Toward the end of that century, experiments became popular in manufacturing to improve production and quality. At their early stages, especially in firms that focused on product design and engineering, experiments were tremendously costly and often involved the destruction of expensive prototypes, such as in automotive crash testing. Nowadays, the digitalization of value chains has created a data-rich environment that offers both new challenges and new opportunities to managers, policy makers, and researchers, as also recognized in the recent (2014–2016) research priorities of the Marketing Science Institute (MSI). In such an environment, it is possible to measure market response at a much faster speed, allowing managers to track key economic parameters. These tracking skills allow companies to develop more effective business strategies to increase customer retention and loyalty or spending on products and/or services. This increased digitalization has also turned experiments into an economically feasible way to improve marketing decisions. Many marketers are embracing a *test and learn* philosophy with the aid of several platforms, such as Optimizely, Adobe Target, Applied Predictive Technologies (APT), Visual Website Optimizer

(VWO), Oracle Maxymiser, and Google Content Experiments, providing easy-to-use software to perform rigorous field experiments in the online and offline environments.

The primary scope of this chapter is to provide an answer to those readers who may be asking themselves: "why should I consider setting-up a field experiment to answer my research or business question?"

As a first answer, bear in mind the following hallmarks of well-designed field experiments:

- Field experiments are one of the most reliable ways to test a theory or to prove that a business action results in a desired outcome.
- Findings from field experiments have direct implications for business operations. In the language of experimentation, we say that they generalize well and have high external validity. On the other hand, lab experiments are acknowledged to have higher internal validity.
- Field experiments are easy to explain to business leaders and policy makers.

Throughout the following pages, we are going to explain each of the aforementioned points in depth advocating a major focus on business-related field experiments and online experiments (A/B tests).

Defining a Field Experiment

Field experimentation represents the conjunction of two methodological strategies: *experimentation* and *fieldwork*.

Defining an Experiment

Experimentation is a form of investigation in which units of observation are randomly assigned to treatment groups. Ex ante randomization ensures that the experimental groups have the same expected outcomes, which is fundamental to achieve an unbiased estimate of the causal effect of the treatment. Experimentation stands opposite to *observational investigations*, in which researchers attempt to draw inference from naturally occurring variations, as opposed to variations generated through random assignment (Gerber and Green 2008). However, some authors (e.g., Teele 2014) prefer to not exclude nonrandomized studies from the group of experiments, while others refer to studies without randomization as quasi-experiments (cf. Campbell and Stanley 1963).

An experiment involves the manipulation of the *independent* (or *explanatory*) variables in a systematic way which is then followed by the observation and measurement of the effect on the *dependent* (or *response*) variable, while any other variables that might affect the treatment are controlled or randomized over (Aaker et al. 2011; Iacobucci and Churchill 2010). For instance, in testing the impact of a 20% off promotion on sales, the researcher manipulates the independent variable of promotion between the two levels of 20% and zero and measures customer purchases as the response variable.

From the perspective of Dunning (2012), true experiments (either in the lab or in the field) show three identifiable aspects:

1. The responses of experimental subjects assigned to receive one treatment are compared to the responses of subjects assigned to another treatment (often a control group which receives some type of baseline treatment that is essentially *no treatment* or the *state-of-the-art* condition). In the case of multivariate experiments, there are several treatment groups, which are all compared among each other.
2. The assignment of subjects to each group is done through a randomization device, such as a coin flip, a dice roll, or a digital algorithm.
3. The manipulation of the treatment is under the control of an experimental researcher.

Some *observational studies* share attribute number 1 of true experiments, in that treatment conditions' outcomes are compared. However, they do not share attributes number 2 and 3 as there is no randomization of treatment assignment and there is no treatment manipulation. On the other side, *natural experiments* share attribute 1 and partially attribute 2 since assignment is random or as-if random. However, in such cases, data comes from naturally occurring phenomena, and therefore the manipulation of treatment variables is not generally under the researcher's control. Natural experiments consider the treatment itself as an experiment and employ naturally occurring variations as a proxy for random assignment. In particular, the treatment is not assigned by a researcher but by some rule-based process that can be mathematically modeled (Teele 2014). Without it, other *confounder* variables could easily explain ex post differences between observed units (Dunning 2012).

Lab Versus Field Experiments

Depending on the setting employed, one can distinguish between laboratory and field experiments (Homburg 2015). In *laboratory experiments*, participants are tested in an environment which is created by the researcher and which thus differs from reality (Aaker et al. 2011). This unreal environment allows the experimenter to control other potential influences on the response but has the main drawback of making the respondent feel observed, which can lead to several kinds of response bias. In addition, the respondents who are willing to participate in a lab experiment may not represent the target population as a whole, and then findings might not be generalizable.

Outside of the lab environment, it is possible to run *field experiments*, in which the setting is an everyday life situation, often the exact same setting where the findings from the experiment will be deployed (Gerber and Greene 2012). In most field experiments, participants are not even conscious of taking part in an experiment (Aaker et al. 2011; Gneezy 2017) eliminating the risk of incurring a response bias.

Just as experiments are designed to test causal claims with minimal reliance on assumptions, experiments conducted in real-world settings are designed to make generalizations less dependent on assumptions (Gerber and Green 2012). Further, especially in digital environments such as websites, adequate sample sizes can be much more easily reached than in offline settings or labs, and randomization over large samples protects against the possibility that a variable other than the treatment is causing the response. Since the aim of this chapter is to provide a complete overview of the topic, a few issues discussed (e.g., issues related to causality, treatment effects, randomization, sources of bias, etc.) apply to experiments in general and therefore to both field and lab experiments. The reader will excuse the unavoidable overlap of some content with other chapters in this book.

Key Features of Field Experiments

Field experiments, either online or offline, can take many forms, but all have four key features that make them a field experiment: authenticity of treatments, representativeness of participants, real-world context, and relevant outcome measures. Indeed, the degree of fieldness of an experiment can vary dramatically; some field experiments may seem naturalistic on all dimensions, while others may be more dependent on assumptions. In a nutshell, what constitutes a field experiment depends on how the field itself is defined (Gerber and Green 2012). Harrison and List (2004) offer a classification system ranking field experiments depending on their degree of realism. The taxonomy they propose is based on six dimensions: (1) nature of the subject pool, (2) nature of the information that the subjects bring to the task, (3) nature of the commodity, (4) nature of the task, (5) nature of the stakes, and (6) nature of the environment that the subject operates in. Harrison and List (2004) propose the following terminology:

- The *conventional lab experiment* employs a convenient subject pool (typically students[2]), an abstract framing, and an imposed set of rules.
- The *artifactual field experiment* is akin to the lab experiment but involving a nonstandard (i.e., non-students) subject pool. With the term artifactual, the authors want to denote studies with an empirical approach that is artificial or synthetic in certain dimensions.
- The *framed field experiment* is akin to the artifactual field experiment but involving a realistic task and the natural environment of the tested subjects that are conscious of being tested. The term framed denotes the fact that the experiment is organized in the field context of the subjects (e.g., social experiments).
- The *natural field experiment* is akin to the framed field experiment involving the environment where subjects naturally undertake the tasks but with the subjects being unaware of participating in an experiment, that is, either online or offline depending on the nature of the setting under examination. Since participants in

---

[2]For an interesting discussion on the choice of participants for an experiment and the questionability of employing students, refer to Koschate-Fisher and Schandelmeier (2014).

this kind of experiments are a representative, randomly chosen, and non-self-selected subset of the treatment population of interest, the causal effect obtained from this type of experiment is the average causal effect for the full population, not for a nonrandom subset that chooses to participate (List 2011).

Online Experiments

Online experiments are a special form of field experiments and their simplest form is commonly referred to as *A/B test*. As shown in Fig. 1, this method involves random assignment of users to two different treatments, typically the current (or A) version and the new (or B) version (Kohavi et al. 2009). In particular, it involves the following steps:

- Randomly divide customers into groups.
- Expose each group to a different treatment.
- Measure one or more selected response variables (also called overall evaluation criteria or key performance indicators, such as conversion rates, click-through rate, revenues, etc.) for both groups.
- Compare groups by mean of data analysis to determine which treatment is better.

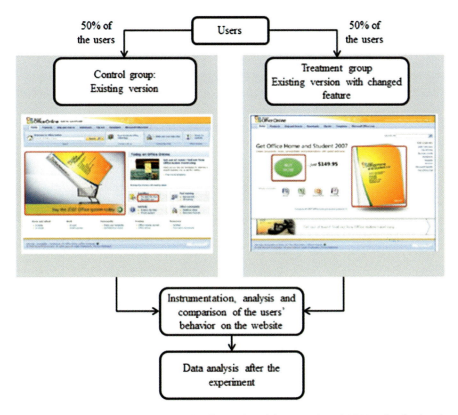

Fig. 1 Example of A/B test on Microsoft Office (Adapted from Crook et al. 2009 and Kohavi et al. 2009)

Field experiments did not start with digital marketing, and they are certainly not limited to digital marketing, but the digital environment has made testing easier and more popular as a way to inform managers' decisions. Managers are slowly accepting that carefully observing how customers respond to changes in marketing is more reliable than their experience and intuition.

Experimentation: Causal Inference and Generalizability

Whether it is a simple A/B test to choose the subject line for an email or a complex field experiment to test an economic theory, there are two main issues that the researcher must consider in designing an experiment. The first is whether the experiment has successfully measured the causal effect of the treatment within the context that the experiment is conducted (called *internal validity*). The second is whether the specific findings of the experiment can be generalized to other settings (called *external validity*). In this section, we discuss these two main issues in turn.

Estimating the Causal Effect of a Treatment

The Average Treatment Effect

Field experiments such as A/B tests allow managers to reveal the causal relationship between actions the company might take, such as price promotions (the *cause*), and consumers' purchase decisions (the *effect*). In other words, the goal of a field experiment is to determine whether a particular cause (such as a 20% price promotion) is responsible for an effect (such as a consumer's increased likelihood to purchase a particular product) and to exclude the reverse. Estimating the causal effect of an action has been a golden standard in the social sciences and in economic research for decades, and, as John List (2011) reminds us, economists have long worked on approaches that seek to separate cause and effect in naturally occurring data. For instance, instrumental variable regression aims at isolating cause-effect relationships. Field experiments use randomization as an instrumental variable, which, by construction, is uncorrelated with other variables that might affect the outcome (List 2011). However, there are a few key assumptions that must be met in order for experiments to provide reliable assessments of cause and effect (Gerber and Green 2012, Imbens and Rubin 2015). First, we provide a definition of *causal effect*: a causal effect is the difference between two potential outcomes, one in which a subject receives the treatment and the other in which the subject does not receive the treatment. In formulas:

$$\tau_i \equiv Y_i(1) - Y_i(0)$$

where (τ_i) is the causal effect of the treatment and $Y_i(1)$ is the potential outcome if the ith subject receives the treatment while $Y_i(0)$ is the potential outcome if the ith subject does not receive the treatment. For example, $Y_i(1)$ might be an indicator for whether the customer would make a purchase if she receives the promotion, and $Y_i(0)$ would be an indicator for whether the customer would make a purchase without the promotion.

Of course, it is typically not possible to directly observe both conditions for any given subject, but it is possible to estimate the average treatment effect (ATE) among all subjects, when certain assumptions are met. The ATE is defined as the sum of the subject-level treatment effects, $Y_i(1) - Y_i(0)$ divided by the total number of subjects. In formulas:

$$ATE \equiv \frac{1}{N} \sum_{i=1}^{N} \tau_i$$

The challenge in estimating the ATE is that at a given point in time, subject i is either treated or non-treated, and therefore either $Y_i(1)$ or $Y_i(0)$ is observed, but not both. Some statisticians conceptualize this as a missing data problem where either $Y_i(1)$ or $Y_i(0)$ is unobserved for each subject (Imbens and Rubin 2015).

Experiments, both in the lab and in the field, provide unbiased estimates of the ATE when the following assumptions are met (Gerber and Green 2012):

1. *Random assignment*: treatments are allocated such that all units have an equal probability between 0 and 1 of being assigned to the treatment group.
2. *Excludability*: the treatment must be defined clearly so that one can assess whether subjects are exposed to the intended treatment or to something else.
3. *Noninterference*: no matter which subjects the random assignment allocates to treatment or control, a given subject's potential outcomes remain the same.

Let us consider the three assumptions in more depth.

Random assignment is fundamental in experimentation, with roots that go back as far as Neyman (1923) and Fisher (1925). It implies that treatment assignments are statistically independent of the subjects' potential outcomes and addresses the missing data issue that challenges the estimate of the ATE, that is, the issue that at a given point in time, subject i is either treated or non-treated and therefore either $Y_i(1)$ or $Y_i(0)$ is observed, but not both. In fact, when treatments are allocated randomly, the treatment group is a random sample of the population in the experiment, and therefore the expected potential outcomes among subjects in the treatment group are identical to the average potential outcomes among the control group. Therefore, in expectation, the treatment group's potential outcomes are the same as the control group. When units are randomly assigned to treatment and control, a comparison of average outcomes in treatment and control groups, the so-called *difference-in-means* estimator, is an unbiased estimator of the ATE. In formulas, the estimator is:

$$\frac{1}{N} \sum_{i \in \text{treated}} Y_i - \frac{1}{M} \sum_{i \in \text{control}} Y_i$$

where N is the number of subjects in the treatment group and M is the number of subjects in the control group. We can see that the expected value of the estimator is equal to the ATE, meaning it is unbiased:

$$E\left[\frac{1}{N} \sum_{i \in \text{treated}} Y_i - \frac{1}{M} \sum_{i \in \text{control}} Y_i\right] = E\left[\frac{1}{N} \sum_{i \in \text{treated}} Y_i\right]$$

$$-E\left[\frac{1}{M} \sum_{i \in \text{control}} Y_i\right] = E[Y_i(1)] - E[Y_i(0)] = E[\tau_i] = ATE$$

When random assignment is not used, there is always potential for a *selection bias*, where the treatment assignment is systematically related to potential outcomes. For example, if we want to measure the effect of a call from a sales agent and we do not randomize calls between customers, the sales agent may choose to call those customers that she/he feels are most likely to buy. This will produce an upward bias in our estimate of the ATE. The key idea is that randomized assignment allows us to use simple averages of the outcome for the treatment and control group to estimate the average treatment effect.

Excludability refers to the fact that each potential outcome depends *solely* on whether the subject *itself* receives the treatment and not on some other feature of the experiment. Therefore, when conducting an experiment, we must define the treatment and distinguish it from other factors with which it may be correlated. Specifically, we must distinguish between d_i, the treatment, and z_i, a variable that indicates which observations have been allocated to treatment or control. We seek to estimate the effect of d_i, and we assume that the treatment assignment z_i has no effect on the outcomes. In other words, the exclusion restriction refers to the assumption that z_i can be omitted from the potential outcomes for $Y_i(1)$ and $Y_i(0)$, and this restriction fails when random assignment sets in motion causes of Y_i other than the treatment. In real life, and therefore in field experiments in particular, it can become difficult to ensure excludability. Consider, for example, an A/B test investigating the impact of a discount on purchase decisions. If being assigned to receive a discount also means that the customer will get an email and customers in the treatment group do not get an email, then the excludability assumption is not met, and any observed difference between the treatment and control groups may be due to the email and not to the discount. A straightforward example of a research design that attempts to isolate a specific cause is a pharmaceutical trial in which the treatment group is given an experimental pill while the control group is given an esthetically identical sugar pill. The aim of administering a pill to both groups is to isolate the pharmacological effects of the ingredients, holding constant the effect of merely taking some sort of pill (*placebo effect*).

How can we make sure that the excludability assumption is met and that we are able to isolate the specific cause we intend to? Basically, by ensuring uniform handling of treatment and control groups, for instance, with double blindness, neither the subjects nor the researchers charged with measuring outcomes are aware of which treatments the subjects receive, so that they cannot consciously or unconsciously distort the results. Another procedure is parallelism when administrating an experiment: the same procedures should be used for both treatment and control groups, and both groups' outcomes should be gathered at approximately the same time and under similar conditions (Gerber and Green 2012). In online experiments, meeting excludability assumptions might seem easier; however, consider, for instance, a test of several versions of the same webpage showing prices and promotions for a given brand. Randomization algorithms ensure that different customers shopping from different laptops and IP addresses see different versions. But if, unluckily, two people sitting one next to the other and surfing the same webpage from different terminals but in the same location see different versions (having been assigned to different treatment groups), we might incur in a violation of the exclusion restriction, as recognizing the different versions can confound the causal effect we set out to estimate. In such cases, precise geolocalization and a randomization procedure that considers such geographical information could help solve the problem.

Noninterference refers to the fact that potential outcomes are defined over the set of treatments that the subject *itself* receives, not the treatments assigned to other subjects. This assumption is sometimes called the Stable Unit Treatment Value Assumption (SUTVA). Considering that each observational unit is either treated or not treated, the number of potential outcomes to take into account can quickly increase if we allow the outcome for subject i to depend on the treatment assignment of another subject j. The noninterference assumption cuts through this complexity by assuming that the outcome for i is not affected by the treatment of other subjects (Gerber and Green 2012; Imbens and Rubin 2015). Consider, for instance, when an A/B test is conducted on an e-commerce website offering promotions to a targeted subsample of existing customers and not to some others. Noninterference would assume that purchase decisions of subject i were only affected by his/her personal assignment to treatment or control group. But what if, for instance, two subjects belonging to the same household, say two sisters, are shopping from the same website and one falls into the treatment but the other one falls into the control? Then, we might have violation of noninterference as the treatment received by one sister can affect the other that therefore no longer constitutes an untreated control group. To prevent this from happening, researchers should try to design experiments in ways that minimize interference between units by spreading them out temporally or geographically or to design experiments in ways that allow researchers to detect spillover between units. Instead of treating interference as a nuisance, these more complex experimental designs aim to detect evidence of communication or strategic interaction among units.

Causality and Internal Validity

The previous section described the issues involved in estimating the causal effects as they are typically discussed in economics (Gerber and Green 2012) and statistics (Imbens and Rubin 2015). Psychologists also have a rich tradition of describing problems that can occur in experiments and have coined the term *internal validity* which refers to the extent to which we can say the observed effect in our study was caused by our treatment (Campbell 1957; Campbell and Stanley 1963; Shadish et al. 2002). Many of the ideas in this section are closely related to the previous discussion of the conditions necessary to estimate the causal average treatment effects, but using a different set of terms. Since both perspectives on experiments are common in marketing, we present both.

To achieve high internal validity, laboratory experiments are generally more suitable. This is because the controlled environment allows for better control of confounders. However, depending on the field considered, the natural environment can be highly controlled as well, especially in digital settings. In general, when considering studies that go beyond the randomized controlled experiment, there are many threats to internal validity, some of which we have discussed previously and most of which apply to both field and lab experiments:

- *Selection bias*: when assignment to treatment is not random and certain types of people are more likely to receive one of the treatments, in other words the experimental groups systematically differ from each other either because of self-selection (e.g., by voluntary choosing whether to receive the treatment) or by incorrect assignment (Campbell 1957; Iacobucci and Churchill 2010; Shadish et al. 2002). For example, when running an offline field experiment to test the effect of marketing actions on purchase intentions, a selection bias could emerge due to self-selection of respondents into treatments. When treatments are not randomly assigned, the subjects or the experimenters may assign certain types of subjects to treatment and other types to the control. For example, if we are studying the effect of receiving emails on customer's purchase rate using observational data collected by the company, we have to consider that customers get to self-select whether to sign up for the mailing list, and so those who sign up may be systematically more likely to purchase than those who do not sign up. This is less likely to happen in online field experiments, as assignment to treatment groups is handled by the computer systems and mostly unnoticed by users who are often completely unaware of being tested.
- *Differential attrition*: when certain types of subjects drop out of one of the treatments. It implies that certain types of participants leave during the run of the experiment or do not take part in the final measurement (Aaker et al. 2011; Shadish et al. 2002), and this attrition is different for the treatment and the control groups. For instance, if you were testing an increase in the frequency of direct marketing, customers who have less affinity for the brand may be more likely to ask to be put on a "do not call" list when they are in the high-frequency condition. These participants would not complete the treatment and so typically would not

be counted in the analysis of the response. The direct consequence of differential attrition is that the average of the experimental group might differ if the exited participants were still involved (Iacobucci and Churchill 2010; Shadish et al. 2002).

- *Time effects*: when treatments are administered at two different times, outside events, learning, or other changes are confounded with the treatment (Shadish et al. 2002).
- *Confounding variables*: when other variables are correlated with the treatment and have an effect on the outcome, a cause-effect relationship between the confounder and the dependent variable can be mistakenly assumed to be a causal effect of the treatment.
- *Noncompliance*: subjects assigned to the experiment do not get the specified treatment. This can happen because of individuals' voluntary decision to use a different treatment than the one they were assigned, because they do not like it or they think another treatment would be better.
- *Diffusion of the treatment across groups*: subjects assigned to one treatment find out about the other treatment.
- *Demand effects*: participants guess hypothesis of the experiment and try to cooperate by exhibiting behavior that confirms the hypothesis.
- *Experimenter bias*: experimenter makes subjective measurements and inadvertently favors the hypothesis in those measurements. An experimenter bias may exist when the mere presence or interaction with the interviewer has an effect on the respondent's responses. Being interviewed about personal purchase intentions might arouse a sense of self-exposure that could lead to biased responses not reflecting the private true intentions. This is more often the case in face-to-face interviews and is quite unlikely to happen in lab experiments or in online field experiments.
- *Hawthorne effect*: it is also possible that individuals being part of an experiment and being monitored change their behavior due to the attention they are receiving from researchers rather than because of the manipulation of the independent variables. The Hawthorne effect was first described in the 1950s by researcher Henry A. Landsberger during his analysis of experiments conducted during the 1920s and 1930s at the Hawthorne works electric company in Illinois. His findings suggested that the novelty of being research subjects and the increased attention deriving from this could lead to temporary increases in workers' productivity. This is sometimes also referred to as the *John Henry effect* and is closely related to the *placebo effect* in medicine. This issue is easily overcome in many field experiments where subjects are unaware of being a subject in a test but is more likely to happen in lab experiments (Landsberger 1958).
- *Ambiguous temporal precedence*: In some experiments, it can be unclear whether the treatment was administered before or after the effect was measured. For instance, if purchases and promotional emails are tracked at a daily level, it can be difficult to discern if a customer who received an email on a particular day and also made a purchase that same day received the email before she made the

purchase. If the treatment does not occur before the outcome is measured, then the causality may be reversed.

Generalizability of Findings and External Validity

Often, we are interested in whether the conclusions of our experiment can be applied to a specific business decision. For instance, if we test a new product display in 30 stores within a chain and find that the new product display increases sales, then we want to know whether this finding will generalize to other stores in the chain or to other retailers. *External validity* refers to the extent to which the specific findings of the experiment can be generalized to other target populations or other similar situations (Campbell 1957; Shadish et al. 2002). If the study shows high external validity, we can say that the results can be *generalized*. Field experiments are largely acknowledged to better generalize to real situations than lab experiments because of the real setting in which they are deployed, although some have cautioned that field experiments conducted in one setting cannot always be generalized to other settings (Gneezy 2017).

The major threat to external validity is that some idiosyncrasy of the test situation (*context effect*) produced the effect, but the effect goes away in the target business environment. For instance, while an ad may perform well in a copy test where customers are brought into a lab setting and exposed to the ad and then surveyed on their purchase intent, those results may not generalize to ad exposures in the real world, perhaps because people do not pay as much attention to ads in the real world as they do in the lab. Or a finding from a field experiment showing that price promotions increase sales of packaged goods may not extend to a different product category. For those familiar with regression, another way to conceptualize context effects is that there is an interaction between the treatment and some context variable that was held fixed in the experiment, such that the effect of the treatment is different depending on the value of that context variable (Campbell and Stanley 1963).

Another key element in designing an experiment with good external validity is determining which subjects to include in the experiment. Note that the assignment of subjects to treatments is closely related to the internal validity of the test, while the selection of subjects to include in the experiment is closely related to the external validity. The best way to enhance external validity is to test the research hypotheses on the entire population that the researcher hopes to learn about, e.g., all the customers in a CRM system or all the stores in a chain. This approach also maximizes the power of the test to detect differences between treatments, which we will discuss in the next section. Obviously, this is rarely possible outside of some digital marketing contexts either because of the high costs of applying treatments and measuring outcomes and/or the riskiness of the treatment.

To reduce risks and costs, researchers frequently rely on samples of subjects from the target population. Some sampling strategies that are available to use are (from ideal to worst):

- *Simple random sample:* take a random draw from the target population using, for instance, a coin flip or a dice roll. This gives to each subject an identical probability of entering the sample, ensuring that the sample will be representative of the target population.
- *Cluster sample*: when it is easy to measure groups or clusters of subjects, randomly sample from among the clusters.
- *Stratified sample*: use a procedure to make sure that the sample contains different types of subjects.
- *Convenience sample*: sample in some way that is easy for the researcher, e.g., an academic might conduct the experiment with students or a company might conduct the experiment using store locations that are nearby.

For instance, if a publishing company wants to evaluate whether a given promotion strategy works better than another and decides to run a field experiment, they have to consider the target population from which to sample. If their goal is to learn how their current customers respond, they might focus on customers from their current mailing list. However, if they hope to learn about how *potential* customers respond to the promotions, they might choose to sample customers from a larger list of avid readers. In either case, once the target population is identified, the ideal strategy for selecting a group of customers to include in the experiment is to either use all the customers in the target population, assigning some to treatment and some to control, or to select smaller treatment and control groups randomly from the mailing list. The simple random sample ensures that the subjects in the study represent the target population. A convenience sample, by contrast, may not properly represent the target population; for example, students may not behave in the same way as other types of customers. If the company plans to study separate subgroups within the target population, they may find a stratified sample useful for ensuring that there is sufficient sample size within each sub-group. Another potential threat to generalizability is the representativeness of the subjects in the test. A common criticism of experiments conducted with students, for instance, through surveys or lab experiments, is that the results may not reliably extend to the entire population of reference. Similarly, in online experiments the researcher should keep in mind that mostly heavy users of the website or app are more likely to be included in field experiments than light users. Most online tests include in the sample all the visitors in a fixed period, and this group will naturally include more frequent users than infrequent users. To overcome such issues, companies should consider test designs that assign treatments to users (rather than to sessions), track users across visits, and cap the number of times each user is exposed to the treatment.

Sample Size

A key question in designing any experiment is determining how many subjects to include in the test. Sample sizes for an A/B test are typically determined by considering the hypothesis test comparing the two groups. The typical A/B test in marketing estimates the average treatment effects by comparing the proportions of people who respond to two different stimuli. Following the traditional one-tailed test for comparing proportions, we begin with a null hypothesis that the proportion of people who respond will be the same in both groups versus an alternative that the A group responds in greater proportion than the B group:

$$H_0 = \pi_A = \pi_B = \pi$$
$$H_1 = \pi_A - \pi_B = \delta > 0$$

Our goal is to plan the number of subjects to include in the treatment and control groups so that we will be able to correctly retain the null hypothesis if there is no difference between treatments and reject the null if there is a difference of at least δ. In the extreme, if we have no subjects, then we clearly will always retain the null hypothesis no matter what. There are four aspects of the experiment that influence the expected required sample size for an A/B test:

- The expected proportion π
- The expected (minimum) difference between the two groups δ
- The desired confidence 1-α (where α is the significance)
- The desired power 1-β

The *confidence* is the likelihood that you will retain the null hypothesis and decide that there is no difference when there really is no difference. *Power* is the likelihood that you will reject the null and detect a difference when indeed there is a difference of at least δ. Both should be considered carefully in the design of an experiment. Consider, for example, an A/B test designed to determine the effect of an ad on the proportion of people who buy. In this case, we want high confidence to prevent the possibility of concluding that the ad has a positive effect when it, in fact, does not. We also want high power, to prevent concluding that that the ad does not work when, in fact, it does. For a given sample size, power and confidence can be traded off. Lewis and Rao (2015) find that for display advertisements, even A/B tests with very large sample size conducted at a traditional confidence level of 0.95 do not have sufficient power to detect whether an ad has positive ROI. Thus, it is critical to consider power when planning an A/B test.

The sample size for each group in a comparative A/B test can be accurately estimated by (Ledolter and Swersey 2007):

$$N \approx \frac{2\pi(1 - \pi)\left[z_{1-\alpha} + z_{1-\beta}\right]^2}{\delta^2}$$

where z_x is the cumulative normal distribution evaluated at x. This can be computed, for example, using the Excel formulas: $z_{1-\alpha} = NORM . S . INV(1 - \alpha)$ and $z_{1-\beta} = NORM . S . INV(1 - \beta)$.

One can see from this formula that if the researcher wants to detect a small difference, δ, in the response rate between the A and B groups, then a larger sample size is required. Similarly, if the researcher wishes to reduce the chance of an erroneous conclusion (i.e., that there is a difference when there is not or that there is not a difference when there is), then $z_{1-\alpha}$ and $z_{1-\beta}$ will be larger and the required sample sizes will be higher.

Note that this formula depends on the size of the difference that the marketer wishes to detect. In practice, it is very important to consider δ carefully. When a very large amount of data is available (for instance, from e-commerce websites), generating large datasets and big samples is much easier than few years ago. In such cases, it might happen that very negligible effects become significant (e.g., WTP is $10 in treatment group and $9.99 in control). While this effect is statistically significant, it does not really tell much about our business/research question and may not be useful for making decisions. So, in situations where N is not limited by the budget, it may be sensible to choose a smaller N so that the difference to detect, δ, is a difference that would be meaningful to the business. This is sometimes referred to as aligning practical and statistical significance.

Experimental Design and Multivariate Experiments

Managers frequently want to measure the effect of several different marketing actions (i.e., they are interested in more than one treatment). For instance, a publisher might be interested in assessing how different discount levels perform in combination with different ways of communicating the discount. They might be interested in measuring the effect of two levels of discount (say 5€ and 10€) while at the same time understanding the effect of communicating the price reduction in terms of price discount (e.g., "subscribe for one month and save x €!") or in terms of bonus time (e.g., "subscribe for 1 month and get x weeks free!"). A multivariate experiment can be used to simultaneously measure the effect of the discount level and the message type while also determining if there is any additional effect of combining two treatments together. When the combined effect of two treatments is better than the sum of the individual effects, there is an *interaction* effect. Detecting interactions is the main reason why companies conduct multivariate tests. In addition, multivariate tests can reduce required sample sizes and increase the amount that can be learned in the time frame of a single test.

Before approaching the technicalities of multivariate testing, we define some useful terminology. The *factors* are those variables (continuous or categorical) whose effect we want to study, e.g., ad copy, font, photo, and color in an advertisement or seed type, fertilizer, and amount of water for an agricultural experiment. In the experiment, each factor is tested at multiple *levels*, the different versions we want to test. The simplest A/B test comparing two treatments has 1 factor with two levels.

Multivariate tests are experiments where two or more factors are tested. Multivariate tests should be carried out when the researcher wants to know the relative effects of the different factors or when there might be combinations of levels that perform especially well together. If the effect of the two factors together is more (or less) than the sum of their separate effects, we say the two factors interact with each other. For instance, the text color and the background color of a call-to-action button typically interact: when the colors are the same, customers cannot read the button and do not respond.

For a better understanding of multivariate experiments, consider the following experiment (adapted from Ledolter and Swersey 2007) that was conducted by a credit card company who wanted to increase the response rate, that is, the number of people who respond to a credit card offer. The marketing team decided to study the effects of interest rates and fees, using the four factors shown in the following table.

	Factor	Level 1 ($-$)	Level 2 ($+$)
A	Annual fee	Current	Lower
B	Account-opening fee	No	Yes
C	Initial interest rate	Current	Lower
D	Long-term interest rate	Low	High

We could choose to study these factors with a series of A/B tests. Suppose we all agree that factor A (annual fee) is likely to be most important. Then we can run an A/B test on annual fee, holding the other factors at the control levels. The combination of factors and levels is clearly summarized in the following *design matrix*:

Run	A Annual fee	B Account-opening fee	C Initial interest rate	D Long-term interest rate	Sample
1	$-$	$-$	$-$	$-$	20,000
2	$+$	$-$	$-$	$-$	20,000

Suppose our first test found that the lower annual fee increased the response rate. So, we can fix the factor A to "$+$" and in our next A/B test, we can look at factor B:

Run	A Annual fee	B Account-opening fee	C Initial interest rate	D Long-term interest rate	Sample
3	$+$	$-$	$-$	$-$	20,000
4	$+$	$+$	$-$	$-$	20,000

Putting a sequence of these A/B tests together, we might end up with the following runs:

Run	A Annual fee	B Account-opening fee	C Initial interest rate	D Long-term interest rate	Sample
1	$-$	$-$	$-$	$-$	20,000
2	$+$	$-$	$-$	$-$	20,000
3	$+$	$-$	$-$	$-$	20,000
4	$+$	$+$	$-$	$-$	20,000
5	$+$	$-$	$-$	$-$	20,000
6	$+$	$-$	$+$	$-$	20,000
7	$+$	$-$	$-$	$-$	20,000
8	$+$	$-$	$-$	$+$	20,000

Looking back at the resulting set of runs, we might notice several serious problems:

- Before we run the first A/B tests, we do not really know which factor is most influential, so it is difficult to know where to start.
- We could be wasting time with the sequential process.
- We are sometimes running the same condition more than once, which is inefficient (runs 2, 3, 5, and 7 are all the same).
- Because we have not tested all combinations of factors, we have little information about the interactions between factors.
- If there are interactions, testing the factors in a different sequence could lead to different conclusions about which combination is best.

To overcome these issues, it is recommended to make use of a proper experimental design (commonly referred to as design of experiment, or DOE). In this example, a better approach creates a single test that includes every possible combination of levels (*full factorial design*) which allows us to see if there are certain combinations of factors which are particularly good and to reduce the sample sizes for each run. The full factorial design matrix, in this case, looks like this:

Run	A Annual fee	B Account-opening fee	C Initial interest rate	D Long-term interest rate	Sample
1	−	−	−	−	7500
2	+	−	−	−	7500
3	−	+	−	−	7500
4	+	+	−	−	7500
5	−	−	+	−	7500
6	+	−	+	−	7500
7	−	+	+	−	7500
8	+	+	+	−	7500
9	−	−	−	+	7500
10	+	−	−	+	7500
11	−	+	−	+	7500
12	+	+	−	+	7500
13	−	−	+	+	7500
14	+	−	+	+	7500
15	−	+	+	+	7500
16	+	+	+	+	7500

Note that the number of possible combinations for a design can be computed by multiplying together the number of levels (2) for each of the four factors ($2 \times 2 \times 2 \times 2 = 2^4 = 16$ combinations). It has become common to describe an experiment with multiple factors using this shorthand. For example, a $2^3 \times 5^1$ full factorial experiment has three factors that have two levels and one factor that has five levels, which is a total of 40 different combinations of the factors.

A full factorial design allows us to estimate the *main effects* of the factors and all *interactions* between factors. The *main effect* of a factor is defined as the change in the response variable when the level of the factor is changed from low to high and corresponds to the average treatment effect for an A/B test that we discussed in "Motivation". For a full factorial design, we can compute the main effect, by averaging the response rate across the runs when the level is at the high level and comparing that to the average across the runs at the low level. A two-way *interaction* occurs when the effect of one factor depends on the level of another factor (e.g., does the impact of having an annual fee depend on whether or not there is an account-opening fee?). *Three-* and *four-way interactions* are similar to two-way interactions, but are difficult to think about (e.g., is the effect of C different when both A and B are at their high levels?). Luckily, those higher-order interactions are usually negligible in most business settings. To estimate main effects and interactions for multivariate experiments, most researchers use *regression analysis*, fitting a model that relates the outcome measure to the various factors. If the subjects in a multivariate test are assigned to conditions randomly, the estimates of main effects and interactions that we get from this regression represent the *causal* effect of those treatments, just as in single-factor experiments.

In the example above, we show a full factorial test, where all the possible combinations of factors are tested. However, as the number of factors increases, the number of combinations increases rapidly. Therefore, researchers who use multivariate tests frequently spend a lot of time thinking about which combinations of factors they should include in their experiment and which they can leave out. One approach is *fractional factorial* design, which reduces the number of combinations to a half or a quarter of the possible combinations, by eliminating the possibility of estimating high-order (three-way and higher) interactions. A newer approach for determining which combinations of factors to include in a multivariate test is *optimal design*, which characterizes how much we learn from an experiment by considering how precisely we will be able to estimate the parameters of our regression model. Optimal designs choose the design matrix so as to get the best possible standard errors and covariance matrix for the parameter estimates. (See Goos and Jones 2011 for more detail.) Optimal design typically requires specialized software (e.g., JMP from SAS or the AlgDesign package in R) where the user inputs the factors and levels and the software finds the best combination of factors to test.

An important feature of good multivariate experimental designs is *orthogonality*. When two variables are orthogonal in an experiment, it means that the various combinations of the two factors occur exactly the same number of times. A nice property of orthogonal design is that the estimate of the effect of one factor will not depend on whether or not the other factor is controlled for in the regression. When the two factors are always set at the same level (e.g., the account opening fee is always paired with the annual fee), it is impossible to estimate separate effects for each factor, and this is called a *confound* in the multivariate design, which is the opposite of orthogonality. Full and fractional factorial designs maintain orthogonality, while optimal designs are not necessarily orthogonal, but are usually nearly orthogonal.

One common application of multivariate testing in marketing is in testing various features of direct mail offers: from the color of the envelope to the celebrity endorser's appeal. In this type of experiment, the direct marketer typically sends out a number of different direct marketing offers with varying levels of the features and then measures the number of customers who respond. In this context, additional cost is incurred for each different version of the mailing, and so fractional factorial and optimal design approaches, which reduce the number of required combinations, are valuable. Applying an optimal design or an orthogonal, fractional factorial design instead of a one-factor-at-a-time method increases the efficiency at evaluating the effects and possible interactions of several factors (independent variables).

Another important application of multivariate experimental design is *conjoint analysis*. In conjoint analysis, customers are asked to evaluate or to choose from a set of hypothetical products, where the products vary along a set of features. These product features become the factors in a multivariate experimental design. A common approach to creating the questions to include in a conjoint survey is to use optimal design (Sándor and Wedel 2001).

Examples of Field Experiments

Case Studies

Field Experiments in Business

Field experiments are rapidly becoming an important part of business practice, and many marketing-oriented firms now employ a testing manager, who is responsible for designing, executing, and reporting on field experiments to answer important questions. These testing managers often specialize in a particular part of the business or communication channel. For instance, one might find different specialists in website testing, email testing, and direct marketing experiments, all within the same company. Regardless of the specific platform, the goal of these testing managers is to find treatments to test, to determine how to measure the response to the treatments, to ensure that the test is designed so that it can be interpreted causally, and to analyze and report on the results. In the next subsection, we describe the testing program employed by the donation platform for the 2012 US presidential campaign for Barack Obama.

A major focus for the 2012 US presidential campaigns was fundraising. Several changes in regulation had made donations to political campaigns more important than ever, and so there was a major focus on the web platform where potential donors were encouraged to make small- and medium-sized donations. In their ongoing efforts to improve the platform, the team conducted more than 240 A/B tests over 6 months to determine which marketing messages worked best (Rush 2012a).

An important consideration for any testing team is deciding which features of the website platform to test. The ultimate determination of which features are worth testing should depend on the potential returns the firm can gain by acting on the findings of the test. The potential returns depend both on how much better the new treatments perform (which is of course unknown before the test) and how many customers will be affected by the treatment. Consequently, most testing teams choose to test features of their marketing that are seen by many customers and that they believe have a large potential to increase sales or other desired outcomes.

The team managing the donation platform for the Obama campaign tested several areas of the website including imagery, copy, and the donation process. Figure 2 shows an example of an image test that was used on the splash page, where potential donors arrived after clicking on a link describing a special campaign where donors could win a "Dinner with Barack" (adapted from Rush 2012b). The objective of the test was to learn whether the focused shot showing the candidate smiling (which they labeled as *control*) would perform better than the wide shot showing several attendees at a previous event chatting with the candidate and his wife (which they labeled as *variation*). Previous tests had shown that large images of the smiling candidate increased the donation rate, so the team hypothesized that the control image would perform better. The images were assigned randomly in real time to all visitors who clicked on a link to the splash page. The team used the Optimizely web-testing platform, which, like other web-testing platforms, handles the random assignment of treatments automatically and integrates with the web analytics platform to measure the response. The team assessed the performance of the two images, by comparing the percentage of people who made donations in the control group relative to the variation group. The team found that the wider shot showing previous guests at the table with the candidate resulted in a 19% increase in donations. Based on this finding, they quickly decided to change the splash page to the variation image for the remaining duration of the campaign.

Figure 3 shows another example of a test described by Rush (2012b) that involved website copy. The website had a feature that invited donors to store their payment information so that they could make donations in the future with one click. This was a very successful tool – by the end of the campaign more than 1.5 million

Fig. 2 Image test for Obama campaign (Adapted from Rush 2012b)

Field Experiments

Fig. 3 Copy test for Obama campaign (Adapted from Rush 2012b)

Quick Donate users donated $115 million – and so the team was anxious to find ways to get more donors to sign up for Quick Donate.

Figure 3 shows two versions of the page that donors saw just after making their donation. The control page asked customers: "save your payment information for next time," while the treatment page made it seem as if saving the payment information was part of the current process by saying: "now, save your payment information." When users were randomly assigned to the two treatments, the percentage of customers who saved their payment information was 21% greater among those who saw the *segue copy*.

This example raises a key issue that testing managers face in practice: how to measure the effect of the treatment. In this case, the team chose to compare treatments based on how many customers signed up for the Quick Donate program, and this is a logical choice as that is the immediate goal of these marketing treatments. However, Quick Donate sign-ups do not result in an immediate monetary gain for the campaign. One might also legitimately prefer to compare these two treatments based on how many actual donations are received in the subsequent month for those in each group, although this would require more time and tracking capability to measure effectively.

In field experiments in digital marketing, it is common to measure a variety of outcomes within the same experiment, both those that are directly related to the short- and long-term effects of the treatment and potential side effects such as increased costs or increased complaints. (Medical experiments face a similar challenge in defining response measures: in testing a new cancer treatment, researchers must decide whether to compare treatments based on a near-term outcome such as the recurrence of cancer in the subsequent 5 years or a longer-term outcome such as mortality in the next 20 years.)

The straightforward randomization and measurement available on the web platform allow for easy causal interpretation of the results, which in turn makes it easy for decision makers to act immediately on the findings without much risk of paralysis by analysis. As Rush describes, "In looking at the overall results I think you could say our efforts paid off. We increased donation conversions by 49%, sign up conversions by 161% and we were able to apply our findings to other areas and products." And this sort of result is not unique: spurred on by a number of popular business books with titles like *Always Be Testing* (Eisenberg and Quarto-von Tivadar 2009), *Experiment!* (McFarland 2012), and *A/B Testing* (Siroker and Koomen 2013) where other examples of the Obama campaign's optimization are reported, many firms are finding ways to making field experiments a regular part of how they make decisions.

Field Experiments in the Academic Literature

Field experiments are becoming popular as a tool for exploring marketing theory (Gneezy 2017), and there are many online and offline field experiments reported in the academic literature.

Offline field experiments can, for instance, be run in retail stores like Chen et al. (2012) did to test how different types of promotions can impact the volume of purchases. They tested whether the bonus pack or an equivalent price decrease of a product has an impact on the sales figures changing the promotion type on a weekly basis for 16 weeks. The employment of only one store allowed keeping all external factors constant (e.g., store layout, employees, background of customers, neighboring environment), increasing internal validity at the expense of external validity.

Furthermore, field experiments are often conducted over a long period of time in order to identify long-term effects. For example, Bawa and Schoemaker (2004) conducted two field experiments each one over a 2-year time frame aimed at estimating the long-run effect of free sampling on sales. In both cases, they recorded the sales data of the customers over 1 year (panel data). After delivering the sample at the end of the first year, the volumes were registered for another year. Of course, the longer the time frame, the higher the probability that external factors can influence the participants. In general, problematic marketing-related extraneous factors depend on the respective context and on the research topic.

Online-controlled experiments have gained popularity because of the increased digitalization of companies that are more and more engaging in a test and learn mentality. As we have discussed, A/B tests can easily be implemented to examine how users react to different webpage layouts and designs. An example is Yang and Ghose (2010), who measured the impact of different search advertising strategies on the click through rate, conversion rate, and revenues. All of these measures give an indication of how the customers use the website.

A study revealing how the use of field experiments can shed new light on existing and well-established theories is the recent paper by Anderson and Simester (2013). Standard models of competition predict that firms will sell less when competitors target their customers with advertising. This is particularly true in mature markets with many competitors that sell relatively undifferentiated products. However, the authors present findings from a large-scale randomized field experiment that contrast sharply with this prediction. The field experiment examines the effect of competitors' advertising on sales at a private label apparel retailer. To examine this effect, the researchers sent competitive advertisement mailings to the treatment group. As customers normally have no comparison of whether other people receive the same or different mailings, they do not realize that they are part of an experiment. Results show that, surprisingly, for a substantial segment of customers, the competitors' advertisements increased sales at this retailer.

Recommended readings for those interested in online advertising are the field tests employed by Goldfarb and Tucker (2011a, c). In the same area, Blake et al. (2015) and Kalyanam et al. (2015) published large-scale field experiments aimed at studying the causal effectiveness of paid search ads. They find somewhat contradictory results: Blake et al. (2015) showed that returns from paid search ads for eBay are minimal, while Kalyanam et al. (2015) find that search ads are effective for other retailers. In a recent working paper, Simonov et al. (2015) have also confirmed that search advertising does have some benefit for less-well-established brands. They use a large-scale, fully randomized experiment on Bing data studying 2500 brands. These experiments rely on treatment and control groups made up of various geographic regions where advertising can be turned on or off; using such *geo-experiments* to measure ad effectiveness has also been suggested by researchers at Google (Vaver and Koehler 2011).

Randomized holdouts take this idea of non-exposure to customer-level experiments and are rapidly becoming popular in many industries. In a randomized holdout experiment, the marketer selects a group of customers at random to not receive planned marketing communication, such as an email, a catalog, or a promotional offer. Comparing the treated and the holdout group allows the marketer to make a causal measurement of the treatment effect, i.e., the incremental sales lift of the marketing. Hoban and Bucklin (2015) report on randomized holdout experiments in display advertising, Zantedeschi et al. (2016) report on randomized holdouts for catalog and email campaigns, and Sahni et al. (2015) report on randomized holdouts for discount offers. All of these studies find positive incremental effects of marketing. However, Lewis and Rao (2015) report similar experiments on display advertising and find effect sizes that are so small that it would be difficult to accurately measure the returns on advertising.

Lambrecht and Tucker (2013) run a field experiment with an online travel firm to examine whether *dynamic retargeting*, a new form of personalized advertising that shows consumers ads that contain images of products they have looked at before on the firm's own website, is more effective than simply showing generic brand ads. Even if this new strategy integrates the usage of both internal and external browsing data, results revealed that dynamic retargeted ads are on average less effective than traditional retargeting.

Ascarza et al. (2016) analyze retention campaigns based on pricing plan recommendations, and the results emerging from their field experiment surprisingly show that being proactive and encouraging customers to switch to cost-minimizing plans can increase rather than decrease customer churn.

As the MSI-Tier 1 priorities suggest, the customer journey is developing into a multimedia, multiscreen, and multichannel era (mobile = physical + digital worlds). Considering multichannel customer management literature, Montaguti et al. (2016) test the causal relationship between multichannel purchasing and customer profitability. Within a field experiment, they show that multichannel customers are indeed more profitable than they would be if they were single-channel customers providing insights on how multichannel shopping leads to higher profit.

Andrews et al. (2015) had the opportunity to collaborate with one of the world's largest telecom providers managing to gauge physical crowdedness in real time in terms of the number of active mobile users in subway trains. Their research examines the effects of hyper-contextual targeting with physical crowdedness on consumer responses to mobile ads, and results based on a massive field experiment counting a sample of 14,972 mobile phone users suggest that, counterintuitively, commuters in crowded subway trains are about twice as likely to respond to a mobile offer by making a purchase vis-à-vis those in non-crowded trains.

Dubé et al. (2015) implemented another massive field experiment to test an information theory of prosocial behavior. A long literature in behavioral economics has generated a collection of empirical examples where economic incentives counterintuitively reduce the supply of prosocial behavior. The data comes from two field experiments involving a consumer good bundled with a charitable donation. Considering a population of 15 million subscribers living 2 km from a theater and who purchased a ticket via phone in the previous 6 months, the sample consisted of 4200 randomly chosen individuals. Results suggest that price discounts crowd out consumer self-inference of altruism.

Nevertheless, the aforementioned papers are only some of those interesting works published involving the use of field experiments. We leave to the reader's curiosity the task to look for other field experiments!

Conclusions

As can be seen from the previous section, there are numerous examples of both companies and academics using field experiments to answer tactical questions and test marketing theory. The increasing use of field experiments in marketing is also enhancing the collaboration between firms and academia. The big challenge and opportunity here are the reconciliation of academics doing "big stats on small data" with practitioners doing "small stats on big data."

This chapter has laid out the key ideas one should think about when designing field experiments. For the reader interested in more detail, a major author of reference is John A. List, who focuses on field experiments in economics. In List (2004) the author presents a series of field experiments he conducted about theories of discrimination, and in a slightly more recent paper (2006), he reviews a broad set of field experiments to explore the implications of behavioral and neoclassical theories as well as of topics ranging from the economics of charity to the measurement of preferences. Furthermore, in 2011 he proposed 14 tips to follow for improving academic's chances of executing successful field experiments in collaboration with companies. We suggest practitioners to refer to this checklist, before implementing their experiment ideas.

Of course, it is unavoidable to meet some challenges in the implementation and use of field experiments. First of all, as pointed out by Levitt and List (2009), field experiments do not provide the same extent of control as laboratory experiments. Therefore, internal validity is often lower, and, because of a lower level of control, potential confounding variables should be identified before starting and recorded during the experiment in order to control for them using statistical methods (Homburg 2015; Gneezy 2017). Pre-testing and continuous monitoring during the experiment are helpful to identify excluded effects and record general trends like a change of the general market conditions which can impact the sales volume independently of the experiment (Gerber and Green 2012; Gneezy 2017). This issue further reveals that researchers should put much effort and time into the planning stage and in the experimental design. On top of that, a relatively high level of knowledge of the whole experimental design and of the underlying constructs is required upfront (Levitt and List 2009). Other challenges concern privacy and security regulations that unavoidably tend to limit collection/retention of data (Goldfarb and Tucker 2011b). Future researchers should focus on the development of analytics that can overcome such limitations and on the proactive development of methods for protection of customer privacy.

In summary, this chapter outlines and argues that field experiments are, next to big data analytics, one of the major advances of the digital age which allow firms to reveal the causality between two processes, actions or observations. Managers and researchers have now to accept the challenge by ensuring that the causal inferences of their field experiments are both correct and useful in terms of advancing management and marketing practice. We hope this chapter encourages and helps managers in considering field experiments as a state-of-the-art market research approach for collection, analysis, and interpretation of market-related information.

Cross-References

▶ Analysis of Variance
▶ Experiments in Market Research

References

Aaker, D. A., Kumar, V., Day, G. S., & Leone, R. P. (2011). *Marketing research*. Hoboken: Wiley.
Anderson, E. T., & Simester, D. (2013). Advertising in a competitive market: The role of product standards, customer learning, and switching costs. *Journal of Marketing Research, 50*(4), 489–504.
Andrews, M., Luo, X., Fang, Z., & Ghose, A. (2015). Mobile Ad effectiveness: Hyper-contextual targeting with crowdedness. *Marketing Science, 35*(2), 1–17.

Ascarza, E., Iyengar, R., & Schleicher, M. (2016). The perils of proactive churn prevention using plan recommendations: Evidence from a field experiment. *Journal of Marketing Research, 53*(1), 46–60.

Bawa, K., & Shoemaker, R. (2004). The effects of free sample promotions on incremental brand sales. *Marketing Science, 23*(3), 345–363.

Blake, T., Nesko, C., & Tadelis, S. (2015). Consumer heterogeneity and paid search effectiveness: A large scale field experiment. *Econometrica, 83*(1), 155–174.

Campbell, D. T. (1957). Factors relevant to the validity of experiments in social settings. *Psychological Bulletin, 54*(4), 297–312.

Campbell, D. T., & Stanley, J. C. (1963). *Experimental and quasi-experimental designs for research*. Boston: Houghton Mifflin.

Chen, H., Marmorstein, H., Tsiros, M., & Rao, A. R. (2012). When more is less: The impact of base value neglect on consumer preferences for bonus packs over price discounts. *Journal of Marketing, 76*(4), 64–77.

Crook, T., Brian, F., Ron, K., & Roger, L. (2009). *Seven pitfalls to avoid when running controlled experiments on the web*. In Proceedings of the 15th ACM SIGKDD international conference on knowledge discovery and data mining.

Dubé, J.-P., Luo, X., & Fang, Z. (2015). *Self-signaling and pro-social behavior: A cause marketing experiment*. Fox school of business research paper no. 15-079. Available at SSRN: http://ssrn.com/abstract=2635808 or https://doi.org/10.2139/ssrn.2635808

Dunning, T. (2012). *Natural experiments in the social sciences: A design-based approach*. Cambridge: Cambridge University Press.

Eisenberg, B., & Quarto-von Tivadar, J. (2009). *Always be testing: The complete guide to Google website optimizer*. New York: Wiley.

Fisher, R. A. (1925). *Statistical methods for research workers*. London: Oliver and Boyd.

Gerber, A. S., & Green, D. P. (2008). Field experiments and natural experiments. In J. M. Box-Steffensmeier, H. E. Brady, & D. Collier (Eds.), *The Oxford handbook of political methodology, Oxford handbooks online* (pp. 357–381). Oxford: Oxford University Press.

Gerber, A. S., & Green, D. P. (2012). *Field experiments. Design, analysis, and interpretation*. New York: Norton.

Gneezy, A. (2017). Field experimentation in marketing research. *Journal of Marketing Research, 46*, 140–143.

Goos, P., & Jones, B. (2011). *Optimal design of experiments: A case study approach*. New York: Wiley.

Goldfarb, A., & Tucker, C. E. (2011a). Online display advertising: Targeting and obtrusiveness. *Marketing Science, 30*(3), 389–404.

Goldfarb, A., & Tucker, C. E. (2011b). Privacy regulation and online advertising. *Management Science, 57*(1), 57–71.

Goldfarb, A., & Tucker, C. E. (2011c). Advertising bans and the substitutability of online and offline advertising. *Journal of Marketing Research, 48*(2), 207–227.

Harrison, G. W., & List, J. A. (2004). Field experiments. *Journal of Economic Literature, 42*(4), 1009–1055.

Hoban, P. R., & Bucklin, R. E. (2015). Effects of internet display advertising in the purchase funnel: Model-based insights from a randomized field experiment. *Journal of Marketing Research, 52*(3), 375–393.

Homburg, C. (2015). *Marketingmanagement. Strategie – Instrumente – Umsetzung – Unternehmensführung. Lehrbuch*. Wiesbaden: Springer Gabler.

Homburg, C., Kuester, S., & Krohmer, H. (2013). *Marketing management. A contemporary perspective*. London: McGraw-Hill Higher Education.

Iacobucci, D., & Churchill, G. A. (2010). *Marketing research. Methodological foundations*. Mason: South-Western Cengage Learning.

Imbens, G. W., & Rubin, D. B. (2015). *Causal inference for statistics, social and biomedical sciences: An introduction*. New York: Cambridge University Press.

Kalyanam, K., McAteer, J., Marek, J., Hodges, J., & Lin, L. (2015). *Cross channel effects of search engine advertising on brick and mortar retail sales: Meta analysis of large scale field experiments on Google.com*. Working paper.

Kohavi, R., Longbotham, R., Sommerfield, D., & Henne, R. M. (2009). Controlled experiments on the web: Survey and practical guide. *Data Mining and Knowledge Discovery, 18*(1), 140–181.

Koschate-Fischer, N., & Schandelmeier, S. (2014). A guideline for designing experimental studies in marketing research and a critical discussion of selected problem areas. *Journal of Business Economics, 84*, 793–826.

Landsberger, H. A. (1958). *Hawthorne revisited.* Ithaca: Cornell University.

Lambrecht, A., & Tucker, C. E. (2013). When does retargeting work? Information specificity in online advertising. *Journal of Marketing Research, 50*(5), 561–576.

Ledolter, J., & Swersey, A. J. (2007). *Testing 1-2-3. Experimental design with applications in marketing and service operations.* Standford: Standford University Press.

Levitt, S. D., & List, J. A. (2009). Field experiments in economics: The past, the present, and the future. *European Economic Review, 53*(1), 1–18.

Lewis, R. A., & Rao, J. M. (2015). The unfavourable economics of measuring the returns to advertising. *The Quarterly Journal of Economics*, 1941–1973.

List, J. A. (2004). The nature and extent of discrimination in the marketplace: Evidence from the field. *Quarterly Journal of Economics, 119*(1), 48–89.

List, J. A. (2011). Why economists should conduct field experiments and 14 tips for pulling one off. *Journal of Economic Perspectives, 25*(3), 3–16.

McFarland, C. (2012). *Experiment! Website conversion rate optimization with A/B and multivariate.* Berkeley: New Riders.

Montaguti, E., Neslin, S. A., & Valentini, S. (2016). Can marketing campaigns induce multichannel buying and more profitable customers? A field experiment. *Marketing Science, 35*(2), 201–217.

Neyman, Jerzy. (1923[1990]). On the application of probability theory to agricultural experiments: Essay on principles. Section 9. *Statistical Science*, 5 (4), 465–472. Translated by Dabrowska, Dorota M. and Terence P. Speed.

Rush, K. (2012a). *Meet the Obama campaign's $250 million fundraising platform.* Blog post 27 Nov 2012.

Rush, K. (2012b). *Optimization at the Obama campaign: a/b testing.* Blog post 12 Dec 2012.

Sahni, N., Dan, Z., & Pradeep, C. (2015). *Do targeted discount offers serve as advertising? Evidence from 70 field experiments.* Stanford University Graduate School of Business research paper no. 15-4. Available at SSRN: http://ssrn.com/abstract=2530290 or https://doi.org/10.2139/ssrn.2530290

Sándor, Z., & Wedel, M. (2001). Designing conjoint choice experiments using managers' prior beliefs. *Journal of Marketing Research, 38*(4), 430–444.

Shadish, W. R., Cook, T. D., & Campbell, D. T. (2002). *Experimental and quasi-experimental designs for generalized causal inference.* Belmont: Wadsworth Cengage Learning.

Simonov, A., Nosko, C., & Rao J. M. (2015). *Competition and crowd-out for brand keywords in sponsored search.* Available at SSRN: http://ssrn.com/abstract=2668265 or https://doi.org/10.2139/ssrn.2668265

Siroker, D., & Pete K. (2013). A/B testing. Wiley.

Teele, D. L. (2014). *Field experiments and their critics: Essays on the uses and abuses of experimentation in the social sciences.* New Haven & London: Yale University Press.

Vaver, J., & Koehler, J. (2011). *Measuring ad effectiveness using geo experiments.* Google Research working paper.

Yang, S., & Ghose, A. (2010). Analyzing the relationship between organic and sponsored search advertising: Positive, negative, or zero interdependence? *Marketing Science, 29*(4), 602–623.

Zantedeschi, D., McDonnell Feit, E., & Bradlow, E. T. (2016). Modeling multi-channel advertising response with consumer-level data. *Management Science*, Articles in Advance. http://pubsonline.informs.org/doi/abs/10.1287/mnsc.2016.2451

Crafting Survey Research: A Systematic Process for Conducting Survey Research

Arnd Vomberg and Martin Klarmann

Contents

Introduction: Relevance of Survey Research	68
Understanding Survey Bias	70
Fundamentals of Survey Research	70
Psychology of Survey Response	71
Measurement Theory	72
Sources of Systematic Errors in Survey Research: Measurement Errors	74
Sources of Systematic Errors in Survey Research: Representation Errors	85
Survey Research Process	89
Selection of Research Variables	89
Selection of Survey Method	91
Questionnaire Design	93
Data Collection	104
Measurement Evaluation	105
Data Analysis	106
Endogeneity in Survey Research	106
Conclusion	110
Cross-References	110
References	111

Abstract

Surveys represent flexible and powerful ways for practitioners to gain insights into customers and markets and for researchers to develop, test, and generalize theories. However, conducting effective survey research is challenging. Survey researchers must induce participation by "over-surveyed" respondents, choose

---

A. Vomberg (✉)
Marketing Department, University of Groningen, Groningen, The Netherlands
e-mail: A.E.Vomberg@rug.nl

M. Klarmann
Department of Marketing & Sales Research Group, Karlsruhe Institute of Technology (KIT),
Karlsruhe, Germany
e-mail: martin.klarmann@kit.edu

© Springer Nature Switzerland AG 2022
C. Homburg et al. (eds), *Handbook of Market Research*,
https://doi.org/10.1007/978-3-319-57413-4_4

appropriately from among numerous design alternatives, and need to account for the respondents' complex psychological processes when answering the survey. The aim of this chapter is to guide investigators in effective design of their surveys. We discuss state-of-the-art research findings on measurement biases (i.e., common method bias, key informant bias, social desirability bias, and response patterns) and representation biases (i.e., non-sampling bias and non-response bias) and outline when those biases are likely to occur and how investigators can best avoid them. In addition, we offer a systematic approach for crafting surveys. We discuss key steps and decisions in the survey design process, with a particular focus on standardized questionnaires, and we emphasize how those choices can help alleviate potential biases. Finally, we discuss how investigators can address potential endogeneity concerns in surveys.

Keywords

Survey research · Biases · Survey design · Survey research process · Measurement theory · Common method bias · Key informant bias · Social desirability · Response styles · Non-sampling bias · Non-response bias · Item reversal · Order bias

Introduction: Relevance of Survey Research

Surveys are ubiquitous, used to inform decision makers in every walk of life. Surveys provide practitioners with deeper insights into the attitudes of their customers (e.g., Hohenberg and Taylor (chapter ▶ "Measuring Customer Satisfaction and Customer Loyalty") in this handbook) and employees (e.g., employee satisfaction surveys). Surveys are also helpful in exploring theoretical mechanisms for theory testing and development, as survey research can contribute to generalizing experimental findings to different persons and settings (Krosnick 1999; MacKenzie and Podsakoff 2012). Many relevant and important research questions would be difficult to study without relying on survey data (Hulland et al. 2018). Often, adequate secondary data are not available and experimental manipulations are not feasible. Thus, unsurprisingly, marketing research has a "rich tradition...in survey research" (Rindfleisch and Heide 1997, p. 30).

Surveys represent a versatile and powerful research instrument that is applicable in various contexts. For instance, investigators rely on surveys to study:

- Customer attitudes (e.g., customer satisfaction, customer loyalty, voice of the customer surveys)
- Employee attitudes (e.g., employee satisfaction, employee commitment)
- Service quality (e.g., surveys about hotel service)
- Product quality (e.g., surveys with package inserts)
- Performance evaluations (e.g., training evaluation surveys)
- Product feedback (e.g., new product/concept testing surveys)

Recent findings demonstrate the superiority of survey research over other methods. For instance, a recent meta-analysis reveals that direct survey-based techniques more validly indicate consumers' willingness-to-pay than indirect methods (Schmidt and Bijmolt 2019). Similarly, survey research might deliver the most valid results in studies of sensitive topics (John et al. 2018).

However, despite its important benefits, survey research is in decline (Hulland et al. 2018). Possibly, awareness of potential biases that can occur in survey research may have nurtured skepticism toward surveys, rendering findings less trustworthy or credible. Thus, a critical challenge for survey research lies in separating noise and bias from a survey. As an understanding of how biases emerge will help investigators enhance the validity of their surveys, we discuss the most commonly identified biases in survey research.

Researchers need to make various decisions when developing their surveys. We introduce a systematic process to survey research design that will help investigators organize and structure survey development by answering guiding questions for each stage of the survey research process. In addition, we outline how those decisions can help to alleviate potential biases – an important consideration, as biases from survey research can to a large extent be attributed to "haphazard decisions" (Schwarz 2003, p. 588), investigators make when constructing surveys. While we focus primarily on procedural remedies to avoiding biases (ex ante bias prevention), we also briefly address statistical techniques (ex post bias corrections) and direct readers to further literature. Such statistical techniques represent important supplements to effective survey design.

After reading this chapter, researchers will have an in-depth understanding of the various biases that may affect the results of survey research. In addition, researchers will comprehend the general survey process and know which decisions in survey development will help to reduce potential biases. Figure 1 shows how we have

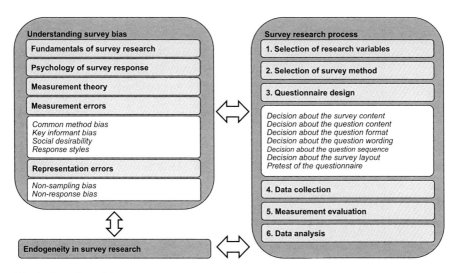

Fig. 1 Overview of chapter structure

structured this chapter. We first foster an understanding of survey bias (section "Understanding Survey Bias") by discussing the psychology of survey response (section "Psychology of Survey Response") and measurement theory (section "Measurement Theory"). We then discuss in detail important sources of systematic errors in survey research, which we classify into measurement errors (section "Sources of Systematic Errors in Survey Research: Measurement Errors") and representation errors (section "Sources of Systematic Errors in Survey Research: Representation Errors"). We subsequently outline the survey research process (section "Survey Research Process"), with a particular focus on how to design the questionnaire (section "Questionnaire Design"). We briefly address the issue of endogeneity (section "Endogeneity in Survey Research") and end by summarizing and aligning the sections (section "Conclusion").

Understanding Survey Bias

Fundamentals of Survey Research

A survey comprises a "cross-sectional design in relation to which data are collected predominantly by questionnaire or by structured interview on more than one case (usually quite a lot more than one) and at a single point in time" (Bryman and Bell 2015, p. 63). Surveys can be categorized by several aspects, such as

1. The method in which they are administered to the participant: written, online, telephone, or personal surveys
2. Time horizon: cross-sectional versus longitudinal surveys
3. The role of the respondent: self-reports versus key informants

Survey administration can be classified into personal, telephone, written, and online surveys. We discuss these different forms when outlining the selection of the survey method (section "Selection of Survey Method"), focusing primarily on written and online surveys because these are the dominant forms of survey research (Hulland et al. 2018).

The time horizon can be purely cross-sectional or longitudinal. While cross-sectional surveys are administered at a single point in time, longitudinal surveys comprise repeated observations for different time periods (e.g., Heide et al. 2007; Jansen et al. 2006; Wathne et al. 2018). Cross-sectional surveys are the dominant form of applied research, encompassing 92.1% (Hulland et al. 2018, p. 94) and 94% (Rindfleisch et al. 2008, p. 262). Examples of longitudinal surveys include

- American Customer Satisfaction Index (theacsi.org; Fornell et al. 1996), which tracks the evolution of customers' satisfaction with several companies over time
- Harris Poll EquiTrend study (e.g., Vomberg et al. 2015) or Young & Rubicam Brand Asset Valuator (e.g., Mizik and Jacobson 2008), which gauge consumers' brand perceptions

- The CMO survey, which regularly surveys the opinions of chief marketing officers (e.g., cmosurvey.org)

Longitudinal surveys can be designed in various ways. The American Customer Satisfaction Index and the Harris Poll EquiTrend Study are repeated cross-sectional surveys in which different respondents are sampled each time. Alternatively, researchers can conduct a panel survey in which mostly the same respondents are surveyed each time (chapter ► "Panel Data Analysis: A Non-technical Introduction for Marketing Researchers" by Vomberg and Wies).

Regarding the role of the respondent, survey participants can either provide self-reports or act as key informants. In self-reports, participants assess questions for themselves. For instance, they may indicate their level of satisfaction or their attitude toward a focal brand. In contrast, key informants provide answers for a higher-order social entity. For instance, employees may indicate the strategic orientation of their company. Key informants are commonly relied on in organizational contexts. We elaborate later on a potential bias stemming from the use of key informants (section "Key Informant Bias").

Psychology of Survey Response

Survey researchers need to be aware of the psychological processes that typically occur when participants answer a questionnaire. In business research, participants usually cannot offer predefined responses but form their evaluations when answering the questionnaire. For instance, when customers are asked about their satisfaction with a company, they are not likely to retrieve such an evaluation directly from memory, but instead tend to reflect on their answer when completing the questionnaire. Thus, survey questions trigger a cognitive process of response generation.

It is beyond the scope of this chapter to outline the variety of models that have been proposed to capture these cognitive processes. Therefore, we only briefly summarize the model of Tourangeau et al. (2000), which investigators frequently refer to when studying respondent behaviors (e.g., MacKenzie and Podsakoff 2012; Podsakoff et al. 2003; Weijters et al. 2009).

Tourangeau et al. (2000) argue that respondents pass through five stages when replying to survey questions: (1) comprehension, (2) retrieval, (3) judgment, (4) response selection, and (5) response reporting. In the comprehension stage, participants attend to the survey question and deduce its intent. Respondents then generate a retrieval strategy and search their memories for relevant information. Retrieval thus entails the process of bringing information held in long-term memory to an active state, in which it enters the short-term memory to be used (belief-sampling model). Respondents integrate this information into a judgment (e.g., their satisfaction with a certain product). Finally, when selecting their response, participants map the judgment onto the offered response categories and report their answer (e.g., Krosnick 1999; Tourangeau et al. 2000; Weijters and Baumgartner 2012).

Each of these stages is quite complex and involves a significant amount of cognitive effort by the participant. Thus, during this process, participants may not be motivated to process survey items in sufficient detail to provide a valid statement. However, even motivated respondents may retrieve biased information. The accessibility-diagnosticity theory argues that respondents retrieve information that is accessible to them and has a high diagnosticity (Feldman and Lynch 1988). For instance, very salient but exceptional events (e.g., a specific negative incident with a company) are likely to be more accessible than regular events and thus lead respondents to provide a distorted picture of their true attitudes and opinions. In addition, information provided in earlier questions may represent a source of information that respondents use to form their answers. For instance, the sequence of questions may influence what information respondents retrieve when answering subsequent questions (section "Decisions About the Question Sequence"). Even if consumers retrieve accurate information, they must make substantial efforts to condense this complex information into rather simple answer categories, such as scales from 1 to 7 (Homburg et al. 2012c).

These examples highlight the complexity of survey response. In the following, we outline the consequences of these psychological processes for the interpretation of survey data.

Measurement Theory

Reliability and Validity: Fundamentals

Measurement theory claims that any observed value x for a question (e.g., an observed value for the liking of a brand) is the sum of a true value t (also referred to as trait) and measurement error, which can have a random e and a systematic component s. Hence, any observed value can be understood in the following way (Eq. 1):

$$x = t + s + e \qquad (1)$$

Importantly, the random error component poses threats to the reliability of a survey question, and the systematic error component can affect the question's validity. A survey question can be considered reliable when it produces the same results under the same measurement conditions, whereas the question has validity when it actually measures what it purports to measure. An intuitive example to understand the concept of random and systematic error is the following. Imagine that 100 researchers measure the time it takes for a participant to run a certain distance. Usually, when all researchers compare their results, their observed measurements will differ slightly. Thus, individual measurements likely suffer from random measurement error. However, since this error is assumed to be randomly distributed among participants, its expected value is zero: $E(e) = 0$. Hence, when taking the average value, researchers likely obtain an unbiased measure (Iacobucci 2013).

With respect to survey research, a characteristic such as imprecise wording can raise fundamental threats to reliability: participants could interpret words such as "usually" or "almost" differently, adding noise to the data (section "Decisions About the Question Wording"). However, since the expected value of the random error is zero, survey researchers can ask multiple questions when measuring abstract concepts such as commitment or satisfaction. Just as in the stop watch example, averaging multiple measurements may help to safeguard against reliability concerns (section "Decisions About the Question Content").

In contrast, systematic errors affect the validity of survey questions. Validity refers to the degree to which a measure really measures what it is supposed to measure. Since the expected value of the systematic error is not zero ($E(s) \neq 0$), repeated measurements cannot alleviate potential validity concerns. Intuitively, this can be explained by continuing with the stop watch example. If all researchers had received stop watches that systematically add 10 s, even the average of the individual measurements will be biased. We discuss sources of systematic errors in survey research in sections "Sources of Systematic Errors in Survey Research: Measurement Errors" and "Sources of Systematic Errors in Survey Research: Representation Errors."

Reliability and Validity: Implications for Survey Research

A natural follow-up question is the extent to which random and systematic errors influence the results of survey research. Many times survey researchers are interested in establishing relationships between variables. In the simplest case, investigators can focus on bivariate correlation coefficients, and in the following we discuss the bivariate correlation coefficient between a variable x (e.g., customer satisfaction (CS)) and a variable y (e.g., word-of-mouth behavior (WOM)). In line with Eq. 1, we assume that both variables are measured with error. We apply two common assumptions in deriving the correlation coefficient: we assume (1) uncorrelated random measurement errors (i.e., $Cov(e,t) = 0$; $Cov(e,s) = 0$; $Cov(e_x, e_y) = 0$) and (2) no correlation between the true value and the systematic measurement error ($Cov(t,s) = 0$). These assumptions lead to the following correlation coefficient (Eq. 2) (e.g., Baumgartner and Steenkamp 2001; Homburg and Klarmann 2009):

$$r(x,y) = \frac{Cov(CS; WOM)}{\sqrt{Var(CS) \cdot Var(WOM)}} = \frac{Cov(x; y)}{\sqrt{Var(x) \cdot Var(y)}} =$$

$$= \frac{Cov(t_x + e_x + s_x; t_y + e_y + s_y)}{\sqrt{Var(t_x + e_x + s_x) \cdot Var(t_y + e_y + s_y)}} = \tag{2}$$

$$= \frac{Cov(t_x, t_y) + Cov(s_x, s_y)}{\sqrt{[Var(t_x) + Var(e_x) + Var(s_x)] \cdot [Var(t_y) + Var(e_y) + Var(s_y)]}}.$$

Equation 2 offers three important insights. First, a common concern regarding survey research is that participants may provide inflated answers that bias the results (e.g., De Jong et al. 2015). For instance, managers may be tempted to exaggerate their performance. However, while these over- or understatements affect mean values, mean values do not directly affect Eq. 2. Thus, (systematic) over- or understatements do not bias the relationships between variables in survey research.

Second, in many research applications, investigators are interested in the direction of a relationship rather than in the size of the coefficient. Since the denominator in Eq. 2 contains only variances that cannot become negative, only the numerator is responsible for the direction of the correlation coefficient. Increased variances in the denominator can only reduce the size of the correlation coefficient. Consequently, Eq. 2 reveals that random measurement errors cannot change the sign of the correlation coefficient since the random error is only part of the denominator. From the perspective of a survey researcher, Eq. 2 implies that random measurement errors can lead to only conservative results by decreasing statistical power. Thus, random measurement errors may obscure an effect that is present, leading to Type II errors. However, random measurement errors cannot artificially create relationships.

Third, the impact of systematic measurement errors (also referred to as method error) can be twofold since the systematic error is part of both the numerator and the denominator in Eq. 2. If sources of systematic errors affect both variables independently (i.e., $\text{cov}(s_x, s_y) = 0$), then systematic errors have the same impact as random errors: they can lower statistical power but cannot artificially create effects. However, more likely sources of systematic errors (e.g., key informant bias) affect both variables simultaneously (i.e., $\text{cov}(s_x, s_y) \neq 0$). Thus, systematic errors can affect not only the strength but also the direction of an effect. Systematic errors could be responsible for either detecting artificial relationships in cases in which there is no true relationship (i.e., Type I error) or masking existing relationships (i.e., Type II error) (Baumgartner and Steenkamp 2001; Homburg et al. 2012c). Huang and Sudhir (2021) provide compelling empirical evidence for the latter. They show that systematic biases in survey research can lead to conservative estimates, that is, an underestimation of true effect sizes.

Sources of Systematic Errors in Survey Research: Measurement Errors

In this section, we review key sources of systematic biases that may affect the validity of survey research. A bias is "any force, tendency, or procedural error in the collection, analysis, or interpretation of data which provides distortion" (Crisp 1957, cited in Tortolani 1965, p. 51). Knowledge regarding these threats is important because, to a certain extent, researchers can safeguard against them when designing the survey instrument.

In the following, we describe the most commonly discussed biases in survey research. Following prior investigators, we categorize those biases into measurement errors and representation errors (e.g., Baumgartner and Steenkamp 2006). Measurement errors reflect tendencies of respondents to answer to survey questions on some grounds other than the item content. Specifically, we discuss common method bias (section "Common Method Bias"), key informant bias (section "Key Informant Bias"), social desirability bias (section "Social Desirability"), and response patterns (section "Response Styles"). Representation errors reflect biases due to the selection of the sample of respondents. These biases could follow from unrepresentative sampling frames – non-sampling bias (section "Non-sampling Bias") – or participants' unwillingness or inability to respond – unit non-response bias (section "Non-response Bias").

Common Method Bias

Conceptualization. Common method bias (CMB) – one of the most frequently discussed threats to survey research – can largely undermine the validity of a study's findings (Hulland 2019; Palmatier 2016). However, no agreement on a definition of CMB presently exists. CMB definitions differ widely in scope. Podsakoff et al. (2003, p. 880) favor a broad definition and refer to CMB as "variance that is attributable to the measurement rather than the construct of interest." Under this definition, CMB can be regarded as an umbrella term for various biases that can be classified into four categories (Podsakoff et al. 2003, p. 882):

- *Common source rater*: for example, consistency motif, social desirability (Section "Social Desirability"), response patterns (section "Response Styles"), or a tendency toward satisficing
- *Item characteristics*: for example, item ambiguity (section "Decisions About the Question Wording"), common scale formats or anchors (section "Decision About the Question Format")
- *Effects due to item context*: for example, item embeddedness (section "Decisions About the Question Sequence")
- *Measurement context*: for example, independent and dependent variables measured at the same point in time

A narrow definition of CMB focuses on the last category and attributes the distortion of the sample's covariance structure to the use of the same data source to measure both independent and dependent variables (e.g., Klarmann 2008; Rindfleisch et al. 2008). We adopt this definition and discuss other biases that Podsakoff et al. (2003) mention separately.

CMB can emerge when a single informant provides information on the independent and dependent variables. As we elaborate below, the severity of CMB will then depend on various factors, such as the type of collected measure (lower CMB threat for objectively verifiable measures), the complexity of the tested relationships (lower CMB threat for quadratic and interactive relationships), whether a time lag occurs in data collection (lower CMB threat when independent and dependent variables are collected at different points in time), or the response format (lower CMB threat if the independent and dependent variables are measured in different scale formats).

CMB can undermine the validity of survey research in two ways. First, it can lead to biases in estimates of construct reliability and validity, as it can inflate reliability and validity measures by 18 to 32% (Podsakoff et al. 2012, p. 543). Thus, CMB can lead researchers to mistakenly believe that they have validly measured the constructs of interest when in reality they have captured method artifacts.

Second, CMB can bias the parameter estimates between two constructs. Notably, however, investigators document vastly different results when quantifying the impact of CMB: some evidence indicates that, on average, CMB inflates correlation coefficients between constructs by approximately 45%, with a range of 27% to 304% (MacKenzie and Podsakoff 2012, p. 543; Podsakoff et al. 2012, p. 545). However, a meta-analysis of 42,934 correlation coefficients showed correlations based on single-source self-reports to be on average only 0.02 higher than correlation coefficients from different sources (Crampton and Wagner 1994).

Reasons for occurrence. To effectively address CMB, understanding the reasons for its occurrence is important. Given the pivotal role CMB assumes in marketing research projects, the literature not surprisingly offers plenty of explanations for why CMB may occur (Podsakoff et al. 2003 provide a detailed discussion). In the following, we highlight selected explanations.

First, when reading the questions, respondents may start developing implicit theories of the relationships between the constructs. In effect, their answers then represent reflections of these theories. For instance, managers might be asked to evaluate the innovativeness of their business unit and their competitive position. If the participating managers develop the implicit theory that innovativeness represents a focal driver of performance, then their answers referring to the business unit's innovativeness might be influenced by prior answers on the unit's competitive position (e.g., Podsakoff et al. 2003).

Second, respondents strive for consistency in their cognitions. Therefore, they may try to provide answers that they think are consistent. They may search for similarities in the questions and adapt their answers accordingly. As a consequence, stated answers may not truly reflect their behaviors or opinions.

While these two explanations in general outline why CMB can emerge, an important question is, in which situation is CMB more likely to occur? Empirical evidence suggests that two factors drive potential CMB concerns: (1) the nature of the constructs under investigation and (2) the complexity of the investigated relationships.

The literature rather consistently states that the likelihood of CMB to occur depends on the nature of the questions. For example, the percentage of common method variance is lower in marketing (16%) than in psychology or sociology (35%) (Cote and Buckley 1987). Constructs investigated in psychology or sociology are likely to be abstract and complex and thus be harder to answer and may trigger cognitive processes that increase covariation between systematic error components (MacKenzie and Podsakoff 2012; Podsakoff et al. 2012; section "Psychology of Survey Response"). Empirical evidence confirms these expectations. In general, concrete, externally oriented, and verifiable constructs are less prone to CMB than are abstract, internally oriented, and non-verifiable constructs (Chang et al. 2010; Rindfleisch et al. 2008).

Second, with increasing complexity of the investigated relationships, CMB is less likely to occur. Analytical evidence demonstrates that CMB can deflate quadratic and moderating relationships but cannot create them (Siemsen et al. 2010). For such complex relationships, participants are unlikely to develop corresponding implicit theories that affect their responses. Therefore, if the main interest of research lies in identifying quadratic relationships or interaction effects, CMB is not likely to undermine researchers' findings (Vomberg et al. 2020).

Procedural remedies. A general recommendation is that investigators should favor procedural remedies over statistical remedies when addressing potential biases in survey research. While statistical controls are rather symptom-based – that is, they target the consequences of CMB only in the analysis stages – procedural remedies try to eliminate sources of CMB in the moment of collecting the data. Naturally, in many situations researchers will not be able to completely alleviate CMB concerns with procedural remedies, and in these cases, statistical remedies can help to elevate the credibility of the findings. In the following, we discuss four procedural remedies: (1) use of different data sources, (2) temporal separation, (3) proximal separation, and (4) psychological separation of scale of scale formats.

(1) *Different data sources.* An investigator nullifies the risk of CMB when relying on different data sources for the independent and dependent variables (Rindfleisch et al. 2008, p. 274; Ostroff et al. 2002). This approach makes it impossible for participants to develop implicit theories between independent and dependent variables.

First, researchers can survey different respondents to evaluate the independent and dependent variables (Gruner et al. 2019) – that is, use dyadic data: one portion of the sample is used to estimate the independent variables and the remaining portion evaluates the dependent variables. Empirical evidence supports the effectiveness of dyadic data to attenuate CMB. Correlations of independent and dependent variables when rated by one respondent ($r = 0.359$) dropped by 49% when different respondents evaluated them ($r = 0.184$) (Podsakoff et al. 2012).

Although this procedure appears promising, it requires large sample sizes, and therefore is not appropriate for all kinds of surveys. Particularly in organizational research, researchers observe generally declining response rates, making it especially challenging to recruit additional respondents (section "Non-response Bias"). It might also be problematic in small companies where the owner is in charge of most of the decisions (Rindfleisch et al. 2008).

Second, researchers can rely on a combination of secondary data and survey data. Most commonly, researchers collect independent variables via a survey study and evaluate performance outcomes from profit and loss statements (e.g., Vomberg et al. 2020). Research suggests that this approach is also effective. Obtaining independent and dependent variables from different data sources can reduce their correlations by 49% (Podsakoff et al. 2012, p. 548).

However, relying on different sources might not be feasible in several settings. For instance, use of different data sources is not viable when the two variables cannot be validly inferred from different sources (e.g., self-referential attitudes and perception constructs; Johnson et al. 2011), when archival data cannot adequately represent the construct, or when such data are available only for prohibitively high costs in terms of money or time.

(2) *Temporal separation of measurement.* An alternative might be to separate the collection of independent and dependent variables temporally by including a

time lag (e.g., Homburg et al. 2020; Jansen et al. 2005; Vomberg et al. 2020). Empirical research indicates that temporal separation of measurement can be effective for reducing potential CMB. However, effectiveness depends on the length of the time lag, with longer time lags triggering the possibility that intervening events might introduce new sources of biases (Podsakoff and Organ 1986; Chang et al. 2010). While some research indicates that temporal separation is effective for same point in time versus two weeks later (Johnson et al. 2011) and same point in time versus one month later (Ostroff et al. 2002), other work finds no significant improvement with relatively long time lags (30 vs. 36 months) (Rindfleisch et al. 2008).

(3) *Proximal separation*. Researchers can increase the proximal distance between independent and dependent variables in the questionnaire. As we elaborate in section "Decisions About the Question Sequence," separating measures significantly reduces shared variance (Weijters et al. 2009). For instance, concern regarding CMB can be alleviated by first measuring the dependent and then the independent variables.

(4) *Psychological separation of scale formats*. Researchers frequently rely on common scale formats for a variety of questions within a questionnaire. While common scale formats make answering the survey questions easier, they enhance the probability that cognitions formed when answering one question may be retrieved when answering another question. However, relying on different scale formats when assessing the independent and dependent variables reduces potential CMB (e.g., Vomberg et al. 2020), as different formats disrupt potential consistency bias (Feldman and Lynch 1988; Podsakoff et al. 2012; Rindfleisch et al. 2008).

Initial empirical evidence supports the effectiveness of using different scale formats. For instance, labeling anchor points differently for independent and dependent variables shrinks CMB by 18% (Johnson et al. 2011). Even larger decreases of 38% or 60% occur when the scale format is changed completely (Arora 1982; Kothandapani 1971).

Statistical remedies. The literature contains discussions of several statistical remedies for reducing CMB. Since these remedies are beyond the scope of the article, we briefly mention only a few. Podsakoff, MacKenzie, and Podsakoff (2012) provide a detailed overview of several statistical techniques, and Hulland et al. (2018) outline how to test for CMB. Hulland et al. (2018) discuss the correction-based marker variable technique, which is one of the most frequently applied approaches to address CMB in marketing research. This approach suggests that a marker variable that is theoretically unrelated to the constructs under investigation resembles the amount of CMB (Lindell and Whitney 2001). Grayson (2007, Appendix B) intuitively summarizes this approach.

Other approaches include (1) the measured latent factor technique, or measured response style technique, in which the researcher directly measure sources of CMB (e.g., Wathne et al. 2018), (2) the unmeasured latent factor technique, in which researchers model a method factor in structural equation models (e.g., Homburg et al. 2011), and (3) endogeneity-correction approaches, in which researchers employ instrument-free techniques (e.g., Vomberg et al. 2020).

Key Informant Bias

Conceptualization. Survey participants can act either as respondents providing self-reports or as key informants. While respondents describe their own beliefs, attitudes, opinions, or feelings, key informants generalize about patterns for a higher social unit (e.g., a company's culture) on the basis of their experiences (Seidler 1974). For example, in an employee satisfaction survey, employees act as respondents when they evaluate their own job satisfaction level. However, they act as key informants when they assess an organizational culture (higher social entity). Key informant bias can occur in the latter case; it comprises the distortion of the sample's covariance structure that arises because the data collection has taken place through key informants. As we elaborate below, the severity of key informant bias will depend on various factors, most pressingly on the expertise of the key informant (less bias if the key informant is knowledgeable, has a higher hierarchical position, and has longer job tenure) and the type of collected data (less bias for objectively verifiable measures).

To the best of our knowledge, only two studies systematically evaluate the occurrence of key informant bias (Homburg et al. 2012b; Kumar et al. 1993), and the two studies deliver conflicting conclusions. Kumar, Stern and Anderson (1993, p. 1646) report high levels of key informant *dis*agreement, whereas Homburg et al. (2012c, p. 605) find in their meta-analytical study high levels of key informant agreement (0.872).

In addition, Homburg et al. (2012c) investigate how large the systematic error provoked by key informant bias needs to be to create artificial effects or to mask true effects. They demonstrate that the requisite size depends largely on the study's sample size and the strength of the effect, and conclude that in the studies of their meta-analysis there is a risk that small and medium-sized effects were not correctly identified.

Reasons for occurrence. Key informant bias can emerge if investigators have unrealistic expectations about the key informant's knowledge. For instance, it might not be feasible for key informants to provide complex judgment about organizational characteristics that may result in random measurement error. In addition, key informant bias may emerge owing to positional bias or knowledge deficiencies (Phillips 1981). For instance, key informants' backgrounds can substantially influence the answers they provide (Homburg et al. 2005). When marketing and sales managers were asked to evaluate the marketing function (same higher social entity), mean values differed considerably between key informants from the two departments (Fig. 2). Sales managers perceive marketing managers (on a scale from 0 to 100) to have a rather low level of customer know-how (mean value = 37), whereas marketing managers on average consider themselves to have rather high levels customer know-how (mean value = 59).

In addition, in line with empirical findings on CMB, the risk of key informant bias largely hinges on the nature of the studied constructs. Key informant reports are reliable for objective and salient issues from the present (e.g., performance outcomes). However, for more abstract measures (e.g., organizational culture) key informants tend to be less accurate. Furthermore, a higher hierarchical position and tenure also increase reliability (Homburg et al. 2012c; Kumar et al. 1993).

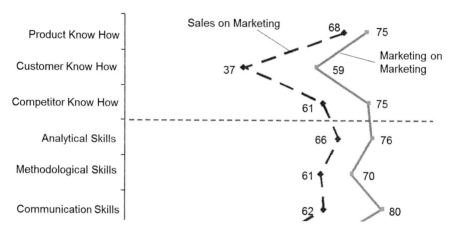

Fig. 2 Marketing and sales managers' evaluations of the marketing function – comparison of mean values (Homburg et al. 2005, p. 14, reproduced with the kind permission of the publisher)

Procedural remedies. The most important and effective remedy to alleviate concerns regarding key informant bias is the careful selection of key informants. The investigator needs to carefully align the contacted key informants with the objective of the study. Typically, key informants are not chosen randomly and are not deemed representative for the population. Instead, researchers select respondents who have special qualifications, such as their position in the company or their knowledge (Phillips 1981; Kumar et al. 1993).

The question of whom to contact as key informants depends primarily on the research context. For instance, if the research objective focuses on strategic issues, high-ranked key informants are probably appropriate. However, if the study investigates operational aspects, such as specific sales approaches used, then key informants with regular customer contact are more promising.

In addition, questions that require less demanding social judgments and instead are impersonal and focus on objective and observable phenomena seem preferable (Phillips 1981; Homburg et al. 2012c; Klarmann 2008). However, whether this condition is realistic depends largely on the context of the study. Nevertheless, even if more complex or abstract constructs are the focus of the study, the researcher might lower the risk of key informant bias with careful wording of the questionnaire items (section "Decisions About the Question Wording").

Finally, if key informant response accuracy is expected to be low or empirical evidence for reliability is scarce in the particular research domain, the researcher may use triangulation – that is, combining methods in the study of the phenomenon. For instance, investigators can try to survey multiple key informants per company. However, since triangulation is costly, sometimes difficult to implement (Rindfleisch et al. 2008), and devoid of substantial additional value if the responses of the first respondent have been accurate (Homburg et al. 2012c), this option should be carefully chosen.

Statistical remedies. Statistical procedures address either the reliability or validity of the key informant study. They aim either to establish or enhance reliability or validity (Homburg et al. 2012c) provide a systematic overview of various approaches). For instance, authors can establish reliability by demonstrating key informants' job tenure or experience with the company (Kumar et al. 1993) or by measuring their perceived knowledge level (e.g., Ghosh and John 2005; Kumar et al. 2011). In the case of triangulated data, researchers can also employ correlational approaches, such as intraclass correlation ICC(1) (Bliese 2000; chapter ▶ "Multi-level Modeling" Haumann et al. in this handbook) or the absolute deviation agreement index (Burke and Dunlap 2002; LeBreton and Senter 2008). To enhance validity, researchers can integrate factors representing the data sources into a structural equation model, allowing estimation of trait relationships while controlling for systematic error (e.g., Cote and Buckley 1987).

Social Desirability

Conceptualization. As one researcher noted over 20 years ago, "One well-known phenomenon in survey research is overreporting of admirable attitudes and behaviors and underreporting of those that are not socially respected" (Krosnick 1999, p. 545). This phenomenon is called social desirability and represents the distortion of the sample's covariance structure that arises owing to the tendency of respondents to reply in a manner that others will view favorably (e.g., De Jong et al. 2010). For instance, in a study on consumer innovativeness, 41% of the respondents indicated they owned, had repurchased, or had seen products that did not actually exist in the market (Tellis and Chandrasekaran 2010).

While social desirability is often considered a source of bias in survey research (e.g., Podsakoff et al. 2003), surprisingly few investigators explicitly address it in their studies (Steenkamp et al. (2010) and Tellis and Chandrasekaran (2010) represent some notable exceptions). As a consequence, knowledge about the impact of social desirability on survey results is scarce.

Reasons for occurrence. Theory proposes two factors to explain the occurrence of socially desirable responding: the level of awareness (self-deception vs. impression management) and the domain of content (agency-based vs. communion-based contexts). Self-deception occurs when participants *unconsciously* dissemble, and impression management occurs when participants *consciously* dissemble (e.g., Krosnick 1999; Paulhus 1984).

Regarding the domain of content, some respondents are more likely to engage in socially desirable responding because they have a need to be perceived as more powerful than others (egoistic response tendencies, arising in agency-based settings). Other respondents offer socially desirable responses because they have a need to be perceived as exceptionally good members of society (moralistic response tendencies, emerging in communion-based contexts) (Paulhus and John 1998; Paulhus 2002; Steenkamp et al. 2010).

Procedural remedies. Self-deception and impression management are particularly important in controlling or reducing potential social desirability bias. Socially desirable responding owing to self-deception might be part of a respondent's personality, and therefore should not be controlled for to prevent elimination of a central component of individual differences in personality. However, the impression management component should be controlled for because this component embodies a conscious bias (Paulhus 1984).

Several methods are available to prevent or at least reduce socially desirable responses to questionnaires. Survey researchers should assure respondents that their answers are anonymous, reinforce that the items have no right or wrong answers, emphasize that people hold different opinions about the issues addressed in the questionnaire, and encourage respondents to answer as honestly as possible. Paradoxically, socially desirable responding remains an issue under anonymous conditions when there is no one to impress (Mick 1996).

Another remedy is to allow respondents to report on the external world rather than answering questions about themselves. The solution is to ask indirect questions in the neutral third-person form that are not affected by the social desirability bias. This approach is based on the assumption that respondents project their opinion onto others and consequently give more honest answers, an assumption that Fisher (1993) demonstrates empirically. In addition, the social distance between interviewer and respondent should be reduced (Nederhof 1985), and socially sensitive questions should be eliminated or placed at the end of the questionnaire to avoid carry-over effects (Baumgartner and Steenkamp 2006).

Finally, a third way to deal with a social desirability bias is through randomized response techniques (e.g., De Jong et al. 2010, 2015; Himmelfarb and Lickteig 1982; Warner 1965). In this approach, respondents are asked a sensitive question (e.g., "Are you willing to pay higher prices for sustainable products?") with response options of "yes" and "no." Prior to answering the question, they flip a coin and adapt their answers following the outcome of the coin flip. If the coin flip returns "heads," respondents should answer the question with "no" regardless of whether they truly engaged in the questioned behavior. However, if the flip returns "tails," respondents should answer the question truthfully with "yes" or "no." Since investigators cannot see the outcome of the coin flip, they cannot tell whether a particular "no" response denotes a negative answer that reveals the respondent's true attitude or a coin flip that has come up heads (or both). Note that in this simplistic illustration, only the socially less desirable answer (i.e., "no") is concealed (De Jong et al. (2010) describe more advanced designs). In theory, this technique should counteract a social desirability bias. However, initial empirical evidence indicates that randomized response techniques can also deliver worse results than directly asking participants (Holbrook and Krosnick 2010; John et al. 2018).

Statistical remedies. The literature offers two main approaches to check or control for social desirability: (1) including a measured latent factor capturing social desirability in the empirical model (e.g., Podsakoff et al. 2003) or (2) correlating separate survey measures with a measured social desirability score (Steenkamp et al. (2010) develop a systematic process to check for social desirability concerns). The latter approach demonstrates whether a social desirability bias likely affects the constructs in the study and the first approach is intended to control for social desirability in empirical models. However, both approaches require the investigator to measure the social desirability construct. To do so, literature suggests relying on Paulhus's (2002) *Balanced Inventory of Desirable Responding* (e.g., Steenkamp et al. 2010).

Response Styles

Response styles lead to a distortion of the sample's covariance structure that arises because, regardless of the question content, respondents favor certain response categories (e.g., Van Rosmalen et al. 2010). The most frequently discussed response styles are respondents' tendency to select specific subsets of response options such as disproportionately favoring the positive side of a response scale (acquiescence response style, or yay-saying).

Response styles can compromise the comparability of the data: the same responses can have different meanings for different respondents. Participants may display different response styles between countries (e.g., Tellis and Chandrasekaran 2010) or between different modes of data collection. Response style biases are higher in telephone interviews than in written and online surveys (Weijters et al. 2008). Response styles thus undermine the ability to validly compare mean values. Furthermore, response styles can also influence construct variances and correlations between constructs. For instance, researchers found that response styles account for 8% of construct variance in their sample and for 27% of the variance in the observed correlations (Baumgartner and Steenkamp 2001).

However, despite their potentially biasing effects, response styles have not received much attention in the marketing literature. In the following, we discuss two common groupings of response styles: (1) acquiescence, disacquiescence, and net acquiescence and (2) extreme responding, midpoint responding, and response range.

Acquiescence, disacquiescence, and net acquiescence. Acquiescence, also called yay-saying, is the respondent's tendency to agree with items regardless of their content, whereas disacquiescence, or nay-saying, is the respondent's tendency to disagree with items regardless of their question content (Baumgartner and Steenkamp 2001; Tellis and Chandrasekaran 2010). Net acquiescence is acquiescence minus disacquiescence and reflects the tendency to show greater yay- than nay-saying (Baumgartner and Steenkamp 2001; Tellis and Chandrasekaran 2010). However, many researchers do not distinguish between acquiescence and net acquiescence (e.g., Greenleaf (1992) uses the label acquiescence but actually measures net acquiescence). We focus on acquiescence and disacquiescence.

Acquiescence poses problems for segmentation research because it can lead to the emergence of clusters that reflect response styles rather than attitudinal information (Greenleaf 1992). In addition, it may falsely heighten correlations among items that are worded in the same direction (Winkler et al. 1982). Remarkably, although acquiescence and disacquiescence appear to be opposites, empirical evidence demonstrates only small- to medium-sized negative correlations between them (Baumgartner and Steenkamp 2001: $r = -0.16$; Tellis and Chandrasekaran 2010: $r = -0.31$).

Dispositional (e.g., personality traits) and situational factors (e.g., item ambiguity) may explain why the three response styles occur (Knowles and Condon 1999).

Regarding dispositional factors, research has demonstrated inconsistent results for demographic variables (particularly gender). For instance, research shows that respondents with an acquiescence response style tend to be extroverted, impulsive, emotional, and undercontrolled. Respondents prone to a disacquiescence response style are likely to be introverted, cautious, rational, and overcontrolled. Acquiescence may be evoked by a desire to please, to be agreeable in social situations, or to display deference to the researcher (e.g., Krosnick 1999).

However, findings on the participants' cultural backgrounds are more consistent. Respondents from countries scoring high on collectivism (uncertainty avoidance) tend to display more (less) acquiescence in their response style (Tellis and Chandrasekaran 2010).

Regarding situational factors, participants are more likely to display an acquiescence response style if response categories are fully labeled (Weijters et al. 2010a), if response categories contain a neutral point (Weijters et al. 2010a), or if items are ambiguous (Podsakoff et al. 2003). Similarly, the personal situation of the participant can provoke an acquiescence response style. An acquiescence response style is likely to occur if participants read items uncritically (Messick 2012), if they experience time pressure (Baumgartner and Steenkamp 2006), or if their cognitive capabilities are exceeded (e.g., items at the end of a long questionnaire) (MacKenzie and Podsakoff 2012).

Extreme responding, midpoint responding, and response range. A respondent with an extreme response style tends to favor the most extreme response categories regardless of the item content. Midpoint responding refers to the tendency to use the middle-scale category regardless of the question content. Response range refers to the tendency to use a wide or narrow range of response categories around the mean response (Baumgartner and Steenkamp 2001).

Thus far, few conceptual and empirical investigations have focused on midpoint responding and response range. Current knowledge suggests that response ranges (and also an extreme response style) may relate to the characteristics of the respondent; they concern rigidity, intolerance of ambiguity, and dogmatism and are associated with higher levels of anxiety and possibly deviant behavior (Hamilton 1968).

In the last few years, investigators have become increasingly interested in extreme responding, with research linking it to personality (Cabooter et al. 2012; Naemi et al. 2009), scale format (Weijters et al. 2020), language (De Langhe et al. 2011; Weijters et al. 2013), and culture (De Jong et al. 2008) – although these papers do not necessarily use the term extreme response style (e.g., De Langhe et al. (2011) talk about "anchor contraction"). In addition, a recent literature stream on item response trees (IRTree) models investigated extreme (and midpoint) responding (e.g., Böckenholt 2012, 2017; Zettler et al. 2015).

Procedural remedies. Thus far, few procedural remedies have been identified for addressing biases from response styles. To the best of our knowledge, the literature provides only initial remedies for midpoint responding and for an acquiescence and a disacquiescence response style.

First, to address midpoint responding, some authors suggest eliminating the middle response category or including a "don't know" category (Baumgartner and

Steenkamp 2006; Schuman and Presser 1996). Second, since acquiescence is more likely for positively worded items and disacquiescence for negatively worded items (Baumgartner and Steenkamp 2001), investigators suggest introducing doubly balanced scales (Tellis and Chandrasekaran 2010). However, researchers need to carefully evaluate this option since negatively worded items may lead to misresponse (Weijters et al. 2010b; section "Decisions About the Question Wording").

Finally, response patterns are often problematic in international market research. Our recommendation is that researchers should make sure that all respondents receive a similar response format with equally familiar labels, preferably in their native language.

Statistical remedies. To investigate whether response styles likely bias the survey results, investigators should correlate the focal constructs of interest with measures of the different response styles – that is, use a measured response style technique. If this analysis does not demonstrate potential biases, then the investigators should proceed as planned. However, if potential threats to validity emerge, the authors should include measures of different response styles in their models (e.g., Weijters et al. 2008).

The literature proposes various ways in which response styles can be measured. For example, response styles can be calculated on the basis of items that are included in the survey – it is not necessary to add items to specifically measure response styles (Weijters et al. 2008, 2010b; Tellis and Chandrasekaran 2010). Alternatively, a latent-class model can identify different response styles (Rosmalen et al. 2010).

Sources of Systematic Errors in Survey Research: Representation Errors

Non-sampling Bias

Conceptualization. Investigators in many research projects are interested in generalizing findings to an overall population. Therefore, representativeness of the sample is important. That is, the sample needs to display approximately the same characteristics as the overarching population. However, as Fig. 3 illustrates, two biases may threaten representativeness: non-sampling bias and nonresponse bias. Non-sampling bias refers to the distortion of the sample's covariance structure that arises because the population is not adequately represented in the original sample (i.e., the sample that received the questionnaire does not resemble the overall population). Nonresponse bias is a distortion of the sample's covariance structure that arises because the structure of the final sample does not correspond with the structure of the original sample. We discuss non-sampling bias and nonresponse bias in section "Nonresponse Bias."

Whether non-sampling bias represents an important threat to a study depends on the research objective. If the researcher is interested in making generalizations to a particular target group, then non-sampling bias represents a severe threat. Thus, in the language of experimental research, if the research objective focuses on external validity, representative heterogeneous samples are required. However, if the

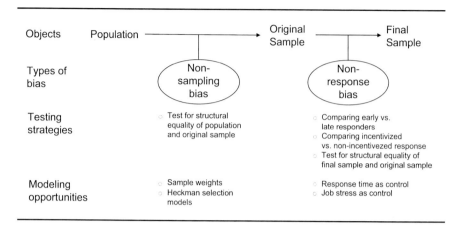

Fig. 3 Illustration of non-sampling and nonresponse bias. (Adapted from Homburg and Krohmer 2008)

researcher is interested in testing the veracity of proposed theoretical effects, non-sampling bias is a lesser issue. Stated differently, when the emphasis lies on internal validity, homogeneous samples can be adequate.

Short, Ketchen, and Palmer (2002) study the effects of non-sampling bias systematically. They link CEO duality, in which a firm's CEO concurrently chairs the board of directors, to a company's return on equity. The authors draw on different sampling frames, for which they observe substantially different effects: no effects in two cases, a positive effect in one case, and a negative effect in one case.

While sampling biases can have important consequences for research findings, the issue of sampling is often not systematically addressed. A review of studies published in leading management journals revealed that less than 40% of the studies included a discussion of representativeness (Short et al. 2002). Similarly, a review of marketing studies found that only 55% used an explicit sampling frame (Hulland et al. 2018). Finally, an important finding is that in general, samples chosen in social science are biased toward Western, educated, industrialized, rich, and democratized countries (Henrich et al. 2010).

Reasons for occurrence. Like resource constraints, the lack of suitable sampling frames can be a principal reason for non-sampling bias. For instance, while past consumer research could rely on telephone books for sampling frames, telephone books no longer validly resemble the population of interest (Iacobucci and Churchill 2010).

Similarly, for organizational studies, identification of adequate sampling frames can be challenging. For example, companies can be classified along numerous criteria (McKelvey 1975). In addition, the question arises regarding the organizational level at which the study should be conducted. A focus on strategic business units or product groups may present additional challenges for identifying adequate sampling frames (Sudman and Blair 1999).

Procedural remedies. The only procedural remedy is to base the sample on a sampling frame that is representative of the overall population. However, as mentioned, various reasons may obstruct knowledge of the overall population. Investigators may rely on sampling frames provided by data bases (e.g., COMPUSTAT), commercial mailing lists (e.g., Heide et al. 2014), or releases from Federal Statistical Offices regarding industry compositions (e.g., Vomberg et al. 2020). Nexis Uni (previously LexisNexis) may also serve to define the population for a study (Homburg et al. 2020). Nexis Uni has the advantage of including private companies, which are common for the business-to-business sector.

Statistical remedies. Statistical remedies can comprise methods to establish and to enhance representativeness. First, researchers can establish representativeness of their sample by comparing the structural equivalence of the original sample and the population (e.g., Vomberg et al. 2020). For instance, a χ^2 test may demonstrate the representativeness of the sample (Homburg et al. 2020).

Even if the distribution in the population is not known, researchers may compare the composition of two samples. For instance, Homburg et al. (2015b) compared the structural equivalence of samples obtained in two waves of data collection (years 1996 and 2013) in terms of industry sectors, sales volume, and number of employees.

Second, researchers may rely on Heckman selection models to control for non-sampling bias (Vomberg et al. 2020). Certo et al. (2016) provide a detailed discussion of Heckman selection models in the context of strategic management and also provide Stata code. Third, researchers may rely on sampling weights to enable the generalizability of their findings (Andreß et al. 2013; McElheran 2015; Raval 2020).

Non-response Bias

Conceptualization. In contrast to non-sampling bias, which refers to structural differences between the population and the original sample, non-response bias refers to structural differences between the original and the final sample (Fig. 3). Non-response bias may result from participants' failure to answer the survey (i.e., unit nonresponse) or from return of incomplete questionnaires (i.e., item nonresponse) (Klarmann 2008).

Analysis of reported response rates from leading management and organizational journals for the years 1975, 1985, and 1995 showed that the average response rate reported in these journals was 55.6% (with a large standard deviation of 19.7%) (Baruch 1999). However, responses have declined substantially over time – a trend that has been observed in various settings such as household studies (De Heer and De Leeuw 2002) or online surveys (Cook et al. 2000). Since the average US consumer receives more than 550 unsolicited surveys per year (compared with 50 to 100 for Germany, the UK, or France) (Iacobucci and Churchill 2010, p. 192), "oversampling" likely (partly) explains the dramatic reduction in response rates since Baruch's study. Today, response rates over 20% in organizational studies constitute the exception (Heide et al. 2007, 2014) and response rates around 10% represent the rule (Klarmann 2008).

In addition, response rates differ substantially between target groups. Top management studies in particular typically yield low response rates (Anseel et al. 2010).

However, participant drop-out does not necessarily threaten the results of a study. Non-response bias is a threat only when the reason for drop-out is related to the survey content (e.g., customers take part in a customer satisfaction survey depending on their satisfaction levels, or people with less discretionary time are less satisfied and less likely to respond to a satisfaction survey) and when sources that positively and negatively relate to survey content are not balanced (e.g., only unsatisfied customers do not reply in a customer satisfaction survey) (Thompson and Surface 2007).

Reasons for occurrence. Unit non-response is typically the result of respondents' refusal to participate in a survey. A review of factors that may drive unit non-response revealed personal factors, organizational factors, and survey-related factors (Klarmann 2008):

- *Personal factors*: Personal attitudes toward the survey (e.g., Helgeson et al. 2002; Rogelberg et al. 2001), involvement with the research topic (e.g., Groves et al. 2004), authorization (e.g., Tomaskovic-Devey et al. 1994; Gupta et al. 2000), and demographic criteria (e.g., Gannon et al. 1971; Gupta et al. 2000) have a strong impact on response rates.
- *Organizational factors*: Organizational factors such as industry profitability, dependence (i.e., subsidiary), and company size also influence the response rate (Tomaskovic-Devey et al. 1994).
- *Survey-related factors*: Number of contacts with participants (i.e., pre-notifications and reminder) (e.g., Yu and Cooper 1983), personalization of the survey (Yu and Cooper 1983), incentives (Church 1993; Yu and Cooper 1983; Yammarino et al. 1991), and length of the questionnaire (Yammarino et al. 1991) affect respondents' decisions to participate.

Procedural remedies. In the literature, four measures are discussed to diminish unit non-response bias (e.g., Klarmann 2008; Rogelberg and Stanton 2007; Anseel et al. 2010 for an in-depth review and evaluation of which techniques are effective for a particular target group):

- *Activities that increase the opportunity to participate in the survey*: These measures include (1) a deadline that can be determined by the participant (e.g., have the survey run for sufficient time so that vacation time does not impede response), (2) reminder notes, and (3) different modes of participation (e.g., written, online, per telephone)
- *Activities that emphasize the importance of the survey*: Emphasis can be achieved by (1) pre-notifying participants personally that they will receive a survey in the future, (2) reflecting participants' interests (e.g., an engaging title), (3) informing the participants about the survey goals.
- *Activities that decrease the perceived costs of the participation*: Researchers should (1) manage survey length and (2) carefully consider the survey design

- *Activities that raise the perceived utility of participation*: Researchers may provide incentives to participants. Common incentives in business-to-business contexts include social incentives (e.g., researchers donate of 10–15€ per participant for a social cause; Vomberg et al. 2020) and reports which outline the study results or benchmark a firm to sample averages; the latter two are more suitable incentives if participants are interested in the survey content. In business-to-consumer contexts payments (e.g., 5€ per participant; Homburg et al. 2019b), advance incentives (e.g., small gift included with the survey such as a pen), or a raffle (e.g., ten randomly chosen participants win a gift coupon from Amazon.com) represent commonly selected incentives. Thereby, the former two are likely effective even if participants are not involved with the survey content.

Statistical remedies. Researchers can use several different approaches to detect and to address a potential nonresponse bias (Rogelberg and Stanton 2007; Klarmann 2008). To establish that the final sample resembles the original sample, investigators can conduct a χ^2 goodness-of-fit test (Homburg et al. 2012b). If incentives are used for only a subset of respondents, then investigators could compare the answers of incentivized to non-incentivized participants. Researchers can also conduct follow-up interviews with non-respondents using a short version of the questionnaire (i.e., focal constructs) to determine the reasons for non-response (e.g., Groves 2006; Homburg et al. 2007). Finally, if researchers suspect that factors like job stress influence a participant's likelihood to respond, then they should also measure such variables and add them as control variables in their statistical models (Homburg et al. 2010).

Survey Research Process

In this section, we outline the general phases of survey research. Figure 4 shows that the typical survey research process starts with selection of research variables and ends with data analysis. Since we focus on the design of survey research in this section, we discuss questionnaire design in greater detail and comment only briefly on issues such as data analysis.

Selection of Research Variables

Which Relationships Are of Particular Interest?

In the first stage, the most important question is which relationships should be investigated. The answer is obviously determined by the research question the investigator wants to address. For instance, researchers might be interested in the role of formal and informal organizational elements for reacquiring customers (Vomberg et al. 2020). In this case, their conceptual model could contain formal reacquisition policies and an informal failure-tolerant organizational culture (Fig. 5).

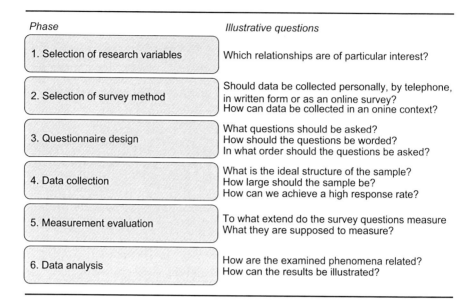

Fig. 4 Phases of the typical survey process

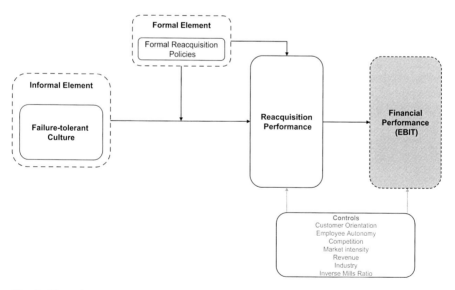

Fig. 5 Illustrative conceptual model (Vomberg et al. 2020, p. 121, reproduced with the kind permission of the publisher)

Importantly, the identification of variables requires familiarity with the research topic and is informed by prior research, conceptual considerations, or, for instance, in-depth interviews with practitioners. The conceptual model should be as coherent and complete as possible, encompassing potential mediating and/ or moderating effects if they are of interest for the subsequent analysis (e.g., Koschate-Fischer and Schwille (chapter ▶ "Mediation Analysis in Experimental Research") in this handbook).

Selection of Survey Method

Should Data be Collected Personally, by Telephone, in Written Form, or as an Online Survey?

We discuss data collection modes only briefly because our focus is on written and online surveys. The personal interview takes place face-to-face between the interviewer and the interviewee. The interviewer reads out the items on the questionnaire to the interviewees and collects their answers. The telephone interview can be a short, cold-call interview or a planned interview. The written survey usually involves sending questionnaires to the respondent by mail, with the respondent then returning the completed questionnaire. The online survey can be conducted in various ways – as a questionnaire attached to an e-mail or as a link provided on a website, in an e-mail, or in a QR-code.

Table 1 which is based on Homburg (2020) systematically compares the appropriateness of the four survey methods with regard to the (1) suitability for the object of study, (2) extent of data, (3) quality of data, and (4) length and costs of the project. These general evaluations may differ according to the survey context. In addition, the four forms of survey method likely differ in the sources of biases that may relate with them. Usually, personal interviews and telephone surveys are more prone to social desirability bias or acquiescence compared to self-administered questionnaires (i.e., written and online surveys) (Krosnick 1999; MacKenzie and Podsakoff 2012). In telephone interviews, midpoint response styles are less common than in mail or online surveys. In addition, telephone surveys tend toward acquiescence. Compared to mail surveys, online surveys display fewer disacquiescence and extreme response styles (Weijters et al. 2008; section "Response Styles").

How Can Data Be Collected in an Online Context?

Current trends in consumer research suggest that researchers increasingly rely on crowdsourcing platforms to obtain convenient and inexpensive samples. Mechanical Turk (MTurk), which was launched by Amazon in 2005, currently is the prevalent option. On MTurk, researchers act as employers and hire and compensate workers for participation in surveys, giving MTurk several likely advantages. Since incentives are comparably low on MTurk, researchers can conduct studies at lower costs without necessarily compromising data quality. In addition, participants likely have strong incentives to fill in the survey with due diligence, since they receive compensation only after passing screening and attention questions. Finally, MTurk allows researchers to implement their studies quickly (e.g., Chandler and Paolacci 2017; Levay et al. 2016).

However, skepticism regarding the use of MTurk is increasing. First, while MTurk samples are likely more heterogeneous than student samples, they are not

Table 1 Comparison of different survey methods

Criteria	Standardized verbal survey	Standardized telephone survey	Standardized written survey	Standardized online survey
Suitability for the object of study				
Possibility to explain a complex issue	Very good	Good	Rather low	Rather low
Possibility to use complex scales and filter questions in the questionnaire	Only when computer-aided	Only when computer-aided	Low	Very good
Possibility to demonstrate trial product samples	Very good	Rather low	Rather low	Rather low
Possibility to include multimedia (e.g., video and sound)	Rather good	Medium	Low	Very good
Extent of data				
Subjective length of the survey evaluated by the interviewee	Short	Medium	Long	Very long
Possibility to question a large sample	Low	Medium	Very high	High
Response rate	High	Medium	Low	Low
Risk of aborting the interview	Low	Medium	High	Very high
Quality of data				
Possibility of inquiries when comprehension problems occur	Very good	Good	Very low	Very low
Possibility of distortion due to the social interaction with the interviewer	Very high	High	None	None
Possibility to modify the research instruments during the field phase	Very good	Good	Low	Good
Length and costs of the project				
Length of the field phase	Medium	Short	Long	Long
Costs	Very high	High	Low	Low

necessarily representative of the overall consumer population. Second, participants on MTurk can be experienced survey takers who answer differently than less experienced survey respondents. Third, participants on MTurk can misrepresent themselves to participate in attractive studies with high payouts. However, misrepresentation is a general threat to online research (Goodman et al. 2013; Goodman and Paolacci 2017; Hulland and Miller 2018; Wessling et al. 2017).

TurkPrime and Prolific Academic (ProA) have recently emerged as alternatives to MTurk. TurkPrime is a website that utilizes MTurk but claims to overcome potential disadvantages of MTurk (e.g., participant misrepresentation) (Litman et al. 2017).

Graduate students from Oxford and Sheffield Universities launched ProA (http://www.prolific.co) in 2014. ProA provides several demographic details about its participant pool. Peer et al. (2017) who compare ProA with MTurk note that ProA participants are less experienced with research paradigms and provide more honest answers than MTurk participants. Marketing researchers increasingly rely on ProA for their studies (e.g., Castelo et al. 2019; Hagen 2020).

Qualtrics, Survey Sampling, Inc. (SSI), or Critical Mix, whose samples are likely more representative than MTurk samples, are other potential ways to collect data. However, these platforms are also more expensive. Finally, for short surveys (up to 10 questions) Google Surveys may offer a valid option. On Google Surveys, respondents take part because they want to read an article, lowering the likelihood of misrepresentation threats (Wessling et al. 2017; Hulland and Miller 2018).

Questionnaire Design

The design of the questionnaire usually represents the crucial stage in the collection of survey data. Mistakes that occur in this stage are normally hard to revise in later stages. Figure 6 outlines the phases of questionnaire design and presents examples of questions during the different phases.

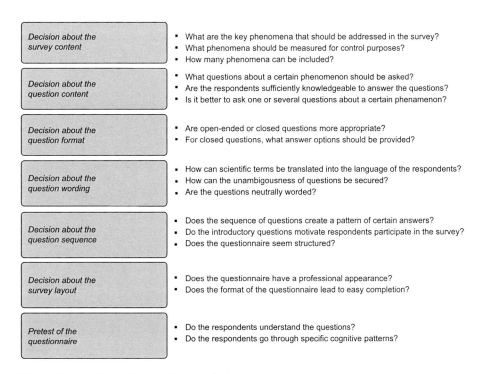

Fig. 6 Phases of the typical questionnaire design process

Decision About the Survey Content

Three fundamental questions determine survey content: What key phenomena should the survey address? What phenomena should be measured for control purposes? How many phenomena can be included in the survey?

What Are the Key Phenomena that Should Be Addressed in the Survey?

The key phenomena are provided by the research questions and the formulated hypotheses. Drawing on the conceptual framework (section "Selection of Research Variables"), investigators decide on the phenomena/constructs that should be included in the survey. In our example (Fig. 5), investigators would include variables that capture formal reacquisition policies, failure tolerance, and reacquisition performance. If financial performance cannot be obtained from archival data bases, then measures of financial performance should also be collected.

What Phenomena Should Be Measured for Control Purposes?

Besides including variables for substantive reasons, researchers should include theoretically motivated control variables to reduce "noise" in the independent and dependent variables. More importantly, however, survey researchers rely on control variables to account for non-randomness in their data. In contrast to experimental data, survey data are a form of observational data, and thus effects observed from survey data might be correlational and not causal in nature. To increase survey researchers' ability to infer causality, control variables serve to rule out rival explanations (section "Endogeneity in Survey Research"). For instance, in our example (Fig. 5), customer orientation may represent an important control variable. Theory suggests that customer-oriented companies might be more successful in winning customers back (i.e., customer orientation may affect the dependent variable) and also are more likely to have formal reacquisition policies in place (i.e., customer orientation may influence the independent variable). However, additional variables have been included to account for further potential differences.

To systematically collect control variables, researchers should review prior literature, follow theoretical considerations, and rely on their own plausibility considerations. They should then store the identified variables in a long list, such as an Excel sheet containing potentially relevant variables. However, in many cases, researchers end up with a list that captures too many variables to be assessed in one questionnaire and have to make a trade-off between questionnaire length and the completeness of the variables.

How Many Phenomena Can Be Included?

Consideration of questionnaire length is essential to reducing potential biases. Excessive length of the questionnaire can lead to respondent fatigue, resulting in careless and biased responses (MacKenzie and Podsakoff 2012) and contributing to an acquiescence response style (section "Response Styles"). In addition, long questionnaires can lead to survey non-response (section "Non-response Bias"), which may threaten the representativeness of the survey or lead to sample sizes that are too small for statistical analysis. As rules of thumb, we recommended the following:

- Telephone interview: 20–30 mins (planned interview; less for a cold call)
- Pop-up online survey: 25 questions
- Written survey: 100 questions

Researchers should also carefully evaluate options discussed in section "Sources of Systematic Errors in Survey Research: Measurement Errors" on how to control for biasing effects, such as using dedicated variables to account for potential CMB through the measured latent factor approach. However, this approach requires that the questionnaire becomes longer and that other substantially important variables be dropped from the questionnaire. Therefore, when designing their surveys, researchers need to critically reflect which biases are likely to present threats to the validity of their findings.

However, we point out that these rules of thumb are general, as situational factors also influence the length of questionnaires. For instance, questionnaires for high-level corporate decision makers need to be shorter, whereas surveys of lower-level employees might be longer. In addition, whether participants are willing to answer longer questionnaires depends heavily on their involvement with the research topic. If participants consider the survey interesting, they may be willing to answer longer questionnaires (section "Nonresponse Bias" discusses measures to stimulate involvement).

Decisions About the Question Content

A next critical step is to decide on the question content. Typical questions in this step are: What questions about a certain phenomenon should be asked? Are the respondents sufficiently knowledgeable to answer the questions? Is it better to ask one question or more about a certain phenomenon? Which questions should be selected?

What Questions about a Certain Phenomenon Should Be Asked?

To determine which questions are appropriate for certain phenomena, researchers first need to conceptually define their constructs of interest. These definitions logically precede the operationalization of the construct – that is, the process of coming up with items for their measurement.

The next important decision is whether to rely on new or established scales to measure the constructs. For many constructs, various established scales already exist in the literature. Researchers can find scales in the following ways:

- Manuals such as the *Handbook of Marketing Scales* (Bearden and Netemeyer 1999) provide an overview of established scales.
- The website inn.theorizeit.org allows online search for established measurement scales
- Articles published in leading journals typically provide the items for the scales they used (e.g., Homburg et al. 2011).

Researchers can systematically collect these established questions with appropriate references in an Excel sheet.

An important advantage of relying on existing scales is that they enjoy wide acceptance in the academic community because prior research has rigorously demonstrated their psychometric properties (e.g., Homburg et al. 2015a). In addition, development of original questions can sometimes lead to problems in evaluating their reliability and validity in later stages (section "Measurement Evaluation"), as even after rigorous pretesting, newly developed scales may not display required psychometric properties in this handbook).

However, a middle way is possible: researchers can combine newly developed items with established items to better fit their research context. In addition, researchers can adapt established items to the context of their study. For instance, Kumar et al. (1995) relied on established items from Price and Mueller (1986) but adapted them to context of their study (e.g., established item: "To what extent are you fairly rewarded for the amount of effort you put forth" vs. adapted item: "How fair are your firm's outcomes and earnings compared to the contributions we make to this supplier's marketing effort").

Are the Respondents Sufficiently Knowledgeable to Answer the Questions?

When selecting questions for the constructs of interest, researchers need to have their target respondent characteristics in mind (e.g., educational background). Researchers should especially evaluate whether respondents are sufficiently knowledgeable to respond to the questions – a pivotal concern in key informant studies (section "Key Informant Bias"). If respondents lack the ability to answer the particular questions, they may take on an acquiescence response style (section "Response Styles").

Is it Better to Ask One Question or Several about a Certain Phenomenon?

When deciding about the questions' content, researchers need to determine the number of questions they intend to ask per variable because adding redundant or unnecessary questions increases the questionnaire's length, perhaps squeezing out questions to collect information on other constructs or evoking the respondent's refusal to participate in the survey (Bergkvist and Rossiter 2007). However, relying on too few questions may result in problems regarding the reliability or validity of the measurement (section "Reliability and Validity: Fundamentals").

In the marketing literature, debate is ongoing as to whether and when single items can be used (Bergkvist and Rossiter 2007; Diamantopoulos et al. 2012). Usually, single items are sufficient when a construct can be precisely captured (e.g., demographic information, revenues). However, in the case of less concrete constructs (e.g., customer satisfaction, company culture, and leadership styles) multiple-item scales offer several benefits. First, multiple-item scales help to control random measurement error. Addition of further items to the measurement of one construct typically increases the overall reliability of the scale (section "Measurement Theory"). Second, multiple-item measures are more likely to capture all facets of the construct of interest (Baumgartner and Homburg 1996). For instance, the construct transformational leadership, which captures leader behaviors that make followers more aware of the importance of their job and that inspire employees to strive for the benefit of the company, is composed of facets such as "identifying and articulating a vision," "providing an appropriate model," or intellectually stimulating employees, thus requiring multiple items for its measurement (Podsakoff et al. 1990). Third, multiple-item measures enable evaluation of the psychometrics properties for the respective scales (section "Measurement Evaluation," in this handbook).

In the following, we provide analytical evidence that increasing the number of items can enhance the overall reliability of a construct (Moosbrugger 2008). Equation 3 formally defines the reliability of a construct (x) measured with a single item (e.g., the researcher measures customer satisfaction with a single question).

$$\text{Rel}(x) = \frac{Var(t)}{Var(x)} = \frac{Var(t)}{Var(t + e)}. \tag{3}$$

The observed variance of the construct x (customer satisfaction) is split into a true value t and a random error component e. Recall that reliability refers to random but not to systematic errors (section "Reliability and Validity: Fundamentals"). Therefore, we do not include a systematic error in Eq. 3. The resulting reliability measure from Eq. 3 ranges from 0 to 1, with larger values indicating higher levels of reliability.

When measuring a construct with multiple items (x_1, x_2, ..., x_k), the overall reliability of the scale (e.g., reliability of the overall customer satisfaction measure) can be calculated according to Eq. 4. For simplicity, Eq. 4 assumes that each individual item has the same individual reliability Rel(x).

$$\text{Rel}_{k \times x} = \frac{k \times \text{Rel}(x)}{1 + (k - 1) \times \text{Rel}(x)}. \tag{4}$$

Table 2 is based on Eq. 4 and demonstrates that the overall reliability of a construct increases with the number of items. To be more precise, Table 2 demonstrates the reliability of a scale depending on the number of items and individual reliability of an item (i.e., Rel(x) = 0.40 and Rel(x) = 0.60). For instance, if an individual item has a reliability of Rel = 0.40 and the researcher uses this single item

Table 2 Illustration of how number of items increases construct reliability

| | Scale reliability | |
| | Individual item reliability | |
# Items	0.40	0.60
1	0.40	0.60
2	0.57	0.75
3	0.67	0.82
4	0.73	0.86
5	0.77	0.88
6	0.80	0.90
7	0.82	0.91
8	0.84	0.92
9	0.86	0.93
10	0.87	0.94

to measure a construct, then the overall reliability of the scale is also $Rel_{1 \times x} = 0.40$. However, if the investigator asks five items to measure one construct (i.e., the questionnaire contains five different questions that all measure customer satisfaction) and each item has an individual reliability of $Rel(x) = 0.40$, the overall reliability of the scale increases to $Rel_{5 \times x} = 0.77$ – a result that clearly demonstrates the advantage of using multiple items. In addition, Table 2 demonstrates that scale reliability does not increase linearly with the number of items (i.e., moving from one to two items increases scale reliability more than moving from nine to ten items).

Diamantopoulos et al. (2012) replicate the analytical evidence in a simulation study and demonstrate that in most instances multiple-item scales outperform single-item scales. Situations in which single items outperform multiple items are not realistic in applied research, as researchers would not have a priori knowledge about which item is most adequate in the specific context.

Against these observations, we recommend relying on single items for concrete constructs (e.g., Carson and Ghosh 2019) but using multiple items for complex constructs (Diamantopoulos et al. 2012; Hulland et al. 2018). In the case of multiple items, as a general rule, researchers should select between four to six items (Table 2). In addition, to avoid reactance from respondents when evaluating similar questions, in the beginning of the survey researchers should point out the necessity of repeating similar questions.

Which Questions Should Be Selected?

A final and important decision is which questions should be selected. The domain-sampling model addresses this question theoretically. The domain-sampling model postulates that a given construct has a broad universe of possible items, behaviors, and responses that can serve as its observable markers or indicators (Nunnally 1967). Relying on concepts from sample selection theory (e.g., the concept of representativeness), the domain sampling model proposes that a valid representation of a construct is achieved when representative items are selected. Representative items can be identified through random sampling – that is, researchers randomly pick items from their list of items that could be used to measure the construct. However, when a given domain is adequately specified (e.g., through prior research or conceptual considerations), the researcher can deliberately select (rather than sample) a set of items (Little et al. 1999).

Decision About the Question Format

The important issue in this step is whether open-ended or closed questions are more appropriate, and for closed questions, what answer options should be provided?

Are Open-Ended or Closed Questions More Appropriate?

Open-ended questions allow participants to freely articulate their thoughts and opinions, while closed questions require participants to choose answers from a given list. Closed questions can have important advantages particularly for written and online surveys. First, the meaning of provided answers to closed questions might be clearer to the researcher than answers to open-ended questions, which likely require subjective interpretation. Relatedly, many statistical techniques (e.g., regression analysis) require quantitative and structured data (however, the automated analysis of qualitative data is evolving; e.g., Humphreys (chapter ▶ "Automated Text Analysis") in this handbook). Second, open-ended questions require great effort on the part of the respondent and may lead to participant refusal. Third and as a consequence of the aforementioned, researchers typically are able to ask more closed questions than open-ended questions – an aspect particularly relevant in organizational studies, for which participants are hard to recruit.

However, open-ended questions offer two potential benefits. First, participants can provide unusual and spontaneous answers to open-ended questions whereas their ability to respond is constrained by closed questions – if the investigator's list of questions and answer options omits important aspects, participants cannot deliver insights in this regard. Second, open-ended questions require less in-depth knowledge than closed questions, and participants can provide insights into topics the investigator has not considered.

However, we question whether these potential benefits arise for written or online surveys. First, we doubt that in all domains participants can better evaluate than the investigator what could be relevant for the research question (Schuman and Presser 1981). Second, investigators can rely on pretesting to discover and fix omissions in their closed questions. Schuman and Presser (1979) demonstrate that answers to closed and open-ended questions are comparable when closed questions are adapted to insights from pretests (section "Pre-test of the Questionnaire").

Our experience mirrors this discussion. We have noted that the quality of answers to open-ended questions in written surveys tends to be low. Consequently, we recommend focusing on closed questions in written and online surveys. However, we recommend that if possible, researchers change scales between dependent and independent variables to alleviate potential CMB (section "Common Method Bias"). We also recommend including an open-ended question at the end of the questionnaire allowing participants to provide further insights (e.g., "Are there additional issues you want to address?").

Relatedly, including an open-ended question has an additional advantage: it lowers the probability that respondents engage in response substitution, which occurs when respondents want to express attitudes and beliefs that the researcher has not asked about. Informing respondents at the beginning of the questionnaire that they will have an opportunity to express any other thoughts in an open-ended format can reduce the biasing effects of response substitution (Gal and Rucker 2011).

For Closed Questions, What Answer Options Should Be Provided?

When selecting answer categories for closed questions, researchers have various options. For instance, closed questions can be multichotomous (e.g., automotive industry, financial industry, consumer durables), dichotomous (e.g., purchase vs. no purchase), or measured on a scale (e.g., Likert scale, frequency scale). When a Likert scale is chosen, a frequently asked question is how many response categories should be provided. The empirical evidence on this matter demonstrates that reliability tends to increase with an increasing number of scale options. However, the marginal utility also tends to decrease. For instance, the quality of the provided answers is better for six than for four response categories (Preston and Colman 2000), and indicators with more response categories tend to display higher reliability (Alwin and Krosnick 1991). However, for more than seven response categories very few additional gains are observed. Thus, we recommend relying on five to seven answer categories.

In addition, participants can adapt their responses to seemingly arbitrary choices of scale labeling. For instance, Schwarz et al. (1991a) relied on two different labels for the same scale. In the first case, the scale ranged from 0 ("not at all successful") to 10 ("extremely successful"). In the second, the anchor values ranged from -5 ("not at all successful") to $+5$ ("extremely successful"). The result was that 34% of the respondents selected values between -5 and 0 on the scale from -5 to $+5$, but only 13% chose the equivalent values between 0 and 5 on a scale from 0 to 10. Since such behaviors are hard to anticipate, this example emphasizes the need for conducting pretests (section "Pretest of the Questionnaire").

Decisions about the Question Wording

Ambiguous question formulations can obviously bias the responses to questionnaires. If respondents do not comprehend the question, they cannot provide adequate information (Baumgartner et al. 2018). Thus, to ensure comprehension, question wording should be (1) simple, (2) unambiguous, and (3) neutral.

Simplicity is important, as complex items likely encourage respondents to develop their own idiosyncratic understanding of questions and/or to use biased response styles. In this regard, researchers need to decide whether to rely on item reversals. Item reversal can be achieved in two ways (Baumgartner et al. 2018; Weijters and Baumgartner 2012; Weijters et al. 2009):

- *Negations:* using "not" ("I see myself as someone who is. . ." talkative vs. *not* talkative), affixal negation of adjectives (e.g., *dis*honest), or using negative adjectives or adverbs (e.g., seldom) or the negation of a noun with "no."
- *Polar opposite items:* e.g., "I enjoy taking chances in buying new products" versus "I am very cautious in buying new products" or "talkative" versus "quiet."

We recommend that researchers avoid negations and use polar opposite items carefully. Reversed items can offer advantages: they can inhibit stylistic responding (e.g., acquiescence bias; section "Response Styles"), act as cognitive "speed bumps," and disrupt non-substantive response behaviors. However, and more pressingly, they might also lead to respondent confusion, lowering the quality of the collected data (e.g., Baumgartner et al. 2018; Weijters et al. 2009; Wong et al. 2003).

Simplicity can also be achieved when investigators

- Use rather short sentences and refrain from pyramiding (e.g., through relative clauses), as pyramiding or longer sentences can lead to complexity
- Avoid unnecessary variations in the format and structure of the questions
- Translate scientific language into the participants' language

- Avoid requiring participants to do computations: for example, instead of directly asking "how much do you spend on average in a focal supermarket per month," investigators should ask two simpler questions (e.g., "how often do you go to the focal supermarket per month?" and "How much do you spend on average per shopping trip at the focal supermarket?")

Unambiguousness also avoids biases. Item ambiguity impairs the respondent's ability to comprehend the question's meaning and clearly undermines the respondent's ability to provide accurate answers. When respondents are uncertain about how to respond to the item's content, systematic response patterns are likely evoked and respondents are more likely to rely on their own implicit theories.

Strategies to avoid item ambiguity include the use of precise and concise language. For instance, universal expressions (e.g., "all," "always") or vague quantifiers (e.g., "often," "many") mean different things to different respondents. Thus, expressions such as "I read many books" would be less valid than "I read ten books a year" (Johnson 2004). Churchill and Iacobucci (2005, p. 248) summarize further aspects which need to be considered in this regard (e.g., "about" could mean "somewhere near" or "almost," "like" distracts the attention of participants to the specific examples, and answers to the word "often" largely depend on the respondent's frame of reference).

Importantly, researchers should use the same words for the same issues. In addition, they should clearly define terms that respondents might interpret differently. For instance, in research on customer reacquisition management in business-to-business markets, in-depth interviews revealed that customer defections can be defined differently. For some companies, only customers who completely stopped purchasing qualified as defected. For other companies, customers that had lowered their purchasing volume represented defectors. Thus, in designing a subsequent questionnaire, the researchers defined customer defection in the beginning of the questionnaire to avoid ambiguity (Homburg et al. 2019a).

Neutrality is also important when formulating questions. To achieve neutrality, researchers should avoid suggestive formulations and anticipations of answers (e.g., "Do you also agree?"). Finally, researchers should avoid loaded words (e.g., market economy vs. capitalism) that are likely to bias participants' answers.

Decisions about the Question Sequence

Does the Sequence of Questions Foster a Pattern of Certain Answers?

As noted earlier, participants may form their opinions while answering the questionnaire (section "Psychology of Survey Response"). That is, answers provided to initial questions may activate information to answer questions at later points in the questionnaire (Schwarz 2003). Thus, researchers need to avoid generating survey data that yields only "self-generated validity" (Feldman and Lynch 1988, p. 421).

A prominent example from the field of political science that has been repeatedly affirmed since 1948 illustrates the effects of question sequence. In this example, participants were asked two questions:

- *Question A:* Do you think the United States should let Communist newspaper reporters from other countries come in here and send back to their papers the news as they see it?
- *Question B:* Do you think a Communist country like Russia should let American newspaper reporters come in and send back to America the news as they see it?

In randomized experiments, the share of "yes" answers pertaining to *Question A* largely depended on the order of the two questions. The group who saw *Question A* and then *Question B* agreed to question *Question A* in 44% of the cases. However, the group that was asked in reversed sequence (first *Question B* then *Question A*) had higher agreement with *Question A* (70% agreement) (Schuman et al. 1983; Schwarz et al. 1991b report similar examples).

These sequence effects also become important in customer satisfaction surveys. A central decision in customer satisfaction surveys usually is at which point the investigator should ask participants to rate their overall level of satisfaction (e.g., "Overall, please indicate how satisfied you are with the company"). Should the rating be solicited before or after asking specific customer satisfaction questions (e.g., "Please indicate your satisfaction regarding the products," "Please indicate your satisfaction regarding the after-sales service")?

Researchers observed that depending on the sequence, different psychological processes set in. If overall customer satisfaction is measured at the beginning of the survey, emotions typically dominate the assessment (e.g., gut feeling). However, if total customer satisfaction is measured at the end of the survey, the same question will trigger cognitive rather than emotional processes. Particularly in this case, the answers to the overall customer satisfaction question will likely depend on the replies to the specific customer satisfaction responses participants provided before.

Which order is the most appropriate largely depends on the research context. Researchers may measure overall customer satisfaction at the beginning (end) of the questionnaire for low (high) involvement products. As emotions (cognitions) are likely to be an important factor when purchasing low (high) involvement products, a more emotional (cognitive) response to overall customer satisfaction might be more insightful.

The literature discusses some measures researchers can employ to reduce the effects of question sequence. One approach could be to randomize the question order, which can easily be achieved in online surveys: researchers present the same questions in different orders to participants. Although this approach might seem intuitively appealing, the downside is that it cannot prevent order effects from occurring on the individual level. In addition, randomization may disrupt the logical order of the questions. An alternative might be to simply tell respondents that the order of presentation is random and therefore of no relevance (Krosnick et al. 1990).

The inclusion of buffer questions might also help to reduce sequence effects. For instance, researchers can include buffer questions between items they expect to evoke a large sequence effect – a tactic that likely lowers artificial correlations among items (Weijters et al. 2009).

Do the Introductory Questions Motivate Respondents to Participate in the Survey? Does the Questionnaire Seem Structured?

In general, we recommend that researchers start with an interesting opening question. This question should motivate participants to take part in the survey, and its importance increases in light of the declining response rates for questionnaires (section "Non-sampling Bias"). After the opening question, researchers should move from general to specific questions and ask sensitive questions later in the survey. Rapport is established as respondents answer general and nonthreatening questions early in the survey. Finally, when researchers cannot access different sources for evaluating independent and dependent variables, they should first assess the dependent and then the independent variables. Thereby, they lower potential demand effects (section "Common Method Bias").

Decisions About the Survey Layout and Pretest of the Questionnaire

Does the Questionnaire Have a Professional Appearance? Does the Format of the Questionnaire Lead to Easy Completion?

The layout of the questionnaire is a critical success factor. Participants perceive the questionnaire to represent the net of the asked questions, layout and design, and logical structure and architecture. All these aspects may affect the effort participants put into answering the survey and thus affect the likelihood of biases to occur (Presser et al. 2004).

In general, the questionnaire "should look as sharp as your résumé" (Iacobucci and Churchill 2010, p. 221). A clean appearance signals interest for the topic and also emphasizes the researcher's trustworthiness. A questionnaire's layout may also create the impression of short processing time and thereby increase response rates, lowering the threat of non-response bias (section "Non-response Bias"). Finally, the instructions should be clearly articulated and the question flow should be evident and supportive.

Pretest of the Questionnaire

Do Respondents Understand the Questions? Do Respondents Engage in Specific Cognitive Patterns?

While textbooks on the development of a survey are plentiful, there are "no silver bullets of questionnaire design" (Schwarz 2003, p. 593), and even experts struggle to anticipate all potential difficulties that arise when participants address the survey questions. Thus, "there is no substitute for in-depth pretesting" (Weijters and Baumgartner 2012, p. 565) and "*all* researchers should use pretests prior to running their main studies" (Hulland et al. 2018, p. 104, emphasis in original).

The goals an investigator may want to achieve when running a pretest are varied and include the following:

- Identification of ambiguous questions and problems of understanding
- Detection of incompleteness of answer categories
- Identification of potential information gaps of respondents
- Verification of the time required to complete the questionnaire

- A preliminary indication of validity and reliability of the measurement (but taking the pretest sample size into account)

Three methods usually pertain to pretests. First, the debriefing method permits pre-testers to complete the questionnaire and then discuss potential issues (for instance, online surveys allow participants to make notes that can be discussed afterwards). Online pretests allow investigators to track pre-tester behaviors, which they can discuss in debriefing meetings. For instance, they could track response time or employ eye-tracking software to identify problematic survey sections (Baumgartner et al. 2018). Second, the protocol method allows pre-testers to raise questions when filling out the questionnaire. Third, the think-aloud method (also referred to as cognitive interviews) require pre-testers to verbalize their thoughts when filling out the questionnaire (Ericsson and Simon 1980; Presser et al. 2004; Weijters et al. 2009).

Data Collection

As our focus is on the design aspect of survey research, we do not discuss in detail various data collection methods but confine our discussion to the importance of sample structure, sample size, and sample response rate. In this handbook, Bornemann and Hattula (chapter ▸ "Experiments in Market Research") provide a more detailed discussion of sampling procedures.

What Is the Ideal Structure of the Sample?

Sampling designs can be divided into probability and non-probability samples. Probability samples are random samples. For instance, a simple random sample assumes that observations are selected by chance from the population. While most statistical tests assume probability sampling, applied researchers often rely on non-probability sampling since random samples are often hard to obtain (Short et al. 2002). As already mentioned, in many situations the population of interest is hard to define (section "Non-sampling Bias"), which limits investigators' ability to draw random samples.

Literature distinguishes four principal ways of non-probability sampling. First, researchers might rely on convenience samples – that is, they select a sample on the basis of accessibility. Convenience samples are the most typical sampling form in marketing and management research (Short, Ketchen, and Palmer (Short et al. 2002) report 42%, and Hulland et al. (2018) report 43%). However, convenience samples are likely to be unrepresentative of the overall population. Importantly, in consumer research debate is ongoing about the use of a particular type of convenience sample – student samples (Peterson 2001).

Second, researchers may apply quota sampling where units are drawn to approximate known proportions found in a population. Third, investigators may rely on snowball sampling, in which researchers identify a few participants from the population of interest and ask them to forward the questionnaire. This technique is useful when determining the population of interest is highly challenging (e.g., as when market research focuses on extreme sports). Fourth, sampling may be based on typicality. Here, researchers do not focus on representative participants but on participants from whom they expect valuable input. This sampling approach is often used during pretests (section "Pretest of the Questionnaire"; Iacobucci and Churchill 2010; Short et al. 2002).

How Large Should the Sample Be?

The question of sample size is hard to answer without considering the specific research setting. A rule of thumb for regression analysis is to rely on 10 observations per parameter (Hair et al. 2010). However, in applied research projects, this ratio is usually larger. For instance, the ratio of sample size to variables could be 70.63 (Short et al. 2002).

Small samples can have important disadvantages. Smaller samples can lead to less reliable test statistics, as standard errors may increase. In addition, small samples may limit the types of statistical techniques that can be applied effectively. However, large samples can also be problematic, as negligible effects might become statistically significant owing to high statistical power.

Finally and importantly, no clear relationship exists between sample size and the sample's representativeness. Opinion polls have revealed that if researchers invest substantial effort in acquiring large samples, representativeness of the final sample might suffer. Therefore, sampling should prioritize representativeness over sample size (Assael and Keon 1982; Krosnick 1999; Rogelberg and Stanton 2007).

How Can we Achieve a High Response Rate?

In section "Non-response Bias," we discussed several techniques for countering potential non-response bias. As the same techniques should help to increase the response rate (Anseel et al. 2010), we do not describe these actions here. However, we note that the size of a response rate does not indicate the representativeness of a sample. In some instances, lower response rates can lead to more accurate results than higher response rates (Visser et al. 1996). Recent evidence confirms this observation and emphasizes that the assumed positive relationship between response rate and survey quality does not always hold (The American Association for Public Opinion Research 2016).

Measurement Evaluation

To What Extent Do the Survey Questions Measure What they Are Supposed to Measure?

After the questionnaires have been returned to the researcher, the quality of their measurement can be evaluated. In-depth discussions of how survey researchers can demonstrate the reliability and validity of their constructs appear elsewhere in this handbook (chapter ▶ "Structural Equation Modeling" by Baumgartner and Weijters).

In the following, we briefly mention which statistics researchers typically report to provide initial guidance. All of the presented techniques require researchers' use of multiple-item scales (section "Decisions About the Question Content").

Researchers can demonstrate the reliability of their constructs by reporting Cronbach's alpha and/or composite reliability values (both have threshold values of >0.70). Both estimate the squared correlation between a construct and an unweighted sum of its items; composite reliability represents a generalization of Cronbach's alpha because it does not assume equal loading across items.

Through confirmatory factory analysis, investigators can demonstrate convergent and discriminant validity. Convergent validity (which affirms that the items correlate with other concepts they should be related to) can be established for individual items by squaring the individual standardized factor loadings (threshold value: >0.40). At the construct level, researchers calculate the average variance extracted (threshold value: >0.50) (Baumgartner and Weijters (chapter ▶ "Structural Equation Modeling") offer more flexible cut-off values).

Researchers can rely on the Fornell-Larcker criterion (1981) to establish discriminant validity (which affirms the items are uncorrelated with concepts they are not related to). For each pair of constructs, the square root of the average variance extracted for each construct needs to exceed the correlation between them.

Data Analysis

How Are the Examined Phenomena Related? How Can the Results Be Illustrated?

Analysis of the acquired data is the final step in the typical survey research process. We mention this step only briefly for two reasons. First, important decisions in survey research precede the statistical analyses. Hence, the careful design of the questionnaire is a necessary condition for the empirical analysis to yield valid results. Second, many statistical techniques can be used to analyze survey data and their in-depth discussions appear in designated method chapters of this handbook: most commonly, researchers rely on regression analysis (chapter ▶ "Regression Analysis" by Skiera et al.), structural equation modeling (Baumgartner and Weijters 2017), partial least squares structural equation modeling (chapter ▶ "Partial Least Squares Structural Equation Modeling" by Sarstedt et al.), or analysis of variance (chapter ▶ "Analysis of Variance" Landwehr).

Endogeneity in Survey Research

Addressing endogeneity concerns is typically important when investigators rely on observational data such as survey data (Sande and Ghosh 2018). For instance, the study of Huang and Sudhir (2021) demonstrates the need for survey researchers to address endogeneity concerns. Their study shows that not accounting for endogeneity leads to an underestimation of the true effect of service satisfaction on customer loyalty. Such underestimation likely leads to less than optimal investment decisions in business practice. While an in-depth discussion of endogeneity is provided elsewhere in this handbook (chapter ▶ "Dealing with Endogeneity: A Nontechnical Guide for Marketing Researchers" by Ebbes et al.), we highlight several aspects that might be particularly important for survey researchers.

Conceptually, endogeneity concerns refer to alternative or rival causal explanations of the findings. Statistically, endogeneity concerns arise if the explanatory variables correlate with the error terms, for example in regression analyses. Literature distinguishes three sources of endogeneity: (1) omitted variables, (2) measurement error, and (3) simultaneity (e.g., Cameron and Trivedi 2005; Kennedy 2008; Rossi 2014).

First, with regard to omitted variables, survey research has an important advantage over secondary data. In principle, survey researchers can rule out omitted variable bias by including control variables (section "Decision About the Survey Content"). If researchers are able to identify all potentially omitted variables when collecting the data, they can estimate a "rich data model," through which they directly address endogeneity concerns and meet the "standard recommendation for limiting omitted variable bias" (Rossi 2014, p. 657). However, although these endeavors in theory may lower or rule out concerns of omitted variable bias, the success of a rich data approach depends on the researchers' ability to identify all relevant control variables. If all potentially omitted variables cannot be identified or if such variables cannot be measured, survey researchers can employ the procedures Ebbes et al. (chapter ▶ "Dealing with Endogeneity: A Nontechnical Guide for Marketing Researchers") outline.

Second, while measurement error in the dependent variable is absorbed in the residual error term, measurement error in the independent variables represents a principal form of endogeneity (Kennedy 2008; Vomberg and Wies (chapter ▶ "Panel Data Analysis: A Non-technical Introduction for Marketing Researchers") in this handbook). If survey researchers rely on multiple-item measures of their independent variables, they are able to directly evaluate measurement error and through structural equation modeling can directly rule out such concerns (e.g., Grewal et al. 2013; Baumgartner and Weijters (chapter ▶ "Structural Equation Modeling") in this handbook).

Measurement error may also arise in the form of biases in surveys. For instance, CMB (section "Common Method Bias") or key informant bias (section "Key Informant Bias") also lead to correlation between the independent variables and the residual error term. Therefore, the procedures we outlined in the previous sections can also serve as ways to account for endogeneity (e.g., procedural remedies to deal with CMB in section "Common Method Bias").

Third, simultaneity – for instance, in the form of reverse causality – may affect cross-sectional survey data. Potential simultaneity concerns should be considered in the development stage of the questionnaire. In this regard, potential instrumental variables can be included. For instance, Homburg et al. (2012a) studied the influence of comprehensive market performance measurement systems on market knowledge. To alleviate simultaneity concerns (i.e., market knowledge drives companies' use of

Table 3 Linking biases with steps of the survey research process: In which steps can researchers address potential biases?

Name	Definition of bias	Reasons for occurence	Remedies	Steps in survey research process
Common method bias (section "Common Method Bias")	Distortion of the samples covariance structure... ...that arises due to the fact that the same data source was used for measuring both independent and dependent variables	Plenty of explanations, e.g.: implicit theories consistency motif satisficing	Different sources for independent and dependent variables; Collect independent and dependent variables at different points in time; Increase distance between independent and dependent variables; Different scales for independent and dependent variables; Inclusion of marker variable or direct measure of source of common method variance	Data collection; Data collection; Decision about question sequence; Decision abou the question format; Decision about the survey content
Key informant bias (section "Key Informant Bias")	...that arises due to the fact that the data collection has taken place through key informants providing information about a larger social unit	Positional bias; Knowledge deficiencies	Adequate selection of key informants; Triangulation; Avoid demanding evaluations of complex social judgments (if possible in the particular research context); Report average job and company experience of participants	Data collection; Decision about survey content; Decision about survey content
Social desirability (section "Social Desirability")	...that arises due to the tendency of respondents to reply in a manner that will be viewed favorably by others	Level of awareness: unconcious self-deception versus deliberate impression management; Content domain: egoistic responde tendencies versus moralistic response tendencies	Ensuring anonymity of respondents; Reinforce that there are no right or wrong answers; Encourage honest answers; Indirect questioning; Distance between respondent and researcher; With caution: Inclusion of negatively valenced items; Social sensitive questions asked at the end of the questionnaire	Decision about question sequence and; Decision about survey layout; Decision about question wording; Selection of research method; Decision about question wording; Decision about question sequence

Response styles (section "Response Styles")	… that arises due to the fact that respondents, regardless of the question content, favor certain response categories	Plenty of explanations, e.g.: Confirmation bias, Satisficing, Impression management, Item ambiguity, Personality traits of respondent	*With* caution: Inclusion of balanced scales (i.e., negative and positive items) *Potentially*: Additional items for deriving measures of response styles	Decision about question wording, Decision about research variables
Non-sampling bias (section "Non-sampling Bias")	… that arises due to the fact that the population is not adequately represented in the original sample	Lack of knowledge about population	Relying on sampling frame, Inclusion of variables on which selection likely appear in the questionnaire	Data collection, Decision about research variables
Non-response bias (section "Nonresponse Bias")	… that arises due to the fact that the structure of the final sample does not coincide with the structure of the original sample	Participant declines survey due to (1) personal, (2) organizational, or (3) survey factors, Inability to reach participant	Increase opportunity to participate, Emphasize importance of the survey, Decrease perceived costs of participation, Raise perceived utility of participation	Data collection, Selection of survey method, Cover Letter, Decision about survey layout, Decision about question content, Decision about survey layout, Pretest of the questionnaire, Data collection

comprehensive market performance measurement systems), the authors relied on an instrumental variable approach and directly measured an instrumental variable in their questionnaire.

Conclusion

Surveys are flexible and powerful ways to address research questions. Indeed, in many situations it is hard to imagine how topics can be studied without directly asking participants questions. However, effective survey research requires careful survey design. As respondents usually develop answers to surveys in the course of completing a survey, investigators must craft their surveys meticulously to avoid potential biases.

To help researchers construct their surveys, we first outlined the psychology of survey response and discussed important biases. Awareness of these biases helps survey researchers develop surveys that are less susceptible to biases. We have also described the general survey process and discussed important decisions investigators face in each step, and in Table 3, we connect those insights: we delineate the types of biases and link these biases to steps in the survey process where researchers can alleviate these biasing effects.

In closing, we note that many of the issues we discussed arise in other forms of research. For example, decisions regarding question content and data collection are equally important for experimental studies (chapter ▶ "Experiments in Market Research" by Bornemann and Hattula; chapter ▶ "Field Experiments" by Valli et al.), and our discussion of CMB is applicable when experimental studies measure mediating variables (chapter ▶ "Mediation Analysis in Experimental Research" by Koschate-Fischer and Schwille).

Cross-References

▶ Analysis of Variance
▶ Automated Text Analysis
▶ Challenges in Conducting International Market Research
▶ Dealing with Endogeneity: A Nontechnical Guide for Marketing Researchers
▶ Experiments in Market Research
▶ Measuring Customer Satisfaction and Customer Loyalty
▶ Mediation Analysis in Experimental Research
▶ Partial Least Squares Structural Equation Modeling
▶ Regression Analysis
▶ Structural Equation Modeling

References

Alwin, D. F., & Krosnick, J. A. (1991). The reliability of survey attitude measurement: The influence of question and respondent attributes. *Sociological Methods & Research, 20*(1), 139–181.

Andreß, H. J., Golsch, K., & Schmidt, A. W. (2013). Applied panel data analysis for economic and social surveys. Springer-Verlag Berlin Heidelberg.

Anseel, F., Lievens, F., Schollaert, E., & Choragwicka, B. (2010). Response rates in organizational science, 1995–2008: A meta-analytic review and guidelines for survey researchers. *Journal of Business and Psychology, 25*(3), 335–349.

Arora, R. (1982). Validation of an SOR model for situation, enduring, and response components of involvement. *Journal of Marketing Research, 19*, 505–516.

Assael, H., & Keon, J. (1982). Nonsampling vs. sampling errors in survey research. *Journal of Marketing, 46*, 114–123.

Baruch, Y. (1999). Response rate in academic studies – A comparative analysis. *Human Relations, 52*(4), 421–438.

Baumgartner, H., & Homburg, C. (1996). Applications of structural equation modeling in marketing and consumer research: A review. *International Journal of Research in Marketing, 13*(2), 139–161.

Baumgartner, H., & Steenkamp, J. B. E. (2001). Response styles in marketing research: A cross-national investigation. *Journal of Marketing Research, 38*(2), 143–156.

Baumgartner, H., & Steenkamp, J. B. E. (2006). Response biases in marketing research. In R. Grover & M. Vriens (Eds.), *The handbook of marketing research. Uses, misuses, and future advances* (pp. 95–109). Thousand Oaks: Sage.

Baumgartner, H., & Weijters, B. (2017). Measurement models for marketing constructs. In B. Wierenga & R. Van der Lans (Eds.), *Handbook of marketing decision models* (International series in operations research & management science) (Vol. 254). Cham: Springer.

Baumgartner, H., Weijters, B., & Pieters, R. (2018). Misresponse to survey questions: A conceptual framework and empirical test of the effects of reversals, negations, and polar opposite core concepts. *Journal of Marketing Research, 55*(6), 869–883.

Bearden, W. O., & Netemeyer, R. G. (1999). *Handbook of marketing scales: Multi-item measures for marketing and consumer behavior research*. Thousand Oaks, Calif: Sage.

Bergkvist, L., & Rossiter, J. R. (2007). The predictive validity of multiple-item versus single-item measures of the same constructs. *Journal of Marketing Research, 44*(2), 175–184.

Bliese, P. D. (2000). Within-group agreement, non-independence, and reliability: Implications for data aggregation and analysis. In K. J. Klein & S. W. J. Kozlowski (Eds.), *Multilevel theory, research, and methods in organizations: Foundations, extensions, and new directions* (pp. 349–381). San Francisco: Jossey-Bass.

Böckenholt, U. (2012). Modeling multiple response processes in judgment and choice. *Psychological Methods, 17*(4), 665–678.

Böckenholt, U. (2017). Measuring response styles in Likert items. *Psychological Methods, 22*(1), 69.

Bryman, A., & Bell, E. (2015). *Business research methods* (4th ed.). Oxford University Press.

Burke, M. J., & Dunlap, W. P. (2002). Estimating interrater agreement with the average deviation index: A user's guide. *Organizational Research Methods, 5*(2), 159–172.

Cabooter, E., Millet, K., Pandelaere, M., & Weijters, B. (2012). The 'I' in extreme responding. Paper presented at the European Marketing Academy Conference, Lisbon.

Cameron, A. C., & Trivedi, P. K. (2005). *Microeconometrics – Methods and applications*. New York: Cambridge University Press.

Carson, S. J., & Ghosh, M. (2019). An integrated power and efficiency model of contractual channel governance: Theory and empirical evidence. *Journal of Marketing, 83*(4), 101–120.

Castelo, N., Bos, M. W., & Lehmann, D. R. (2019). Task-dependent algorithm aversion. *Journal of Marketing Research, 56*(5), 809–825.

Certo, S. T., Busenbark, J. R., Woo, H. S., & Semadeni, M. (2016). Sample selection bias and Heckman models in strategic management research. *Strategic Management Journal, 37*(13), 2639–2657.

Chandler, J. J., & Paolacci, G. (2017). Lie for a dime: When most prescreening responses are honest but most study participants are impostors. *Social Psychological and Personality Science, 8*(5), 500–508.

Chang, S. J., Van Witteloostuijn, A., & Eden, L. (2010). From the editors: Common method variance in international business research. *Journal of International Business Studies, 41*, 178–184.

Church, A. H. (1993). Estimating the effect of incentives on mail survey response rates: A meta-analysis. *Public Opinion Quarterly, 57*(1), 62–79.

Churchill, G. A., & Iacobucci, D. (2005). *Marketing research. Methodological foundations* (9th ed.). Mason: South-Western Cengage Learning.

Cook, C., Heath, F., & Thompson, R. L. (2000). A meta-analysis of response rates in web-or internet-based surveys. *Educational and Psychological Measurement, 60*(6), 821–836.

Cote, J. A., & Buckley, M. R. (1987). Estimating trait, method, and error variance: Generalizing across 70 construct validation studies. *Journal of Marketing Research, 24*, 315–318.

Cote, J. A., & Buckley, M. R. (1988). Measurement error and theory testing in consumer research: An illustration of the importance of construct validation. *Journal of Consumer Research, 14*(4), 579–582.

Crampton, S. M., & Wagner, J. A., III. (1994). Percept-percept inflation in microorganizational research: An investigation of prevalence and effect. *Journal of Applied Psychology, 79*(1), 67.

De Heer, W., & De Leeuw, E. (2002). Trends in household survey nonresponse: A longitudinal and international comparison. In *Survey nonresponse* (p. 41). New York: Wiley.

De Jong, M. G., Steenkamp, J. B. E., Fox, J. P., & Baumgartner, H. (2008). Using item response theory to measure extreme response style in marketing research: A global investigation. *Journal of Marketing Research, 45*(1), 104–115.

De Jong, M. G., Pieters, R., & Fox, J. P. (2010). Reducing social desirability bias through item randomized response: An application to measure underreported desires. *Journal of Marketing Research, 47*(1), 14–27.

De Jong, M. G., Fox, J. P., & Steenkamp, J. B. E. (2015). Quantifying under-and overreporting in surveys through a dual-questioning-technique design. *Journal of Marketing Research, 52*(6), 737–753.

De Langhe, B., Puntoni, S., Fernandes, D., & Van Osselaer, S. M. J. (2011). The anchor contraction effect in international marketing research. *Journal of Marketing Research, 48*(2), 366–380.

Diamantopoulos, A., Sarstedt, M., Fuchs, C., Wilczynski, P., & Kaiser, S. (2012). Guidelines for choosing between multi-item and single-item scales for construct measurement: a predictive validity perspective. *Journal of the Academy of Marketing Science, 40*(3), 434–449.

Ericsson, K. A., & Simon, H. A. (1980). Verbal reports as data. *Psychological Review, 87*(3), 215–251.

Evans, M. G. (1985). A Monte Carlo study of the effects of correlated method variance in moderated multiple regression analysis. *Organizational Behavior and Human Decision Processes, 36*(3), 305–323.

Feldman, J. M., & Lynch, J. G. (1988). Self-generated validity and other effects of measurement on belief, attitude, intention, and behavior. *Journal of Applied Psychology, 73*(3), 421.

Fisher, R. J. (1993). Social desirability bias and the validity of indirect questioning. *Journal of Consumer Research, 20*(2), 303–315.

Fornell, C., & Larcker, D. F. (1981). Structural Equation Models with Unobservable Variables and Measurement Error: Algebra and Statistics. *Journal of Marketing Research, 18*(3):382–388. https://doi.org/10.1177/002224378101800313

Fornell, C., Johnson, M. D., Anderson, E. W., Cha, J., & Bryant, B. E. (1996). The American customer satisfaction index: nature, purpose, and findings. *Journal of Marketing, 60*, 7–18.

Gal, D., & Rucker, D. D. (2011). Answering the unasked question: Response substitution in consumer surveys. *Journal of Marketing Research, 48*(February), 185–195.

Gannon, M. J., Nothern, J. C., & Carroll, S. J. (1971). Characteristics of nonrespondents among workers. *Journal of Applied Psychology, 55*(6), 586.

Ghosh, M., & John, G. (2005). Strategic fit in industrial alliances: An empirical test of governance value analysis. *Journal of Marketing Research, 42*(3), 346–357.

Goodman, J. K., & Paolacci, G. (2017). Crowdsourcing consumer research. *Journal of Consumer Research, 44*(1), 196–210.

Goodman, J. K., Cryder, C. E., & Cheema, A. (2013). Data collection in a flat world: The strengths and weaknesses of Mechanical Turk samples. *Journal of Behavioral Decision Making, 26*(3), 213–224.

Grayson, K. (2007). Friendship versus business in marketing relationships. *Journal of Marketing, 71*(4), 121–139.

Greenleaf, E. A. (1992). Measuring extreme response style. *Public Opinion Quarterly, 56*(3), 328–351.

Grewal, R., Kumar, A., Mallapragada, G., & Saini, A. (2013). Marketing channels in foreign markets: Control mechanisms and the moderating role of multinational corporation headquarters–subsidiary relationship. *Journal of Marketing Research, 50*(3), 378–398.

Groves, R. M. (2006). Nonresponse rates and nonresponse bias in household surveys. *Public Opinion Quarterly, 70*(5), 646–675.

Groves, R. M., Presser, S., & Dipko, S. (2004). The role of topic interest in survey participation decisions. *Public Opinion Quarterly, 68*(1), 2–31.

Gruner, R. L., Vomberg, A., Homburg, C., & Lukas, B. A. (2019). Supporting new product launches with social media communication and online advertising: Sales volume and profit implications. *Journal of Product Innovation Management, 36*(2), 172–195.

Gupta, N., Shaw, J. D., & Delery, J. E. (2000). Correlates of response outcomes among organizational key informants. *Organizational Research Methods, 3*(4), 323–347.

Hagen, L. (2020). Pretty healthy food: How and when aesthetics enhance perceived healthiness. *Journal of Marketing*, forthcoming.

Hair, J. F., Jr., Black, W. C., Babin, B. J., & Anderson, R. E. (2010). *Multivariate data analysis* (7th ed.). Upper Saddle River: Prentice Hall.

Hamilton, D. L. (1968). Personality attributes associated with extreme response style. *Psychological Bulletin, 69*(3), 192.

Heide, J. B., Wathne, K. H., & Rokkan, A. I. (2007). Interfirm monitoring, social contracts, and relationship outcomes. *Journal of Marketing Research, 44*(3), 425–433.

Heide, J. B., Kumar, A., & Wathne, K. H. (2014). Concurrent sourcing, governance mechanisms, and performance outcomes in industrial value chains. *Strategic Management Journal, 35*(8), 1164–1185.

Helgeson, J. G., Voss, K. E., & Terpening, W. D. (2002). Determinants of mail-survey response: Survey design factors and respondent factors. *Psychology & Marketing, 19*(3), 303–328.

Henrich, J., Heine, S. J., & Norenzayan, A. (2010). Most people are not WEIRD. *Nature, 466*(7302), 29.

Himmelfarb, S., & Lickteig, C. (1982). Social desirability and the randomized response technique. *Journal of Personality and Social Psychology, 43*, 710–717.

Holbrook, A. L., & Krosnick, J. A. (2010). Measuring voter turnout by using the randomized response technique: Evidence calling into question the method's validity. *Public Opinion Quarterly, 74*(2), 328–343.

Homburg, C. (2020). *Marketingmanagement: Strategie – Instrumente – Umsetzung – Unternehmensführung* (7th ed.). Heidelberg: Springer.

Homburg, C., & Klarmann, M. (2009). Multi informant-designs in der empirischen betriebswirtschaftlichen Forschung. *Die Betriebswirtschaft, 69*(2), 147.

Homburg, C., & Krohmer, H. (2008). Der Prozess der Marktforschung: Festlegung der Datenerhebungsmethode, Stichprobenbildung und Fragebogengestaltung. In A. Herrmann, C. Homburg, & M. Klarmann (Eds.), *Handbuch Marktforschung*. Heidelberg: Springer Gabler.

Homburg, C., Jensen, O., & Klarmann, M. (2005). *Die Zusammenarbeit zwischen Marketing und Vertrieb-eine vernachlässigte Schnittstelle* (Vol. 86). Mannheim: Inst. für Marktorientierte Unternehmensführung, Univ. Mannheim.

Homburg, C., Grozdanovic, M., & Klarmann, M. (2007). Responsiveness to customers and competitors: The role of affective and cognitive organizational systems. *Journal of Marketing, 71*(3), 18–38.

Homburg, C., Klarmann, M., & Schmitt, J. (2010). Brand awareness in business markets: When is it related to firm performance? *International Journal of Research in Marketing, 27*(3), 201–212.

Homburg, C., Müller, M., & Klarmann, M. (2011). When should the customer really be king? On the optimum level of salesperson customer orientation in sales encounters. *Journal of Marketing, 75*(2), 55–74.

Homburg, C., Artz, M., & Wieseke, J. (2012a). Marketing performance measurement systems: Does comprehensiveness really improve performance? *Journal of Marketing, 76*(3), 56–77.

Homburg, C., Jensen, O., & Hahn, A. (2012b). How to organize pricing? Vertical delegation and horizontal dispersion of pricing authority. *Journal of Marketing, 76*(5), 49–69.

Homburg, C., Klarmann, M., Reimann, M., & Schilke, O. (2012c). What drives key informant accuracy? *Journal of Marketing Research, 49*(August), 594–608.

Homburg, C., Schwemmle, M., & Kuehnl, C. (2015a). New product design: Concept, measurement, and consequences. *Journal of Marketing, 79*(3), 41–56.

Homburg, C., Vomberg, A., Enke, M., & Grimm, P. H. (2015b). The loss of the marketing department's influence: Is it really happening? And why worry? *Journal of the Academy of Marketing Science, 43*(1), 1–13.

Homburg, C., Gwinner, O., & Vomberg, A. (2019a). *Customer reacquisition in business-to-business contexts*. Working paper.

Homburg, C., Lauer, K., & Vomberg, A. (2019b). The multichannel pricing dilemma: Do consumers accept higher offline than online prices? *International Journal of Research in Marketing, 36*(4), 597–612.

Homburg, C., Vomberg, A., & Muehlhaeuser, S. (2020). Design and governance of multichannel sales systems: Financial performance consequences in business-to-business markets. *Journal of Marketing Research, 57*(6), 1113–1134.

Huang, G., & Sudhir, K. (2021). The Causal Effect of Service Satisfaction on Customer Loyalty. *Management Science, 67*(1), 317–341.

Hulland, J. (2019). In through the out door. *Journal of the Academy of Marketing Science, 47*(1), 1–3.

Hulland, J., & Miller, J. (2018). Keep on Turkin? *Journal of the Academy of Marketing Science, 46*(5), 789–794. https://doi-org.proxy-ub.rug.nl/10.1007/s11747-018-0587-4

Hulland, J., Baumgartner, H., & Smith, K. M. (2018). Marketing survey research best practices: Evidence and recommendations from a review of JAMS articles. *Journal of the Academy of Marketing Science, 46*(1), 92–108.

Iacobucci, D. (2013). *Marketing models: Multivariate statistics and marketing analytics* (International Edition). South-Western: Cengage Learning.

Iacobucci, D., & Churchill, G. A. (2010). *Marketing research. Methodological foundations* (10th ed.). Mason: South-Western Cengage Learning.

Jansen, J. J., Van Den Bosch, F. A., & Volberda, H. W. (2005). Managing potential and realized absorptive capacity: How do organizational antecedents matter? *Academy of Management Journal, 48*(6), 999–1015.

Jansen, J. J., Van Den Bosch, F. A., & Volberda, H. W. (2006). Exploratory innovation, exploitative innovation, and performance: Effects of organizational antecedents and environmental moderators. *Management science, 52*(11), 1661–1674.

John, L. K., Loewenstein, G., Acquisti, A., & Vosgerau, J. (2018). When and why randomized response techniques (fail to) elicit the truth. *Organizational Behavior and Human Decision Processes, 148*, 101–123.

Johnson, J. A. (2004). The impact of item characteristics on item and scale validity. *Multivariate Behavioral Research, 39*(2), 273–302.

Johnson, R. E., Rosen, C. C., & Djurdjevic, E. (2011). Assessing the impact of common method variance on higher order multidimensional constructs. *Journal of Applied Psychology, 96*(4), 744.

Kennedy, P. (2008). *A guide to econometrics* (6th ed.). Cambridge, MA: Wiley-Blackwell.

Klarmann, M. (2008). *Methodische Problemfelder der Erfolgsfaktorenforschung: Bestandsaufnahme und empirische Analysen* (Doctoral dissertation).

Knowles, E. S., & Condon, C. A. (1999). Why people say "yes": A dual-process theory of acquiescence. *Journal of Personality and Social Psychology, 77*(2), 379.

Kothandapani, V. (1971). Validation of feeling, belief, and intention to act as three components of attitude and their contribution to prediction of contraceptive behavior. *Journal of Personality and Social Psychology, 19*(3), 321.

Krosnick, J. A. (1999). Survey research. *Annual Review of Psychology, 50*(1), 537–567.

Krosnick, J. A., Li, F., & Lehman, D. R. (1990). Conversational conventions, order of information acquisition, and the effect of base rates and individuating information on social judgments. *Journal of Personality and Social Psychology, 59*(6), 1140.

Kumar, N., Stern, L. W., & Anderson, J. C. (1993). Conducting interorganizational research using key informants. *Academy of Management Journal, 36*(6), 1633–1651.

Kumar, N., Scheer, L. K., & Steenkamp, J. B. E. (1995). The effects of supplier fairness on vulnerable resellers. *Journal of Marketing Research, 32*, 54–65.

Kumar, A., Heide, J. B., & Wathne, K. H. (2011). Performance implications of mismatched governance regimes across external and internal relationships. *Journal of Marketing, 75*(2), 1–17.

LeBreton, J. M., & Senter, J. L. (2008). Answers to 20 questions about interrater reliability and interrater agreement. *Organizational Research Methods, 11*(4), 815–852.

Levay, K. E., Freese, J., & Druckman, J. N. (2016). The demographic and political composition of mechanical Turk samples. *SAGE Open, 6*(1), 2158244016636433.

Lindell, M. K., & Whitney, D. J. (2001). Accounting for common method variance in cross-sectional research designs. *Journal of Applied Psychology, 86*(1), 114.

Litman, L., Robinson, J., & Abberbock, T. (2017). TurkPrime. com: A versatile crowdsourcing data acquisition platform for the behavioral sciences. *Behavior Research Methods, 49*(2), 433–442.

Little, T. D., Lindenberger, U., & Nesselroade, J. R. (1999). On selecting indicators for multivariate measurement and modeling with latent variables: When "good" indicators are bad and "bad" indicators are good. *Psychological Methods, 4*(2), 192.

MacKenzie, S. B., & Podsakoff, P. M. (2012). Common method bias in marketing: Causes, mechanisms, and procedural remedies. *Journal of Retailing, 88*(4), 542–555.

McElheran, K. (2015). Do market leaders lead in business process innovation? The case (s) of e-business adoption. *Management Science, 61*(6), 1197–1216.

McKelvey, B. (1975). Guidelines for the empirical classification of organizations. *Administrative Science Quarterly, 20*, 509–525.

Messick, S. (2012). Psychology and methodology of response styles. In R. E. Snow & D. E. Wiley (Eds.), *Improving inquiry in social science: A volume in honor of Lee J. Cronbach* (pp. 161–200). Hillsdale: Lawrence Erlbaum.

Mick, D. G. (1996). Are studies of dark side variables confounded by socially desirable responding? The case of materialism. *Journal of Consumer Research, 23*(2), 106–119.

Mizik, N., & Jacobson, R. (2008). The financial value impact of perceptual brand attributes. *Journal of Marketing Research, 45*(1), 15–32.

Moosbrugger, H. (2008). Klassische Testtheorie (KTT). In *Testtheorie und Fragebogenkonstruktion* (pp. 99–112). Berlin/Heidelberg: Springer.

Naemi, B. D., Beal, D. J., & Payne, S. C. (2009). Personality predictors of extreme response style. *Journal of Personality, 77*(1), 261–286.

Nederhof, A. J. (1985). Methods of coping with social desirability bias: A review. *European Journal of Social Psychology, 15*(3), 263–280.

Nunnally, J. C. (1967). *Psychometric theory.* New York: McGraw-Hill.

Ostroff, C., Kinicki, A. J., & Clark, M. A. (2002). Substantive and operational issues of response bias across levels of analysis: An example of climate-satisfaction relationships. *Journal of Applied Psychology, 87*(2), 355.

Palmatier, R. W. (2016). Improving and publishing at JAMS: Contribution and positioning. *Journal of the Academy of Marketing Science, 44*(6), 655–659.

Paulhus, D. L. (1984). Two-component models of socially desirable responding. *Journal of Personality and Social Psychology, 46*(3), 598.

Paulhus, D. L. (2002). Socially desirable responding: The evolution of a construct. In H. Brand, D. N. Jackson, D. E. Wiley, & S. Messick (Eds.), *The role of constructs in psychological and educational measurement* (pp. 49–69). Mahwah: L. Erlbaum.

Paulhus, D. L., & John, O. P. (1998). Egoistic and moralistic biases in self-perception: The interplay of self-deceptive styles with basic traits and motives. *Journal of Personality, 66*(6), 1025–1060.

Peer, E., Brandimarte, L., Samat, S., & Acquisti, A. (2017). Beyond the Turk: Alternative platforms for crowdsourcing behavioral research. *Journal of Experimental Social Psychology, 70*, 153–163.

Peterson, R. A. (2001). On the use of college students in social science research: Insights from a second-order meta-analysis. *Journal of Consumer Research, 28*(3), 450–461.

Phillips, L. W. (1981). Assessing measurement error in key informant reports: A methodological note on organizational analysis in marketing. *Journal of Marketing Research, 18*, 395–415.

Podsakoff, P. M., & Organ, D. W. (1986). Self-reports in organizational research: Problems and prospects. *Journal of Management, 12*(4), 531–544.

Podsakoff, P. M., MacKenzie, S. B., Moorman, R. H., & Fetter, R. (1990). Transformational leader behaviors and their effects on followers' trust in leader, satisfaction, and organizational citizenship behaviors. *The Leadership Quarterly, 1*(2), 107–142.

Podsakoff, P. M., MacKenzie, S. B., Lee, J. Y., & Podsakoff, N. P. (2003). Common method biases in behavioral research: A critical review of the literature and recommended remedies. *Journal of Applied Psychology, 88*(5), 879.

Podsakoff, P. M., MacKenzie, S. B., & Podsakoff, N. P. (2012). Sources of method bias in social science research and recommendations on how to control it. *Annual Review of Psychology, 63*, 539–569.

Presser, S., Couper, M. P., Lessler, J. T., Martin, E., Martin, J., Rothgeb, J. M., & Singer, E. (2004). Methods for testing and evaluating survey questions. *Public Opinion Quarterly, 68*(1), 109–130.

Preston, C. C., & Colman, A. M. (2000). Optimal number of response categories in rating scales: Reliability, validity, discriminating power, and respondent preferences. *Acta Psychologica, 104*(1), 1–15.

Price, J. L., & Mueller, C. W. (1986). *Handbook of organizational measurements.* Marshfield: Pittman.

Raval, D. (2020). Whose voice do we hear in the marketplace? Evidence from consumer complaining behavior. *Marketing Science, 39*(1), 168–187.

Rindfleisch, A., & Heide, J. B. (1997). Transaction cost analysis: Past, present, and future applications. *Journal of marketing, 61*(4), 30–54.

Rindfleisch, A., Malter, A. J., Ganesan, S., & Moorman, C. (2008). Cross-sectional versus longitudinal survey research: Concepts, findings, and guidelines. *Journal of Marketing Research, 45*(3), 261–279.

Rogelberg, S. G., & Stanton, J. M. (2007). Introduction: Understanding and Dealing With Organizational Survey Nonresponse. *Organizational Research Methods, 10*(2):195–209. https://doi.org/10.1177/1094428106294693

Rogelberg, S. G., Fisher, G. G., Maynard, D. C., Hakel, M. D., & Horvath, M. (2001). Attitudes toward surveys: Development of a measure and its relationship to respondent behavior. *Organizational Research Methods, 4*(1), 3–25.

Rossi, P. E. (2014). Even the rich can make themselves poor: A critical examination of IV methods in marketing applications. *Marketing Science, 33*(5), 655–672.

Sa Vinhas, A., & Heide, J. B. (2015). Forms of competition and outcomes in dual distribution channels: The distributor's perspective. *Marketing Science, 34*(1), 160–175.

Sande, J. B., & Ghosh, M. (2018). Endogeneity in survey research. *International Journal of Research in Marketing, 35*(2), 185–204.

Schmidt, J., & Bijmolt, T. H. (2019). Accurately measuring willingness to pay for consumer goods: A meta-analysis of the hypothetical bias. *Journal of the Academy of Marketing Science, 48*(3), 499–518.

Schuman, H., & Presser, S. (1979). The open and closed question. *American Sociological Review, 44*, 692–712.

Schuman, H., & Presser, S. (1981). The attitude-action connection and the issue of gun control. *The Annals of the American Academy of Political and Social Science, 455*(1), 40–47.

Schuman, H., & Presser, S. (1996). *Questions and answers in attitude surveys: Experiments on question form, wording, and context.* New York: Sage.

Schuman, H., Kalton, G., & Ludwig, J. (1983). Context and contiguity in survey questionnaires. *Public Opinion Quarterly, 47*(1), 112–115.

Schwarz, N. (1999). Self-reports: How the questions shape the answers. *American Psychologist, 54*(2), 93.

Schwarz, N. (2003). Self-reports in consumer research: The challenge of comparing cohorts and cultures. *Journal of Consumer Research, 29*(4), 588–594.

Schwarz, N., & Scheuring, B. (1992). Selbstberichtete Verhaltens-und Symptomhäufigkeiten: Was Befragte aus Antwortvorgaben des Fragebogens lernen. Zeitschrift für klinische Psychologie.

Schwarz, N., Knäuper, B., Hippler, H. J., Noelle-Neumann, E., & Clark, L. (1991a). Rating scales numeric values may change the meaning of scale labels. *Public Opinion Quarterly, 55*(4), 570–582.

Schwarz, N., Strack, F., & Mai, H. P. (1991b). Assimilation and contrast effects in part-whole question sequences: A conversational logic analysis. *Public Opinion Quarterly, 55*(1), 3–23.

Seidler, J. (1974). On using informants: A technique for collecting quantitative data and controlling measurement error in organization analysis. *American Sociological Review, 39*, 816–831.

Short, J. C., Ketchen, D. J., Jr., & Palmer, T. B. (2002). The role of sampling in strategic management research on performance: A two-study analysis. *Journal of Management, 28*(3), 363–385.

Siemsen, E., Roth, A., & Oliveira, P. (2010). Common method bias in regression models with linear, quadratic, and interaction effects. *Organizational Research Methods, 13*(3), 456–476.

Steenkamp, J. B. E., De Jong, M. G., & Baumgartner, H. (2010). Socially desirable response tendencies in survey research. *Journal of Marketing Research, 47*(2), 199–214.

Sudman, S., & Blair, E. (1999). Sampling in the twenty-first century. *Journal of the Academy of Marketing Science, 27*(2), 269–277.

Tellis, G. J., & Chandrasekaran, D. (2010). Extent and impact of response biases in cross-national survey research. *International Journal of Research in Marketing, 27*(4), 329–341.

The American Association for Public Opinion Research. (2016). *Standard definitions: Final dispositions of case codes and outcome rates for surveys* (9th ed.). AAPOR. https://www.aapor.org/AAPOR_Main/media/publications/Standard-Definitions20169theditionfinal.pdf

Thompson, L. F., & Surface, E. A. (2007). Employee surveys administered online: Attitudes toward the medium, nonresponse, and data representativeness. *Organizational Research Methods, 10*(2), 241–261.

Tomaskovic-Devey, D., Leiter, J., & Thompson, S. (1994). Organizational survey nonresponse. *Administrative Science Quarterly, 39*, 439–457.

Tortolani, R. (1965). Introducing bias intentionally into survey techniques. *Journal of Marketing Research, 2*, 51–55.

Tourangeau, R., Rips, L. J., & Rasinski, K. (2000). *The psychology of survey response*. Cambridge: Cambridge University Press.

Van Rosmalen, J., Van Herk, H., & Groenen, P. J. (2010). Identifying response styles: A latent-class bilinear multinomial logit model. *Journal of Marketing Research, 47*(1), 157–172.

Visser, P. S., Krosnick, J. A., Marquette, J., & Curtin, M. (1996). Mail surveys for election forecasting? An evaluation of the Columbus Dispatch poll. *Public Opinion Quarterly, 60*(2), 181–227.

Vomberg, A., Homburg, C., & Bornemann, T. (2015). Talented people and strong brands: The contribution of human capital and brand equity to firm value. *Strategic Management Journal, 36* (13), 2122–2131.

Vomberg, A., Homburg, C., & Gwinner, O. (2020). Tolerating and managing failure: An organizational perspective on customer reacquisition management. *Journal of Marketing, 84* (5), 117–136.

Warner, S. L. (1965). Randomized response: A survey technique for eliminating evasive answer bias. *Journal of the American Statistical Association, 60*, 63–69.

Wathne, K. H., Heide, J. B., Mooi, E. A., & Kumar, A. (2018). Relationship governance dynamics: The roles of partner selection efforts and mutual investments. *Journal of Marketing Research, 55*(5), 704–721.

Weijters, B., & Baumgartner, H. (2012). Misresponse to reversed and negated items in surveys: A review. *Journal of Marketing Research, 49*(5), 737–747.

Weijters, B., Schillewaert, N., & Geuens, M. (2008). Assessing response styles across modes of data collection. *Journal of the Academy of Marketing Science, 36*(3), 409–422.

Weijters, B., Geuens, M., & Schillewaert, N. (2009). The proximity effect: The role of inter-item distance on reverse-item bias. *International Journal of Research in Marketing, 26*(1), 2–12.

Weijters, B., Cabooter, E., & Schillewaert, N. (2010a). The effect of rating scale format on response styles: The number of response categories and response category labels. *International Journal of Research in Marketing, 27*(3), 236–247.

Weijters, B., Geuens, M., & Schillewaert, N. (2010b). The individual consistency of acquiescence and extreme response style in self-report questionnaires. *Applied Psychological Measurement, 34*(2), 105–121.

Weijters, B., Geuens, M., & Baumgartner, H. (2013). The effect of familiarity with the response category labels on item response to Likert scales. *Journal of Consumer Research, 40*(2), 368–381.

Weijters, B., Millet, K., & Cabooter, E. (2020). Extremity in horizontal and vertical Likert scale format responses. Some evidence on how visual distance between response categories influences extreme responding. *International Journal of Research in Marketing*. https://doi.org/10.1016/j.ijresmar.2020.04.002.

Wessling, K. S., Huber, J., & Netzer, O. (2017). MTurk character misrepresentation: Assessment and solutions. *Journal of Consumer Research, 44*(1), 211–230.

Williams, L. J., & Brown, B. K. (1994). Method variance in organizational behavior and human resources research: Effects on correlations, path coefficients, and hypothesis testing. *Organizational Behavior and Human Decision Processes, 57*(2), 185–209.

Winkler, J. D., Kanouse, D. E., & Ware, J. E. (1982). Controlling for acquiescence response set in scale development. *Journal of Applied Psychology, 67*(5), 555.

Wong, N., Rindfleisch, A., & Burroughs, J. E. (2003). Do reverse-worded items confound measures in cross-cultural consumer research? The case of the material values scale. *Journal of Consumer Research, 30*(1), 72–91.

Yammarino, F. J., Skinner, S. J., & Childers, T. L. (1991). Understanding mail survey response behavior a meta-analysis. *Public Opinion Quarterly, 55*(4), 613–639.

Yu, J., & Cooper, H. (1983). A quantitative review of research design effects on response rates to questionnaires. *Journal of Marketing Research, 20*, 36–44.

Zettler, I., Lang, J. W., Hülsheger, U. R., & Hilbig, B. E. (2015). Dissociating indifferent, directional, and extreme responding in personality data: Applying the three-process model to self-and observer reports. *Journal of Personality, 84*(4), 461–472.

Challenges in Conducting International Market Research

Andreas Engelen, Monika Engelen, and C. Samuel Craig

Contents

Introduction 122
Challenges in the Research Process 123
    Conceptual Framework (Phase 1) 124
    Research Units and Drivers of Differences (Phase 2) 127
    International Data Collection (Phase 3) 133
    Data Analysis (Phase 4) 138
    Interpretation (Phase 5) 140
Summary 141
References 141

Abstract

This chapter explains the need to conduct international market research, identifies the main challenges researchers face when conducting marketing research in more than one country and provides approaches for addressing these challenges. The chapter examines the research process from the conceptual design of the research model to the choice of countries for data collection, the data collection process itself, and the data analysis and interpretation. Challenges identified include differentiating between etic and emic concepts, assembling an adequate research unit, ensuring data collection equivalence, and reducing ethnocentrism

---

A. Engelen ($\boxtimes$)
TU Dortmund University, Dortmund, Germany
e-mail: andreas.engelen@tu-dortmund.de

M. Engelen
TH Köln, Cologne University of Applied Science, Köln, Germany
e-mail: monika.engelen@th-koeln.de

C. Samuel Craig
New York University, Stern School of Business, New York, NY, USA
e-mail: scraig@stern.nyu.edu

© Springer Nature Switzerland AG 2022
C. Homburg et al. (eds), *Handbook of Market Research*,
https://doi.org/10.1007/978-3-319-57413-4_6

of the research team. We draw on the extant literature to determine methods that address these challenges, such as an adapted etic or linked emic approach, to define the concept of the culti-unit, and to identify prominent approaches to cultural dimensions and collaborative and iterative translation and statistical methods for testing equivalence. This chapter provides researchers with the methods and tools necessary to derive meaningful and sound conclusions from research designed to guide international marketing activities.

> **Keywords**
>
> International research · Cross-cultural research · Emic/etic constructs · National indicators · National culture · Data equivalence · Culti-unit · Ethnocentrism · Back-translation

Introduction

Multinational companies are increasingly finding major opportunities for expansion outside their home markets. The transformation of planned economies into market economies and increasing demand from emerging middle classes in transition countries present new opportunities for firm growth, and rapid advances in technology facilitate access to these markets. As a consequence, many companies generate a large portion of their sales abroad. For example, the US giant Intel generated more than 80% of its overall sales in 2014 outside the US, BMW generated 81% of its sales outside Germany, and Sony generated 72% of its sales outside Japan. In the first quarter of 2012, Porsche sold more cars in China than in its German home market for the first time. Many start-up companies today are even "born global," generating substantial sales outside their home nations from their founding or soon after (Knight and Cavusgil 2004).

These developments have important implications for marketing science. Practitioners expect advice about whether marketing knowledge and practices that are successful in their home markets (such as how to facilitate a firm's market orientation, how consumers make purchasing decisions, and how promotion messages work) work in other nations (Katsikeas et al. 2006), as some highly successful companies (e.g., Disney with Disneyland Paris and Walmart in Germany) have experienced problems and even failures in expanding outside their home markets. These blunders have been traced back to failure to understand the new context and to adapt marketing activities to the host country, among other causes (Ghauri and Cateora 2010).

What, then, must marketing science do so it can provide useful recommendations? Single-country studies may be a first step, but they do not permit sound comparisons of phenomena between countries (Craig and Douglas 2005). Instead, multi-country studies that involve data collection in two or more nations are necessary to identify the generalizable similarities and differences in marketing-related insights between countries that marketing managers can use as guidelines for international marketing decisions.

Multi-country studies also contribute to marketing as an academic discipline. Steenkamp (2005) points out that marketing research has traditionally been driven by US researchers, so its constructs, theories, and relationships implicitly reflect the cultural predispositions of these researchers and the respondents in their empirical studies. Steenkamp claims that marketing science has to get out of the "US silo" and either show the cross-national generalizability of marketing phenomena or identify the contingencies that are related to national characteristics. National characteristics are valuable for marketing science since they allow constructs, theories, and relationships to be tested in diverse settings, similar to those that natural scientists create in their experiments (Burgess and Steenkamp 2006). Two nations, such as the US (a highly developed nation) and Cambodia (a developing nation), can provide extreme situations for testing constructs, theories, and relationships that other frequently used external contingency factors, such a firm's industry, cannot provide. If constructs, theories, or relationships hold in such diverse conditions as those offered in the US and Cambodia, a high level of generalizability can be assumed (Triandis 1994), and differences can be incorporated into theories and research models to make them more complete.

As a result, increasing numbers of multi-country studies have been published in leading marketing journals like *Journal of Marketing* (e.g., Petersen et al. 2015) and in journals that are dedicated to international marketing topics, such as *Journal of International Marketing* and *International Marketing Review*. While growing in number, multi-country marketing studies are often criticized for how they address the challenges that emerge when data is collected from more than one country (Cadogan 2010; Engelen and Brettel 2011; He et al. 2008; Nakata and Huang 2005). A multi-country research project has much in common with a project that focuses on one country (e.g., in terms of choice between primary and secondary data), but additional challenges render multinational studies more complex. From the conceptual design of the research model to the choice of countries for data collection, the actual data collection process, the data analysis and interpretation, pitfalls must be circumvented, and challenges faced in order to avoid limitations that can render an international marketing study all but useless. When differences in constructs, theories, or relationships between nations emerge, marketing researchers must ensure that they reflect the phenomena of interest and are not artifacts of poor research design and execution. The present article presents an overview of the challenges along the steps of the research process and state-of-the-art approaches to addressing these challenges so international marketing studies provide sound recommendations to practitioners and sound conclusions for marketing science.

Challenges in the Research Process

In order to capture comprehensively and in a structured way the particular challenges of international research projects in marketing, we break the typical research process into five steps, as depicted in Fig. 1: finding a conceptual framework (Phase 1), defining the research unit and identifying the unit's drivers (Phase 2), conducting the

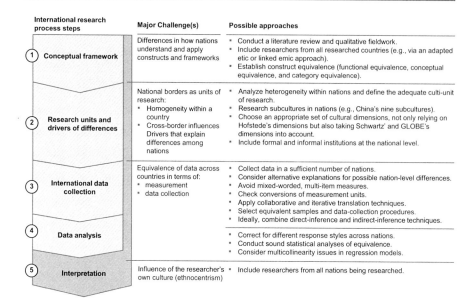

Fig. 1 Summary of challenges along the international research process; own illustration

data collection in multiple nations (Phase 3), performing the data analyses (Phase 4), and interpreting the findings (Phase 5). The concept of data equivalence, in addition to other issues, assumes a major role in each of these steps, manifesting in terms of various facets of the concept (Hult et al. 2008). Data equivalence ensures that the differences between nations that are identified are actual differences in terms of the phenomena of interest and not artifacts that are due to conceptual and methodological shortcomings that ignore the particularities of multi-country studies.

Conceptual Framework (Phase 1)

A typical starting point of a multi-country study in marketing is the particular constructs, theories, or relationships to be tested. For example, a marketing researcher of Western origin might want to investigate whether the relationship between a firm's market orientation and the firm's performance, measured as the firm's profitability, holds across national contexts. Before collecting data for the research model, the researcher should determine whether the constructs and theories that link them are universal across nations, as the theory that guides the research might not be salient in all research contexts, and even if it is, the constructs might not hold the same meaning in one country as they do in another (Douglas and Craig 2006).

If this challenge is ignored at the beginning of a research process, implications drawn from findings in later phases can be misleading. In our example, while firm profitability might be the primary performance measure in the Western nations,

Asian cultures put more emphasis on group-oriented harmony than on achievement and consider employee satisfaction an important outcome of a market orientation, maybe even at the expense of some degree of profitability (Braun and Warner 2002). Leaving out this effect of a firm's market orientation would lead to an incomplete research model from the Asian perspective.

The degree to which research models, including their constructs, theories, and relationships, allow for country-specific adaptations is captured in the differentiation between an etic and emic approach (Berry 1989). These terms were coined by the linguistic anthropologist Pike (1967), who draws on an analogy with the terms "phon*emic*" (referring to language-specific sounds) and "phon*etic*" (referring to sounds that exist in multiple languages). An etic approach in cross-national research assumes that a research model from one national or cultural background can be applied and replicated in other nations and cultures, so it views the elements of the research model as universally valid. The emic view proposes that theories and constructs are specific to the context in which they are applied and are not universal. By using their own domestic situations as frames of reference that are then, without due reflection, applied to and tested in other nations, researchers often implicitly apply an "imposed-etic" approach. While this approach often leads more easily to comparable results ("comparing apples to apples"), the results might be influenced by a pseudo-etic perspective or bias (Triandis 1972) ("apples only relevant in country A, but not in country B") that leads to misguided or prejudiced findings. Schaffer and Riordan (2003) find that more than 80% of all published multi-country studies implicitly take such an "imposed-etics" approach.

Douglas and Craig (2006) propose two alternative approaches to designing the conceptual framework of a research model in a multi-country study: the adapted etic model and the linked emic model, whose differences are illustrated in Fig. 2. The adapted etic model starts with a conceptual model from a base culture and adapts it to other nations, while the linked emic model uses the various nations as a starting point and then incorporates the insights gained from the nations into one overall conceptual framework. Both approaches decenter the research perspective from the researchers' own national perspective by requiring extensive study of local literature on the topic, an international research team, and close consultation with researchers from the other nations.

The "adapted etic model" assumes that the conceptual framework applies to all nations, with some adaptations to local contexts. As a first step, the conceptual framework, its constructs, theories, and relationships are tested in terms of their applicability and relevance to other national contexts. For example, a market orientation may not be relevant in a planned economy. Next, the relevant constructs and hypotheses are checked with support from local researchers. For example, when a researcher is interested in determining whether a particular kind of corporate culture fosters a market orientation across nations (Deshpandé and Farley 2004), it may be necessary to ask local researchers to identify the values (as elements of a corporate culture) that are particularly relevant in their nations. This approach focuses on the similarities among nations, as even when modifications are made, it is likely that

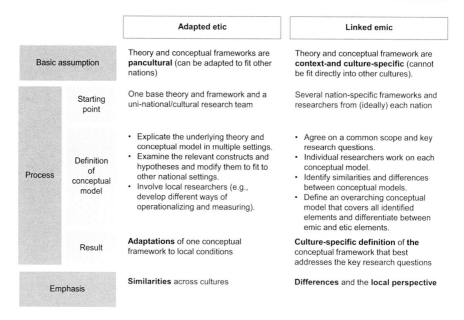

Fig. 2 Adapted etic and linked emic research approaches; own illustration based on Douglas and Craig (2006)

the base nation's perspective dominates, while the unique specifics of other nations may be ignored.

The "linked emic model" addresses this weakness by starting the process of defining a conceptual research model in multiple countries simultaneously, ideally with the support of a host country-based researcher for each setting. As a first step, the researchers from the various nations agree on the scope of the conceptual framework, which serves as input for the subsequent individual work on a conceptual model for each researcher in his or her national setting. Next, the researchers identify similarities among the locally developed models and factors at the national level that explain differences. Ideally, an overarching conceptual model is derived that covers all identified elements and differentiates between emic and etic elements. Nation-specific factors can be integrated into the model as contingencies to capture the nations' emic particularities. Assuming a researcher is interested in understanding what drives a firm's market orientation, collaboration among departments may be more important in collectivistic cultures than in individualistic cultures. This process puts a strong emphasis on the local perspective and is facilitated by effective cooperation among researchers from the nations in which the research takes place.

The efforts required in developing the adapted etic or linked emic model are targeted toward ensuring construct equivalence, a major facet of data collection equivalence that refers to whether constructs, theories, and relationships have the same purpose and meaning in all of the nations under investigation. Construct equivalence has three facets (Bensaou et al. 1999): functional equivalence, conceptual equivalence, and category equivalence. Functional equivalence refers to the degree to which phenomena or objects have the same function across nations. For example, a car provides family transportation in a highly developed country while a motor bike performs the same function in an emerging economy. Conceptual equivalence relates to the degree to which the phenomena are interpreted similarly across nations. For example, in a study of the antecedents of market orientation, local interpretations of the "amount of market-related information transferred between departments" can be tested in exploratory fieldwork. Category equivalence captures the degree to which the same classification scheme can be applied to a phenomenon across nations. For example, a particular market orientation's primary stakeholder group can be customers in one nation and government institutions in another.

Research Units and Drivers of Differences (Phase 2)

Once the conceptual framework has been established, the next step is to identify a research unit and the drivers of the differences between research units. We investigate the concept of the unit of research (section "Definition of the Unit of Analysis") and discuss potential drivers of differences between units of research (section "Identifying Drivers of Differences Between Nations").

Definition of the Unit of Analysis

In cross-national research, a unit of analysis must be established that defines the geographic scope and the group of the people or organizations to be examined within it. A good research unit has a high degree of homogeneity in terms of the members' behaviors and values among the members of this group, which are heterogeneous to other groups and is as free of influence by other groups as possible (Craig and Douglas 2006; Lytle et al. 1995).

Literature reviews on international marketing research indicate (e.g., Engelen and Brettel 2011; Nakata and Huang 2005) that nations are the primary unit of research. Some of the reasons for a focus on nation as the unit are practical and pragmatic. Nations have clear and defined boundaries, and sampling frames are available at the nation level or for defined geographic areas in countries, such as regions and cities. In addition, multinational firms are often organized on a country basis and are interested in formulating strategies in multiple countries, for which they must assess the similarities and differences among countries. This focus carries through to academic researchers' interest. For example, empirical cross-national marketing research often focuses on comparing phenomena of interest between the Western nations – often the US – and Asian countries – often China (Sheng et al. 2011). However, whether national borders are the best criterion with which to define the unit of research in international marketing may be questioned.

Nations and cultures are increasingly influenced by other nations and cultures. A primary mechanism is the global flows identified by Appadurai (1990). Five primary global flows blur the borders between nations: mediascapes (flow of images and communication, such as by screening US-made films in other countries), ethnoscapes (flows of tourism, student exchanges, and migrants), ideoscapes (flows of political impacts and ideologies, such as democratization and views of equality), technoscapes (flows of technology and expertise), and finanscapes (flows of capital and money). These global flows, which will only grow because of the increasing ease and decreasing cost of data transfers and travel, lead to multicultural marketplaces (Demangeot et al. 2015), so the view of cultures as localized and determined only by national boundaries has lost much of its validity. These flows can cause changes in a country's cultural elements through cultural contamination (adopting foreign cultural elements), pluralism (individuals in one culture exhibiting features of multiple cultures), and hybridization (fusion of two cultural elements into one new) (Craig and Douglas 2006). For example, the US culture is presented to customers in most other countries via products that are seen as typical of the American lifestyle (e.g., McDonalds, Levis, Marlboro), and it exerts cultural influence via a globally dominant movie industry. Consequently, at least part of many countries' populations adopt these cultural elements and values, leading to the "Americanization" of other nations' cultures.

Further, many nations and their cultures are not homogeneous units but contain subgroups (Cheung and Chow 1999) that may be driven by migration, ethnic heritage (e.g., Chinese in Malaysia, the Dutch heritage of South African immigrants), religious beliefs (e.g., US Jews, Chinese Catholics), or the nation's size (e.g., Russia, China, India). For example, studies find cultural subgroups in Singapore (Chen 2008) and several South American nations (Lenartowicz and Johnson 2002). The frequent presence of such subgroups poses a challenge to international marketing research that seeks specificity in the differences between nations, as findings will depend on the subgroup sampled in such heterogeneous nations.

Given the influences that nations exert on each other and the heterogeneity in most nations, it follows that researchers must examine the homogeneity of the nations or regions they want to analyze. While some countries, such as Belgium, India, and Switzerland, are inherently heterogeneous in terms of behaviors, attitudes, and/or language, some studies provide concrete empirical evidence of this heterogeneity. Based on World Values Survey data, Minkov and Hofstede (2012) identify 299 in-country regions in terms of cultural values in twenty-eight countries that cluster on national borders, even for potentially heterogeneous countries like Malaysia and Indonesia. Intermixtures across borders are rare, even in cases of culturally similar African neighbors, such as Ghana and Burkina Faso. While this study validates empirically that nations can be good approximations for cultures, other studies that focus on a single nation find that there are substantial cultural differences within one nation. For example, Cheung and Chow (1999) use empirical research to find nine distinct subcultures in China, and Dheer et al. (2015) identify nine distinct subcultural regions in India and provide guidance on how these subcultures differ. (For example, the far-eastern and southwestern regions are lower in male dominance than the other parts of India.)

Given these diverse findings, it follows that researchers should consider whether using national borders is an appropriate way to define a unit of research. If there is no homogenous national culture or if there is doubt that homogeneity is present, researchers should focus instead on subcultures, or "culti-units," as the units of research (Douglas and Craig 1997). Naroll (1970) introduces the concept of culti-units as the relevant unit for studying cultural phenomena when homogeneous nations cannot be assumed, while a prominent definition is presented by Featherstone (1990; p. 385):

> A culti-unit is [...] defined in terms of the racial, ethnic, demographic or social-economic characteristics or specific interests (e.g., ecologically concerned consumers) of its members which provide a common bond and establish a common ethnie, a core of shared memories, myths, values and symbols woven together and sustained in popular consciousness.

A commonly shared ethnie distinguishes the members of one culti-unit from others. This ethnie can be a national culture, a shared religion (e.g., Jewish heritage), or a strong interest (e.g., the hacker community of Anonymous). A major merit of the culti-unit concept is that it incorporates the concept of nation when the nation is sufficiently homogeneous, but it can also be applied to other ethnies. Researchers can benefit from the culti-unit construct since it makes ruling out alternative explanations for a theory or relationship easier than does a broader concept like nations. The ethnie core can be revealed by means of qualitative research. By taking the culti-unit as a starting point in defining the unit of research, researchers are forced to define their units of research unit cautiously and not to use national borders without careful reflection.

Sometimes the country or larger region is the appropriate sampling frame and serves as the culti-unit, particularly when culture has relatively little influence on the product or topic being researched. For example, compared to food and clothing, automobiles and consumer electronics do not have a strong cultural component. However, whenever there is likely to be considerable within-country heterogeneity or when the researcher is interested in understanding culture's influence on a particular outcome, the researcher should either sample from the culti-unit or be able to identify the various cultural or ethnic groups and conduct analysis to determine their affect. For example, Petruzzellis and Craig (2016) examine the concept of Mediterranean identity across three European countries (Spain, France, and Italy) and find elements of an ethnie core related to Mediterranean identity that transcends national borders.

Research on subcultures within a larger culture illustrates the importance of a culti-unit. For example, Vida et al. (2007) conduct research in Bosnia and Herzegovina, where there are three major cultural/ethic groups: Croats, Serbs, and Bosnians. The research analyzes responses by cultural group and finds that ethnic identity influences the dependent variables. Studies that examine a particular subculture face challenges in obtaining a sampling frame, but they can view a homogeneous group of respondents. Within-country differences can also be examined geographically. Lenartowicz et al. (2003) find significant within-country and between-county differences among managers on the Rokeach Value Survey, suggesting that using the country as the unit of analysis would mask important within-country variations.

Ultimately, the selection of the unit of analysis will be a function of practical considerations and the research's theoretical underpinnings. If a particular theory is being tested in multiple countries, the respondents in each country must reflect the ethnie core of the culture of interest. Ideally, the research would be able to locate appropriate sampling frames to focus on the specific groups, but if such sampling frames are not available, questions should be included that allow for a fine-grained examination so the entire sample can be analyzed and then broken down by specific cultural/ethnic groups. If there are significant differences between groups, the one (s) most relevant to the research can be examined more closely. A related concern is determining what factors account for the observed differences, whether they are contextual factors like the level of economic development or the influence of other cultures. The use of covariates in the analysis will often help in identifying which factors affect the culture.

Identifying Drivers of Differences Between Nations

When several nations are compared,[1] one of the key questions that arises concerns the underlying drivers between nations that account for the difference and that may even be generalized to explain variations from other nations. Assuming that nations are appropriate units of research for a particular purpose and we find differences (e.g., in the strength of the relationship between market orientation and firm performance between the US and Indonesia). An explanation for these differences can lie in the differing degrees of cultural individualism versus collectivism (Hofstede 2001), but the US and Indonesia also have differences in their economic (e.g., GPD per capita) and development levels (e.g., Human Development Indicator or HDI), which may be the key drivers of the observed differences.

In their review of empirical cross-national and cross-cultural research, Tsui et al. (2007) find that national culture – typically defined as the values and norms that guide a group's behavior (Adler 2002) – is the most frequently investigated driver of differences between nations. National culture can be conceptualized along national cultural dimensions that relate to how societies resolve the problems that all societies face (e.g., whether the individual person is more important than group equality and harmony and how much privacy is granted to individuals). Various schemes of cultural dimensions have been proposed, but the four original dimensions from Hofstede (2001) – power distance, individualism versus collectivism, uncertainty avoidance, and masculinity versus femininity – are the most prominent. Later, Hofstede and colleagues added the dimensions of long-term orientation and indulgence versus restraint. The latter, originally proposed by Minkov (2007), has been identified by means of World Value Survey items (Hofstede et al. 2010). Societies that are strong on indulgence allow free gratification of natural human desires, while

---

[1] For the sake of simplicity, we will subsequently refer to nations as the unit of research, acknowledging that other culti-units may be more appropriate as outlined in section "Conceptual Framework (Phase 1)."

societies that are strong on restraint prefer strict norms that regulate such gratification.

International marketing research focuses on Hofstede's dimensions, as the literature review from Engelen and Brettel (2011) indicates. One might argue that the country scores that Hofstede initially developed at the end of the 1960s/beginning of the 1970s are outdated, but Beugelsdijk et al. (2015) show that cultural change is absolute, rather than relative. By replicating Hofstede's dimensions for two birth cohorts using data from the World Values Survey, Beugelsdijk et al. (2015) find that most countries today score higher on individualism and indulgence and lower on power distance compared to Hofstede's older data, but cultural differences between country pairs are generally stable. Further, to circumvent the threat of using outdated country data, international marketing researchers can apply the updates provided on Hofstede's website (http://geert-hofstede.com/). These updated data have been used in some recent cross-national marketing studies, such as Samaha et al. (2014). Other studies, such as the meta-analytical review from Taras et al. (2012), also provide updated country scores for Hofstede's dimensions.

Several authors criticize Hofstede's approach in terms of its theoretical foundation and the limited number of cultural dimensions (Sondergaard 1994). Schwartz (1994) and the GLOBE study address some of these criticisms. Siew Imm et al. (2007) find that the cultural dimensions from Schwartz (1994) are broader than those from Hofstede (2001), as Schwartz (1994) covers all of Hofstede's dimensions and adds the dimensions of egalitarianism and hierarchy. Steenkamp (2001) also highlights Schwartz' (1994) theoretical foundations, concluding that "given its strong theoretical foundations, [Schwartz's approach] offers great potential for international marketing research" (p. 33).

Javidan et al. (2006) point out that the GLOBE study adopts a theory-based procedure and formulate a priori dimensions based on Hofstede (2001) dimensions, values that Kluckhohn (1951) and McClelland (1961) described, and the interpersonal communication literature (Sarros and Woodman 1993). In addition to Hofstede's cultural dimensions of power distance and uncertainty avoidance, the GLOBE study adds performance orientation, assertiveness, future orientation, human orientation, institutional collectivism, in-group collectivism, and gender egalitarianism (House et al. 2001). Some of these novel dimensions are more fine-grained than are Hofstede's (2001) dimensions. For example, the dimensions of assertiveness and gender egalitarianism reflect two major facets of Hofstede's masculinity dimension (Hartog 2004). Cross-cultural marketing studies often neglect or even ignore the potential offered by Schwartz (1994) and the GLOBE study. International marketing researchers should be sure to justify their choices of national cultural dimensions as the most appropriate for their purposes.

A marketing researcher who needs to choose one approach should consider the following thoughts: Hofstede's and GLOBE's dimensions and country scores have been derived theoretically and/or empirically in the workplace setting, so organizational marketing topics might rather build on their dimensions. Schwartz' dimensions have their theoretical origin in psychological research on individual values and have been empirically analyzed by Schwartz in a cross-national sample of teachers and students. Therefore, these dimensions are rather appropriate when investigating the decisions of private persons across cultures (such as in international consumer studies).

Further, the targeted nations in an international marketing study can lead to the use of the one or other approach. Schwartz generated data in some regions which have not been covered to the same extent in Hofstede's and the GLOBE survey (e.g., some former Eastern European bloc countries and some countries in the Middle East). There are also some countries (e.g., some African countries) which have been covered by GLOBE and not the other approaches. So, the individually targeted countries in a research project may determine the choice of dimensions.

In addition, researchers should take into consideration that the cultural dimensions differ between the approaches. Steenkamp (2001) factor analyzes the dimensions from Hofstede (the original four dimensions) and Schwartz and identifies four factors – three related to both Hofstede's and Schwartz's dimensions and one, a factor related to egalitarianism versus hierarchy that refers to how people coordinate with other people and to what degree they take the other people's interests into account, that emerged in the Schwartz data. Steenkamp (2001) argues that, when a researcher investigates cross-nationally whether the consumption of products that could harm other nonusers is accepted (e.g., cigarettes), this factor is represented in Schwartz's dimensions, not in Hofstede's dimensions, and is highly relevant. Therefore, Schwartz's dimensions might be the best choice. The GLOBE dimensions are also broader than Hofstede's dimensions, breaking down Hofstede's dimension of masculinity versus femininity into gender egalitarianism and assertiveness and differentiating between two versions of Hofstede's individualism versus collectivism dimension (in-group and institutional collectivism), which enables more fine-grained analysis on this dimension. Building on the GLOBE scores, Waldman et al. (2006) differentiate between in-group and institutional collectivism and find that institutional collectivism is positively related to corporate social responsibility in a firm's decision-making, while in-group collectivism has no impact. Using one score for a broader collectivism dimension may have masked these cultural dependencies, so depending on what a marketing researcher wants to examine, the more fine-grained GLOBE dimensions might be more appropriate. Figure 3 provides a summary of the three approaches to cultural dimensions.

In their literature review on cross-national and cross-cultural research, Tsui et al. (2007) conclude that extant research has focused too much on national cultural dimensions while neglecting other drivers of the differences between nations. As a result, the findings of multination studies that focus only on national cultural dimensions may be misleading. Tsui et al. (2007) and researchers like Glinow et al. (2004) call for a *polycontextualization* of international research in order to accommodate the complexity of the context and avoid misleading conclusions about what drives the differences between nations. Beyond national culture, the physical context (e.g., climate, typology), the historic context (e.g., sovereignty, colonization), the political context (e.g., the political and legal systems), the social context (e.g., religion, family structure), and the economic context (e.g., economic system, technology) may be the reason for differences (Saeed et al. 2014). Sound

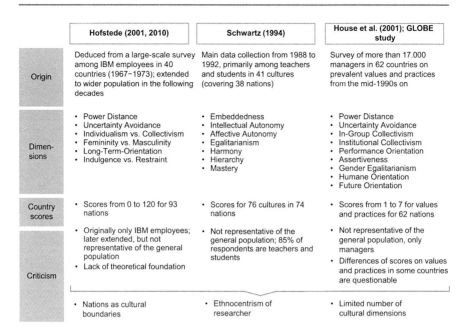

Fig. 3 Comparison of prominent approaches to cultural dimensions; own illustration based on Hofstede (2001), Schwartz (1994), and House et al. (2001)

international marketing research must not neglect these contextual drivers (see Douglas and Craig (2011) for a discussion of the role of contextual factors).

International Data Collection (Phase 3)

After the conceptual framework and the research unit are defined, data collection can begin. A key decision for the researcher is to decide in which and how many nations to collect empirical data. The key challenge is to take steps to ensure that the data are comparable and equivalent across all countries. This is a critical step as sound data provide the foundation for inferences and interpretation. The three pillars that guide data collection relate to the constructs that underlie the research, the actual measurement of the constructs and other variables of interest, and the procedures used to collect the data across multiple countries. These steps are summarized in Fig. 4. In addition, steps need to be taken to ensure translation equivalence, sampling frame equivalence, and data collection procedure equivalence (Hult et al. 2008).

Extant international marketing research is often built on data from only two nations (Cadogan 2010; Engelen and Brettel 2011). However, this approach has serious limitations, particularly since countries typically differ in terms of more than one cultural dimension, as well as in such contextual areas as the macroeconomic development stage or the educational system (Geyskens et al. 2006). As a positive example, Steenkamp et al. (1999) draw on responses from more than 8000

	Type of equivalence	Possible approaches
Con-structs	Functional Conceptual Category	Literature review, qualitative fieldwork, and adapted etic or linked emic approach
Measure-ment	Translation	Collaborative and iterative translation techniques
	Configural, metric, and scalar	Multiple group confirmatory factor analysis
Data collection	Sampling frame	Selection of equivalent samples across nations
	Data collection procedure	Similar data-collection time and procedures, allowing for different levels of literacy and infrastructure
	Sampling comparability	Statistical control with socio-demographic variables as covariates

Fig. 4 Overview of types of data collection equivalence; own illustration based on Hult et al. (2008)

consumers in 23 countries to isolate the effects of the regulatory system, the moral system (national identity), and the cultural system (degree of individualism) on the perceived value of websites. These effects could not have been separated on the national level with a two-country comparison.

To address what is a meaningful number of nations in which data should be collected and how these nations should be chosen, Sivakumar and Nakata (2001) develop an approach to guide researchers in defining the number of nations for data collection. In their approach, when cultural differences are expected to be due to one cultural dimension (e.g., the degree of power distance), two nations that have strong differences in terms of this dimension and few differences in the other cultural dimensions should be chosen, and when differences are expected to be due to two cultural dimensions, four national cultures should be used to represent all four combinations of the two levels (high and low) for each cultural dimension, while the four national cultures are similar in terms of the remaining cultural dimensions.

While this approach can help researchers determine the appropriate number of nations for identifying the role of cultural dimensions, the procedure does not provide guidance on how to deal with rival and confounding drivers at the national level, such as the stage of macroeconomic development (Ralston et al. 1997). In order to exclude rival explanations for differences between nations, even more nations should be included. For example, Tan (2002) creates a hybrid, quasi-experimental design to determine whether national cultural or contextual effects prevail by drawing on three samples from two subcultures and two countries: mainland Chinese, Chinese Americans, and Caucasian Americans.

In order to identify the roles that national cultural or contextual factors at the national level play, the number of nations for data collection must be extended, as long as identified differences can be traced back to either one of the national cultural or contextual factors, while controlling for alternative explanations at the national level.

Once the national settings are defined but before the data collection begins, three equivalence challenges must be addressed in order to generate sound empirical findings: translation equivalence, sampling frame equivalence, and data collection procedure equivalence (Hult et al. 2008). Collecting data in several countries in which more than one language is involved requires ensuring translation equivalence. Simple back-translation is the dominant approach in international marketing studies, where a questionnaire in the researcher's native language is translated into another language by a bilingual person (Brislin 1980). This translated questionnaire is then back-translated to English by another bilingual person. Only when the researcher compares the original and the back-translated questionnaire and finds no relevant differences can translation equivalence be assumed. While this approach is the most widely applied in international marketing literature, it has some limitations, as it does not necessarily ensure equivalence in meaning in each language (Douglas and Craig 2007). Referring to the "emic versus etic" debate, assuming that a simple translation from the base language that does not take the particularities of the other language into account (e.g., words or idioms that exist in only one language) is inherently etic or even "imposed-etic."

Douglas and Craig (2007) propose a collaborative, iterative approach that finds meanings of the source language in the other languages, thereby integrating emic elements into the questionnaires. Given the complexity of languages, the authors hold that researchers and translators with linguistic skills and skills in questionnaire design collaborate for this purpose. This approach has five major steps, as Fig. 5 shows.

The process starts with the translation, where a questionnaire in one language is translated independently to all target languages by at least two translators. Translators should especially pay attention to items that deal with attitudes since linguistic research indicates that the connotations of words like "happiness" and "mourning" can differ from language to language. The translation of mix-worded multi-item measures – that is, measures that contain positive-worded statements and reverse-worded statements – is a major challenge since empirical studies have found problems with the internal consistency and dimensionality of these measures, which are mostly of US origin, when applied cross-nationally. Wong et al. (2003) identify two reasons for these problems: how languages indicate negation differ such that reverse-worded statements may be difficult or even impossible to translate appropriately, and respondents' cultural predeterminations affect how they respond to reverse-worded statements. When the dominant norm is to be polite and agreeable, as is the case in some Asian cultures (Child and Warner 2003), respondents may tend to agree with any statement, leading to low internal consistency and disruption of the dimensionality of mixed-worded measures. Therefore, Wong et al. (2003) suggest employing only positively worded statements cross-nationally or replacing Likert statements with questions.

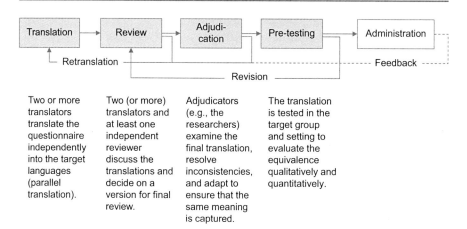

Fig. 5 Collaborative and iterative translation; own illustration based on Douglas and Craig (2007)

The second step of Douglas and Craig's (2007) approach is a review meeting with the translators and an independent researcher in order to agree on a preliminary version of the questionnaire in each language. In the third step, adjudication, inconsistencies are resolved and whether the questionnaire actually measures the same meaning in each country is determined. In the fourth step, the questionnaire is pretested with native respondents in each language to ensure comprehension, and issues are referred to the team of researchers and translators to start a new round of iterations. Finally, in the fifth step, if more than one round of data collection is planned, such as may be the case with longitudinal data collected yearly, insights gained during the initial data collection are reported to the team of researchers and translators so they can improve the questionnaires for successive rounds of data collection (without compromising year-to-year comparability).

Sampling frame equivalence refers to the extent to which the samples drawn from the various nations parallel one another (Hult et al. 2008). For example, if high school students from the middle class in India are compared to public high school students from all social classes in the US, the discrepancy in social class could distort the findings. Researchers must select equivalent samples among the various research units while allowing variations in the sample on the factors to be analyzed. For example, individuals of similar income, education level, and gender (equality of sample) are selected from nations whose cultural values (variation to be researched) differ. Hult et al. (2008) consider sample equivalence a major prerequisite for sound cross-cultural comparisons and recommend that organization-level studies match samples in terms of potentially confounding factors like company age, size, and industry sector. Although sample equivalence does not guarantee that findings can be generalized to the participating countries, it helps to ensure that comparisons are not confounded by other factors and that differences can be traced back to the cultural dimensions or contexts under study (van Vijver and Leung 1997).

Data collection procedure equivalence combines administrative equivalence (e.g., telephone, face-to-face, email) and time equivalence in terms of the time between data collection in the participating countries (Hult et al. 2008). While a completely standardized and parallel data collection procedure in all units of research is ideal, regulations (e.g., national rules and regulations against telephone interviews), cultural norms (e.g., nonconformity of impersonal surveys with the cultural preferences related to personal interactions), and infrastructure (e.g., availability of high-speed internet lines) often prevent data collection procedures from being perfectly equal (Hult et al. 2008). Even so, researchers must seek equivalent data collection procedures and keep unavoidable differences (e.g., different survey settings and different times) in mind as a possible explanation for findings.

Finally, in the international data collection phase, researchers must decide on which level to measure cultural properties. Cultural properties can either be directly measured in the surveyed sample at the individual level of each respondent ("direct value inference") or captured by means of typically nation-related secondary data (e.g., the Hofstede country scores) according to the surveyed individuals' or firms' national identity ("indirect value inference"). Direct value inference measures individuals' cultural properties and derives cultural properties for data analyses by aggregating these cultural properties to the relevant group level (e.g., the national level). Researchers can directly measure the surveyed individuals' individual values or ask about their perceptions of their environment's cultural values. This approach ensures that the actual culture of the surveyed individuals is measured. However, the questions concerning whether the surveyed individual can assess the cultural properties correctly and whether there are any bias in the assessments remain. Indirect value inference assigns existing values on cultural dimensions (e.g., from the Hofstede data) to surveyed individuals according to their group membership – that is, surveyed individuals from Germany receive the score for Germany on the relevant cultural dimension as reported by Hofstede or other researchers. In this case, however, a measurement error might occur since the researcher assumes that the surveyed sample's cultural properties comply with the cultural properties of the samples used in the earlier studies that report country scores (Soares et al. 2007). Given the benefits and perils of both approaches, Soares et al. (2007) recommend a multi-method approach that combines the indirect and direct value inference approaches.

Whether direct or indirect value inference is pursued, Brewer and Venaik (2014) recommend that researchers that are determining the right level of analysis ensure a fit between the levels at which the constructs (e.g., cultural properties) are theorized and empirically validated. Conceptualization of theories, measurement of constructs, and data collection should be conducted consistent with the underlying research question. Brewer and Venaik (2014) refer to the danger of an ecological fallacy when researchers assume that group-level relationships automatically apply to the individual level. Some recent studies use cultural dimensions explicitly at the individual level (e.g., individual power orientation) to make clear that cultural properties at the level of the surveyed individual are theorized and measured (e.g., Auh et al. 2015; Kirkman et al. 2009). When only group-level data on cultural properties is available,

Brewer and Venaik (2014) recommend that higher-level constructs (e.g., cultural dimensions at the national level) be cross validated with measures at the level at which the construct is theorized (e.g., at the individual level of a consumer).

Data Analysis (Phase 4)

Data analysis starts with analyses which are not specific to international marketing research but have to be done in any data analysis. Such checks and tests include establishing the reliability and validity of the measures and ruling out biases in the survey data like common-method bias, nonresponse bias, and informant bias (Bagozzi et al. 1991; Podsakoff et al. 2003). However, the particularities of international marketing research impose additional challenges related to the data analysis based on how differences in national response styles can affect findings. A response style refers to a person's tendency to respond systematically to questionnaire items on some basis other than what the items are designed to measure (Jong et al. 2008). For example, in the US school grading systems range from A+ (best) to F (worst) or points up to 100 (best) and down to 0 (worst), while the German grading system is the other way around, ranging from 1 (best) to 5 or 6 (worst). Therefore, Germans who are used to "lower is better" might unwittingly answer incorrectly on US surveys that range from 1 (worst) to 5 (best). While these scale definition issues might be resolved easily, national cultural predeterminations based on deeply rooted values and preferences may have more subtle effects on a participant's response style (Clarke III 2001).

Two major response styles have been shown to be subject to the respondent's national culture: An extreme response style (ERS) is the tendency to favor the end points of rating scales, regardless of the item's content, while an acquiescence response style (ARS) refers to the tendency to agree with all items, regardless of the item's content. Chen (2008) reports that US respondents are much more inclined to show an ERS than are respondents from China. In cultural terms, respondents from low-ERS cultures may wish to appear modest and nonjudgmental, whereas members of high-ERS cultures may prefer to demonstrate sincerity and conviction. Regarding ARS, Riordan and Vandenberg (1994) report that a response of 3 on a 5-point Likert-type scale means "no opinion" to American respondents but "mild agreement" to Korean respondents, so a Korean's "3" may be equivalent to an American's "4," and a Korean's "4" may be equivalent to an American's "5." A strong response bias is problematic because whether differences are caused by differences in response styles or differences in the factor of interest remains uncertain. If relationships are compared, differences in response styles lead to variances in the dependent and independent variables that result in unintended and confounding differences in correlations.

Differences in response styles belong to a larger group of issues when measurement models are applied in more than one nation. A major threat to sound multination marketing research occurs when respondents do not interpret the constructs that link relevant relationships or that build theoretical frameworks similarly such that identified differences in relationships are actually due to systematically different interpretations of constructs and measurement models (Mullen 1995). While some countermeasures can be taken in the pre-data collection phase, such as ascertaining translation equivalence, quantitative tests on the actual data collected are necessary.

In particular, measurement equivalence, which relates to whether measurement models are understood similarly across nations, must be established. Steenkamp and Baumgartner (1998) provide a multigroup confirmatory factor analysis approach for reflective multi-item measurement models, which approach consists of configural, metric, and scalar equivalence analyses (for applications, see, e.g., Homburg et al. (2009) and Zhou et al. (2002)). Configural equivalence indicates that respondents from all nations under analysis conceptualize and understand the basic structure of measurement models similarly. Metric equivalence indicates that groups of respondents understand scale intervals similarly. Scalar equivalence indicates that the systematic response style among respondents from the nations under study does not differ.

Configural equivalence, which is tested by running a multigroup confirmatory factor analysis that allows all factor loadings to be free across the national samples, is given when the factor loadings are significant in all samples and the model's fit is satisfactory. Partial metric equivalence is given when at least one item (in addition to a marker item) for each measurement model has equivalent factor loadings across nations. Metric equivalence models must be specified with at least two factor loadings per measurement model that are kept equal across nations while not constraining the remaining factor loadings. Full metric equivalence is given when all factor loadings are equal across groups, although Steenkamp and Baumgartner (1998) indicate that partial metric equivalence is sufficient in most cases. By means of a χ^2-difference test, this metric equivalence model is compared with a model in which all factor loadings are free across samples, and metric equivalence is confirmed when the two models do not differ significantly. Finally, scalar equivalence, which is tested by comparing means, ensures that differences in observed and latent means between national samples are comparable. The procedure for testing scalar equivalence is the same as the χ^2-difference test for metric equivalence except that item intercepts are constrained across national samples. Steenkamp and Baumgartner (1998) point out that, in most cross-national comparisons, only partial scalar invariance is realistic.

Since establishing measurement equivalence across a high number of countries would require extremely large sample sizes, some studies have created set of countries with similar cultural and economic conditions between which measurement equivalence is established (e.g., Hohenberg and Homburg 2016; Tellis et al. 2009). For example, Hohenberg and Homburg (2016) cluster their 38 surveyed countries into four categories, differentiating among English-speaking countries, European countries, Asian countries, and Latin American countries.

Once measurement equivalence is established, the relationships of interest can be empirically investigated. When national constructs are integrated as moderators in theoretical frameworks, group comparisons (e.g., in structural equation modeling) and interaction term models (e.g., in regression models) can be applied (Engelen and

Brettel 2011), although some challenges specific to international marketing projects must be considered. Most multinational studies investigate a particular relationship (e.g., the effect of top management's attention on a firm's market orientation) in multiple nations, for which the researchers have a national dependency in mind, such as a particular national cultural dimension (e.g., the degree of national cultural power distance). However, to accommodate the multiplicity of possible drivers at the national level (section "Identifying Drivers of Differences Between Nations"), researchers should add controls for alternative explanations in their models, an approach that is particularly feasible in regression models (Becker 2005). For example, by integrating a broad set of national cultural dimensions into their model, Samaha et al. (2014) show that national culture has a more multifaceted role in relationship marketing than earlier studies that focus on just one national cultural dimension suggest. Adding several cultural dimensions into a regression model is likely to lead to multicollinearity since the cultural dimensions are often correlated. Individualism versus collectivism and power distance are often strongly correlated. Samaha et al. (2014) circumvent this problem by not adding these two dimensions simultaneously in their regression models, leaving out the individualism versus collectivism dimension in their power distance model and leaving power distance out of all other models.

Interpretation (Phase 5)

While interpretation is an important element in all five steps of the research process – before, during, and after data collection – it manifests particularly at the end of the research process, when the actual findings are available. Of course, interpretation is by no means a particularity of international marketing research projects, but one particular challenge emerges with these kinds of studies. A major assumption of cross-national research projects is that drivers at the national level can lead to differences in marketing relationships, constructs, and theories, and since national drivers, especially national culture, affect everyone living in a nation or culture (Hofstede 2001), the researcher himself or herself is also subject to national or cultural predetermination. Thus, the researcher's cultural values can affect his or her interpretation of the findings (Berry 1980). This bias, called ethnocentrism, occurs when one person's or group's frame of reference is applied in interpreting other groups' responses without adaptation to other national cultures. If, in our example, we find that the attention of top management to market-related issues drives a firm's market orientation more strongly in Asia than in Western nations, coming from a Western perspective, we could easily assume that power distance, which is particularly strong in Asian cultures, is the driving force. However, Asian researchers might relate this finding to particularities of the Confucian teachings. To exclude such an ethnocentric bias, researchers in international studies should build and use cross-national research teams during the entire research process, but especially in the last step of interpreting the findings (Hofstede and Bond 1988), and document nation- or culture-specific interpretations of findings.

Summary

As firms from developed and developing economies continue to expand outside their home markets, marketing research is essential to guide development and execution of marketing strategy. An implicit challenge is for management to appreciate that there are potentially a wide range of differences between their home market and the foreign markets they currently operate in or are planning to enter. Well-constructed research will not only identify differences but also reveal important similarities. Regardless of the specific purpose of the research, it is essential that valid and reliable research be designed and executed. This is the critical challenge and applies whether the research is to guide management decisions or test the applicability of theories and constructs across multiple countries.

However, international marketing research is more complex and time consuming than single country research. Advances in technology, particularly ready access to internet samples in multiple countries has greatly facilitated rapid collection of multi-country data. However, unless careful attention is paid to the design and execution of the research to achieve equivalence on all dimensions across the units studies, the results may be misleading or meaningless. Careful attention to all the steps outlined in this chapter is essential to ensure that the results of international marketing research are reliable and valid and can be used to make meaningful inferences and advance the state of our knowledge about markets outside our own.

References

Adler, N. (2002). *International dimensions of organizational behavior*. Cincinnati: South-Western College Publishing.

Appadurai, A. (1990). Disjuncture and difference in the global cultural economy. *Public Culture, 2*, 1–24.

Auh, S., Menguc, B., Spyropoulou, S., Wang, F. (2015). Service employee burnout and engagement: The moderating role of power distance orientation. *Journal of the Academy of Marketing Science*, 1–20. https://doi.org/10.1007/s11747-015-0463-4.

Bagozzi, R., Yi, Y., & Phillips, L. (1991). Assessing construct validity in organizational research. *Administrative Science Quarterly, 36*(3), 421–458.

Becker, T. E. (2005). Potential problems in the statistical control of variables in organizational research: A qualitative analysis with recommendations. *Organizational Research Methods, 8*(3), 274–289.

Bensaou, M., Coyne, M., & Venkatraman, N. (1999). Testing metric equivalence in cross-national strategy research: An empirical test across the. *Strategic Management Journal, 20*(7), 671–689.

Berry, J. (1980). Introduction to methodology. In H. Triandis & J. Berry (Eds.), *Handbook of cross-cultural psychology* (pp. 1–28). Boston: Allyn & Bacon.

Berry, J. (1989). Imposed etics-emics-derived etics: The operationalization of a compelling idea. *International Journal of Psychology, 24*(6), 721–734.

Beugelsdijk, S., Maseland, R., & van Hoorn, A. (2015). Are scores on Hofstede's dimensions of national culture stable over time? A cohort analysis. *Global Strategy Journal, 5*(3), 223–240.

Braun, W., & Warner, M. (2002). The "Culture-Free" versus "Culture-Specific" management debate. In M. Warner & P. Joynt (Eds.), *Managing across cultures: Issues and perspectives* (pp. 13–25). London: Thomson Learning.

Brewer, P., & Venaik, S. (2014). The ecological fallacy in national culture research. *Organization Studies, 35*(7), 1063–1086.

Brislin, R. (1980). Translation and content analysis of oral and written materials. In H. Triandis & J. Berry (Eds.), *Handbook of cross-cultural psychology* (pp. 389–444). Boston: Allyn and Bacon.

Burgess, S., & Steenkamp, J.-B. (2006). Marketing renaissance: How research in emerging markets advances marketing science and practice. *International Journal of Research in Marketing, 23*(4), 337–356.

Cadogan, J. (2010). Comparative, cross-cultural, and cross-national research: A comment on good and bad practice. *International Marketing Review, 27*(6), 601–605.

Chen, F. F. (2008). What happens if we compare chopsticks with forks? The impact of making inappropriate comparisons in cross-cultural research. *Journal of Personality and Social Psychology, 95*(5), 1005–1018.

Cheung, G. W., & Chow, I. H.-S. (1999). Subcultures in Greater China: A comparison of managerial values in the People's Republic of China. *Asia Pacific Journal of Management, 16*(3), 369–387.

Child, J., & Warner, M. (2003). Culture and management in China. In M. Warner (Ed.), *Culture and management in Asia* (pp. 24–47). London: Routledge.

Clarke III, I. (2001). Extreme response style in cross-cultural research. *International Marketing Review, 18*(3), 301–324.

Craig, C. S., & Douglas, S. P. (2005). *International marketing research* (3rd ed.). Chichester: Wiley.

Craig, C. S., & Douglas, S. P. (2006). Beyond national culture: Implications of cultural dynamics for consumer research. *International Marketing Review, 23*(3), 322–342.

Demangeot, C., Broderick, A., & Craig, C. S. (2015). Multicultural marketplaces. *International Marketing Review, 32*(2), 118–140.

Deshpandé, R., & Farley, J. (2004). Organizational culture, market orientation, innovativeness, and firm performance: An international research odyssey. *International Journal of Research in Marketing, 21*(1), 3–22.

Dheer, R. J. S., Lenartowicz, T., & Peterson, M. F. (2015). Mapping India's regional subcultures: Implications for international management. *Journal of International Business Studies, 46*(4), 443–467.

Douglas, S. P., & Craig, C. S. (1997). The changing dynamic of consumer behavior: Implications for cross-cultural research. *International Journal of Research in Marketing, 14*(4), 379–395.

Douglas, S., & Craig, C. (2006). On improving the conceptual foundations of international marketing research. *Journal of International Marketing, 14*(1), 1–22.

Douglas, S. P., & Craig, C. S. (2007). Collaborative and iterative translation: An alternative approach to back translation. *Journal of International Marketing, 15*(1), 30–43.

Douglas, S. P., & Craig, C. S. (2011). The role of context in assessing international marketing opportunities. *International Marketing Review, 28*, 150–162.

Engelen, A., & Brettel, M. (2011). Assessing cross-cultural marketing theory and research. *Journal of Business Research, 64*(5), 516–523.

Featherstone, M. (1990). *Global culture: Nationalism, globalism and modernism*. London: Sage.

Geyskens, I., Steenkamp, J., & Kumar, N. (2006). Make, buy, or ally: A transaction cost theory meta-analysis. *Academy of Management Journal, 49*(3), 519–543.

Ghauri, P., & Cateora, P. (2010). *International marketing* (3rd ed.). New York: McGraw-Hill.

von Glinow, M. A., Shapiro, D. L., & Brett, J. M. (2004). Can we talk, and should we? Managing emotional conflict in multicultural teams. *Academy of Management Review, 29*(4), 578–592.

Hartog, D. (2004). Assertiveness. In R. House, P. Hanges, M. Javidan, P. Dorfman, & V. Gupta (Eds.), *Culture, leadership, and organizations: The GLOBE study of 62 societies* (pp. 395–436). Thousand Oaks: Sage.

He, Y., Merz, M. A., & Alden, D. L. (2008). Diffusion of measurement invariance assessment in cross-national empirical marketing research: perspectives from the literature and a survey of researchers. *Journal of International Marketing, 16*(2), 64–83.

Hofstede, G. (2001). *Culture's consequences: Comparing values, behaviors, institutions, and organizations across nations.* Thousand Oaks: Sage.

Hofstede, G., & Bond, M. (1988). The confucius connection: From cultural roots to economic growth. *Organizational Dynamics, 16*(4), 5–21.

Hofstede, G., Hofstede, J., & Minkov, M. (2010). *Cultures and organizations – software of the mind: Intercultural cooperation and its importance for survival.* New York: Mcgraw-Hill.

Hohenberg, S., & Homburg, C. (2016). Motivating sales reps for innovation selling in different cultures. *Journal of Marketing, 80*(2), 101–120.

Homburg, C., Cannon, J. P., Krohmer, H., & Kiedaisch, I. (2009). Governance of international business relationships: A cross-cultural study on alternative governance modes. *Journal of International Marketing, 17*(3), 1–20.

House, R., Javidan, M., & Dorfman, P. (2001). Project GLOBE: An introduction. *Applied Psychology. An International Review, 50*(4), 489–505.

Hult, T., Ketchen, D., Griffith, D., Finnegan, C., Gonzalez-Padron, T., Harmancioglu, N., et al. (2008). Data equivalence in cross-cultural international business research: Assessment and guidelines. *Journal of International Business Studies, 39*(6), 1027–1044.

Javidan, M., House, R., Dorfman, P., Hanges, P., & Luque, M. d. (2006). Conceptualizing and measuring culture and their consequences: A comparative review of GLOBE's and Hofstede's approaches. *Journal of International Business Studies, 37*, 897–914.

de Jong, M. G., Steenkamp, J.-B. E. M., Fox, J.-P., & Baumgartner, H. (2008). Using item response theory to measure extreme response style in marketing research: A global investigation. *Journal of Marketing Research (JMR), 45*(1), 104–115.

Katsikeas, C. S., Samiee, S., & Theodosiou, M. (2006). Strategy fit and performance consequences of international marketing standardization. *Strategic Management Journal, 27*(9), 867–890.

Kirkman, B. L., Chen, G., Farh, J.-L., Chen, Z. X., & Lowe, K. B. (2009). Individual power distance orientation and follower reactions to transformational leaders: A cross-level, cross-cultural examination. *Academy of Management Journal, 52*(4), 744–764.

Kluckhohn, C. (1951). The study of culture. In D. Lerner & H. Lasswell (Eds.), *The policy standard* (pp. 393–404). Stanford: Stanford University Press.

Knight, G. A., & Cavusgil, S. T. (2004). Innovation, organizational capabilities, and the born-global firm. *Journal of International Business Studies, 35*, 124–141.

Lenartowicz, T., & Johnson, J. P. (2002). Comparing managerial values in twelve Latin American countries: An exploratory study. *Management International Review (MIR), 42*(3), 279–307.

Lenartowicz, T., Johnson, J. P., & White, C. T. (2003). The neglect of intracountry cultural variation in international management research. *Journal of Business Research, 56*(12), 999–1008.

Lytle, A., Brett, J., Barsness, Z., Tinsley, C., & Janssens, M. (1995). A paradigm for confirmatory cross-cultural research in organizational behavior. *Research in Organizational Behavior, 17*, 167–214.

McClelland, D. (1961). *The achieving society.* Princeton: Van Nostrand Co.

Minkov, M. (2007). *What makes us different and similar: A new interpretation of the world values survey and other cross-cultural data.* Sofia: Klasika y Stil Publishing.

Minkov, M., & Hofstede, G. (2012). Is national culture a meaningful concept? Cultural values delineate homogeneous national clusters of in-country regions. *Cross-Cultural Research, 46*, 133–159.

Mullen, M. (1995). Diagnosing measurement equivalence in cross-national research. *Journal of International Business Studies, 26*(3), 573–596.

Nakata, C., & Huang, Y. (2005). Progress and promise: The last decade of international marketing research. *Journal of Business Research, 58*(5), 611–618.

Naroll, R. (1970). The culture-bearing unit in cross-cultural surveys. In R. Naroll & R. Cohen (Eds.), *A handbook of methods in cultural anthropology* (pp. 721–765). New York: Natural History Press.

Petersen, J. A., Kushwaha, T., & Kumar, V. (2015). Marketing communication strategies and consumer financial decision making: The role of national culture. *Journal of Marketing, 79*(1), 44–63.

Petruzzellis, L., & Craig, C. S. (2016). Separate but together: Mediterranean identity in three countries. *Journal of Consumer Marketing, 33*(1), 9–19.

Pike, K. (1967). *Language in relation to a unified theory of the structure of human behavior.* The Hague: Mouton & Co.

Podsakoff, P., MacKenzie, C., Lee, J., & Podsakoff, N. (2003). Common method biases in behavioral research: A critical review of the literature and recommended remedies. *Journal of Applied Psychology, 88*(5), 879–903.

Ralston, D. A., Holt, D. H., Terpstra, R. H., & Yu, K.-C. (1997). The impact of national culture and economic ideology on managerial work values: A study of the United States, Russia, Japan, and China. *Journal of International Business Studies, 28*(1), 177–207.

Riordan, C. M., & Vandenberg, R. J. (1994). A central question in cross-cultural research: Do employees of different cultures interpret work-related measures in an equivalent manner? *Journal of Management, 20*(3), 643–641.

Saeed, S., Yousafzai, S. Y., & Engelen, A. (2014). On cultural and macroeconomic contingencies of the entrepreneurial orientation–performance relationship. *Entrepreneurship Theory and Practice, 38*(2), 255–290.

Samaha, S. A., Beck, J. T., & Palmatier, R. W. (2014). The role of culture in international relationship marketing. *Journal of Marketing, 78*(5), 78–98.

Sarros, J., & Woodman, D. (1993). Leadership in Australia and its organizational outcomes. *Leadership and Organization Development Journal, 14*, 3–9.

Schaffer, B. S., & Riordan, C. M. (2003). A review of cross-cultural methodologies for organizations research: A best-practices approach. *Organizational Research Methods, 6*(2), 169.

Schwartz, S. (1994). Beyond individualism/collectivism: New cultural dimensions of values. In U. Kim, H. Triandis, C. Kagitcibasi, S. Choi, & G. Yoon (Eds.), *Individualism and collectivism: Theory, methods and applications* (pp. 85–119). Thousand Oaks: Sage.

Sheng, S., Zhou, K. Z., & Li, J. J. (2011). The effects of business and political ties on firm performance: Evidence from China. *Journal of Marketing, 75*(1), 1–15.

Siew Imm, N., Lee, J. A., & Soutar, G. N. (2007). Are Hofstede's and Schwartz's value frameworks congruent? *International Marketing Review, 24*(2), 164–180.

Sivakumar, K., & Nakata, C. (2001). The stampede toward Hofstede's framework: Avoiding the sample design pit in cross-cultural research. *Journal of International Business Studies, 32*(3), 555–574.

Soares, A., Farhangmehr, M., & Shoham, A. (2007). Hofstede's dimensions of culture in international marketing studies. *Journal of Business Research, 60*, 277–284.

Sondergaard, M. (1994). Research note: Hofstede's consequences: A study of reviews, citations and replications. *Organization Studies, 15*(3), 447–456.

Steenkamp, J. (2001). The role of national culture in international marketing research. *International Marketing Review, 18*(1), 30–44.

Steenkamp, J. (2005). Moving out of the U.S. Silo: A call to arms for conducting international marketing research. *Journal of Marketing, 69*(4), 6–8.

Steenkamp, J.-B., & Baumgartner, H. (1998). Assessing measurement invariance in cross-national consumer research. *Journal of Consumer Research, 25*, 78–90.

Steenkamp, J., Hofstede, F., & Wedel, M. (1999). A cross-national investigation into the individual and national cultural antecedents of consumer innovativeness. *Journal of Marketing, 63*(2), 55–69.

Tan, J. (2002). Culture, nation, and entrepreneurial strategic orientations: Implications for an emerging economy. *Entrepreneurship Theory and Practice, 26*(4), 95–111.

Taras, V., Steel, P., & Kirkman, B. L. (2012). Improving national cultural indices using a longitudinal meta-analysis of Hofstede's dimensions. *Journal of World Business, 47*(3), 329–341.

Tellis, G. J., Prabhu, J. C., & Chandy, R. K. (2009). Radical innovation across nations: The preeminence of corporate culture. *Journal of Marketing, 73*(1), 3–23.

Triandis, H. (1972). *The analysis of subjective culture.* New York: Wiley.

Triandis, H. (1994). *Culture and social behavior.* New York: McGraw-Hill.

Tsui, A. S., Nifadkar, S. S., & Ou, A. Y. (2007). Cross-national, cross-cultural organizational behavior research: Advances, gaps, and recommendations. *Journal of Management, 33*(3), 426–478.

Vida, I., Obadia, C., & Kunz, M. (2007). The effects of background music on consumer responses in a high-end supermarket. *The International Review of Retail, Distribution and Consumer Research, 17*(5), 469–482.

van Vijver, F., & Leung, K. (1997). *Methods and data analysis for cross-cultural research*. Thousand Oaks: Sage.

Waldman, D. A., de Luque, M. S., Washburn, N., House, R. J., Adetoun, B., Barrasa, A., et al. (2006). Cultural and leadership predictors of corporate social responsibility values of top management: A GLOBE study of 15 countries. *Journal of International Business Studies, 37*(6), 823–837.

Wong, N., Rindfleisch, A., & Burroughs, J. (2003). Do reverse-worded items confound measures in cross-cultural consumer research?: The case of the material values scale. *Journal of Consumer Research, 30*(1), 72–91.

Zhou, K. Z., Su, C., & Bao, Y. (2002). A paradox of price-quality and market efficiency: A comparative study of the US and China markets. *International Journal of Research in Marketing, 19*(4), 349–365.

Fusion Modeling

Elea McDonnell Feit and Eric T. Bradlow

Contents

Introduction	148
The Classic Data Fusion Problem in Marketing	148
Mixed Levels of Data Aggregation	151
Developing and Estimating Fusion Models	153
Ex. 1: Fusing Data Using a Multivariate Normal Model	153
Ex. 2: Fusing Data Using a Multivariate Probit Model	163
Summary of the Process for Developing a Fusion Model	165
Summary of Related Literature	167
Literature on Data Fusion	167
Related Missing Data Problems	169
Conclusion	170
Appendix	171
R Code for Generating Synthetic Data and Running Ex. 1 with Stan	171
Stan Model for Ex. 2 (Split Multivariate Probit Data)	175
R Commands for Ex. 2	178
References	179

Abstract

This chapter introduces readers to applications of data fusion in marketing from a Bayesian perspective. We will discuss several applications of data fusion including the classic example of combining data on media viewership for one group of customers with data on category purchases for a different

---

E. M. Feit (✉)
LeBow College of Business, Drexel University, Philadelphia, PA, USA
e-mail: efeit@drexel.edu

E. T. Bradlow
The Wharton School, University of Pennsylvania, Philadelphia, PA, USA
e-mail: ebradlow@wharton.upenn.edu

© Springer Nature Switzerland AG 2022
C. Homburg et al. (eds), *Handbook of Market Research*,
https://doi.org/10.1007/978-3-319-57413-4_9

group, a very common problem in marketing. While many missing data approaches focus on creating "fused" data sets that can be analyzed by others, we focus on the overall inferential goal, which, for this classic data fusion problem, is to determine which media outlets attract consumers who purchase in a particular category and are therefore good targets for advertising. The approach we describe is based on a common Bayesian approach to missing data, using data augmentation within MCMC estimation routines. As we will discuss, this approach can also be extended to a variety of other data structures including mismatched groups of customers, data at different levels of aggregation, and more general missing data problems that commonly arise in marketing. This chapter provides readers with a step-by-step guide to developing Bayesian data fusion applications, including an example fully worked out in the Stan modeling language. Readers who are unfamiliar with Bayesian analysis and MCMC estimation may benefit by reading the chapter in this handbook on Bayesian Models first.

Keywords

Data fusion · Data augmentation · Missing data · Bayesian · Markov-chain Monte Carlo

Introduction

The Classic Data Fusion Problem in Marketing

Like many other fields, numerous situations arise in marketing where the ideal data for analysis is not readily available. For example, in media planning, marketers want to know whether viewers of a particular media (e.g., television channels or shows, magazines, websites, etc.) purchase a particular product (e.g., breakfast cereal or video games), so that they can decide where to place advertising or estimate the association between exposures to ads and purchases. (See the chapter in this handbook on Return on Media Models for more on marketing response modeling.) Ideally, we would like a data set where the media consumption and purchase behavior are tracked for the same set of customers. However, such data is seldom available. Typically, a media tracking firm (e.g., Comscore, Rentrak) collects data on media usage for one set of consumers, while another firm tracks data on product purchases (e.g., IRI, Niesen, or Dunnhumby for CPG products, Polk for automobiles in the USA, or IMS Health for pharmaceuticals in the USA). Even when media and purchase data are collected by the same firm, it is often impractical to collect that data for the same group of customers, and so firms like Nielsen and Kantar, which collect both purchase and media usage data, typically maintain separate panels for media tracking and purchase tracking. Thus, fusing these separate data sources is a classic problem in marketing analytics (cf. Kamakura and Wedel 1997; Gilula et al. 2006).

Fig. 1 The traditional data fusion problem is to combine two multivariate data sets with different, but overlapping, sets of variables. This data structure occurs in a number of marketing settings and can be addressed as a Bayesian missing data problem

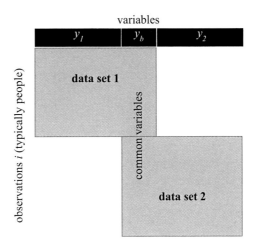

While the goal is to measure the relationship between media usage and product purchase, the data structure that we are faced with is like that shown in Fig. 1, where each row (indexed by i) in data set 1 represents a user in the media panel and the variables in data set 1 describe which content (e.g., channels, shows or websites) user i views. (We let y_{i1} denote the vector of observed variables for each user in data set 1). Data set 2 describes a different set of customers in a purchase panel with observed variables describing which products each consumer has purchased (denoted as y_{i2}). The marketing objective is to estimate what types of products the viewers of some content purchase. The key that makes this possible is a vector of common linking variables which are observed both for customers in data set 1 and customers in data set 2 (y_{ib}), where the subscript b indicates "both." These variables are often demographics that are collected for users in both data sets. Typically, these demographics are correlated with both media consumption and product purchases (i.e., new parents may be more likely to visit a parenting website and more likely to buy diapers), which enable data fusion.

Beyond the media and purchase data fusion problem, the data structure depicted in Fig. 1 arises in many other contexts in marketing where we observe one set of variables for one group of customers and another set of variables for another group of customers. For example, two retailers considering a co-branding agreement might want to fuse their separate customer lists to estimate how often customers purchase both brands. And even within companies, growing privacy concerns have led firms to avoid maintaining data sets with personal identifiers (e.g., names or addresses) for individual customers. The data fusion methods we describe here can be used to link two data sets which have been de-identified to protect user privacy (Qian and Xie 2014).

In some cases marketing analysts may even plan to create such unmatched data; for instance, in split questionnaire design, marketing researchers minimize the burden on survey respondents by creating a pair of complementary surveys which each can be answered by a subset of the respondents and later fused back together

(Adigüzel and Wedel 2008). Beyond marketing, in educational testing, the data structure in Fig. 1 occurs when data set 1 is students who take the SAT in 2015, data set 2 is those who take it in 2016, and linking variables are test questions (items) that overlap between the two tests.

In all of these examples, the analysis goal is to understand the multivariate relationships between y_{i1} and y_{i2}. The key to linking the two sets of survey data is a set of questions that is common to both surveys, providing the linking variables described in Fig. 1 (y_{ib}).

There are also several closely related data settings where similar methods can be employed including survey subsampling and time sampling (cf. Kamakura and Wedel 2000). In subsampling, some of variables are only collected for a subset of the population, often because those variables are more difficult to collect, e.g., expensive medical tests in population health surveys. In time sampling, a subset of respondents answer a repeated survey at each point in time, avoiding potential respondent fatigue while still collecting data at the desired time interval.

Early approaches to data fusion tackled it as a database integration problem, where in a first stage we match records in data set 1 with records in data set 2 to create a complete database. Statistical modeling and estimation can then proceed as usual with the now-complete data set. For example, the hot deck procedure (Ford 1983), and its more sophisticated variants, can be used to match records in the two data sets using a set of ad hoc rules to match customer i in data set 1 with a customer j in data set 2 who has the same values of y_{ib}. If there are more than one candidate match, the match is selected randomly. If there are a large number of common variables y_{ib}, such that a perfect match to customer i is not always available, then a nearest neighbor approach can be used to match to customers who are similar. In both hot deck and nearest neighbor, once all the customers i in data set 1 are matched to a customer j in data set 2, analysis proceeds as if y_{i1} and y_{j2} were observed from the same customer.

A challenging and often ignored aspect of these two-step imputation-then-analysis approaches is that the uncertainty in the imputation is not propagated forward to the statistical modeling stage (Andridge and Little 2010). In marketing, two-step approaches have become largely superseded by approaches which cast data fusion as a Bayesian missing data problem (Kamakura and Wedel 1997; Gilula et al. 2006; Qian and Xie 2014), which is the approach we will focus on in this chapter.

We focus on analyzing data like that in Fig. 1 as a Bayesian missing data problem: y_{i2} are missing for individuals in data set 1 and y_{i1} are missing for data set 2. Thus, while this chapter resides in the section of this book on data, the approach is more of "a modeling method to handle data that is less than ideal."

A critical step in analyzing any missing data problem is to consider the process by which the missing data came to be missing. Ideally, data is Missing Completely at Random (MCAR), which means that missingness is unrelated to the observed data or the values of the missing data. When data is MCAR, we can ignore the missing data mechanism in data fusion problems.

In data fusion, this assumption would be violated if one or both of the data sets was a biased sample from the target population. For instance, if a media usage data set contains mostly lower-income respondents and the relationship between media usage and product usage is different for low- and high-income respondents, then the missing data in Fig. 1 would not be ignorable for overall population-level inferences. This can happen due to poor sampling methods or survey non-response in one or both of the panels. Respondents frequently avoid answering sensitive questions particularly when the true answer is socially undesirable, e.g., viewing content that one might be embarrassed to admit watching. In these instances, the likelihood of a particular survey response being missing depends on the missing response. In these cases, the process that created the missingness can be modeled to avoid bias (Bradlow and Zaslavsky 1999; Ying et al. 2006).

When fusing two data sets that have been carefully sampled from the same target population, we can assume the data is missing by design, which is a special case of Missing Completely at Random (Little and Rubin 2014, Chap. 1). In this case, inference can proceed without explicitly modeling the process that led to the missingness. We are not aware of any published examples of data fusion in marketing where sampling bias or non-response is modeled, although this is a potential area for future research.

The procedure for handling the missing data in Fig. 1 is as follows. If $f(y_i|\theta)$ is the model for the complete vector of responses $y_i = (y_{i1}, y_{i2}, y_{ib})$ with parameters θ, our inference is based on the likelihood of the observed data y^{obs}, which is given by:

$$f(y^{\text{obs}}|\theta) = \int_{y_1^{\text{mis}}} \int_{y_2^{\text{mis}}} \prod_i f(y_i|\theta) dy_2^{\text{mis}} dy_1^{\text{mis}} \qquad (1)$$

where y_1^{mis} is the missing observation of y_{i2} in data set 1 and y_2^{mis} is the missing observation of y_{i1} in data set 2.

One way to estimate θ in Eq. 1 is to create a Bayesian MCMC sampler that samples simultaneously from the posterior of θ and the posteriors of the missing data elements y_1^{mis} and y_2^{mis}. This approach is referred to as data augmentation (Tanner and Wong 1987). We will illustrate data augmentation for two alternative specifications of $f(y|\theta)$ in section "Developing and Estimating Fusion Models," but first we introduce another closely related missing data problem that occurs when merging data from separate sources.

Mixed Levels of Data Aggregation

A second problem that can arise when trying to combine data from two data sources is that the data is provided for individual customers in one data set but is only available in aggregate in another. In analyzing media usage data, this problem occurs because usage of some media channels like websites and mobile apps are easily tracked and linked at the user level, while data on exposure to broadcast media like radio, television, or outdoor signage is only available in aggregate. For example, we might know from a representative panel (e.g., Nielsen People Meter) that approximately 5.3% of a group of users watched a television show, but we do not know exactly which users those were. Media planners would like to understand the co-usage of media channels – are users who watch some content on TV also likely to watch it on mobile or the web – but we cannot directly observe the co-usage at the consumer level (Feit et al. 2013).

The resulting mixed aggregate-disaggregate data structure is depicted in Fig. 2 where we observe one set of disaggregate variables, y_{i1t} at the individual-level and only totals, Y_{2t}, for a set of aggregate variables. The managerial goal is to infer the correlations across users between the aggregate and the disaggregate variables, which requires repeated observations of y_{i1t} and Y_{2t} over t.

Beyond the media-planning problem described above, this mixed aggregate-disaggregate data structure occurs in other marketing settings, often due to the limitations of tracking systems. For example, a retailer may have detailed customer-level data on visits to an online store, but only aggregate counts of customer visits in physical stores. Even though this data is deficient, one can still use it to infer how many multichannel customers there are and often which customers those are. Similarly, retailers often have customer-level data on coupon redemption (tracked as part of the transaction), but only aggregate data on how many coupons are in circulation. Musalem et al. (2008) show how to use a Bayesian missing data approach with this data to infer "who has the coupon?," in turn leading to more accurate inference about the effect of coupons on purchases.

Inference for the mixed aggregate-disaggregate data structure described in Fig. 2 can also be viewed as a missing data problem, where the individual-level observations for the aggregated variables, y_{i1t}, are missing; we only observe a total $Y_{2t} = \sum y_{i2t}$ for each period t. As with the traditional data fusion problem, the y_{i2t} is missing by design, and inference can be based on specifying a likelihood for the complete data and then integrating out the missing observations. Specifically, if $f(y_{i1t}, y_{i2t}|\theta)$ is

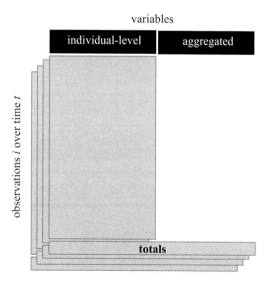

Fig. 2 In mixed aggregate and disaggregate data, only marginal totals are observed for some variables. Repeated observations of the marginal totals make it possible to identify the individual-level correlations, even when they are not directly observed

the likelihood for the complete individual-level observations that we do not observe, then inference is based on:

$$f(y_{1t}, Y_{2t}|\theta) = \prod_i \int_{y_{i2t}} f(y_{i1t}, y_{i2t}|\theta) dy_{i2t} \quad \text{s.t.} \sum_i y_{i2t} = Y_{2t} \qquad (2)$$

The key nuance in Eq. 2 is that the integral over the missing data must conform to the constraint implied by the observed marginal totals $\sum y_{i2t} = Y_{2t}$. By observing covariation between media channels over *time*, and posing a model limiting the covariation structure in the model so that it is driven by user-level behavior, one can estimate the user-level covariation in media usage and make inference about which customers are most likely to have been consuming the aggregated media channel on a given day. By contrast, if we were to aggregate all the data and fit an aggregate time-series model with $\sum y_{i1t} = Y_{1t}$ and $\sum y_{i1t} = Y_{1t}$, it would be impossible to attribute covariation in *aggregate* media usage to co-usage by individual users.

An MCMC sampler can be developed to sample from the posterior of the model in Eq. 2 by developing a way to sample the missing individual-level y_{i2t} such that they conform to the constraint. Thus the method is closely related to the approach used to estimate choice models from aggregate data proposed by Chen and Yang (2007) and Musalem et al. (2008). In fact, in this case, the aggregated data (i.e., constraint) provides information that makes the imputed y_{i2t} even more plausible.

Developing and Estimating Fusion Models

This section provides readers with a step-by-step guide to developing and estimating fusion models by walking the reader through the computation for two examples. These examples are intentionally simplified to allow the reader to focus on the core ideas in data fusion. Our hope is that readers who master these examples will be well-prepared to move on to the more sophisticated examples we discuss in the literature review in section "Summary of Related Literature."

Ex. 1: Fusing Data Using a Multivariate Normal Model

We begin with an example of data like that in Fig. 1, where a vector of K_1 variables, y_{i1}, are only observed in the first data set, while another vector of K_2 variables, y_{i2}, are only observed in second data set. As we discussed in the introduction, this is the data structure for split questionnaire designs (where data set 1 and data set 2 represent sub-surveys administered to separate people) and for the classic problem of fusing media consumption data with product purchase data. While creating a complete fused data set (i.e., imputing the missing data in Fig. 1) is often an intermediate step in the analysis, it is important to recognize the ultimate inferential goal in both of these examples is to understand the association between y_{i1} and y_{i2}

despite the fact that those variables are never observed together for the same respondent.

The key to making this inference is that there is a vector of K_b variables that are observed in both data sets, y_{ib}. As we will illustrate, it is vital that these linking variables be correlated with y_{i1} and y_{i2}. If they are independent, then the observed data provide no information about the association between y_{i1} and y_{i2}.

The first step in building a fusion model is to specify a likelihood for the complete observation that we wish we had for all respondents $y_i = (y_{i1}, y_{i2}, y_{ib})$. One simple model for a vector response like this is a multivariate normal distribution:

$$y_i \sim N_{(K_1+K_2+K_b)}(\mu, \Sigma) \tag{3}$$

where N_K denotes the multivariate normal distribution of dimension K and μ and Σ are the mean vector and covariance matrix to be estimated from the data. The multivariate normal model is computationally convenient to work with and so is commonly used in the statistical literature (Little and Rubin 2014; Rässler 2002). It also allows us to estimate correlations between elements of y_i through the covariance matrix Σ. In data fusion problems, we are particularly interested in the correlations between elements of y_{i1} and y_{i2}, which are never observed for the same subject. For example, when combining media consumption and purchase data, these correlations tell us that users who use a particular media channel are likely to purchase a particular product.

While we begin with the simpler multivariate normal model, we should note that the variables we observe in marketing are often binary or discrete, which may not be suitably modeled with a multivariate normal model. In most real cases, an appropriate model is chosen such as a latent cut point model. However, these other models are a relatively straightforward extension of the multivariate model as we will show in Ex. 2.

The core idea of fusion modeling is to estimate the model in (3) using Bayesian methods. Bayesian inference readily handles missing data, including the missing data that is created here due to the fact that some elements of y_i are unobserved for each respondent in the data set. Of course, it would be impossible to follow the approach of estimating the model in (3) using only complete cases, as there are no complete cases.

While our goal is to evaluate the likelihood in Eq. 1, we handle the integral by treating the missing data as unknown and computing the joint posterior of the missing data and the model parameters. In Bayesian inference, all unknown parameters, missing data, and latent variables are treated similarly. Conditional on the model and priors, we compute a posterior distribution for each unknown quantity based on Bayes theorem. Once this joint posterior is obtained, the marginal posteriors of the parameter Σ can be evaluated to understand the correlations in the data. The posteriors of the missing data elements in y_i can also be used to generate a fused data set, if that is desired.

It should be emphasized that by fitting a Bayesian fusion model, we *simultaneously* obtain estimates for both the parameters of interest – in this case μ and

Fusion Modeling

Σ – and impute the missing values in y_i for each respondent, i. Unlike other approaches to missing data which impute in a first stage (often using ad hoc methods) and then estimate parameters in a second stage, the posteriors obtained using Bayesian inference use all the information available in the data and reflect all of the posterior uncertainty resulting from the imputing the missing data.

For all but the most simple Bayesian models, the posterior is obtained by developing an algorithm that will generate random draws from the joint posterior distribution of all unknown parameters. These random samples are then analyzed to estimate the posterior distributions for both the model parameters and the missing data. There are a variety of algorithms for sampling from the posterior distribution that can be adapted to any model including the broad class of Markov-chain Monte Carlo (MCMC) algorithms. When writing MCMC samplers for a fusion model, it is necessary to work out the full conditionals for the missing data and create Gibbs steps to explicitly draw them. An alternative to building the sampler directly is to use a tool like Stan (Carpenter et al. 2016), which allows the user to specify a likelihood using a modeling language and then automatically produces an MCMC algorithm to generate posterior draws from that model. We will illustrate this example using Stan. This code can be run in R, after the Stan software and the `RStan` R package are installed; see the RStan Getting Started guide (Stan Core Development Team 2016) for installation instructions.

The first step in estimating the fusion model using Stan is to lay out the Stan model code, which describes the data and the likelihood. We provide this code in Fig. 3.

The `data` block in the code in Fig. 3 tells Stan what data is observed: `N1` observations of a vector of length `K1` called `y1`, `N2` observations of a vector of length `K2` called `y2`, and `N1 + N2` observations of a vector of length `Kb` called `yb`. These correspond to the variables observed only in data set 1, the variables observed only in data set 2, and the common linking variables.

The `parameters` block in Fig. 3 defines the variables for which we want to obtain a posterior. This includes the parameters `mu`, `tau`, and `Omega`, where `mu` is the mean vector for y_i, `tau` is a vector of variances, and `Omega` is the correlation matrix. (This is the preferred parameterization of the multivariate normal in Stan. Note that other MCMC tools like WinBUGS (Spiegelhalter et al. 2003) parameterize the multivariate normal with a precision matrix, the inverse of the covariance matrix.) The `parameters` block also defines the missing elements of y_i: `y1mis` for the missing variables in data set 1 and `y2mis` for the missing variables in data set 2. In Stan, the term `parameters` is used for any unknown quantity including both traditional parameters and missing data; following the Bayesian approach to inference, Stan makes no distinction between these two types of unknowns.

In the `transformed parameters` block, there is a bit of code that maps the observed data and the missing data into the full `y` array. This is simply bookkeeping; the known and unknown elements of `y` from the `data` and `parameters` blocks are mapped into a single vector. (Note that WinBUGS does not require this step and instead simply assumes that any declared data that is not provided is missing data.)

```
data {
  int<lower=0> N1;   //observations in data set 1
  int<lower=0> N2;   //observations in data set 2
  int<lower=0> K1;
  int<lower=0> K2;
  int<lower=0> Kb;
  vector[K1] y1[N1];
  vector[K2] y2[N2];
  vector[Kb] yb[N1 + N2];
}
parameters {
  // mean of complete vector
  vector[K1 + K2 + Kb] mu;
  // correlation matrix for complete vector
  corr_matrix[K1 + K2 + Kb] Omega;
  // variance of each variable
  vector<lower=0>[K1 + K2 + Kb] tau;
  // missing elements in data set 1 (observed in y2)
  vector[K2] y1mis[N1];
  // missing elements in data set 2 (observed in y1)
vector[K1] y2mis[N2];
}
transformed parameters{
  // create the complete data
  vector[K1 + K2 + Kb] y[N1 + N2];
  for (n in 1:N1) {
    for (k in 1:K1) y[n][k] = y1[n][k];
    for (k in 1:K2) y[n][K1 + k] = y1mis[n][k];
    for (k in 1:Kb) y[n][K1 + K2 + k] = yb[n][k];
  }
  for (n in 1:N2) {
    for (k in 1:K1) y[N1+n][k] = y2mis[n][k];
    for (k in 1:K2) y[N1+n][K1+k] = y2[n][k];
    for (k in 1:Kb) y[N1+n][K1+K2+k] = yb[N1+n][k];
  }
}
model {
  //priors
  mu ~ normal(0, 100);
  tau ~ cauchy(0,2.5);
  Omega ~ lkj_corr(2);
  //likelihood
  y ~ multi_normal(mu, quad_form_diag(Omega, tau));
}
```

Fig. 3 Stan code for multivariate normal data fusion model

Stan requires the user to explicitly declare the observed and missing data and then use the `transformed parameters` block to define the combined "wished for" data.

Fusion Modeling

In the final `model` block, the model is specified, along with priors for the parameters. The complete y vector is modeled as a multivariate normal with mean vector mu and covariance matrix `quad_form_diag(Omega, tau)`, which transforms `Omega` and `tau` to the covariance matrix Σ. The prior on mu is the conjugate normal prior, and the priors on `tau` and `Omega` are the Cauchy and the LKJ prior for correlation matrices, as recommended by the Stan Modeling Language User's Guide and Reference Manual (Stan Development Team 2017). Note that Stan provides a wide variety of other possible models and priors, and the code in Fig. 3 can be easily modified. More details on how Stan models are specified can be found in the User's Guide.

To estimate the model, the Stan code above is saved in a file and then called using the `stan` function from the `RStan` package in R. (Alternatively, Stan can be called from other languages including Python, MATLAB, Mathematica, and Stata.) In R, the data is passed to Stan as an R list object of elements with the same names and dimensions as defined in the `data` block in the Stan model code, i.e., d1 is a list with N1, N2, K1, K2, Kb, y1, y2, and yb. For example, if the data is stored in the R object `d1$data`, its structure would be as follows:

```
> str(d1$data)
List of 8
 $ K1: num 1
 $ K2: num 1
 $ Kb: num 2
 $ N1: num 100
 $ N2: num 100
 $ y1: num [1:100, 1] 1.037 -0.798 0.318 -0.322 0.323 ...
 $ y2: num [1:100, 1] 0.401 -1.821 -1.701 0.726 -0.228 ...
 $ yb: num [1:200, 1:2] 0.607 0.53 1.759 0.49 0.406 ...
```

In this example, the combined vector y_i consists of four variables where the y_{1i} vector is a single variable observed for 100 respondents, y_{2i} is a second single variable observed for a different 100 respondents, and y_{bi} consists of two variables observed for all 200 respondents. Complete code to generate synthetic data and run this example is included in the Appendix and is available online at https://github.com/eleafeit/data_fusion.

If the code above is saved in the file Data_Fusion.stan in the working directory of R, then we can obtain draws from the posterior distribution of all unknowns with the following command in R:

```
library(rstan)
m1 <- stan(file="Data_Fusion.stan", data=d1, iter=10000,
           warmup=2000, chains=1)
```

The result is a set of samples from the posterior distribution for mu, tau, Omega, and the missing values of y_i, which are called `y1mis` and `y2mis`. Note the inputs `iter` and `warmup`, which specify that Stan should throw away the first 2000 draws (`warmup`) and then treat the next $10,000 - 2000 = 8000$ draws as samples from the posterior. See the chapter in this handbook on Bayesian models for more details.

Once this call to Stan from R is completed, the posterior draws are stored in the `m1` object in R. Note the computation may take minutes or hours depending on the size of the data set and the speed of the computer; MCMC algorithms tend to be quite computationally intensive. These draws can be analyzed (typically within R) to make statements about the posteriors of the parameters and the missing data. For instance, a summary of the estimated correlations can be produced with the command:

```
> summary(m1, par=c("Omega"))
```

which results in the output:

```
$summary
            stats
parameter          mean           sd         2.5%          25%          50%          75%        97.5%
   Omega[1,1]  1.00000000 0.000000e+00  1.00000000   1.00000000   1.00000000   1.00000000   1.0000000
   Omega[1,2]  0.41684930 2.061013e-01  0.02423465   0.26268973   0.41374668   0.57872494   0.7835050
   Omega[1,3] -0.28081755 7.906684e-02 -0.42740820  -0.33640737  -0.28380772  -0.22730667  -0.1226349
   Omega[1,4]  0.64837176 5.226765e-02  0.53581533   0.61582170   0.65217926   0.68441334   0.7424671
   Omega[2,1]  0.41684930 2.061013e-01  0.02423465   0.26268973   0.41374668   0.57872494   0.7835050
   Omega[2,2]  1.00000000 8.368726e-17  1.00000000   1.00000000   1.00000000   1.00000000   1.0000000
   Omega[2,3] -0.69550156 4.772961e-02 -0.77889871  -0.72881140  -0.69929899  -0.66573197  -0.5916050
   ...
```

In this example, the primary inferential goal is to understand the correlation between y_{1i} and y_{2i}, which are the first two elements in the vector y. This corresponds to the `Omega[1,2]` correlation reported in the second row of the above summary. The summary shows that the correlation has a posterior mean of 0.417 with a standard deviation of 0.206, suggesting that the correlation is between 0.024 and 0.784, which is fairly diffuse, but clearly suggests a positive correlation between y_{i1} and y_{i2}. While this correlation is the key parameter of interest in the data fusion problem, posterior summaries of other parameters can be obtained with similar commands. See the R code in the Appendix for details.

The posterior distributions for μ and Σ are shown graphically in Figs. 4 and 5, and code to produce these graphs is included in the Appendix. The posterior distribution of the key correlation between y_{i1} and y_{i2} is shown in the bottom of the plot in Fig. 5, labeled `Omega.12`. Again, the figure clearly shows that the posterior of this correlation is quite diffuse. However, despite the fact that we never observe y_{1i} and y_{2i} for the same individual, we can infer that that y_{1i} and y_{2i} are positively correlated, which was precisely the goal of our data fusion. Since we generated this data synthetically, we happen to know that the true correlation is 0.3, which the model has recovered reasonably well, despite the fact that y_{1i} and y_{2i} are never observed for the same i and the data set is rather small.

Another important feature to notice in Fig. 5 is that the posterior for the correlation between y_{i1} and y_{i2} (labeled `Omega.12`) is much more diffuse than the other correlations. Since the first two elements of y_i are never directly observed together,

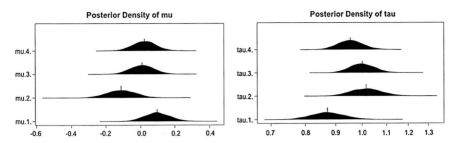

Fig. 4 Posterior distribution of mu (means of multivariate normal for y_i) and tau (variances of y_i) in Ex. 1

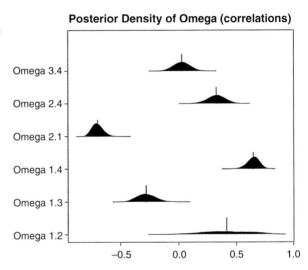

Fig. 5 Posterior distribution of Omega (correlations in the multivariate normal for y_i) in Ex. 1

the data contains only *indirect* information about the correlation. The other correlations are directly observed and therefore better identified resulting in narrower posteriors for the other correlations in Fig. 5. This can be understood by noting that for the correlations where the variables are never observed together, the MCMC sampler is integrating over possible missing values which creates greater diffuseness (appropriately so) in the posterior.

Although our primary goal is to understand the association between y_{i1} and y_{i2} which can be assessed with the posterior of Omega.12, the MCMC sampler also produces posterior samples for the missing elements of y_i. An example of one of these posterior distributions is shown in Fig. 6. Although the overall mean of y_{i1} across all respondents (observed and unobserved) is around 0.1 (see Fig. 4), the posterior for this particular respondent is substantially lower and is centered at -1.22 (2.5%-tile $= -2.45$, 97.5%-tile $= 0.00$). Even though we don't observe y_{i1} for this respondent, the posterior for the missing data tells us the likely range of reasonable values of y_{i1} *for this respondent*, based on his or her observed values for y_{i2} and y_{ib}. The posterior of y_{i1} can be summarized by the mean or median to obtain a "best

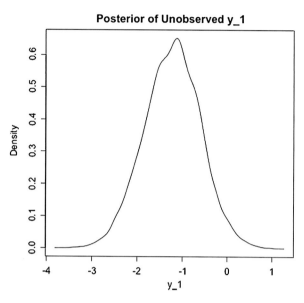

Fig. 6 Posterior distribution for one of the unobserved elements of y

estimate" of the missing data for this respondent. These estimates depend on the observed data for individual i, as well as the estimated mean and covariance across the population.

Importantly, because the posterior for the unobserved elements of y_i and the parameters are evaluated simultaneously, the posterior uncertainty in the missing elements of y_i fully accounts for the posterior uncertainty in μ and Σ, and, similarly, the posterior uncertainty in μ and Σ fully accounts for posterior uncertainty in the unobserved elements of y_i. That is, we can say that there is a 95% chance that the missing value of y_{i1} for this respondent is between -2.45 and 0.00, conditional on the model and our priors.

The MCMC sampler has produced posterior samples for all 100 missing values of y_{i1} and 100 missing values of y_{i2}, and the posterior draws could be summarized to produce a fused data set where the missing values are imputed with posterior means or medians. Although this is unnecessary, if the inferential goal was to measure the correlations in Σ, we can interpret the posteriors for Σ directly. If the goal is to produce a fused data set, then to carry forward the posterior uncertainty into any future analysis, the missing values should be multiply imputed (Rubin 1996), simply by sampling a subset of the posterior draws to create multiple fused data sets. We strongly recommend this approach as opposed to plugging in posterior means or medians (even when appropriately obtained) as biased estimates of nonlinear parameters would occur.

Depending on the context, the imputed individual-level data may also be used to target individual customers. For instance, if y_{2i} represents usage of a particular product, then the imputed values of y_{2i} could be used to target specific customers who are likely to use the product, even if we have never observed those customers' product usage. This scoring application is useful in any CRM application where the

Fusion Modeling

customers in the data set can be re-targeted, such as fusing the product purchase data between two retailers to identify customers that are good prospects for cross-selling.

To summarize the overall ability of the model to recover the unobserved values in y_{i1}, we plot the posterior medians for all 100 missing observations of y_{i1} against the true value used to generate the data in Fig. 7. (We know the true values because when we generated the data, we drew y_i from a multivariate normal distribution and then removed the "unobserved" elements of y_i.) Figure 7 also shows the posterior uncertainty in the imputation by plotting error bars representing the 2.5 and 97.5%- tiles of the posterior distribution, illustrating the full range of values that the missing data might take. The posterior medians are generally consistent with the true values, and the true value is always contained within the posterior interval. Thus, the fusion model is able to accurately recover the unobserved value of y_{i1}.

Figure 7 shows that the posterior medians for the unobserved y_{1i} tend to be somewhat closer to zero than the true values. (The slope of a best-fit line thorough the points in Fig. 7 is somewhat less than 1.) This is an example of Bayesian shrinkage, where Bayesian posteriors for individuals tend to be closer to the overall mean and should be expected.

With this example, we have illustrated that fusion modeling is straightforward to execute; however, a word of caution is due. Inference about unobserved values of y_{1i} and y_{2i} and the correlation between them (including non-Bayesian inference) depends critically on their being correlations between the linking variables and y_{1i} and y_{2i}. To illustrate this, we re-estimated the fusion model with two other synthetic data sets that were identical in dimension to the first. One was generated where Σ was diagonal (i.e., no correlations in y_i) and one generated where all correlations in Σ were 0.9. Complete R code for replicating these analyses is included in the Appendix.

When the correlations are high, as shown on the bottom panel in Fig. 8, the missing elements of y_{1i} can be recovered very precisely. The posterior medians are

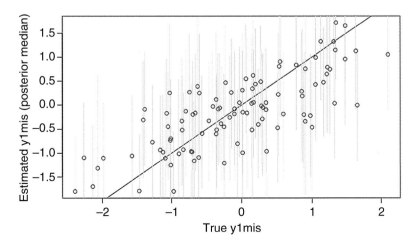

Fig. 7 Posterior estimates of missing elements of y_1 are accurately recovered by the fusion model

close to the true values and the posteriors are quite narrow, which reflects the fact that when there are high correlations the data is more informative about the unobserved elements of y_{1i} than our first example, where the correlations were moderate. However, when the correlations are zero, the data is completely uninformative of the missing observations of y_{1i}. As shown in the top panel of Fig. 8, there is no discernible relationship between the posterior medians and the true values, and the posteriors are so wide that they run off the edges of the plot. This extends to inference about the correlation between y_{i1} and y_{i2}, which has a posterior that is close to uniform between −1 and 1 – which is essentially the same as the prior, reflecting that fact that the data contains no information about the correlation between y_{i1} and y_{i2}. So, even with a substantial number of observations, it is possible

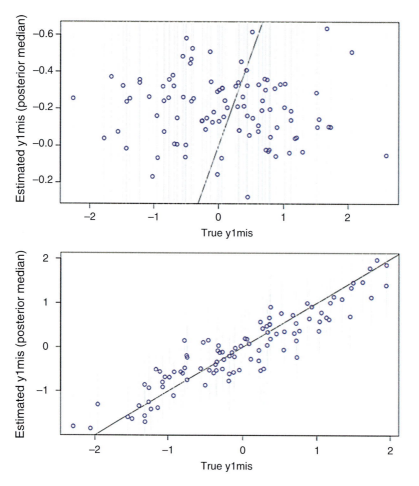

Fig. 8 Inference about missing elements of y_1 depends critically on the correlations between the elements of y. When Σ is diagonal, there is no information in the data about the missing elements of y_{1i} (top). When correlations between elements of y_i are high, unobserved elements of y_{1i} are precisely recovered (bottom)

that the missing elements of y_{i1} and y_{i2} cannot be recovered if the linking variables y_{ib} are not correlated with y_{i1} and y_{i2}.

This discussion relates to the clear distinction between the fraction of missing data and fraction of missing information in the missing data literature (Little and Rubin 2014) where the number of rows that are incomplete may be a poor indicator of how much missing information there is.

The two cases presented in Fig. 8 illustrate why it is extremely important when doing data fusion to carefully choose the linking variables in y_{ib}. For example, in designing a split questionnaire survey, it is important that responses to the questions that are answered by all respondents are correlated with responses to the questions that are only answered by some respondents. (See Adigüzel and Wedel (2008) for more extensive discussion of split questionnaire design.) In fusing media consumption and product purchase data – the classic data fusion example – demographics are usually used as the linking variables. This will work best when demographics are correlated with media consumption (which is very likely but perhaps less so in today's highly fragmented media landscape) and product purchase (which is likely at the category level but perhaps not at the brand level).

However, even if a poor choice is made for the linking variables, the Bayesian posteriors for the parameters and the missing data will always reflect whatever uncertainty remains. Thus, unlike ad hoc imputation approaches, Bayesian fusion modeling will identify when the linking variables are weak by reporting diffuse posteriors for the individual-level imputations.

Ex. 2: Fusing Data Using a Multivariate Probit Model

As we mentioned earlier, the multivariate normal model is inappropriate for most marketing data, where there are many binary or categorical variables. This is easily accommodated by specifying a latent variable model where an underlying latent vector is normally distributed and then each element of that vector is appropriately transformed to suit the observed data. For example, if the data is binary, which is quite common in marketing, for instance, with "check-all-that-apply"-type questions in a survey or with behavioral variables that track incidence, one can use a multivariate probit model. Assuming that $y_i = (y_{1i}, y_{2i}, y_{bi})$ contains all binary variables, the model for the complete data is:

$$y_{ik} = \begin{cases} 1 & \text{if } z_{ik} > 0 \\ 0 & \text{if } z_{ik} < 0 \end{cases} \tag{4}$$

$$z_i = (z_{1i}, \ldots, z_{Ki}) \sim N_K(\mu, \Sigma) \tag{5}$$

where k indexes the elements in y_i from 1 to $K = K_1 + K_2 + K_b$. Complete Stan model code for this model is provided in the Appendix. Note that the variances in Σ are not identified in the multivariate probit model, but associated correlations (`Omega`) are identified.

We estimated this model using a data set with similar structure as that in Ex. 1. As in the previous example, there is one observed variable in the first data set (y_{i1}), one in the second (y_{i2}), and two linking variables in y_{ib}; however, these variables are now all binary. As in the previous example, the key inferential goal is to estimate the correlation between y_{i1} and y_{i2}.

Complete R code for running this model is provided in the Appendix; we focus here on the resulting posterior inference. The posterior distribution for the correlations are shown in Fig. 9 which shows that the correlation between y_{i1} and y_{i2} has a posterior mean of 0.368 with a rather wide posterior relative to our first example (2.5%-tile $= 0.024$, 97.5%-tile $= 0.784$). This is unsurprising as in the previous example y_{i1} and y_{i2} are never observed for the same subject and, in addition, the binary data used in this example is less informative than the data used in Ex. 1.

For each of the unobserved y_{1i}, we obtain a set of posterior draws that is either 0 or 1. Summarizing these, we can get a probability that a particular missing value is 1. For example, the first missing element of data set 1 is equal to one in 0.296 of the posterior draws, indicating that there is a 0.296 probability that $y_{1,1}$ is one. Consequently, our best estimate of the missing value of $y_{1,1}$ is that it is equal to zero.

We can summarize these best estimates across all individuals in the data set. Comparing these to the true values that generated the data, we get the confusion matrix in Table 1.

So, even with binary data, which is less informative, it is still possible to estimate a fusion model and recover the unobserved variables from each data set reasonably well.

The multivariate probit sampler also produces draws for the underlying continuous normal variables, z_i. In Fig. 10 we plot the posterior means of those estimated

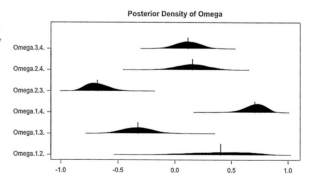

Fig. 9 Posterior distribution of correlations (Omega) from a data fusion model for binary data in Ex. 2

Table 1 Confusion matrix for estimated missing values of y_{1i} in fusion model for binary data

		True value of y_{1i}	
		0	1
Estimated y_{1i}	0	38	17
	1	14	31

Fusion Modeling

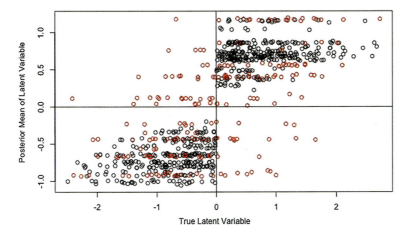

Fig. 10 Posterior means latent variable z for missing binary values y (red) show some confusion where the imputed value is inconsistent with the true value

latent variables. Those z which are associated with an observed binary y are plotted in black, and those z for which the y is missing are plotted in red. In Fig. 10 all of the black points are in the upper right or lower left quadrants, reflecting the fact that when the associated binary variable y is observed, the posterior means for z are consistent with the observed y which is in turn consistent with the sign of the true z. In contrast, the red points appear in all four quadrants, reflecting the same "confusion" we saw in Table 1. However, the points in Fig. 10 do generally follow a diagonal line, reflecting the model's ability to recover the missing values of y_i for most users and the latent z_i.

Examples 1 and 2 illustrate simple data fusion models for continuous data and binary data. Example 2 uses a continuous normal latent variable to model a binary observation, and this strategy can be extended to allow for ordinal responses, truncated continuous responses or a combination of different variable types. These models can also be extended to allow for mixed levels of aggregation as we discussed in the "Introduction." Additionally, one could build any number of model structures to relate the data in both data sets. The Bayesian framework and tools like Stan allow analysts the flexibility to build models that reflect the data-generating process.

Summary of the Process for Developing a Fusion Model

To summarize, the general process for developing a fusion model is as follows:

1. Cast the fusion problem as one of missing data.
2. Consider how the missing data came to be missing. In most data fusion problems, the missing data is *missing by design*, which means we do not need to model the process by which the data became missing as in other missing data settings.
3. Specify a parametric model for the complete "wished-for" or "fused" data.

4. Develop an MCMC sampler for the model. In these examples, we have used Stan which automatically produces a MCMC sampler based on a specified model. Programs similar to Stan include WinBUGS and JAGS. One may also code the sampler directly in a statistical language like R, MATLAB, Python, or Gauss.
5. Treat the missing data as unknowns and estimate them using data augmentation. In the above example, we used Stan to define the missing data as a Stan `parameter`, which resulted in Stan producing a posterior sample for the missing data. When building a Gibbs sampler from scratch, one would find a way to draw the missing parameters from their full conditional distributions based on the model parameters and the observed data.
6. Analyze the posterior samples to make inferences about the model parameters. Often those model parameters correspond directly to the inferential goals of the project.
7. If desired, create a multiply-imputed "fused" data set by taking several random draws from the posterior for the imputed missing data. The fused data can be used as a basis for targeting individual customers.

A point that should be emphasized is that this approach, like all Bayesian inference, conditions on the specified model for the fused data. Our first example used a multivariate normal model and our second used a multivariate probit model. Models based on the multivariate normal are computationally convenient and common in the literature. For instance, in the context of split questionnaires, Raghunathan and Grizzle (1995) and Adigüzel and Wedel (2008) use a cut point model with an underlying multivariate normal distribution. Rässler (2002) also focuses primarily on data fusion with the multivariate normal. However, as with all model-based inference, a model should be chosen that is appropriate for the data and obtaining a posterior based on that model, and the observed data is generally easy to do using modern Bayesian computational methods.

We focused here on methods that propose a model for the joint distribution of the fused data, (y_1, y_2, y_b), but Gilula et al. (2006) point out that it is actually only necessary to specify the joint distribution of y_1 and y_2 *conditional* on y_b. They further point out that most of the two-stage matching approaches implicitly assume independence of y_1 and y_2 conditional on y_b, i.e., $f(y_1, y_2|y_b) = f(y_1|y_b)f(y_2|y_b)$. Relying on this assumption, one can specify and estimate models for $f(y_1|y_b)$ and $f(y_2|y_b)$ directly and then integrate over the observations of y_b in the data to find the joint distribution of y_1 and y_2. This simplifies the modeling task, eliminating the need to specify a model for the linking variables, y_b. The likelihood of $f(y_1|y_b)$ and $f(y_2|y_b)$ can be modeled using off-the-shelf methods such as generalized linear models. Qian and Xie (2014) expand on this approach by proposing an alternative nonparametric model for $f(y_1|y_b)$ and $f(y_2|y_b)$ that is highly flexible and suitable for both continuous and discrete data.

By contrast, the approaches like that illustrated in Exs. 1 and 2 model the full vector (y_1, y_2, y_b) and do not make the assumption of conditional independence directly. Instead, they identify the conditional dependence through the prior which yields dependence in the marginal distribution. As we illustrated in Ex. 1, the empirical identification of the full joint distribution can be weak, that is, some parameters of the joint distribution are only identified by the prior. The level of identification depends, sometimes in subtle ways, on the data; in our example identification was weak when y_{ib} was not correlated with y_{i1} and y_{i2}. Empirical identification should always be checked by comparing the prior to the posterior uncertainty; if they are the same, then the data has not provided any information.

Summary of Related Literature

We conclude with a brief summary of the literature in marketing on data fusion and then expand to a number of related papers that use Bayesian missing data methods. Our hope is that the examples provided in the previous section will provide a solid base from which students can tackle the more challenging data fusion problems described in the literature.

Literature on Data Fusion

Table 2 organizes several key papers on data fusion into three related problem domains: (1) the classic data fusion problem, (2) split questionnaires, and (3) mixed aggregate-disaggregate data.

The classic problem of fusing media and purchase data (see Fig. 1) was first recognized by Kamakura and Wedel (1997). They cast the problem as a Bayesian missing data problem, recognizing that the missing data mechanism is missing by design and so is ignorable. They propose a joint model for the fused categorical data (y_{i1}, y_{i2}, and y_{ib}) that is a discrete mixture model where incidence is independent across y_i within each latent group. They also show that it is important to account for the uncertainty caused by the data fusion process and propose a multiple imputation approach that is a predecessor to the Bayesian posterior samples we have described in this chapter. Kamakura and Wedel (2000) build on this work by proposing an alternative factor model which can be used in data fusion. They also point out there are a number other related problems where data is missing by design (including subsampling and time sampling, which we discussed in section "Introduction") where the same Bayesian missing data approach may be employed.

Gilula et al. (2006) simplified the data fusion problem by making the assumption of conditional independence between the fused variables. If $p(y_{i1}|y_{ib})$ is assumed to be independent of $p(y_{i2}|y_{ib})$, then it becomes unnecessary to specify the full joint distribution of y_{i1}, y_{i2}, and y_{ib}. Instead, the $p(y_1|y_b)$ and $p(y_2|y_b)$ can be estimated separately (using standard models), and then the joint distribution can be approximated by averaging over the observed empirical distribution of y_{ib}, i.e.,

Table 2 Summary of key data fusion papers

	Paper	Fusion	Contribution
Media and purchase	Kamakura and Wedel (1997)	Joint	Recognizing data fusion as a missing data problem and a discrete mixture model for data fusion with categorical variables
	Kamakura and Wedel (2000)	Joint	Factor model for data fusion with continuous and categorical variables
	Gilula et al. (2006)	Direct	Direct approach to data fusion applied with several off-the-shelf models
	Qian and Xie (2014)	Direct or joint	Nonparametric odds ratio model for data fusion with continuous and categorical variables
Split quest.	Raghunathan and Grizzle (1995)	Joint	Split questionnaire as a missing data problem and a model for continuous and discrete data
	Adigüzel and Wedel (2008)	Joint	Method to *design* a split questionnaire and a normal multivariate cut point model for data fusion
Agg.	Feit et al. (2013)	Joint	Fusion model for mixed aggregate-disaggregate binary data

$$p(y_{i1}, y_{i2}|D) \approx E_{\theta|D}\left[\frac{1}{N}\sum_{obs} p(y_{i1}|y_{ib}, \theta) p(y_{i2}|y_{ib}, \theta)\right] \qquad (6)$$

where D is the observed data and N is the number of observations in the complete data set. This so-called direct approach to data fusion reduces the potential for misspecification and is computationally simpler than the joint modeling approach. This approach works well for the standard data fusion problem, yet the joint modeling approach is often desirable when the data fusion problem is embedded within a more complex model (e.g., Musalem et al. 2008; Feit et al. 2010).

Most recently, Qian and Xie (2014) developed a nonparametric odds ratio model, which they show performs better than the parametric models typical of the prior literature and applies this model using both the direct and the joint modeling approaches. They also identify a new application area for data fusion: combining data collected anonymously on a sensitive behavior with data collected non-anonymously on other behaviors. In their specific application, they fuse data on customer's use of counterfeit products with other shopping and product attitudes.

At about the same time the data fusion was recognized as an important problem in marketing, Raghunathan and Grizzle (1995) proposed similar techniques for analyzing split questionnaires in the statistics literature. They propose a model for combined continuous and categorical data and analyze that model with a fully Bayesian approach, using a Gibbs sampler, as we described in section "Developing and Estimating Fusion Models." Adigüzel and Wedel (2008) extend the work on split questionaires, focusing on the problem of split questionnaire *design*, using a pilot sample of complete data to determine which questions should be included in each block of the split questionnaire to obtain the most precise posteriors for the missing (by design) data. They use a normal multivariate cut point model for the data fusion.

Building on this prior work on data fusion, Feit et al. (2013) brought the problem of combining mixed aggregate and disaggregate data into the marketing literature. Their approach involves building a posterior sampler for the complete individual-level data that is constrained to be consistent with the aggregate data.

Related Missing Data Problems

The application of the Bayesian approach to missing data extends far beyond the data fusion problem. Since the reader of this chapter has, by this point, become familiar with the Bayesian approach to missing data, in this section, we provide a brief overview of other applications of this approach. Table 3 lists a few key papers in this area.

Both Feit et al. (2010) and Qian and Xie (2011) propose solutions to the common problem that the analyst wishes to estimate a regression model but has some missing regressors. Regressors are not typically included in the probability model, and so Feit et al. (2010) illustrate how these missing regressors can be handled by including a model specification for them. Inference then proceeds by simulating from the joint posterior for the regression model parameters, regressor model parameters, and the missing regressors. Their work illustrates how, under the Bayesian framework, the posterior for missing regressors is informed by the observed regression outcomes. Specifically, they show that you can impute consumers product needs (typically modeled as a regressor) from their observed choices in a conjoint study. While Feit et al. (2010) use a standard multivariate probit model for the missing regressors, Qian and Xie (2011) propose a more flexible nonparametric model that can handle a variety of missing regressors. Both papers illustrate the point that researchers should specify a model that reflects their beliefs about the data-generating process, whether that model is one of those proposed in the papers in Table 2 specifically for data fusion or a regression model or a more complex structural model. Once the model is specified, model parameters and missing data are estimated simultaneously, rather than treating missing data as a problem that should be handled prior to data analysis.

Table 3 Summary of related work on Bayesian missing data problems

Problem	Paper	Missing data mechanism
Missing regressors	Feit et al. (2010)	Ignorable
	Qian and Xie (2011)	Ignorable
Aggregated regressors	Musalem et al. (2008)	Ignorable
Survey selection	Bradlow and Zaslavsky (1999)	Non-ignorable
	Ying et al. (2006)	Non-ignorable
	Cho et al. (2015)	Non-ignorable
Anonymous visits	Novak et al. (2015)	Non-ignorable

Musalem et al. (2008) develop a model and estimation routine for a similar problem where individual-level regressors are missing but are observed in aggregate. The specific problem they study is the situation where purchase histories are observed for individual customers, and those customers are observed redeeming coupons, but we don't know which customers have a coupon that they chose not to redeem. Instead, we only observe how many coupons were distributed in aggregate. They simultaneously estimate a model that relates the (unobserved) coupon availability to purchases and imputes "who has the coupon" in a way that is consistent with the aggregate observation.

All the previously discussed literature deals with situations where data is missing by design. That is, the data is missing because the researcher planned not to collect it, and the missingness is therefore ignorable. But many missing data problems in marketing address situations where the missingness is stochastic and related to the missing value, which is non-ignorable. The classic example of this is survey non-response. Bradlow and Zaslavsky (1999) impute individual users' missing satisfaction ratings under the assumption that a user will be less likely to answer a satisfaction question when they do not hold a strong opinion. Similar, Ying et al. (2006) study individual users' movie ratings under the assumption that the likelihood that a user will not rate a movie (probably because they didn't watch it) is related to their (unobserved) rating for that movie. Ying et al. (2006) illustrate that when the correlation between a movie being not-rated and the likely rating is ignored, predicted ratings are less accurate, leading to less a less effective movie recommendation system. More recently, Cho et al. (2015) have revisited missing data in customer satisfaction surveys.

Finally, in a recent application of Bayesian missing data methods, Novak et al. (2015) estimate a model of repeat transactions using customer relationship management (CRM) data, which often has the problem that there are a number of visits where the customer is not identified. These transactions may have been made by an existing customer or by a new customer. They show that when there are so-called anonymous visits, a Bayesian missing data approach can be used to impute the missing user ids and identify the customer who made the anonymous visit.

Conclusion

As readers can see, the general problem of missing data in marketing is very broad. The Bayesian framework can be used for missing Ys, missing Xs, data sets where there is individual and aggregate data, and so on. In fact, the broad class of missing data and data fusion problems, we would argue, is one of the most prevalent among practitioners today who want to leverage all the data that they have even when disparate data sources cannot be directly linked. However, as a final note, we warn again that for those who use these sophisticated methods, one should always pay attention to the mechanism (or hopefully lack thereof) that generated the missing data. If the mechanism is non-ignorable, then one would have to build a likelihood for the missing data process, and that process is often hard to observe and verify.

Fusion Modeling

While much research has been done for over 30 years in this area, as new data sets emerge, we expect this area to remain one of high activity going forward.

Acknowledgments We would like to thank the many co-authors with whom we have had discussions while developing and troubleshooting fusion models and other Bayesian missing data methods, especially Andres Musalem, Fred Feinberg, Pengyuan Wang, and Julie Novak.

Appendix

This appendix provides the code used to generate all examples in this chapter. It is also available online at https://github.com/eleafeit/data_fusion. Note that the results in the chapter were obtained with Stan 2.17. If you use a different version of Stan, you may obtain slightly different results even when using the same random number seed.

R Code for Generating Synthetic Data and Running Ex. 1 with Stan

R Commands for Ex. 1 (Requires Utility Functions Below to Be Sourced First)

```
library(MASS)
library(coda)
library(beanplot)
library(rstan)

# Example 1a: MVN =====================================
# Generate synthetic data
set.seed(20030601)
Sigma <- matrix(c(1, 0.3, -0.2, 0.7, 0.3, 1, -0.6, 0.4, -0.2,
                  -0.6, 1, 0.1, 0.7, 0.4, 0.1, 1), nrow=4)
d1 <- data.mvn.split(K1=1, K2=1, Kb=2, N1=100, N2=100,
                     mu=rep(0,4), Sigma=Sigma)
str(d1$data)
# Call to Stan to generate posterior draws
m1 <- stan(file="Data_Fusion_MVN.stan", data=d1$data,
           iter=10000, warmup=2000, chains=1, seed=12)
# Summaries of posterior draws for population-level parameters
summary(m1, par=c("mu"))
summary(m1, par=c("tau"))
summary(m1, par=c("Omega"))
plot.post.density(m1, pars=c("mu", "tau"), prefix="Ex1",
                  true=list(d1$true$mu, sqrt(diag(d1$true$Sigma)),
                            returncov2cor(d1$true$Sigma)))
```

```r
draws <- As.mcmc.list(m1, pars=c("Omega"))
png(filename="Ex1PostOmega.png", width=600, height=600)
beanplot(data.frame(draws[[1]][,c(2:4, 7:8, 12)]),
         horizontal=TRUE, las=1, what=c(0, 1, 1, 0),
         side="second", main=paste("Posterior Density of Omega
         (correlations)", log=""), cex.axis=0.5)
dev.off()
# Summaries of posterior draws for missing data
summary(extract(m1, par=c("y1mis"))$y1mis[,3,])
png("Ex1y13mis.png")
plot(density(extract(m1, par=c("y1mis"))$y1mis[,3,]),
     main="Posterior of Unobserved y_1", xlab="y_1")
dev.off()
summary(m1, par=c("y")) # posteriors of observed data place a
point mass at the observed value
plot.true.v.est(m1, pars=c("y1mis", "y2mis"), prefix="Ex1",
                true=list(d1$true$y1mis, d1$true$y2mis))

# Example 1b: MVN with zero correlations ==================
# Generate synthetic data
set.seed(20030601)
Sigma <- matrix(0, nrow=4, ncol=4)
diag(Sigma) <- 1
# Call to Stan to generate posterior draws
d2 <- data.mvn.split(K1=1, K2=1, Kb=2, N1=100, N2=100,
                     mu=rep(0,4), Sigma=Sigma)
m2 <- stan(file="Data_Fusion_MVN.stan", data=d2$data,
           iter=10000, warmup=2000, chains=1, seed=12)
# Summarize posteriors of population-level parameters
summary(m2, par=c("mu"))
summary(m2, par=c("tau"))
summary(m2, par=c("Omega"))
plot.post.density(m2, pars=c("mu", "tau"), prefix="Ex2",
                  true=list(d1$true$mu, sqrt(diag(d1$true$Sigma)),
                            cov2cor(d1$true$Sigma)))
draws <- As.mcmc.list(m2, pars=c("Omega"))
png(filename="Ex2PostOmega.png", width=600, height=400)
beanplot(data.frame(draws[[1]][,c(2:4, 7:8, 12)]),
         horizontal=TRUE, las=1, what=c(0, 1, 1, 0), side="second",
         main=paste("Posterior Density of Omega", log=""),
         cex.axis=0.5)
dev.off()
# Summaries of posterior draws for missing data
plot.true.v.est(m2, pars=c("y1mis", "y2mis"), prefix="Ex2",
                true=list(d2$true$y1mis, d2$true$y2mis))
# Example 1c: MVN with strong positive correlations ==========
```

Fusion Modeling

```
# Generate synthetic data
set.seed(20030601)
Sigma <- matrix(0.9, nrow=4, ncol=4)
diag(Sigma) <- 1
# Call to Stan to generate posterior draws
d3 <- data.mvn.split(K1=1, K2=1, Kb=2, N1=100, N2=100,
                     mu=rep(0,4), Sigma=Sigma)
m3 <- stan(file="Data_Fusion_MVN.stan", data=d3$data,
           iter=10000, warmup=2000, chains=1, seed=12)
# Summaries of population-level parameters
summary(m3, par=c("mu"))
summary(m3, par=c("tau"))
summary(m3, par=c("Omega"))
plot.post.density(m3, pars=c("mu", "tau"), prefix="Ex3",
                  true=list(d1$true$mu, sqrt(diag(d1$true$Sigma))))
draws <- As.mcmc.list(m3, pars=c("Omega"))
png(filename="Ex3PostOmega.png", width=600, height=400)
beanplot(data.frame(draws[[1]][,c(2:4, 7:8, 12)]),
         horizontal=TRUE, las=1, what=c(0, 1, 1, 0), side="second",
         main=paste("Posterior Density of Omega", log=""))
dev.off()
# Summaries of posterior draws for missing data
plot.true.v.est(m3, pars=c("y1mis", "y2mis"), prefix="Ex3",
                true=list(d3$true$y1mis, d3$true$y2mis))
```

Utility Functions for Ex. 1

```
data.mvn.split <- function(K1=2, K2=2, Kb=3, N1=100, N2=100,
                           mu=rep(0, K1+K2+Kb),
                           Sigma=diag(1, K1+K2+Kb))
{
  y <- mvrnorm(n=N1+N2, mu=mu, Sigma=Sigma)
  list(data=list(K1=K1, K2=K2, Kb=Kb, N1=N1, N2=N2,
                 y1=as.matrix(y[1:N1, 1:K1], col=K1),
                 y2=as.matrix(y[N1+1:N2, K1+1:K2], col=K2),
                 yb=as.matrix(y[,K1+K2+1:Kb], col=Kb)),
       true=list(mu=mu, Sigma=Sigma,
                 y1mis=y[1:N1, K1+1:K2],
                 y2mis=y[N1+1:N2, 1:K1]))
}
data.mvp.split <- function(K1=2, K2=2, Kb=3, N1=100, N2=100,
                           mu=rep(0, K1+K2+Kb),
                           Sigma=diag(1, K1+K2+Kb))
```

```r
{
  z <- mvrnorm(n=N1+N2, mu=mu, Sigma=Sigma)
  y <- z
  y[y>0] <- 1
  y[y<0] <- 0
  y1mis <- y[1:N1, K1+1:K2]
  y2mis <- y[N1+1:N2, 1:K1]
  y[1:N1, K1+1:K2] <- NA
  y[N1+1:N2, 1:K1] <- NA
  true=list(mu=mu, Sigma=Sigma, z=z, y=y, y1mis=y1mis,
            y2mis=y2mis)
  y[is.na(y)] <- 0
  data=list(K1=K1, K2=K2, Kb=Kb, N1=N1, N2=N2, y=y)
  list(data=data, true=true)
}

plot.post.density <- function(m.stan, pars, true, prefix=NULL){
  for (i in 1:length(pars)) {
    draws <- As.mcmc.list(m.stan, pars=pars[i])
    if (!is.null(prefix)) {
      filename <- paste(prefix, "Post", pars[i], ".png", sep="")
      png(filename=filename, width=600, height=400)
    }
    beanplot(data.frame(draws[[1]]),
             horizontal=TRUE, las=1, what=c(0, 1, 1, 0),
             side="second", main=paste("Posterior Density of",
                                       pars[[i]]))
    if (!is.null(prefix)) dev.off()
  }
}

plot.true.v.est <- function(m.stan, pars, true, prefix=NULL){
  for (i in 1:length(pars)) {
    draws <- As.mcmc.list(m.stan, pars=pars[i])
    est <- summary(draws)
    if (!is.null(prefix)) {
      filename <- paste(prefix, "TrueVEst", pars[i], ".png", sep="")
      png(filename=filename, width=600, height=400)
    }
    plot(true[[i]], est$quantiles[,3], col="blue",
         xlab=paste("True", pars[i]),
         ylab=paste("Estiamted", pars[i], "(posterior median)"))
    abline(a=0, b=1)
    arrows(true[[i]], est$quantiles[,3], true[[i]],
           est$quantiles[,1], col="gray90", length=0)
```

Fusion Modeling

```
  arrows(true[[i]], est$quantiles[,3], true[[i]],
       est$quantiles[,5], col="gray90", length=0)
  points(true[[i]], est$quantiles[,3], col="blue")
  if (!is.null(prefix)) dev.off()
  }
}
```

Stan Model for Ex. 2 (Split Multivariate Probit Data)

```
functions {
  int mysum(int[,] a) {
    int s;
    s = 0;
    for (i in 1:size(a))
      s = s + sum(a[i]);
    return s;
  }
}
data {
  int<lower=0> K1;    // number of vars only observed in data set 1
  int<lower=0> K2;    // number of vars only observed in data set 2
  int<lower=0> Kb;    // number of vars observed in both data sets
  int<lower=0> N1;    // number of observations in data set 1
  int<lower=0> N2;    // number of observations in data set 2
  int<lower=0,upper=2> y[N1+N2, K1+K2+Kb];    // should contain
       zeros in missing positions
}
transformed data {
  int<lower=1, upper=N1+N2> n_pos[mysum(y)];
  int<lower=1, upper=K1+K2+Kb> k_pos[size(n_pos)];
  int<lower=1, upper=N1+N2> n_neg[(N1+N2)*(K1+K2+Kb) - K2*N1
                                   - K1*N2 - mysum(y)];
  int<lower=1, upper=K1+K2+Kb> k_neg[size(n_neg)];
  int<lower=0> N_pos;
  int<lower=0> N_neg;
  N_pos = size(n_pos);
  N_neg = size(n_neg);
  {
    int i;
    int j;
```

```
i = 1;
j = 1;
for (n in 1:N1) {                      //positions in observed y1
  for (k in 1:K1) {
    if (y[n,k] == 1) {
      n_pos[i] = n;
      k_pos[i] = k;
      i = i + 1;
    } else {
      n_neg[j] = n;
      k_neg[j] = k;
      j = j + 1;
    }
  }
  for (k in (K1+K2+1):(K1+K2+Kb)) {
    if (y[n,k] == 1) {
      n_pos[i] = n;
      k_pos[i] = k;
      i = i + 1;
    } else {
      n_neg[j] = n;
      k_neg[j] = k;
      j = j + 1;
    }
  }
}
for (n in (N1+1):(N1+N2)) {       //positions in observed y2
  for (k in (K1+1):(K1+K2+Kb)) {
    if (y[n,k] == 1) {
      n_pos[i] = n;
      k_pos[i] = k;
      i = i + 1;
    } else {
      n_neg[j] = n;
      k_neg[j] = k;
      j = j + 1;
    }
  }
}
}
```

```
parameters {
  vector[K1 + K2 + Kb] mu;
  corr_matrix[K1 + K2 + Kb] Omega;
  vector<lower=0>[N_pos] z_pos;
  vector<upper=0>[N_neg] z_neg;
  vector[K2] z1mis[N1];
  vector[K1] z2mis[N2];
}
transformed parameters{
  vector[K1 + K2 + Kb] z[N1 + N2];
  vector[K2] y1mis[N1];
  vector[K1] y2mis[N2];
  for (i in 1:N_pos)
    z[n_pos[i], k_pos[i]] = z_pos[i];
  for (i in 1:N_neg)
    z[n_neg[i], k_neg[i]] = z_neg[i];
  for (n in 1:N1) {
    for (k in 1:K2) {
      z[n, K1 + k] = z1mis[n, k];
      if (z1mis[n, k] > 0)
        y1mis[n, k] = 1;
      if (z1mis[n, k] < 0)
        y1mis[n, k] = 0;
    }
  }
  for (n in 1:N2) {
    for (k in 1:K1) {
      z[N1 + n, k] = z2mis[n, k];
      if (z2mis[n, k] > 0)
        y2mis[n, k] = 1;
      if (z2mis[n, k] < 0)
        y2mis[n, k] = 0;
    }
  }
}
model {
  mu ~ normal(0, 3);
  Omega ~ lkj_corr(1);
  z ~ multi_normal(mu, Omega);
}
```

R Commands for Ex. 2

```
# Generate synthetic data
set.seed(20030601)
Sigma <- matrix(c(1, 0.3, -0.2, 0.7, 0.3, 1, -0.6, 0.4, -0.2,
                  -0.6, 1, 0.1, 0.7, 0.4, 0.1, 1), nrow=4)
d1 <- data.mvp.split(K1=1, K2=1, Kb=2, N1=100, N2=100, mu=rep
(0,4), Sigma=Sigma)
# Call to Stan to generate posterior draws
m1 <- stan(file="Data_Fusion_MVP.stan", data=d1$data,
           iter=10000, warmup=2000, chains=1, seed=35)
# Summaries of posteriors of population-level parameters
summary(m1, par=c("mu", "Omega"))
plot.post.density(m1, pars=c("mu"), prefix="Ex1MVP", true=list
(d1$true$mu))
png(filename="Ex1MVPPostOmega.png", width=600, height=400)
draws <- As.mcmc.list(m1, pars=c("Omega"))
beanplot(data.frame(draws[[1]][,c(2:4, 7:8, 12)]), horizontal=TRUE,
         las=1, what=c(0, 1, 1, 0), side="second",
         main=paste("Posterior Density of Omega", log=""))
dev.off()
# Summarize posteriors for one of missing values
y1mis.draws <- extract(m1, par=c("y1mis"))[[1]][,1,1] # draws for
    third respondent
mean(y1mis.draws > 0)
# Confusion matrix for missing data
y1mis.est <- summary(m1, par=c("y1mis"))$summary[, "50%"]>0
xtabs(y1mis.est + (d1$true$y1mis>0))
y2mis.est <- summary(m1, par=c("y1mis"))$summary[, "50%"]>0
xtabs(y2mis.est + (d1$true$y2mis>0))
z.est <- data.frame(z.true=as.vector(t(d1$true$z)),
                    y=as.vector(t(d1$true$y)),
                    z.postmed=summary(m1, pars=c("z"))
                    $summary[,"50%"])
png(filename="Ex1MVPTrueVEstz.png", width=600, height=400)
plot(z.est[,c(1,3)], xlab="True Latent Variable",
     ylab="Posterior Mean of Latent Variable")
points(z.est[is.na(z.est$y), c(1,3)], col="red")
abline(h=0, v=0)
dev.off()
```

References

Adigüzel, F., & Wedel, M. (2008). Split questionnaire design for massive surveys. *Journal of Marketing Research, 45*(5), 608–617.

Andridge, R. R., & Little, R. J. (2010). A review of hot deck imputation for survey nonresponse. *International Statistical Review, 78*(1), 40–64.

Bradlow, E. T., & Zaslavsky, A. M. (1999). A hierarchical latent variable model for ordinal data from a customer satisfaction survey with no answer responses. *Journal of the American Statistical Association, 94*(445), 43–52.

Carpenter, B., Gelman, A., Hoffman, M., Lee, D., Goodrich, B., Betancourt, M., Brubaker, M. A., Guo, J., Li, P., & Riddell, A. (2016). Stan: A probabilistic programming language. *Journal of Statistical Software, 76*.

Chen, Y., & Yang, S. (2007). Estimating disaggregate models using aggregate data through augmentation of individual choice. *Journal of Marketing Research, 44*(4), 613–621.

Cho, J., Aribarg, A., & Manchanda, P. (2015). *The value of measuring customer satisfaction.* Available at SSRN 2630898.

Feit, E. M., Beltramo, M. A., & Feinberg, F. M. (2010). Reality check: Combining choice experiments with market data to estimate the importance of product attributes. *Management Science, 56*(5), 785–800.

Feit, E. M., Wang, P., Bradlow, E. T., & Fader, P. S. (2013). Fusing aggregate and disaggregate data with an application to multiplatform media consumption. *Journal of Marketing Research, 50*(3), 348–364.

Ford, B. L. (1983). An overview of hot-deck procedures. *Incomplete Data in Sample Surveys, 2*(Part IV), 185–207.

Gilula, Z., McCulloch, R. E., & Rossi, P. E. (2006). A direct approach to data fusion. *Journal of Marketing Research, 43*(1), 73–83.

Kamakura, W. A., & Wedel, M. (1997). Statistical data fusion for cross-tabulation. *Journal of Marketing Research, 34*, 485–498.

Kamakura, W. A., & Wedel, M. (2000). Factor analysis and missing data. *Journal of Marketing Research, 37*(4), 490–498.

Little, R. J., & Rubin, D. B. (2014). *Statistical analysis with missing data.* Hoboken: Wiley.

Musalem, A., Bradlow, E. T., & Raju, J. S. (2008). Who's got the coupon? Estimating consumer preferences and coupon usage from aggregate information. *Journal of Marketing Research, 45*(6), 715–730.

Novak, J., Feit. E. M., Jensen, S., & Bradlow, E. (2015). *Bayesian imputation for anonymous visits in crm data.* Available at SSRN 2700347.

Qian, Y., & Xie, H. (2011). No customer left behind: A distribution-free bayesian approach to accounting for missing xs in marketing models. *Marketing Science, 30*(4), 717–736.

Qian, Y., & Xie, H. (2014). Which brand purchasers are lost to counterfeiters? An application of new data fusion approaches. *Marketing Science, 33*(3), 437–448.

Rässler, S. (2002). *Statistical matching: A frequentist theory, practical applications, and alternative Bayesian approaches* (Vol. 168). New York: Springer Science & Business Media.

Raghunathan, T. E., & Grizzle, J. E. (1995). A split questionnaire survey design. *Journal of the American Statistical Association, 90*(429), 54–63.

Rubin, D. B. (1996). Multiple imputation after 18+ years. *Journal of the American Statistical Association, 91*(434), 473–489.

Spiegelhalter, D., Thomas, A., Best, N., & Lunn, D. (2003). WinBUGS User Manual Version 1.4, January 2003 at https://faculty.washington.edu/jmiyamot/p548/spiegelhalter%20winbugs%20user%20manual.pdf.

Stan Development Team. (2017). *Stan modeling language user's guide and reference manual, version 2.17.0.* http://mc-stan.org

Tanner, M. A., & Wong, W. H. (1987). The calculation of posterior distributions by data augmentation. *Journal of the American Statistical Association, 82*(398), 528–540.

Stan Development Team (2016). *Rstan getting started.* https://github.com/stan-dev/rstan/wiki/RStan-Getting-Started

Ying, Y., Feinberg, F., & Wedel, M. (2006). Leveraging missing ratings to improve online recommendation systems. *Journal of Marketing Research, 43*(3), 355–365.

Dealing with Endogeneity: A Nontechnical Guide for Marketing Researchers

P. Ebbes, D. Papies, and H. J. van Heerde

Contents

Introduction	182
What Is Endogeneity?	183
Why and When Does Endogeneity Matter?	187
Price Endogeneity	188
Advertising Endogeneity	189
Detailing Endogeneity	190
Firm Strategies	190
CMO Presence	190
Digital Piracy	190
Summary	191
How to Address Endogeneity in a Regression Model	192
Implementing IV Estimation	199
What Happens in an IV Regression When Using Poor IVs?	205
Extensions of the Basic IV Approach	207
Control Function	207
Multiple Endogenous Regressors	209
Interaction Terms	210
The Benefit of Panel Data	211
Conclusions	214
References	216

P. Ebbes (✉)
HEC Paris, Jouy-en-Josas, France
e-mail: ebbes@hec.fr

D. Papies
School of Business and Economics, University of Tübingen, Tübingen, Germany
e-mail: dominik.papies@uni-tuebingen.de

H. J. van Heerde
School of Communication, Journalism and Marketing, Massey University, Auckland, New Zealand
e-mail: heerde@massey.ac.nz

© Springer Nature Switzerland AG 2022
C. Homburg et al. (eds), *Handbook of Market Research*,
https://doi.org/10.1007/978-3-319-57413-4_8

> **Abstract**
>
> This chapter provides a nontechnical summary of how to deal with endogeneity in regression models for marketing research applications. When researchers want to make causal inference of a marketing variable (e.g., price) on an outcome variable (e.g., sales), using observational data and a regression approach, they need the marketing variable to be exogenous. If the marketing variable is driven by factors unobserved by the researcher, such as the weather or other factors, then the assumption that the marketing variable is exogenous is not tenable, and the estimated effect of the marketing variable on the outcome variable may be biased. This is the essence of the endogeneity problem in regression models. The classical approach to address endogeneity is based on instrumental variables (IVs). IVs are variables that isolate the exogenous variation in the marketing variable. However, finding IVs of good quality is challenging. We discuss good practice in finding IVs, and we examine common IV estimation approaches, such as the two-stage least squares approach and the control function approach. Furthermore, we consider other implementation challenges, such as dealing with endogeneity when there is an interaction term in the regression model. Importantly, we also discuss when endogeneity matters and when it does not matter, as the "cure" to the problem can be worse than the "disease."

> **Keywords**
>
> Endogeneity · Bias · Regression · Instrumental variables · IV · 2SLS · Omitted variables · Causal inference

Introduction

Suppose a firm sells a product, and at some point the firm anticipates that the product will be in higher demand. For example, the product is likely to be in higher demand due to events such as seasonality, promotions, or free publicity. To benefit from this anticipated positive "demand shock," the firm decides to raise its price. Despite the rise in price, demand is so strong that there is an increase in sales. A researcher who is examining price and sales data from this firm now observes price increases going together with sales increases. If the researcher is unaware of the demand shock, then (s)he may falsely conclude that an increase in price causes an increase in sales. That is, when the researcher attempts to estimate a price elasticity in a regression model, but does not control for the demand shock in the model, the estimated elasticity of price will be biased. In such circumstances, price is said to be endogenous, and the subsequent optimization of the price level results in suboptimal decision-making.

More formally, endogeneity problems arise when the independent variables in a regression model are correlated with the error term in the model. In the example, the unobserved (to the researcher) demand shock is part of the model's error term, which is now correlated with the independent variable price. Endogeneity problems are common in marketing studies that use observational data. Observational data are data where the researcher just records or observes what happens in the marketplace, without interference or experimentation. Observational data includes transaction data (e.g., scanner data, online purchase data) and survey data. In observational data, it is not unlikely that there is some unobserved factor that is part of the model's error term that is correlated with the marketing variable of interest, which is the essence of the endogeneity problem. To address the problem, good practice calls for instrumental variable (IV) estimation techniques. However, to avoid an endogeneity problem altogether, the best approach would be to use experimental data, where the researcher experimentally manipulates the marketing variable.

This chapter provides a nontechnical summary of dealing with endogeneity in market research applications via instrumental variable (IV) estimation. IV methods were developed to overcome the endogeneity problem, but finding suitable IVs is challenging. We discuss good practice in finding instrumental variables and in using these to estimate the model, such as at the two-stage least squares approach and the control function approach. Furthermore, we discuss other implementation challenges, such as dealing with endogeneity when there is an interaction term in the regression model. Importantly, we discuss when endogeneity matters and when not, as the "cure" to the problem can be worse than the "disease."

What Is Endogeneity?

Regression modelling in marketing often centers around the estimation of the effects of marketing activities, such as price or advertising, on a performance metric (e.g., sales or profit). However, managers are strategic in their use of marketing activities and adapt these activities in response to factors that are related to demand, but that are often unobserved by and unknown to the researcher. Regression models in marketing that seek to estimate the causal effect of marketing instruments need to account for such deliberate planning of marketing activities or otherwise may suffer from an endogeneity problem, leading to biased estimates of the effects of the marketing activities on performance.

To illustrate the problem with a simple example, we consider an ice-cream vendor who is selling ice creams on the beach. She is the only ice-cream vendor in the near vicinity. Her main decision is centered on pricing of the ice creams. She knows that when the weather is warm, there are more people on the beach, and they are willing to pay more for the ice creams. To take advantage of this, she increases prices on days with higher temperature and sets prices lower on days with lower temperature.

She asks a researcher to estimate a linear demand model which would help her for her decision-making (e.g., pricing, purchasing ingredients). While she kept daily records of sales and prices for about 2 years, she did not inform the researcher about her price setting strategy using temperature. Hence, the researcher observes a data set consisting of daily dates, prices, and sales for the (let's say) 500 days of observations.

The researcher may now fit a simple linear[1] regression model of the following form:

$$Y_i = \beta_0 + \beta_1 P_i + \varepsilon_i \qquad (1)$$

Here, Y_i indicates the i-th sales observation (e.g., number of ice creams sold on day i), P_i indicates the price on day i, and ε_i is the model error term capturing (among other things) all unobserved factors that also affect sales[2]. The coefficient β_1 is the coefficient of interest: the effect of price on sales.

When a researcher estimates model (1) using the ordinary least squares (OLS) approach, (s)he is unlikely to estimate the causal effect of price on sales, i.e., β_1. The reason is that by using OLS, we implicitly assume that price is exogenous. Price is "exogenous" in this regression model when it does not correlate with the error term ε_i. In other words, OLS estimation requires that the covariance between price and error is zero: i.e., cov $(P_i, \varepsilon_i) = 0$.

However, in the ice-cream example, we have a problem: the temperature that the ice-cream vendor used to set prices also affects sales. Therefore, temperature is part of the model error term ε_i. Because she used temperature information to set prices, prices and temperature are correlated, i.e., cov $(P_i, \varepsilon_i) \neq 0$, and prices P_i are said to be "endogenous." In fact, as she increases price with higher temperature, we tend to see in the data that price increases go together with sales increases as higher temperature also leads to higher sales. In the absence of data on temperature, the increase in price is positively associated with the increase in sales, which could make the estimated price coefficient less negative or even positive.

This is the essence of the endogeneity problem: the estimated effect of a marketing variable (e.g., price) on the dependent variable (e.g., sales) is distorted (biased), because there is a correlation between one or more independent variables (price in the example) and one or more unobserved factors that are part of the regression model's error term (temperature in the example).

We now consider the problem of endogeneity in the above model a bit more formally. For illustration sake, we assume that prices can be described by a normal distribution with mean μ_p and variance σ_p^2. We can write $P_i = \mu_P + \nu_i$, where ν_i is normally distributed with mean 0 and variance σ_p^2. We also assume that the error term ε_i has a normal distribution with mean 0 and variance σ_ε^2. Because prices are

---

[1]Many demand models in marketing are nonlinear. At the end of this chapter, we briefly discuss nonlinear models. A popular nonlinear demand model to estimate price elasticities is the log-log demand model, where both the dependent and independent variables are the natural logs of the original variables, which can be estimated using standard approaches for linear regression models. Log-log models are also prone to an endogeneity problem.

[2]We use the cross-sectional setup in Eq. 1 as the leading example in this chapter. A similar logic applies to a time series setup (e.g., when we would view Eq. 1 as a time series model). However, this would require an additional discussion of dealing with potential autocorrelation in the model error terms, which is beyond the scope of this chapter. Therefore, we assume that the error terms ε_i are independent and identically distributed in this chapter.

correlated with the errors, ε_i and v_i have a non-zero covariance, $\text{cov}(\varepsilon_i, v_i) = E(\varepsilon_i v_i) = \sigma_{\varepsilon p}$. Viewing the distribution of Y_i and P_i as a bivariate normal distribution, the conditional mean and variance of Y_i given $P_i = p_i$ are (e.g., Lindgren 1993, p. 423)

$$E(Y_i|\, P_i = p_i) = \beta_0 + \beta_1 p_i + \frac{\sigma_{\varepsilon p}}{\sigma_p^2}\left(p_i - \mu_p\right)$$

$$= \left(\beta_0 - \frac{\sigma_{\varepsilon p}}{\sigma_p^2}\mu_p\right) + \left(\beta_1 + \frac{\sigma_{\varepsilon p}}{\sigma_p^2}\right)p_i \qquad (2)$$

$$\text{Var}(Y_i|\, P_i = p_i) = \sigma_\varepsilon^2\left(1 - \rho_{\varepsilon p}^2\right) = \sigma_\varepsilon^2 - \frac{\sigma_{\varepsilon p}^2}{\sigma_p^2} \qquad (3)$$

where $\rho_{\varepsilon p} = \frac{\sigma_{\varepsilon p}}{\sigma_\varepsilon \sigma_p}$ is the correlation between prices and the error term. If the endogeneity in prices is ignored, then standard OLS produces the coefficients $\beta_0^r = \left(\beta_0 - \frac{\sigma_{\varepsilon p}}{\sigma_p^2}\mu_p\right)$ and $\beta_1^r = \left(\beta_1 + \frac{\sigma_{\varepsilon p}}{\sigma_p^2}\right)$ instead of the true parameters β_0 and β_1. That is, in the previous ice-cream example, where prices were positively correlated with the error term (because she increases prices when temperature is higher), the estimated price coefficient is higher than the true value because $\frac{\sigma_{\varepsilon p}}{\sigma_p^2}$ is positive. As we may expect that the true value β_1 is negative, the OLS estimated price coefficient $\hat{\beta}_1^r$ is "less negative" or potentially positive depending on the magnitude of β_1 and $\frac{\sigma_{\varepsilon p}}{\sigma_p^2}$.

Furthermore, from Eq. 3, we can see that the conditional variance of Y_i given price is less than the true unobserved variance σ_ε^2. In other words, OLS produces an estimate of the residual variance that is smaller than the actual variance. Hence, using OLS, we are led to believe that the model "fits" better than it actually does. We return to this below when it comes to predictions in the presence of endogenous regressors.

Figure 1 shows a scatterplot for 500 hypothetical daily observations of price and sales for the ice-cream seller from the example above. The solid black line represents the incorrectly estimated demand curve by OLS, whereas the dashed line is the true demand curve (in this case the "curve" is a straight line given that we use linear regression). Indeed, as the equations above suggest, the OLS line is less "steep" than the true line. We discuss how to estimate the correct demand curve using an instrumental variable approach below.

In this stylized example, we have an endogeneity problem because the temperature variable was omitted from the model. If the researcher had known the price setting behavior and had observed the temperature variable in the data set, then (s)he should have included this variable as a covariate in the model in Eq. 1, and this would have taken care of this particular endogeneity problem. Then an OLS regression using both prices and temperature as covariates would have estimated the correct price effect. Unfortunately, in many real-world applications, it is impossible to enumerate all relevant demand drivers, measure them, and include them in the model. Thus, we often cannot fully address the endogeneity problem by just including a set of control

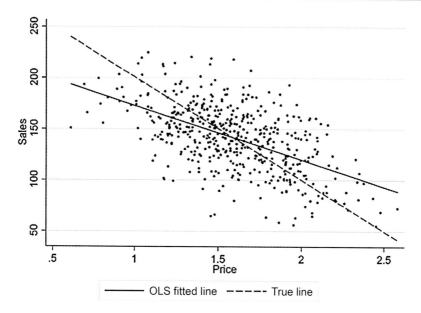

Fig. 1 Scatterplot of sales versus price in the presence of an omitted variable

variables. Nevertheless, we do recommend to always include a rather complete set of control variables as they do make the endogeneity problem less severe.

In sum, if models of consumer demand do not account for marketing instruments (e.g., price, advertising, sales force) that are set strategically, an endogeneity bias is likely present in the estimated regression coefficients (e.g., Petrin and Train 2010; Villas-Boas and Winer 1999). This leads to flawed decisions in determining optimal levels of the marketing instruments, as we show next.

Before we proceed, we would like to highlight two additional aspects. First, the stylized ice-cream vendor example above, as well as most examples that we discuss below, considers transaction data in which endogeneity arises because managers or consumers exhibit strategic (nonrandom) behavior, which is not captured by the regression model. We would like to emphasize, however, that endogeneity concerns are also relevant for survey research. Unobserved respondent characteristics often correlate with the dependent as well as the independent variables in regression models that are estimated using survey data. Hence, causal inferences in cross-sectional survey analyses are only possible if we can rule out these unobserved components. This problem is similar to the common-method bias that is often presented as a serious concern for survey research (Podsakoff et al. 2003).

Second, in marketing models, a regressor may be correlated with the error term, not only because of omitted variables (e.g., temperature) but also because of measurement error. Measurement error in econometrics refers to situations where one or more regressors cannot be measured exactly and are observed with an error. Another cause for an endogeneity problem is when price and demand are determined simultaneously, as is the case, e.g., in an auction for commodities.

In the case of the ice-cream seller example, measurement error and simultaneity problems may happen, for instance, in the following case. Suppose that the ice-cream seller has the goal of selling all ice cream she has in her cart on any given day, e.g., because the ice cream is less fresh the next day. If at the same time, she is afraid of losing customers during a stock-out situation, she may use price to control supply and demand during the day, e.g., increase prices when she observes long queues and decrease prices when there are no queues. If she now reported daily average price, the OLS approach would not capture that price and demand are formed simultaneously. Besides, the average daily price would be a proxy for actual price charged, leading to potential measurement error in price. Similar to omitted variables (e.g., temperature), both measurement error and simultaneity may result in regressor-error dependencies, such that $cov(P_i, \varepsilon_i) \neq 0$, and standard OLS suffers from an endogeneity problem. For technical details on measurement error and simultaneity, see, e.g., Verbeek (2012) or Greene (2011).

Why and When Does Endogeneity Matter?

From a practical perspective, it may be tempting to dismiss the problem of endogeneity as an academic exercise that is of little relevance to managers. Indeed, many applied textbooks on empirical methods rarely touch upon the issue of endogeneity at all, which may seem to support this argument. We, however, argue the opposite: the problem of endogeneity is of high managerial relevance because obtaining correct effect estimates is essential.

Bijmolt et al. (2005) analyze 1851 estimated price elasticities at the brand level that were published across 40 years in 81 articles. They find that the estimated price elasticity when endogeneity is controlled for is, on average, -3.74. In contrast, the estimated price elasticity when endogeneity is ignored is, on average, -2.47, which is quite a strong difference. In other words, when we do not control for endogeneity, the price elasticity estimate is biased toward zero (less negative), similar to the ice-cream vendor example above.

Moreover, there can be endogeneity in other important marketing variables as well. Sethuraman et al. (2011) investigate in a meta-analysis of advertising effectiveness the potential endogeneity bias in the estimated advertising elasticity. They find that the estimated advertising elasticity is lower when endogeneity is not accounted for than when it is accounted for. Albers et al. (2010) analyze 506 estimated personal selling elasticities from 75 articles and find that the estimated elasticity when endogeneity is not taken into account is, on average, 0.37, while it is, on average, 0.28 when endogeneity is accounted for. Hence, the personal selling elasticity is overestimated when endogeneity is not incorporated in model estimation.

Are these empirical findings on endogeneity biases something that managers need to worry about? Yes, we believe so, and here is why. Going back to the ice-cream vendor example, suppose that the ice-cream vendor wanted to change her price strategy from using temperature to profit maximization. She asks the researcher to calculate the optimal price, given a marginal cost (c) for ice cream of, say, €1. The researcher estimates a demand model using the data described above with a standard estimation approach (e.g., OLS) and finds that the estimated price elasticity of ice cream is -2. Following the Amoroso-Robinson theorem[3], we find that the optimal price would be €2. This optimal price is not correct, because the true price elasticity is underestimated. Suppose that the true price elasticity is -3. Using this number, we find that the optimal price is €1.5. Hence, in this example, ignoring endogeneity in estimating price elasticity leads to an "optimal" price of €2 instead of €1.5. Clearly, this is suboptimal. We therefore believe that it is of critical importance to managers and decision-makers to be aware of potential endogeneity problems in estimating marketing regression models.

What are typical situations in which researchers and managers must be aware of potential endogeneity problems? We now consider several examples in detail.

Price Endogeneity

Many retailers such as supermarkets have to decide which items to include and which items to exclude from their assortments. To offer guidance for these decisions, Rooderkerk et al. (2013) develop a model to optimize retailer assortment of laundry detergents. As part of the analysis, they estimate demand models using supermarket scanner data to understand the effect of price on demand, while controlling for price endogeneity. In essence, they estimate a regression model for sales of an SKU (stock keeping unit) in week t as a function of its price. Why may price be endogenous in this case? In the case of laundry detergents, there may be time-varying unobserved demand shocks such as promotional (e.g., coupons) or advertising activities. If these effects are not included in the model, an endogeneity bias in the estimated effect of price is likely.

The same is true if there are brand-specific time-varying shocks in brand popularity and managers use this information to adjust prices. These shocks may arise, for instance, from online buzz or media coverage. One product category in which these variations seem quite natural is experiential goods, such as music or movies.

In cross-sectional analyses, unobserved product characteristics pose a problem. Managers may set prices based on product characteristics such as style, quality, durability, status, service levels, or brand strength. If these factors are not observed by the researcher (which is often the case), an endogeneity bias may occur in the estimated regression parameters (Berry 1994). On the other hand, if we observe variation across brands and across time as in standard panel data applications, these

---

[3]For the sake of simplicity in this example, we assume that the researcher estimates a constant elasticity model (e.g., using a log-log regression). The optimal price can then be computed as $p^* = c(\beta/(\beta + 1))$, where c is marginal cost and β is the estimated price elasticity (Amoroso-Robinson theorem, e.g., Homburg et al. 2009, p. 181).

Advertising Endogeneity

Similar arguments apply to non-price marketing instruments. Consider the following example in Dinner et al. (2014). They address the question of whether advertising in one channel (e.g., online) affects sales in the other channel (e.g., offline or brick-and-mortar sales). They are in particular interested in the direction and magnitude of these effects. Dinner et al. (2014) analyze retailer data to test for the presence of "own-channel" effects (e.g., online display advertising on online sales) versus "cross-channel effects" (e.g., online display advertising on store sales). They estimate the following regression models for online and offline sales in week t:[4]

$$\ln \text{Online Sales}_t = \beta_0 + \beta_1 \ln \text{Online Advertising}_t \\ + \beta_2 \ln \text{Offline Advertising}_t + \varepsilon_{1t} \tag{4}$$

$$\ln \text{Offline Sales}_t = \gamma_0 + \gamma_1 \ln \text{Online Advertising}_t \\ + \gamma_2 \ln \text{Offline Advertising}_t + \varepsilon_{2t} \tag{5}$$

Online advertising includes expenditures on online banner ads and offline advertising expenditures on TV, print, or radio advertising. Since Eqs. 4 and 5 are log-log models, the response parameters can be interpreted as advertising elasticities. For example, β_1 is the own-channel online advertising elasticity (the percentage increase in online sales due to a 1% increase in online advertising), and β_2 is the cross-channel elasticity for the offline advertising on online sales. An endogeneity problem arises when the managers use unobserved demand shocks to adjust their advertising budgets. For instance, a manager may anticipate seasonal shocks in demand. If the manager then allocates her advertising budget accordingly, then this may lead to an overestimation of the advertising elasticity using a standard estimation approach. Dinner et al. (2014) control for endogeneity in model estimation.

As an another example, consider an artist who sells records and downloads. If this artist experiences a surge in popularity (e.g., because of online word of mouth or a TV show), the artist may decide to cut down on advertising because she feels that the product does not need the advertising. This would potentially lead to an underestimation of the advertising elasticity if endogeneity is not accounted for, because we tend to observe high demand with relatively low advertising expenditures.

---

[4]We simplified their model here for sake of exposition. The full model of Dinner et al. (2014) splits online advertising into search advertising and banner ads, allows for advertising carryover effects, and for the effects of other covariates.

Detailing Endogeneity.

Pharmaceutical companies typically spend a substantial amount of their marketing budget on detailing, i.e., sales reps visiting doctors to influence the doctors' prescription behavior. A well-recognized pattern in this domain is that high-volume doctors (i.e., those that often prescribe the drug of the focal brand) receive more detailing. When this is not considered in the regression model, the estimation approach may produce a positive estimated detailing effect, even in the complete absence of a causal effect of detailing on prescription behavior (Manchanda et al. 2004). Accordingly, the meta-analysis by Albers et al. (2010) on personal selling elasticities (that includes detailing) finds that estimation approaches that do not account for endogeneity in detailing studies overestimate the personal selling elasticity.

Firm Strategies

"Firms choose strategies based on their attributes and industry conditions" (Shaver 1998). These attributes may represent a general strategic orientation, management background, or other characteristics that affect firm performance, but are generally difficult to observe for the researcher. Furthermore, firms deliberately choose those strategies that are most likely to increase profit. Hence, most empirical models, in which firm performance is modelled as a function of strategic choices made by firms, are likely to suffer from an endogeneity problem (Shaver 1998).

CMO Presence

Germann et al. (2015) estimate the effect of the presence of a chief marketing officer (CMO) on firm performance. Similar to the point made by Shaver (1998), Germann et al. (2015) argue that the presence or absence of a CMO is likely an endogenous regressor in a regression model because firms do not randomly decide to have a CMO. Rather, the decision to employ a CMO is a strategic choice that will be related to other firm characteristics (e.g., management style, strategic orientation, beliefs about the effect of a CMO). Hence, the variable that captures the presence and absence of the CMO will be correlated with unobserved firm characteristics that also drive firm performance, which will potentially induce an endogeneity bias in the estimated effect of CMO on firm performance, which Germann et al. (2015) address in their analyses.

Digital Piracy

Since the rise of digital distribution of media products, a strong debate has developed on the extent to which digital piracy hurts music sales (see Liebowitz 2016 for an overview). A naïve approach would be to use OLS to estimate a regression model with artist's sales as dependent variable and piracy (e.g., the number of illegal downloads) as an independent variable. However, in such a regression model, the popularity of the artist would be an omitted variable. We expect that an artist's popularity affects both the piracy level as well as music sales. As both piracy and sales are likely positively correlated with popularity, the OLS estimated effect of piracy on sales will be biased (probably less negative than the true effect of piracy on sales).

An endogeneity problem may also occur when *survey data* are used to estimate the effect of piracy on music sales. We could, for instance, survey a random sample of 10,000 respondents and measure the extent to which they illegally download music as well as their expenditures for music. Respondents highly involved with music are probably more likely to download music illegally, whereas at the same time, they are also more likely to purchase music. Hence, if we would correlate the survey responses of the illegal download and music expenditure questions, we probably would find a rather positive and significant correlation. This estimated positive correlation between music expenditures and illegal download activity is likely to be spurious and should not be interpreted as causal, because the estimated correlation is largely driven by unobserved involvement of the respondents with music.

Summary

Researchers and managers must be aware of the problem of endogeneity whenever they are interested in the causal effect of a marketing (or other) variable on an outcome variable. And, very often managers are interested in causal effects. For instance, the statement "If you change the marketing variable by 1%, the performance changes by $\beta_1\%$" requires an estimate of the causal effect of the marketing variable on performance. Such a statement is useful for making predictions about the consequences of changing a marketing policy or the value of a marketing instrument. It would tell the manager what would happen in an alternative scenario (Angrist and Pischke 2008).

To avoid endogeneity all together, we would need to run field experiments. In the ice-cream vendor example, for instance, we could run a field experiment where we set prices randomly every day for a period of time. In such an experiment, the random assignment of prices would likely guarantee that there is no correlation between price and other drivers of demand that are unobserved by the researcher. For instance, because of the randomization, we would sometimes observe high prices with high temperatures, but also sometimes observe high prices with low temperatures (and vice versa). Prices are no longer strategically set. This would allow us to use a straightforward (OLS) regression of sales on price to unbiasedly estimate the causal effect of price. Similarly, we could randomly allocate advertising budgets across brands, or we could randomly assign some firms a CMO, while other firms would have to work without a CMO, and observe the effect on sales or firm performance.

Unfortunately, in most marketing applications, such field experiments are not feasible, and we would have to resort to nonexperimental approaches that can be used with observational data. Fortunately, in studies with observational data, we can often develop an identification strategy to estimate the effect of interest (Angrist and Pischke 2008; Germann et al. 2015), as we discuss next.

How to Address Endogeneity in a Regression Model

The goal of a regression analysis is to estimate the causal effect of the regressor (e.g., price) on the dependent variable (e.g., demand). For the reasons discussed above, there is often reason to believe that price and other regressors may be correlated with the error term in the regression equation (e.g., ε_i in Eq. 1). To address the endogeneity problem, a popular approach is to find one or more additional variables, called instrumental variables (IVs), which correlate with the price variable but not with the unobserved determinants of sales (that are part of the error term). This IV approach is the classical approach to address endogeneity in linear regression models (e.g., Greene 2011; Wooldridge 2010). To identify potential IVs, the researcher must have a deep understanding of the practical context of the study, because IVs must meet two requirements (e.g., Angrist and Pischke 2008):

1. The *relevance criterion*, i.e., the IVs must have a strong relation with the endogenous regressors.
2. The *exclusion restriction*, i.e., the IVs must be unrelated to the error of the main Eq. 1.

If one of these two criteria is *not* fulfilled, the IV approach, which we outline in more detail next, *will fail*.

The idea behind IV estimation is to use exogenous variation in the independent variable to estimate the causal effect of the independent variable on the dependent variable. Returning to the ice-cream example, we have to augment the demand equation in (1) with an auxiliary equation for price, where price is modelled as:

$$P_i = \gamma_0 + \gamma_1 Z_i + \nu_i \qquad (6)$$

Here Z_i is the IV that must be uncorrelated with ε_i in Eq. 1. Thus, P_i is partitioned into a part $\gamma_0 + \gamma_1 Z_i$ that is exogenous (i.e., uncorrelated with ε_i in Eq. 1) and a random part ν_i that is endogenous (i.e., correlated with ε_i in Eq. 1). The exogenous part is used to estimate the regression parameters of Eq. 1, as we argue below. Thus, the IV enables us to "partition the variation [in prices] into that which can be regarded as clean or as though generated via experimental methods, and that which is contaminated and could result in an endogeneity bias" (Rossi 2014, p. 655). This decomposition of price in an exogenous and endogenous part is schematically represented in Fig. 2.

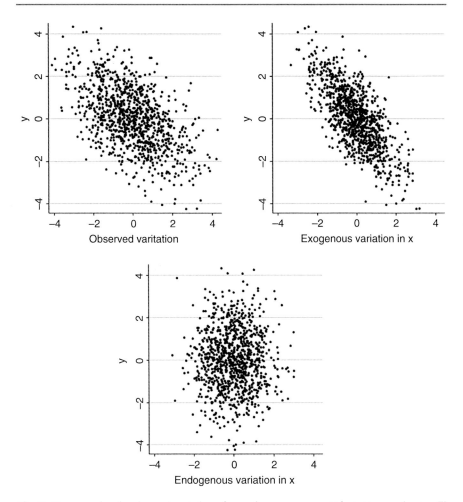

Fig. 2 Decomposing the observed variation of an endogenous regressor in exogenous ($\gamma_0 + \gamma_1 Z_i$) and endogenous (v_i) variation

How can we use the exogenous and "clean" variation in prices to estimate β_0 and β_1 in Eq. 1? The answer is to isolate the exogenous variation through the auxiliary regression model (6), which is typically referred to as the first-stage regression. From this first-stage regression, we obtain the predicted prices, given values for Z. Then, the predicted prices are used instead of the original prices as regressor in Eq. 1. More specifically, this stepwise approach goes as follows:

1. Estimate Eq. 6 using OLS to obtain the estimated parameters $\hat{\gamma}_0$ and $\hat{\gamma}_1$. Compute the predicted values for prices using the estimated parameters, i.e., compute $\hat{P}_i = \hat{\gamma}_0 + \hat{\gamma}_1 Z_i$.

2. Use the predicted values $\hat{P}_i$ in Eq. 1, instead of observed prices P_i, and estimate the resulting equation with OLS. That is, estimate the following equation with OLS:

$$Y_i = \beta_0 + \beta_1 \hat{P}_i + \varepsilon_i \tag{7}$$

The resulting estimate for β_1 is now the causal effect of prices on sales, and this estimation approach results in a "consistent estimate for β_1." A consistent estimate means the estimate converges (in probability) to the true value as the sample size tends to infinity. This stepwise approach is called the two-stage least squares (2SLS) approach.

Many software packages implement the 2SLS approach, and we would caution against doing these steps manually in a research study (see also next section). However, from this stepwise approach, we can get a better intuition as to why IV estimation works. We can see that in step 1, we predict prices using only the exogenous information contained in Z_i. Thus, by construction, $\hat{P}_i$ is exogenous (under the assumption that Z_i is exogenous, i.e., uncorrelated with ε_i). Subsequently, in step 2, the endogenous variable P_i is replaced by its exogenous "alter ego" $\hat{P}_i$, which is not correlated with the error term ε_i. Thus, we can simply apply OLS in step 2 to estimate Eq. 7 because all regressors are now exogenous.

Importantly, from this stepwise approach, we can also get a better intuition for what criteria an IV must satisfy for this to work. Firstly, Z_i needs to be able to predict the endogenous variable P_i well, i.e., it needs to satisfy the relevance criterion. This criterion can be tested, as we discuss below. When the IV has little explanatory power, the IV is a "weak" IV (Bound et al. 1995), and the predicted values from step 2 above are bad "alter egos" that have little to do with the original price variable. Estimating the resulting Eq. 7 with OLS is not going to give a very precise estimate for β_1. In the worst case, there is no explanatory power of Z_i at all, i.e. $\gamma_1 = 0$, and the predicted values for P_i would all be the same (and equal to the average value of prices) for $i = 1, 2, \ldots, N$, and the price effect β_1 cannot be estimated.

The second requirement is the exclusion restriction. This means that Z_i must be exogenous: uncorrelated with the error term ε_i from the main Eq. 1. Otherwise $\hat{P}_i$ is also endogenous, and we have not solved the endogeneity problem in P_i. This requirement implies that Z_i must be unrelated to all unobserved factors that drive demand and that may be correlated with price. Going back to the example of the ice-cream seller, the Z_i must be uncorrelated with weather and other unobserved factors that are part of the model's error term. Unfortunately, and this is often the biggest challenge in the implementation of IV, the exogeneity assumption for Z cannot be tested directly. Hence, researchers must rely on the knowledge of the empirical context (i.e., the data generating process), and theory, to argue that their IV meets this criterion.

In the ice-cream example, the cost of ingredients (e.g., milk) may serve as an IV, because these costs will influence consumer prices, but they are unrelated with other unobserved factors that drive consumer demand. In the CMO example above

(Germann et al. 2015), we need a variable that predicts the presence of a CMO, but that is not related to unobserved firm characteristics that drive the decision to appoint a CMO and affect firm performance. For the piracy example, we need a variable that is correlated with an artist's piracy level, but unrelated to shocks in the artist's popularity. We discuss possible IVs for these contexts below.

Hence, two conditions are central to IV estimation: (1) Z_i correlates with P_i, but (2) is uncorrelated with the errors ε_i. Without these two conditions, the IV estimate for β_1 is not consistent, and we cannot interpret the IV estimate as the causal effect of prices on sales. Good IVs can be difficult to find (e.g., Germann et al. 2015, p. 8). The reason is that the two conditions are very hard to meet simultaneously: when the IV is very strongly correlated with the endogenous regressor, it is often hard to argue that the IV is not a direct driver of demand (i.e., it does not satisfy the exclusion restriction). When the IV is completely exogenous (it does satisfy the exclusion restriction), it often is a rather weak IV.

Finding IVs requires "a combination of institutional knowledge and ideas about processes determining the variable of interest" (Angrist and Pischke 2008, p. 117). Likewise, Rossi (2014) notes that "good IVs need to be justified using institutional knowledge because there is no true test for the quality of IVs." Thus, substantive knowledge about the marketing context is needed to identify and argue which variables may be proper candidates for an IV.

To assess whether a candidate IV (or a set of candidate IVs; more on that below) is an appropriate IV, the researcher is advised to perform the following two tasks (see also Germann et al. 2015, pp. 8–9):

1. *Demonstrate* relevance of the IV (i.e., that the IV is not weak).
2. *Argue* that the IV meets the exclusion restriction (i.e., the IV is exogenous).

To perform the first task, the researcher needs to make the case that the IV correlates with the endogenous variable. The arguments should provide a prediction of why and how the IV affects the endogenous variable. This task also includes a discussion of the first-stage regression estimation results (Eq. 6) and assessing whether the estimates make sense in the light of the theoretical context. For instance, do the magnitude and signs of the estimated effects for the IVs (e.g., γ_1) make sense (see also Angrist and Pischke 2008, p. 173)? If these do not make sense, perhaps the hypothesized mechanism for the IVs is not correct or is incomplete. In addition, the researcher should report the R^2 or the F-statistic of the excluded IVs. That is, the researcher needs to run *two* first-stage regressions. The first one includes the IVs and other exogenous variables in the main regression equation, and the second one only includes the exogenous variables but excludes the IVs (note that in the ice-cream vendor example, there are no other exogenous regressors in Eq. 1). Then, the change in R^2 and value of the F-statistic for the comparison of the two models is indicative of the strength of the IVs and should routinely be reported with an IV regression. The bigger the change in R^2 and the higher the F-statistic, the stronger the IVs are.

The second task involves providing arguments for the exclusion restriction of the IV. That is, why is the IV uncorrelated with the omitted variables that affect the dependent variable? Unfortunately, this assumption cannot be tested for, which is arguably the biggest drawback of IV estimation. Therefore, it is important to develop valid theoretical arguments that support this assumption, as the consistency of the IV approach depends on whether this assumption is met or not. Thus, any IV analysis must be accompanied by such a discussion.

How could we develop such arguments? Often it is useful to think of an endogeneity problem in a marketing model as an omitted variable problem, as in the ice-cream vendor example where temperature was an omitted variable. Here, the omitted variable explains variation in both the dependent variable and the endogenous independent variable. For example, temperature drives sales, but also prices, as the merchant used temperature to set prices. When we try to argue for an IV in a marketing regression model, the argument has to make a case that the IV is uncorrelated with the key unobserved factors driving demand. For example, the cost of ingredients (e.g., milk) as an IV is unlikely to be related to the unobserved factors that drive demand for ice creams on the beach, such as the temperature that day, and hence the IV may be valid in the sense that it is uncorrelated with the error term.

Formally speaking, the second task examines the assumption $E(Z_i \varepsilon_i) = 0$. When the researcher has provided arguments in favor of this assumption, and also argued and demonstrated that the IV is not weak (first task), then we may continue with estimating the regression parameters in model (1) using an IV approach. The key to IV estimation is thus to decompose the endogenous regressor into an exogenous part, which is independent of the model error term ε, and an endogenous part v, which is correlated with the error in the regression model for Y. The exogenous part is used to estimate the regression parameters of Eq. 1. As should be clear from this discussion, while there are some empirical checks, the validity of the IV(s) is an assumption that ultimately cannot be tested for.

We would like to add a note on the relation between the criteria of IV strength and IV exogeneity. Consider the following thought experiment. Imagine an IV Z_i that leads to an R^2 in the first-stage regression in Eq. 6 of 0.98. Under the assumption that the IV is truly exogenous, this implies that the endogeneity bias cannot be large in the first place because almost all variation in P_i is exogenous given this very high R^2. If, in contrast, theory suggests that there is a sizeable endogeneity problem, then such a high R^2 in a first-stage regression makes it implausible that the IV is uncorrelated with the error (Rossi 2014). In general, stronger IVs are less likely to be exogenous, and vice versa, which is unfortunate because an IV needs to be both at the same time.

We have one more remark regarding the underlying assumptions of IVs. Occasionally one can hear or read the statement that "a valid, exogenous IV must be unrelated with the dependent variable Y." For a demand model with endogenous price, this statement would mean that we need an IV "that is correlated with price but uncorrelated with demand." These statements are generally *not correct*. Here is why. Consider Eqs. 1 and 6. If we substitute Eq. 6 into Eq. 1, we obtain:

$$Y_i = \beta_0 + \beta_1(\gamma_0 + \gamma_1 Z_i + \nu_i) + \varepsilon_i$$
$$= (\beta_0 + \beta_1\gamma_0) + \beta_1\gamma_1 Z_i + \beta_1\nu_i + \varepsilon_i = \pi_0 + \pi_1 Z_i + u_i \qquad (8)$$

where π_0, π_1, and u_i are defined accordingly. For explanation sake, imagine we estimate an OLS regression with Z_i as the independent variable and Y_i as the dependent variable (we note that this regression is typically not performed in practice). We would expect that π_1 is *non-zero*, because π_1 is zero only if $\gamma_1 = 0$, if $\beta_1 = 0$, or if both are 0. In a demand model, we would expect that $\beta_1 < 0$, in general. Furthermore, as argued above, γ_1 has to be non-zero for an IV approach to be valid. Hence, in general, when using an IV approach for a demand model, we are actually expecting π_1 to be non-zero. In other words, the IV likely has an effect on demand in Eq. 8. But, this effect is an indirect effect through the endogenous regressor P_i. For example, assuming that cost is a strong and an exogenous IV (i.e., it meets the exclusion restriction), it must affect demand in (8) ($\pi_1 \neq 0$), because prices are affected by cost ($\gamma_1 \neq 0$) and we expect that prices affect demand ($\beta_1 \neq 0$). In fact, we would expect $\pi_1 < 0$. Hence, it is important to recognize that the assumption for an IV to be exogenous is *not* that the IV is unrelated to demand. Rather, the assumption is that the IV is uncorrelated with the *error term* from the demand equation in (1) (i.e., it meets the exclusion restriction)[5].

To conclude the discussion on endogeneity and potential remedies, Table 1 gives several examples of endogeneity problems in academic marketing studies. For each example, we point the reader to some ideas of where to find potential good IVs. We briefly outline the rationale for the choice of some of these IVs.

In line with the discussion about the endogenous price of ice cream, a considerable number of studies treat price as endogenous. In many cases, the researchers manage to obtain cost data that they use as an IV. For example, the study by Rooderkerk et al. (2013) in Table 1 uses the costs of ingredients of liquid laundry detergents and transportation costs as IVs. The idea is that these costs should affect the price of the consumer product, but they should be unrelated to brand-specific unobserved demand shocks.

Nevo (2001) proposes to use the prices in other cities (markets) as an IV for price in the focal market. The argument is that these prices (e.g., on the US west coast) capture common cost shocks, but they are unrelated to specific demand shock in the focal city (e.g., on the US east coast). Nevo (2001) highlights potential limitations of these IVs and discusses in great detail the relevant assumptions underlying their validity. Readers interested in an example of how to build a case supporting the validity of an IV should turn to Nevo (2001).

A similarly detailed discussion to build a case for an IV can be found in Germann et al. (2015) regarding the choice of CMO prevalence among peer firms as an instrument for CMO presence in a focal firm. The argument is that the CMO prevalence captures the extent to which it is common among a group of firms to have a CMO, but CMO

---

[5]This discussion is similar in spirit to the rationale behind mediation analysis. We refer the reader to chapter ▶ "Mediation Analysis in Experimental Research" in this handbook for more details.

Table 1 Examples of endogeneity problems and potential IVs

	Dependent variable	Potentially endogenous regressor	Potential causes for endogeneity	Potential IVs (the pages that are cited offer arguments for the suitability of the IVs)
Managers' behavior is source of endogeneity	Demand	Price	Managers set prices based on factors that are related to demand but are unobserved by the researcher: • Promotional activities • Changes in popularity • Product characteristics (for cross-sectional analyses)	Costs of ingredients and transportation (Rooderkerk et al. 2013, p. 706); prices in other markets (Nevo 2001, p. 320)
	Demand	Advertising	Managers set advertising based on factors that are related to demand but are unobserved by the researcher: • Price changes • Changes in preferences or popularity • (Expected) sales volume	Advertising expenditures of other (noncompeting) firms (Dinner et al. 2014, p. 534); Advertising cost
	Demand	Detailing	Managers set advertising based on factors that are related to demand but are unobserved by the researcher, e.g., large accounts receive more detailing than small accounts	Costs for detailing (e.g., wages; Chintagunta and Desiraju 2005, p. 74)
	Firm performance	CMO presence	Firms strategically choose to have a CMO, and this choice depends on unobserved firm characteristics as well as expected performance effects	CMO prevalence among peer firms (Germann et al. 2015, p. 8)
Consumers' behavior is source of endogeneity	Demand	Piracy	Unobserved factors (e.g., popularity) affect both a music album's sales as well as piracy	RIAA announcement to start legal actions against file sharing (Bhattacharjee et al. 2007, p. 1364)
	Demand offline channel	Demand online channel	Preferences for channels are correlated	Ease of access to online channel (Gentzkow 2007, p. 726)
	Consumer share of wallet	Membership in loyalty program	Consumers with high intrinsic preference for a firm have a higher share of wallet and are more likely to join the firm's loyalty program	General inclination to join a loyalty program (Leenheer et al. 2007, p. 36)

prevalence among peers is likely unrelated to the focal firm's optimization considerations. In that sense, their argument for the IV's exclusion restriction is similar to the argument provided by Nevo (2001) for prices in demand models.

As a last example, consider the case of piracy and demand for music. Here, unobserved factors such as an artist's popularity will drive both sales and piracy. Bhattacharjee et al. (2007) investigate whether illegal downloads hurt album sales. As a proxy for album sales, they measure how long the album stays in the billboard top charts. They use an announcement of the Recording Industry Association of America (RIAA) to start legal actions against file sharers as the IV for illegal downloads. That is, their IV is a dummy variable that varies for albums observed before and after the announcement. Their motivation for this IV is that the perceived legal cost of file sharing and illegal downloading increases substantially as a result of this announcement. Consequently, we would expect that the IV has a negative effect on illegal downloads. At the same time, it can be argued that the RIAA announcement is unrelated to an album's specific unobserved factors, such as the artist's popularity.

Naturally, researchers must develop arguments whether their IVs fulfill the criteria of relevance and exogeneity. We highlight these studies as examples, as the authors go in great length to build a theoretical case for the validity of their IVs. Without such a discussion of instrument validity, we would not be able to judge whether the IV analyses have merit. We include in Table 1 several references to studies (including the page numbers) that offer arguments for the suitability of the IVs mentioned in Table 1.

We next discuss practical matters of how to implement IV estimation using Stata.

Implementing IV Estimation

We assume that the researcher has one or more valid IVs for the endogenous regressor (we briefly discuss the case of multiple endogenous regressors in the next section). We also assume that the researcher has provided the arguments to demonstrate (i) relevance of the IVs, and (ii) that the IVs meet the exclusion restriction, i.e., there is strong theoretical evidence that the IVs are uncorrelated with the error from the main Eq. 1.

The standard approach to estimate Eq. 1 using IV(s) is to use the two-stage least squares (2SLS) approach. This approach is available in most statistical software packages. For instance, in Stata, researchers can use the ivreg or the (higher optioned) ivreg2 command (Baum et al. 2007, 2015). In R, researchers may use, for instance, the packages ivmodel, ivpack, or sem (tsls).

We suggest that the researcher who uses 2SLS, in addition to providing the theoretical argumentation to support the IVs that she uses, discusses the outcomes of the following six empirical tasks (see also Angrist and Pischke 2008):

1. Report both the standard OLS results (i.e., ignoring endogeneity) and the 2SLS results. At the minimum, the estimated coefficients and standard errors from both approaches should be reported. Furthermore, the direction of the bias in OLS as

suggested by 2SLS should be in the expected direction as predicted by theory. For instance, in the ice-cream example, we expected OLS to be biased upward, and 2SLS should therefore give a more negative price effect estimate.

2. Report the complete results of the first-stage regression. The first-stage regression is basically the OLS regression of Eq. 6, including all IVs Z *and all other exogenous regressors that are in* Eq. 1 (note that in the ice-cream vendor example, there are no other exogenous regressors in Eq. 1). As in the previous step, both the estimated coefficients and the standard errors should be reported. Do the estimated coefficients have the correct sign and magnitude, particularly the coefficient(s) of Z?

3. Report the R^2 of the first-stage regression *and report the R^2 of the same regression excluding all IVs*. How big is the difference? The smaller the difference, the worse, because it means that the IVs have little incremental explanatory power. Some researchers suggest reporting the incremental F-statistic of the excluded IVs and argue that this number should be at least 10 (e.g., Stock et al. 2002, Rossi 2014). However, this number should not be seen as standalone threshold that needs to be passed. Rossi (2014) argues that this number may be seen as an absolute minimum requirement. While it is important to discuss the R^2 (or F-statistic) of the *first-stage* regression Eq. 6, however, as we discuss below, we caution against a comparison of the R^2 of OLS to the R^2 of 2SLS of the *second-stage regression* (the main Eq. 1) as this comparison is usually meaningless (e.g., Ebbes et al. 2011).

4. When there is more than one IV in the case of one endogenous regressor, we suggest the researcher estimates the model with the best IV (based on theory) and compares the results to the model with all IVs included. Are the results stable in the sense that the main conclusions stay the same? If so, that is good news (more on that below when we discuss Sargan's test). If not, what can explain the difference? The theoretical arguments of IV validity may have to be revisited.

5. Report the results for a test for the presence of endogeneity. This test formally compares the OLS estimates to the 2SLS estimates and tests whether OLS is consistent or not (the latter is the null hypothesis). If the null hypothesis is rejected, then the 2SLS estimates should be used for inferences. In contrast, if the test does not reject the null hypothesis, then the OLS results should be used for inference. This test can be carried out in a few different ways. One way is through a Hausman test (e.g., Verbeek 2012, p. 152; Wooldridge 2010, p. 130). The other way is by estimating the IV regression model through a control function approach (see next section). Regardless of the outcome of the test, we recommend that all previous tasks (1–6) are reported in an IV regression analysis.

We note that sometimes researchers may add an additional task to this list. This additional task involves carrying out a Sargan test, which attempts to test whether the IVs that we use are exogenous. This test is an overidentification test which can only be used if there are more IVs than endogenous regressors. The idea behind this test is as follows. In case we have more IVs than endogenous variables (i.e., we have overidentification), we can regress the fitted residuals from Eq. 7 on the IVs. That is, we run an OLS regression with the fitted residuals as dependent variable and all IVs (as well as all other exogenous regressors in the regression model, if present) as independent variables. If the set of IVs is exogenous, then they should be jointly unrelated to the residuals, i.e., the R^2 from this regression should be close to zero. If that is not the case, then we have to reject the *entire* set of IVs. The reason is that this test cannot tell which of the IV or IVs are problematic – we can only assess the set of IVs as a whole. The test is usually referred to as the Sargan test (Wooldridge 2010, p. 135), and it is available in packages such as ivreg2 in Stata. When there are more IVs than endogenous regressors, this test can be used as *additional* evidence besides the theoretical arguments that we develop to choose the IVs. We advise against this test as a substitute for theoretical arguments. For more information on this test, we refer to Wooldridge (2010, p. 135) or Bascle (2008).

We now demonstrate the above six tasks for the ice-cream example. We provide a simulated dataset that contains ice-cream sales and prices for 500 days. We generate the data with a true price coefficient of -100 and a true intercept of 300. In generating the data, we create a correlation between price and the error term such that we have an endogeneity problem. Table 2 contains descriptive statistics for this hypothetical dataset.

The average sales is about 131 servings of ice cream per day, and the average daily price is €1.69. Table 3 contains the estimation results of a simple OLS regression that does not account for endogeneity. The estimated coefficient for price is -62.88, while the true coefficient in the data generating process (DGP) is -100. Hence, it becomes apparent that OLS severely underestimates the true price sensitivity of consumers, which is in line with previous research (e.g., Bijmolt et al. 2005). We note that these numbers are the marginal effects of a €1 price change on sales; these are not price elasticities.

We now attempt to solve the endogeneity bias using an IV approach. The IV Z_1 is the sum across the costs for all ingredients that are used for the ice-cream production (e.g., milk, sugar, fruits). The costs do not vary every day as the ice-cream seller often makes bulk purchases for several days. Because the ice-cream seller does not use local produce, the prices of the ingredients that she uses do not depend on local short-term temperature fluctuations. We therefore can accept the assumption that costs are exogenous. In other words, using costs in this example as the IV results in

Table 2 Descriptive statistics of example data set

	Mean	Std. dev.	Min	Max
Sales (units)	130.69	34.15	35.60	226.19
Price (€)	1.69	0.33	0.72	2.63
Instrument 1 (Z_1)	0.99	0.29	0.50	2.00

Table 3 OLS estimation results of example data set

Sales	True β	Estimate for β	se	t	p
Price	-100	-62.88	3.71	-16.96	0.00
Intercept	300	236.99	6.39	37.12	0.00

an IV that meets the exclusion restriction. Table 4 contains the first-stage regression of price on Z_1.

Here, we expect that the IV (cost) has a positive effect on price, which is the case as the estimate is 0.50 and significant. Such an empirical examination of the sign and magnitude of the estimated effect of the IV on the endogenous regressor is important, as it provides face validity for the theoretical arguments supporting the IV. The R^2 of this regression is 0.20. Because Z is the only regressor in the first-stage regression model, we can conclude that 20% of the variance in price is explained by the IV. Table 4 also reports an F-test, which assesses the joint significance of the IVs. In this case the F-test for the excluded IV is 125.07 and highly significant ($p < 0.0001$). This provides support for the strength of the cost variable as IV.

We now use the IV to estimate Eq. 1 with 2SLS, which we could do by estimating Eq. 7 with OLS, but it is better to rely on a command from the shelf (e.g., ivreg in Stata), because otherwise there is a risk that the standard errors of the second stage are not correct (more on that below). Table 5 summarizes the IV results from the 2SLS procedure.

The results indicate that 2SLS accurately estimates the true regression coefficient (-100). Note, however, the large standard error (9.05) compared to the OLS standard error in Table 3 (3.71), which is a typical outcome of an IV regression, i.e., IV is known to be less efficient (have a higher asymptotic variance) than OLS.

In Stata, rather than using ivreg, we can also use ivreg2, which provides a comprehensive set of additional statistics and diagnostics that are important to examine. For example, the Stata command would be:

ivreg2 sales (price = Z1), first.

Please note that running this command for this example does not give the Sargan test for the exogeneity of the IV. This makes sense because the Sargan test cannot be conducted if there is exactly the same number of IVs (one here) as endogenous regressors (one here).

We now turn to the Hausman test for endogeneity, which compares the IV estimate to the potentially inconsistent OLS estimate. In case of systematic differences between the IV and OLS estimates, the null hypothesis of no difference between the two will be rejected, and we would conclude that endogeneity is present. In Stata, we can implement this test by first running an OLS regression, storing the

Table 4 First-stage regression results with the IV Z_1

Price	Estimate for γ	se	t	p
Z_1	0.40	0.04	8.95	0.00
Intercept	1.19	0.05	25.78	0.00
F-test excluded IV	df $= 498$, $F = 125.07$, $p < 0.0001$			

Table 5 2SLS estimation results of example data set

Sales	True β	Estimate for β	se	t	p
Price	-100	-99.99	9.05	-11.05	0.00
Intercept	300	299.73	15.36	19.51	0.00

estimation results, then running an IV regression, and again storing the estimation results. After that we can run the Hausman test. We then tell Stata to compare both estimates:

reg sales price
estimates store ols
ivreg sales (price = Z1), first
estimates store iv
hausman iv ols, sigmamore[6]

For the ice-cream example, we find a Hausman χ^2 test statistic of 25.17 (d.f. = 1), which leads to a strong rejection of the null hypothesis of no endogeneity ($p < 0.001$). We therefore conclude that endogeneity is present in the demand model for ice cream and the 2SLS results should be used for interpretation of the effect of price on sales.

It is important to recognize that the validity of the Hausman test depends on the assumption that we used valid IVs. If we use weak or endogenous IVs, the results of the test are likely to be meaningless. Second, we recommend researchers to complement this test with an assessment of the managerial and economic relevance of the difference between the estimated coefficients of OLS and IV. For instance, there may be cases where the test indicates a statistically significant difference, but the difference in estimated coefficients is managerially or economically not relevant.

Recall that for the ice-cream example, we argued that the endogeneity issue arises because the ice-cream seller sets prices based on weather, which was unobserved by the researcher. Let us now assume that we managed to collect information on this variable. We may add the variable that captures weather into the main Eq. 1 as an additional covariate. Table 6 summarizes the results of the OLS regression with both price *and* temperature as covariates in the model.

The results indicate that controlling for the previously omitted variable eliminates the endogeneity problem. The standard error of the estimated price effect (1.15) is also *much* smaller than in the OLS model where temperature is omitted (3.71), as well as in the IV model where price endogeneity is corrected for using 2SLS (9.05). Hence, it is our advice to develop a regression model that controls for relevant covariates, such that no important covariate (e.g., temperature) that correlates with both the dependent (e.g. sales) and key independent variables (e.g., price) is omitted.

Table 6 OLS estimation results of example data set

Sales	True β	Estimate for β	se	t	p
Price	−100	−100.62	1.15	−87.78	0.00
Temperature	30	29.98	0.39	76.74	0.00
Intercept	300	300.88	1.97	152.89	0.00

---

[6]The option sigmamore specifies that the covariance matrices are based on the estimated error variance from the efficient OLS estimator. Stata's online help provides more information ("help Hausman").

This approach is also discussed in Germann et al. (2015, p. 4), who refer to such an approach as the "data-rich approach" to endogeneity correction.

Are there ways to assess whether the endogeneity correction was successful by examining in-sample model fit criteria or carrying out holdout-sample validation? For many advances in market response models, (e.g., unobserved parameter heterogeneity, nonlinear functional forms), we can use model fit criteria to assess how well the model performs. Unfortunately, however, this is *not* possible in general for endogeneity correction. The reason is that any endogeneity correction in a linear regression model will tilt the fitted line away from the best fitting OLS line, both in and out of sample. We illustrate this point in Fig. 3, which displays the same scatterplot of price and sales as before, along with the fitted regression lines for IV (dashed) and OLS (solid).

Figure 3 shows that the OLS line fits right through the scatter of sales and price observations. The IV line, however, has a more negative slope because the IV approach estimates the correct (more negative) price effect compared to OLS. However, this does mean that the IV fitted line is tilted away from the OLS fitted line. The OLS line minimizes the sum of squared residuals, and thus the OLS fitted line has the better fit to the observed data, as shown in Fig. 3.

The same principle holds both in an estimation sample and in a holdout sample, as long as the underlying data generating process in the holdout sample has not changed from the data generation process in the estimation sample. In other words, the OLS fitted line will predict better in a holdout sample than the IV fitted line, even though the OLS fitted line is based on biased parameter estimates. For instance, going back to the ice-cream example, suppose that the ice-cream vendor

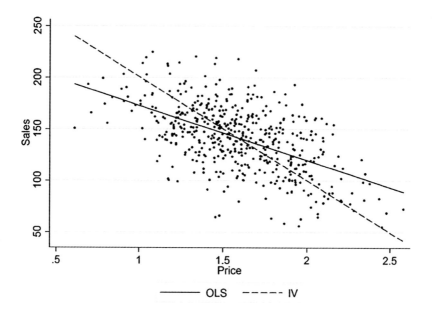

Fig. 3 OLS and IV regression fitted lines for the ice-cream example

wants to predict tomorrow's demand. Suppose also that tomorrow's temperature can be predicted quite accurately and that she is planning to set her prices using tomorrow's temperature information, as is usual practice for her. What would be the best prediction for tomorrow's sales? Looking at the lines in Fig. 3, we are better off using the OLS fitted line (solid line) than the "true" IV fitted line describing the causal effect of price on sales (dashed line) to predict tomorrow's sales, given price.

Ebbes et al. (2011) formalize this discussion and conclude with two main recommendations. First, if the model has a descriptive or normative purpose, consistent estimates for the regression effects are key, and an estimation approach that corrects for endogeneity is required. Descriptive models are developed to provide statements about the effectiveness of marketing instruments (Franses 2005), and normative models are developed to offer a recommended course of action (Leeflang et al. 2000). For either descriptive or normative models, comparisons of in- and out-of-sample fit of OLS versus 2SLS, or any other method that corrects for endogeneity, *are not useful*. Second, if prediction is the primary model objective, Ebbes et al. (2011) recommend to *not* correct for endogeneity. Particularly, if the data generating process in the estimation or holdout samples are the same, then the fitted line obtained from estimating Eq. 1 with OLS will predict as well or better as a model that corrects for endogeneity.

Hence, when considering potential endogeneity in a regression model, the researcher should first decide on the model objective, before attempting to correct for endogeneity. Importantly, we should not use the standard R^2 measure for model fit to assess the success of an endogeneity correction compared to OLS: OLS will typically perform better, despite its biased estimates.

What Happens in an IV Regression When Using Poor IVs?

As we saw above, the IV approach can be an effective way of addressing an endogeneity problem in a linear regression model *if the IVs used are strong and exogenous*. However, the quality of an IV regression deteriorates quickly when one or both of these key requirements are violated. To demonstrate this, we run two IV regressions, one with an endogenous IV and another one with a weak IV, continuing from the earlier hypothetical example.

Suppose we have two additional IVs available, Z_2 and Z_3, where Z_2 is not exogenous and Z_3 is weak. What would be an example for Z_2 such that it is an endogenous IV? Rossi (2014) argues that lagged marketing variables, such as lagged prices, are often invalid IVs, as they are likely to be endogenous, and should thus not be used as IVs. For instance, in the ice-cream vendor example, using lagged price as IV (e.g., price of the previous day, or P_{t-1}) would likely result in an endogenous IV, because today's temperature is likely correlated with yesterday's temperature, while yesterday's price (the proposed IV) is also correlated with yesterday's temperature, because of the ice-cream vendor's price setting behavior. Hence, corr(ε_t, P_{t-1}) $\neq 0$, making the IV $Z_{2t} = P_{t-1}$ endogenous and thus invalid.

An example for a weak IV (Z_3) in the ice-cream vendor case would be, for instance, gasoline prices. The price of gasoline is potentially an exogenous IV because gasoline prices are unlikely to be correlated with today's temperature or other demand shocks. However, while gasoline prices are part of the cost of producing ice creams (e.g., transporting ingredients), these prices will probably be only a small fraction of total cost and thus are expected to only weakly correlate with the price of ice creams. Hence, we would expect corr(P, Z_3) $\approx$ 0, making the IV Z_3 a weak IV and thus inappropriate.

Table 7 contains the first-stage OLS estimation results using the (invalid) instrument Z_2. Table 8 shows the IV results for the main Eq. 1, using only Z_2 as an IV.

From Table 7, we can see that the instrument is clearly not weak, as it explains a significant portion of the variation in prices as indicated by the F-test of the excluded IV. However, the results in Table 8 show that the 2SLS estimate for the price effect is severely biased. Interestingly the IV estimate (-47.95) is similarly biased compared to the true value (-100) as the OLS estimate (-62.88, Table 3), while the IV estimate has a much larger standard error. Applying the Hausman test here to test for the presence of endogeneity would give us X^2 test statistic of 1.42 (d.f. $= 1$) and a p-value of 0.23. Hence, the researcher would believe that there is no endogeneity problem in estimating Eq. 1 with OLS, which is clearly a wrong conclusion.

We now turn to the case of using the weak IV Z_3. Table 9 contains the first-stage estimation results using OLS, and Table 10 displays the results for the main equation using only Z_3 as a weak IV.

From the first-stage regression results in Table 9, we can conclude that Z_3 is a weak IV, because it is not a significant predictor for price. Consequently, the F-test statistic of the excluded IV is very low ($F = 1.54$). As the results in Table 10 show,

Table 7 First-stage regression with the strong but endogenous instrument Z_2

Price	True γ	Estimate for γ	se	t	p
Z_2: strong but endogenous IV	0.3	0.32	0.05	6.60	0.00
Intercept	0	1.36	0.05	26.10	0.00
F-test excluded IV	df $= 498$, $F = 43.50$, $p < 0.001$				

Table 8 2SLS estimation results with the strong but endogenous instrument Z_2

Sales	True β	Estimate for β	se	t	p
Price	-100	-47.95	13.27	-3.61	0.00
Intercept	300	211.76	22.46	9.43	0.00

Table 9 First-stage regression with the exogenous but weak IV Z_3

Price	True β	Estimate for γ	se	t	p
Z_3: exogenous but weak IV	.3	-0.02	0.01	-1.24	0.22
Intercept	0	1.69	0.01	115.11	0.00
F-test excluded IV	df $= 498$, $F = 1.54$, $p = 0.22$				

Dealing with Endogeneity: A Nontechnical Guide for Marketing Researchers 207

Table 10 2SLS estimation results with the exogenous but weak IV Z_3

Sales	True β	Estimate for β	se	t	p
Price	-100	-19.65	75.31	-0.26	0.79
Intercept	300	163.90	127.33	1.29	0.20

the estimated coefficients from the main equation using the IV approach with only Z_3 as IV are now severely biased and have huge standard errors.

Unlike using Z_2 as IV, which is an endogenous IV, we could have identified that Z_3 is inappropriate as an IV because of its weakness, by examining the first-stage regression (Bound et al. 1995). This example illustrates that it is important that researchers assess the strength of the IV by examining the first-stage regression. When the IV is not strong, we should resist the temptation to interpret and use the IV estimation results, as the ones presented in Table 10. Unfortunately, for the endogenous IV Z_2, an examination of the first-stage regression (Table 7) did not reveal any problems with this IV, and only theoretical arguments would have served to dismiss Z_2 as an appropriate IV.

In sum, when the assumptions underlying the validity of IVs are violated, as was the case for Z_2 and Z_3, the IV estimates are potentially severely biased, and we would be better off to not use an IV approach to correct for endogeneity, as the "cure" to the problem is worse than the "disease."

Extensions of the Basic IV Approach

Many empirical regression applications in marketing cannot be addressed by a simple linear market response model with just one independent variable. More likely, we encounter applications where there are multiple endogenous regressors, other regressors (covariates) that are not endogenous, interaction terms with endogenous regressors, or there is endogeneity in the presence of binary dependent or independent variables. We now provide a discussion of several common extensions of the basic IV approach, which may be useful to address an endogeneity problem in a marketing application. We continue using a linear regression model for our discussion; if the original model is a model that can be linearized (e.g., a multiplicative model using the log transform), then the extensions that we discuss next will still apply.

Control Function

There is an alternative way of estimating Eq. 1 using IVs. Instead of using the 2SLS approach, we could use the control function (CF) approach (e.g., Petrin and Train 2010; Ebbes et al. 2011; Wooldridge 2015). Recall that in the 2SLS approach, we replace the observed values of the endogenous regressor by its predictions obtained from the first-stage regression. In contrast, in the control function approach, we add the *residuals* of the first-stage regression as an *additional regressor* into the main Eq. 1.

We can implement the control function approach by using the same first-stage regression (6) as in 2SLS. After estimating the first-stage regression with OLS, we compute the fitted residuals

$$\hat{\nu}_i = P_i - \hat{P}_i \tag{9}$$

Then, we include these fitted residuals *as an additional regressor in the main regression* Eq. 1 *for the dependent variable*, resulting in

$$Y_i = \beta_0 + \beta_1 P_i + \beta_2 \hat{\nu}_i + \varepsilon_i \tag{10}$$

Subsequently, this "augmented" regression equation can be estimated using standard estimation approaches (e.g., OLS). It can be shown that 2SLS and CF give identical estimates for the regression parameters in the linear regression model (e.g., Verbeek 2012). Note that the original P_i is used in Eq. 10 and not $\hat{P}_i$. The idea is that the term $\hat{\nu}_i$ captures the "omitted" variables that make P_i endogenous. By including this term in Eq. 1, we "control" for endogeneity. Interestingly, a standard t-test for the significance of β_2 would be a fairly straightforward way to test for the presence of endogeneity, i.e., it is a computationally easy version of the Hausman test (step 6 in the previous section).

One note of caution regarding the use of the CF approach is the following. While in linear models the estimated coefficients using the CF approach are identical to the 2SLS estimates, the standard errors when estimating Eq. 10 using OLS are incorrect, because $\hat{\nu}_i$ is an estimated quantity. One way to address this is to use bootstrapping techniques to estimate the correct standard errors. The procedure to compute the correct standard errors using bootstrapping is given in Karaca-Mandic and Train (2003) and Papies et al. (2017).

We illustrate the control function approach using the same data as above. We first estimate Eq. 6, then store the residuals (e.g., in Stata by using the command predict new_variable, res), and use these residuals as an additional regressor in the main regression equation. The estimated coefficient (-99.99) using the CF approach is identical to the one obtained from 2SLS (Table 5). Importantly, the control function requires the exact same conditions for the IVs as before. That is, the IVs must be strong and exogenous. Thus, in the linear regression model, there is little reason to use the CF approach. In fact, it is harder to implement the CF approach than the 2SLS approach, as we need to bootstrap to obtain the correct standard errors.

However, the CF approach is often the more straightforward way of correcting for endogeneity when the dependent variable in Eq. 1 is *not continuous*. We may have a dependent variable that is, e.g., binary (e.g., purchased an ice cream or not), a discrete variable (e.g., how many scoops of ice creams were purchased), or a choice variable (e.g., which ice-cream flavor is chosen); see, e.g., Petrin and Train (2010),

Ebbes et al. (2011), and Andrews and Ebbes (2014). In those cases, the model in Eq. 1 would not be a linear regression model, but rather a binomial logit or probit model for a binary dependent variable, a Poisson regression model for a discrete count dependent variable, or a multinomial regression model for a nominal (choice) dependent variable (Andrews and Ebbes 2014; Petrin and Train 2010). We can control for endogeneity in these models by including the control function term $\hat{v}_i$ as an additional regressor and bootstrapping the standard errors of the estimated regression coefficients.

Multiple Endogenous Regressors

Many marketing applications have more than one potentially endogenous regressor. Suppose we have two regressors, price and advertising, in a regression model that we suspect are both endogenous because of strategic planning. In addition, we have one other regressor X_i, which we believe is exogenous. That is, let us consider the following extension of Eq. 1:

$$Y_i = \beta_0 + \beta_1 P_i + \beta_2 A_i + \beta_3 X_i + \varepsilon_i \tag{11}$$

Here, A_i is the endogenous advertising variable, and X_i is the exogenous regressor. We now need at least two IVs to correct for endogeneity in Eq. 11. In general, when there are K endogenous regressors, we need $L \geq K$ IVs. For each IV, the researcher needs to develop theoretical arguments to argue that (1) the IV is relevant (i.e., is not weak) and (2) the IV meets the exclusion restriction.

Once we have identified appropriate IVs, we could then think of the IV approach as estimating a separate first-stage regression for each endogenous regressor. But, there is an important practical matter: each first-stage regression needs to have the *same set of right-hand-side variables*. That is, all available exogenous information (IVs and exogenous regressors) belong to the right-hand side of each first-stage regression equation, as in the following two first-stage regression equations for price P and advertising A:

$$P_i = \gamma_0 + \gamma_1 Z_{1i} + \gamma_2 Z_{2i} + \gamma_3 X_i + v_i^P \tag{12}$$

$$A_i = \eta_0 + \eta_1 Z_{1i} + \eta_2 Z_{2i} + \eta_3 X_i + v_i^A \tag{13}$$

where v_i^P and v_i^A are the error terms of the first-stage regression equations. Another important matter concerns the theoretical development of the IVs: we must ensure that *each* endogenous variable is identified by *at least one unique IV*. That is, we only address the endogeneity problem adequately if at least one IV is related to P_i and the other IV is related to A_i. We cannot have that Z_1 is correlated with both P and A, while Z_2 is correlated with none. We can also not have that Z_1 and Z_2 are both correlated with P and neither is correlated with A.

To test for the strength of the instruments in case of multiple endogenous variables, we can use a multivariate F-test (e.g., the Sanderson-Windmeijer F-test). This test is implemented in Stata's ivreg2 (Baum et al. 2007, 2015; Sanderson and Windmeijer 2016).

In case we want to address an endogeneity problem with multiple endogenous regressors using the CF approach, the procedure is quite similar as before. Using the first-stage regressions (12) and (13), we can compute the fitted OLS residuals from Eqs. 12 and 13 and include both as two additional regressors in the main Eq. 11. Subsequently, the augmented Eq. 11 may be estimated by OLS. As before, we need to bootstrap to obtain the correct standard errors of the estimated regression coefficients.

Interaction Terms

In many marketing applications, the effect of one independent variable on the dependent variable depends on the level of a second independent variable. In that case, we need an interaction term in the regression equation, i.e., the product of the two independent variables enters the regression as an additional covariate. Consider the following example in which the effect of the endogenous regressor price depends on the level of the exogenous variable X_i:

$$Y_i = \beta_0 + \beta_1 P_i + \beta_2 X_i + \beta_3 P_i X_i + \varepsilon_i \tag{14}$$

To use 2SLS, we must treat the interaction as a separate endogenous regressor that needs its own IV(s) and its own first-stage regression equation. As a second IV, we could use the interaction $X_i Z_i$ between the exogenous regressor X_i and Z_i:[7]

$$P_i = \gamma_0 + \gamma_1 Z_i + \gamma_2 X_i Z_i + \gamma_3 X_i + \nu_i^p \tag{15}$$

$$P_i X_i = \eta_0 + \eta_1 Z_i + \eta_2 X_i Z_i + \eta_3 X_i + \nu_i^{px} \tag{16}$$

Here, ν_i^p and ν_i^{px} are the error terms of the two first-stage regression equations. The regression coefficients in Eq. 14 should be estimated with 2SLS. As before, we would need to support the IV analyses with the six tasks discussed above, including a discussion of the first-stage regressions and the strength of the instruments (which now includes the constructed instrumental variable $X_i Z_i$).

A potentially more straightforward and parsimonious way to address an endogeneity problem in an interaction term is through the CF approach (Wooldridge

---

[7]In case the variables are mean centered before they enter the product, i.e., $(P_i - \overline{P})(X_i - \overline{X})$, we need to use the mean-centered interaction term on the left-hand side of (16) and on the right-hand side of (14), instead of $P_i X_i$. The IVs do not require mean centering as the first-stage predictions will not be affected by mean centering.

2015). It is sufficient to estimate the following first-stage regression and add the fitted residuals as an additional regressor to (14):

$$P_i = \gamma_0 + \gamma_1 Z_i + \gamma_2 X_i + v_i^p \tag{17}$$

By including the residuals from Eq. 17 in the main Eq. 14, we can directly address the endogeneity problem, without having to specify a second first-stage equation for the interaction term (Wooldridge 2015, p. 428). However, a potential downside is that the standard errors need to be computed using a bootstrapping approach.

The Benefit of Panel Data

As the discussion above highlights, correcting for potential endogeneity in a market response model is important but not straightforward. In fact, when the IVs are poor (e.g., weak, endogenous, or both), the IV estimator is potentially more biased than the OLS estimator. Hence, the "cure" to the problem can be worse than the "disease" (see also Rossi 2014). Therefore, the researcher should only resort to IV estimation if there is a serious concern of an endogeneity problem and when it cannot be solved by adding other covariates (e.g., Germann et al.'s (2015) rich data approach).

However, another opportunity to correct for endogeneity arises when the researcher has panel data (e.g., Wooldridge 2010; Verbeek 2012). Panel data means multiple observations per response unit across time, such as tracking the sales of a set of stores over time. In some cases, the panel structure of the data can be leveraged to correct for endogeneity. In the literature, these models are often labeled "unobserved effects models" (Wooldridge 2010; Germann et al. 2015). The idea behind such models is that they control for omitted variables by using fixed effects dummy variables as control variables. To illustrate this idea, suppose we have daily data not only for one ice-cream vendor but for multiple vendors. We extend model (1) for panel data as follows:

$$Y_{it} = \beta_0 + \beta_1 P_{it} + \alpha_i + \lambda_t + \varepsilon_{it} \tag{18}$$

Here $i = 1, \ldots, N$ indicates ice-cream vendor i, and $t = 1, \ldots, T$ indicates day t. In addition, there are two new terms in the model: α_i and λ_t. The first term, α_i, is a term specific to ice-cream vendor i and does not vary over time. This term represents all factors that we cannot observe that are particular to this ice-cream vendor and which do not change during the observation window. As examples we could think of the location of the vendor or the quality of the vendor's ice cream. If they are not accounted for in model estimation, these unobserved, time-constant effects could lead to an endogeneity problem: if the ice-cream vendors realize the potential of their location, they may be tempted to charge higher prices on premium locations, regardless of which day it is. When this price setting behavior is unobserved to the researcher, P_{it} will correlate with the (composite) error term $u_{it} = \alpha_i + \varepsilon_{it}$ through α_i, and we have an endogeneity problem.

The second term, λ_t, is a time-specific term that affects all ice-cream vendors in the same way. Here, we could think of, say, weather (assuming the same weather applies to all ice-cream vendors), industry-wide changes, economic cycles, government policy, etc. Following similar reasoning, when ice-cream vendors take these "time" shocks into consideration for setting their prices, then we may have an endogeneity problem if the model estimation does not account for these time shocks. Hence, when the factors α_i and λ_t are not explicitly accounted for in the estimation, they will be part of the composite error term $u_{it} = \alpha_i + \lambda_t + \varepsilon_{it}$, and price (or other regressors) may be correlated with u_{it}, leading to biased estimates using standard estimation approaches such as OLS.

Fortunately, the panel structure of the data allows us to eliminate these two unobserved components α_i and λ_t and any endogeneity problem arising from these two components, *without needing IVs*. This is done by leveraging a two-way fixed effects model (Baltagi 2013, p. 39) that uses fixed effects to control for systematic differences between cross-sectional units (e.g., ice-cream vendors) and for factors that are common to all cross-sectional units but vary by time period.

As fixed effects for the cross-sectional units, we could include a set of dummy variables for each ice-cream vendor in the model. However, this can potentially lead to many more parameters to estimate. Instead, we could calculate the average demand and average price across t for each i, by averaging (18) across time, resulting in:

$$\overline{Y}_i = \beta_0 + \beta_1 \overline{P}_i + \alpha_i + \overline{\lambda} + \overline{\varepsilon}_i \tag{19}$$

with $\overline{Y}_i = \frac{1}{T} \sum_{t=1}^{T} Y_{it}$, and the other averages $\overline{P}_i$, $\overline{\lambda}$, and $\overline{\varepsilon}_i$ defined similarly. Then, subtracting Eq. 19 from Eq. 18 results in the following regression equation:

$$\left(Y_{it} - \overline{Y}_i \right) = \beta_1 \left(P_{it} - \overline{P}_i \right) + \left(\lambda_t - \overline{\lambda} \right) + \left(\varepsilon_{it} - \overline{\varepsilon}_i \right) \tag{20}$$

Examining (20), we see that the unobserved time constant effect α_i dropped out of the model, and the concern about it inducing an endogeneity problem is gone. We may estimate (20) with OLS, using $Y_{it} - \overline{Y}_i$ as the "new" dependent variable and $P_{it} - \overline{P}_i$ as the "new" independent variable and including time-fixed effects dummies $\tilde{\lambda}_1, \ldots, \tilde{\lambda}_T$ (alternatively, we can include $T - 1$ time-fixed effects dummies and an intercept). This estimator for β_1 is called the "within estimator" because it only uses within-cross-section variation to estimate β_1.

However, as Germann et al. (2015, p. 4) note, we do need the assumption that prices are uncorrelated with the error term ε_{it} across all time periods (this assumption is sometimes called "strict exogeneity"). Thus, the identifying assumptions underlying the fixed effects model (20) are that (i) the omitted variable(s) is (are) time invariant (i.e., the individual-specific intercept captures the omitted variable(s)) and (ii) there is enough variance in the dependent variable as well as the focal endogenous variable within one specific individual (ice-cream vendor) to allow for the estimation of its effect (the endogenous variable is identified only through the within-individual variation). The effects of time-invariant independent variables (e.g., quality of the location of the ice-cream vendor) cannot be estimated in the fixed effects approach and are thus eliminated from the fixed effects model during estimation.

How about the time unobserved effects? In estimating Eq. 20 with OLS, we already suggested to include time-fixed effects dummies. These dummies capture any unobserved time-specific effects. Thus, any endogeneity concern arising from unobserved time-specific shocks that are common to all ice-cream vendors are now no longer present.

However, if we have daily data, this would lead to the inclusion of many time dummies in (20), which may complicate the estimation of Eq. 20 with OLS. As an alternative, we could subtract the average across cross section (per time period) from both the dependent and independent variables. That is, we average (18) across cross-sectional units, for each time period $t = 1, 2, \ldots, T$, resulting in

$$\overline{Y}_t = \beta_0 + \beta_1 \overline{P}_t + \overline{\alpha} + \lambda_t + \overline{\varepsilon}_t \tag{21}$$

with $\overline{Y}_t = \frac{1}{N} \sum_{i=1}^{N} Y_{it}$, and the other averages $\overline{P}_t$, $\overline{\alpha}$, and $\overline{\varepsilon}_t$ defined similarly. In addition, we average (18) across cross section and time, giving

$$\overline{Y} = \beta_0 + \beta_1 \overline{P} + \overline{\alpha} + \overline{\lambda} + \overline{\varepsilon} \tag{22}$$

with $\overline{Y} = \frac{1}{NT} \sum_{t=1}^{T} \sum_{i=1}^{N} Y_{it}$, and the other averages $\overline{P}$, $\overline{\alpha}$, $\overline{\lambda}$, and $\overline{\varepsilon}$ defined similarly. Now we subtract Eqs. 19 and 21 from Eq. 18 and add Eq. 22 (Baltagi 2013, p. 40), to obtain

$$\left(Y_{it} - \overline{Y}_i - \overline{Y}_t + \overline{Y}\right) = \beta_1 \left(P_{it} - \overline{P}_i - \overline{P}_t + \overline{P}\right) + \left(\varepsilon_{it} - \overline{\varepsilon}_i - \overline{\varepsilon}_t + \overline{\varepsilon}\right) \tag{23}$$

We can now run a standard OLS regression on (23) to estimate β_1 as both α_i and λ_t are dropped out of the model. Here, we would *not* include an intercept and use as dependent variable the "new" variable $Y_{it} - \overline{Y}_i - \overline{Y}_t + \overline{Y}$ and as independent variable the "new" variable $P_{it} - \overline{P}_i - \overline{P}_t + \overline{P}$. There would be neither time dummies nor vendor-specific dummies in this regression. We believe that in many panel data applications in marketing, such an approach can already address most of the endogeneity problems and should routinely be carried out.

We note that another approach commonly discussed in panel applications is the random effects estimator that treats the unobserved intercepts α_i in (18) as random variables. We would like to stress that this approach does *not* account for endogeneity, and it has even slightly stronger exogeneity assumptions regarding the identification of the regression effects in (18) than OLS. Hence, if the researcher believes that there is an endogeneity problem arising from unobserved, time-constant effects, then including random intercepts in the model, as in a random effects regression approach, does *not* address the endogeneity problem (see also Ebbes et al. (2004) for a discussion). A discussion on the main identifying assumptions of panel data model applications in marketing is given by Germann et al. (2015, Table 2).

Conclusions

Many marketing research professionals and consultants are interested in estimating regression models to understand the effect of one variable (e.g., price or a marketing investment) on another (e.g., sales or market share). If the goal is to find the causal effect based on observational data such as transaction data or survey data, endogeneity is a serious challenge in achieving this goal. Endogeneity occurs if the independent variable is set deliberately and strategically by managers in order to capitalize on factors causing shocks in demand that are observable to the manager but not to the researcher. Similarly, consumers may be strategic and make decisions based on factors not observable to the researcher. As a result, these unobserved factor(s) can become part of the error term in the regression model. If one or more such factors are used to set the independent variable, then the variable is endogenous, which means that the estimated effect of the independent variable will be biased in standard estimation approaches such as OLS.

The bias can be substantial in practical applications, and therefore considering endogeneity issues is important both in marketing academia and marketing practice. However, this is more easily said than done. As a first step, we recommend researchers to expand the regression model with covariates that could capture the unobserved factors. In the ice-cream vendor example, once the temperature variable was added to the regression model, the OLS estimates were very close to the true parameter values and were estimated with high precision (low standard errors).

In a panel data setting, unobserved factors may be concentrated in unobserved cross-sectional differences between firms or consumers. In this case, adding fixed effects (dummies for each cross-sectional unit) as additional covariates adequately addresses the endogeneity problem. If the endogeneity problem arises because of time-related demand shocks, adding fixed time effects (time dummies) as additional covariates solves the problem. Equivalently, we can use the within estimators presented in the previous section.

If we have a single time series or a single cross section of observations or if we have a panel data setting and the fixed effects approach does not fully solve the endogeneity problem (e.g., Germann et al. 2015; Ebbes et al. 2004), then we need to split the exogenous variation in the independent variable from the endogenous variation and only use the exogenous variation to estimate the causal effect. This is the essence of the IV (or 2SLS) approach. It is, however, challenging to find IVs that satisfy two seemingly contradictory conditions: they need to be strong (explain the endogenous independent variable) yet be uncorrelated with the error term of the main regression equation. While the first condition (IV strength) can be investigated empirically, the second condition (IV exogeneity) can only be supported with theoretical arguments.

The difficulty of finding suitable IVs has sparked researchers' interest in finding ways of accounting for endogeneity in observational data without the need to use observed instruments. In the marketing literature, two approaches have been proposed. Firstly, Ebbes et al. (2005) develop the method of latent instrumental variables (LIV) that provides identification through latent, discrete components in the endogenous regressors. Similar to the observed IV approach, the LIV approach shares the underlying idea that the endogenous regressor is a random variable that can be separated into two components, one which represents the exogenous variation and one which represents the endogenous variation. The endogenous component is correlated with the error term of the main regression equation through a bivariate normal distribution. The LIV model may be estimated using, e.g., a maximum likelihood approach. Secondly, Park and Gupta (2012) introduce a method that directly models the correlation between the endogenous regressor and the model error term using Gaussian copulas. This approach can be implemented through a control function approach. Both the LIV and the Gaussian copulas approaches require non-normality in the endogenous regressor and normality of the error term of the main regression equation. We refer to Papies et al. (2017) for a detailed discussion of these two approaches.

Since exogenous variation in the independent variable of interest is essential for the estimation of causal effects, perhaps the best way to estimate causal effects is through *field experiments* (e.g., Ledolter and Swersey 2007; Ascarza et al. 2017). In a field experiment, we randomly set the values of the independent variable(s). After observing the realizations of the dependent variable, we can estimate the causal effect of the independent variable(s) on the dependent variable with a standard OLS regression approach[8], as the variation in the independent variable is exogenous because of the randomization. Field experiments are suitable in business applications where there are many potential customers, who can be accurately targeted and randomized into two or more treatment groups and whose outcomes or responses can be measured. But even in those settings, the implementation can be a challenge. For instance, a field experiment that attempts to randomly manipulate prices in an online setting can be detected by consumers, who realize that their price changes from one online session to another or notice that their price is different from the price of another consumer who is purchasing the same product. This may lead to a potential backlash, especially in today's world of online connectivity (see, e.g., Verma 2014).

This chapter is deliberately written rather informally, as a way to introduce the problem of endogeneity in regression models to marketing researchers. For a more formal, econometric treatment of endogeneity problems in regression models, we refer to the excellent textbooks by Wooldridge (2010) and Verbeek (2012) and the article by Bascle (2008). We hope that this chapter has clarified the issue of endogeneity and has provided some perspective on approaches to address endogeneity.

---

[8]Ascarza et al. (2017) leverage a field experiment to address endogeneity concerns in the context of a customer relationship management (CRM) campaign, customer targeting, and social influence.

References

Albers, S., Mantrala, M. K., & Sridhar, S. (2010). Personal selling elasticities: A meta-analysis. *Journal of Marketing Research, 47*(5), 840–853.

Andrews, R. L., & Ebbes, P. (2014). Properties of instrumental variables estimation in logit-based demand models: Finite sample results. *Journal of Modelling in Management, 9*(3), 261–289.

Angrist, J. D., & Pischke, J. S. (2008). *Mostly harmless econometrics. An empiricist's companion.* Princeton: Princeton University Press.

Ascarza, E., Ebbes, P., Netzer, O., & Danielson, M. (2017). Beyond the target customer: Social effects in CRM campaigns. forthcoming in the *Journal of Marketing Research*.

Baltagi, B. H. (2013). *Econometric analysis of panel data* (5th ed.). Chichester: Wiley.

Bascle, G. (2008). Controlling for endogeneity with instrumental variables in strategic management research. *Strategic Organization, 6*(3), 285.

Baum, C. F., Schaffer, M. E., & Stillman, S. (2007). Enhanced routines for instrumental variables/GMM estimation and testing. *Stata Journal, 7*(4), 465–506.

Baum, C. F., Schaffer, M. E., & Stillman, S. (2015). *IVREG2: Stata module for extended instrumental variables/2SLS and GMM estimation.* Boston College Department of Economics. Retrieved from https://ideas.repec.org/c/boc/bocode/s425401.html

Berry, S. T. (1994). Estimating discrete-choice models of product differentiation. *The Rand Journal of Economics, 25*(2), 242–262.

Bhattacharjee, S., Gopal, R. D., Lertwachara, K., Marsden, J. R., & Telang, R. (2007). The effect of digital sharing technologies on music markets: A survival analysis of albums on ranking charts. *Management Science, 53*(9), 1359–1374.

Bijmolt, T. H. A., van Heerde, H. J., & Pieters, R. G. M. (2005). New empirical generalizations on the determinants of price elasticity. *Journal of Marketing Research, 42*(2), 141–156.

Bound, J., Jaeger, D. A., & Baker, R. M. (1995). Problems with instrumental variables estimation when the correlation between the instruments and the endogenous explanatory variable is weak. *Journal of the American Statistical Association, 90*(430), 443–450.

Chintagunta, P. C., & Desiraju, R. (2005). Strategic pricing and detailing behavior in international markets. *Marketing Science, 24*(1), 67–80.

Dinner, I. M., van Heerde, H. J., & Neslin, S. A. (2014). Driving online and offline sales: The cross-channel effects of traditional, online display, and paid search advertising. *Journal of Marketing Research (JMR), 51*(5), 527–545.

Ebbes, P., Böckenholt, U., & Wedel, M. (2004). Regressor and random-effects dependencies in multilevel models. *Statistica Neerlandica, 58*(2), 161–178.

Ebbes, P., Wedel, M., Böckenholt, U., & Steerneman, T. (2005). Solving and testing for regressor-error (in)dependence when no instrumental variables are available: With new evidence for the effect of education on income. *Quantitative Marketing & Economics, 3*(4), 365–392.

Ebbes, P., Papies, D., & van Heerde, H. J. (2011). The sense and non-sense of holdout sample validation in the presence of endogeneity. *Marketing Science, 30*(6), 1115–1122.

Franses, P. H. (2005). On the use of econometric models for policy simulation in marketing. *Journal of Marketing Research, 42*, 4–14.

Gentzkow, M. (2007). Valuing new goods in a model with complementarity: Online newspapers. *American Economic Review, 97*(3), 713–744.

Germann, F., Ebbes, P., & Grewal, R. (2015). The chief marketing officer matters! *Journal of Marketing, 79*(3), 1–22.

Greene, W. H. (2011). *Econometric analysis.* Upper Saddle River: Prentice Hall.

Homburg, C., Kuester, S., & Krohmer, H. (2009). *Marketing management: A contemporary perspective.* London: Mcgraw-Hill Higher Education.

Karaca-Mandic, P., & Train, K. (2003). Standard error correction in two-stage estimation with nested samples. *The Econometrics Journal, 6*(2), 401–407. https://doi.org/10.1111/1368-423X.t01-1-00115.

Ledolter, J., & Swersey, A. J. (2007). *Testing 1-2-3 experimental design with applications in marketing and service operations.* Stanford, California: Stanford Business Books.

Leeflang, P., Wittink, D. R., Wedel, M., & Naert, P. A. (2000). *Building models for marketing decisions*. Dordrecht: Kluwer.

Leenheer, J., Van Heerde, H. J., Bijmolt, T. H. A., & Smidts, A. (2007). Do loyalty programs really enhance behavioral loyalty? An empirical analysis accounting for self-selecting members. *International Journal of Research in Marketing, 24*, 31–47.

Liebowitz, S. J. (2016). How much of the decline in sound recording sales is due to file-sharing? *Journal of Cultural Economics, 40*(1), 13–28.

Lindgren, B. W. (1993). *Statistical theory*. London: Chapman and Hall.

Manchanda, P., Rossi, P. E., & Chintagunta, P. K. (2004). Response modeling with nonrandom marketing-mix variables. *Journal of Marketing Research (JMR), 41*(4), 467–478.

Nevo, A. (2001). Measuring market power in the ready-to-eat cereal industry. *Econometrica, 69*(2), 307–342.

Papies, D., Ebbes, P., Van Heerde, H. J. (2017). Addressing endogeneity in marketing models. In P. S. H. Leeflang, J. E. Wieringa, T. H. A. Bijmolt, & K. H. Pauwels (Eds.), *Advanced methods for modelling marketing*. Switzerland: Springer. http://www.springer.com/de/book/9783319534671

Park, S., & Gupta, S. (2012). Handling endogenous regressors by joint estimation using copulas. *Marketing Science, 31*(4), 567–586.

Petrin, A., & Train, K. (2010). A control function approach to endogeneity in consumer choice models. *Journal of Marketing Research (JMR), 47*(1), 3–13.

Podsakoff, P. M., MacKenzie, S. B., Lee, J.-Y., & Podsakoff, N. P. (2003). Common method biases in behavioural research: A critical review of the literature and recommended remedies. *Journal of Applied Psychology, 88*(5), 879–903.

Rooderkerk, R. P., van Heerde, H. J., & Bijmolt, T. H. A. (2013). Optimizing retail assortments. *Marketing Science, 32*(5), 699–715.

Rossi, P. (2014). Even the rich can make themselves poor: A critical examination of IV methods in marketing applications. *Marketing Science, 33*(5), 655–672.

Sanderson, E., & Windmeijer, F. (2016). A weak instrument -test in linear IV models with multiple endogenous variables. *Journal of Econometrics, 190*(2), 212–221.

Sethuraman, R., Tellis, G. J., & Briesch, R. A. (2011). How well does advertising work? Generalizations from meta-analysis of brand advertising elasticities. *Journal of Marketing Research, 48*(3), 457–471.

Shaver, J. M. (1998). Accounting for endogeneity when assessing strategy performance: Does entry mode choice affect. *Management Science, 44*(4), 571–585.

Stock, J. H., Wright, J. H., & Yogo, M. (2002). A survey of weak instruments and weak identification in generalized method of moments. *Journal of Business Statistics and Economic Statistics, 20*, 518–529.

Verbeek, M. (2012). *A guide to modern econometrics* (4th ed.). Hoboken: Wiley.

Verma, I. M. (2014). Editorial expression of concern: Experimental evidence of massive scale emotional contagion through social networks. *Proceedings of the National Academy of Sciences, 111*(29), 10779–10779.

Villas-Boas, J. M., & Winer, R. S. (1999). Endogeneity in brand choice models. *Management Science, 45*(10), 1324–1338.

Wooldridge, J. M. (2010). *Econometric analysis of cross section and panel data* (2nd ed.). Cambridge, MA: MIT Press.

Wooldridge, J. M. (2015). Control function methods in applied econometrics. *Journal of Human Resources, 50*(2), 420–445.

Part II

Methods

Cluster Analysis in Marketing Research

Thomas Reutterer and Daniel Dan

Contents

Introduction 222
An Overview of Clustering Methods 223
    Data Quality and Proximity Measures 224
    Distance-Based Cluster Algorithms 227
Cluster Analysis of Market Basket Data 229
    Data Characteristics and Choice of Distance Measure 229
    Hierarchical Clustering 232
    K-Medoid Clustering 236
    K-Centroids Cluster Analysis 240
Conclusions 244
Cross-References 246
References 246

Abstract

Cluster analysis is an exploratory tool for compressing data into a smaller number of groups or representing points. The latter aims at sufficiently summarizing the underlying data structure and as such can serve the analyst for further consideration instead of dealing with the complete data set. Because of this data compression property, cluster analysis remains to be an essential part of the marketing analyst's toolbox in today's data rich business environment. This chapter gives an overview of the various approaches and methods for cluster analysis and links them with the most relevant marketing research contexts. We also provide

---

T. Reutterer (✉)
Department of Marketing, WU Vienna University of Economics and Business, Vienna, Austria
e-mail: thomas.reutterer@wu.ac.at

D. Dan
Department of New Media, Modul University Vienna, Vienna, Austria
e-mail: daniel.dan@modul.ac.at

© Springer Nature Switzerland AG 2022
C. Homburg et al. (eds), *Handbook of Market Research*,
https://doi.org/10.1007/978-3-319-57413-4_11

pointers to the specific packages and functions for performing cluster analysis using the R ecosystem for statistical computing. A substantial part of this chapter is devoted to the illustration of applying different clustering procedures to a reference data set of shopping basket data. We briefly outline the general approach of the considered techniques, provide a walk-through for the corresponding R code required to perform the analyses, and offer some interpretation of the results.

Keywords

Cluster analysis · Hierarchical clustering · k-centroid clustering · k-medoid clustering · Marketing analysis · Marketing research

Introduction

Cluster analysis is a generic term for exploratory statistical techniques and methods aiming at detecting groupings in data sets that are internally more homogeneous than the entities across the categorized groups. One of the primary goals of clustering is data compression, i.e., to summarize the original entities by a smaller number of groups or representing points instead of considering the complete data set. Cluster analysis has a long history and emerged as a major topic in the 1960s and 1970s under the label "numerical taxonomy" (cf., Sokal and Sneath 1963; Bock 1974). The origins of cluster analysis appeared in disciplines such as biology for deriving taxonomies of species or psychology to study personality traits (Cattell 1943). Over the years, a large variety of clustering techniques has been proposed for numerous types of applications in diverse fields of research. From a historical perspective, excellent books on cluster analysis have been written by Anderberg (1973), Hartigan (1975), Späth (1977), Aldenderfer and Blashfield (1984), Jain and Dubes (1988) or Kaufman and Rousseeuw (1990). Additionally, Arabie and Lawrence (1996) provide an extensive compilation of contributions on various aspects of cluster analysis; for more development updates in the field, see Everitt et al. (2011) or Hennig et al. (2015). From a marketing researcher's perspective, Punj and Stewart (1983) or Arabie and Lawrence (1994) provide comprehensive reviews of cluster analysis.

The "classical" marketing problems involving the application of clustering methods are market segmentation (Wedel and Kamakura 2000; Dolnicar et al. 2018) and competitive market structure (CMS) analysis (DeSarbo et al. 1993). The former entails deriving segments of customers who either react homogeneously to various marketing mix variables (response-based segmentation) or are more homogeneous with respect to some psychometric constructs such as product attitudes or product images, perceived value, or preferences (construct-based segmentation); see Mazanec and Strasser (2000) or Reutterer (2003) for this distinction and an overview of corresponding clustering methods.

The task of CMS analysis is to derive a configuration of brands in a specific product class which adequately reflects inter-brand competitive relationships as perceived by consumers (DeSarbo et al. 1993). This is typically accomplished via an arrangement of the rivaling brands in ultrametric trees, overlapping or fuzzy cluster structures (Rao and Sabavala 1981; Srivastava et al. 1981, 1984). Because they utilize identical data structures but just differ in the mode of data compression, segmentation (compression of the consumer mode) and CMS (compression of the brand mode) turn out to be "reverse sides of the same analysis" (Grover and Srinivasan 1987; Reutterer 1998). Yet another very similar data structure arises when companies keep record of their customer transactions (e.g., by tracking them over time in customer relationship management systems). Such data sets tend to be huge and accrue as clickstreams of visitation and corresponding purchasing patterns on a website or as sequences of shopping baskets comprising jointly purchased items or product categories. The data compression tasks involved in the so-called exploratory market basket analysis (Mild and Reutterer 2003; Boztuğ and Reutterer 2008; Reutterer et al. 2017) are analogous to those in market segmentation vs. CMS analysis and also entail some suitable clustering method. The marketing literature refers to the task of discovering subgroups of distinguished cross-category interrelationship patterns among jointly purchased items or product categories also as "affinity analysis" (Russell et al. 1999; Manchanda et al. 1999; Russell and Petersen 2000).

The remainder of this chapter is organized as follows: In the next section, we provide a brief overview of the various clustering methods and focus on how to proceed when conducting distance-based clustering in more detail. We also present the most popular distance/proximity measures and algorithms as well as the most commonly used software implementations in the computational environment R available to analysts. To demonstrate the application and the results obtained from using various clustering methods, we then provide a couple of hands-on examples on how to put cluster analysis into action. Using one and the same data set, we demonstrate the specific quality of data compression achieved when utilizing a specific type of cluster analysis. While most textbooks use market segmentation as the standard case for illustrating cluster analysis in marketing (see, e.g., Chapman and McDonnell Feit (2019) and Dolnicar et al. (2018) for excellent examples), we focus in our demonstration on the exploratory analysis of shopping basket data representing customers' joint purchase decisions across a wide range of product categories.

An Overview of Clustering Methods

We can distinguish between two major groups of clustering methods: model-based clustering and distance-based clustering. While model-based methods explicitly assume some statistical probability model as an underlying data generating process, the latter are more exploratory by nature. The idea behind model-based methods is that the observations arise from a probability distribution which is a mixture of two

Fig. 1 Steps to conduct cluster analysis

or more components (i.e., clusters). Each of these components is a density function with an associated weight in the mixture (e.g., a mixture of multivariate normal distributions) and the task is to determine the mixture distribution which fits the data best. This is usually done by varying the number of components and optimizing some fit or information criterion. A specific variant of model-based clustering is discussed in the chapter ▶ "Finite Mixture Models" of this handbook. For more technical details on model-based clustering, see Titterington et al. (1985), McLachlan and Basford (1988), Fraley and Raftery (2002), and Frühwirth-Schnatter (2006).

In the following, we will focus on distance-based clustering. The aim of distance-based clustering is to find groupings in the data such that the distance between entities within a group is minimized, while it is maximized for entities between groups for some predefined distance measure. The steps required to employ a distance-based clustering procedure are shown in Fig. 1. After the objects and variables of interest are selected from an available data base, the second step involves the choice of an appropriate proximity measure to quantify the (dis-)similarity between the objects to be clustered. In the next step, a specific cluster algorithm is selected, and once the results are obtained, the number of clusters is determined and the cluster solution interpreted accordingly. Because of their crucial impact on the resulting cluster solutions, we next discuss some of the most popular proximity measures and clustering algorithms used in research practice.

Data Quality and Proximity Measures

The choice of a proximity measure depends on the nature of the data to be clustered, more specifically, the scaling properties of the variables at hand. Generally speaking, we can distinguish between numerical (quantitative, metric) and categorical (qualitative, nonmetric) data. Metric data is characterized by a scale with numerically equal distances representing values of the underlying characteristic being measured, such as age, income, or the number of units sold over a month. With this kind of data, any mathematical operation can be performed, it can be displayed from the greatest to the least and vice versa. In contrast, categorical data include binary and nominal data with no natural order, for example: product choice, gender, ethnicity, etc. If categorical data imply an order relationship (such as preference rankings) of the measured objects, the scale is denoted as being ordinal. The latter include rating scales (e.g., brand attitudes measured using itemized scales), which occasionally are

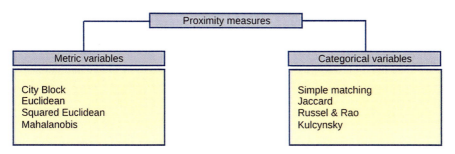

Fig. 2 Common examples of proximity measures

called pseudometric as they are treated as numerical data despite their ordinal properties. For a detailed discussion of measurement issues and data quality see, e.g., Mooi et al. (2018). Given the scaling properties of the data and the type of (dis-)similarity desired, the choice of a proximity measure determines how close/similar or how far/dissimilar objects in a data set are situated. A major distinction of alternative measures arises when we distinguish between metric and nonmetric data, see Fig. 2. In the case of metric data, most of the proximity measures are based on the summed distances of the objects with respect to all variables or dimensions of the data.

In an n-dimensional space, the most well-known and widely used distance measure between two data points $X = (x_1, x_2, \cdots, x_n)$ and $Y = (y_1, y_2, \cdots, y_n)$ arises as a family of metrics denoted as Minkowski distance or L_p norm (Adams and Fournier 2003), i.e., a metric where the distance between two vectors is given by the norm of their difference. The outcome of this metric is given by Eq. 1:

$$d_p(X,Y) = \left(\sum_{i=1}^{n} |x_i - y_i|^p \right)^{1/p} \tag{1}$$

The distance is a metric if $p \geq 1$. The most commonly used norms are L_1 known as the Manhattan norm and L_2 known as the Euclidean norm. The distances derived from these norms are called Manhattan distance

$$d_1(X,Y) = \sum_{i=1}^{n} |x_i - y_i|, \tag{2}$$

and Euclidean distance

$$d_2(X,Y) = \sqrt{\sum_{i=1}^{n} |x_i - y_i|^2}, \tag{3}$$

respectively. In cases where more weight should be put on the measurement of very distant data objects, the squared Euclidean distance can be used:

$$d_2^2(X,Y) = \sum_{i=1}^{n} |x_i - y_i|^2 \tag{4}$$

If the data is nonmetric (i.e., nominal, binary, or ordinal scales), the most common way of quantifying the (dis)similarity between data points is based on a two-way cross-classification of objects which counts for having a binary attribute: present or absent (note that ordinal data can be transformed into a series of binary variables accordingly). The corresponding similarity coefficients mentioned in Fig. 2 mainly differ in their assumptions on whether the common absence of a characteristic reflects similarity (such as the simple matching coefficient) or not and how much weight they put on the matched presence of an attribute.

Since we will use the Jaccard (dis)similarity coefficient in the following applications of cluster analysis using shopping basket data, we briefly illustrate the construction of the Jaccard index. The latter is used to assess the similarity s between two sets A, B or categories c_A, c_B. Formally, it measures the size ratio of their intersection $c_A \cap c_B$ divided by their union $c_A \cup c_B$ and can be written as follows:

$$s_{c_{AB}} = \frac{c_A \cap c_B}{c_A \cup c_B} = \frac{c_A \cap c_B}{c_A + c_B - c_A \cap c_B} \tag{5}$$

As discussed below in more detail, in the context of market-basket analysis the analyst's interest is in quantifying the (dis)similarity of products or product categories depending on whether they are jointly purchased in a set of transactions or not. In doing so, the product purchases are represented as binary elements with (1) denoting presence and (0) denoting absence of the specific product in a shopping basket. By cross-classifying a pair of products, we can calculate the Jaccard coefficient with the help of the following contingency table (cf. Sneath 1957; Kaufman and Rousseeuw 1990; Leisch 2006).

		Product 1		
		1	0	sum
Product 2	1	a	b	a+b
	0	c	d	c+d
	sum	a+c	b+d	p

For a set of p shopping baskets, the Jaccard similarity coefficient (also often referred to as the Tanimoto similarity coefficient (Anderberg 1973)) for products 1 and 2 can be calculated as:

$$s_{\mathrm{prod1,prod2}} = \frac{a}{a+b+c}, \tag{6}$$

and the corresponding dissimilarity coefficient is:

$$d_{\mathrm{prod1,prod2}} = \frac{b+c}{a+b+c}, \tag{7}$$

with the elements in the contingency table representing:

- a, the number of transactions with purchases of both product 1 and 2
- b, the number of incidences of product 2 but no product 1 purchases
- c, the number of incidences of product 1 but not product 2 purchases
- d, the number of transactions with neither product 1 nor product 2 purchases

Note that $s_{\text{prod1, prod2}} = 1 - d_{\text{prod1, prod2}}$ and in practice d in the above contingency table is usually the cell with the (by far) highest counts. This particularly applies to the context of shopping basket analysis but is not limited to this case. In such situations, any proximity measure that treats co-incidences of common zeros (in our case: nonpurchases of two specific products or categories) the same way as common ones would be biased towards the absence of two characteristics. For example, this is the case for the simple matching coefficient (which is $s_{\text{prod1},\text{prod2}} = \frac{(a+d)}{p}$) or the Hamming distance (i.e., the number of different bits $d_{\text{prod1, prod2}} = b + c$). Thus, in many scenarios it makes sense to use asymmetric proximity measures like the abovementioned Jaccard coefficient which gives more weight to common ones than to common zeros.

Distance-Based Cluster Algorithms

Regarding the choice of a cluster algorithm (step three in the above by Fig. 1), one popular way to distinguish variations of distance-based clustering methods is to

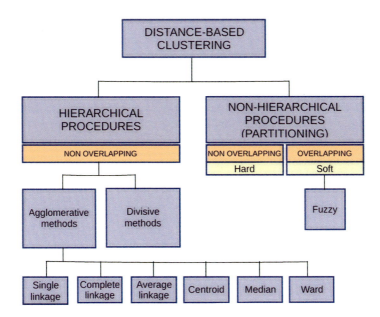

Fig. 3 Overview of distance-based clustering algorithms

divide them into hierarchical and nonhierarchical procedures. As illustrated by Fig. 3, the former can be split into agglomerative and divisive, while the later can be branched into nonoverlapping, overlapping, or fuzzy clustering methods (Hruschka 1986; Wedel and Kamakura 2000).

While in the case of nonoverlapping clustering each entity is assigned to one single group, overlapping clustering techniques allow for the simultaneous membership of objects to multiple groups. For example, depending on the consumption, brands and/or consumers might belong to more than one cluster of products or to several segments, respectively (see, e.g., Arabie et al. 1981). Fuzzy clustering abandons the idea of a "hard" partitioning of the data and replaces fixed cluster assignments by a degree of membership assigned to each entity and cluster (Hruschka 1986). Note that despite similar in idea but different in conception and interpretation, the notion of a "soft" group membership assignment becomes also apparent in model-based clustering methods when probabilities of cluster memberships are estimated and thus each data point can be assigned to more than one cluster. In this case, the inclusion of a data point in multiple clusters is due to a probabilistic approach, not of a distance.

Nonoverlapping clustering approaches can be further classified into hierarchical and nonhierarchical methods (Punj and Stewart 1983). Techniques for hierarchical clustering either start out with all entities in a single cluster (divisive algorithms or top down) or with each entity in its own cluster (agglomerative algorithms or bottom up). The latter approach is more popular among marketing researchers and successively links pairs of clusters (or still isolated entities) from a previous stage based on their shortest mutual distance. The agglomeration schedule stops when all entities are combined into one single cluster. We illustrate the application of some common hierarchical clustering procedures below in section "Hierarchical Clustering."

Nonhierarchical clustering starts with a (typically randomly initialized) grouping of the data for a prespecified number k of clusters and aims to gradually improve the partition by optimizing a "minimum variance criterion," i.e., by minimizing the inner (within-group) dispersion of the k-partition (cf. Bock 1974; Strasser 2000). The k-means algorithm was first proposed by MacQueen (1967) and its many variations (see, e.g., Jain and Dubes 1988; Kaufman and Rousseeuw 1990) are popular examples for such nonhierarchical distance-based clustering procedures. There is a huge variety of clustering procedures available in packages and functions provided by the R (R Core Team 2019) ecosystem for statistical computing. The most commonly used packages are the following:

- `stats`: The base R package provides a number of implementations for both partitioning and hierarchical clustering techniques. Function `kmeans()` comprises several algorithms for computing Euclidean distance-based partitions, while `hclust()` provides agglomerative hierarchical clustering algorithms. The `stats` package also provides various auxiliary functions like `dendrogram()` for visualizing cluster hierarchical solutions.
- `cluster`: This package provides R implementations of methods introduced in Kaufman and Rousseeuw (1990) and comprises a number or both partitioning (`pam()`, `clara()`, and `fanny()`) and hierarchical cluster algorithms (`agnes()`,

`diana()`, and `mona()`). The package also contains many extensions of these base methods and visualization functions (Struyf et al. 1996).

- `mclust`: A set of model-based clustering methods for fitting Gaussian finite mixture models using an expectation maximization (EM) algorithm is provided by the `mclust` package. It also provides numerous functions to assist cluster validation and evaluating the number of mixture components using the Bayesian Information Criterion (BIC) (Fraley and Raftery 2003).
- `flexclust`: This package provides an environment for partitioning cluster analysis with non-Euclidean distance measures using *k*-centroids cluster algorithms (KCCA) (Leisch 2006). There are also functions for deriving neighborhood graphs and image plots for visualization of partitions.

A comprehensive list of R packages for performing model-based or distance-based clustering is maintained by Friedrich Leisch and Bettina Grün and made available via the following CRAN task view: https://CRAN.R-project.org/view= Cluster.

Cluster Analysis of Market Basket Data

We next illustrate three different clustering procedures applied to a reference data set of shopping basket data. In doing so, we briefly outline the data used and the general approach of the selected procedure, then provide a walk-through for the corresponding R code required to perform the analyses and give some interpretation of the results. The three clustering procedures under consideration are: hierarchical clustering using the function `hclust()` and two prototype generating clustering methods: function `pam()` from the `cluster` package and function `kcca()` from the `flexclust` package.

Data Characteristics and Choice of Distance Measure

To illustrate the clustering methods, we use one month (30-days) of real-world point-of-sale transaction data from a local grocery outlet. The data set is included in the widely used R package `arules` and consists of an easy-to-handle set of 9835 retail transactions representing purchases in 169 different categories. The data come as a sparse matrix with each observation (row) representing a retail transaction and each column a binary variable with 1 denoting that a specific grocery category is present in the transaction and 0 otherwise. Thus, the row-wise sums indicate the number of categories purchased together in each transaction. A typical transaction is expressed as a list of categories such as: {tropical fruit, yogurt, coffee}, {citrus fruit, semifinished bread, margarine, ready soups}, and so on.

To obtain the data, in the R console, we add the `arules` package and activate the `Groceries` data set included in the library. To get a first visual impression of the proposed data set, we plot a histogram for the basket sizes, see Fig. 4, which

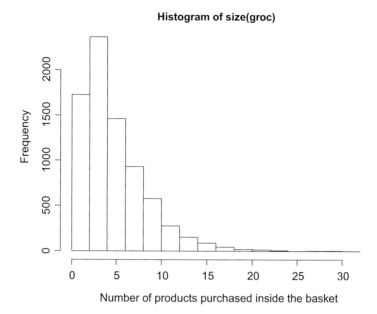

Fig. 4 Histogram of basket sizes

shows a right-skewed pattern we typically observe in supermarket transaction data: the majority of baskets are composed of only a few categories. Thus, the binary basket data are extremely sparse, with a mean basket size mean(size(Groceries)) of only 4.41 categories per shopping trip. Note that throughout the chapter, we will omit the category "shopping bags" because the latter does not reflect any specific consumption preference but in a grocery shopping context merely serves to carry the bought items around. The arules library, the Groceries data and the groc variable indicated below will be the same throughout all the further examples and will be reported only once in the R code examples.

To get a better understanding about which categories are purchased most frequently, we can plot the frequency distribution of categories exceeding a threshold (support) of 5%. As we can see from Fig. 5, the most frequently purchased categories are typical grocery products such as whole milk, other vegetables, rolls/buns, soda, yogurt, etc.

```
library("arules")
data("Groceries")
groc <- Groceries[size(Groceries)>1,
which(itemLabels(Groceries) != "shopping bags")]
hist(size(groc), xlab =
"Number of products purchased inside the basket")
```

With the itemFrequencyPlot function, we plot the most frequent items.

Cluster Analysis in Marketing Research

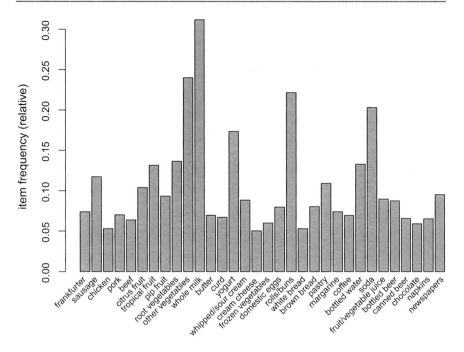

Fig. 5 Histogram of the most frequent items purchased

```
itemFrequencyPlot(groc, support = 0.05)
```

As we discussed in the previous section, in order to perform distance-based clustering, we need to specify a proximity measure which quantifies the distance between the objects to be clustered. Two aspects need to be considered in our present application. Firstly, an appropriate distance measure needs to adequately account for the data sparsity we observe for our market basket data at hand. Secondly, from a more substantive perspective, we are typically interested in finding groupings in the data which reflect jointly purchased categories, i.e., we aim at detecting complementary cross-purchase incidences. Thus, an asymmetric distance measure giving more weight to joint purchases than to common zeros (i.e., nonpurchases) is preferred in such situations. The previously discussed Jaccard coefficient (cf. Kaufman and Rousseeuw 1990) has such properties and is used in the present application.

For a given data set of market baskets $X^T = [x_n]$, $n = 1, \ldots, N$ containing binary purchase incidences $x_n \in \{1, 0\}^J$ we can compute a frequency matrix $X^T \times X = C = [c_{ij}]$ of pairwise co-purchases of categories $i, j = 1, \ldots, J$ and derive the Jaccard distance as follows (cf. Sneath 1957):

$$d_{ij} = 1 - \frac{c_{ij}}{c_{ii} + c_{jj} - c_{ij}}, \forall i,j = 1, \ldots, J \qquad (8)$$

Note that in the present context, the corresponding Jaccard similarity $s_{ij} = 1 - dij$ measures the percentage of joint purchases in all baskets which contained at least one of the two categories.

Hierarchical Clustering

In our first example, we employ hierarchical clustering to the described set of shopping basket data. In such a setting, the task is to explore subgroups of jointly purchased product categories based on pairwise co-purchase "affinities" across the categories included in the data set. Thus, we aim at detecting clusters of product categories which tend to be purchased together more often by the customers of the local supermarket.

As already mentioned in section "Distance-Based Cluster Algorithms," the most popular hierarchical clustering method is agglomerative clustering, which can be performed by using the function `hclust()`. In this family of clustering methods, the agglomeration procedure initially considers each singleton object (here: product category) as a cluster and then, step by step, merges the objects iteratively into groups of clusters until one final cluster is generated. The merging mechanism is directed by (i) the proximity or (dis)similarity measure and (ii) a linking criterion.

In our example, we use the Jaccard distance as defined above. As a starting point, we thus compute a dissimilarity matrix $D = [d_{ij}]$ according to Eq. 8:

```
diss <- dissimilarity(groc[, itemFrequency(groc) > 0.02], method =
"jaccard", which = "items")
```

Note that for simplicity reasons and to keep the resulting tree structure easy to inspect, we only select categories which are contained in more than 2% of the retail transactions at hand. This is done by specifying `itemFrequency (Groceries) > 0.02`.

The choice of a linking criterion determines how the distance between two groups of observations is calculated during the agglomeration procedure. It uses the previously computed (dis)similarity measure and one of the many available methods for measuring the distance between two clusters or between a cluster and a singleton object. The most popular linkage methods are represented in Fig. 6. While single linkage uses the distance between the two closest elements of two clusters, complete linkage measures the distance between the two farthest or most distant elements in two sets. The average linkage criterion compromises between the two previously mentioned ones and takes the mean distance between the elements of each cluster. Ward's method aims at minimizing the within-cluster variance and at each step merges the pair of clusters that leads to a minimum increase in total within-cluster variance after merging (cf. Kaufman and Rousseeuw 1990).

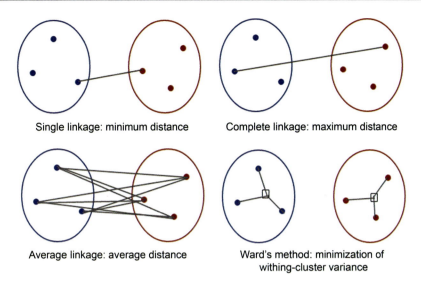

Fig. 6 A selection of popular linkage criteria in hierarchical clustering

Note that the choice of a cluster linkage method has a decisive impact on the resulting cluster solution. To illustrate this, consider the following two cases using single linkage clustering and the minimum variance method proposed by Ward (1963). Using the function hclust(), single linkage clustering can be performed as follows:

```
# Single linkage method
hc.single <- hclust(diss, method = "single")
plot(hc.single, cex=0.7)
abline(h = c(0.75, 0.80, 0.85, 0.90, 0.95),
col = "gray", lty = 3)
```

One common way to visualize the outcome of hierarchical clustering is by using a so-called dendrogram. The word dendrogram comes from the combination of two ancient Greek words: déndron ("tree") and grámma ("written character, letter, that which is drawn.") The analogy with a reversed tree is obvious, each leaf represents one object (in our case a product category), each branch represents one cluster at a certain point of the agglomeration process, and the root encompasses all the clusters. Notice that at a certain "height" of the cluster dendrogram, the branches are merged together. The height of the fusion, also known as the *cophenetic distance* (Farris 1969), is inversely proportional to the similarity of the objects. A common way to assess how the generated dendrogram reflects the data is to compare the cophenetic distances with the original distances by correlating them.

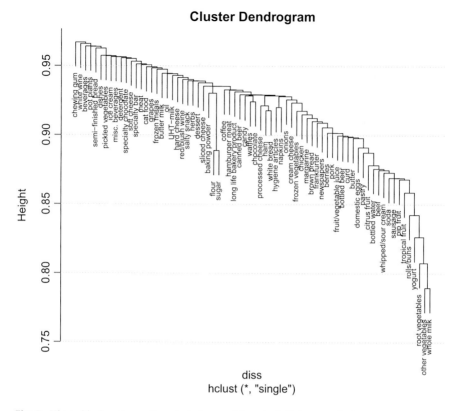

Fig. 7 Hierarchical agglomerative clustering applying single linkage method

A strong correlation indicates a good linking of the objects in the dendrogram (Saraçli et al. 2013).

The dendrogram derived for our market basket data is obtained by the `plot()` command for object `hc.simple`. It is given in Fig. 7 and depicts a typical property inherent to single linkage clustering, namely that very "similar" categories (i.e., those which are purchased together very often, here whole milk, other vegetables, followed by root vegetables, yogurt, etc.) are merged at a very early stage of the agglomeration process and those categories which rarely appear in the same shopping baskets (chewing gum, beverages, etc.) at a later stage.

The single linkage criterion employs a "nearest neighbor" rule to merge sets and thus is able to reveal rather complex, elongated, or snake-shaped data structures (Kaufman and Rousseeuw 1990; Dolnicar et al. 2018). On the other hand, single linkage typically induces a chaining effect in the hierarchical agglomeration procedure, which can be clearly seen in Fig. 7 in the creation of long straggling "clusters." This is due to the fact that objects are added sequentially to clusters, and at each stage, the "closest distant" (or most similar) object is merged with the already existing configuration. Because of this property, single linkage cluster is also sometimes used for outlier detection (i.e., those entities merged with the configuration towards the end of the agglomeration process).

In contrast, Ward's linking method aims at forming minimum inner variance partitions. To achieve this, at each step, the pair of clusters which minimizes the incremental increase in within-cluster variance is merged. Ward's method can be called in the R code by specifying the ward.D option. As we see from the dendrogram in Fig. 8, using this method, the categories are merged more evenly from the start, and thus we have a more balanced distribution of clusters.

```
# Ward linkage method
hc.wardd <- hclust(diss, method = "ward.D")
plot(hc.wardd, cex=0.7)
rect.hclust(hc.wardd, k = 5, border = 2:7)
```

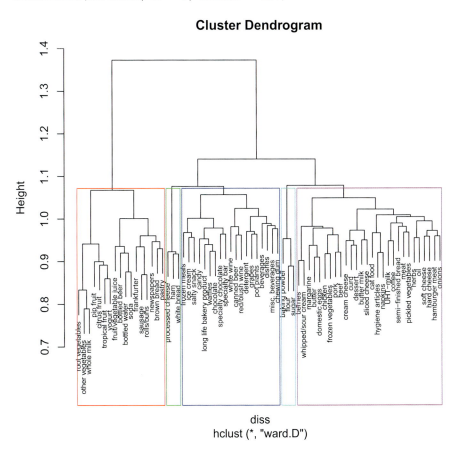

Fig. 8 Hierarchical agglomerative clustering applying Ward's method

As we move up from the leaves to the root, we notice that the branches get linked together at a variable height. The height of the linkage, indicated on the vertical axis, measures the (dis)similarity between two objects or clusters. The more we move towards the root of the dendrogram, the more dissimilar the merged objects are. In our illustrative example, we can see that several branches merge frequently co-purchased categories from the assortment of fresh products (e.g., vegetables, whole milk, fruits, yogurt) at the left-hand side of the tree, which are later linked with drinks (e.g., bottled beer, juices, water, soda, etc.) and a combination of categories associated with snacks (e.g., frankfurter, sausage, rolls, etc.) into one cluster marked by a red box. In the other (right-hand side) branch from the root, other distinct category combinations (such as salty and sweet snacks, candies and chocolate categories, etc.) are represented.

Notice that at any horizontal "cut" of the tree structure a specific cluster solution consisting of groups of product categories with internally more intense cross-category purchase relationships emerge. For example, in Fig. 8, we marked a solution with $k = 5$ clusters: three larger clusters and two smaller, each representing only three categories which are purchased together very frequently (i.e., {processed cheese, ham, white bread} and {baking powder, four, sugar}). Such formations of "supra-categories" can be helpful for store managers to design shelf placements of categories within the store but also to consider the representation of categories in leaflets or promotional activities.

K-Medoid Clustering

Hierarchical clustering is a useful tool for data compression and visualization if the number of objects used for clustering is reasonably small. For example, this is the case if we are interested in analyzing the joint purchase affinities among the product categories J represented in a matrix X of shopping baskets as just illustrated above. However, as J increases, the dimensionality of the to-be-derived distance-matrix reaches computational limits and/or visualization of the dendrogram for the linkage procedure becomes intractable and interpretation cumbersome. The latter also applies to the task of deriving a segmentation of the shopping baskets or the households behind the observed retail transactions. From a substantive perspective, such a focus also implies moving away from studying category purchase interdependencies for a pooled set of transaction data. When we compress the shopping baskets into a smaller number of representing basket classes, we aim at finding a partition of the data set at hand with outstanding or more distinguished complementary cross-category purchase incidences within the detected classes (for more details, see Boztuğ and Reutterer 2008; Reutterer et al. 2006, 2017).

For such tasks, nonhierarchical or partitioning clustering is a feasible alternative. Formally, the task is to find a partition $P = \{P_1, \ldots, P_K\}$ of the data set into a fixed number of K basket classes which fulfills the following objective function:

$$\sum_k \sum_{n \in P_k} d(x_n, c(x_n)) \rightarrow \min_{P,C} \tag{9}$$

where $C = (c_1, \ldots, c_K)$ is a set of centroids or prototypes and $d(\cdot)$ a distance measure, such as the Jaccard distance in Eq. 8, we are using in the present application. In the clustering and classification literature, the "minimum dispersion criterion" in Eq. 9 is also known as the principal point or k-centroids problem (Jain and Dubes 1988; Leisch 2006). One important property of resolving Eq. 9 is that for any optimum configuration (P^*, C^*), the condition $c^*(x_n) = arg\ min\ \{d(x_n, c_k), \forall k\}$ holds, which warrants that each basket x_n is mapped onto its minimum distant or closest centroid. With the notable exception of Ward's method (which follows a similar objective function), this is in sharp contrast to the way most linkage procedures proceed in forming clusters. Instead of minimizing a global objective function, agglomerative hierarchical clustering aims at minimizing a distance function at each step of the cluster fusion but can result in a potentially suboptimal global solution.

Before we illustrate using a generic method for solving the k-centroids problem in the next section, we first employ an iterative, easy-to-implement, relocation-based heuristic proposed by Kaufman and Rousseeuw (1990) under the name Partitioning Around Medoids (PAM). Combined with clustering objective function (Eq. 9), this algorithm requires from the centroid to have the property $c_k \in \{x_n\}_n \in P_k\ \forall\ k$, i.e., the "medoid" is defined as the shopping basket which minimizes the mean distance with all other transactions in the same cluster P_k. This medoid property guarantees that the centroids are real shopping baskets, which tend to result in more robust cluster solutions in the presence of outliers and facilitates interpretation. On the other hand, PAM is suitable for relatively small- to medium-sized data sets, but this problem can be overcome by selecting randomly from the available data or following other resampling methodologies.

For clustering larger data sets using the medoid approach, one may use CLARA (Clustering LARGE Applications; see Kaufman and Rousseeuw 1990) or CLARANS (Clustering Large Applications based upon RANdomized Search; see Ng and Han 2002). The former does not use the entire data, but it randomly chooses multiple samples with fixed size and repeatedly applies PAM to each of these samples and selects the representative k-medoids. Afterwards, the objects in the data set are assigned to the closest medoid. CLARA finds the best clustering if the sampled medoid is among the best k-medoids by calculating the mean of the dissimilarities of the data to their closest medoid. CLARANS interprets the search space as a hypergraph, where each node represents a set of k-medoids. The algorithm randomly chooses a set of neighbor nodes as new medoids in an iterative manner. If the neighbor discovered is better than the previous one, a local optimum is discovered. The whole process is repeated until the whole graph is sufficiently explored and an optimal solution is found.

We apply the k-medoid partitioning to the `Groceries` data set by taking into account only transactions that contain at least two different product categories.

After this preselection, we are left with 7,676 transactions and 168 categories. To retain a dissimilarity matrix of moderate size, we randomly select 2,000 transactions and use the Jaccard coefficient as distance measure. The cluster solutions for a sequence of $K = 1, \ldots, 8$ clusters are generated using the function pam ( ). Setting a seed value to secure reproducibility of the obtained results completes the following code for performing k-medoid clustering of the available shopping basket data:

```
library("cluster")
set.seed(42)
samp <- sample(groc, 2000)
diss <- dissimilarity(samp, method = "Jaccard")
clust <- lapply(1:8, function (x) pam(diss, k= x))
```

Determining a suitable number of clusters based on distance-based clustering methods is an open issue and the relevant literature offers a huge variety of "validity" metrics to assist the analyst with this task. Popular metrics include the cluster separation measure proposed by Davies and Bouldin (1979) or indices based on the agreement of repeated cluster solutions like the measures proposed by Rand (1971). An overview and detailed performance comparisons of alternative metrics for determining the number of clusters is provided by Milligan and Cooper (1985) or Dimitriadou et al. (2002). Among these heuristics is also the easy-to-use silhouette coefficient proposed by Rousseeuw (1987) which takes into consideration the discrepancies of the average within-cluster dissimilarities and the nearest data points of each neighboring cluster. Based on this heuristic, we opt for a solution of $K=5$ clusters (see also the discussion in Reutterer et al. 2007 or Reutterer et al. 2017).

As discussed before, the derived clusters should reflect classes of shopping baskets with more distinguished complementary cross-category purchase incidences within the detected basket classes. To explore these particular patterns, we select two exemplary clusters, namely cluster number 2 and 5, and characterize their specific properties using the function itemFrequencyPlot(). The resulting plots exhibited in Figs. 9 and 10 represent the relative purchase frequencies across categories in the complete data set as continuous lines and contrast them with the respective cluster-specific distributions. Note that for space and illustrative reasons, we include only categories which are present in at least 5% of transactions.

```
itemFrequencyPlot(samp[clust[[5]]$clustering == 2],
population = groc, support = 0.05)


set.seed(42)
inspect(samp[clust[[5]]$medoids[2]])
##          items
##     [1] {citrus fruit,
##          tropical fruit,
##          root vegetables,
```

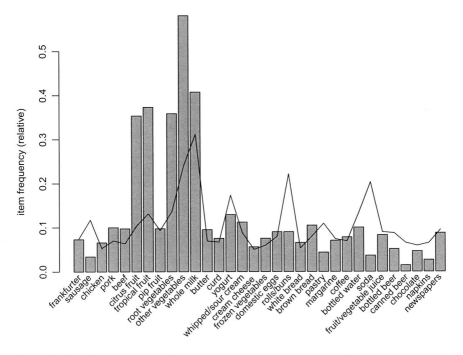

Fig. 9 Profile of relative purchase frequencies across categories in cluster 2

```
##            other vegetables,
##            whole milk}
```

Comparing the two clusters, they clearly point to considerable differences between the shopping baskets summarized by them. The transactions represented by cluster 2 are characterized by a shopping pattern with elevated purchase likelihood in fruits (citrus fruit, tropical fruit) and vegetables (root vegetables, other vegetables) categories as well as whole milk. In contrast, the purchase behavior behind cluster 5 transactions is clearly dominated by remarkably high purchase incidences in certain beverage categories (bottled water, soda, bottled beer) and only moderate class-conditional choice probabilities in the remaining categories.

The inspect() function returns us the respective medoid shopping baskets for these two clusters which confirm the above interpretation (i.e., {citrus fruit, tropical fruit, root vegetables, other vegetables, whole milk} for cluster 2 and {bottled water, soda, bottled beer} for cluster 5).

```
itemFrequencyPlot(samp[clust[[5]]$clustering == 5],
population = groc, support = 0.05)
```

```
set.seed(42)
```

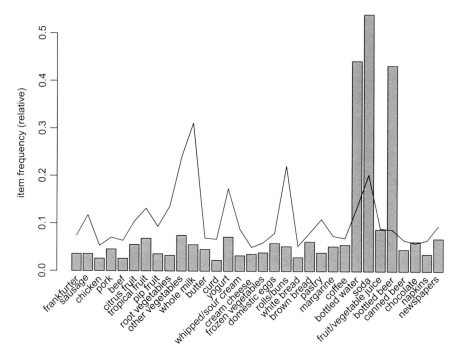

Fig. 10 Profile of relative purchase frequencies across categories in cluster 5

```
inspect(samp[clust[[5]]$medoids[5]])
##         items
##     [1] {bottled water,soda,bottled beer}
```

K-Centroids Cluster Analysis

A more flexible approach to solve the *k*-centroids problem introduced in the previous section is offered by the function kcca() in package flexclust (Leisch 2006). The R package flexclust includes a multitude of functions for various cluster algorithms. The main function in this package is kcca() which implements generalizations of *k*-means clustering for arbitrary distance measures. Thus, it can be used as a unifying partitioning framework for finding canonical centroids in both metric and nonmetric spaces including binary data (Hartigan and Wong 1979). Like the previous PAM application, once applied to the data structure at hand and using the same distance measure (i.e., Jaccard), this method also derives clusters of retail transactions with internally more homogeneous and pronounced cross-category dependencies.

To illustrate this approach, we use again the Groceries data set from the arules library and apply the same preselection for categories (threshold of being present in more than 2% of all transactions) as we did in the above application of hierarchical clustering. In order to be able to perform the necessary computations, we transform the remaining data set into a matrix `grc` with logical values structure and then just add a zero to transform the result into a usable numerical values container.

The `flexclust` family provides, among others, the Jaccard coefficient option as a distance measure for binary data and the `kcca()` function returns a set of real-valued centroids representing class conditional expectations which are directly accessible for the interpretation of the derived cluster solution. The issue of choosing a suitable number of clusters follows the same line of arguments as discussed in the previous subsection and is usually addressed by generating cluster solutions for a sequence of increasing K numbers of clusters and applying some internal "validity" metrics or by systematically studying the stability of alternative solutions using ensemble clustering techniques (Hornik 2005). Here, to exemplify and simplify our illustration, we use five clusters like in the above illustration of the PAM method (`num_clusters` = 5).

One way to inspect the separation of the derived clusters is by visualizing a lower-dimensional representation of the cluster solution. This can be accomplished by applying a data projection method, such as principal component analysis to the data set at hand. We note that principal components or factor analysis is problematic for non-Gaussian (here binary) data, but following Leisch (2006) we consider using it as appropriate for the mere purpose as a simple and easy-to-use data projection device used to visualize a cluster solution (we are not interested in the underlying interpretation of the derived dimensions). Other appropriate methods would be, for example, correspondence or homogeneity analysis.

Combining the results of `kcca()` and `prcomp()`, the projection of the data points together with indicators of their cluster membership on the first two dimensions can be done by using the `plot()` function. In Fig. 11, the centroids of the five clusters solution are plotted as numbers and connected by a neighborhood graph, which thickness represents the degree of connectedness. Even though the projected clusters apparently overlap, the scatter plot suggests an underlying structure of five diagonally separated groups of data points.

```
library("ggplot2")
library("flexclust")
Gr <- groc[, itemFrequency(groc) > 0.02]
grc <- as(Gr, "matrix")
grc <- grc +0

# flexclustControl object holds the "hyperparameters"

fxc <- new("flexclustControl")
lc <- list(iter.max=500, tol=0.001, verbose=0)
fxc <- as(lc, "flexclustControl")
fc_seed <- 100
num_clusters <- 5
```

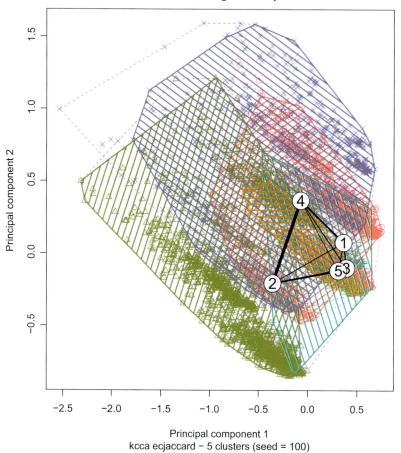

Fig. 11 Neighborhood plot of the Groceries data using the Jaccard distance on the two principal components

```
set.seed(fc_seed) }

# verbose > 0 will show iterations
vol.cl <- kcca(grc, k = num_clusters, save.data = TRUE,
control = fxc, family = kccaFamily("ejaccard"))
main_text1 <- "Groceries Basket"
sub_text <- "kcca ejaccard - 5 clusters (seed = 100)"

# plot on first two principal components
vol.pca <- prcomp(grc)
plot(vol.cl, data = grc, project = vol.pca, which = 1:2,
```

```
main = paste0(main_text1, " - Segment Separation Plot"),
xlab = "Principal component 1",
ylab = "Principal component 2",
points = TRUE, hull.args = list(density=10),
sub = sub_text)


barchart(vol.cl, strip.prefix = "# ",
shade = TRUE, layout = c (vol.cl@k, 1),
main = paste0(main_text1, " - Cluster Profile Plot"),
which = hc.wardd$order)
```

Similar to the cluster-specific barplots for the relative category purchase frequencies of the k-medoid cluster solution, the `barchart()` function allows for a graphical representation of the cluster solution contained in a `kcca()` object and thus helps interpreting the findings (see Dolnicar et al. 2014). The argument `shade = TRUE` detects and displays the `marker variables` in colors. The argument `which` defines the order of the variables. In our case, we chose the order of the product categories such that it corresponds to the order in the dendrogram represented in Fig. 8.

Figure 12 shows in the header the absolute number (i.e., the number of shopping baskets assigned to the respective cluster) and the percentage size of each cluster. The individual barplots help to compare the overall against the cluster-specific centres or mean values per category, which in the present context can be interpreted as the respective percentage of transactions containing a specific category. The line with the full dot represents the relative purchase frequencies over the complete sample. Thus, as we already know from above, the categories with highest shares in the shopping baskets are whole milk, other vegetables, rolls/buns, etc. The bars represent the respective within-cluster purchase shares for each category. They are colored if the difference to the overall mean exceeds a certain threshold value, the bar has a gray contour if this difference is not relevant for interpretation but might be a relevant characteristic of the cluster.

From the visual inspection of Fig. 12, it becomes obvious that the five derived basket classes differ in their basket composition from the overall "average" shopping basket by only a few categories, which makes them distinctive from each other. For example, the shopping baskets represented by cluster 4 are characterized by an outstanding share of rolls/buns and clearly above average purchase incidences in the sausage and frankfurter categories (the three categories together representing typical items demanded for making snacks). A slightly different variation of this cluster is represented by segment 3, in which drinks are represented by the bottled beer and food by sausages and bread. In contrast, the 36% of shopping baskets represented by cluster 2 contain typical grocery shopping categories, such as whole milk, other vegetables, root vegetables, butter, and domestic eggs above average.

From a managerial perspective, knowledge of such behavioral segments is an important prerequisite for designing customized target marketing actions (see Reutterer et al. 2006). For example, categories with distinguished purchase propensities within a specific segment (such as beer in segment 3 or water and soda

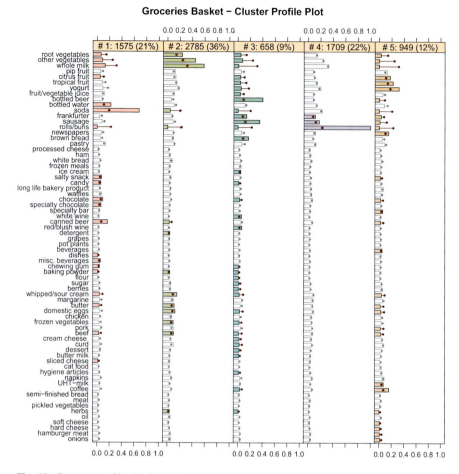

Fig. 12 Segment profile plot for the five-segment solution based on the *K*-centroids algorithm

in segment 1) are promising candidates for deriving targeted promotions to increase store traffic. On the other hand, direct marketers could also aim at promoting categories which are systematically underrepresented in certain segments by cross-promoting them in combination with certain "draw" categories; for example, in segment 3, customers could be stimulated to purchase more vegetables or milk by cross-promoting bottled beer in a way similar to "get a bottle of beer free if you purchase one liter of milk" (Breugelmans et al. 2010; Dréze and Hoch 1998).

Conclusions

As demonstrated in the previous section, the cluster solutions and corresponding interpretations vary considerably depending on the applied clustering procedure. This clearly reflects the exploratory nature of cluster analysis which implies that there is no single "correct" or natural solution for a specific data set at hand. The achieved data compression effect and thus the specific data structure uncovered by a particular approach to cluster analysis rather depends on a number of factors under the analyst's control. The main factors are the choice of the cluster analysis procedure, the distance measure, the number of clusters, and the data mode to be clustered.

While there is some more or less sophisticated methodological guidance available to decide on some of these factors, it merely depends on the specific research objective for others. For example, there is extensive research on the determination of the number of clusters (Milligan and Cooper 1985; Dimitriadou et al. 2002) or on the stability properties of cluster solutions (Hornik 2004; Hornik 2005). However, the choice of an appropriate clustering procedure or the specific focus on a particular data mode to be compressed is a decision that is determined by the substantive research question or the analysts subjective judgement. Generally speaking, hierarchical linkage methods have their merits when the task is to explore differences and commonalities among objects on a more fine-granular level (e.g., by "zooming in" the representing deondrogram) and the number of clusters is not fixed a priori. On the other hand, partitioning methods like k-centroid clustering tend to be the preferred method when the analyst aims at compressing larger data sets into a smaller number of representing points (centroids or prototypes), each characterizing a subset of the data as accurately as possible and simultaneously are distinctive from the other cluster centroids.

Using a widely used benchmark set of market basket data, we demonstrated in this chapter that the analytical task of exploring the specific structures of cross-category purchase relationships can be achieved by reducing the dimensionality of the data set using hierarchical clustering (i.e., by analyzing the (dis)similarity structure among the variables of the data matrix). We have also shown that the derived structural patterns strongly depend on the specific method applied and they would also vary if we chose a different distance metric. On the other hand, compressing the number of baskets using nonhierarchical partitioning methods results in a set of specific classes of shopping baskets with distinguished complementary cross-category purchase incidences within the classes. The latter effect is obtained by choosing an appropriate distance measure (in our case Jaccard distances) and the partitioning as well as the interpretation of the classes which would be different for other distance metrics. All these examples demonstrate the generic idea behind cluster analysis as an exploratory data compression tool. This "idea" is to uncover structure in the data, which in the case of distance-based clustering is based on a specific conceptual understanding of quantifying proximity between data points.

The field of cluster analysis is a very dynamic one and the analysts' toolbox is constantly growing. New methods which aim to cope with the specific challenges of today's data-rich environments are emerging. Such challenges are not limited to but include real-time (online) updating of cluster solutions for data streams (Ghesmoune et al. 2016), clustering of very high dimensional data sets (Strehl and Ghosh 2003), bootstrap aggregated clustering (Dolnicar and Leisch 2003), and other ensemble methods to improve the quality and robustness of cluster solutions (Hornik 2004;

Hornik 2005); see also the extension package `clue` for R (R Core Team 2019) which provides a computational environment for cluster ensembles.

Modern clustering methods also comprise a variety of unsupervised machine learning methods (for an overview, see Hastie et al. 2009). Marketing applications of such machine learning methodologies include the employment of vector quantization techniques (e.g., Decker 2005; Reutterer et al. 2006), neural networks (e.g., Hruschka and Natter 1986; Mazanec 1999; Reutterer and Natter 2000), topic models for "soft-clustering" unstructured texts (e.g., Tirunillai and Tellis 2014; Büschken and Allenby 2016), or graph partitioning methods (Netzer et al. 2012).

Cross-References

▶ Finite Mixture Models
▶ Market Segmentation

References

Adams, R. A., & Fournier, J. J. (2003). *Sobolev spaces* (Pure and applied mathematics) (Vol. 140). Amsterdam: Elsevier.

Aldenderfer, M. S., & Blashfield, R. K. (1984). *Cluster analysis*. Beverly Hills: Sage.

Anderberg, M. R. (1973). *Cluster analysis for applications*. New York: Academic.

Arabie, P., & Lawrence, J. H. (1994). Cluster analysis in marketing research. In R. P. Bagozzi (Ed.), *Advanced methods of marketing research* (pp. 160–189). Cambridge, MA: Blackwell.

Arabie, P., & Lawrence, J. H. (1996). *An overview of combinatorial data analysis. Clustering and classification* (pp. 5–63). Singapore: World Scientific.

Arabie, P., Carroll, J. D., DeSarbo, W., & Wind, J. (1981). Overlapping clustering: A new method for product positioning. *Journal of Marketing Research, 28*(3), 310–317.

Bock, H. H. (1974). *Automatische Klassifikation*. Göttingen: Vandenhoeck & Ruprecht.

Boztuğ, Y., & Reutterer, T. (2008). A combined approach for segment-specific market basket analysis. *European Journal of Operational Research, 187*(1), 294–312.

Breugelmans, E., Boztuğ, Y., & Reutterer, T. (2010). A multistep approach to derive targeted category promotions. Working paper series of the Marketing Science Institute, MSI report no. 10-118, Cambridge, MA.

Büschken, J., & Allenby, G. M. (2016). Sentence-based text analysis for customer reviews. *Marketing Science, 35*(6), 953–975.

Cattell, R. B. (1943). The description of personality: Basic traits resolved into clusters. *Journal of Abnormal and Social Psychology, 38*(4), 476–506.

Chapman, C., & McDonnell Feit, E. (2019). *Segmentation: Clustering and classification. R for marketing research and analytics* (pp. 299–338). New York: Springer.

Davies, D. L., & Bouldin, D. W. (1979). A cluster separation measure. *IEEE Transactions on Pattern Analysis and Machine Intelligence, 1*(2), 224–227.

Decker, R. (2005). Market basket analysis by means of a growing neural network. *The International Review of Retail, Distribution and Consumer Research, 15*(2), 151–169.

DeSarbo, W. S., Ajay, K. M., & Lalita, A. M. (1993). Non-spatial tree models for the assessment of competitive market structure: An integrated review of the marketing and psychometric literature. In J. Eliashberg & G. L. Lilien (Eds.), *Handbooks in operations research and management science* (Vol. 5, pp. 193–257). Amsterdam: Elsevier.

Dimitriadou, E., Dolničar, S., & Weingessel, A. (2002). An examination of indexes for determining the number of clusters in binary data sets. *Psychometrika, 67*(1), 137–159.

Dolnicar, S., & Leisch, F. (2003). Winter tourist segments in Austria: Identifying stable vacation styles using bagged clustering techniques. *Journal of Travel Research, 41*(3), 281–292.

Dolnicar, S., Grün, B., Leisch, F., & Schmidt, K. (2014). Required sample sizes for data-driven market segmentation analyses in tourism. *Journal of Travel Research, 53*(3), 296–306.

Dolnicar, S., Grün, B., & Leisch, F. (2018). *Market segmentation analysis. Understanding it, doing it, and making it useful.* Singapore: Springer.

Dréze, X., & Hoch, S. J. (1998). Exploiting the installed base using cross-merchandising and category destination programs. *International Journal of Research in Marketing, 15*(5), 459–471.

Everitt, B. S., Landau, S., Leese, M., & Stahl, D. (2011). *Cluster analysis: Wiley series in probability and statistics.* New York: Wiley.

Farris, J. S. (1969). On the cophenetic correlation coefficient. *Systematic Zoology, 18*(3), 279–285.

Fraley, C., & Raftery, A. E. (2002). Model-based clustering, discriminant analysis, and density estimation. *Journal of the American Statistical Association, 97*(458), 611–631.

Fraley, C., & Raftery, A. E. (2003). Enhanced model-based clustering, density estimation, and discriminant analysis software: MCLUST. *Journal of Classification, 20*(2), 263–286.

Frühwirth-Schnatter, S. (2006). *Finite mixture and Markov switching models.* New York: Springer Science & Business Media.

Ghesmoune, M., Lebbah, M., & Azzag, H. (2016). State-of-the-art on clustering data streams. *Big Data Analytics, 1*(13), 1–27.

Grover, R., & Srinivasan, V. (1987). A simultaneous approach to market segmentation and market structuring. *Journal of Marketing Research, 24*, 139–153.

Hartigan, J. A. (1975). *Clustering algorithms.* New York: Wiley.

Hartigan, J. A., & Wong, M. A. (1979). Algorithm AS 136: A k-means clustering algorithm. *Journal of the Royal Statistical Society: Series C: Applied Statistics, 28*(1), 100–108.

Hastie, T., Tibshirani, R., & Friedman, J. (2009). Unsupervised learning. In *The elements of statistical learning* (pp. 485–585). New York: Springer.

Hennig, C., Meila, M., Murtagh, F., & Rocci, R. (2015). *Handbook of cluster analysis.* Boca Raton/London/New York: CRC Press.

Hornik, K. (2004). Cluster ensembles. In C. Weihs, W. Gaul (Eds.), *Classification – The ubiquitous challenge. Proceedings of the 28th annual conference of the Gesellschaft für Klassifikation E.V* (pp. 65–72). Heidelberg: University of Dortmund/Springer.

Hornik, K. (2005). A clue for cluster ensembles. *Journal of Statistical Software, 14*(12), 1–25.

Hruschka, H. (1986). Market definition and segmentation using fuzzy clustering methods. *International Journal of Research in Marketing, 3*(2), 117–134.

Hruschka, H., & Natter, M. (1986). Comparing performance of feedforward neural nets and K-means for cluster-based market segmentation. *European Journal of Operational Research, 114*(2), 346–353.

Jain, A. K., & Dubes, R. C. (1988). *Algorithms for clustering data.* Upper Saddle River: Prentice-Hall.

Kaufman, L., & Rousseeuw, P. J. (1990). *Finding groups in data: An introduction to cluster analysis.* Hoboken: Wiley.

Leisch, F. (2006). A toolbox for k-centroids cluster analysis. *Computational Statistics & Data Analysis, 51*(2), 526–544.

MacQueen, J. (1967). Some methods for classification and analysis of multivariate observations. *Proceedings of the Fifth Berkeley Symposium on Mathematical Statistics and Probability, 1*(14), 281–297.

Manchanda, P., Ansari, A., & Gupta, S. (1999). The "shopping basket": A model for multicategory purchase incidence decisions. *Marketing Science, 18*(2), 95–114.

Mazanec, J. A. (1999). Simultaneous positioning and segmentation analysis with topologically ordered feature maps: A tour operator example. *Journal of Retailing and Customer Services, 6*(4), 219–235.

Mazanec, J. A., & Strasser, H. (2000). *A nonparametric approach to perceptions-based market segmentation: Foundations* (Vol. 1). Wien: Springer.

McLachlan, G. J., & Basford, K. E. (1988). *Mixture models: Inference and applications to clustering.* New York: Marcel Dekker.

Mild, A., & Reutterer, T. (2003). An improved collaborative filtering approach for predicting cross-category purchases based on binary market basket data. *Journal of Retailing and Consumer Services, 10*(3), 123–133.

Milligan, G. W., & Cooper, M. C. (1985). An examination of procedures for determining the number of clusters in a data set. *Psychometrika, 50*(2), 159–179.

Mooi, E., Sarstedt, M., & Mooi-Reci, I. (2018). Data. In *Market research* (pp. 27–50). Singapore: Springer.

Netzer, O., Feldman, R., Goldenberg, J., & Fresko, M. (2012). Mine your own business: Market-structure surveillance through text mining. *Marketing Science, 31*(3), 521–543.

Ng, R. T., & Han, J. (2002). CLARANS: A method for clustering objects for spatial data mining. *IEEE Transactions on Knowledge and Data Engineering, 14*(5), 1003–1016.

Punj, G., & Stewart, D. W. (1983). Cluster analysis in marketing research: Review and suggestions for application. *Journal of Marketing Research, 20*(2), 134–148.

R Core Team. (2019). *R: A language and environment for statistical computing. R Foundation for Statistical Computing.* Vienna: R Development Core Team.

Rand, W. M. (1971). Objective criteria for the evaluation of clustering methods. *Journal of the American Statistical Association, 66*, 846850.

Rao, V. R., & Sabavala, D. J. (1981). Inference of hierarchical choice processes from panel data. *Journal of Consumer Research, 8*(1), 85–96.

Reutterer, T. (1998). Competitive market structure and segmentation analysis with self-organizing feature maps. In P. Anderson (Ed.), *Proceedings of the 27th EMAC conference. Track 5: Marketing research* (pp. 85–105). Stockholm: EMAC.

Reutterer, T. (2003). Bestandsaufnahme und aktuelle Entwicklungen bei der Segmentierungsanalyse von Produktmarkten. *Journal für Betriebswirtschaft, 53*(2), 52–74.

Reutterer, T., & Natter, M. (2000). Segmentation-based competitive analysis with MULTICLUS and topology representing networks. *Computers & Operations Research, 27*(11–12), 1227–1247.

Reutterer, T., Mild, A., Natter, M., & Taudes, A. (2006). A dynamic segmentation approach for targeting and customizing direct marketing campaigns. *Journal of Interactive Marketing, 20*(3–4), 43–57.

Reutterer, T., Hahsler, M., & Hornik, K. (2007). Data mining und marketing am beispiel der explorativen warenkorbanalyse. *Marketing ZFP, 29*(3), 163–180.

Reutterer, T., Hornik, K., March, N., & Gruber, K. (2017). A data mining framework for targeted category promotions. *Journal of Business Economics, 87*(3), 337–358.

Rousseeuw, P. J. (1987). Silhouettes: A graphical aid to the interpretation and validation of cluster analysis. *Journal of Computational and Applied Mathematics, 20*, 53–65.

Russell, G. J., & Petersen, A. (2000). Analysis of cross category dependence in market basket selection. *Journal of Retailing, 76*(3), 367–392.

Russell, G. J., Ratneshwar, S., Schocker, A. D., Bell, D., Bodapat, A., Degeratu, A., Hildebrandt, L., Kim, N., Ramaswami, S., & Shankar, V. H. (1999). Multiple-category decision-making: Review and synthesis. *Marketing Letters, 10*(3), 319–332.

Saraçli, S., Doğan, N., & Doğan, I. (2013). Comparison of hierarchical cluster analysis methods by cophenetic correlation. *Journal of Inequalities and Applications, 2013*(1), 203.

Sneath, P. H. (1957). Some thoughts on bacterial classification. *Journal of General Microbiology, 17*, 184–200.

Sokal, R. R., & Sneath, P. H. A. (1963). *Principles of numerical taxonomy* (A series of books in biology). San Francisco: W.H. Freeman.

Späth, H. (1977). *Cluster-analyse – Algorithmen zur Objektklassifizierung und Datenreduktion* (2nd ed.). München/Wien: Oldenbourg Wissenschaftsverlag.

Srivastava, R. K., Leone, R. P., & Shocker, A. D. (1981). Market structure analysis: Hierarchical clustering of products based on substitution-in-use. *Journal of Marketing, 45*(3), 38–48.

Srivastava, R. K., Alpert, M. I., & Shocker, A. D. (1984). A customer-oriented approach for determining market structures. *Journal of Marketing, 48*(2), 32–45.

Strasser, H. (2000). Reduction of complexity. In J. Mazanec & H. Strasser (Eds.), *A nonparametric approach to perceptions-based market segmentation: Foundations* (pp. 99–140). Wien/New York: Springer.

Strehl, A., & Ghosh, J. (2003). Relationship-based clustering and visualization for high-dimensional data mining. *INFORMS Journal on Computing, 15*(2), 208–230.

Struyf, A., Hubert, M., & Rousseeuw, P. (1996). Clustering in an object-oriented environment. *Journal of Statistical Software, 1*(4), 1.

Tirunillai, S., & Tellis, G. J. (2014). Mining marketing meaning from online chatter: Strategic brand analysis of big data using Latent Dirichlet allocation. *Journal of Marketing Research, 51*(4), 463–479.

Titterington, D. M., Smith, A. F. M., & Makov, U. E. (1985). *Statistical analysis of finite mixture distributions*. Chichester: Wiley.

Ward, J. H. (1963). Hierarchical grouping to optimize an objective function. *Journal of the American Statistical Association, 58*, 236–244.

Wedel, M., & Kamakura, W. A. (2000). *Market segmentation – Conceptual and methodological foundations*. New York: Springer.

Finite Mixture Models

Sonja Gensler

Contents

Introduction 252
Basic Idea of Finite Mixture Models 253
   Illustrative Example 253
   Finite Mixture Model and Likelihood Function 254
   Probability to Observe a Specific Value of the Segmentation Variable and Mixed
   Density Function 256
   Assignment of Consumers/Objects to Segments Within Finite Mixture Models 257
   Determining the Number of Segments 258
Popular Applications of Finite Mixture Models in Multivariate Methods of Analysis 260
Conclusion 261
References 263

Abstract

Finite Mixture models are a state-of-the-art technique of segmentation. Next to segmenting consumers or objects based on multiple different variables, Finite Mixture models can be used in conjunction with multivariate methods of analysis. Unlike approaches combining multivariate methods of analysis and cluster analysis, which require a two-step approach, the parameters are then directly estimated at the segment level. This also allows for inferential statistical analysis. This book chapter explains the basic idea of Finite Mixture models and describes some popular applications of Finite Mixture models in market research.

S. Gensler (✉)
Marketing Center Münster – Institute for Value-based Marketing, University of Münster, Münster, Germany
e-mail: s.gensler@uni-muenster.de

© Springer Nature Switzerland AG 2022
C. Homburg et al. (eds), *Handbook of Market Research*,
https://doi.org/10.1007/978-3-319-57413-4_12

Keywords

Finite Mixture models · Latent class analysis · Segmentation · Maximum likelihood estimation · Multivariate methods

Introduction

Finite Mixture models are segmentation approaches (in this article, we make no distinction between Finite Mixture and Latent Class models). Segmentation considers heterogeneity among consumers/objects and is crucial for developing marketing strategies. For example, marketing managers may want to know whether there are groups of consumers who exhibit similar shopping behaviors or share particular preferences for product features. Such knowledge offers opportunities to target specific groups of consumers and to develop targeted products and services.

Cluster analysis has traditionally been used to identify groups of consumers who are similar with respect to some specified variables (e.g., shopping behavior, attitude, preferences) – either on its own or in combination with multivariate methods of analysis in a two-step procedure. An example for the latter is the use of a conjoint study to elicit consumers' preferences and the subsequent implementation of a cluster analysis with the estimated preferences as segmentation variables (Green and Krieger 1991).

In recent years, Finite Mixture models have gained popularity as alternative approaches for segmentation. What are advantages of Finite Mixture models compared to traditional clustering approaches? A Finite Mixture model is a *model-based approach*. This means that a statistical model is assumed for the population from which the data stems from. Specifically, it is postulated that a *mixture* of underlying probability distributions generates the data. The assumption of an underlying statistical model has important consequences. Finite Mixture models aim to recover the actual observations in the dataset, while traditional cluster approaches just intent to find homogenous groups of consumers/objects that are distinct from each other (heterogeneity across groups). Thus, *goodness-of-fit measures* for Finite Mixture models are available and support the confidence in the obtained solution. Moreover, *rigorous statistical criteria* help the researcher to identify the most appropriate segment structure in the market. In contrast, researchers use rather arbitrary criteria (e.g., dendrogram) to decide on the number of segments when using traditional cluster analyses (Magidson and Vermunt 2002). Another advantage of Finite Mixture models is that they reduce the experiment-wise error. If traditional cluster approaches are combined with multivariate methods of analysis, a two-step approach is implemented (see example above). Such two-step processes inflate experiment-wise error since there are two different objective functions that are optimized. Finite Mixture models allow for formulating a model that incorporates the identification of segments in the original analysis. That means, instead of separately conducting two different types of analysis and optimizing two different objective functions, one objective function is formulated (*one-step approach*). Finally, Finite Mixture models are flexible in the sense that variables measured at different scales can be considered. These advantages have contributed to the increasing popularity of Finite Mixture models in market research.

It is the aim of this book chapter to illustrate the basic idea of Finite Mixture models and to discuss how Finite Mixture models can be combined with different multivariate methods of analysis. Finally, the book chapter refers to some specific applications in academic literature.

Basic Idea of Finite Mixture Models

Illustrative Example

A simple example should help to illustrate the basic idea of Finite Mixture models. We observe the purchase frequency of chocolate bars for 450 consumers (see Fig. 1; example adapted from Dillon and Kumar 1994).

Before considering the Finite Mixture model approach, we have a look at the solution derived from traditional cluster analysis.

In this example, the observed purchase frequency serves as the segmentation variable. Traditionally, the researcher would start with running a hierarchical cluster analysis to determine the number of segments. When we use Ward's algorithm, we conclude that there are three segments in the data. We use this information to conduct a K-means clustering, and we find that the three segments have purchase frequencies of 0.74, 4.64, and 12.50, respectively. With K-means clustering each consumer is assigned to one specific segment based on his/her purchase frequency. In this example, the relative segment sizes are 45%, 41%, and 14%. Figure 2 illustrates the result graphically. Obviously, the K-means solution does not represent the observed purchase frequencies well. One reason is the deterministic assignment of consumers to segments.

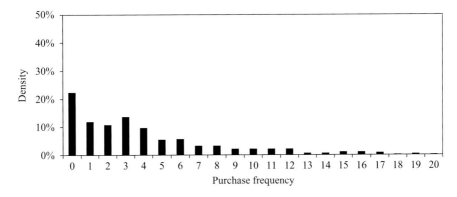

Fig. 1 Density function of the observed purchase frequencies of chocolate bars

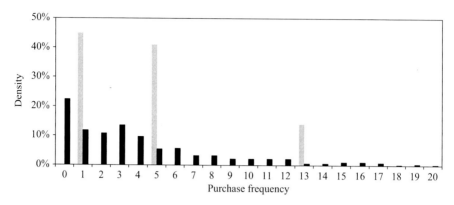

Fig. 2 Density function of the observed purchase frequencies and K-means result for three segments (chocolate bar example)

Finite Mixture Model and Likelihood Function

In the following, the basic idea of the Finite Mixture approach is illustrated. The Finite Mixture approach is a model-based approach and assumes that any observation of one or more variables of interest (i.e., segmentation variable(s)) stems from an underlying density function. In this example, we use again the purchase frequency for the segmentation. Purchase frequency is a count variable, and, thus, the Poisson distribution serves as the underlying density function. The observed density function (see Fig. 1) results from two or more segment-specific density functions that are *mixed*. The segment-specific density functions stem from the same distribution and only differ in their characteristic parameters. That means, we observe multiple Poisson distributions that differ in their means. The objective is now to *unmix* (separate) the density functions of the observations to identify the segment-specific density functions (Green et al. 1976).

The density function of the Poisson distribution is:

$$g(y|\mu) = \frac{\mu^y}{y!} \cdot \exp(-\mu) \tag{1}$$

where

g(): density function
y: value of the variable of interest (here: observed purchase frequency)
μ: mean value of the Poisson distribution

In order to identify the segment-specific density functions of the Finite Mixture model, we formulate a likelihood function:

$$L = \prod_{h \in H} \prod_{s \in S} \hat{\eta}_s^{\lambda_{h,s}} \hat{g}_{h|s}(y_h|\hat{\mu}_s)^{\lambda_{h,s}} \tag{2}$$

where

$\hat{\eta}_s$: estimated relative size of segment s

$\lambda_{h,s}$: indicator variable for segment membership of consumer h to segment s

$$\lambda_{h,s} = \begin{cases} 1, \text{if consumer } h \text{ belongs to segment } s, \\ 0 \text{ otherwise.} \end{cases}$$

$\hat{g}_{h|s}(\ )$: estimated conditional density function of consumer h if this consumer is a member of segment s

y_h: value of the variable of interest for consumer h (here: purchase frequency of consumer h)

$\hat{\mu}_s$: estimated mean of Poisson distribution for segment s

H: index set of consumers

S: index set of segments

The likelihood function represents the mixture of distributions, and the relative segment size serves as a weighting variable. Moreover, the likelihood function considers an indicator variable that indicates to which segment a consumer belongs. The likelihood function is maximized using iterative optimization algorithms such as the Newton-Raphson algorithm or expectation-maximization (EM) algorithm (Wedel and Kamakura 2000; Wedel and DeSarbo 1994).

The different algorithms require starting values. In this example, we need to set starting values for the segment-specific means of the Poisson distributions and the relative segment sizes. This implies that we also have to specify the number of segments we want to consider. Since we do not know how many segments represent our data, we estimate models with different numbers of segments. To define the starting values for the means of the Poisson distribution and the relative segment sizes, we can use the result of the K-means clustering. However, since the likelihood function is multimodal in nature, we might find a local and not the global maximum of the likelihood function. To circumvent this issue, one should use different starting values.

Table 1 shows the result for a three-segment solution from the maximization of the likelihood function (2), and Fig. 3 shows the segment-specific density functions. (An Excel spreadsheet for the "chocolate bars" example using the Newton-Raphson algorithm can be request from the author).

The estimated means of the segment-specific Poisson distributions and the relative segment sizes differ from the K-means results. A comparison of the

Table 1 Mean values of the segment-specific Poisson distributions and their relative sizes in the "chocolate bars" example

	Mean value of Poisson distribution	Relative size (%)
Segment 1	0.3	27.7
Segment 2	3.5	54.3
Segment 3	11.2	18.0

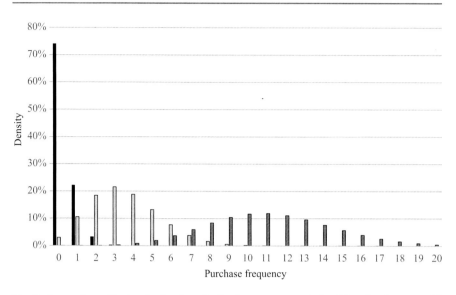

Fig. 3 Segment-specific density functions for the three-segment solution (chocolate bar example)

ln-likelihood values (natural logarithm of the value of Eq. 2) for each solution allows assessing which set of estimated parameters reflects the observed purchase frequencies better. The K-means solution leads to an ln-likelihood of −1,147.70 for Eq. 2, while the Finite Mixture solution results in an ln-likelihood of −1,132.04. Thus, the Finite Mixture solution fits the observed data better.

Probability to Observe a Specific Value of the Segmentation Variable and Mixed Density Function

The segment-specific (conditional) density functions weighted by the estimated relative segment sizes allow deriving the probability to observe a certain value of the purchase frequency. For any individual consumer in the above example, the *unconditional* individual probability to observe his/her purchase frequency is as follows:

$$\hat{g}_h(y_h|\hat{\mu}) = \sum_{s \in S} \hat{\eta}_s \cdot \hat{g}_{h|s}(y_h|\hat{\mu}_s)$$
$$= 0.277 \cdot \frac{0.3^{y_h}}{y_h!} \cdot \exp(-0.3) + 0.543 \cdot \frac{3.5^{y_h}}{y_h!} \cdot \exp(-3.5) \quad (3)$$
$$+ 0.18 \cdot \frac{11.2^{y_h}}{y_h!} \cdot \exp(-11.2) \qquad \forall h \in H$$

For an individual consumer who buys two chocolate bars, this yields, for example, a probability of 0.11. That means, the probability to observe a purchase frequency of

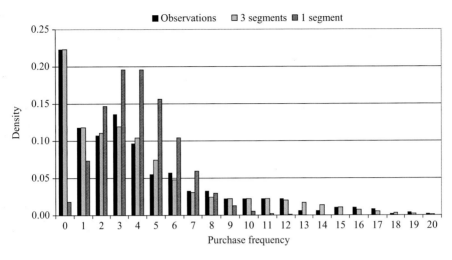

Fig. 4 Density function of the observed purchase frequencies and mixed density functions with one and three segments (chocolate bar example)

two chocolate bars equals 11%. This way, we can compute the probability for every observed value of the purchase frequency. We can use these probabilities to construct the mixed density function (Fig. 4). Figure 4 illustrates that the three-segment solution provides a very good fit with the observed purchase frequencies. Figure 3 also shows the density function for the one-segment solution. In this case, the estimated mean of the Poisson distribution equals 3.99. The one-segment solution does not capture the heterogeneity in purchase frequencies adequately.

Assignment of Consumers/Objects to Segments Within Finite Mixture Models

In contrast to traditional clustering approaches, Finite Mixture models assign consumers to a segment with a certain probability (probabilistic assignment). That means each consumer has a certain probability to belong to a specific segment. This probability is determined based on the estimated relative segment sizes and means of the Poisson distribution. Specifically, the a posteriori probability of segment membership equals

$$\omega_{h,s} = \frac{\hat{\eta}_s \hat{g}_{h|s}(y_h|\hat{\mu}_s)}{\sum_{s \in S} \hat{\eta}_s \hat{g}_{h|s}(y_h|\hat{\mu}_s)} \qquad \forall h \in H, s \in S \qquad (4)$$

where

$\omega_{h,s}$: probability that consumer h belongs to segment s

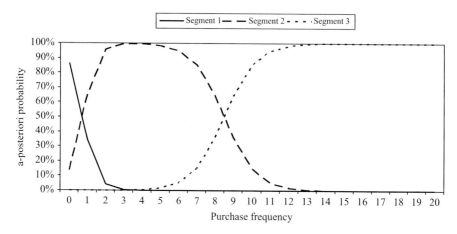

Fig. 5 Relation between purchase frequency and a posteriori probability of segment membership

The following conditions need to hold:

$$0 \leq \omega_{h,s} \leq 1 \qquad \forall h \in H, s \in S \qquad (5)$$

$$\sum_{s \in S} \omega_{h,s} = 1 \qquad \forall h \in H \qquad (6)$$

The a posteriori probability considers the probability to observe the actual purchase frequency given that a consumer belongs to a specific segments and weighs this probability with the relative size of the segment. For managerial purposes, the consumer is 'assigned' to the segment for which he/she has the highest a posteriori probability of segment membership.

Figure 5 shows the relationship between the observed purchase frequency of a consumer and his/her a posteriori probability of segment membership. For example, Fig. 5 illustrates that a consumer who buys four chocolate bars has a posteriori probability of segment membership that is close to one for segment 2. Thus, this consumer would be assigned to segment 2, which is characterized by a mean purchase frequency of 3.5 ("medium buyers"). In contrast, a consumer who buys 14 chocolate bars belongs to segment 3 with probability almost equal to one. Segment 3 represents the "heavy buyers" of chocolate bars (mean = 11.2).

Determining the Number of Segments

The most critical decision when conducting a segmentation analysis is to determine the number of segments. Traditional clustering approaches use rather arbitrary criteria to make this decision. In Finite Mixture models, statistical decision criteria are available. These criteria use the model fit and a posteriori segment membership probability to determine the number of segments.

The most prominent criteria are the so-called *information criteria*. The information criteria use the deviance (i.e., $-2\ln L$ of the estimated model) which reflects the model fit and a *penalty factor*. The penalty factors take the number of estimated parameters and/or observations into account. The lower the value for the information criterion the better. Thus, when comparing two models that differ with respect to the number of segments, the researcher selects the model with the lower value for the information criterion. The idea behind is that the deviance decreases when more segments are considered since an increasing number of segments improves the flexibility, that is, it becomes easier to capture the nature of the observed data. However, increasing the number of segments results in an increasing number of parameters and less degrees of freedom. The decreasing degrees of freedom should be taken into account when making a decision of which model is most appropriate (similar to adjusted R^2 in OLS regression analysis). In the following, different popular information criteria are described.

The Akaike's information criterion (AIC) suggests using two times the number of estimated parameters as a penalty factor (Bozdogan 1987; McLachlan and Peel 2001, p. 203):

$$AIC(S) = -2\ln L + 2|K| \tag{7}$$

where

$|K|$: number of elements in the index set of estimated parameters

The modified Akaike information criterion (also called AIC3) uses a penalty factor of three. The number of estimated parameters has a stronger negative effect (Andrews and Currim 2003a):

$$AIC3(S) = -2\ln L + 3|K| \tag{8}$$

Consistent Akaike information criterion (CAIC) and the Bayesian information criterion (BIC) consider the number of observations in addition to the number of estimated parameters (Wedel and Kamakura 2000, p. 92):

$$CAIC(S) = -2\ln L + (\ln(|H||I|) + 1)|K| \tag{9}$$

$$BIC(S) = -2\ln L + (\ln(|H||I|))|K| \tag{10}$$

where

$|H|$: number of elements in the index set of consumers

$|I|$: number of elements in the index set of observations for each consumer

There is no single best information criterion. Several simulation studies indicate the weaknesses of the different information criteria in certain settings. The studies suggest that the AIC tends to overestimate the number of segments (Ramaswamy et al. 1993). Andrews and Currim (2003a, b) suggested that AIC3 is an appropriate criterion in many settings – especially with smaller sample sizes. With large samples ($n > 300$), BIC and CAIC perform well (Andrews and Currim 2003a). Sarstedt et al. (2011) find that AIC4 (penalty factor of 4) performs generally better than BIC and

CAIC. Given these ambiguous results, a researcher may want to discuss multiple information criteria and argue for a certain solution using also alternative criteria.

An alternative criterion is the entropy. The entropy metric considers the a posteriori segment membership probability:

$$\text{Entropy} = 1 + \frac{\sum_{h \in H}\sum_{s \in S} \omega_{h,s} \ln \omega_{h,s}}{|H| \ln |S|} \tag{11}$$

where
$|S|$: number of segments

The entropy measure ranges between zero and one. If the a posteriori segment membership probabilities are very similar across all segments, the solution is fuzzy, and the entropy measure would be close to zero. Imagine a three-segment solution and the a posteriori segment membership probability is one third for all consumers for all three segments. In this specific case, the resulting value for the entropy measure equals zero. If the a posteriori segment membership probability is exactly one for one specific segment for all consumers, entropy equals one (Ramaswamy et al. 1993). Thus, the closer the value of the entropy to one, the better solution in the sense that the segments are better separated. A good separation is critical for deriving managerial implications later on.

In addition to these model-based criteria, one should evaluate whether the identified segments are actionable, differentiable, and substantial (e.g., Kotler and Keller 2012). Hence, the finally chosen segment solution might not always be the "best" one in statistical terms.

Popular Applications of Finite Mixture Models in Multivariate Methods of Analysis

A main reason for the popularity of Finite Mixture models is that they can easily be implemented within other multivariate methods of analysis. While segment-level solutions are attractive from a managerial standpoint, multivariate methods of analysis inherently assume either an individual- (e.g., conjoint analysis, multi-dimensional scaling) or aggregate-level of analysis (e.g., logit models, structural equation models).

For multivariate methods that originally perform an individual estimation of the parameters, employing a Finite Mixture model will reduce the variance of the estimated parameters through segment-based estimation. For multivariate methods that originally estimate the parameters at aggregate level (i.e., assuming homogeneity), incorporating the inherent heterogeneity of the consumers into the model can reduce systematic biases in the estimated parameters. Note that ultimately there will always be a trade-off between variance and systematic bias: segment-based estimation rather than individual estimation leads to some systematic bias, as the heterogeneity of the consumers is less accurately captured. On the other hand, performing segment-based estimation rather than aggregate estimation has a negative effect on the variance of the estimated parameters. Nevertheless, a segment-level analysis is attractive from a managerial perspective and builds the basis of many marketing strategies.

Before the advent of Finite Mixture models, researchers used two-step procedures to derive results at the segment level. In case of an original analysis at the individual level, the researcher used the individual-level parameters as segmentation variables in traditional clustering approaches (see, e.g., Green and Krieger 1991). However, this approach ignores that the segmentation variables are estimates in themselves. Moreover, two objective functions are optimized independently, for example, minimizing the squared errors in a regression and minimizing the within-group variance in K-means clustering. In case of an original analysis at the aggregate level, the researcher used a priori segmentation and then estimated the parameters for the predefined segments. This approach requires a thorough knowledge of the source of heterogeneity when defining the segmentation variables.

Implementing the Finite Mixture approach in multivariate methods of analysis leads to the specification of one likelihood function. Thus, there is only one single optimization step and no need of optimizing multiple functions with different and maybe conflicting objectives.

The most popular applications of Finite Mixture models in combination with multivariate methods of analysis are regression analysis (special case: conjoint analysis), logit models (special case: choice-based conjoint analysis), multi-dimensional scaling, and structural equation models. Table 2 lists the advantage of using the Finite Mixture model in combination with the multivariate method of analysis and refers the interested reader to articles that describe the approach in more detail or represent some recent applications of the approach.

Conclusion

Segment-level analyses are particularly useful to managers, as it enables them to target consumers effectively. Finite Mixture models are therefore highly relevant in practice, and software developments, such as LatentGold®, Sawtooth®, or SmartPLS® have supported the increasingly widespread adoption.

Finite Mixture models provide a flexible framework for performing model-based estimations of segment-specific parameters. Combining Finite Mixture models with multivariate methods of analysis makes it possible to estimate segment-specific parameters, segment sizes, and the a posteriori probability of segment membership simultaneously for each consumer. Thus, for multivariate methods of analysis that traditionally operate at an aggregate level (i.e., assuming homogeneity across consumers), a reduction in systematic bias in the estimated parameters can be achieved by considering consumer heterogeneity. For multivariate methods of analysis that traditionally operate at an individual level, estimating segment-specific parameters instead can yield more stable estimates.

Table 2 Overview of main applications of Finite Mixture models in multivariate methods

Multivariate method of analysis	Original level of aggregation	Advantage of using a Finite Mixture model	Description of approach	Exemplary applications
Regression analysis	Aggregate	Reduced systematic bias in the estimated utility parameters	Wedel and DeSarbo (1994)	Decker and Trusov (2010)
				Petersen and Kumar (2015)
				Srinivasan (2006)
Conjoint analysis	Individual	Reduced variance of the estimated utility parameters	DeSarbo et al. (1992)	DeSarbo et al. (1992)
			Kamakura et al. (1994)	
Logit models (choice-based conjoint analysis)	Aggregate	Reduced systematic bias in the estimated utility parameters	DeSarbo et al. (1995)	Papies et al. (2011)
			Natter and Feurstein (2002)	Steiner et al. (2016)
			Kamakura et al. (1994)	Ailawadi et al. (2014)
Multidimensional scaling	Individual	Reduced variance of the estimated utility parameters	DeSarbo et al. (1994)	Natter et al. (2008)
			DeSarbo et al. (1991)	
			DeSarbo and Wu (2001)	
			Wedel and DeSarbo (1996)	
Structural equation modelling	Aggregate	Reduced systematic bias in the estimated utility parameters	Jedidi et al. (1997)	DeSarbo et al. (2006)
			Sarstedt and Ringle (2010)	Haapanen et al. (2016)
				Wilden and Gudergan (2015)

Finite Mixture models are based on a fuzzy partition of the consumers into segments, and they assume that there exists a finite number of segments that are homogenous in themselves. Yet, this assumption is a weakness of the Finite Mixture model approach and has been addressed in research (e.g., Lenk and DeSarbo 2000).

References

Ailawadi, K. L., Gedenk, K., Langer, T., Ma, Y., & Neslin, S. A. (2014). Consumer response to uncertain promotions: An empirical analysis of conditional rebates. *International Journal of Research in Marketing, 31*(1), 94–106.

Andrews, R., & Currim, I. (2003a). A comparison of segment retention criteria for finite mixture logit models. *Journal of Marketing Research, 40*(2), 235–243.

Andrews, R., & Currim, I. (2003b). Retention of latent segments in regression-based marketing models. *International Journal of Research in Marketing, 20*(4), 315–321.

Bozdogan, H. (1987). Model selection and Akaike's Information Criterion (AIC). The general theory and its analytical extensions. *Psychometrika, 52*(3), 345–370.

Decker, R., & Trusov, M. (2010). Estimating aggregate consumer preferences from online product reviews. *International Journal of Research in Marketing, 27*(4), 293–307.

DeSarbo, W., Howard, D., & Jedidi, K. (1991). MULTICLUS: A new method for simultaneously performing multidimensional scaling and cluster analysis. *Psychometrika, 56*(1), 121–136.

DeSarbo, W., Wedel, M., Vriens, M., & Ramaswamy, V. (1992). Latent class metric conjoint analysis. *Marketing Letters, 3*(3), 273–288.

DeSarbo, W., Manrai, A., & Manrai, L. (1994). Latent class multidimensional scaling. A review of recent developments in the marketing and psychometric literature. In R. P. Bagozzi (Ed.), *Advanced methods of marketing research* (pp. 190–222). Cambridge, MA: Blackwell Publishers.

DeSarbo, W., Ramaswamy, V., & Cohen, S. (1995). Market segmentation with choice-based conjoint analysis. *Marketing Letters, 6*(2), 137–147.

DeSarbo, W. S., & Wu, J. (2001). The joint spatial representation of multiple variable batteries collected in marketing research. *Journal of Marketing Research, 38*(2), 244–253.

DeSarbo, W., Di Benedetto, C., Jedidi, K., & Song, M. (2006). Identifying sources of heterogeneity for empirically deriving strategic types: A constrained finite-mixture structural-equation methodology. *Management Science, 52*(6), 909–924.

Dillon, W. R., & Kumar, A. (1994). Latent structure and other mixture models in marketing: An integrative survey and overview. In R. P. Bagozzi (Ed.), *Advanced methods for marketing research* (pp. 295–351). Cambridge, MA: Blackwell Publishers.

Green, P., & Krieger, A. (1991). Segmenting markets with conjoint analysis. *Journal of Marketing, 55*(4), 20–31.

Green, P., Carmone, F., & Wachspress, D. (1976). Consumer segmentation via latent class analysis. *Journal of Consumer Research, 3*(3), 170–174.

Haapanen, L., Juntunen, M., & Juntunen, J. (2016). Firms' capability portfolios throughout international expansion: A latent class approach. *Journal of Business Research, 69*(12), 5578–5586.

Jedidi, K., Jagpal, H., & DeSarbo, W. (1997). Finite mixture structural equation models for response-based segmentation and unobserved heterogeneity. *Marketing Science, 16*(1), 39–59.

Kamakura, W. A., Wedel, M., & Agrawal, J. (1994). Concomitant variable latent class models for conjoint analysis. *International Journal of Research in Marketing, 11*(5), 451–464.

Kotler, P. T., & Keller, K. L. (2012). *Marketing Management*. Pearson.

Lenk, P., & DeSarbo, W. (2000). Bayesian inference for finite mixtures of generalized linear models with random effects. *Psychometrika, 65*(1), 93–119.

Magidson, J., & Vermunt, J. K. (2002). Latent class models for clustering: A comparison with K-means. *Canadian Journal of Marketing Research, 20*, 36–43.

McLachlan, G., & Peel, D. (2001). *Finite mixture models*. New York: Wiley.

Natter, M., & Feurstein, M. (2002). Real world performance of choice-based conjoint models. *European Journal of Operational Research, 137*(2), 448–458.

Natter, M., Mild, A., Wagner, U., & Taudes, A. (2008). Planning new tariffs at tele.ring: The application and impact of an integrated segmentation, targeting, and positioning tool. *Marketing Science, 27*(4), 600–609.

Papies, D., Eggers, F., & Wlömert, N. (2011). Music for free? How free ad-funded downloads affect consumer choice. *Journal of the Academy of Marketing Science, 39*(5), 777–794.

Petersen, A., & Kumar, V. (2015). Perceived risk, product returns, and optimal resource allocation: Evidence from a field experiment. *Journal of Marketing Research, 52*(2), 268–285.

Ramaswamy, V., DeSarbo, W., Reibstein, D., & Robinson, W. (1993). An empirical pooling approach for estimating marketing mix elasticities with PIMS data. *Marketing Science, 12*(1), 103–124.

Sarstedt, M., & Ringle, C. M. (2010). Treating unobserved heterogeneity in PLS path modeling: A comparison of FIMIX-PLS with different data analysis strategies. *Journal of Applied Statistics, 37*(8), 1299–1318.

Sarstedt, M., Becker, J.-M., Ringle, C., & Schwaiger, M. (2011). Uncovering and treating unobserved heterogeneity with FIMIX-PLS: Which model selection criterion provides an appropriate number of segments? *Schmalenbach Business Review, 63*, 34–62.

Srinivasan, R. (2006). Dual distribution and intangible firm value: Franchising in restaurant chains. *Journal of Marketing, 70*(3), 120–135.

Steiner, M., Wiegand, N., Eggert, A., & Backhaus, K. (2016). Platform adoption in system markets: The roles of preference heterogeneity and consumer expectations. *International Journal of Research in Marketing, 33*(2), 276–296.

Wedel, M., & DeSarbo, W. (1994). A review of recent developments in latent class regression models. In R. P. Bagozzi (Ed.), *Advanced methods of marketing research* (pp. 352–388). Cambridge, MA: Blackwell Publishers.

Wedel, M., & DeSarbo, W. (1996). An exponential-family multidimensional scaling mixture methodology. *Journal of Business & Economic Statistics, 14*(4), 447–459.

Wedel, M., & Kamakura, W. (2000). *Market segmentation. Conceptual and methodological foundations*. Norwell: Kluwer.

Wilden, R., & Gudergan, S. (2015). The impact of dynamic capabilities on operational marketing and technological capabilities: Investigating the role of environmental turbulence. *Journal of the Academy of Marketing Science, 43*(2), 181–199.

Analysis of Variance

Jan R. Landwehr

Contents

Introduction 266
Between-Subjects: One Observation per Person 268
    Two Means: One-Factorial ANOVA or Independent-Samples *t*-Test 268
    More Than Two Means: One-Factorial ANOVA 274
    Multiplicative Effects: Factorial ANOVA 277
Within-Subjects: Two or More Observations per Person 285
    Two Means: One-Factorial RM-ANOVA or Paired-Samples *t*-Test 286
    More Than Two Means: One-Factorial RM-ANOVA 288
    Multiplicative Effects: Factorial RM-ANOVA/Mixed-ANOVA 289
Extensions 291
    Analysis of Covariance (ANCOVA) 291
    Multivariate Analysis of Variance (MANOVA) 292
Conclusion 293
References 296

Abstract

Experiments are becoming increasingly important in marketing research. Suppose a company has to decide which of three potential new brand logos should be used in the future. An experiment in which three groups of participants rate their liking of one of the logos would provide the necessary information to make this decision. The statistical challenge is to determine which (if any) of the three logos is liked significantly more than the others. The adequate statistical technique to

---

Electronic supplementary material: The online version of this chapter (https://doi.org/10.1007/978-3-319-57413-4_16) contains supplementary material, which is available to authorized users.

J. R. Landwehr (✉)
Marketing Department, Goethe University Frankfurt, Frankfurt, Germany
e-mail: landwehr@wiwi.uni-frankfurt.de

© Springer Nature Switzerland AG 2022
C. Homburg et al. (eds), *Handbook of Market Research*,
https://doi.org/10.1007/978-3-319-57413-4_16

assess the statistical significance of such mean differences between groups of participants is called analysis of variance (ANOVA). The present chapter provides an introduction to the key statistical principles of ANOVA and compares this method to the closely related t-test, which can alternatively be used if exactly two means need to be compared. Moreover, it provides introductions to the key variants of ANOVA that have been developed for use when participants are exposed to more than one experimental condition (repeated-measures ANOVA), when more than one dependent variable is measured (multivariate ANOVA), or when a continuous control variable is considered (analysis of covariance). This chapter is intended to provide an applied introduction to ANOVA and its variants. Therefore, it is accompanied by an exemplary dataset and self-explanatory command scripts for the statistical software packages R and SPSS, which can be found in the Web-Appendix.

Keywords

ANOVA · ANCOVA · RM-ANOVA · MANOVA · Mixed-ANOVA · Split-plot ANOVA · t-test · GLM · Experimental design · F-distribution · Between-subjects · Within-subjects · Mean comparison · Sum of squares · Effect size · Confidence intervals · Effect coding · Simple effects · Disordinal interaction · Crossover interaction · R · SPSS

Introduction

The term analysis of variance (ANOVA) refers to a family of statistical methods that are closely linked to the analysis of experimental data where a continuous outcome variable (i.e., dependent variable, DV) is explained by one or more experimental factors with discrete levels (i.e., independent variable(s), IVs). For instance, if a company conducts an experiment in which consumers have to rate their liking of an emotional advertisement or a reason-based advertisement for the same product, ANOVA can be used to determine whether the mean liking ratings (the DV) of the two types of advertisements (the IV) differ significantly. To determine whether a significant mean difference is present, ANOVA follows an indirect testing strategy rather than directly comparing the means. In particular, it compares the explained part of the variance in the data (i.e., the systematic variance) to the unexplained part of the variance (i.e., the error variance) and determines whether the explained part of the variance is significantly larger. ANOVA thus compares the relative size of the variances, which gives the approach its name.

The general structure of the present chapter follows a crucial distinction of experimental design: between-subjects and within-subjects. In a between-subjects design, the experimental variable is manipulated such that each participant is only exposed to one level of the independent variable. In the earlier advertisement example, this would mean that a participant is randomly assigned to either the emotional or the reason-based advertisement, and the means of these two groups of participants are compared. In contrast, in a within-subjects design, the independent variable is manipulated within each participant such that a participant is exposed to both versions of the advertisement and must provide two judgments. These judgments are compared across all participants using an extension of ANOVA called repeated-measures analysis of variance (RM-ANOVA). The differences between these two approaches and their respective statistical advantages and disadvantages are discussed in the second part of this chapter.

For both between- and within-subjects designs, three versions of ANOVA models will be discussed: a simple comparison of two means, a slightly more complicated version with three means, and the simultaneous examination of two IVs and their interactive effect on a DV (each IV with two levels, resulting in $2 \times 2 = 4$ means to compare). It is important to note that the naming of an ANOVA model depends on the number of factors considered (in the terminology of ANOVA, the terms factor and IV can be used interchangeably). A model with just one factor is called a one-way ANOVA, a model with two factors is called a two-way ANOVA, and so forth (there are few ANOVA models with more than three factors because such models are very hard to interpret). After an extensive discussion of these ANOVA models, this chapter ends with a brief introduction to two variants of ANOVA: analysis of covariance (ANCOVA), where in addition to IVs with discrete levels, continuous IVs are included in the ANOVA model, and multivariate analysis of variance (MANOVA), which is used to analyze several DVs at the same time.

To provide an easy access to these ANOVA models, the presentation of the theory behind these models will be accompanied by an exemplary dataset. The dataset is simulated and is based on a series of hypothetical market research experiments. The parameters used to simulate the data ensure that we obtain statistically significant results throughout the chapter. It is important to note that real studies do usually not produce such a perfect pattern of results. Moreover, for ease of presentation, the results of all market research experiments are saved within only one dataset, as if each participant took part in all experiments. In reality, one would rather use different samples of participants for different experiments and would hence save the data to different data files. Throughout the chapter, names printed in *italics* refer to the variable names of this exemplary dataset.

All analyses described in this chapter were conducted using the statistical software R. This powerful statistical software is free of charge and is continuously improved and extended by world-leading statisticians on an open-access basis. The downside is that it is not as easy to use as menu-based statistical software, such as SPSS. To provide a versatile applied introduction to ANOVA, the Web-Appendix contains the simulated dataset and all R scripts used for the analyses described in this chapter in addition to a corresponding SPSS syntax file with explanatory comments.

Table 1 Experimental conditions of Study 1

Condition (1) Simple font	Condition (2) Complex font
BUYCYCLE	BUYCYCLE

Note: All imaginary bicycle brand logos used in this text are designed by Veronika König (www.nachtundtag.com)

For ease of recognition, the R commands used throughout this chapter are printed in `Courier New`.

Between-Subjects: One Observation per Person

Two Means: One-Factorial ANOVA or Independent-Samples *t*-Test

Let us start with a simple comparison between two means. Suppose a company would like to launch a new brand of exclusive bicycles targeted at successful businesspeople. The brand is to be called "BUYCYCLE." The brand manager considers a simple reduced font and a more complex font as candidates for printing the brand name (see Table 1). To explore which of these two versions is preferred by their target group of consumers, he decides to conduct a market research experiment to compare the liking of the two fonts. He randomly splits a sample of 120 potential consumers into two groups. Each group is shown one of the font versions of the brand name and is asked to rate their liking of the brand name. The aim of this research is to determine whether there is a difference in the mean liking of the simple-font group compared to the complex-font group.

A typical data matrix for this type of study would look like the matrix shown in Table 2, where the first six cases and the last case of a sample of 120 participants are shown (the full dataset can be found in the Web-Appendix). The experimental factor is named *iv_2*, and the dependent variable liking is named *dv_2*.[1] Before computing inferential test statistics, the first reasonable step is to visually display the key patterns in the data. In the current example, we are interested in the statistical significance of the mean difference between the two experimental groups. Hence, we are interested in displaying the two means, which is usually done by a barplot for discrete IVs[2] (see Fig. 1). Moreover, to gain an impression of the random noise in the data, we would like to include an indicator of random variation. Usually, either the standard error of the mean or, more often and hence recommended, a 95% confidence interval is used (which is, for sufficiently large samples of $N > 30$, equal to approximately 1.96 times the standard error, Field et al. 2012, pp. 45–46).

---

[1] The naming of the variables throughout the chapter follows the key characteristic of the respective experimental scenario. "_2" refers to the two factor levels employed in the present experiment. All variable names are constructed following the same logic.

[2] All barplots in this chapter were produced using the `ggplot2`-library in R (Wickham 2009).

Table 2 Data matrix for the first few participants of Study 1

id	gender	age	iv_2	dv_2
1	male	28	complex	7
2	male	23	simple	1
3	male	20	simple	3
4	male	24	complex	6
5	female	25	simple	4
6	female	25	simple	7
⋮	⋮	⋮	⋮	⋮
120	female		23	complex	3

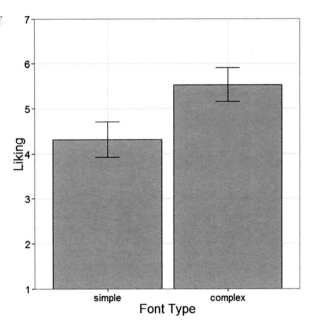

Fig. 1 Mean liking ratings of Study 1 with 95% confidence intervals

Interestingly, in a between-subjects design, the statistical significance of a mean difference can easily be inferred from a mere visual inspection of the means and their 95% confidence intervals ("inference by eye"; Cumming and Finch 2005). When the 95% confidence intervals do not overlap (as in Fig. 1), the mean difference is significant at the $p < 0.01$ level. When they overlap by less than half the length of the intervals' whiskers (i.e., half the length between the upper/lower bound of the interval and the mean), the mean difference is significant at the $p < 0.05$ level. This technique is an efficient way to obtain a quick but solid impression of the data pattern. A more precise way to assess the statistical significance in terms of an exact probability estimate (i.e., p-value) is to conduct either a t-test or an ANOVA. In practice, only the

t-test would be conducted and reported for the given research question because it is the more parsimonious technique for a comparison of just two means. However, I will also introduce the key ideas of ANOVA using this simple dataset.

An independent-samples t-test can compare a maximum of two means. It evaluates the ratio of the mean difference between the two experimental groups and the standard error (SE) of the mean difference:

$$t_{emp} = (M_1 - M_2)/\text{SE}(M_1 - M_2) \tag{1}$$

The higher the empirical t-value, the less likely is a purely random mean difference. The theoretical t-distribution can be used to compute the exact likelihood of observing an empirical mean difference given the null hypothesis that both means are the same, which is denoted as the p-value. For the present example, the mean is 4.32 for the simple font condition and 5.53 for the complex font condition. The empirical t-value for the difference between these two means is -4.53 (the negative sign indicates that the first mean is smaller than the second). To derive the corresponding p-value from the theoretical t-distribution, the degrees of freedom for estimating the difference between two means are calculated. The total sample size is 120. Since two means need to be estimated, two degrees of freedom are "consumed" and 118 degrees of freedom remain for the analysis. The p-value corresponding to a t-value of -4.53 with 118 degrees of freedom can be looked up in a t-table and is smaller than 0.001. In practice, the statistical software package automatically provides the p-value, and there is no need to find a classical statistics book that still contains tables with exact values for the t-distribution. When reporting the result of a t-test in a scientific manuscript, one would write that the difference in means between the simple font condition ($M = 4.32$) and the complex font condition ($M = 5.53$) is statistically significant (t(118) $= -4.53; p < 0.001$).

Alternatively, we could also run an ANOVA model to estimate whether there is a significant mean difference between the two experimental groups. Since ANOVA is the key topic of the present chapter, I will present the theoretical background of this method in greater detail. When considering ANOVA in general, it is important to note that it is not a unique statistical method but is closely linked to many other statistical techniques. In particular, as is almost every method of inferential statistics, ANOVA is a special case of the general linear model (GLM) underlying regression analysis (Rutherford 2001). Hence, the model formula of a one-way ANOVA is similar to the usual regression model, with y_{ig} indicating the DV of participant i in condition g, $\bar{y}$ indicating the grand mean across all observations, α_g indicating the impact of the experimental manipulation with g levels, and e_{ig} indicating the residual:

$$y_{ig} = \bar{y} + \alpha_g + e_{ig} \tag{2}$$

As the name analysis of variance suggests, the aim of ANOVA is to examine the sources of variation in the data. In particular, the total amount of variance in the data

Analysis of Variance

is partitioned into an explained and an unexplained part of the total variance. A reasonable ANOVA model should explain more variance than is left unexplained by the model, that is, the ratio of explained to unexplained variance should be greater than 1. How much greater it must be to reach statistical significance is determined based on the F-distribution, which is a probability density function of the ratios of variances.

To provide a better understanding of these different parts of variance and the necessary steps to determine F- and p-values, we consider the first six cases of the dataset featured in the Web-Appendix. As hopefully will become clear, ANOVA is a mathematically simple technique that can be easily computed by hand (although it would be quite annoying for larger datasets). Figure 2 shows the key elements necessary to understand the mechanics of ANOVA: the computation of the total sum of squares (SS_T) in Fig. 2a, the computation of the model sum of squares (SS_M) in Fig. 2b, and the computation of the residual sum of squares (SS_R) in Fig. 2c. All three figures depict the same three key elements: first, the observed liking evaluations of the first six participants (participant ID is shown on the x-axis). The dark gray circles indicate that the person is in the simple font condition, and the light gray diamonds indicate that the person is in the complex font condition; second, the mean evaluation across all 120 participants (independent of the experimental group), as indicated by the horizontal black line, which is also called the "grand mean"; and third, the mean evaluation of the 60 observations of the simple font (horizontal dark gray line at 4.32) and the mean evaluation of the 60 observations of the complex font condition (horizontal light gray line at 5.53).

The dashed vertical lines differ between the three figures and indicate three different sources of variation in the data. In Fig. 2a, the dashed lines indicate the deviation of each individual observation from the grand mean. As shown in formula (3a), the sum of these deviations squared is defined as SS_T. Because the magnitude of this measure directly depends on the number of observations (i.e., every additional participant will add a squared deviation from the mean), it has no meaningful interpretation. To obtain meaning, we can calculate the total mean squares (MS_T), as shown in formula (4a), by dividing SS_T by the corresponding degrees of freedom. Since the grand mean needs to be estimated from the data, one degree of freedom is "consumed." Hence, the degrees of freedom are computed as the sample size minus one (df: $N - 1$; here: $120 - 1 = 119$). Consequently, MS_T is the average squared deviation from the grand mean, which is better known by the term "variance" (i.e., MS_T = the total variance in the data).

The SS_T can be decomposed into two components: the part of the variation in the data that is explained by the statistical model SS_M and the part that is unexplained SS_R (i.e., $SS_T = SS_M + SS_R$). Figure 2b shows how SS_M is computed. The ANOVA model defines the two experimental groups as sources of systematic variation. Hence, the mean of the simple and complex group, respectively, is the part of the variation in the data that is explained by the statistical model. SS_M is defined as the sum of the squared deviations of the group means from the grand mean (see formula (3b)). As indicated by the vertical dashed lines in Fig. 2b, there are as many squared deviations entering SS_M as there are participants. We can compute the average SS_M by dividing SS_M by the

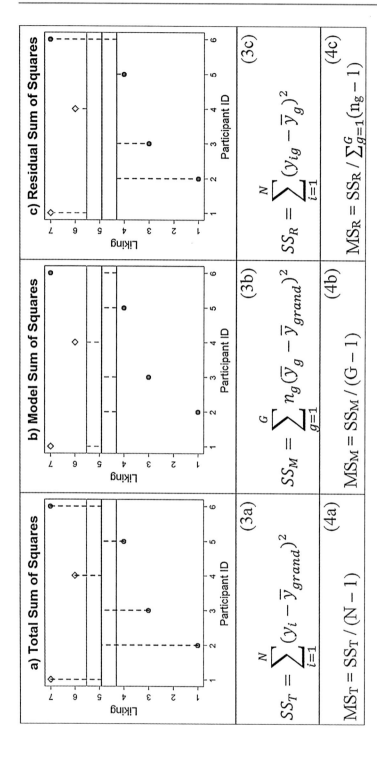

Fig. 2 Visualization of the different sources of variation in a one-factorial ANOVA with two groups. *Note*: The figures show the first six cases of the exemplary dataset. The *dark gray circles* (*light gray diamonds*) indicate individual observations from the simple (complex) font condition. The *horizontal black line* indicates the grand mean across all observations, and the *dark* (*light*) *gray line* indicates the mean of the simple (complex) font condition. The sum of the squares of the *vertical dashed lines* is computed in the formulas below the figures

Analysis of Variance

corresponding df (i.e., the number of factor levels minus 1; here: $2 - 1 = 1$; see formula (4b)). The resulting MS_M is the systematic variance in the data.

Finally, Fig. 2c shows how the unsystematic variance in the data is computed. The vertical dashed lines indicate the deviation of individual observations from the mean of the group the observation belongs to. As defined in formula (3c), the sum of these squared deviations across all observations is called SS_R. To compute the residual variance, we again divide SS_R by the corresponding df (i.e., the sum of the $n - 1$ participants per experimental group; here: $59 + 59 = 118$; see formula (4c)).

Given the variances computed by formulas (4b) and (4c), we are ready to perform the test of statistical significance. To this end, we compute the empirical F-value:

$$F_{emp} = MS_M/MS_R \qquad (5)$$

Hence, F_{emp} represents the ratio of the systematic and the unsystematic variance in the data. Clearly, if F_{emp} is smaller than 1, there cannot be a significant effect in the data because the unsystematic variance is larger than the systematic variance. When F_{emp} is larger than 1, the question arises of how much larger than 1 F_{emp} must be to call the effect statistically significant. To compute the precise level of statistical significance (i.e., the p-value), the empirical F-value F_{emp} is compared to the theoretical probability density function of F-values. This distribution describes how ratios of variance are distributed and provides the critical thresholds that have to be exceeded to infer that the systematic variance is so much larger than the unsystematic variance that a mere random difference between the variances is unlikely (i.e., less than 5%). In contrast to the previously discussed t-distribution with only one parameter, the F-distribution has two parameters that determine the shape of the distribution. The first parameter is the degrees of freedom of the systematic variance (i.e., MS_M); the second parameter is the degrees of freedom of the unsystematic variance (i.e., MS_R). As in the previous t-test example, classic textbooks on ANOVA contain tables of critical F-values ordered by the model degrees of freedom and the residual degrees of freedom. Nowadays, statistical software packages do the tedious job of computing the exact probability for a given F_{emp} with its two corresponding degrees of freedom. For the given dataset, the ANOVA output of R, including all discussed elements, is shown in Fig. 3.

In the figure, MS_M is 44.41, MS_R is 2.17, and F_{emp} is $44.41/2.17 = 20.48$. The model degrees of freedom is 1. The residual degrees of freedom is 118. R computed that an F_{emp} of 20.48 given 1 and 118 degrees of freedom is very unlikely (Pr $(>F) = p = 0.0000145$).[3] In a scientific text, the results of the present ANOVA would commonly be described as follows: An ANOVA showed that the factor font type has a significant influence on participants' liking evaluations (F $(1, 118) = 20.48$; $p < 0.001$). In particular, the complex font ($M = 5.53$) is systematically liked better than the simple font ($M = 4.32$).

---

[3] R denotes the p-value by "Pr($>F$)," which refers to the probability of observing the empirical F-value given the null hypothesis. R uses exponential notation to show small numbers. Hence, the value 1.45e-05 in Fig. 3 is equivalent to 0.0000145.

```
> summary(aov(dv_2 ~ iv_2, data=Data.Anova))
            Df Sum Sq Mean Sq F value   Pr(>F)
iv_2         1  44.41   44.41   20.48 1.45e-05 ***
Residuals  118 255.92    2.17
---
Signif. codes:  0 '***' 0.001 '**' 0.01 '*' 0.05 '.' 0.1 ' ' 1
```

Fig. 3 R output of a one-way ANOVA with two factor levels (Study 1)

Table 3 The third condition of the second study that is added to the two conditions shown in Table 1

Condition (3) Super-complex font

More Than Two Means: One-Factorial ANOVA

The example described in the previous section did not require an ANOVA model but could have been analyzed by a *t*-test because only two means were compared. We turn now to the key strength of ANOVA: situations where more than two means are involved. Since the *t*-test is limited to a comparison of two means, it cannot be applied to such situations. In what follows, we extend the two group example of the previous section by a third experimental group.

When the brand manager of our imaginary company sees the results of the first study, he gets excited about complex fonts. He asks his team of designers to find an even more complex font, expecting an even higher liking due to the increased complexity. However, the head of market research is skeptical and proposes a second study where all three fonts are compared. She sets up a study with one factor (font type) that has three levels: the two levels of the first study plus a third level, the "super-complex font" condition (see Table 3).

For ease of data handling, the dataset in the Web-Appendix contains the data of this second experiment, too.[4] The experimental factor of this second study is named iv_3, and the dependent variable is named dv_3. A total of 120 participants

---

[4] In real data collections, we would collect a second independent dataset from new participants. Please assume that although the data for the second experiment (and all further studies) are stored in the same dataset, these datasets are independent and come from different participants.

completed this study, with 40 participants per experimental condition. Before conducting statistical tests, we inspect the descriptive pattern of the results by plotting the means and their 95% confidence intervals (see Fig. 4). The pattern of means suggests that the medium complex font still performs best.

To formally confirm this "inference by eye," we conduct a one-factorial ANOVA. The model formula is identical to formula (2), and the approach to compute the variances and the empirical F-value is identical to Fig. 2. The only difference is that the group index g now has three levels instead of two. Before running the actual analysis, it is important to note that ANOVA compares the variance explained by one factor (in the present case with three levels) to the unexplained variance and computes one F-value and one p-value per factor, that is, the ANOVA shows whether the factor as a whole explains a significant amount of variance. However, one does not learn which levels of the factor are responsible for the effect. Consider the ANOVA output produced by R for the given dataset (Fig. 5).

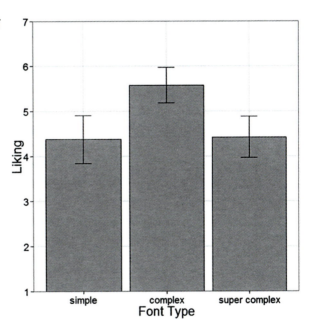

Fig. 4 Mean liking ratings of Study 2 with 95% confidence intervals

```
> summary(aov(dv_3 ~ iv_3, data=Data.Anova))
             Df Sum Sq Mean Sq F value  Pr(>F)
iv_3          2  36.87  18.433   8.664 0.00031 ***
Residuals   117 248.92   2.128
---
Signif. codes:  0 '***' 0.001 '**' 0.01 '*' 0.05 '.' 0.1 ' ' 1
```

Fig. 5 R output of a one-way ANOVA with three factor levels (Study 2)

The ANOVA shows that the factor "font type" has a significant influence on participants' liking evaluations ($F(2, 117) = 8.66; p < 0.001$).[5] This result tells us that, according to the presented rationale, at least one of the three means is significantly different from at least one other mean. However, this result alone does not inform the researcher which of the three potential pairwise mean comparisons is significant. This is a very important characteristic of ANOVA that, when ignored, leads to unjustified claims about statistically significant mean differences. To assess the significance of the pairwise mean differences, it is necessary to compare each pair of means separately using a priori contrasts, post hoc tests, or inference by eye.

Which of these techniques should a researcher use? A priori contrasts require that one knows prior to the analysis the exact means or group of means one would like to compare. Given that market researchers are usually interested in novel phenomena, it is unlikely that exact hypotheses about specific mean differences can be derived a priori. Moreover, it is usually difficult to convince a critical reader that a contrast was actually proposed prior to the analysis and is not simply declared as being a priori (Rodger and Roberts 2013). Hence, convincing theorizing is required to justify a priori contrasts.[6] Post hoc contrasts perform an exploratory comparison of all pairwise group means. One problem associated with such post hoc tests is that the same data are used to perform multiple statistical tests, which increases the likelihood of falsely rejecting a null hypothesis (also known as Type I error inflation or alpha inflation). Over the years, countless post hoc procedures have been proposed to counter alpha inflation, and it has become difficult for a market researcher to make an informed decision about which of these methods to select. They differ mainly with respect to the severity of the alpha correction, which has the downside of reducing statistical power (overlooking a significant effect that is actually present, i.e., Type II error). A test is called liberal if it adjusts the alpha level only slightly, and it is called conservative if it adjusts the alpha level considerably.

The most prominent liberal test is called Fisher's least significant difference test (LSD, Fisher 1935). This test consists of a sequential two-step test procedure. First, the global significance of the ANOVA is assessed, which is called the omnibus test. If this omnibus test is not significant, the test procedure stops. If it is significant, uncorrected t-tests are performed for all pairs of means. An even simpler version of this test procedure is to inspect the means and their confidence intervals based on the inference by eye technique if, and only if, the global F-test of the ANOVA is significant. A conservative procedure was proposed by a statistician named Carlo Bonferroni (although there is no traceable publication), which adjusts the alpha level by the number of conducted pairwise tests m ($\alpha_{Bonferroni} = \alpha/m$). A less-conservative version of the Bonferroni correction was proposed by Holm (1979) that tests the mean differences in the order of their magnitude and uses increasingly more relaxed

---

[5]Please note how the df of the ANOVA changed compared to Fig. 3 due to three rather than two factor levels.

[6]The interested reader can find more information about a priori contrasts (also called planned contrasts) in the textbooks of Field (2013), Field et al. (2012), and of Klockars and Sax (1986).

Analysis of Variance

alpha values for smaller mean differences. Which of these tests to select mainly depends on the consequences of falsely accepting/rejecting a null hypothesis. In most market research applications, the research examines potential business opportunities, where it is preferable to give an alternative a try rather than miss a potentially valuable business opportunity. Hence, in most market research applications, Fisher's LSD (or even simpler, the inference by eye technique as a follow-up on a globally significant ANOVA omnibus test) is a reasonable choice. However, in other disciplines (such as medicine), falsely rejecting a null hypothesis may have very negative consequences; hence, conservative tests are better suited in such instances. The implementation of the three post hoc tests described in the present section can be found in the Web-Appendix.

Multiplicative Effects: Factorial ANOVA

After the brand manager learns that his idea of a super-complex font does not work as intended, he comes up with a new idea: He wants to examine whether the influence of font type on liking depends on the positioning of the brand. In addition to the brand name "BUYCYCLE," which is targeted at business people, he creates the brand name "EASYCYCLE," which is targeted at leisure-oriented consumers. He asks his market researchers to test whether the optimal font depends on the brand positioning. An experimental design with two factors with two levels each is implemented, as shown in Table 4, and data are collected from 30 people per cell ($N_{\text{total}} = 120$). In the dataset of the Web-Appendix, the factor "font type" is named *iv_fac_a*, the factor "brand name" is named *iv_fac_b*, and the corresponding liking judgments are stored in a variable named *dv_fac*.

The key idea of the two-way experimental design is to go beyond simple main effects (i.e., A is better than B) and examine conditional effects (i.e., A is only better than B when C). Statistically speaking, the basic one-way ANOVA formula (2) is extended by the second experimental factor and by the interaction (i.e., multiplication) of both factors:

$$y_{\text{igh}} = \bar{y} + \alpha_g + \beta_h + \left(\alpha_g{}^*\beta_h\right) + e_{\text{igh}} \tag{6}$$

Table 4 Experimental conditions of Study 3

		Factor (1) Font type	
		Simple font	Complex font
Factor (2) Brand name	Business	**BUYCYCLE**	**BUYCYCLE**
	Leisure oriented	**EASYCYCLE**	**EASYCYCLE**

Table 5 Comparison of a balanced and an unbalanced experimental design

(a) Balanced experimental design: factors are uncorrelated				(b) Unbalanced experimental design: factors are correlated			
		Factor A				Factor A	
		-1	1			-1	1
Factor B	-1	$n = 30$	$n = 30$	Factor B	-1	$n = 45$	$n = 15$
	1	$n = 30$	$n = 30$		1	$n = 15$	$n = 45$

Accordingly, the two-way ANOVA considers four sources of variation: the variance produced by factor α, the variance produced by factor β, the variance produced by the interaction of α and β, and finally the residual variance e, against which the significance of all three effects is evaluated.

Before conducting the two-way ANOVA, we need to consider three important aspects that are relevant for ANOVA with more than one factor: (1) coding of the factors, (2) different ways of computing the model sum of squares, and (3) the interpretation of main effects when an interaction is present.

The coding of the factors refers to the numeric coding that is used to represent the categorical factor levels. For the example provided in Table 4, the factor levels are denoted by verbal labels (i.e., "simple font" versus "complex font" and "business" versus "leisure oriented"). However, a statistical procedure, such as ANOVA, cannot handle verbal information but requires numeric information. Although most statistical software packages automatically transform verbal codes into numeric codes internally, it is important to keep in mind what is going on under the surface of the statistical software package. Readers familiar with regression analysis are used to so-called "dummy coding," which refers to a coding scheme in which a base category is denoted by 0 and the other category by 1 (for k factor levels, k-1 dummy-coded variables are needed). This is the default internal coding R uses when a verbally labeled factor is processed. However, in the context of ANOVA with more than one factor, dummy coding leads to an incorrect evaluation of the main effects because this type of coding dismisses one experimental cell from the mean comparison.[7] Therefore, effect coding must be used, where one factor level is coded as -1 and the other factor level as 1 (see Table 5a).

Effect coding ensures that for a given factor, both cells corresponding to the value -1 are compared to both cells corresponding to the value 1. This is the default coding scheme SPSS uses in its ANOVA procedure. Hence, when using SPSS, the defaults of the software take care of the coding issue. However, when using R, it is important to change the coding scheme from dummy to effect coding to obtain

---

[7]For the example with 2×2 experimental cells provided in Table 4, dummy-coding Factor 1 (simple = 0; complex = 1) and Factor 2 (business = 0; leisure = 1) would mean that the effect of Factor 1 compares the cell denoted by {0,0} (i.e., "simple and business") to the two cells for which Factor 1 has the value 1 (i.e., "complex and business" and "complex and leisure"). The cell "simple and leisure" would be omitted from the test of the main effect, which is an undesirable feature of dummy coding when applied to ANOVA models.

Analysis of Variance

meaningful results (see lines 24–41 of the Web-Appendix R script on how to specify effect coding in R).

The second important issue concerning ANOVA with more than one factor is how the model sum of squares is computed. This issue is only relevant when the experimental design is unbalanced (i.e., an unequal number of observations per experimental cell; see Table 5b), which leads to a correlation between factors. To understand this point, let us consider the key characteristic of a bivariate correlation in the present context: knowing the value of one factor provides information about the other factor. In the balanced design in Table 5a, this is not the case. If I know that a person is in condition "1" of Factor A, the likelihood of being in condition "-1" or "1" of Factor B is exactly the same (50% or $n = 30$ in each). In contrast, when considering the unbalanced design in Table 5b, things are different: If I know that a person is in condition "1" of Factor A, the likelihood of being in condition "1" of Factor B is 75% ($n = 45$) and the likelihood of being in condition "-1" is only 25% ($n = 15$). Hence, in unbalanced experimental designs, the factors are correlated, meaning that they share common variance. This issue is known as multicollinearity between predictor variables in regression analysis and poses the problem of assigning explained variance in the DV to the IVs. Before we dig deeper into this problem, it is important to note that in practice, unbalanced designs are much more common than perfectly balanced designs due to dropouts. The exemplary dataset in the Web-Appendix, however, contains a perfectly balanced design, as shown in Table 5a. As shown in the lower figure of Table 6, this situation is unproblematic in terms of assigning explained variance to the factors.

When confronted with an unbalanced design, however, it is important to distinguish between three ways of computing the model sum of squares. In Type I,[8] the explained variance is assigned to the experimental factors in the order of their specification in the model. Hence, the first factor in the model formula can potentially explain more variance than factors occurring later in the formula. Table 6 visualizes this situation using Venn diagrams. In these Venn diagrams, the dashed black circle symbolizes the total variance of the DV, the black circle the total variance of Factor A, the light gray circle the total variance of Factor B, and the dark gray circle the total variance of the interaction of Factors A and B. When circles overlap, they share common variance (i.e., they are correlated). In particular, the area of the dashed black circle covered by the other circles is the explained part of the variance of the DV.

Given that the factors are entered into the ANOVA according to the following formula (DV $= A + B + A * B$) using Type I sum of squares, Factor A explains the black area in the DV, Factor B the light gray area, and the interaction the dark gray area. If the order of the factors in the formula is changed, the explained parts of the

---

[8]It is important to note that the term "Type I" is used to denote more than just one statistical concept, which can be confusing. We already encountered the term in the context of the statistical p-value, where falsely rejecting the null hypothesis is called an alpha or Type I error. In the present context, "Type I" refers to a specific way of computing the sum of squares in an ANOVA model, which is completely unrelated to the "Type I error" in statistical hypothesis testing.

Table 6 Visualization of different ways of computing the model sum of squares

	Type I Sum of squares	Type II Sum of squares	Type III Sum of squares
Correlated factors			
Uncorrelated factors			

Analysis of Variance

variance also change, which is a disadvantageous characteristic of Type I sum of squares because the order of the factors in the model formula is rarely meaningful. The second way of computing the sum of squares is Type II, where the explained variance is assigned to the main effects first and the interaction explains the leftover variance. This way of assigning the explained variance in the DV to the factors can only be applied when no significant interaction is present. In such a situation, Type II sum of squares tests the main effects with high statistical power (i.e., high likelihood of detecting significant effects). However, two-way experimental designs are usually conducted because the researcher is particularly interested in the interaction, which brings us to the third way of computing the sum of squares: Type III, where each factor only explains that part of the variance in the data that is uniquely produced by that factor. The shared explained variance of several factors is not assigned to a particular factor when using Type III sum of squares but is nevertheless counted as explained variance in the computation of the total R^2. Type III sum of squares allows a meaningful interpretation of main effects and interactions when interactions are present and is usually the best choice in the analysis of experimental designs.

Common statistical packages, such as SPSS, use Type III sum of squares as the default option. R uses Type I as its default in the `aov` function. Because there is rarely a natural order of factors in an ANOVA model, using Type I sum of squares may lead to biased results because the arbitrary order of specifying the model in the statistical software can influence the significance of the factors. Hence, I recommend using Type III sum of squares to avoid such biases. The Web-Appendix shows how to use Type III in R using the `Anova` function of the `car` library (Fox and Weisberg 2011).

The third general issue concerning ANOVA with more than one factor is the question of how the main effects can be interpreted when an interaction is present. This is a particularly important point since the mere significance of a main effect can lead to misleading conclusions when the pattern of an existing interaction is ignored. To clarify this point, Fig. 6 shows four prototypical mean patterns of a two-way experimental design. In Fig. 6a, we see a meaningful main effect of Factor A ("1" is better than "−1") but no other effects. In Fig. 6b, we see two main effects of Factors A and B (for both factors "1" is better than "−1"), which are both meaningful, but there is no interaction. In Fig. 6c, we see the same two main effects but in addition also an interaction such that the effect of Factor B is stronger for level "1" of Factor A than for level "−1" of Factor A. This situation is called an ordinal interaction because the order of the means is not changed by the interaction. Therefore, both main effects remain meaningful and can be interpreted, that is, the claim that factor level "1" is better than "−1" is true for both factors, independently of the other factor.

Now let us consider Fig. 6d, which features a disordinal interaction (also called "crossover interaction"). On average, level "1" of Factor A is better than level "−1." Given the exemplary mean pattern, this effect would most likely show up as a significant main effect in an ANOVA model. However, this effect would not be meaningful because the claim that factor level "1" of Factor A is better than factor level "−1" is not true unconditionally. This claim only holds in condition "1" of

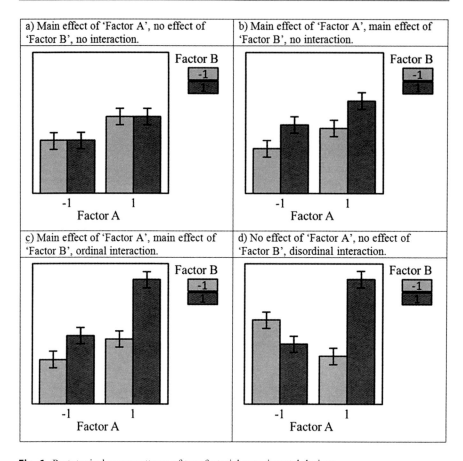

Fig. 6 Prototypical mean patterns of two-factorial experimental designs

Factor B. However, in condition "−1" of Factor B, the effect reverses, that is, the order of the means changes, conditional on the other factor, which makes it a disordinal interaction. Therefore, it is not sufficient to inspect the ANOVA output to judge the significance of main effects; the pattern of means must also be considered because a statistically significant effect can lack substantial meaning when a disordinal interaction is present. When a disordinal interaction is present, the main effects are meaningless and should not be the basis of conclusions.

With the understanding of these three general aspects of ANOVA with more than one factor, we can start to examine the exemplary dataset of the Web-Appendix. When running the model in R (see Fig. 7), we find no effects of font type (F(1,116) = 0.47; p = 0.49) and brand name (F(1,116) = 1.44; p = 0.23) but a significant interaction between the factors (F(1,116) = 32.05; p < 0.001). Thus, in the present example, only the interaction is significant. However, even if one or both of the main effects were statistically significant, they would not be meaningful in the present scenario since we observe a disordinal interaction (see Fig. 8).

```
> Anova(aov(dv_fac ~ iv_fac_a * iv_fac_b, data=Data.Anova), type="III")
Anova Table (Type III tests)

Response: dv_fac
                 Sum Sq  Df   F value    Pr(>F)
(Intercept)     3040.13   1 2683.8316 < 2.2e-16 ***
iv_fac_a           0.53   1    0.4708    0.4940
iv_fac_b           1.63   1    1.4419    0.2323
iv_fac_a:iv_fac_b 36.30   1   32.0457 1.107e-07 ***
Residuals        131.40 116
---
Signif. codes:  0 '***' 0.001 '**' 0.01 '*' 0.05 '.' 0.1 ' ' 1
```

Fig. 7 R output of a two-way ANOVA with two factor levels for each factor (Study 3) (R denotes the multiplicative interaction of two factors by ":")

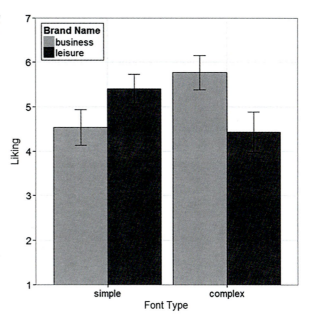

Fig. 8 Mean liking ratings of Study 3 with 95% confidence intervals

How can we interpret the results of an ANOVA with interaction(s)? A significant interaction indicates that the effect of at least one of the factors is dependent on at least one other factor. A disordinal interaction indicates that the effect of each factor is dependent on the other factor, that is, in the present example, any effect is conditional on the other effect. For a substantial interpretation of the interaction, one needs to know which conditional effects are significant. To this end, we can compute so-called "simple effects." To introduce the idea of simple effects, let us first recap the types of effects we have encountered thus far using Table 7. The main effect of Factor A compares the mean of [*$\{-1,-1\}$* and °$\{1,-1\}$°] with the mean of [^$\{-1,1\}$^ and #$\{1,1\}$#]. Accordingly, the main effect of Factor B compares the mean of [*$\{-1,-1\}$* and ^$\{-1,1\}$^] with the mean of [°$\{1,-1\}$° and #$\{1,1\}$#]. The interactive effect of Factors A and B tests whether the mean of $[*\{-1,-1\}*$ and $\#\{1,1\}\#]$ differs from the mean of $[°\{1,-1\}°$ and $^\wedge\{-1,1\}^\wedge]$.

In contrast, simple effects do not compare combinations of experimental cells but directly compare experimental cells for one factor level of the other factor. For the exemplary design in Table 7, four simple effects can be computed: the simple effect of Factor A conditional on Factor B's "−1" level (i.e., $*\{-1,-1\}*$ vs. $^\wedge\{-1,1\}^\wedge$), the simple effect of Factor A conditional on Factor B's "1" level (i.e., $°\{1,-1\}°$ vs. $\#\{1,1\}\#$), the simple effect of Factor B conditional on Factor A's "−1" level (i.e., $*\{-1,-1\}*$ vs. $°\{1,-1\}°$), and the simple effect of Factor B conditional on Factor A's "1" level (i.e., $^\wedge\{-1,1\}^\wedge$ vs. $\#\{1,1\}\#$).

How do we compute these simple effects? The attentive reader would probably suggest that the current chapter started with a situation where two means need to be compared. A t-test for independent samples or a one-way ANOVA applied to a subset of the dataset (i.e., just those experimental cells involved in the respective simple effect) appears to be a natural solution. Simple effects are, however, a bit more complicated because they make use of the information contained in all experimental cells (i.e., also those cells that are not involved in the respective simple effect). In particular, simple effects estimate the residual variance based on the full dataset and the model variance based on only the cells involved in the simple effect (Field 2013; Field et al. 2012). This approach increases the residual degrees of freedom for the evaluation of the empirical F-value and hence increases the statistical power of the simple effects. Thus, simple effects are a variant of ANOVA that are conducted as a follow-up analysis after a significant interaction has been observed. As with any follow-up technique in the ANOVA world (cf. post hoc contrasts), it is important to only run the follow-up analyses if, and only if, the omnibus test is significant. Therefore, simple effects are only computed if a significant interaction is present in the initial factorial ANOVA. Otherwise, an inflation of the alpha error is likely to occur, and the obtained results would be questionable.

Unfortunately, neither SPSS nor R offers a straightforward, convenient way of testing simple effects (Field 2013; Field et al. 2012). In SPSS, simple effects are not available from the menu but need to be requested by a self-written command in the syntax. In R, simple effects need to be computed by extracting the residual sum of squares and residual degrees of freedom from the initial factorial ANOVA and the model sum of squares and model degrees of freedom from a follow-up ANOVA applied to only the involved experimental cells. Own code must be written to apply the formulas of Fig. 2 to compute the empirical F-value and the corresponding

Table 7 Distinguishing main effects, interaction effects, and simple effects

		Factor (A)	
		−1	1
Factor (B)	−1	$*\{-1,-1\}*$	$^\wedge\{-1,1\}^\wedge$
	1	$°\{1,-1\}°$	$\#\{1,1\}\#$

Note: The symbols $*^\wedge°\#$ are used to facilitate the recognition of the four different cells in the text

Analysis of Variance

Table 8 Comparison of different data formats commonly used for RM-ANOVA

(a) Wide format					(b) Long format				

id	gender	age	dv_within_2_a	dv_within_2_b
1	male	28	2	1
2	male	23	5	7
3	male	20	5	7
⋮	⋮	⋮	⋮	⋮
120	female	23	4	6

id	gender	age	font.type	liking
1	male	28	simple	2
1	male	28	complex	1
2	male	23	simple	5
2	male	23	complex	7
3	male	20	simple	5
3	male	20	complex	7
⋮	⋮	⋮	⋮	⋮
120	female	23	simple	4
120	female	23	complex	6

p-value. Examples for how to compute simple effects in SPSS and R can be found in the Web-Appendix.

In the present example, the market researcher is most likely interested in the question of whether the effect of font type is significant in each of the brand name groups, that is, whether the difference between the two light gray bars in Fig. 8 is statistically significant and whether the difference between the two dark gray bars in Fig. 8 is statistically significant. Thus, we will focus on the two managerially most relevant simple effects described above (i.e., the effect of "font type" for the "business brand name" and the effect of "font type" for the "leisure brand name") and will discard the managerially less relevant effects (i.e., the effect of brand name conditional on font type). The simple effects indicate that a complex font works better for a business brand name ($F(1, 116) = 20.14$; $p < 0.001$) and a simple font works better for a leisure brand name ($F(1, 116) = 12.37$; $p = 0.001$).[9]

Within-Subjects: Two or More Observations per Person

The standard ANOVA covered in the first part of this chapter requires that all observations are independent from each other and hence come from different individuals. However, there are situations where it is preferable to collect more than one measurement per person, which requires the application of a different type of ANOVA: repeated-measures ANOVA (RM-ANOVA). If a market researcher would like to compare the effectiveness of two advertisement campaigns, he or she is usually not only interested in the short-term effects but also in the long-term effects. To this end, one could survey the same participants immediately after viewing an advertisement and 1 month later. The time between these two measurements is a within-subjects factor. In the last dataset of this chapter (Study 6), we will consider an example of a longitudinal dataset, where time is the within-subjects factor. Another field of application for RM-ANOVA is the manipulation of a "normal"

---

[9]Please note that the residual degrees of freedom (i.e., 116) for the simple effects are the same as in the initial factorial ANOVA. This is the reason why simple effects have higher statistical power than other post hoc approaches that would just compare the two means, such as an independent-samples t-test.

experimental factor within-subjects instead of between-subjects. If there is no reason to expect that participants respond in a biased way (e.g., demand artifact[10]) once they know all factor levels of an experimental factor, it is statistically much more powerful (and hence more efficient) to manipulate an experimental factor within-subjects instead of between-subjects. We will consider examples of such situations in the next two sections (studies 4 and 5).

Two Means: One-Factorial RM-ANOVA or Paired-Samples *t*-Test

In the fourth study of the present chapter, we revisit the first between-subjects study of this chapter (Study 1), where "font type" was manipulated with two levels: simple vs. complex. If we assume that participants can provide an unbiased answer even if they know both levels of the factor "font type," it would be more efficient to conduct a within-subjects manipulation of this factor because half the number of participants is sufficient to gather the same number of measurements as in the between-subjects scenario. In fact, a key advantage of a within-subjects experiment is that even less than half the number of participants is sufficient to reach a comparable level of power compared to a between-subjects scenario because the random differences between individuals are "pulled out" of the analysis. Let us consider how this is achieved using the dataset provided in the Web-Appendix. In the dataset, a sample of 120 participants rated the simple font (*dv_within_2_a*) and the complex font (*dv_within_2_b*), and each rating is stored in a separate variable (i.e., a separate column in the data matrix). This type of data storage is called "wide format." We will see later that some types of analyses require a different type of storage called "long format," where a second row instead of a second column is used to store the second measurement (see Table 8).

To illustrate the mechanics of RM-ANOVA, we again compare the *t*-test approach with the ANOVA approach.[11] A paired-samples *t*-test can be used to analyze repeated measures with a maximum of two measurements. The key idea of this type of *t*-test is that it is not the means per se that are analyzed but the differences between pairwise means within an individual. That is, the difference D_i is first computed per participant i by subtracting measurement$_{i2}$ from measurement$_{i1}$. Then, the mean of all D_i is computed and divided by its standard error to derive an empirical *t*-test statistic:

$$T_{emp} = mean(D_i)/SE(D_i) \qquad (7)$$

---

[10]The term demand artifact indicates that participants guess the hypothesis of an experiment and demonstrate behavior that is consistent with their guess instead of their natural behavior. Therefore, the occurrence of a demand artifact destroys the external validity of the observed effects. Sawyer (1975) provides an excellent discussion of this problem and potential solutions.

[11]A third possible approach would be an extension of the regression framework called linear mixed models (LMM; for an applied introduction, see West et al. 2015).

Following this approach, the absolute differences between participants are omitted from the analysis; therefore, this source of random noise does not reduce the precision of the estimated mean difference. This key idea of excluding the between-subjects variance when evaluating the significance of the within-subjects effect of interest is part of all repeated-measures techniques and is responsible for their high level of statistical power. The present example finds a significant difference (D = −0.59) between the simple (M = 3.92) and complex (M = 4.51) fonts (t(119) = −4.34; p < 0.001).

For illustrative purposes, we evaluate the same mean difference using RM-ANOVA. In practice, however, when only one factor with two levels is present, the paired-samples *t*-test would be the method of choice. The RM-ANOVA explicitly disentangles the within- and between-subjects variance and uses only the within-subjects portion to evaluate significance. This approach of splitting the total sum of squares into the relevant components is illustrated in Fig. 9.

As can be seen in Fig. 9, RM-ANOVA only considers the within-subjects variance to determine the statistical significance by splitting this source of variation into the two components we previously encountered in the normal between-subjects ANOVA model at the outset of this chapter (see Fig. 2): SS_{MW} and SS_{RW}. The between-subjects variance is, however, isolated and does not influence the estimation of the model's statistical significance. Different software packages require different data formats to perform RM-ANOVA (see Table 8). SPSS requires the repeated measures to be stored in separate variables called "wide format," as shown in Table 8a. In R, the required data format depends on the function used: Anova requires "wide format," and ezAnova from the ez library (Lawrence 2015) requires "long format" (Table 8b) where each participant fills as many rows as there are measurements (in the present example, we have two repeated measures and hence two rows per person). The output shown in Fig. 10 is produced by running the Anova procedure on the wide-format data. The results of the RM-ANOVA replicate the findings of the paired-samples *t*-test by showing a significant effect of "font type" on liking (F(1,119) = 18.87; $p < 0.001$).

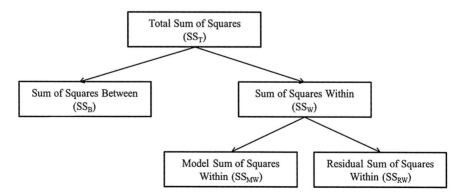

Fig. 9 Sources of variation in a RM-ANOVA

```
> summary(Anova(mod.Rm.2, idata=idata.Rm.2, idesign=~font.type, type="III"), multivariate=F)

Univariate Type III Repeated-Measures ANOVA Assuming Sphericity

                 SS num Df Error SS den Df       F    Pr(>F)
(Intercept) 4258.8      1   898.66    119 563.951 < 2.2e-16 ***
font.type     21.0      1   132.50    119  18.865 2.968e-05 ***
---
Signif. codes:  0 '***' 0.001 '**' 0.01 '*' 0.05 '.' 0.1 ' ' 1
```

Fig. 10 R output of a one-way RM-ANOVA with two factor levels (Study 4)

More Than Two Means: One-Factorial RM-ANOVA

The key concept of RM-ANOVA introduced in the previous section can be extended to more than two within-subjects factor levels. Suppose we would like to repeat the second study described in the between-subjects part of this chapter using a within-subjects design, where each participant rates all three font types (simple, complex, and super-complex). In the exemplary dataset, 120 participants participated in this study (Study 5). Their answers are stored in the variables *dv_within_3_a* (= simple), *dv_within_3_b* (= complex), and *dv_within_3_c* (= super-complex). This type of dataset with one within-subjects factor with three levels cannot be analyzed by a paired-samples *t*-test; it requires RM-ANOVA.

The existence of more than two factor levels challenges a key assumption of RM-ANOVA called sphericity. Sphericity means that all the differences between pairwise repeated measures have equal variance. This issue arises when more than two repeated measures are involved, such as in Study 5. When the assumption of sphericity is harmed, the *F*-test is too liberal and needs to be corrected. Most statistical software packages (like SPSS and R) automatically check the sphericity assumption using Mauchly's test of sphericity. If the test is significant, the sphericity assumption is violated, and the *F*-test must be corrected using either the Greenhouse-Geisser (Greenhouse and Geisser 1959) or the Huynh-Feldt (Huynh and Feldt 1976) correction, which applies a correction factor to the degrees of freedom of the empirical *F*-value. These two approaches usually differ only slightly, and it is up to the researcher to report either the more conservative Greenhouse-Geisser or the slightly more liberal Huynh-Feldt correction. However, when Mauchly's test of sphericity is significant, one of the two corrections must be applied and reported.

For the present dataset, we observe the highest liking rating for the complex font ($M = 5.10$), followed by the simple ($M = 4.23$) and the super-complex font ($M = 4.03$). The RM-ANOVA produces a significant Mauchly's test ($p < 0.001$). Hence, we report the corrected degrees of freedom for the *F*-test. We use the Huynh-Feldt correction and observe a significant effect of font type on liking (F(1.78, 211.47) = 25.39; $p < 0.001$). The R output of this analysis is shown in Fig. 11. The degrees of freedom in the first output have been multiplied by the "HF eps" (i.e., Huynh-Feldt) correction factor (i.e., $2 \times 0.8885498 = 1.78$; $238 \times 0.8885498 = 211.47$). Post hoc LSD contrasts reveal that the complex font condition is significantly different from the other two ($p < 0.001$), but the simple and super-complex font conditions do not differ from each other ($p = 0.19$). Hence, the complex font is the best-liked option.

Analysis of Variance

```
> summary(Anova(mod.Rm.3, idata=idata.Rm.3, idesign=~font.type, type="III"), multivariate=F)

Univariate Type III Repeated-Measures ANOVA Assuming Sphericity

                SS num Df Error SS den Df      F      Pr(>F)
(Intercept) 7137.8       1 1181.86     119 718.69 < 2.2e-16 ***
font.type     77.6       2  363.73     238  25.39 1.012e-10 ***
---
Signif. codes:  0 '***' 0.001 '**' 0.01 '*' 0.05 '.' 0.1 ' ' 1


Mauchly Tests for Sphericity

           Test statistic    p-value
font.type          0.8591 0.00012837


Greenhouse-Geisser and Huynh-Feldt Corrections
 for Departure from Sphericity

             GG eps Pr(>F[GG])
font.type 0.8765  1.107e-09 ***
---
Signif. codes:  0 '***' 0.001 '**' 0.01 '*' 0.05 '.' 0.1 ' ' 1


               HF eps    Pr(>F[HF])
font.type 0.8885498 8.764784e-10
```

Fig. 11 R output of a one-way RM-ANOVA with three factor levels (Study 5)

Multiplicative Effects: Factorial RM-ANOVA/Mixed-ANOVA

The RM-ANOVA approach introduced in the previous two sections is easily extended to two or more within-subjects factors. The key ideas of RM-ANOVA and the handling of interactions in an ANOVA framework have already been described; therefore, we will focus on a slightly more complex situation: the combination of between- and within-subjects factors within one analysis. If these two types of factors are combined within one analysis, the analysis is called either a mixed-ANOVA or a split-plot ANOVA (both terms can be used interchangeably). To illustrate this type of analysis, we revisit the study introduced at the outset of this chapter, in which the simple font was compared to the complex font (Study 1). Market researchers are usually interested not only in the immediate effects but also in the long-term effects of their marketing efforts. Suppose that the participants of the first study were instructed to provide an immediate liking judgment for the brand name printed in one of the fonts and to take a look at the brand name once per day for a 1-month period (Study 6). After the month is over, they are asked to provide a second liking judgment. It then becomes possible to examine the temporal stability of the liking judgment and to determine whether one of the fonts is more prone to habituation.

Technically, such a study has a 2 (between: font type) $\times$ 2 (within: time) mixed factorial design. In the exemplary dataset, the between-subjects factor is named iv_2, the immediate liking judgment is dv_2, and the follow-up liking judgment is dv_2_within. A total of 120 participants were randomly assigned to the two between-subjects conditions (60 per factor level). To understand the mechanics of a mixed-ANOVA, we first look at the decomposition of the total sum of squares provided in Fig. 12.

The key concept of RM-ANOVA is also applied to the mixed-ANOVA: The residual variance is decomposed into a between- and a within-subjects part, and each effect is only tested against the relevant part of the residual variance. In particular, the main effect of the between-subjects factor (i.e., font type) SS_{MB} is tested against the between-subjects residual variance SS_{RB}. The main effect of the within-subjects factor (i.e., time) SS_{MW} is tested against the within-subjects residual variance SS_{RW}. Finally, the interaction of the between- and the within-subjects factor SS_{MB*W} is only tested against the within-subjects residual variance SS_{RW}. This testing procedure is evident from the output of the described mixed-ANOVA provided in Fig. 13 (note the column denoted by "Error SS").

The results of the mixed-ANOVA reveal that "font type" ($F(1, 118) = 42.45$; $p < 0.001$), time ($F(1, 118) = 27.80$; $p < 0.001$), and the interaction of the factors ($F(1, 118) = 26.04$; $p < 0.001$) all have a significant influence on liking. The barplot of the means provided in Fig. 14 shows that the interaction is caused by the complex font being equally liked immediately after seeing it the first time and 1 month later,

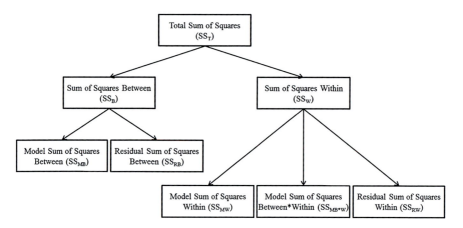

Fig. 12 Sources of variation in a mixed-ANOVA

```
> summary(Anova(mod.Mixed, idata=idata.Mixed, idesign=~Time, type="III"), multivariate=F)

Univariate Type III Repeated-Measures ANOVA Assuming Sphericity

                      SS num Df Error SS den Df        F    Pr(>F)
(Intercept)        5226.7     1   491.52    118 1254.783 < 2.2e-16 ***
Data.Anova$iv_2     176.8     1   491.52    118   42.449 1.864e-09 ***
Time                 16.0     1    67.98    118   27.800 6.166e-07 ***
Data.Anova$iv_2:Time 15.0     1    67.98    118   26.036 1.296e-06 ***
---
Signif. codes:  0 '***' 0.001 '**' 0.01 '*' 0.05 '.' 0.1 ' ' 1
```

Fig. 13 R output of a mixed-ANOVA with two factors (Study 6)

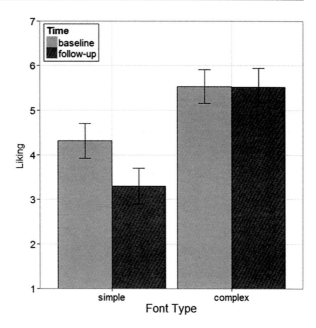

Fig. 14 Mean liking ratings of Study 6 with 95% confidence intervals

whereas the liking of the simple font decreases over time, which is arguably due to boredom.

Extensions

The standard (RM-)ANOVA approach described thus far is limited to discrete independent variables (i.e., predictors) and to a single dependent variable (i.e., outcome). We will now cover two variants of the standard approach that extend the ANOVA framework to continuous predictors (ANCOVA) and to more than one dependent variable (MANOVA).

Analysis of Covariance (ANCOVA)

Analysis of covariance (ANCOVA) refers to an ANOVA model in which at least one continuous predictor variable is included. The key idea of ANCOVA is to include continuous control variables that are independent of the experimental factors but are related to the dependent variable. Such a control variable reduces the residual variance of the model and hence increases the likelihood of discovering a significant effect of the experimental factors. Before conducting ANCOVA, it is essential to ensure that the covariates are not correlated with the experimental factors (see Miller and Chapman 2001 for more details on this issue). If a correlation is present, the effects of the experimental factors are difficult to interpret since the covariate is confounded with the experimental effect. To avoid such a correlation, researchers should either use only trait/person variables (e.g., age, education) rather than state variables (e.g., mood, motivation) as covariates or if a state variable is really needed, it must be measured before the experimental manipulation occurs. Moreover, researchers should refrain from including too many covariates in the ANCOVA model. A covariate can only reduce the residual variance if it is highly correlated with the dependent variable and not correlated with the experimental factors. Furthermore, the included covariates should not be correlated with each other. Usually, it is difficult to find a lot of variables that fulfill these criteria. Therefore, ANCOVA often employs a single covariate and rarely more than two to three covariates.

As an example of the application of ANCOVA, consider the one-way ANOVA study at the outset of this chapter. It is reasonable to assume that the general liking of a business bicycle brand differs between people, independent of the employed font. For instance, participants' age could influence the general liking, such that the general preference for a business bicycle brand increases with age. If age is added to the first ANOVA model of this chapter (Study 1) as a covariate, the model becomes an ANCOVA. Thereby, the residual variance can be reduced. The Web-Appendix contains an exemplary application of such an ANCOVA. Please note that in R, the covariate needs to be mean centered (i.e., x_i – mean(x) for each individual observation i of variable x) before it can be included in the ANCOVA. In SPSS, mean centering is automatically executed by the ANCOVA procedure.

Multivariate Analysis of Variance (MANOVA)

Suppose that in this chapter's first study, participants were not only asked to provide a liking judgment (variable name in the dataset, *dv_2*) but also a willingness-to-buy judgment (*dv_2_manova*). In this situation, there is more than one dependent variable that could be analyzed by ANOVA. One could be tempted to run two univariate ANOVAs sequentially for the two variables. However, it is likely that these two variables are correlated with each other, and this information would be lost when running two separate analyses. Furthermore, as previously discussed in the context of post hoc contrasts, this approach would be an example of multiple statistical testing using the same data, which leads to an inflation of Type I error (i.e., alpha inflation).

There are two potential solutions to this problem. First, if the two (or more) variables are statistically highly correlated and, based on their theoretical meaning, are highly related, it would be advisable to treat them as items of an overarching scale and to aggregate the sores to form a single value (i.e., the mean of the two or more scores). This approach follows the logic of latent constructs that are measured by multiple indicators. Then, one can simply run a univariate ANOVA on the aggregated score and follow the steps described thus far.

Second, if the two variables measure theoretically different concepts that cannot be summarized by one overarching construct, one would perform MANOVA. The key idea of MANOVA is that the dependent variables are not analyzed in isolation but a linear combination of all dependent variables (called a "variate") serves as the outcome to be analyzed. Moreover, MANOVA accounts for the correlation between the dependent variables using information present in the error terms. A significant effect in MANOVA means that at least one experimental group differs from one other group on at least one of the considered dependent variables. To determine which group mean/means differs/differ, one usually conducts separate univariate ANOVAs and respective post hoc tests. In this sense, MANOVA serves as a global omnibus test that guards against alpha inflation. The follow-up analyses are only conducted if the MANOVA indicates significant effects; otherwise, the analysis stops. The Web-Appendix contains an exemplary application of MANOVA.

Conclusion

Managers often need to make discrete decisions: Should I run advertisement A or B? Should I launch product A or B? Should I position my brand as A or B? These types of decisions require marketing research to evaluate the effect of a discrete predictor (i.e., experimental factor) on a continuous outcome variable (such as consumers' liking, willingness to buy, or willingness to pay). ANOVA is the method of choice to analyze such datasets because it determines whether there are differences in the means of different groups of observations. The data entered into an ANOVA are usually produced through experimental research, which has major advantages in terms of causal interpretation of effects. Since ANOVA provides answers to some of the most important types of questions (marketing) managers have in mind, it is not surprising that ANOVA is one of the most important techniques in marketing research. Accordingly, a comprehensive review of articles published in one of the world-leading scientific marketing journals, the *Journal of Marketing Research*, found that ANOVA is the most frequently used statistical technique across all papers published by the journal (Malhotra et al. 1999).

The present book chapter was intended to provide an applied introduction to this important statistical technique. Instead of covering all statistical details and all the different options to run the analysis (see Field 2013 and Field et al. 2012 for a more detailed introduction to the different types of ANOVA), the key intention of this book chapter was to provide clear guidance for how to apply this technique without making mistakes. To this end, the book chapter is accompanied by a comprehensive Web-Appendix covering an exemplary dataset and complete scripts of commands for R and SPSS to conduct all the analyses covered in this chapter. These scripts can be used as blueprints to conduct these analyses on the readers' own datasets. To close this chapter, I would like to summarize some recommendations for applying ANOVA:

– *Coding of factors*: The main effects of ANOVA are only meaningful when effect coding (i.e., -1 vs. 1) instead of dummy coding (i.e., 0 vs. 1) is implemented for the experimental factors because only effect coding evaluates the main effects relative to the grand mean (see Table 7 and the corresponding explanations). SPSS uses effect coding by default for ANOVA models, and the user does not need to consider this issue. However, R uses dummy coding by default, and the user needs to actively specify effect coding to make the main effects in ANOVA models meaningful (see lines 24–41 of the Web-Appendix R Script on how to specify effect coding in R). This is a serious issue because the type of coding has a substantial impact on the estimated effects. Incorrect coding can lead to completely wrong inferences.

- *Sum of squares (SS):* As long as only one experimental factor is involved or if all experimental cells contain exactly the same number of observations, one does not have to consider the different ways of computing the SS. If these conditions do not hold, Type III SS is highly recommended. Type I SS suffers from the fact that the order in which the factors are entered into the model determines how much of the explained variance is ascribed to the factors (the first factor gets more than the later factors). However, there is rarely a meaningful order for the factors. SPSS uses Type III SS by default. However, the `aov` function in R uses Type I SS, and the `Anova` function is required to estimate Type III SS. It is highly recommended to change the default when using R and to base the analysis on Type III SS (see, e.g., line 156 of the Web-Appendix R Script on how to change to Type III SS).

- *Linear mixed models (LMMs)*: Recent discussions on the sphericity assumption and the treatment of missing values in RM-ANOVA designs have led researchers to conclude that in situations where three or more within-factor levels and/or missing values are present, an alternative analytical technique is superior: LMMs (see West et al. 2015 for an applied introduction). LMMs are an extension of the regression framework and were developed to model any type of multilevel data. Repeated measures on the same participants are one potential field of application for this type of model. The key idea of this class of models when applied to repeated measures is that the between-subjects variance is treated as a random effect. As in RM-ANOVA, this part of the variation is excluded from the evaluation of the experimental effects. However, LMMs can also explicitly model deviations from the sphericity assumption and can easily handle missing values within participants (in contrast to RM-ANOVA). However, LMMs are theoretically and computationally more difficult to understand and more difficult to apply than RM-ANOVA. Nevertheless, LMMs have become increasingly popular in many fields. Recent research (e.g., Westfall et al. 2014) recommends the use of such models for any ANOVA procedure where random stimulus replicates are used within participants.[12]

- *Effect size*: Scientists and practitioners are not only interested in the existence of an effect but in addition also in the magnitude of the effect. For large datasets, very small effects can be statistically significant without having any practical

---

[12]For example, when the effect of funny vs. rational advertisement is examined, one usually shows several funny and several rational advertisements and compares the aggregated mean evaluations. The random variation between advertisements can be controlled by LMM.

meaning. To quantify the magnitude of an effect, it has become good scientific practice to report the effect size in addition to F- and p-values (Lakens 2013).[13] In the context of ANOVA, the most common effect size measure is the partial eta squared, reported as η_p^2. For a Factor A, it is defined as $SS_A/(SS_A + SS_{Residual})$. Hence, it measures a factor's share of the variance not explained by other factors in the model. According to Cohen (1988, pp. 285–288), a value of 0.01 is regarded as a small effect, a value of 0.06 is regarded as a medium effect, and a value of 0.14 and larger is regarded as a large effect (see also Richardson 2011). The Web-Appendix contains an exemplary computation of this effect size measure using the `BaylorEdPsych` library in R (Beaujean 2012) and the option menu of SPSS.

– *Extensions of ANOVA*: The present chapter exclusively focused on the application of ANOVA to experimental data. We learned that by comparing two portions of variance (systematic vs. unsystematic), ANOVA can determine whether the means of experimental groups significantly differ. The basic principle of ANOVA can, however, be extended to any situation in statistical data analysis where the sizes of variances need to be compared. For instance, many statistical techniques require homogeneity of variances across different groups of observations to fulfill the distributional assumptions of the technique. ANOVA itself makes the assumption that the error variance is homogenous across different experimental groups, which can be tested using Levene's test of variance homogeneity (Levene 1960). Interestingly, Levene's test is just a special case of ANOVA. Another example is the modeling of data using regression analysis. When applying regression, one often has to decide how many predictors should be included in the model. In particular, the question whether adding additional predictors to the model sufficiently increases the fit of the model needs to be answered. For this purpose, ANOVA can be used to compare the residual variances of a more parsimonious model and a model with additional predictors. In this context, ANOVA assesses whether the additional predictors significantly decrease the residual variance and should be included or discarded. Hence, ANOVA can also be used to support model selection in the context of regression analysis. The reader of this chapter should thus not be surprised to see applications of ANOVA to problems beyond the analysis of experimental data.

– *Statistical software*: The present chapter is accompanied by an exemplary dataset and command script files for SPSS and R. I selected these two software packages because SPSS is a widespread and easy-to-use statistical software, and the application of ANOVA models is well implemented in SPSS. By default, SPSS uses the correct coding of factors and computes the correct sum of squares, which prevents potential errors. SPSS also provides many helpful additional outputs by default, for instance, checks of the model assumptions. Hence, I would highly recommend SPSS for beginners in the application of ANOVA and for people who

---

[13]An excellent introduction to the use of effect size measures and a comparison of different approaches can be found in the referred article by Lakens (2013).

do not want to focus too much on technical issues in their daily research to make life easier and less error prone. The implementation of ANOVA in R is not user-friendly. As discussed above, the defaults in R with respect to factor coding and sum of squares lead to potentially wrong results. Applying RM-ANOVA and computing simple effects are very difficult in R and require computations by hand. I nevertheless chose R because it is a highly powerful statistical software with a steadily increasing number of users. Moreover, because the implementation of ANOVA in R is so difficult and error prone, I found it particularly important to equip the interested reader with the required knowledge to prevent mistakes when using R for ANOVA. I hope that the exemplary R code will help readers to build their own error-free ANOVA models and that it makes applying ANOVA in R less challenging and more fun.

References

Beaujean, A.A. (2012). *BaylorEdPsych: R package for Baylor University educational psychology quantitative courses*. R package version 0.5.

Cohen, J. (1988). *Statistical power analysis for the behavioral sciences* (2nd ed.). Hillsdale: Lawrence Erlbaum Associates.

Cumming, G., & Finch, S. (2005). Inference by eye: Confidence intervals and how to read pictures of data. *American Psychologist, 60*(2), 170–180.

Field, A. (2013). *Discovering statistics using R* (4th ed.). Los Angeles: Sage.

Field, A., Miles, J., & Field, Z. (2012). *Discovering statistics using R*. Los Angeles: Sage.

Fisher, R. A. (1935). *The design of experiments*. Edinburgh: Oliver & Boyd.

Fox, J., & Weisberg, S. (2011). *An {R} companion to applied regression* (2nd ed.). Thousand Oaks: Sage.

Greenhouse, S. W., & Geisser, S. (1959). On methods in the analysis of profile data. *Psychometrika, 24*(2), 95–112.

Holm, S. (1979). A simple sequentially rejective multiple test procedure. *Scandinavian Journal of Statistics, 6*(2), 65–70.

Huynh, H., & Feldt, L. S. (1976). Estimation of the box correction for degrees of freedom from sample data in randomized block and split-plot designs. *Journal of Educational Statistics, 1*(1), 69–82.

Klockars, A. J., & Sax, G. (1986). *Multiple comparisons*. Newbury Park: Sage.

Lakens, D. (2013). Calculating and reporting effect sizes to facilitate cumulative science: A practical primer for t-tests and ANOVAs. *Frontiers in Psychology*. https://doi.org/10.3389/fpsyg.2013.00863.

Lawrence, M.A. (2015). *ez: Easy analysis and visualization of factorial experiments*. R package version 4.3.

Levene, H. (1960). Robust tests for equality of variances. In I. Olkin et al. (Eds.), *Contributions to probability and statistics* (pp. 278–292). Stanford: University Press.

Malhotra, N. K., Peterson, M., & Kleiser, S. B. (1999). Marketing research: A state-of-the-art review and directions for the twenty-first century. *Journal of the Academy of Marketing Science, 27*(2), 160–183.

Miller, G. A., & Chapman, J. P. (2001). Misunderstanding analysis of covariance. *Journal of Abnormal Psychology, 110*(1), 40–48.

Richardson, J. T. E. (2011). Eta squared and partial eta squared as measures of effect size in educational research. *Educational Research Review, 6*(2), 135–147.

Rodger, R. S., & Roberts, M. (2013). Comparison of power for multiple comparison procedures. *Journal of Methods and Measurements in the Social Sciences, 4*(1), 20–47.

Rutherford, A. (2001). *Introducing ANOVA and MANOVA: A GLM approach*. London: Sage.

Sawyer, A. G. (1975). Demand artifacts in laboratory experiments in consumer research. *Journal of Consumer Research, 1*(4), 20–30.

West, B. T., Welch, K. B., & Galecki, A. T. (2015). *Linear mixed models: A practical guide using statistical software* (2nd ed.). Boca Raton: Chapman & Hall.

Westfall, J., Kenny, D. A., & Judd, C. M. (2014). Statistical power and optimal design in experiments in which samples of participants respond to samples of stimuli. *Journal of Experimental Psychology: General, 143*(5), 2020–2045.

Wickham, H. (2009). *ggplot2: Elegant graphics for data analysis*. New York: Springer.

Regression Analysis

Bernd Skiera, Jochen Reiner, and Sönke Albers

Contents

Introduction	300
Statistical Explanation of the Method	300
Problem Statement	300
Objective Function and Estimation of Regression Coefficients	301
Goodness of Fit	304
Significance Testing	305
Standardization of Coefficients	306
Interpretation of Results	307
Results of Numerical Example	307
Assumptions	309
Procedure	310
Efficiency of Estimators	311
Test for Multicollinearity	311
Test for Autocorrelation	313
Test for Heteroscedasticity	315
Identification of Outliers	317
Transformation of Variables	318
Implications of the Analysis	320
Endogeneity	321
Further Topics	324
Software	325
Summary	326
References	326

B. Skiera (✉) · J. Reiner
Goethe University Frankfurt, Frankfurt, Germany
e-mail: skiera@skiera.de; jreiner@wiwi.uni-frankfurt.de

S. Albers
Kuehne Logistics University, Hamburg, Germany
e-mail: soenke.albers@the-klu.org

© Springer Nature Switzerland AG 2022
C. Homburg et al. (eds), *Handbook of Market Research*,
https://doi.org/10.1007/978-3-319-57413-4_17

> **Abstract**
>
> Linear regression analysis is one of the most important statistical methods. It examines the linear relationship between a metric-scaled dependent variable (also called endogenous, explained, response, or predicted variable) and one or more metric-scaled independent variables (also called exogenous, explanatory, control, or predictor variable). We illustrate how regression analysis work and how it supports marketing decisions, e.g., the derivation of an optimal marketing mix. We also outline how to use linear regression analysis to estimate nonlinear functions such as a multiplicative sales response function. Furthermore, we show how to use the results of a regression to calculate elasticities and to identify outliers and discuss in details the problems that occur in case of autocorrelation, multicollinearity and heteroscedasticity. We use a numerical example to illustrate in detail all calculations and use this numerical example to outline the problems that occur in case of endogeneity.

> **Keywords**
>
> Regression analysis · Marketing mix modeling · Elasticities · Multicollinearity · Autocorrelation · Outlier detection · Endogeneity · Sales response function

Introduction

Linear regression analysis is one of the most important statistical methods. It examines the linear relationship between a metric-scaled dependent variable (also called endogenous, explained, response, or predicted variable) and one or more metric-scaled independent variables (also called exogenous, explanatory, control, or predictor variable). Often, the dependent variable describes the success of marketing and the independent variables the factors that explain this success. Variables that describe the success of marketing are either "hard" success factors such as profit, sales volume (here referred to as quantity), and market share or "soft" success factors such as customers' attitudes, purchase intention, and satisfaction. Variables that influence this success are frequently marketing instruments such as price, product, distribution, and communication. To illustrate how regression analysis works, we focus here on a numerical example with a hard success factor, namely, the estimation of quantity (i.e., sales volume), which is explained by variables such as advertising budget, price, and number of salespersons.

Statistical Explanation of the Method

Problem Statement

We illustrate the basic idea of linear regression analysis by applying it to data from a (fictitious) company (displayed in Table 1). Their analysis should address the following business problems:

Regression Analysis

Table 1 Distribution of quantity and marketing instruments across districts

District	Quantity	Salespersons	Price	Advertising	Number of mailings
1	81,996	7	49	228,753	7,106
2	91,735	5	46	370,062	4,733
3	70,830	4	50	297,909	3,734
4	101,192	6	45	271,884	6,152
5	78,319	6	51	299,919	5,734
6	105,369	7	47	367,644	6,640
7	68,564	3	47	241,362	3,115
8	95,523	7	46	244,575	6,859
9	88,834	7	49	296,100	6,905
10	89,511	5	46	372,498	5,142
11	107,836	6	45	359,511	6,196
12	83,310	7	50	324,837	6,801
13	67,817	4	50	288,303	3,965
14	59,207	6	54	289,470	5,830
15	81,410	6	52	363,501	6,124
16	71,431	3	46	361,974	2,509
17	119,000	3	45	250,000	–

- What is the optimal price?
- What is the optimal budget for advertising and the sales force?

The data in Table 1 shows quantitiy at one point in time for 16 districts that were randomly selected from a much larger number of districts in which the company operates. The districts differ only in terms of price, advertising budget, and salespersons. For the moment, we ignore district 17 and the marketing instrument "number of mailings."

The company has variable costs per unit sold of \$30 and costs for each salesperson of \$120,000 per year. Moreover, we assume that thus far the company has managed its marketing activities naively and has not systematically selected the value for each of its marketing instruments in each district. With this assumption, we exclude the problem of endogeneity (we do address this topic subsequently).

Objective Function and Estimation of Regression Coefficients

Linear regression analysis investigates the effect of metric-scaled independent variables (here, person, price, and advertising budget) on a metric-scaled dependent variable (here, quantity). We consider each district as one observation. The corresponding regression equation for the linear regression analysis is as follows:

$$y_i = b_0 + \sum_{k \in K} b_k \cdot x_{i,k} + e_i \ (i \in I), \tag{1}$$

where

y_i = value of the ith observation for the dependent variable,
b_0 = intercept of the regression,
b_k = regression coefficient capturing the influence of the kth independent variable,
$x_{i,k}$ = value of the ith observation for the kth independent variable,
e_i = residual of the ith observation,
K = index set of the independent variables, and
I = index set of the observations.

We can observe values of the dependent variable y_i and independent variables $x_{i,k}$ (see the respective values in Table 1), but we need to estimate the coefficients of the regression equation (Eq. 1), b_0 and b_k ($k \in K$), and the resulting residuals e_i ($i \in I$) (sometimes also referred to as "disturbance" or "error term"). The residual e_i describes the deviation between the observed value of the dependent variable y_i for the ith observation and the predicted value for the dependent variable $\widehat{y_i}$. The predicted value of the dependent variable is based on the estimated regression coefficients b_k and the respective observed independent variables $x_{i,k}$, as illustrated in Eq. 2:

$$\widehat{y_i} = b_0 + \sum_{k \in K} b_k \cdot x_{i,k} \ (i \in I). \tag{2}$$

The upper part of Fig. 1 illustrates the deviations of the observed values from the predicted values (for quantity, depending on advertising budget), with the predicted values lying on the regression line.

The aim of linear regression analysis is to estimate the coefficients of the regression equation b_0 and b_k ($k \in K$) so that the sum of the squared residuals (i.e., the sum over all squared differences between the observed values of the ith observation of y_i and the corresponding predicted values $\widehat{y_i}$) is minimized. The lower part of Fig. 1 illustrates this approach, which is called the "least squares method" (Stock and Watson 2015, p. 162). Simply speaking, the least squares method aims to minimize the sum of all rectangular areas displayed in the lower part of Fig. 1. The approach results in the following objective function:

$$\sum_{i \in I} e_i^2 = \sum_{i \in I} (y_i - \widehat{y_i})^2 = \sum_{i \in I} \left(y_i - b_0 - \sum_{k \in K} b_k \cdot x_{i,k} \right)^2 \to \min! \tag{3}$$

Using squared residuals is advantageous in that larger residuals receive a greater weight than smaller residuals and the solution for the objective function (Eq. 3) is algorithmically easy to determine (Pindyck and Rubenfeld 1998, p. 5). We do not derive the solution for the objective function (Eq. 3) here because a wide range of software (such as those presented in section "Software") can perform this operation.

Regression Analysis

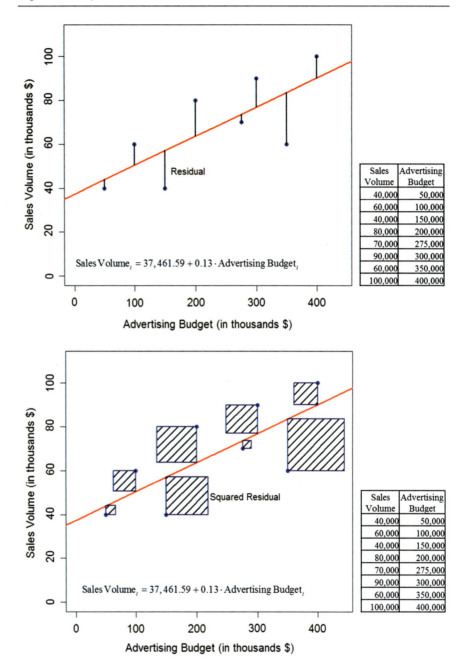

Fig. 1 Regression line with residuals and squared residuals

For more details on deriving the solution, see Wooldridge (2009, p. 27) and Gujarati (2003, p. 58), among many others.

Goodness of Fit

The assessment of goodness of fit for a linear regression analysis builds on the idea that the best estimate of the predicted value of a dependent variable is its mean value if nothing is known about the independent variables. Thus, a linear regression analysis is only meaningful if it can explain deviations from this mean value. More precisely, we determine goodness of fit by evaluating the extent to which considering the independent variables improves the "simple" prediction of just taking the mean value of the dependent variable. The coefficient of determination, called R^2 (see Eq. 4), measures goodness of fit by calculating the proportion of explained variance from the regression equation compared with the variance indicated by simply taking the mean value $\bar{y}$:

$$R^2 = \frac{\sum_{i \in I} (\hat{y}_i - \bar{y})^2}{\sum_{i \in I} (y_i - \bar{y})^2} \tag{4}$$

Thus, the linear regression analysis always explains at least the variance of the simple approach in that even if all independent variables have no explanatory power (the extreme worst case), the intercept captures the mean value of the dependent variable; in other words, the linear regression analysis reduces to simply predicting the mean value. Fortunately, adding one or more independent variables frequently improves this prediction. At the other extreme, the improvement in prediction might be so large that the predicted values of the dependent variable exactly match their observed values. In this case, the regression equation explains the total variance of the simple approach. R^2 can therefore take values between 0% and 100%. Negative values for R^2 can only arise when the researcher estimates the regression equation without an intercept, which is possible with most statistical programs; however, without an intercept, the linear regression analysis does not necessarily explain the variance of the simple approach.

These considerations should also make clear that including an additional independent variable never leads to a reduction of R^2, because the explanatory power of the additional variable is at least zero, even if that variable explains nothing. In the extreme case that the number of observations corresponds to the number of estimated coefficients (more precisely, the intercept b_0 plus the number of regression coefficients b_k), we would essentially estimate a linear system of equations. The estimation of such a linear system always results in $R^2 = 100\%$, its largest possible value. To account for the fact that R^2 can only increase and does not penalize the use of variables that have no explanatory power, researchers frequently use the adjusted R^2 (R^2_{adj}), defined as follows (Wooldridge 2009, p. 200):

$$R^2_{adj} = R^2 - \frac{|K| \cdot \left(1 - R^2\right)}{|I| - |K| - 1}, \tag{5}$$

where

|I| = number of elements in the index set of observations (equivalent to the number of observations) and
|K| = number of elements in the index set of independent variables (equivalent to the number of regression coefficients).

Note that both numerator and denominator of the fraction are positive; therefore, the adjusted R^2 has at best the same value as the (unadjusted) R^2. Large differences indicate that the regression equation contains many independent variables that do not explain the dependent variable (i.e., they have no explanatory power).

Significance Testing

Data are usually available only for a sample and not for an entire population, whether in the context of a large amount of surveys carried out by market research companies or data collected via panels and laboratory or field experiments. In the same vein, the presented 16 districts represent a (randomly selected) sample. In such a situation, it is necessary to determine the extent to which the results drawn from the sample also apply for the entire population. To do so, we must make an assumption about the distribution of the residuals.

For regression analysis (and many other methods), it is common to assume a normal distribution for the residuals. This assumption is based on the central limit theorem, which states that the mean from a random sample for any population (with finite variance), when standardized, has an asymptotic standard normal distribution (Wooldridge 2009, p. 758).

Using this assumption, we can conduct significance tests for the regression coefficients by calculating the error probability (often abbreviated as p-value) that the regression coefficients are nonzero. The significance test compares the determined error probability with a predetermined level of significance (often 5%). If the error probability is less than this predetermined level of significance, then the effect is considered significant.

To test the overall significance of a regression – that is, that all regression coefficients of the independent variables are 0 ($b_1 = b_2 = \ldots = b_k = 0$) – we conduct the following F-Test with $|K|$ and ($|I| - |K| - 1$) degrees of freedom:

$$F_{emp} = \frac{\dfrac{R^2}{|K|}}{\dfrac{1 - R^2}{|I| - |K| - 1}}. \tag{6}$$

If the F-value (F_{emp}) computed from Eq. 6 exceeds the critical F-value from the F table at a predetermined level of significance (often, as mentioned above, 5%), the researcher can reject the null hypothesis that all independent variables have no effect on the dependent variable. Alternatively, many statistical software programs immediately report the error probability (p-value) for the F-value. If the error probability is less than the predetermined level of significance, the researcher can also reject the null hypothesis.

Whereas the F-test verifies the existence of a significant relationship between all independent variables and the dependent variable, the t-test determines the significance of each individual regression coefficient separately. Thus, it tests whether the null hypothesis of the coefficient being equal to 0 cannot be rejected with a certain error probability, frequently 5%. The t-test has $(|I| - |K| - 1)$ degrees of freedom and is calculated as follows:

$$t_{k, emp} = \frac{b_k}{s_k} \quad (k \in K),\tag{7}$$

where

$t_{k, emp}$ = empirical t-value for the kth regression coefficient and
s_k = estimated standard error of the kth regression coefficient.

If the empirical t-value exceeds the critical t-value (from the t-distribution) at the chosen level of significance or, alternatively, the error probability (p-value) is less than the predetermined level of significance, then the coefficient is not equal to 0, and the impact of the kth independent variable is significant.

Standardization of Coefficients

Often, it is necessary to compare the importance of the independent variables against one another. However, directly comparing the regression coefficients is hardly meaningful because the independent variables usually have different orders of magnitude (e.g., in Table 1, the advertising budget is measured in dollar values and person is measured in number of salespersons). The standardized regression coefficients $beta_k$ allow for a meaningful comparison. They are calculated by multiplying the (unstandardized) regression coefficients b_k with the standard deviation σ_{xk} of the associated independent variable and dividing the result by the standard deviation of the dependent variable σ_y:

$$beta_k = b_k \cdot \frac{\sigma_{x_k}}{\sigma_y} \quad (k \in K).\tag{8}$$

If the dependent and independent variables are standardized before running the regression analysis, then the regression coefficients $beta_k$ and b_k will be the same. Thus, comparing the absolute values of all standardized regression coefficient $beta_k$ shows the importance of the influence of the individual independent variables: Higher absolute values indicate a stronger influence.

Note, however, that using the standardized regression coefficient is discouraged when the standard deviations of the independent variables can be influenced. For example, if a company varied its product price to a greater extent than its advertising, then the standardized regression coefficients will indicate a stronger influence of the price due to the high standard deviation of the price (see Eq. 8). Therefore, it is preferable to calculate the elasticities of the independent variables, which are dimensionless and measure the responsiveness of the dependent variable to a change in one of the independent variables. Stated differently, they measure the percentage change of the dependent variable that corresponds to a 1% change of the independent variable. In the case of a linear regression, the elasticity is defined as follows:

$$\varepsilon_{y, x_k} = \frac{\frac{\partial y}{y}}{\frac{\partial x_k}{x_k}} = \frac{\partial y}{\partial x_k} \cdot \frac{x_k}{y} = b_k \cdot \frac{x_k}{y} \quad (k \in K).$$

(9)

Although the elasticity derived from Eq. 9 varies with the value of the independent variables, the common approach to calculate the elasticity for the independent variable x_k is to use the mean values of the independent variable x_k and the dependent variable y.

Interpretation of Results

Substantive insights should guide the interpretation of the results, rather than simply statistical criteria. In other words, researchers should first consider whether the regression equation captures all relevant variables via a meaningful functional relationship and then examine whether the signs of the regression coefficients are plausible. For the company in our example, the regression coefficients for advertising and person should be positive and negative, respectively, with regard to price. Then, to assess the size of the regression coefficients, calculating elasticities is often helpful. For example, advertising elasticities with values greater than 1 usually make little sense. The same holds for price elasticities with absolute values smaller than 1. Next to evaluating the substantive criteria, researcher should inspect statistical criteria such as the R^2, the overall significance of the regression equation (F-test), the significance of the regression coefficients (t-test), and the subsequent assumptions for the least squares method.

Results of Numerical Example

In this section, we use the software program R to estimate the regression equation (codes for R but also other software programs such as STATA and SPSS are available on the authors' website). Figure 2 displays the result for this linear regression analysis with three marketing instruments (person, price, and advertising budget as independent variables and quantity as the dependent variable.

```
Call:
lm(formula = Quantity ~ Person + Price + Advertising, data = regdata)

Residuals:
    Min      1Q  Median      3Q     Max
-7650.1 -3383.9   287.8  3211.0  5047.8

Coefficients:
             Estimate  Std. Error t value Pr(>|t|)
(Intercept) 210159.444  23729.909   8.856    0.000 ***
Person        6723.478     840.997   7.995    0.000 ***
Price        -3832.503     444.013  -8.632    0.000 ***
Advertising      0.069       0.024   2.903    0.013 *
---
Signif. codes:  0 '***' 0.001 '**' 0.01 '*' 0.05 '.' 0.1 ' ' 1

Residual standard error: 4546 on 12 degrees of freedom
Multiple R-squared:  0.9189,     Adjusted R-squared:  0.8986
F-statistic: 45.29 on 3 and 12 DF,  p-value: 8.077e-07


-----------
"standardized coefficients - beta"
   Person         Price      Advertising
    0.665        -0.725            0.242
------------------------------------------------------------------
Elasticities, at average values (not provided by R directly)
   Person         Price      Advertising
    0.446        -2.206            0.257
```

Fig. 2 Results of the linear regression analysis

The number of observations (here 16) is equal to the sum of the degrees of freedom (here 12) and the number of estimated coefficients (here 4). The R^2 ("R-squared") and the adjusted R^2 ("Adjusted R-squared") have values of 91.9% and 89.9%, respectively. The error probabilities determined for the F-test ("p-value") and the t-tests (column "Pr $(>|t|)$") are lower than the predetermined significance level of 5%; thus, the data indicate that all three marketing instruments have a significant effect. For example, the value 0.013 in column "Pr $(>|t|)$" means that if we repeatedly draw samples from the entire population, the probability of not observing a relationship between the advertising budget and the quantity is 1.3%.

The column titled "Estimate" provides the values for the (rounded) regression coefficients; their standard errors are in the column "Std. Error." In contrast to other software programs, R does not automatically calculate the standardized beta values; therefore, separate calculations were necessary (values shown below the regression results in Fig. 2). In line with our expectations, person and the advertising budget have a positive impact, and price has a negative impact on quantity. Yet, we cannot use these regression coefficients to determine the strength of the effects. Instead, we must rely on the standardized beta values, which indicates that price has a slightly higher impact than the salesperson and that both marketing instruments show a considerably higher impact than advertising. Calculating the elasticities using Eq. 9,

Regression Analysis

we find an elasticity of the salespersons of 0.45, a price elasticity of -2.21, and an advertising elasticity of 0.26. All elasticities show plausible signs and proportions (see also the meta-analyses conducted by Hanssens et al. 1990 and Albers et al.'s 2010 as well as Assmus et al. 1984; Bijmolt et al. 2005; Lodish et al. 1995; Sethuraman et al. 2011; Tellis 1988).

Assumptions

Thus far, we have focused on the method and the results of the linear regression. Next, we continue by examining whether the underlying statistical assumptions for a linear regression are fulfilled. These assumptions relate to the residuals; the relationship between dependent and independent variables, between the independent variable and the residuals, or between the independent variables; or the number of observations.

Assumptions for the residuals:

- Normal distribution of the residuals e_i
- Expected value of zero for the residuals $E(e_i) = 0$
- No correlation between residuals and independent variables, i.e., $corr(x_{i,k}, e_i) = 0$
- Constant variance of the residuals (homoscedasticity), i.e., $E(e_i^2) = \sigma^2$
- No correlation between the residuals (missing autocorrelation), i.e., $E(e_i \cdot e_i') = 0$

These assumptions essentially mean that the residuals resulting from the regression equation do not depend on the size of the observed variables (homoscedasticity), any of the independent variables, or the other residuals, particularly not on the residual of the previous period, as often occurs in the presence of time series (autocorrelation). In our example, the residual values should therefore be independent of the values of the three marketing instruments.

Endogeneity refers to the important assumption of the regression analysis that there is no relationship between one of the independent variables and the residuals. This independence should be present in our example because the company was naive in its marketing, which means that the company randomly chose the respective values for the marketing instruments. Therefore, no correlation should exist between the residuals, which reflect high or low level of marketing success, and the marketing instruments.

In reality, this assumption is often not fulfilled, because companies do not set their marketing activities randomly but systematically. These situations suffer from endogeneity. A typical example for such a situation occurs if the company does more marketing in districts where the company expects to be particularly successful. In our regression, "particularly successful" means that the quantity is higher than expected so that residuals are positive. Consequently, the independent variables correlate with the residuals.

Assumptions regarding the relationship between dependent and independent variables

- Consideration of all relevant independent variables
- Linearity of the regression equation (i.e., functional form)

To derive meaningful conclusions, we must ensure that the regression equation includes all relevant independent variables to avoid risking that the regression coefficients reflect the impact of the missing (also called omitted) variables. Furthermore, we assume in our linear regression analysis a linear relationship between the independent and dependent variables.

Assumptions regarding the relationship between the independent variables

- No multicollinearity between the independent variables

The regression analysis assumes that there is no linear relationship between the independent variables, that is, that there is a lack of multicollinearity. If multicollinearity occurs, because, for example, a high correlation exists between two independent variables, then a problem will occur: The effect of neither of the two variables on the dependent variable can be clearly derived.

Number of observations

- Sufficient number of observations

We can only estimate the regression equation in Eq. 1 if a sufficient number of observations are available. More precisely, the number of observations must be at least as large as the number of estimated coefficients (intercept b_o plus the total number of regression coefficients b_k). Yet detecting a significant influence requires that the number of observations is much larger than the number of estimated coefficients. It is difficult to come up with a general statement about the ratio of the number of observations and the number of estimated coefficients, because this ratio always depends on the characteristics of variables in the data set. However, it is advisable that the number of observations is three times, better five times, as large as the number of estimated coefficients.

Procedure

Next, we describe the procedure for conducting a linear regression. We start by discussing the efficiency of the estimators. Afterwards, we discuss the problems that occur in case of multicollinearity, autocorrelation, heteroscedasticity, and outliers. In addition, we describe the transformation of variables often required to create a linear model.

Efficiency of Estimators

The estimated regression coefficient is efficient if it (1) is unbiased and (2) has the least variance of all unbiased coefficients (Gujarati 2003, p. 79). However, the least squares method only yields efficient estimates if the assumptions presented in section "Assumptions" hold. If the assumptions do not hold, then we must use a different estimation method or an alternative specification of the regression equation.

When examining the assumptions of the least squares method, we recommend investigating for the presence of multicollinearity, autocorrelation, and heteroscedasticity. If a sufficiently large number of observations are available, then the assumption of a normal distribution of the residuals is of minor importance, as it is usually fulfilled because of the central limit theorem (Stock and Watson 2015, p. 96). Koutsoyiannis (1977, p. 197) notes that this assumption is even fulfilled when samples have only 10–20 observations. In addition, the absence of a normal distribution signifies only that the F- and t-tests (discussed in section "Significance Testing") are not meaningfully applicable. The estimated regression coefficients are still unbiased (Koutsoyiannis 1977, p. 197).

Test for Multicollinearity

Multicollinearity occurs when the independent variables are mutually linearly dependent. Multicollinearity usually leads to high standard errors of the estimated coefficients such that it is difficult to interpret them adequately. Inspecting the correlation matrix helps detect multicollinearity in the form of a linear dependency between two independent variables. High correlation values, often greater than -0.5 and $+0.5$, indicate multicollinearity, particularly if there are few observations. In this case, it is necessary to test the degree of the multicollinearity problem. We recommend running additional regressions that leave out some of the highly correlated variables. If the regression coefficients of the kept variables change substantially, multicollinearity represents a serious problem.

Running several linear regressions can help diagnose multicollinearity in the form of a linear dependence between more than two independent variables. In each regression, we use one of the original independent variables as a dependent variable and keep the others as independent variables. The difference between 1 and the R^2 for such a regression is called "tolerance," and the inverse of this difference, which most statistical software programs report, is the "variance inflation factor" (VIF value). We can only assume a linear independence of the variables if the R^2 values of these regressions are low, which means that tolerance values are high, i.e., close to 1 and VIF values are low. Lower tolerance and higher VIF values, in contrast, indicate problems with multicollinearity. Although VIF values greater than 10 clearly indicate multicollinearity, even values of greater than 3, particularly with smaller data sets, point to problems with multicollinearity (see Hair et al. 2014, p. 200; for additional tests to uncover multicollinearity, see, e.g., Leeflang et al. 2000, pp. 348, 357).

```
                       Correlation Matrix

             Person   Price  Advertising
Person       *****    0.143  -0.080
Price        0.597    *****  -0.158
Advertising  0.767    0.559  *****

upper diagonal part contains correlation coefficient estimates
lower diagonal part contains corresponding p-values


-------------------------------------------------------------
                       VIF-Values

       Person      Price      Advertising
       1.024       1.044        1.029
```

Fig. 3 Testing for multicollinearity

In our example, the correlation matrix (see Fig. 3) indicates consistently low correlations between the independent variables, which shows there are no linear dependencies between two independent variables present. In addition, the VIF values close to 1 indicate that no linear dependencies between several independent variables exist.

With regard to the three marketing instruments, multicollinearity is thus not a problem for our data. Problems begin to emerge, however, if we also consider mailings (see Table 1), because the number of mailings is highly correlated (0.989) with the number of salespersons. Adding mailings to the linear regression analysis changes the results for the salespersons completely (Fig. 4); they now exert a negative influence on the quantity, while the number of mailings is highly positive. The high VIF values for the variables person and mailings also indicate the presence of multicollinearity.

An econometric solution for multicollinearity is difficult, although ridge regression (see Leeflang et al. 2000, p. 360) and partial least squares (Hair et al. 2017) might help. Increasing the number of observations can also help, in particular if the added observations exhibit a lower degree of linear dependence (here, salespersons and mailings). Alternatively, we could combine the linear dependent variables into a single variable (e.g., using factor analysis). We could also eliminate one or several of these variables from the linear regression analysis. For example, eliminating the salespersons from the regression decreases the parameter for mailings to 6.627 and its elasticity to 0.432.

Usually, however, it is difficult to find a truly satisfying solution for the multicollinearity problem because the number of observations is typically fixed and deleting variables is not helpful because the effects of these variables are often of primary interest. Therefore, in our numerical example, we can only assess the joint effect of both variables but not the specific effect of each variable, salespersons and mailings, on quantity. However, this information would certainly be of interest for the marketing manager in this case because this knowledge would enable her to optimize the marketing mix. For better determining the influence, the marketing manager should vary the number of salespersons and mailings so that a high correlation no longer occurs, ideally in the form of a field experiment.

```
                            Correlation Matrix
                  Person  Price  Advertising  Mailings
Person            *****   0.143  -0.080        0.989
Price             0.597   *****  -0.158        0.120
Advertising       0.767   0.559  *****        -0.115
Mailings          <0.001  0.659   0.672        *****

upper diagonal part contains correlation coefficient estimates
lower diagonal part contains corresponding p-values
------------------------------------------------------------------
                            Model Summary
Call:
lm(formula = Quantity ~ Person + Price + Advertising + Mailings,
    data = regdata)

Residuals:
    Min     1Q  Median      3Q      Max
-5964.3 -3963.1    73.7  2805.2   5867.2

Coefficients:
               Estimate Std. Error t value Pr(>|t|)
(Intercept) 203009.252  23379.266   8.683    0.000  ***
Person       -1372.882   5815.151  -0.236    0.818
Price        -3711.737    435.531  -8.522    0.000  ***
Advertising      0.078      0.024   3.288    0.007  **
Mailings         7.949      5.654   1.406    0.187
---
Signif. codes:  0 '***' 0.001 '**' 0.01 '*' 0.05 '.' 0.1 ' ' 1

Residual standard error: 4372 on 11 degrees of freedom
Multiple R-squared:  0.9312,    Adjusted R-squared:  0.9062
F-statistic: 37.23 on 4 and 11 DF,  p-value: 2.473e-06
------------------------------------------------------------------
                            VIF-Values
      Person        Price   Advertising    Mailings
      52.968        1.086        1.113      52.962
------------------------------------------------------------------
  Elasticities, at average values (not provided by R directly)
      Person        Price   Advertising    Mailings
      -0.091       -2.137        0.291       0.518
```

Fig. 4 Result of the regression analysis with multicollinearity problems

Test for Autocorrelation

Autocorrelation means that the residuals correlate with each other. Such correlation is most common in time series analyses, when the independent variables do not adequately cover the cyclical fluctuations in the time series. Autocorrelation usually leads to a situation where the predicted values are too high for some periods and too low for others. Thus, a series of negative residuals alternates with a series of positive residuals.

Autocorrelation causes an underestimation of the standard errors of the regression coefficients and, thus, an overestimation of the significance level of the t-test. (The standard error appears in the numerator of the t-test; see Eq. 7.) The estimated regression coefficients remain undistorted. However, they are no longer efficient because the standard error is not correctly detected (Wooldridge 2009, p. 408).

Most tests for autocorrelation examine the first-order autocorrelation, that is, the correlation between two consecutive residuals. In addition to graphical inspection of the residuals, the Durbin-Watson statistic (Wooldridge 2009, p. 415) is a common method to identify first-order autocorrelation:

$$dw = \frac{\sum_{i \in I'} (e_i - e_{i-1})^2}{\sum_{i \in I} e_i^2} \tag{10}$$

where

dw = value of the Durbin-Watson test and
I' = index set of observations without the first observation.

If the difference between the two successive residuals is very small (large), positive (negative) autocorrelation is present, and the numerator in Eq. 10 takes small (large) values. The Durbin-Watson value dw approaches 0 (4) in this situation. A value of 2 indicates that no first-order autocorrelation is present. For an accurate representation of the level of significance for the Durbin-Watson test, refer to Wooldridge (2009, p. 415) or Gujarati (2003, p. 970). Also note that tests for autocorrelation often make little sense for cross-sectional data unless the order of observations follows a particular trend.

In time series, the value of the dependent variable of the previous period often can serve as an independent variable, typically called the "lagged variable." In this case, the Durbin-Watson statistic is not suitable for the detection of autocorrelation, and the Durbin h test should be used (see, e.g., Gujarati 2003, p. 503).

In our numerical example, considering autocorrelation is meaningless because we use cross-sectional data, in which temporal correlation cannot be present. At most, a spatial autocorrelation might be present (see Gujarati 2003, p 442, for an explanation). Autocorrelation, however, can be a substantive problem because it is often an indication of missing (i.e., omitted) independent variables. Therefore, we illustrate the problem of autocorrelation with the numerical example in Table 2.

The columns with the x- and y-values describe the relationship between the x- and y-values in the following form:

$$y = 5 + 2 \times x. \tag{11}$$

The columns "True Error1" and "True Error2" provide the true residuals for two examples that illustrate first-order autocorrelation. These two residuals differ only by their signs. We compute the dependent variables y1 and y2 by adding the values of "True Error 1" and "True Error2" to the y-values, that is, y1 = y + True Error1 and y2 = y + True Error2.

Table 3 and Fig. 5 present the results of the linear regression analyses for the two numerical examples with the dependent variables y1 and y2 and the independent variable x. Note that the estimated residuals are systematically

Regression Analysis

Table 2 Numerical example to illustrate the problem of autocorrelation

Case	x	y	y1	y2	True Error1	True Error2
1	2	9	11	7	2	−2
2	3	11	15	7	4	−4
3	4	13	17	9	4	−4
4	5	15	17	13	2	−2
5	6	17	15	19	−2	2
6	7	19	15	23	−4	4
7	8	21	17	25	−4	4
8	9	23	21	25	−2	2

Table 3 Results of the linear regression analyses in the case of autocorrelation

	Regression 1 (with y1 as dep. var.)		Regression 2 (with y2 as dep. var.)	
	Intercept_1	Slope_1	Intercept_2	Slope_2
Value	11.286	0.857	−1.286	3.143
Standard error	1.882	0.316	1.882	0.316
Significance level t-test	0.00	0.03	0.52	0.00
R^2	0.55		0.94	
Significance level F-test	0.03		0.00	
Durbin-Watson value	1.27		1.27	

under- or overestimated in both examples and that the estimated regression equation does not reflect the actual functional relationship stated in Eq. 11. However, the estimated regression coefficients are still unbiased because the coefficients of Eq. 11 can be retained if we use a large number of random samples and run linear regression analyses on each of them. This result is also visible in Table 2 because the mean values of the constants and the regression coefficients of the two regression equations correspond to the coefficients in Eq. 11 $\left(\frac{11.29-1.29}{2} = 5, \text{respectively } \frac{0.86+3.14}{2} = 2\right)$.

We can solve autocorrelation by detecting the factors responsible for the temporal fluctuations. Otherwise, we should consider econometric solutions such as the Cochrane-Orcutt procedure, the Hildreth-Lu procedure, or the Prais-Winsten estimate (Gujarati 2003, p. 482). These econometric methods, however, can only solve the problem if the regression equation is correctly specified.

Test for Heteroscedasticity

Heteroscedasticity means that the residuals do not have a constant variance. For example, the estimation of market shares for companies with high market shares might have a larger error than companies with small market shares (e.g., Gujarati 2003, p. 392). Heteroscedasticity leads to a situation in which the least squares method does not treat all observations equally and instead puts a greater emphasis on

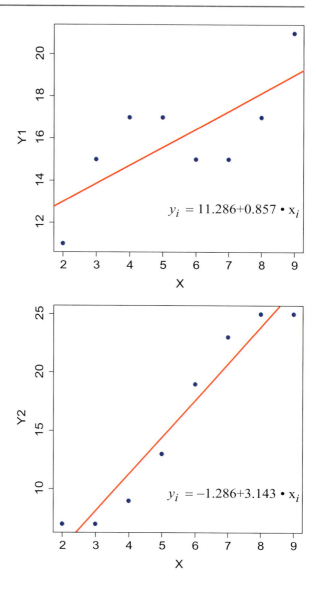

Fig. 5 Graphical representation of the regression equations in the case of the autocorrelation

the prediction of values with a high variance such that these observations receive a greater weight. The coefficients are still unbiased but are no longer efficient because they do not have the smallest estimation error (Stock and Watson 2015, p. 206).

We can detect heteroscedasticity by making a graphical comparison of the residuals with each of the independent variables or the dependent variable or by applying the Goldfeld-Quandt test, the Breusch-Pagan test, or the White test (Gujarati 2003, p. 400; Leeflang et al. 2000, p. 335). In our numerical example, the graphical comparison in Fig. 6 does not show a relationship between the standardized residuals and the standardized predicted values of the dependent variable, which indicates that heteroscedasticity is not present.

Fig. 6 Graphical inspection of heteroscedasticity

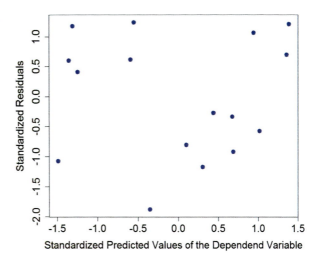

Unfortunately, heteroscedasticity is often not eliminated by collecting additional variables because the assumption of equal variances frequently does not make sense, as in our example of the estimation of market shares. It might help to transform variables in the regression equation (e.g., dividing the regression equation by the independent variable that causes the heteroscedasticity; Leeflang et al. 2000, p. 338). Alternatively, we can use a weighted linear regression analysis ("weighted least squares") because it resolves the different weighting that results from heteroscedasticity (Gujarati 2003, pp. 415). When the data set consists of a large number of observations, calculating heteroscedastic robust standard error (Wooldridge 2009, p. 271) with procedures such as White robust standard errors (Gujarati 2003, pp. 439; White 1980) or the Newey-West estimator (Greene 2008, p. 643; Gujarati 2003, p. 439) also can be effective.

Identification of Outliers

The goal of linear regression analysis is usually that all observations have a comparable influence on the result; thus, it is optimal to avoid situations in which very few observations strongly influence the result. So-called outliers, whose values differ substantially from others in the data set, can cause such disproportional influence. Therefore, to examine for the presence of outliers, the easiest method is a visual inspection of the distribution of the observed values or the distribution of the residuals. In addition, a wide range of statistical methods are also effective. For example, the Mahalanobis distance is based on the standardized squared values of the independent variables, while Cook's distance analyzes changes of the residuals that occur when the considered observation is removed from the regression equation. Chatterjee and Hadi (1986) provide a good overview of these and other statistical methods.

In our numerical example, the inspection of the residuals, the Mahalanobis distance, and the Cook's distance do not show conspicuous values. However, district 17, which we have not yet used, has a much higher quantity than other districts. The

```
                              Model Summary
Call:
lm(formula = Quantity ~ Person + Price + Advertising, data =
regdata_w17, x = TRUE, y = TRUE)

Residuals:
   Min      1Q Median     3Q     Max
-14644   -5243   -1448   3443   29168

Coefficients:
                Estimate Std. Error t value Pr(>|t|)
(Intercept) 286804.698   51573.602   5.561    0.000 ***
Person         4294.625    1864.581   2.303    0.038 *
Price         -4710.844    1024.335  -4.599    0.000 ***
Advertising       0.009       0.054   0.159    0.876
---
Signif. codes:  0 '***' 0.001 '**' 0.01 '*' 0.05 '.' 0.1 ' ' 1

Residual standard error: 10840 on 13 degrees of freedom
Multiple R-squared:  0.6377,    Adjusted R-squared:  0.5541
F-statistic: 7.628 on 3 and 13 DF,  p-value: 0.003423
```

Fig. 7 Results of the linear regression analysis in the presence of an outlier

values of Cook's distance and Mahalanobis distance indicate that district 17 may represent an outlier. Including district 17 in our regression analysis causes a strong change in the coefficients and the significance levels compared with the previous results (Fig. 7). The corresponding elasticities for the number of salespersons, price, and advertising also change significantly (0.27, -2.64, and 0.03, respectively). In addition, the R^2 drops to 63.77%.

If the outliers are due to imputation errors, their values are easy to adjust. Otherwise, the solution is more difficult and depends largely on the question explored with the regression analysis. If the resulting recommendations should hold for all observations, eliminating outliers is not very satisfactory. Typically, however, recommendations are designed for the majority of the observations, so eliminating the outliers is appropriate.

In our example, we recommend eliminating the outlier (district 17) because the marketing manager is probably more interested in making recommendations that apply to the majority of the considered districts. However, at the same time, the marketing manager should carefully think about why district 17 is so different from the other districts. In any case, researchers should always carefully and precisely report which observations are considered outliers to prevent the appearance of data manipulation (Laurent 2013).

Transformation of Variables

When modeling quantity, it is frequently beneficial to estimate nonlinear relationships. The following equation is such a relationship that occurs in a multiplicative regression equation (i.e., a multiplicative sales response function):

$$Q = \alpha \cdot \text{Person}^\beta \cdot \text{Price}^\gamma \cdot \text{Advertising}^\delta \tag{12}$$

In contrast to the linear regression equation outlined in Eq. 1, the characteristics of this multiplicative regression equation are such that it captures interaction effects between the marketing instruments and varying marginal returns for each marketing instrument (see Gujarati 2003, p. 175 for a discussion of other functional forms).

It is still possible to use linear regression analysis to estimate such a nonlinear relationship, but to do so, transforming the variables so that a linear relationship between the independent variables and the dependent variable in the estimated regression equation is necessary. In the multiplicative regression equation, such a linear relation occurs if we take the logarithm of all variables:

$$\ln(Q) = \ln(\alpha) + \beta \cdot \ln(\text{Person}) + \gamma \cdot \ln(\text{Price}) + \delta \cdot \ln(\text{Advertising}). \tag{13}$$

The linear regression equation is then as follows:

$$\text{LN\_Q}_i = a' + \beta \cdot \text{LN\_Person}_i + \gamma \cdot \text{LN\_P}_i + \delta \cdot \text{LN\_AD}_i + e_i \quad (i \in I), \tag{14}$$

where the variables LN_Q_i, LN_Person_i, LN_P_i, and LN_AD_i are defined as follows:

$\text{LN\_Q}_i = \ln(Q_i)$,
$\text{LN\_Person}_i = \ln(\text{Person}_i)$,
$\text{LN\_P}_i = \ln(\text{Price}_i)$,
$\text{LN\_AD}_i = \ln(\text{Advertising}_i)$, and
$\alpha' = \ln(\alpha)$.

We again ignore district 17. Figure 8 displays the results. Although the R^2 and the F-value are high, the R^2 only describes the goodness of fit of the logarithmic model shown in Eq. 14 and not that of the initial multiplicative model (Eq. 13). Therefore, calculating the R^2 of the initial model using the estimated values of the regression coefficients in Eq. 13 presents an alternative. The significance levels of all variables are comparable to those of the linear model. An important advantage of a multiplicative regression equation is that the regression coefficients represent the elasticities of the respective marketing instruments (Gujarati 2003, p. 176), which makes interpreting the results easier.

The results also show that all marketing instruments have the expected signs and plausible values. Inserting the estimated regression coefficients of Eq. 14 into Eq. 13 yields the following (rounded) results for the multiplicative regression equation:

$$\begin{aligned} Q &= \exp(16.98) \cdot \text{Person}^{0.40} \cdot \text{Price}^{-2.34} \cdot \text{Advertising}^{0.22} \\ &= 23{,}676{,}653 \cdot \text{Person}^{0.40} \cdot \text{Price}^{-2.34} \cdot \text{Advertising}^{0.22} \end{aligned} \tag{15}$$

Due to its more plausible properties, the multiplicative regression equation is more popular than the linear regression equation (see, e.g., Tellis 1988).

```
Call:
lm(formula = log(Quantity) ~ log(Person) + log(Price)
            + log(Advertising), data = regdata)

Residuals:
     Min       1Q    Median       3Q      Max
-0.10317 -0.02581  0.01209  0.03504  0.07761

Coefficients:
                 Estimate Std. Error t value Pr(>|t|)
(Intercept)        16.981      1.493  11.372    0.000 ***
log(Person)         0.400      0.047   8.565    0.000 ***
log(Price)         -2.339      0.248  -9.440    0.000 ***
log(Advertising)    0.217      0.082   2.647    0.021 *
---
Signif. codes:  0 '***' 0.001 '**' 0.01 '*' 0.05 '.' 0.1 ' ' 1

Residual standard error: 0.05198 on 12 degrees of freedom
Multiple R-squared:  0.9276,    Adjusted R-squared:  0.9095
F-statistic: 51.23 on 3 and 12 DF, p-value: 4.098e-07
```

Fig. 8 Results for the linear regression of the multiplicative regression equation

Implications of the Analysis

In this section, using our numerical example, we determine the optimal price and the amount of money that should be spend on advertising and salespersons. To do so, we rely on the estimated multiplicative regression equation (i.e., sales response function) shown in Eq. 16. We also ignore the marketing instrument mailings.

$$\text{Quantity} = 23,676,653 \cdot \text{Person}^{0.40} \cdot \text{Price}^{-2.34} \cdot \text{Advertising}^{0.22} \quad (16)$$

The profit function builds on this sales response function. Costs per unit are \$30 and the costs per salespersons are \$120,000 per year. Thus, profit is:

$$\text{Profit} = (\text{Price} - 30) \cdot 23,676,653 \cdot \text{Person}^{0.40} \cdot \text{Price}^{-2.34} \cdot \text{Advertising}^{0.22} \\ - 120,000 \cdot \text{Person} - \text{Advertising} \quad (17)$$

Its derivation leads to:

$$\frac{\partial \text{Profit}}{\partial \text{Price}} = 23,676,653 \cdot \text{Person}^{0.40} \cdot (-1.34) \cdot \text{Price}^{-2.34} \cdot \text{Advertising}^{0.22} \\ -30 \cdot 23,676,653 \cdot \text{Person}^{0.40} \cdot (-2.34) \cdot \text{Price}^{-3.34} \cdot \text{Advertising}^{0.22} \quad (18)$$

$$\frac{\partial \text{Profit}}{\partial \text{Person}} = (\text{Price} - 30) \cdot 23,676,653 \cdot 0.40 \cdot \text{Person}^{-0.60} \cdot \text{Price}^{-2.34} \\ \cdot \text{Advertising}^{0.22} - 120,000 \quad (19)$$

$$\frac{\partial \text{Profit}}{\partial \text{Advertising}} = (\text{Price} - 30) \cdot 23,676,653 \cdot \text{Person}^{0.40} \cdot \text{Price}^{-2.34}$$
$$\cdot 0.22 \cdot \text{Advertising}^{-0.78} - 1 \tag{20}$$

By setting the derivatives to 0 and solving for the three marketing instruments, we can determine the optimal price and spending for salespersons as well as advertising budget. For our example, we obtain the following results (calculation with unrounded values):

$$\text{Price}^* = 3652.40$$
$$\text{Person}^* = 36603,070.53$$
$$\text{Advertising}^* = 36327,402.06.$$

The optimal value leads to (again calculating with unrounded values) a quantity of 67,398 units, revenue of $3,531,459.94, profit contribution (i.e., profit before considering the budget for advertising and salespersons) of $1,509,505.85, and profit of $579,033.27.

Endogeneity

Endogeneity is currently one of the most important topics in linear regression analysis. Endogeneity means that one or more of the independent variables correlate with the residuals and therefore influences the relationship between the dependent variable and the independent variable. Its existence leads to a systematic distortion of the estimated regression coefficient. It can occur for several reasons, such as an omitted independent variable, simultaneity in the variables, measurement error in an independent variable, autocorrelation with delayed dependent variable, or self-selection.

We use our numerical example to discuss this fundamental problem. To do so, we first compute the residuals resulting from the linear regression analysis and the regression coefficients that are depicted in Fig. 2. We then add a column with these residuals to Table 1 and sort all districts according to the size of the residuals, which are defined as the difference between the observed and predicted (also called estimated) value of the dependent variable ($e_i = y_i - \widehat{y_i}$). Positive residuals represent districts in which the company was more successful than an "average" district. Table 4 presents the results. For ease of exposition, we ignore the variable mailings and the outlier district 17 for the subsequent considerations.

A fundamental assumption of the linear regression analysis is that the correlation between each of the independent variables and the residuals is equal to 0 (corr $(x_{i,\ k}, u_i) = 0$). In line with our initial assumption that the company's marketing is naive (i.e., random), this assumption appears realistic.

Now, more realistically, we assume that the company knows in which districts it is particularly successful and also selects its marketing instruments in such a way

Table 4 Districts with sales information sorted by the residuals

District	Quantity	Salespersons	Price	Advertising	Residuals
15	81,410	6	52	363,501	5,047.79
11	107,836	6	45	359,511	4,922.35
3	70,830	4	50	297,909	4,788.31
4	101,192	6	45	271,884	4,341.61
6	105,369	7	47	367,644	2,834.12
5	78,319	6	51	299,919	2,523.77
13	67,817	4	50	288,303	2,439.98
7	68,564	3	47	241,362	1,660.99
9	88,834	7	49	296,100	−1,085.46
2	91,735	5	46	370,062	−1,352.74
8	95,523	7	46	244,575	−2,328.75
1	81,996	7	49	228,753	−3,263.45
10	89,511	5	46	372,498	−3,745.29
14	59,207	6	54	289,470	−4,367.71
12	83,310	7	50	324,837	−4,765.38
16	71,431	3	46	361,974	−7,650.14

that it intensifies its marketing activities in the districts where it is already particularly successful. Thus, the company sets the highest of its 16 advertising budgets in the districts with the highest (positive) residuals, the second highest advertising budget in the district with the second highest residuals, and so on. We assume that the regression coefficients and residuals (see the results in Fig. 2) still apply and consider them the true parameters and the true residuals. Of course, given the newly allocated advertising budgets, the quantities in each district change. Yet, the total quantity of all 16 districts and the total advertising budget remain unchanged. However, the correlation between the true residuals (see Table 5) and the advertising budget is now 0.965.

Running a linear regression analysis with the data presented in Table 5 now leads to the results depicted in Table 6 (in the row "Endogeneity for advertising"). The coefficient for advertising is now more than twice as high (0.149 vs. 0.069; see Table 6). The reason for this increase in value is that the coefficient now reflects its own effect and the effect of the systematic allocation of the advertising budgets to districts with higher quantity. The estimate of the regression coefficient is therefore inconsistent and, thus, biased.

Endogeneity is difficult to detect because we do not observe the true residuals. Stated differently, the true relationship between advertising budget and the true residuals displayed in Table 5 with a correlation of 0.965 is unknown. We only observe the residuals that result from the linear regression analysis with the observations displayed in Table 5. The correlation of these residuals with the advertising budget is, by definition, 0.

The analogous procedure for the other two marketing instruments, price and salespersons, results in similar effects (see Table 6). Here, we assign the lowest

Regression Analysis

Table 5 Quantity of modified allocation of advertising budgets across districts

District	Quantity	Salespersons	Price	Advertising (endogenous)	True residuals
15	82,032.54	6	52	372,498	5,047.79
11	108,566.07	6	45	370,062	4,922.35
3	75,655.24	4	50	367,644	4,788.31
4	107,531.34	6	45	363,501	4,341.61
6	104,976.67	7	47	361,974	2,834.12
5	82,442.41	6	51	359,511	2,523.77
13	70,344.93	4	50	324,837	2,439.98
7	72,615.79	3	47	299,919	1,660.99
9	88,959.17	7	49	297,909	−1,085.46
2	86,617.28	5	46	296,100	−1,352.74
8	98,629.46	7	46	289,470	−2,328.75
1	86,116.50	7	49	288,303	−3,263.45
10	82,549.12	5	46	271,884	−3,745.29
14	56,100.54	6	54	244,575	−4,367.71
12	77,534.03	7	50	241,362	−4,765.38
16	62,212.91	3	46	228,753	−7,650.14

True regression equation:
Quantity $= 210,159.444 + 6723.478 *$ Person $- 3,832.503 *$ Price $+0.069 *$ Advertising+ residual

Table 6 Regression results when endogeneity for the variables advertising, price, and salespersons is present

		Advertising	Price	Salespersons	Intercept
Without	Coefficient	0.069	−3,832.503	6,723.478	210,159.444
Endogeneity	Standard error	0.024	4,44.013	840.997	23,729.909
	p-value	0.013	0.000	0.000	0.000
	R^2	0.919			
Endogeneity	Coefficient	0.149	−3,733.320	6,381.400	182,421.558
For advertising	Standard error	0.005	101.972	195.945	5245.791
	p-value	0.000	0.000	0.000	0.000
	R^2	0.996			
Endogeneity	Coefficient	0.068	−5,318.478	6,579.367	283,245.887
For price	Standard error	0.004	73.352	140.682	3917.548
	p-value	0.000	0.000	0.000	0.000
	R^2	0.999			
Endogeneity	Coefficient	0.072	−3,679.197	9,460.590	186,682.532
For salespersons	Standard error	0.008	144.168	272.228	8040.702
	p-value	0.000	0.000	0.000	0.000
	R^2	0.995			

prices and highest number of salespersons to the district with the highest residuals, and so forth. The correlation between the true residuals and price is -0.984, and between true residuals and the number of salespersons is 0.940. We still assume that the other two independent variables have the values shown in Table 4.

Again, it is clear that the size and significance level of the regression coefficients increase substantially when the values of the respective variables are set systematically, that is, according to the quantities of the districts. Ebbes et al. (chapter ▶ "Dealing with Endogeneity: A Nontechnical Guide for Marketing Researchers") provide a more detailed discussion of solutions in such situations.

Further Topics

As mentioned at the beginning of this chapter, linear regression analysis aims to relate a metric-scaled dependent variable with one or more metric-scaled independent variables. In practice, however, researchers often aim to include nonmetric information – for example, discrete variables such as gender, income groups, or shopping locations – or nonlinear (e.g., U-shaped) relationships.

Dummy variables are frequently used to include discrete information. For representing k characteristics, we require k – 1 dummy variables. The most common type of coding is indicator coding, in which each of the k – 1 dummy variables is represented by 1 (present) or 0 (not present). The kth characteristic that is not represented by 1 is then the reference characteristic. The estimated k – 1 coefficients represent the difference of the respective characteristic with respect to the reference characteristic. We can thus interpret the coefficients as the difference in the intercepts of the characteristics. An alternative approach for the coding of dummy variables is so-called effect coding (for more details, refer to Hair et al. 2014, p. 173).

It is also possible to include nonlinear curve-shaped relationships in the regression by using appropriate transformation of the respective variables (Albers 2012). An example of such a relationship is a diminishing marginal effect of a marketing instrument such as advertising. In many situations, several types of data transformations are appropriate for linearizing a curvilinear relationship (Hair et al. 2014, pp. 174–175). Examples of direct approaches are arithmetic transformations such as taking the square root or the logarithm of a variable. Another method is the use of polynomials, most often, only the first (x_i) and second order (x_i^2) of the independent variables. Polynomials can help represent complex relationships, thereby making it possible to interpret and statistically test each coefficient individually. The independent variables would then describe the overall effect of the polynomial.

The discussion of nonlinear relationships thus far reflects the relationship of the dependent variable and an independent variable; however, situations in which a second independent variable influences the effect of an independent variable on the dependent variable, or a moderating or an interaction effect, are also common. To represent such an interaction effect, it is necessary to create a new variable by multiplying the two independent variables. Thus, if two variables $x_{i,1}$ and $x_{i,2}$ interact – in other words, the variable $x_{i,2}$ moderates the influences of variable $x_{i,1}$ (or vice versa) – then we add the product of the two variables to the regression equation. The coefficient of these two variables ($x_{i,1} \cdot x_{i,2}$), also called the moderator, reflects the change in the effect of the variable $x_{i,1}$ if the variable $x_{i,2}$ changes. For a further discussion of the mis-specification and interpretation of interaction effects, refer to Irwin and McClelland (2001).

For our numerical examples in this chapter, we use either cross-sectional (Table 1) or longitudinal (Table 2) data. However, many marketing studies use panel data (also called pooled data) (Wooldridge 2009, p. 10), which combines longitudinal and cross-sectional data. Their analysis requires the consideration of specific issues (e.g., the consideration of structural differences between the individual cross-sectional data) that are beyond the scope of this chapter. For further details, refer to Hsiao (2014).

Furthermore, researchers should consider whether the data have a hierarchical structure. In that case, hierarchical or multilevel regressions are recommended. Not accounting for a hierarchical data structure in turn leads to an error in the estimation of the coefficients. For a good introduction to the topic of multilevel modeling, see Snijders and Bosker (2012).

Software

Software for estimating a regression analysis is available in many forms. Most spreadsheet programs (e.g., Microsoft Excel) enable the calculation of some simple analyses, but these programs are limited with respect to graphical representation of the results as well as the number of statistical and econometric tests. In addition, they offer only a limited range of functions to transform data easily, examine different variants of the regression analysis, detect heteroscedasticity and autocorrelation, identify outliers, and apply nonlinear regression analysis.

More sophisticated programs such as SPSS (now owned by IBM) allow for performing these analyses easily. Although SPSS is easy to use, it does not include all methods for the detection and management of autocorrelation and hetero-scedasticity (e.g., the Durbin's h statistic). Other statistical programs such as SAS, STATA, EViews, and LIMDEP provide a higher functionality, although they are slightly less user-friendly. Furthermore, none of these programs are available free of charge. An open source program, PSPP, is intended as an alternative to IBM SPSS. In principle, matrix-oriented programs such as R, MATLAB, or Gauss also allow for applying all econometric methods because the user works directly with matrices. However, these programs are less easy to use and have a considerably greater learning curve. R's advantage is that it is open source and available free of charge. In summary, most spreadsheet programs are sufficient for the occasional computation of regression analysis, but for more detailed analyses, researchers should use of one of the aforementioned statistical or matrix-oriented programs.

Summary

We use a numerical example to describe in detail one of the most important statistical methods, linear regression analysis. It examines the linear relationship between a dependent variable and one or more independent variables but can be easily used to also estimate nonlinear relationships if they can be linearized, as is the case for a multiplicative sales response functions (and many other functions). We use an extensive numerical example to illustrate all aspects that we cover in this section (autocorrelation, multicollinearity, heteroscedasticity, outlier detection, endogeneity, optimization of marketing mix), and we provide the code (for R, SPSS, and STATA) that we used to perform all calculations on our website (www.skiera.de). In addition, we also provide an Excel spreadsheet that contains all calculations, which should help in even better understanding of all calculations. Yet, we would like to highlight that Excel is not a good environment to conduct these calculations.

References

Albers, S. (2012). Optimizable and implementable aggregate response modeling for marketing decision support. *International Journal of Research in Marketing, 29*(2), 111–122.

Albers, S., Mantrala, M. K., & Sridhar, S. (2010). Personal selling elasticities: A meta-analysis. *Journal of Marketing Research, 47*(5), 840–853.

Assmus, G., Farley, J. W., & Lehmann, D. R. (1984). How advertising affects sales: A meta-analysis of econometric results. *Journal of Marketing Research, 21*(1), 65–74.

Bijmolt, T. H. A., van Heerde, H., & Pieters, R. G. M. (2005). New empirical generalizations on the determinants of price elasticity. *Journal of Marketing Research, 42*(2), 141–156.

Chatterjee, S., & Hadi, A. S. (1986). Influential observations, high leverage points, and outliers in linear regressions. *Statistical Science, 1*(3), 379–416.

Greene, W. H. (2008). *Econometric analysis* (6th ed.). Upper Saddle River: Pearson.

Gujarati, D. N. (2003). *Basic econometrics* (4th ed.). New York: McGraw Hill.

Hair, J. F., Black, W. C., Babin, J. B., & Anderson, R. E. (2014). *Multivariate data analysis* (7th ed.). Upper Saddle River: Pearson.

Hair, J. F., Hult, G. T. M., Ringle, C. M., & Sarstedt, M. (2017). *A primer on partial least squares structural equation modeling (PLS-SEM)* (2nd ed.). Thousand Oaks: Sage.

Hanssens, D. M., Parsons, L. J., & Schultz, R. L. (1990). *Market response models: Econometric and time series analysis*. Boston: Springer.

Hsiao, C. (2014). *Analysis of panel data* (3rd ed.). Cambridge: Cambridge University Press.

Irwin, J. R., & McClelland, G. H. (2001). Misleading heuristics and moderated multiple regression models. *Journal of Marketing Research, 38*(1), 100–109.

Koutsoyiannis, A. (1977). *Theory of econometrics* (2nd ed.). Houndmills: MacMillan.

Laurent, G. (2013). EMAC distinguished marketing scholar 2012: Respect the data! *International Journal of Research in Marketing, 30*(4), 323–334.

Leeflang, P. S. H., Wittink, D. R., Wedel, M., & Neart, P. A. (2000). *Building models for marketing decisions*. Berlin: Kluwer.

Lodish, L. L., Abraham, M. M., Kalmenson, S., Livelsberger, J., Lubetkin, B., Richardson, B., & Stevens, M. E. (1995). How TV advertising works: A meta-analysis of 389 real world split cable T. V. advertising experiments. *Journal of Marketing Research, 32*(2), 125–139.

Pindyck, R. S., & Rubenfeld, D. (1998). *Econometric models and econometric forecasts* (4th ed.). New York: McGraw-Hill.

Sethuraman, R., Tellis, G. J., & Briesch, R. A. (2011). How well does advertising work? Generalizations from meta-analysis of brand advertising elasticities. *Journal of Marketing Research, 48*(3), 457–471.

Snijders, T. A. B., & Bosker, R. J. (2012). *Multilevel analysis: An introduction to basic and advanced multilevel modeling* (2nd ed.). London: Sage.

Stock, J., & Watson, M. (2015). *Introduction to econometrics* (3rd ed.). Upper Saddle River: Pearson.

Tellis, G. J. (1988). The price sensitivity of selective demand: A meta-analysis of econometric models of sales. *Journal of Marketing Research, 25*(4), 391–404.

White, H. (1980). A heteroskedasticity-consistent covariance matrix estimator and a direct test for heteroskedasticity. *Econometrica, 48*(4), 817–838.

Wooldridge, J. M. (2009). *Introductory econometrics: A modern approach* (4th ed.). Mason: South-Western Cengage.

Logistic Regression and Discriminant Analysis

Sebastian Tillmanns and Manfred Krafft

Contents

Introduction 330
Discriminant Analysis 331
    Foundations and Assumptions of Discriminant Analysis 331
    Discriminant Analysis Procedure 333
Logistic Regression 343
    Foundations and Assumptions of Logistic Regression 343
    Logistic Regression Procedure 348
Applied Examples 357
    Research Question and Sample, Model, Estimation, and Model Assessment 357
    Discriminant Analysis 357
    Logistic Regression 359
Conclusion 364
References 366

Abstract

Questions like whether a customer is going to buy a product (purchase vs. non-purchase) or whether a borrower is creditworthy (pay off debt vs. credit default) are typical in business practice and research. From a statistical perspective, these

---

Dr. Sebastian Tillmanns is an Assistant Professor at the Institute of Marketing at the Westfälische Wilhelms-University Münster. Prof. Dr. Manfred Krafft is Director of the Institute of Marketing at the Westfälische Wilhelms-University Münster. The book chapter is adapted from Frenzen and Krafft (2008). We thank Linda Hollebeek for her copy-editing.

S. Tillmanns (✉)
Westfälische Wilhelms-Universität Münster, Muenster, Germany
e-mail: s.tillmanns@uni-muenster.de

M. Krafft
Institute of Marketing, Westfälische Wilhelms-Universität Münster, Muenster, Germany
e-mail: m.krafft@uni-muenster.de

© Springer Nature Switzerland AG 2022
C. Homburg et al. (eds), *Handbook of Market Research*,
https://doi.org/10.1007/978-3-319-57413-4_20

questions are characterized by a dichotomous dependent variable. Traditional regression analyses are not suitable for analyzing these types of problems, because the results that such models produce are generally not dichotomous. Logistic regression and discriminant analysis are approaches using a number of factors to investigate the function of a nominally (e.g., dichotomous) scaled variable. This chapter covers the basic objectives, theoretical model considerations, and assumptions of discriminant analysis and logistic regression. Further, both approaches are applied in an example examining the drivers of sales contests in companies. The chapter ends with a brief comparison of discriminant analysis and logistic regression.

Keywords

Dichotomous Dependent Variables · Discriminant Analysis · Logistic Regression

Introduction

Decision makers and researchers regularly need to explain or predict outcomes that have only one of two values. For example, practitioners might aim to predict, which customers will respond to their next mailing campaign. In this case, the outcome is either response or no response. Variables with such a nominal scaling can be described as dichotomous or binary. Table 1 lists several marketing-based examples. When approaching these issues systematically, it becomes obvious that traditional ordinary least squares (OLS) regression analyses are not suitable for analyzing these types of problems, because the results that such models produce are generally not dichotomous. For example, if product purchase (coding of the dependent variable $Y = 1$) and non-purchase ($Y = 0$) are considered, an OLS regression could predict purchase probabilities of less than zero or above one, which cannot be interpreted. In addition, a binary dependent variable would violate the assumption of normally distributed residuals and would render inferential statistical statements more difficult (Aldrich and Nelson 1984, p. 13). Discriminant analysis and logistic regression are suitable methodologies for the analysis of problems in which the dependent variable is nominally scaled.

Table 1 Potential applications of discriminant analysis and logistic regression in marketing

Subject of investigation	Grouping
Direct marketing/mail order business	Order (yes – no)
Nonprofit marketing	Donation (yes – no)
Retailing	Purchase/non-purchase (choice)
Staff selection (salespeople, franchisees)	Successful/unsuccessful employee
Customer win-back	Defected customers return (yes – no)
Branding	Repurchase (yes – no)
Product policy	New product success versus failure
Innovation adoption	Adopter versus non-adopter

Although both logistic regression and discriminant analysis are suitable for explaining or predicting dichotomous outcomes, discriminant analysis is optimal for classifying observations when the independent variables are normally distributed (conditional on the dependent variable Y). In this case, the discriminant analysis is more efficient, because it utilizes information about the distribution of the independent variables, which the logistic regression does not (Agresti 2013, p. 569). However, if the independent variables are not normally distributed (e.g., because they are categorically scaled) logistic regression is more appropriate, because it makes no assumptions about the independent variables' distribution. Further, in comparison to discriminant analysis, extreme outliers affect logistic regression less. Generally, logistic regression is preferred to discriminant analysis (e.g., Agresti 2013; Osborne 2008). Nevertheless, one way to validate the results of a logistic regression is to see whether an alternative method can replicate the findings and discriminant analysis can serve as such an alternative (Cambell and Fiske 1959; Anderson 1985).

In section "Discriminant Analysis," we discuss the basic objectives, theoretical model considerations, assumptions, and different steps of discriminant analysis. Analogously, the third section addresses the logistic regression. An applied example is presented in section "Applied Examples," in which both methods are used to explain which factors drive the use of sales contests in companies. This chapter ends with a conclusion and a brief comparison of discriminant analysis and logistic regression.

Discriminant Analysis

Foundations and Assumptions of Discriminant Analysis

Discriminant analysis is a multivariate (separation) method for the analysis of differences between relevant groups. It can help determine which variables explain or predict the observations' membership of specific groups. Depending on the investigation objectives, this enables the approach to undertake either diagnostic or predictive analyses.

The four key objectives of discriminant analysis can be described as follows (Hair et al. 2010, p. 350; Aaker et al. 2011, p. 470):

- Determining the linear combinations of independent variable(s) that lead to the best possible distinction between groups by maximizing the variance *between* the groups relative to the varaince observed *within* the groups. This linear combination is also called a discriminant function or axis. By inserting the independent variables' attribute values into the discriminant function, researchers can calculate a discriminant score for each observation.
- Examining whether, based on the group means obtained through the discriminant scores (centroids), the groups differ significantly from each other.

- Identifying the variables that contribute most effectively to the explanation of intergroup differences.
- Allocating new observations for which the attribute values are known to the relevant group (either classification or prediction).

Based on the distance between the group centroids, it is possible to determine the statistical significance of a discriminant function. Undertaking such analyses requires a comparison of the distribution of the groups' discriminant scores. The less the distributions overlap, the more the groups based on the discriminant function differ. Figure 1 illustrates this basic concept of discriminant analysis according to the distributions of the two groups A and B: besides showing the separation value Y^* (i.e., the critical discriminant score) through which the examined observations can be classified, the discriminant axis is also shown next to the two group centroids $\bar{Y}_A$ and $\bar{Y}_B$. The area of overlap (i.e., the white areas under the curves) between the two distributions corresponds to the proportion of misclassified observations in group A (i.e., to the right-hand side of Y^*) and group B (i.e., to the left-hand side of Y^*).

Discriminant analysis is considered a dependency analysis, which distinguishes between nominally scaled dependent variables and metrically scaled independent variables. When comparing discriminant analysis with regression and analysis of variance (ANOVA), the following analogies and differences are specifically found:

- Discriminant analysis is based on a model structure similar to the one deployed in multiple regression. The main difference lies in the nominal level of the dependent variable's measurement. In regression analysis, a normal distribution of the error terms is assumed, and the independent variables are known or predetermined. In discriminant analysis, the reverse applies: the independent variables are assumed to have a multivariate normal distribution, while the dependent variable is fixed; that is, the groups are defined a priori (Aaker et al. 2011, p. 471).
- If a reverse relationship existed, such that the variables of interest are dependent on a group membership, an approach such as a one-factorial multivariate analysis

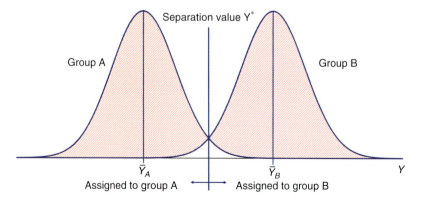

Fig. 1 Distributions of the discriminant scores of two groups A and B

of variance (MANOVA) would be appropriate. Accordingly, discriminant analysis can also be regarded as the reversal of a MANOVA.

To apply discriminant analysis, certain assumptions have to be complied with. For a comprehensive overview of the assumptions of discriminant analysis, see Hair et al. 2010, pp. 354 et seq. and Tabachnick and Fidell 2013, pp. 384 et seq. As in multiple regression analysis, this includes the absence of multicollinearity and autocorrelation. Further, the observed relationships should be of a linear nature. Finally, the independent variables should be normally distributed. Nonetheless, discriminant analysis is relatively robust regarding the violation of the normality assumption, provided the violation is not caused by outliers, but by skewness. If the group sizes are very different, the sample should be sufficiently large to ensure robustness: based on a conservative recommendation, robustness is assumed if the smallest group includes 20 cases and only a few (up to five) explanatory variables (Hair et al. 2010, p. 375; Tabachnik and Fidell 2013, p. 384). The equality of the independent variables' variance-covariance matrices in the different groups is the most important assumption for the application of discriminant analysis. Again, inferential statistics are relatively robust against a violation of this assumption, given that the group sizes are not too small or too uneven. However, the classification accuracy might not be robust even if reasonable group sizes are adopted, because in such cases observations are frequently misclassified into groups with greater variance. If classification is a key objective of the analysis, the homogeneity of the variance-covariance matrices should always be tested (Tabachnik and Fidell 2013, pp. 384 et seq.). Finally, all independent variables are required to be at least interval-scaled, since the violation of this assumption leads to unequal variance-covariance matrices.

Discriminant Analysis Procedure

The application of discriminant analysis involves several steps, which we discuss in the following.

Step 1: Problem and Group Definition As mentioned, discriminant analysis can be used to explain the differences between groups in a multivariate manner. However, it can also serve as a procedure to classify observations with known attribute values, but unknown group membership. To apply discriminant analysis, the dependent variable has to be defined first; that is, the groups to be analyzed need to be determined. The dependent variable can be drawn directly from the specific examination context (e.g., product purchasers vs. non-purchasers) or from the findings of preceding analyses. For example, customer segments identified by means of cluster analysis might be further investigated by undertaking discriminant analysis. The cluster analysis might be used to reveal groups and a subsequent discriminant analysis might use either the same or different variables for further analytical purposes. In the first case, the aim of the investigation would be to verify the clustering variables' adequacy in terms of their discriminatory meaning. In the second case, the groups generated by means of cluster analysis are explored in greater depth. For instance, an initial cluster analysis generates consumer segments based on their purchase behavior. A subsequent discriminant analysis might then be used to explain the segment-specific differences in consumer purchase patterns by means of psychographic variables.

If, in its original form, the dependent variable is based on a metric scale, it can be classified into two or more groups (e.g., low/medium/high), which can be analyzed by the subsequent discriminant analysis. The group definition is also related to the number of groups to be analyzed. The simplest case is two-group discriminant analysis (e.g., ordering vs. non-ordering in mail order businesses). However, if the classification involves more than two groups, a multigroup discriminant analysis should be used. In determining the number of groups, the number of observations per group should be at least 20. Consequently, combining several groups into a single category might be appropriate.

Step 2: Model Formulation As part of discriminant analysis a discriminant function should be estimated, which ensures an optimal separation between the groups and an assessment of the discrimination capability of the applied variables. The discriminant function is a linear combination of the applied variables and generally adheres to the following scheme:

$$Y_i = \beta_0 + \sum_{j=1}^{J} \beta_j X_{ji}, \tag{1}$$

where

Y: Discriminant score
β_0: Constant
β_j: Discriminant coefficient of independent variable j

By using the attribute values X_{ji} for each observation i, the discriminant function generates an individual discriminant score Y_i.

Step 3: Estimation of the Discriminant Function The parameters β_j are estimated such that the calculated discriminant scores provide an optimal separation between the groups. This result requires a discriminant criterion that measures the intergroup differences. The estimation procedure is then carried out such that the discriminant criterion is maximized.

Considering the distance between the group centroids for the purpose of evaluating the differences between the groups might initially seem obvious. However, also the variance of the discriminant scores within a group has to be considered. While a larger distance between two group centroids improves the distinction of the groups, the distinction is made more difficult when the variance of the groups' discriminant scores increases. This situation is illustrated in Fig. 2, where two pairs of groups A and B are represented as distributions on the discriminant axis. The centroids of the pairs of groups A $(\overline{Y}_A = -2)$ and B $(\overline{Y}_B = 2)$ are identical, but the

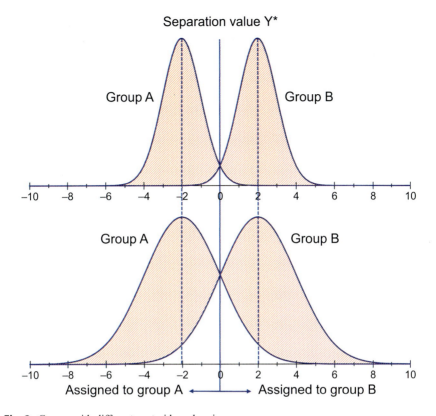

Fig. 2 Groups with different centroids and variances

standard deviations of the discriminant scores differ (standard deviations upper distributions = 1; standard deviations lower distributions = 2). Based on a comparison of the pairs shown at the top and at the bottom of Fig. 2, we can observe that, although the lower groups indicate identical centroids, they also have greater variances – in this case, generating a lower discrimination.

Thus, assessments of discriminant analysis performance should aim at optimizing both the distance of the group centroids and the spread of the observations. To achieve optimal separation efficiency between the groups, we refer to the well-established regression- and ANOVA-based principle of variance decomposition:

$$SS = SS_b + SS_W$$

Total variance = Between − group variance + Within − group variance (2)
= Explained variance + Unexplained variance

Thus, a discriminant function should be determined such that the group means (centroids) differ significantly from one another, if possible. For this purpose, we refer to the following discriminant criterion:

$$\Gamma = \frac{\text{Variance between the groups}}{\text{Variance within the groups}} \qquad (3)$$

This criterion can be made more precise and converted into an optimization problem as follows:

$$\Gamma = \frac{\sum_{g=1}^{G} I_g \left(\overline{Y}_g - \overline{Y}\right)^2}{\sum_{g=1}^{G} \sum_{i=1}^{I_g} \left(Y_{gi} - \overline{Y}_g\right)^2} = \frac{SS_b}{SS_w} \underset{b_j}{\rightarrow} \text{Max!}, \qquad (4)$$

where

G: Number of groups studied
I: Group size

In order to account for different group sizes, the variance between the groups is multiplied by the respective group size I. The discriminant coefficients β_j ($j = 1, \ldots, J$) have to be determined so that the discriminant criterion Γ is maximized. The maximum value of the discriminant criterion

$$\gamma = \text{MAX}\{\Gamma\} \qquad (5)$$

is referred to as the eigenvalue, because it can be determined mathematically by solving the eigenvalue problem (for further details refer to Tatsuoka 1988, pp. 210 et seq.).

In the multigroup case (i.e., with more than two groups), more than one discriminant function and more than one eigenvalue must be determined. The maximum number of discriminant functions is given by $K = \text{Min } \{G\text{-}1, J\}$. Generally, the number of independent variables J exceeds the number of groups, so that the number of groups usually determines the number of discriminant functions to be estimated. The following applies to the order of the respective discriminant functions and their corresponding eigenvalues:

$$\gamma_1 \geq \gamma_2 \geq \gamma_3 \geq \cdots \geq \gamma_K.$$

This way, the first discriminant function explains the majority of the independent variables' variance. The second discriminant function is uncorrelated (orthogonal) to the first and explains the maximum amount of the remaining variance once the first function has been determined. Since additional discriminant functions are always calculated in order to explain the remaining variance's maximum share, the functions' explanatory power declines gradually.

The following measure represents a discriminant function's relative importance by deriving the respective eigenvalue share (ES):

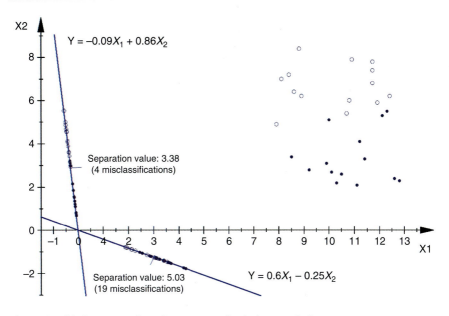

Fig. 3 Graphical representation of a two-group discriminant analysis

$$ES_k = \frac{\gamma_k}{\gamma_1 + \gamma_2 + \ldots + \gamma_K}. \qquad (6)$$

The eigenvalue share equals the share of variance explained by the kth discriminant function relative to the variance explained by all discriminant functions K combined. The eigenvalues always add up to one.

Figure 3 illustrates the discriminant analysis's estimation principle by means of a graphic representation. In this case, the determination is based on a two-group discriminant function. It is assumed that two attribute values X_1 and X_2 are available for each of the subjects examined, which are shown in the scatter plot in Fig. 3, in which filled circles represent the members of group A and empty circles members of group B. In this example the optimal discriminant function is $Y = -0.09X_1 + 0.86X_2$. Based on this function four members of group A are misclassified as members of group B. The arbitrarily selected discriminant function $Y = 0.6X_1 - 0.25X_2$ shows a worse classification performance by having 19 misclassifications in total. A projection of the respective attribute value combinations on the discriminant axes corresponds to the examined subjects' discriminant values.

Step 4: Assessment the Discriminant Function Performance Researchers have two basic approaches at their disposal to assess a discriminant function's performance. The first approach compares the classification of observations with the observations' actual group membership. This approach is explained later in this chapter in relation to logistic regression, where a specific example is also provided. It is also specifically applicable in the context of the discriminant analysis.

A second fundamental way of assessing the discriminant function's quality is based on the discriminant criterion described above. The eigenvalue γ represents the maximum value of the discriminant criterion and, thus, forms a starting point for assessing the discriminant function's quality or discriminant power. Since γ has the disadvantage of not being standardized to values between zero and one, other metrics based on the eigenvalue have been established for quality assessment, including the canonical correlation coefficient (c):

$$c = \sqrt{\frac{\gamma}{1+\gamma}} = \sqrt{\frac{\text{Variance explained}}{\text{Total variance}}} \tag{7}$$

In the two-group case, the canonical correlation equals the simple correlation between the estimated discriminant values and the binary grouping variables. The most common criterion for testing the quality of the discriminant function is Wilks's lambda (Λ):

$$\Lambda = \frac{1}{1+\gamma} = \frac{\text{Unexplained variance}}{\text{Total variance}} \tag{8}$$

As can be seen from the above formula, Wilks's lambda is an inverse measure of goodness; that is, lower (higher) values imply a better (worse) discriminant power of the discriminant function. Wilks's lambda can be transformed into a test statistic, thereby enabling inferential statements on the diversity of groups. By applying the transformation

$$V = -\left[N - \frac{J+G}{2} - 1\right]\ln\Lambda, \tag{9}$$

where

N: Number of observations
J: Number of independent variables
G: Number of groups
Λ: Wilks's lambda

the resulting test statistic is approximately χ^2-distributed with J (G-1) degrees of freedom. Thus, a statistical significance testing of the discriminant function can be performed. Given that the test statistic increases with lower values of Λ, higher values imply a greater diversity between the groups.

In the case of multigroup discriminant analysis, each discriminant function can be evaluated by means of the above measures on the basis of their respective eigenvalue. Here, the kth eigenvalue γ_k measures the proportion of the explained variance which can be attributed to the kth discriminant function. There is a clear analogy to

Logistic Regression and Discriminant Analysis

the principal components analysis procedure in which the components are extracted from the independent variables (like the "main components") in the form of discriminant functions (Tatsuoka 1988).

All discriminant functions and their eigenvalues are considered to assess the overall differences between the groups. The multivariate Wilks's lambda, which is calculated by multiplying the univariate lambdas, is a measure that can capture this:

$$\Lambda = \prod_{k=1}^{K} \frac{1}{1 + \gamma_k}, \tag{10}$$

where

K: Number of possible discriminant functions
γ_k: Eigenvalue of the kth discriminant function

To statistically check whether the groups differ significantly from one another, a χ^2-distributed test statistic can be generated by using transformation (9).

Other test statistics representing approximations of the F-distribution and Wilks's lambda are available and can be applied to test the significance of group-related differences. These statistics cannot only be applied to a MANOVA but also to discriminant analysis (e.g., Hotelling's trace, Pillai's trace, and Roy's GCR). Other measures, such as Rao's V and Mahalanobis's D^2 are particularly applied in the context of stepwise discriminant analyses (Tabachnik and Fidell 2013, p. 399; Hair et al. 2010, p. 435).

As with all statistical tests, a statistically significant test result does not necessarily imply a substantial difference. In a sufficiently large sample size, even small differences are likely to have statistical significance. Consequently, the absolute values of the mean differences between the groups, the canonical correlation coefficients, and Wilks's lambda, should not be overlooked. For the sake of interpretability, it is advisable to limit analyses to two or three discriminant functions, even if further discriminant functions prove to be statistically significant.

Step 5: Examination and Interpretation of the Discriminant Coefficients If testing the discriminant function(s) result(s) in a sufficient discriminatory power between the groups in step 4, the independent variables can be examined. Assessing the importance of individual independent variables can be used to, first, explain the key differences between the groups, thereby contributing to the interpretation of group-based differences. Second, unimportant variables can be removed from the model if the goal is to specify a parsimonious model. As an alternative to simultaneously including all variables into the model for estimation, a stepwise estimation may be undertaken. Here, only variables are included in the discriminant function one at a time, which contribute significantly to the discriminant function's improvement, depending on the level of significance that the researcher specifies.

Individual variables' discriminatory relevance can be checked by using univariate and multivariate approaches. As part of a *univariate* assessment, each of the variables can be tested separately to determine whether their mean values between the groups differ significantly from one another. Likewise, undertaking discriminant analyses of each of the variables based on Wilks's lambda serves to isolate their discriminant power. The F-test can also be used here. The result then corresponds to a one-factorial analysis of variance with the groups as factor levels.

A review of the univariate discriminatory relevance is insufficient if there are potential interdependencies between the variables. For example, while a particular variable may have little discriminatory meaning when viewed in isolation, it may significantly contribute to an increase of discriminant power in combination with other variables.

Multivariate assessments of individual variables' discriminatory power and of their importance as part of the discriminant function can be undertaken by using the standardized discriminant coefficients. These represent the influence of the independent variables on the discriminant variable and are defined as follows:

$$\beta_j^* = \beta_j \cdot s_j, \tag{11}$$

where

β_j: Discriminant coefficient of independent variable j
s_j: Standard deviation of independent variable j

Standardization allows for assessments independent of independent variables' scaling and their meaning. The higher the absolute value of a standardized coefficient, the greater the discriminatory power of the associated variable. The unstandardized discriminants are, however, required to calculate the discriminant scores (Hair et al. 2010, p. 381).

Deriving the correlation coefficients between the values of the respective independent variables and the discriminant scores is another alternative method to interpret the independent variables' influences. These correlation coefficients are called discriminant loadings, canonical loadings, or structure coefficients. Compared to (standardized) discriminant coefficients, potential multicollinearity between the independent variables affects them less. Therefore they often provide benefits in terms of an unbiased interpretation of the independent variables. As a rule of thumb, loadings exceeding a magnitude of 0.4 indicate substantially discriminatory variables (Hair et al. 2010, pp. 389 et seq.). The identification of variables with sufficiently high loadings allows for creating profiles of groups in terms of these variables and to identify differences between the groups. The signs of discriminant weights and loadings reflect the groups' relative average profile.

A sufficiently large sample size is required to obtain stable estimates of the standardized discriminant coefficients and discriminant loadings. As a guiding value, a minimum of 20 observations per independent variable is required (Hair et al. 2010, p. 435; Aaker et al. 2011, p. 477).

Logistic Regression and Discriminant Analysis

Step 6: Prediction In discriminant analysis, several alternative prediction approaches are available. Predictions can be based on classification functions, the distance concept, or the probability concept (Backhaus et al. 2016, pp. 246 et seq.). Classification functions and the probability concept allow the consideration of a priori probabilities. Such probabilities can reflect theoretical knowledge about different group sizes before any prediction is conducted. The consideration of a priori probabilities is especially useful, if the examined groups differ in their size. Furthermore, the probability concept allows to allocate specific costs to the misclassification of observations into a certain group. Specifically, this builds on the distance concept and thus should be addressed last.

Classification Functions

Fisher's classification functions can be used to predict an observation's group-membership. They require the variances in the groups to be homogeneous and one classification function has to be determined for each group. Thus, in a two-group case, two functions have to be determined:

$$
\begin{aligned}
F_{1i} &= \beta_{01} + \sum_{j=1}^{J} \beta_{j1} X_{ji} \\
F_{2i} &= \beta_{02} + \sum_{j=1}^{J} \beta_{j2} X_{ji}
\end{aligned}
\tag{12}
$$

For the classification of an observation, the value of each function F_i has to be calculated. An observation is assigned to the group for which it yields the maximum value.

As mentioned above, classification functions allow the consideration of a priori probabilities $P(g)$. A priori probabilities must add up to one and are implemented in the classification function as follows:

$$
F_g := F_g + \ln P(g)
\tag{13}
$$

It is also possible to determine individual probabilities $P_i(g)$ for each observation i.

Distance Concept

According to the distance concept, an observation i needs to be assigned to a group g, such that the distance to the centroid is minimized (i.e., to which it is closest on the discriminant axis). This corresponds to determining whether an observation lies either left or right of the critical discriminant score Y^* (see Fig. 1). The squared distance is the measure usually deployed in the K-dimensional discriminant space between observation i and the centroid of group g:

$$D_{ig}^2 = \sum_{i=1}^{I} \left(Y_{ki} - \overline{Y}_{kg}\right)^2, \tag{14}$$

where

Y_{ki}: Discriminant score of observation i according to discriminant function k
$\overline{Y}_{kg}$: Centroid of group g regarding discriminant function k

It is, however, not necessary to consider all possible K discriminant functions to execute the classification. Usually, it is sufficient to limit the analysis to the significant or relevant discriminant functions, which substantially facilitates the calculation.

Classification based on the distance concept requires the variances in the groups to be nearly homogeneous. This assumption can, for instance, be checked using Box's M as a test statistic. When the assumption of homogeneous variances in the groups is violated, modified distance measures need to be calculated.

Probability Concept

The probability concept, which builds on the distance concept, is the most flexible approach to the classification of observations. It allows the consideration of a priori probabilities and different misclassification costs in the examined group. Without these modifications, the probability concept generates the same results as the distance concept.

Regarding the classification of observations with the probability concept, a priori probabilities and conditional probabilities are combined in order to derive a posteriori probabilities according to the Bayes theorem:

$$P(g|Y_i) = \frac{P(Y_i|g)P_i(g)}{\sum_{g=1}^{G} P(Y_i|g)P_i(g)}, \tag{15}$$

where

$P(g|\ Y_i)$: A posteriori probability, that an observation is in group g, given a discriminant score Y_i is observed.
$P(Y_i|\ g)$: Conditional probability, that a discriminant score Y_i is observed, given that it appears in group g.
$P_i(g)$: A priori probability, that an observation is in group g

An observation i is assigned to group g, for which the value of $P(g|\ Y_i)$ is maximized. For example, if G = 2, observation i is assigned to group 1 if

$$\frac{P(Y_i|g_1)P_i(g_1)}{\sum_{g=1}^{2} P(Y_i|g)P_i(g)} > \frac{P(Y_i|g_2)P_i(g_2)}{\sum_{g=1}^{2} P(Y_i|g)P_i(g)}. \tag{16}$$

Logistic Regression and Discriminant Analysis 343

The a posteriori probabilities can be calculated on the basis of the observations' distances to the group centroids (see Tatsuoka 1988, pp. 358 et seq. for more details). Another advantage of the probability concept lies in the possibility of explicitly incorporating the *costs of a misclassification* in the decision rule. The field of medical diagnostics can be used as an example: the consequences of not diagnosing a malignant disease are certainly more fatal than coming up with an erroneous diagnosis. Hence, the expected value of the costs involved might be considered in such calculations:

$$E_g(C) = \sum_{h=1}^{G} C_{gh} P(h \mid Y_i). \tag{17}$$

The costs, which are quantified by C_{gh}, arise if an observation is assigned to group g, though it belongs to group h. Thus, an observation i is assigned to the group g with the lowest expected costs $E_g(C)$.

Marketing decisions in which misclassification costs could play a major role are for example new product introductions. In this regard, high costs may arise due to misclassifications of products as a "success" or a "flop" in terms of either their launch or non-launch. Further, in the mail order business, substantial misclassification costs may result from customers either being sent or not sent a catalogue of relevant product assortments.

Logistic Regression

Foundations and Assumptions of Logistic Regression

The application of logistic regression has become increasingly popular in recent years. There is little difference between logistic regression and discriminant analysis with respect to their objectives and applications. On the one hand, logistic regression may be used to examine the variables and the specific degree to which they contribute to explaining group membership (diagnosis). On the other hand, it allows for classifying new observations into groups (prediction). The following section describes the basics underlying logistic regression's estimation method. Initially, the measures with which to assess the entire model are explained only generically, because an example in section "Logistic Regression" is used to clarify the quality measures as well as the options for interpreting the coefficients. This example draws on a study that Mantrala et al. (1998) conducted to address the (non-)adoption of sales contests. The dependent variable takes two values:

$$Y = \begin{cases} 1, \text{if sales contests are used,} \\ 0, \text{if sales contests are not used.} \end{cases} \tag{18}$$

Compared to a linear regression, linking one or more independent variables to a dependent variable that can only take one of two values (i.e., 0 and 1) is more complicated. However, this linkage can be established through a logistic regression model, which can be derived as either a latent variable model or a probability model (see Long and Freese 2014). In the following, both approaches are explained.

In the latent variable model, a non-observed (i.e., latent) variable Y^* is assumed, which is related to the observed independent variables in the following way:

$$Y_i^* = \beta_0 + \sum_{j=1}^{J} \beta_j X_{ji} + \epsilon_i, \tag{19}$$

where

β_0: Constant
β_j: Coefficient of independent variable j
ϵ_i: Error term

Equation 19 is identical to a linear regression, in which the dependent variable can range from $-\infty$ to ∞, but it differs with regard to the dependent variable, which is non-observable. In order to transform the continuous non-observable dependent variable into a dichotomous one (i.e., one that can only take the values 0 and 1), the following linkage is established:

$$Y_i = \begin{cases} 1, \text{if } Y_i^* > 0, \\ 0, \text{otherwise.} \end{cases} \tag{20}$$

Thus, Y_i is assigned a value of 1 if Y_i^* takes positive values and a value of 0 if Y_i^* is smaller or equal to 0. In our abovementioned example, Y_i^* can be viewed as the propensity to adopt (as opposed to the non-adoption of) sales contests.

To illustrate the latent variable model, we assume a single independent variable in the following. For any given value of X of this variable, we can link the observable dependent variable Y_i to its non-observable counterpart through the following equation:

$$P(Y = 1 | X) = P(Y^* > 0 | X) \tag{21}$$

Equation 21 represents the probability of an event occurring (e.g., the use of a sales contest), with either $Y = 1$ or $Y^* > 0$ representing the occurrence of the event, which is conditional on the value X of the independent variable. If Y^* is substituted by Eq. 19 (and restricted to a single independent variable), Eq. 21 results in:

$$P(Y = 1 | X) = P((\beta_0 + \beta_1 X_{1i} + \epsilon_i) > 0 | X) \tag{22}$$

It can be rearranged in:

$$P(Y = 1 \mid X) = P(\epsilon_i > -(\beta_0 + \beta_1 X_{1i}) \mid X) \tag{23}$$

In this equation, the probability of the event occurring depends on the distribution of the error ϵ_i. Depending on the assumptions about this distribution, either a probit or a logit model can be derived. Similar to logit models, probit models are capable of modeling a dichotomous dependent variable. While a normal distribution with a variance of 1 is assumed for the probit model, a logistic distribution with a variance of $\frac{\pi^2}{3}$ is assumed for the logit model. In the logistic regression model, this leads to the following equation:

$$P(Y = 1 \mid X) = \frac{e^{(\beta_0 + \beta_1 X_{1i})}}{1 + e^{(\beta_0 + \beta_1 X_{1i})}} \tag{24}$$

In a more general form, which allows for more than one independent variable, this becomes:

$$P_i = \frac{e^{Z_i}}{1 + e^{Z_i}} = \frac{1}{1 + e^{-Z_i}}, \tag{25}$$

where Z_i serves as a linear predictor of the logistic model for the ith observation with $Z_i = \beta_0 + \beta_1 X_{1i} + \beta_{2i} X_{2i} + \ldots + \beta_J X_{Ji}$.

The probability model is an alternative to the latent variable model, which allows the logistic model to be derived without referring to a latent variable (see Theil 1970; Long and Freese 2014). In order to derive a model with an outcome ranging from 0 to 1, the probabilities of an event occurring have to be transformed into odds:

$$\text{Odds}(Y = 1) = \frac{P(Y = 1)}{P(Y = 0)} = \frac{P(Y = 1 \mid X)}{1 - P(Y = 1 \mid X)} \tag{26}$$

Odds indicate how often something happens relative to how often it does not happen (i.e., $Y = 1$ vs. $Y = 0$). The odds therefore represent the chance of an event occurring. The natural logarithm of the odds is called logit (logistic probability unit), which ranges from $-\infty$ to ∞, and is linear:

$$\ln(\text{Odds}(Y = 1)) = \beta_0 + \sum_{j=1}^{J} \beta_j X_{ji} \tag{27}$$

The logistic function, which is an S-shaped curve, has the advantageous characteristic that even for infinitely small or large values of the logit Z_i the resulting values of P_i are never outside the interval of [0,1] (Hosmer et al. 2013, pp. 6 et seq.).

The nonlinear characteristics of Eq. 25 are represented in Fig. 4, in which the exponent X_i is systematically varied from -9 to +9. The figure shows the prediction of an indifferent result if the sum of the weighted factors (i.e., Z_i) equals zero. Its symmetry at the turning point of $P_i = 0.5$ is another essential feature of the logistic function. The constant β_0 of the linear predictor Z_i moves the function horizontally, while higher coefficients lead to a steeper slope of the logistic function. Negative signs of the coefficient β_j change the origin of the curve, which corresponds to the dotted line in Fig. 4 (Menard 2002, pp. 8 et seq.; Agresti 2013, pp. 119 et seq.).

As mentioned, in empirical research the actual (non-)entry of an event and not its probability of entry is observed. The logistic regression approach regarding the occurrence of an event ($Y_i = 1$) and its opposing event ($Y_i = 0$) can thus be expressed as follows for each observation i:

$$P_i(Y) = \left(\frac{1}{1+e^{-Z_i}}\right)^{Y_i} \left(1 - \frac{1}{1+e^{-Z_i}}\right)^{1-Y_i} \qquad (28)$$

Thus, the information required to establish the probabilities regarding the z-values (logits) can be calculated using Eq. 25.

The coefficients of the logistic model β_j can now be estimated by maximizing the likelihood (L) of obtaining the empirical observation values of all possible cases. Since the observed values Y_i represent realizations of a binomial process with the probability P_i, which vary depending on the expression of X_{ji}, we are able to set up the following likelihood function, which has to be maximized:

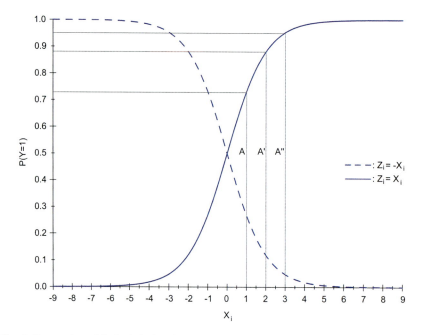

Fig. 4 Progression of the logistic function curves

$$L = \prod_{i=1}^{N} \left(\frac{1}{1 + e^{-Z_i}} \right)^{Y_i} \left(1 - \frac{1}{1 + e^{-Z_i}} \right)^{1-Y_i} \rightarrow \text{Max!} \qquad (29)$$

Compliance with specific assumptions is required to apply logistic regression usefully. Compared to discriminant analysis, logistic regression offers the advantage that the assumptions of multivariate normality and identical variance-covariance matrices between the groups are not required. It should be ensured that the independent variables do not exhibit multicollinearity, errors are independent, and the linearity of the logit is given (Field 2013, pp. 768 et seq. and pp. 792 et seq.).

The Variance Inflation Factor (VIF) is commonly derived to assess multi-collinearity. Empirical research often quotes critical VIF values that must not be exceeded. Nevertheless, it should be noted that multicollinearity problems might already arise with very small VIFs (Baguley 2012). Hence, in order to control for multicollinearity, researchers should exclude their specific independent variables from the model one at a time and verify whether the remaining independent variables experience a substantial change regarding their level of significance or the direction of their effect.

In logistic regression, the outcome variable is categorical and, hence, there is no given linear relationship between independent and dependent variables. Nevertheless, the assumption of linearity in logistic regression assumes a linear relationship between any metric independent variable and the logit of the outcome variable. A significant interaction term between an independent variable and its log transformation indicates that this assumption has been violated (Field 2013, p. 794; for further approaches to test this assumption refer to Hosmer et al. 2013, pp. 94 et seq.).

In addition, one should ensure that outliers and other influential observations do not affect the estimated results. Some statistical packages, like SAS, offer a huge variety of outlier statistics for logistic regression, which might be used to alter results in different directions. Hence, researchers should always report whether substantial changes occur in their results when outliers have been removed.

Finally, a reasonable sample size must be used, since maximum likelihood estimation is adopted with this method and requires a large number of observations based on its asymptotic properties. With respect to a study by Peduzzi et al. (1996) it is recommended that the ratio of the group size to the number of independent variables should be at least 10:1 for the smallest group. For instance, in a sample where 25% of the observations have an outcome of $Y = 1$ (representing the least frequent outcome) and 4 independent variables are available, 160 observations are needed (160 observations * 0.25 (share of the observations with the least frequent outcome) = 40 observations; 40 observations / 4 variables =10 observations for each independent variable). Even though this recommendation is widely accepted in literature, Agresti (2013, p. 208) and Hosmer et al. (2013, p. 408) note that this is merely one guideline and models that violate it should not necessarily be neglected. For example, Vittinghoff and McCulloch (2006) conclude in their simulation study that at least 5-9 observations for each independent variable in the smallest group should be sufficient. A more stringent threshold is provided by Aldrich and Nelson (1984), who view 100 degrees of freedom as a minimum for a valid estimation.

Logistic Regression Procedure

The application of logistic regression comprises different steps, which are addressed in more detail below.

Step 1: Problem and Group Definition As stated, similar to two-group discriminant analysis, logistic regression is suitable for the multivariate explanation of differences between groups or for the classification of group-based observations for prediction purposes. Logistic regression is therefore generally appropriate when a single categorical variable is used as a dependent variable. When more than two groups are given, ordered or multinomial logistic regressions can be applied, which represent generalizations of binary logistic regression. If the dependent variable has a metric scale, either those observations that are furthest from one another can be coded as 0 and 1 or the metric variables can be classified into multiple groups (e.g., low, medium, high). This approach is called the "polar extreme approach" (Hair et al. 2010, p. 352).

Step 2: Model Formulation Model formulation may be used to assess which of the independent variables should be analyzed. In contrast to discriminant analysis, no metric scale is required of the explanatory variables. Rather, dummy or categorical variables can be considered. It is important to clarify whether these nonmetric variables are indicator or effect coded. With indicator coding, the reference category is assigned the value of 0 and the resulting coefficient should be interpreted as a relative effect of a category compared to the reference category. Effect-coded variables may be interpreted as a category's relative influence compared to the average effect of all the categories. Unlike in indicator coding, one of the categories is assigned the value of -1. The coefficients of the categories of effect-coded variables add up to zero, so that the reference category's coefficient can be calculated from the coefficients of the other categories (for further details, see Hosmer et al. 2013, pp. 55 et seq.).

Generally, the selection of the independent variables should be based on sound logical or theoretical considerations. Nevertheless, especially in the context of Big Data, a large number of interdependent independent variables with unknown quality are often available. In this case, theoretical considerations might not be possible. However, a limited set of variables still needs to be selected to avoid overfitting. Overfitting often occurs when a large number of variables are included in a prediction model. This might result in a good prediction performance, if a logistic regression model is applied to the observations used for its estimation. Nevertheless, as soon as a prediction is conducted for observations outside the original sample, the prediction performance is likely to suffer. Thus, researchers and practitioners might therefore reduce the dimensions of their data by applying a principal component analysis and only including a limited number of factors into their logistic regression model. Alternatively, variable selection approaches can be used. Tillmanns et al. (2017) provide an extensive comparison of different approaches that can handle a large number of independent variables in models predicting a binary outcome.

Finally, a sufficiently large number of observations is required (see section "Foundations and Assumptions of Logistic Regression"), which should be distributed as evenly as possible between the analyzed groups. If a sufficiently large sample is given, it also makes sense to split the observations into an estimation sample and a holdout sample. The regression function estimated on the basis of the estimation sample can then be used to cross-validate the results with those from the holdout sample.

Step 3: Function Estimation Before the regression model can be estimated, the assumptions underlying logistic regression need to be checked (see section "Foundations and Assumptions of Logistic Regression"). If these assumptions are met, the model can be estimated. As in multiple regression analysis or discriminant analysis, this can be done by using a stepwise procedure ("forward/backward elimination") or by the simultaneous entry of each of the independent variables into the estimation equation ("enter"). If the logistic regression is used to test hypotheses, the latter method is required. In preliminary estimation runs, the potential presence of influential observations or outliers should also always be checked. In this process, the use of Cook's distance is recommended. In cases where the sample is very unbalanced (i.e., one outcome is very rare), researchers might consider ReLogit (Rare Events Logistic Regression) as an alternative approach (for a detailed explanation see King and Zeng 2001).

The maximization of the likelihood function shown in Eq. 29 is achieved with statistical packages, such as SAS or SPSS, using the Newton-Raphson algorithm. The principle underlying maximum likelihood estimation is to select the estimates of parameter β_j in a stepwise iterative analytical approach, such that the observation of the estimated value is assigned a maximum likelihood.

Figure 5 illustrates two logistic functions fitted to two different samples. On the ordinate, the dependent variable Y is shown, wherein $P(Y = 1)$ represents the probability of occurrence of an event. On the abscissa, the values of an independent variable X_i are represented. The logistic function reflects the predicted (estimated) probabilities for the occurrence of the event under the independent variables' different values. The actual observation values are marked by points. In the upper part (a), the logistic function is suitably adapted to the observed data: high independent variable values correspond to the occurrence of the event, and vice versa. However, in the lower part (b), the logistic function is not suitably adapted to the observed data, which is expressed by the large overlap between the two groups in the central region of the abscissa. Entering a cutoff point of 0.5 for classifying observations shows that, in example (a), four observations are misclassified whereas eight observations are misclassified in example (b).

Step 4: Assessment of the Model Performance Before starting with the interpretation of the individual coefficients, it is important to first investigate whether an estimated logistic regression model is in fact suitable. When reviewing this issue, one cannot rely on the traditional measurements and tests used in linear regression analysis (such as the coefficient of determination or F-values), because the

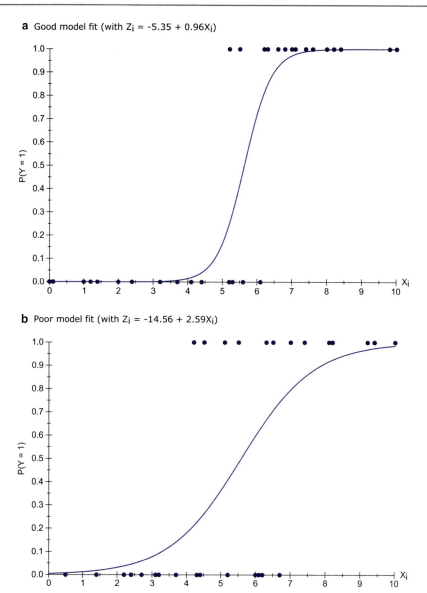

Fig. 5 Fit of the logistic function with different samples

coefficients obtained from logistic regression are determined by using maximum likelihood estimation. Goodness-of-fit in maximum likelihood applications is usually assessed by using *deviance* (or -2LL), which is calculated as -2*log (likelihood). A perfect fit of the parameters is equivalent to a likelihood of 1, corresponding to a deviance of 0 (Aldrich and Nelson 1984, p. 59; Hosmer et al. 2013, p. 155).

Logistic Regression and Discriminant Analysis

In terms of interpretation, the likelihood is comparable to that of least squares errors in conventional regression analysis. Further, -2LL is used, because it is asymptotically χ^2-distributed with (N-p) degrees of freedom, where N is the number of observations, and p the number of the parameters. Good models reflecting a "high" likelihood of close to 1 result in a deviance that is close to 0, while a bad fit is mirrored in high deviance values. Deviance values are unlimited in positive range.

Whether a deviance has to be considered as rather "high" or "low" depends on the particular sample used and the analysis deployed. The value of the deviance can be used to test a hypothesis H_0, which posits that the overall model shows a perfect fit with the data. With either low deviance values or high significance, H_0 cannot be rejected and the model can be deemed as showing a good fit with the data (Menard 2002, pp. 20 et seq.).

In addition to the deviance, *likelihood ratio tests* and pseudo-R^2 statistics can be applied, which provide additional indicators permitting assessments of the full model fit compared to the null model, which only comprises an estimated value for β_0, i.e., the intercept of the linear predictor Z_i. In this process, the deviance is applied, which can also be used for comparing incremental differences of different models. The absolute difference between the deviance of the null model and the full model provides an asymptotically distributed χ^2 value, which can be tested against the null hypothesis that the full model coefficients are not significantly different from 0. Thus, a likelihood-ratio test can be conducted, which is comparable to the F-test in linear regression analysis. This test statistic is called the Model Chi-Square. High χ^2 values and low significance levels suggest that the final model's coefficients are significantly different from 0. For this test, the 5% level is usually set as the critical level of significance (Hosmer et al. 2013, p. 40; Menard 2002, p. 21; Tabachnik and Fidell 2013, pp. 448 et seq.).

In logistic regressions, the deviances of the full and the null model can be used to calculate McFadden's R^2. This pseudo-R^2 metric is expressed in the following equation:

$$\text{McFadden's } R^2 = 1 - \frac{LL_1}{LL_0}, \tag{30}$$

where

LL_1: Natural logarithm of the likelihood of the full model.
LL_0: Natural logarithm of the likelihood of the null model

There are additional pseudo-R^2 statistics, which are also based on a comparative goodness-of-fit of the null model and the full model. Similarly, the R^2 statistics of Cox and Snell, as well as of Nagelkerke suggest that higher values correspond to enhanced model fit, with the maximum value of 1 corresponding to perfect model fit.

Assessments of the model performance can also be undertaken on the basis of the attained classification results, where the predicted values P_i are compared with the actual (observed) values Y_i. As part of the Hosmer-Lemeshow test, the accuracy of predictions is checked against the null hypothesis, which posits that the difference between the predicted and observed values is equal to zero (Hosmer et al. 2013, pp. 157 et seq.). These observations are divided into 10 groups of approximately equal size based on the predicted values P_i. By means of a Chi-Square test, the extent to which the observed and predicted frequencies differ is checked. A low χ^2 value of the test statistic, coupled with a high significance level, implies a good model fit.

Further, to assess the predictive accuracy of logistic models, the confusion matrix or classifications matrix is considered. In this 2*2 matrix, the predicted group memberships on the basis of the logistic regression model are compared to the empirically observed group memberships (Menard 2002, p. 31). The correctly classified items are then available on the main diagonal, while the misclassified observations appear off the main diagonal. The proportion of correctly classified elements – as facilitated by logistic regression (which is called the match quality or the hit ratio) – should be higher than the matches obtained from a random allocation. This is a limitation, since the matches attained by using the model are inflated when the parameter estimation of logistic regression and the calculation of the hit rate are based on the same sample (Morrison 1969, p. 158; Hair et al. 2010, p. 373; Afifi et al. 2012, p. 265). Using the estimated coefficients from a calibration sample is therefore expected to generate lower hit rates for other (holdout) samples. With approximately equal groups represented by the dependent variable, using the maximum chance criterion (MCC) to assess the classification performance is recommended. By applying the MCC metric, the classification performance is based on the share of the larger groups within the total sample (Morrison 1969, p. 158; Hair et al. 2010, p. 384; Aaker et al. 2011, p. 478). Nevertheless, if two groups of rather unequal size are considered, adopting the MCC metric is inadequate.

The proportional chance criterion (PCC) is particularly recommended when analyzing two groups of unequal size or when seeking a classification that is equally as good for both groups. The PCC is equivalent to a random hit rate of $\alpha^2 + (1-\alpha)^2$, where α represents the proportion of a group to the total number of observations (Morrison 1969, p. 158; Hair et al. 2010, p. 384; Aaker et al. 2011, p. 478). Whether to use the PCC, MCC, or a different classification criterion depends on the particular subject of investigation. For example, it may be meaningful to minimize the misclassification of only one of the two groups, when assessing credit risks or failure of new products.

The Receiver Operator Characteristic (ROC) is another well-established measure for assessing a logistic regression model's classification performance (see Hosmer et al. 2013, pp. 173 et seq. for a more detailed discussion). Within this analysis, the sensitivity (i.e., the true positive rate: the probability that a certain outcome is predicted to occur, given that the outcome occurred) and specificity (i.e., the true negative rate: the probability that a certain outcome is predicted not to occur, given that the outcome did not occur) are derived. Classification performance depends on the choice of an appropriate cutoff point (i.e., the probability that is necessary to assign a predicted outcome of either 0 or 1 to an object). Generally, an outcome of 1 is predicted for probabilities greater than 0.5. Nevertheless, the choice of an appropriate cutoff point has implications for the

Logistic Regression and Discriminant Analysis   353

classification performance in terms of sensitivity and specificity. Hence, it is worthwhile deriving a cutoff point that maximizes both sensitivity and specificity. The ROC curve considers all possible cutoff points by plotting sensitivity versus 1 - specificity and represents the likelihood that an object with an actual outcome of 1 has a higher probability than an object with an actual outcome of 0. If the logistic regression model has no predictive power, the curve has a slope of one, resulting in an area under the ROC curve of 0.5. Higher values indicate a good predictive power and typically range between 0.6 and 0.9 (Hilbe 2009, p. 258). Hosmer et al. (2013, p. 177) provide a general rule for evaluating classification performance regarding the area under the ROC curve: ROC $= 0.5$: no discrimination; $0.7 \leq$ ROC < 0.8: acceptable discrimination; $0.8 \leq$ ROC < 0.9: excellent discrimination; ROC ≥ 0.9: outstanding discrimination.

Table 2 provides an overview of the different criterions, which can be used to assess the performance of a logistic regression.

Step 5: Examination and Interpretation of the Coefficients If the total model fit is considered acceptable, one can start testing and interpreting the coefficients in terms of their significance, direction, and relative importance. It should be noted that the parameter estimates of a logistic regression are much more difficult to interpret than those attained with linear regression. In linear regression, the coefficient corresponds to the absolute change in the dependent variables with a one-unit increase in the independent variables. The nonlinear nature of the logistic function makes the interpretation more difficult. For a demonstration, refer to Fig. 4 and suppose two variables X_1 and X_2. For example, Z_i might increase from A to A' or from A' to A" because of an increase of X_1 by one unit. The resulting change of the probability for $Y = 1$ depends heavily on the starting point of the increase – A or A'. These starting points in turn depend on the value of the other variables in the model, like X_2 in our example. Thus, in logistic regression coefficients represent only the change in the dependent variable's logit with a one-unit change in the independent variables (Aldrich and Nelson 1984, p. 41; Hair et al. 2010, p. 422; Agresti 2013, p. 163). The logit is the natural logarithm of the "chance of winning;" that is, the ratio of the probability that the dependent variable

Table 2 Acceptable ranges for logistic regression performance measures

Criterion	Range of (acceptable) values
Deviance (-2LL)	Deviance close to 0; significance level close to 100%
Likelihood-ratio test ("Model χ^2")	Highest possible χ^2 value; significance level $< 5\%$
Hosmer-Lemeshow test	Lowest possible χ^2 value; significance level close to 100%
Proportional chance criterion (PCC)	Classification should be better than the proportional chance: $\alpha^2 + (1\text{-}\alpha)^2$, with α = relative size of a group
Area under the ROC curve	ROC $= 0.5$: no discrimination $0.7 \leq$ ROC < 0.8: acceptable discrimination $0.8 \leq$ ROC < 0.9: excellent discrimination ROC ≥ 0.9: outstanding discrimination

is equal to 1 divided by its counter probability (see Eqs. 26 and 27). For interpretation purposes, it may be easier to use the "odds ratios," or effect coefficients, which are obtained by means of the e^β transformation (Hosmer et al. 2013, pp. 50–51). Specifically, odds ratios show how the odds change with a one-unit increase in the independent variables. The odds describe the ratio of the probability of occurrence of an event to its counter probability (i.e., chance) as displayed in Eq. 26. Odds range from 0 to ∞, whereby values below one indicate that the chance of an event occurring becomes lower with increasing values of the independent variable and values above one indicate the opposite.

To verify the *significance* of the independent variables, either the Wald statistic or the likelihood-ratio test can be used. The confidence interval of individual coefficients can be determined based on the χ^2-distributed Wald statistic, which is calculated from the square of the ratio of the coefficient and the variable's standard error. This formula applies to metric variables with one degree of freedom only. For categorical variables, the variable's degrees of freedom have to be considered in addition. With the likelihood-ratio test, the full model is tested against a reduced model, which is reduced by the variable under consideration. The significance test is performed on the basis of the difference between both models' deviances, which again follows a χ^2-distribution.

The *direction* of the variables' effects with significant coefficients can be interpreted directly. As can be seen in Fig. 4, negative signs imply that the probability P_i decreases, while positive signs imply increasing probabilities with higher values of the variable under consideration. Statements regarding the *relative importance* of each variable can be made based on the aforementioned "odds ratios." Their level is, however, dependent on the scaling of the variables. Furthermore, a constant change in the odds ratios does not result in a constant change in probabilities, and the magnitude of the effect on the probabilities is not symmetric around one (Hoetker 2007). Hence, alternative interpretations are discussed in the following.

In order to derive the relative importance of each predictor, different options are available. First, a *standardized coefficient* can be calculated to reflect the strength of the effect independent from the scaling of the independent variables. This effect strength can be interpreted similar to the standardized coefficients used in linear regression, as this metric specifies the number of standard deviations by which the logit changes when the independent variable increases by one standard deviation (for further details refer to Menard 2002, pp. 51 et seq.).

Marginal effects, i.e., the partial derivative of the logit function for an independent variable X_j, represent another alternative (Leclere 1992, pp. 771 et seq.). The marginal effect of X_j can be derived by applying the following formula:

$$\frac{\partial P_i}{\partial X_j} = \frac{e^{-\left(\beta_0 + \sum_{j=1}^{J} \beta_j X_j\right)}}{\left(1 + e^{-\left(\beta_0 + \sum_{j=1}^{J} \beta_j X_j\right)}\right)^2} \beta_j \tag{31}$$

Equation 31 can be reduced to:

$$\frac{\partial P_i}{\partial X_j} = \beta_j P_i(1 - P_i) \tag{32}$$

Regarding the relative importance of different variables, it has to be considered that marginal effects depend on the scale of the examined variables. Furthermore, marginal effects vary across different values of an independent variable as can be seen easily in our example in Fig. 4. Because of the different gradients of the curve in points A, A', and A", the marginal effects at these points are substantially different. The issue regarding marginal effects' dependence on the scaling of independent variables can be resolved by standardizing the independent variables on the one hand, while on the other hand using their elasticities to interpret the logistic regression coefficients.

Elasticities are easier to interpret than the coefficients' scale-variant partial derivatives, because they are dimensionless and quantify the percentage change in the probability P_i under a 1% change in the respective independent variable of the logistic model. The elasticity of the probability P_i regarding infinitesimally small changes of X_j is obtained by adoption of the following equation (Leclere 1992, p. 772):

$$\varepsilon_{j,i} = \frac{X_j}{P_i} \frac{\partial P_i}{\partial X_j} = \frac{X_j}{P_i} \frac{e^{-\left(\beta_0 + \sum_{j=1}^{J} \beta_j X_j\right)}}{\left(1 + e^{-\left(\beta_0 + \sum_{j=1}^{J} \beta_j X_j\right)}\right)^2} \tag{33}$$

The equation can be simplified to

$$\varepsilon_{j,i} = \frac{X_j}{P_i} \frac{\partial P_i}{\partial Xj} = X_j(1 - P_i) \cdot \beta_j. \tag{34}$$

The elasticity thus results from the multiplication of the partial derivative of probability P_i (with respect to the independent variable X_j) with X_j divided by P_i. For X_j the mean value $\overline{X}_j$ is often applied (Leclere 1992, pp. 773 et seq.). As with partial derivatives, elasticities depend on the initial values of P_i and the independent variables' values. However, the lacking dimensionality of elasticities allows direct comparisons of various independent variables' relative influence on the probability P_i.

From the perspective of non-econometricians, *sensitivity analysis* may be an appealing way of interpreting logistic regression models. In order to conduct a sensitivity analysis, the probability P_i is examined for different values of the independent variable. Usually, the value of a single independent variable is varied systematically (e.g., +10%, +20%, ..., -10%, -20%), while the other variables are kept constant. The difference between the initially estimated and the resulting new probability P_i can then be interpreted as the relative importance of each significant independent variable for P_i. The advantage of sensitivity analysis lies in the visualization of the absolute effect of the independent variables' different values on the probability P_i (Leclere 1992, pp. 772 et seq.). In section "Interpretation of the Coefficients," we provide an example for such a sensitivity analysis.

Several authors emphasize that the interpretation of *interaction effects* in logistic regression is often insufficient, as the marginal effect of an interaction between two variables is not simply the coefficient of their interaction and the associated level of significance (e.g., Hoetker 2007). Ai and Norton (2003) show that the interaction effect of two independent variables X_1 and X_2 is the cross-derivative of P_i with respect to each. For two continuous variables X_1 and X_2 this results in the following equation:

$$\frac{\partial^2 P_i}{\partial X_1 \partial X_2} = \beta_{12} P_i (1 - P_i)$$
$$+ (\beta_1 + \beta_{12} X_2)(\beta_2 + \beta_{12} X_1) (P_i (1 - P_i)(1 - 2P_i)) \tag{35}$$

Based on Eq. 35, Norton et al. (2004, p. 156) emphasize four important implications for the interpretation of interaction effects in logistic regression. First, eq. (35) shows that the interaction effect is not equal to the coefficient of the interaction β_{12} and an interaction can even exist, if $\beta_{12} = 0$. Second, the statistical significance of an interaction must be derived for the entire cross-derivative and not just the coefficient of the interaction. Third, the interaction effect is conditional on the independent variables. Fourth, Eq. 35 consists of two additive terms, which can take different signs. Accordingly, the interaction effect may have different signs for different values of the independent variables and therefore, the sign of the interaction coefficient does not necessarily represent the sign of the interaction effect. Thus, we recommend to derive the interaction effects for each observation and plot it against the predicted values of the dependent variable in order to reveal the full interaction effect (see e.g., Norton et al. 2004 for an example).

Step 6: Prediction At the beginning of section "Logistic Regression," we pointed out that logistic regression can also be used for prediction purposes. As in discriminant analysis, a holdout sample can be applied to validate the prediction performance of a logistic regression. Alternatively, cross-validation can be undertaken by means of the U-method or the jackknife method (Hair et al. 2010, pp. 374 et seq.; Aaker et al. 2011, p. 478). Examples for applying logistic regression in a prediction context include the check of creditworthiness, where financial service providers first analyze good and poor credit agreements, in order to then be in a position to assess current loan applications and their associated risks. The methods presented in the preceding sections are illustrated below in an application to sales contests among sales people.

Applied Examples

Research Question and Sample, Model, Estimation, and Model Assessment

Mantrala et al. (1998) examine the use of sales contests (SCs) in the USA and Germany. Although SCs represent commonly used motivational tools in practice, they are often neglected in research. The authors therefore develop hypotheses based on institutional economics that investigate the influence that the sales force size (x_1), the ease and adequacy of output measurement (x_2), the replaceability of sales people (x_3), and the length of the sales cycle (x_4) has on the probability that SCs are used. This might help managers to determine, whether their firm should use sales contests according to market standards. In addition to 118 observations from the USA, the study considers 270 German cases. Of the 270 original cases, 39 have missing values for at least one of the four variables. The remaining 231 observations are made up of 91 sales forces that do not use SCs (39.39%) and 140 sales forces that do deploy SCs as part of their incentive system (60.61%). The latter data set is also described in Krafft et al. (2004) and forms the basis of the following example. In our example, 231 observations are used to estimate four parameters, such that 226 degrees of freedom remain. The data set thus meets the most stringent criteria in terms of sample size and the ratio of sample size to parameters to be estimated. Table 3 provides an overview of the independent variables' mean values and whether they differ significantly with regard to the use of sales contests. The analyses are based on one-factorial analyses of variances and provide initial evidence that the independent variables can discriminate between the groups in our sample. This initial analysis is especially suitable for a discriminant analysis, which requires a metric scale for the independent variables.

Discriminant Analysis

Model Estimation and Model Assessment
The estimation of the discriminant function yields an eigenvalue of 0.255. As mentioned in section "Discriminant Analysis Procedure," higher values indicate a

Table 3 Determinants of the adoption of sales contests

Independent variable	Means			F	
	Total ($n = 231$)	No SC ($n = 91$)	SC ($n = 140$)		
Sales force size (x_1)	269.16	42.12	416.74	13.58	***
Adequacy of output measures (x_2)	0.51	0.44	0.55	18.99	***
Replaceability of sales people (x_3)	7.98	6.89	8.69	11.83	***
Length of the sales cycle (x_4)	12.27	19.08	7.85	24.85	***

***$p < .001$

higher quality of the discriminant function. Since the measure is not standardized to values between zero and one, Wilks's lambda is a more appropriate measure to indicate a discriminant function's discriminant power. Wilks's lambda is an inverse measure of goodness, such that lower values represent a better discriminant power. In the given application, Wilks's lambda yields a value of 0.797 and indicates that the discriminant function significantly discriminates between companies that use sales contests and those that do not use them (χ^2 (4), $p < 0.001$). A classification matrix can be applied to derive the predictive power of the discriminant function and is depicted in Table 4. Given the group sizes in our example, the proportional chance criterion (PCC) is 52.25% (i.e., $0.61^2 + (1 - 0.61)^2$). In relation to the PCC, the hit rate of 69.70% (i.e., $(61 + 100) / 231$) can be considered sufficient.

Interpretation of the Coefficients

Even though Table 3 provides initial evidence about the discriminatory meaning of the variables in our example, particularly by highly significant F statistics, the interdependencies between the variables are not considered and a multivariate assessment might provide more valuable insights. Examining the standardized discriminant coefficients and the discriminant loadings, which are displayed in Table 5, is one such approach.

In our example, the standardized discriminant coefficients and discriminant loadings indicate that the length of the sale cycle and adequacy of output measures are the best predictors for the use of sales contests. Notably, slight differences can be observed with regard to the relative importance of both variables. Because

Table 4 Classification matrix regarding the (non-)adoption of sales contests after applying a discriminant analysis

Observed group membership	Predicted group membership		
	No sales contests	Adoption of sales contests	Correct classifications (%)
No sales contests	61	30	67.03
Adoption of sales contests	40	100	71.43
Total			69.70

Table 5 Discriminant coefficients and loadings

Independent variable	Standardized discriminant coefficients	Discriminant loadings
Sales force size (x_1)	0.443	0.482
Adequacy of output measures (x_2)	0.531	0.570
Replaceability of sales people (x_3)	0.311	0.450
Length of the sale cycle (x_4)	-0.526	-0.652

Logistic Regression and Discriminant Analysis

discriminant loadings are superior to discriminant coefficients in terms of an unbiased interpretation (see section "Discriminant Analysis Procedure"), we recommend to take them into account for assessing variables' relative importance.

Logistic Regression

Model Estimation and Model Assessment

According to the Cook's distance statistic, we do not find any influential outliers in our data set. After seven iterations of the logistic regression, no further improvement in the model likelihood could be achieved (improvement $< 0.01\%$). The full model has a deviance of 232.109 (-2LL of the null model: 309.761). This relatively low value in combination with a significance level of 1.000 for the deviance indicates a good model fit. This is also confirmed by a high significance level of the Hosmer-Lemeshow test. The logistic model exhibits a likelihood ratio value of 77.652, which is highly significant ($p < 0.001$). Thus, compared to the null model, the inclusion of the four independent variables results in a significantly improved model fit. A LL_1 value of -116.055 is obtained for the full model, while an LL_0 value of -154.880 is observed for the null model. The resulting McFadden's R^2 of 0.2507 for the final model may be viewed as relatively good, given that only four variables are used.

Considering the proportional chance criterion (PCC) of 52.25%, an overall hit rate of 75.32% of correctly classified observations ((58 + 116) / 231) indicates a good prediction performance within the calibration sample. In addition, the hit rate of 63.74% for the (smaller) group of sales forces without SCs indicates a suitable classification performance. Table 6 shows the classification table of the logistic regression in our example.

The predicted group memberships in Table 6 are based on a cutoff point of 0.5 for the predicted probability regarding the use of SCs. Consequently, if the predicted probabilities are larger than or equal to 50%, the observations are assigned to the SC group. In our example, a true positive rate (i.e., sensitivity) of 0.83 (i.e., 116 / (116 + 24)) and a true negative rate (i.e., specificity) of 0.64 (i.e., 58 / (58 + 33)) are achieved. Especially if the groups under consideration are unequal in size or if a misclassification is associated with costs, applying a different cutoff point might be more reasonable. For example, misclassification costs might appear if firms predict households' responses to a direct mailing campaign and

Table 6 Classification matrix regarding the (non-)adoption of sales contests after applying a logistic regression

Observed group membership	Predicted group membership		
	No sales contests	Adoption of sales contests	Correct classifications (%)
No sales contests	58	33	63.74
Adoption of sales contests	24	116	82.86
Total			75.32

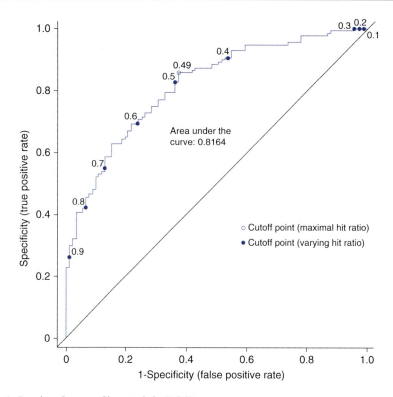

Fig. 6 Receiver Operator Characteristic (ROC) curve

seek to avoid reactance (i.e., costs) by those who are not interested in the offering, but who would be misclassified as potential respondents. In this case, the firm would try to limit the false positive rate. The Receiver Operator Characteristic (ROC) curve in Fig. 6 visualizes the trade-off between the true positive rate and the false positive rate, when different cutoff points are used in our example. If higher cutoff points are chosen, the false positive rate decreases (e.g., from 0.36 (i.e., 33 / (33 + 58)) to 0.24 (i.e., 22 / (22 + 69)) if a cutoff point of 0.6 instead of 0.5 is chosen). Choosing a cutoff point of 0.49 would maximize the hit ratio to 0.77 in the given setting. Generally, the area under the curve is frequently used as a meaningful measure to evaluate the predictive performance of logistic regression models. In the given example, it yields a value of 0.8164, indicating that the logistic regression provides an excellent discrimination.

Interpretation of the Coefficients

Table 7 shows the coefficients of the four variables included in the logistic regression, as well as the constant. With the exception of the significance level and the direction of the effect of each variable, a direct interpretation of the coefficients of the logistic regression model is not possible. As an indicator of the change in odds

Table 7 Elasticities and sensitivity analysis of the significant variables regarding the use of sales contests

Independent variable	Logit-coefficient	SE	Odds Ratio	Means			Elasticity (based on no SC mean)	Probability in % that SCs are used when ... is included in the logistic function[a]		
				No SC	Total	SC		No SC mean	Total mean	SC mean
Sales force size	0.0080[b]	0.002	1.008	42.12	269.16	416.74	0.1977	41.07	80.95	93.23
Adequacy of output measures	3.0574[b]	0.897	21.272	0.44	0.51	0.55	0.7920	41.07	46.09	49.41
Replaceability of sales people	0.1110[b]	0.043	1.117	6.89	7.98	8.69	0.4506	41.07	44.03	45.98
Length of the sales cycle	0.0258[c]	0.012	0.974	19.08	12.27	7.85	-0.2905	41.07	45.38	48.22
Constant	2.3121[b]	0.652								

No SC: Non-deployment of sales contests, *SC*: Deployment of sales contests, *SE*: Standard error
[a]The respective mean value of the SC sample is replaced only for the variable under consideration (*ceteris paribus*)
[b]significant at the 0.1 % level
[c]significant at the 5 % level

resulting from a one unit change in the predictor, the odds ratios (see Table 7) are helpful for interpreting the coefficients (see Field 2013, pp. 766 et seq. for a detailed explanation).

In our example, the odds of the use of SCs are defined as follows:

$$\text{odds} = \frac{\text{probability, that } SCs \text{ are used}}{\text{probability, that no } SCs \text{ are used}} \tag{36}$$

The probability of using SCs (i.e., P(SCs)) is derived by applying the logistic regression coefficients in our example to formula (25), while the probability, that SCs are not used is simply 1-P(SCs):

$$P(SCs) = \frac{1}{1 + e^{-(2.3121 + 0.008x_1 + 3.0574x_2 + 0.1110x_3 - 0.0258x_4)}} \tag{37}$$

The odds ratio represents the odds before and after a one unit change of the predictor variable:

$$\text{odds ratio} = \frac{\text{odds after a one unit change}}{\text{original odds}} \tag{38}$$

In our example, the odds ratio for sales force size is derived by $e^{0.0080} = 1.008$ and indicates that an increase of the salesforce by one salesperson increases the odds of using SCs by 1.008 or 0.8%. If the length of the sales cycle is increased by one month, the odds of using SCs are reduced by 0.974, equivalent to 2.6% ($e^{0.0258}$). As mentioned in section "Logistic Regression Procedure," odds ratios are dependent on the scaling of the variables. This can easily be seen when comparing the magnitude of the odds ratios with the mean values in Table 7. Further, a change of odds ratios does not result in a constant change of probabilities. Thus, in order to derive insights on the relative importance of the determinants of the use of SCs, we calculated the variables' elasticities based on the means of the non-SC observations. If these means are used in the logistic regression function, we observe a probability of $P = 41.07\%$ that SCs are used.

As elasticities are dimensionless, they can be compared directly with each other at the absolute level. However, just like the partial derivatives, they are valid only for a certain point examined in the logistic probability function (e.g., the means of the non-SC observations in our application) and vary when other points (e.g., the means of the SC observations in our application) are examined.

All elasticities shown in Table 7 exhibit absolute values that differ substantially from 0; that is, the influence of the independent variables on the probability that SCs are deployed is comparatively high. However, there are substantial differences between the elasticities: in terms of magnitude, the strongest influence stems from the variable "adequacy of output measures," followed by "replaceability of sales people," "length of the sales cycle," and "sales force size."

Logistic Regression and Discriminant Analysis

In the event that $P = 41.07\%$, it may be deduced that with a 1% increase in the size of the sales force (i.e., from 42.12 to 42.54 sales people), the probability P_i that SCs are used increases by 0.20% to approximately 41.15%. If the length of the 19.08 week sales cycle is increased by 1% to approximately 19.27 weeks, the probability P_i decreases by -0.29% to 40.95%. For the other two significant variables used in our example, the effect of a 1% change in the influencing factors can be calculated analogously.

For sales mangers it might be revealing to know, how the probability that SCs are used changes when the values of the independent variables are changed by a certain level (e.g., "what effect is observed on the probability that SCs are used, when the length of the sales cycle increases from 10 to 15 weeks?"). In our example of a sensitivity analysis in Table 7, the mean values of the non-SC observations are selected as the baseline again. If only the mean values of the non-SC observations are used in the logistic function, we derive a probability of 41.07% that SCs are used. For our sensitivity analysis, we now replace the mean values of the non-SC observations with the mean values of the SC observations one at a time for each independent variable. The values of the other variables are at the same time kept constant at the means of the non-SC observations. The estimated probabilities shown in Table 7 indicate that the largest influence on the probability that SCs are used emanates from "sales force size." If the number of sales people increases from 42.12 (i.e., mean for sales forces that do not use SCs) to 416.74 (i.e., mean value for sales forces that deploy SCs), the estimated probability to use SCs rises from 41.07% to 93.23%. Notably, the variable is ranked as least important with regard to its elasticity. This can be explained by the substantial difference between the means of the non-SCs and SCs observations, which exhibit a ratio of almost 1:10. While elasticities are good at indicating a variable's influence for a rather limited range of values, sensitivity analyses are useful to reveal probability changes for larger changes of the independent variable. The variable "adequacy of output measures" also exerts a substantial, although clearly smaller influence on the change in the probability that SCs are used. If this standardized multiple-item variable (which is normed between 0 and 1) equals 0.55 (i.e., the mean of cases where SCs are used), rather than equaling 0.44, the probability of using SCs increases from 41.07% to 49.41%. While a substantial impact is also exerted by the "length of the sales cycle" on the estimated change in the dependent variables, the variable "replaceability of sales people" exerts the lowest influence on P_i.

Logistic regression can also be used for prediction or cross-validation purposes. As part of cross-validation, the estimated coefficients can be applied to a holdout sample. In this case, only a part of the sample is used for calibrating the logistic function, which is then used to predict the actual outcomes of the remaining sample. Comparing the predicted outcomes with the actual outcomes of the holdout sample provides a good indication about the predictive power of the logistic function. Especially in direct marketing, it is crucial to know which customers will respond

Table 8 Data for a pharmaceutical company regarding the use of sales contests

Independent variable	Logit coefficient	Observation at the sample company
Sales force size	+0.0080	18
Adequacy of output measures	+3.0574	0.39[a]
Replaceability of sales people	+0.1110	5[a]
Length of the sales cycle (in weeks)	-0.0258	20

[a]For further information on these scales refer to Krafft et al. (2004) and the literature cited there

to a direct marketing instrument (e.g., direct mailings) in order to select the most promising customers. In this case, choosing the logistic function with the best out-of-sample prediction performance is pivotal for the success of a marketing campaign. Evaluations of the predictive performance, which are based on the calibration sample, might be particularly misleading when using models that suffer from overfitting (see section "Logistic Regression Procedure" and Tillmanns et al. 2017 for further explanations).

However, the estimated function can also be used to facilitate management decisions: companies considering whether or not to use SCs might use the findings of the logistic regression model presented in our application. Based on the attribute values given in a certain company, managers can derive the probability whether SCs are used by companies with similar attribute values. As an illustration, we use the observed attributes of a pharmaceutical company (see Table 8). The attributes of this company are then applied to Eq. 25 with the coefficients of the logistic regression model, which results in a probability of $P_i = 28.05\%$ that SCs are used. Since the observed company currently does not use SCs, the current (non-)use of sales contests corresponds to the typical practice as observed in the sample.

Conclusion

In the preceding sections, we addressed the fundamentals of discriminant analysis and logistic regression. Table 9 provides a compact overview of both methods in terms of their essential characteristics.

In principle, both methods are suitable for research questions in which the dependent variable has a categorical scale level with two or more groups. They might be applied for either classification or prediction purposes.

Compared to discriminant analysis, logistic regression has a number of key benefits, which relate particularly to the comparatively high robustness of the estimation results. For example, logistic regression allows to conduct analyses even in cases where the assumptions of discriminant analysis are violated, such as for the analysis of nonmetric independent variables (Hosmer et al. 2013, p. 22). As in linear regression, categorical variables can be analyzed using dummy variables, while in discriminant analysis, such variables would violate the assumption of homogeneous variances in the groups (Hair et al. 2010, p. 341 and p. 426).

Logistic Regression and Discriminant Analysis

Table 9 Overview of logistic regression and discriminant analysis

Logistic regression	Discriminant analysis
Objectives	
■ Identification of variables that contribute to the explanation of group membership ■ Prediction of group membership for out-of-sample observations	■ Determination of linear combinations of the independent variables that optimize the separation between the groups and minimize the misclassification of observations ■ Identification of variables that contribute to explaining differences between groups ■ Predicting the group membership for out-of-sample observations
Estimation principle	
Maximum likelihood approach	Maximization of the variance between the groups, relative to the variance within the groups
Scaling of the variables	
■ Dependent variable: nominal scale ■ Independent variables: metric and/or nominal scales	■ Dependent variable: nominal scale ■ Independent variables: metric scales
Assessment of the significance and strength of influence of the independent variables	
■ Wald test, likelihood ratio test ■ Odds ratio, standardized coefficients, partial derivatives, elasticities, sensitivity analyses	■ F-test (univariate ANOVA) ■ Standardized discriminant coefficients, discriminant loadings
Interpretation of the coefficients	
Coefficients represent the effect of a one-unit change in the independent variables on the logit	Discriminant coefficients and weights reflect the relative average group profile
Sample size (recommendations)	
■ A minimum of 10 observations per independent variable in the smallest group ■ Large samples sizes are recommended because of the asymptotic properties of the maximum likelihood estimates in the model parameters	■ A minimum of 20 observations per group ■ A minimum of five observations per independent variable. Better: 20 observations per independent variable to attain stable estimates for the standardized coefficients and weights
Assumptions/recommendations	
■ Nonlinear relationships ■ No multicollinearity ■ Errors are independent ■ Linearity of the logit	■ Linear relationships ■ No multicollinearity ■ Multivariate normal distribution of the independent variables ■ Homogeneity of the variance-covariance matrices of the independent variables

Further, the assumption of multivariate normally distributed independent variables, which is required for the use of discriminant analysis, is frequently not met in practical applications. In these situations, logistic regression is also preferable. The same holds for studies in which the analyzed groups have very different sizes (Tabachnik and Fidell 2013, p. 380). Another important advantage of logistic regression is that through the regression procedure, asymptotic t-statistics can be provided for the estimated coefficients. The confidence intervals obtained in discriminant analysis are, on the other hand, not interpretable (Morrison 1969, pp. 157 et seq.).

Compared to discriminant analysis, logistic regression is thus an extremely robust estimation method. However, it should not be concluded that logistic regression is always the best choice. Discriminant analysis might provide more efficient estimates with higher statistical power if group sizes do not turn out to be too unequal and in cases where the assumptions of discriminant analysis are met (Press and Wilson 1978, p. 701; Tabachnik and Fidell 2013, p. 380 and p. 443). Further, because of the asymptotic properties of the maximum likelihood estimation, the use of logistic regression often requires larger sample sizes than discriminant analysis. Additionally, researchers should examine whether the assumed nonlinear development of the probability P_i is suitable for the specific research context. If, for example, a linear change of P_i is more appropriate, the logistic regression should be avoided. Instead, researchers should check whether linear approaches such as the linear probability model (LPM) or discriminant analysis are more appropriate (Aldrich and Nelson 1984).

References

Aaker, D. A., Kumar, V., Day, G. S., & Leone, R. P. (2011). *Marketing research* (10th ed.). New York: Wiley & Sons.

Afifi, A., May, S., & Clark, V. A. (2012). *Practical multivariate analysis* (5th ed.). Boca Raton: Taylor & Francis.

Agresti, A. (2013). *Categorical data analysis* (3rd ed.). Hoboken: Wiley-Interscience.

Ai, C., & Norton, E. C. (2003). Interaction terms in logit and probit models. *Economics Letters, 80* (1), 123–129.

Aldrich, J., & Nelson, F. (1984). *Linear probability, logit, and probit models*. Beverly Hills: SAGE.

Anderson, E. (1985). The salesperson as outside agent or employee: A transaction cost analysis. *Marketing Science, 4*(3), 234–254.

Backhaus, K., Erichson, B., Plinke, W., & Weiber, R. (2016). *Multivariate Analysemethoden* (14th ed.). Berlin: Springer.

Baguley, T. (2012). *Serious stats: A guide to advanced statistics for the behavioral sciences.* Basingstoke: Palgrave MacMillan.

Campbell, D. T., & Fiske, D. W. (1959). Convergent and discriminant validation by the multitrait-multimethod matrix. *Psychological Bulletin, 56*(2), 81–105.

Field, A. (2013). *Discovering statistics using IBM SPSS* (4th ed.). London: Sage.

Frenzen, H., & Krafft, M. (2008). Logistische Regression und Diskriminanzanalyse. In A. Herrmann, C. Homburg, & M. Klarmann (Eds.), *Handbuch Marktforschung – Methoden, Anwendungen, Praxisbeispiele* (pp. 607–649). Wiesbaden: Gabler.

Hair, Jr, J., Black, W. C., Babin, B. J., Anderson, R. E. (2010). *Multivariate data analysis* (7th ed.). Upper Saddle River: Pearson Prentice Hall.

Hilbe, J. (2009). *Logistic regression models*. Boca Raton: CRC Press.

Hoetker, G. (2007). The use of logit and probit models in strategic management research: Critical issues. *Strategic Management Journal, 28*(4), 331–343.

Hosmer, D., Lemeshow, S., & Sturdivant, R. X. (2013). *Applied logistic regression* (3rd ed.). Hoboken: Wiley.

King, G., & Zeng, L. (2001). Explaining rare events in international relations. *International Organization, 55*(3), 693–715.

Krafft, M., Albers, S., & Lal, R. (2004). Relative explanatory power of agency theory and transaction cost analysis in German salesforces. *International Journal of Research in Marketing, 21*(4), 265–283.

LeClere, M. (1992). The interpretation of coefficients in models with qualitative dependent variables. *Decision Sciences, 23*(3), 770–776.

Long, J. S., & Freese, J. (2014). *Regression models for categorical dependent variables using stata* (3rd ed.). College Station: Stata Press.

Mantrala, M., Krafft, M., & Weitz, B. (1998). Sales contests: An investigation of factors related to use of sales contests using German and US survey data. In P. Andersson (Ed.), Proceedings Track 4 – Marketing management and communication, 27th EMAC conference, Stockholm, pp. 365–375.

Menard, S. (2002). *Applied logistic regression analysis* (2nd ed.). Thousand Oaks: Sage.

Morrison, D. (1969). On the interpretation of discriminant analysis. *Journal of Marketing Research, 6*(2), 156–163.

Norton, E. C., Wang, H., & Ai, C. (2004). Computing interaction effects and standard errors in logit and probit models. *Stata Journal, 4*(2), 154–167.

Osborne, J. W. (2008). Best practices in quantitative methods. Los Angeles: Sage.

Peduzzi, P., Concato, J., Kemper, E., Holford, T. R., & Feinstein, A. R. (1996). A simulation study of the number of events per variable in logistic regression analysis. *Journal of Clinical Epidemiology, 49*(12), 1373–1379.

Press, S. J., & Wilson, S. (1978). Choosing between logistic regression and discriminant analysis. *Journal of the American Statistical Association, 73*(364), 699–705.

Tabachnick, B. G., & Fidell, L. S. (2013). *Using multivariate statistics* (6th ed.). Boston: Pearson.

Tatsuoka, M. M. (1988). *Multivariate analysis: Techniques for educational and psychological research* (2nd ed.). New York: Macmillan.

Theil, H. (1970). On the estimation of relationships involving qualitative variables. *American Journal of Sociology, 76*(1), 103–154.

Tillmanns, S., Ter Hofstede, F., Krafft, M., & Goetz, O. (2017). How to separate the wheat from the chaff: Improved variable selection for new customer acquisition. *Journal of Marketing, 80*(2), 99–113.

Vittinghoff, E., & McCulloch, C. E. (2006). Relaxing the rule of ten events per variable in logistic and cox regression. *American Journal of Epidemiology, 165*(6), 710–718.

Multilevel Modeling

Till Haumann, Roland Kassemeier, and Jan Wieseke

Contents

Introduction: Relevance of Multilevel Modeling in Marketing Research	370
Fundamentals of Multilevel Modeling	372
The Conceptual Relevance of Multilevel Modeling	372
The Statistical Relevance of Multilevel Modeling	375
Types of Constructs and Models in Multilevel Modeling	378
Process of Multilevel Modeling: The Two-Level Regression Model	381
Step 1: Baseline Model	382
Step 2: Adding Independent Variables at Level 1	383
Step 3: Adding Independent Variables at Level 2	383
Step 4: Testing for Random Slopes	384
Step 5: Adding Cross-Level Interaction Effects	385
Assumptions of Multilevel Modeling	386
Model Estimation & Assessing Model Fit	386
Variable Centering	389
Sample Size Considerations	390
Multilevel Structural Equation Modeling	392
Software for Estimating Multilevel Models	396
Example: Building and Estimating a Two-Level Model	398
Conclusions	402
Cross-References	402
Appendix	403
References	404

T. Haumann (✉)
South Westphalia University of Applied Sciences, Soest, Germany
e-mail: haumann.till@fh-swf.de

R. Kassemeier
Marketing Group, Warwick Business School, University of Warwick, Coventry, UK
e-mail: roland.kassemeier@wbs.ac.uk

J. Wieseke
Sales Management Department, University of Bochum, Bochum, Germany
e-mail: jan.wieseke@rub.de

© Springer Nature Switzerland AG 2022
C. Homburg et al. (eds), *Handbook of Market Research*,
https://doi.org/10.1007/978-3-319-57413-4_18

> **Abstract**
>
> Many phenomena in marketing involve multiple levels of theory and analysis. Adopting a multilevel lens to marketing phenomena can often yield richer and more rigorous results. However, the consideration of multiple levels of theory and analysis often leads to the challenge to cope with nested data structures in which a lower level unit of analysis is nested within a higher level unit of analysis. Explicitly acknowledging such nested data structures is important as its analysis with single level analysis techniques may result in biased results and thus incorrect conclusions because nested data structures often violate assumptions of conventional single level analysis techniques. A methodological approach which explicitly accounts for multiple levels of analysis and thus the nested structure of data is referred to as multilevel modeling. This chapter attempts to help researchers and practitioners interested in investigating multilevel phenomena by providing an introduction to multilevel modeling. It therefore describes the theoretic fundamentals of multilevel modeling by outlining the conceptual and statistical relevance of multilevel modeling. Furthermore, it provides guidance how to build a multilevel regression model using a step-by-step approach. The chapter also discusses how to assess the fit of multilevel models, how to center variables at different levels of analysis, and how to determine the sample sizes to adequately estimate multilevel models. Moreover, it offers insights how the logic of multilevel regression analysis could be expanded to multilevel structural equation modeling, discusses different statistical software packages that can be employed to estimate multilevel models, and provides a detailed example of building and estimating a multilevel model.

> **Keywords**
>
> Random coefficient modeling · Hierarchical linear modeling · Nested data structures · Hierarchical data · Between variance · Within variance · Random intercept · Random slope · Cross-level interaction · Intraclass correlation coefficient · Group mean centering · Grand mean centering

Introduction: Relevance of Multilevel Modeling in Marketing Research

Many phenomena in marketing which raise the interest of marketing researchers and practitioners involve multiple levels of theory and analysis. For example, marketing researchers and practitioners may be interested investigating which skills salespeople do need to service their customers best (Homburg et al. 2011), how marketing and/or sales managers may behave to increase their employees' performance (Wieseke et al. 2009), or to determine the effectiveness of different instruments of the marketing mix in managing brands across different countries (Steenkamp et al. 2010). Indeed, all of these questions pertain to multiple levels – i.e., the salesperson and the customer level, the manager and the employee level, and the customer and the country level. Recognizing the multilevel nature of marketing phenomena can be important for at least two reasons.

First, the recognition and inclusion of different levels of theory often has the potential to provide richer and more rigorous insights of the studied phenomenon. It may provide richer insights because acknowledging the multilevel nature of a phenomenon allows the identification of contextual factors which influence the phenomenon under investigation. Or as Hitt et al. (2007, p. 1385) put it: "Using a multilevel lens reveals the richness of social behavior; it draws our attention to the context in which behavior occurs and illuminates the multiple consequences of behavior traversing levels of social organization. For management to continue advancing as a field in which scholars seek to explain the behaviors of individuals, groups, and organizations, we must expand our theories and empirical investigations to encompass these multilevel effects." Originally referring to management, this conclusion also strongly pertains to marketing research. Adopting a multilevel lens may also provide more rigorous insights because it is associated with collecting data at multiple levels. Such multilevel data collections can assure that each variable is measured at the adequate level (e.g., salesperson variables at the salesperson level and customer variables at the customer level) (Klein et al. 1994) and often result in multisource data sets benefiting from advantageous characteristics such as a lower susceptibility to common method bias (Johnson et al. 2014).

Second, it is important to account for the multilevel nature of marketing phenomena because acknowledging multiple levels of analysis may have consequences for the adequate methodological approach. Specifically, multilevel phenomena are characterized by hierarchical data structures in which lower entities are nested within higher entities (e.g., customers nested within salespersons or employees nested within managers) (Heck and Thomas 2015). To acknowledge such nested data structures is important because they may violate assumptions of conventional single level analysis techniques and thus may result in biased standard errors and in spuriously significant results (Hox et al. 2018; Wieseke et al. 2008).

A methodological approach to adequately account for the complexity associated with hierarchical nested data structures is referred to as multilevel or random coefficient modeling (Raudenbush and Bryk 2002; Hox et al. 2018). It can conceptually be regarded as a system of hierarchical regression equations. In such a hierarchical system of regression equations, one equation captures the influence of variables at the lower level, while one or more equations refer to the influences at the higher level (Hox et al. 2018). Thereby, multilevel modeling can help to assure the integrity between multilevel theory and multilevel analysis and thus help to unfold the full potential of a multilevel lens to marketing phenomena.

This chapter attempts to help researchers and practitioners interested in investigating multilevel phenomena by providing an introduction to multilevel modeling. We begin with discussing the "Fundamentals of Multilevel Modeling" and describe its conceptual and statistical relevance. Furthermore, we discuss core types of constructs and models in multilevel contexts. Then, the section "Process of Multilevel Modeling: The Two-Level Regression Model" begins with offering a detailed description of the steps of estimating a two-level regression model and provides information on how the model fit of a multilevel model is assessed. Afterwards, we discuss different approaches of centering variables at lower and higher levels and provide insights into sample size requirements for adequately analyzing multilevel models. The Section "Multilevel Structural Equation Modeling" extends the multilevel regression approach and explains how to apply multilevel structural equation modeling. In Section "Software for Estimating Multilevel Models" we provide information on core software packages for multilevel analysis and in section "Example: Building and Estimating a Two-Level Model" we offer a detailed example of building and estimating a multilevel model. Finally, we conclude this chapter by offering an overview of the most important terms introduced in this chapter together with their definitions.

Fundamentals of Multilevel Modeling

The Conceptual Relevance of Multilevel Modeling

The adequate analysis of nested data structures is important because such data structures permeate marketing research (Wieseke et al. 2008). Specifically, marketing research in fields such as relationship marketing, international marketing, personal selling, sales management, services, organizational research in marketing, research based on secondary data (e.g., research at the interface of marketing and finance), longitudinal marketing phenomena, or meta-analyses attempts to address research questions which involve nested data structures and multiple level of analysis. Table 1 provides an overview of exemplary nested data structures in the aforementioned fields of marketing research and additionally offers examples of papers that conducted a multilevel approach to analyze their data.

Most of the nested data structures presented in Table 1 and thus the conceptual relevance of multilevel modeling primarily stems to large extent from the hierarchical structure of (marketing) organizations. In this respect Klein et al. (1994, p. 198) state that "By their very nature, organizations are multilevel. Individuals work in dyads, groups, and teams within organizations that interact with other organizations both inside and outside the industry. [...]. To examine organizational phenomena is thus to encounter levels issues." In the following, we outline the conceptual relevance of multilevel modeling in marketing research by highlighting how different entities are integrated in the conceptual structure of a marketing organization and how they are thus nested in higher level entities (e.g., Hitt et al. 2007; Wieseke et al. 2008). Figure 1 illustrates an exemplary hierarchical structure in marketing organizations.

Figure 1 visualizes customers as the centroid of the exemplary multilevel structure. As salespeople's behavior is crucial for customer perceptions of the selling interaction (e.g., Homburg et al. 2009a), the company's products (e.g., Goff et al. 1997), and the organization as a whole (e.g., Homburg et al. 2011), customers are nested within salespeople. Consequently, the aforementioned customer perceptions depend in part on the salespeople by whom they are served. The study of Mikolon

Multilevel Modeling

Table 1 Exemplary nested data structures in marketing research

	Exemplary nested data structures[a]		
Research area	Lower level	Higher level	Exemplary papers
Relationship Marketing	Customers	Organizations	Homburg et al. 2009b; Maxham et al. 2008; Netemeyer et al. 2012; Palmatier 2008
International Marketing	Individuals (e.g., salespeople, customers)	Countries Cultures	Hohenberg and Homburg 2016; Steenkamp et al. 2010; Walsh et al. 2014
Personal Selling	Customers	Salespeople	Homburg et al. 2011; Mikolon et al. 2020; Wieseke et al. 2014
Sales Management	Salespeople	Leaders Territories Sales Teams	Ahearne et al. 2010; Auh et al. 2014; Mathieu et al. 2007; Wieseke et al. 2009; Van der Borgh et al. 2019
Service Research	Customers Frontline Employees	Service Providers Organizations	Brady et al. 2012; Donavan et al. 2004; Mikolon et al. 2015
Organizational Research in Marketing	Frontline Employees	Work Groups Subsidiaries	de Jong et al. 2004; Homburg et al. 2011; Liao and Chuang 2007; Wieseke et al. 2012
Marketing-Finance Interface	Firms	Industries	Anderson et al. 2004; Groening et al. 2016; Gruca and Rego 2005; Josephson et al. 2016; Larivière et al. 2016; Misangyi et al. 2006
Longitudinal Marketing Phenomena	Observations in Time	Individuals (e.g., salespeople, customers)	Boichuk et al. 2014; Fu et al. 2010 Lam et al. 2013
Meta-Analysis in Marketing Research	Effect Sizes/ Relationships	Samples/ Studies	Edeling and Fischer 2016; Krasnikov and Jayachandran 2008; Roschk and Hosseinpour 2020; Troy et al. 2008

Note: [a]Included levels of analysis (i.e., nestings) are only exemplary and for illustrative purposes. The cited article may include further other levels of analysis.

et al. (2015), for example, investigates data from customers nested within service provides. The study uses dyadic data of 310 customers that interacted with 108 service providers to explore the role of complexity in professional service encounters.

Further, Figure 1 illustrates salespeople's complex integration within their organization. First, salespeople work in sales teams which are part of larger organizational units (e.g., departments), which in turn are nested in organizations which are nested in environments (e.g., industries). Consequently, salespeople are part of a larger collective that may share values, attitudes, cognitions, experiences, perceptions or behaviors (Kozlowski and Klein 2000). The study of Ahearne et al. (2010) provides an example of such a nested structure by investigating a data set comprising 1070 sales representatives nested within 185 selling teams.

Second, sales managers are usually responsible for sales teams and department managers for company departments. Therefore, salespeople are nested in their

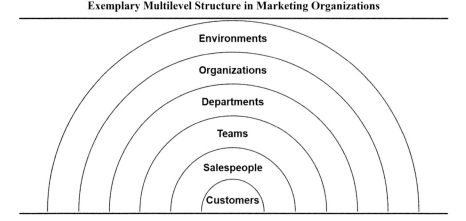

Fig. 1 Exemplary multilevel structure in marketing organizations. (Note: Adapted from Hitt et al. (2007))

direct supervisors, who again may be nested in their department managers. Department managers in turn may have to report to the organization's chief marketing officers at the top of the organization. As supervisors oftentimes have an enormous impact on their subordinate employees (e.g., Bass and Bass 2009), it is important to account for important supervisor characteristics when investigating processes at lower organizational levels. An example yielding support for the importance of supervisors in affecting their subordinates is provided by the study of Wieseke et al. (2009).

Furthermore, Figure 1 illustrates that customers, salespeople, sales teams, and departments are nested in organizations. Thus, researchers that are interested in investigating inter-organizational differences of organizational entities or customers will be confronted with the nesting of these entities in organizations. Palmatier's (2008) investigation of interfirm relational drivers of customer value reflects an example of the analysis of such data where business-to-business customers ($n = 466$) are nested in different organization ($n = 27$).

Finally, Figure 1 shows that organizations are nested in environments. Environments could be the industry, country, culture or market in which an organization operates. The study of Gruca and Rego (2005) provides an example as it investigates how consequences of customer satisfaction on shareholder value differentiate between industries. The authors' analyze data of 840 firm-year observations in 23 industries.

In addition to the hierarchical structure of marketing organizations, there are further study designs that are associated with a nested data structure (Deadrick et al. 1997). For example, longitudinal data or data of repeated measures can be considered as hierarchical because repeated measurements are nested within individuals (Hox et al. 2018). When investigating longitudinal data employing a multilevel modeling approach, the series of repeated measures can be modeled at the lower level and the individual subjects at the higher level. The consideration of repeated measures of individuals over time allows researchers to investigate "the existence, nature, and causes of within-person [. . .] changes over time" (Deadrick et al. 1997, p. 748).

The study of Fu et al. (2010) provides an example for the application of multilevel modeling for the examination of longitudinal data. The study comprises survey data of 534 salespeople and corresponding performance data of salespeople's daily sales during two product's first several months in the market. The authors employ a growth curve model to examine how the continuous outcome daily sales changes over time and how it is affected by salesperson variables.

Another study design in which multilevel modeling can yield richer and more accurate results refers to meta-analytical investigations (a general introduction to meta-analyses in marketing research is provided by Bijmolt (2021) in the online version of this handbook). A meta-analysis reflects a systematic approach towards synthesizing a larger number of results from empirical studies to summarize findings of a specific research question (Glass 1976; Hox et al. 2018; Lipsey and Wilson 2001). Meta-analyses may be characterized by nested data structures as multiple effect sizes of relationships under investigation are nested within studies (Bijmolt and Pieters 2001). Adopting a multilevel approach recognizes these nestings and additionally allows to include differences between studies (e.g., research operational factors such as measurement approaches, environmental factors such as industries or cultures, or sample or manuscript related factors such as socio-demographical differences between samples or manuscript statuses [e.g., published vs. unpublished]). Methodologically, a multilevel approach to meta-analysis includes effect sizes of relationships under investigation at the lower level and between study characteristics at the higher level (Hox et al. 2018). Thereby, the study characteristics can be used as explanatory variables to explain differences in the investigated relationships between studies (Hox et al. 2018).

An example for applying multilevel modeling to conduct a meta-analysis reflects the study of Troy et al. (2008). In this study, the authors analyze 146 correlations of 25 studies of cross-functional integration and new product success. They use multilevel modeling to investigate moderating influences under which the examined relationship of cross-functional integration and new product success varies.

Thus, in sum, focusing solely on a single level of theory often impedes a profound understanding of complex phenomena prevalent in marketing research (Wieseke et al. 2008). Returning to the introductory thoughts, including the (multiple) relevant levels of analysis into one's theoretical framework has the potential to increase the validity of its findings and thus its contribution to academic marketing research and to provide richer insights for marketing practitioners.

The Statistical Relevance of Multilevel Modeling

The following section describes the methodological challenges that exist when analyzing hierarchical data structures. Figure 2 illustrates a hierarchical data

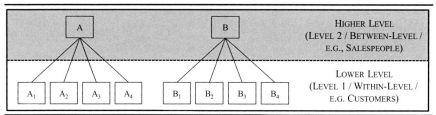

Fig. 2 Hierarchical data structure

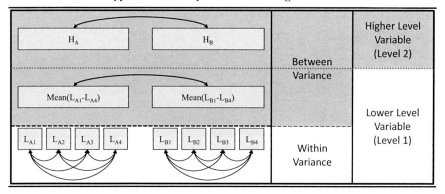

Fig. 3 Different types of variability of lower and higher level variables

structure with two levels. In hierarchical data structures, usually one entity at the higher level (A; e.g., a salesperson) relates to multiple entities at the lower level (A_1-A_4; e.g., consumers served by the same salesperson). In such nested data structures, the association between a specific higher level entity (A) and its nested lower level entities (A_1-A_4) is referred to as a cluster (cluster A).

In hierarchical data structures, in which multiple entities from the lower level are nested within a specific entity at the higher level, one can distinguish between different types of variability of variables at the lower and the higher level. Figure 3 visualizes the different types of variability of lower and higher level variables.

Specifically, in a two level context, lower level variables (L) are characterized by two types of variability, variability at the lower level (Level 1) which captures the variability of a variable within a cluster (*within variance* between L_{A1}-L_{A4} and L_{B1}-L_{B4} at Level 1) and variability at the higher level which captures the variability of the lower level variable between clusters (*between variance* between the cluster mean of cluster A and B at Level 2). In contrast, higher level variables (H) only possess variance at the higher level (*between variance* between H_A and H_B at Level 2).

Turning to a mathematical formulation, these types of variability can be expressed by decomposing the total variance of a variable in its parts at the lower level (i.e., the within variance) and the higher level (i.e., the between variance). Consequently, the variance of a variable x can be written as:

$$V_T(x) = V_W(x) + V_B(x) \tag{1}$$

If x denotes a variable at the higher level, $V_T(x)$ equals $V_B(x)$ since higher level variables possess no lower level variability. However, variables at the lower level often possess meaningful variability at both levels.

This complex variance structure of lower and higher variables can have consequences for the analysis of data. First, lower level observations belonging to different clusters may not be independent from each other (which would be reflected in a meaningful between variance of the lower level variable). However, independence of observations is a core assumption of many single-level methods and a violation of this assumption could lead to biased standard errors and incorrect hypothesis tests (e.g., Hox et al. 2018; Wieseke et al. 2008).

Second, if one is interested in modeling the influence of a higher level variable at a lower level variable using a disaggregated approach (i.e., by disaggregating the higher level variable to the lower level), conventional single-level methods would erroneously assume the disaggregated higher level observations to be independent information and use the larger lower level sample size for hypothesizing testing rather than the adequate higher level sample size. Erroneously using the larger sample size may lead to downward-biased standard errors and thus again to incorrect hypotheses tests (e.g., Hox et al. 2018; Wieseke et al. 2008).

These potential biases of using single-level methods to analyze hierarchical, nested data structures clearly highlight the importance of adopting a methodological approach that is able to adequately handle such multilevel data structures. This is especially true if one is interested in analyzing models with variables from multiple levels.

If one is only interested in analyzing relationships between lower level variables which are however part of a nested data structure, the biases associated with employing a single level method depends on the degree of non-independence of observations and thus of the proportion of between variance of the lower level variables. This proportion of between variance (V_B) compared to the total variance (V_T) of a lower level variable is often referred to as intraclass correlation (ρ; also referred to as intraclass correlation coefficient [ICC]) and is especially helpful in evaluating the necessity of adopting a multilevel modeling technique for investigating single level models testing relationships between lower level variables from a nested data structure. Using mathematical notation, the intraclass correlation for a two-level data structure can be expressed as:

$$\rho = \frac{V_B}{V_T} = \frac{V_B}{(V_W + V_B)} \tag{2}$$

where V_T reflects the total variance, V_B the between variance, and V_W the within variance of a lower level variable (to compute intraclass correlations for three-level models see for example Hox et al. (2018)). The higher the intraclass correlation the higher the non-independence of observation, the higher the potential biases, and thus the more important it is to employ a multilevel modeling approach. Hox (2010) suggests 0.05, 0.10, and 0.15 as small, medium, and large values for the intraclass correlation. However, even for small intraclass correlations biases may be substantial if cluster sizes are large. Therefore, a second helpful metric to determine the necessity to adopt a multilevel modeling approach is the design effect which additionally includes information about the average cluster sizes.

The design effect reflects "the ratio of the variance of estimation obtained with the given sampling design, to the variance of estimation obtained for a simple random sample from the same population, and with the same total sample size" (Snijders and Bosker 2012, p. 287). The higher the design effect, the higher the variation between clusters and the more relevant it is to employ a multilevel modeling approach. Design effects can be calculated as a function of the intraclass correlation (ρ) and the average cluster size (c) (Muthén and Satorra 1995):

$$\text{deff} = 1 + (c - 1) * \rho \qquad (3)$$

A commonly used rule of thumb is that a design effect greater than 2 indicates that the considered variable varies substantially between clusters and, thus, a multilevel approach is necessary to analyze the data. However, as it is only a rule of thumb, Lai and Kwok (2015) have shown that researchers should refrain from using this rule if they are interested in effects of higher-level predictors or investigate data with a cluster size that is less than 10.

Types of Constructs and Models in Multilevel Modeling

Depending on the specific research question, one may distinguish between different types of constructs and models in multilevel modeling. We first discuss constructs referring to individuals and collectives and then distinguish between different types of multilevel models.

Types of constructs in multilevel modeling. In multilevel modeling, one can distinguish between constructs that refer to an individual and constructs that refer to a larger collective. Individual-level constructs refer to characteristics, experiences, attitudes, perceptions, values, cognitions, or behaviors of individuals (e.g., a customer's satisfaction or a salesperson's customer orientation) and can be relevant at different levels of a multilevel model (Kozlowski and Klein 2000). For example, in a context with sales managers supervising multiple salespeople one may be interested whether a sales manager's organizational identification at the higher level may affect the salespeople's level of organizational identification at the lower level (Wieseke et al. 2009).

Beyond individual level constructs, multilevel models are especially helpful for studying larger collectives (e.g., teams, departments, organizations, or industries). Constructs describing such larger collectives can refer to their (1) global, (2) shared, or (3) configural properties (Kozlowski and Klein 2000).

First, global properties refer to descriptive or easily observable characteristics of a collective (e.g., the number of salespersons in a sales team or the type of sales context [B2C vs. B2B]). Such information can be retrieved from archival data or measured using a key informant approach (e.g., the sales manager responsible for the respective sales team).

Second, shared properties emerge from experiences, attitudes, perceptions, values, cognitions, or behaviors that are held in common by a collective of individuals (e.g., a service- or team-climate within a sales team) (Kozlowski and Klein 2000). Such constructs are typically assessed at the individual level and then aggregated to the adequate level of theory and analysis, i.e., the higher level. When employing shared properties it is important to assure that the theoretical foundation resides at the higher level, that the measurement refers to the entity at the higher level (e.g., the group), and that the empirical aggregation of the individual observations is justified. To justify the aggregation of lower level observations to a higher level, researchers often refer to the level of within group or agreement, r_{wg} or $r_{wg(J)}$ (James et al. 1984, 1993), the proportion of within to between variance of the variable, i.e., the intraclass correlation (ICC1), and the reliability of the group mean (ICC2) (Bliese 2000). A description of these criteria and their specific formulas appears in the Appendix. More detailed discussions about these and further criteria to justify aggregation can for example be found in Woehr et al. (2015), LeBreton and Senter (2008), LeBreton, James, and Lindell (2005), or Bliese (2000).

Third, configural properties also refer to experiences, attitudes, perceptions, values, cognitions, or behaviors. However, in contrast to shared properties, configural properties do not reflect agreement or common understanding but describe a pattern or variability between the individuals of the respective collective. A typical example for a configural property is a form of consensus within a collective. Ahearne et al. (2010), for instance, study how interpersonal climate consensus and the consensus regarding leadership empowerment behaviors in sales teams influence the effect of the respective shared properties (i.e., both group-level perceptions) on team potency. Another typical example for a configural property from service research refers to the consensus of service climate within a group of service employees (e.g., Schneider et al. 2002).

Types of models in multilevel modeling. Multilevel models may focus on relationships between constructs on a single level or on relationships across levels (Kozlowski and Klein 2000). In single-level models, researchers are solely interested in the relationships between constructs of one level of a nested data structure. Despite this focus on a single level, it might yet be advantageous to adopt a multilevel modeling approach. Specifically, even if one is solely interested in relationships between lower level variables (e.g., how individual salespersons' customer orientation affect their individual level of sales performance), it can be worthwhile to adopt a multilevel modeling approach. First, as mentioned before the nested data structure may violate the assumption of independence between observations of conventional single level analysis techniques. Second, if observations are not independent from each other, adopting a multilevel modeling approach can account for unobserved heterogeneity between the lower level observations (e.g.,

Hamaker and Muthén 2020). However, if one wants to analyze a single-level model and is solely interested in relationships between higher level variables and if the level of theory and analysis of the included constructs reside at this level and no higher levels exist, a single-level analysis technique can be employed (Kozlowski and Klein 2000).

In contrast to single-level models, cross-level models include relationships between variables of different levels. In cross-level models, a higher level predictor variable may either directly affect an outcome variable at the lower level or moderate a relationship between two variables at the lower level, which is typically referred to as a cross-level interaction. For example, a sales manager's empowering leadership may affect her/his followers' self-efficacy using a new sales technology system and may additionally moderate the relationship between salespersons' prior work experience and their technology self-efficacy (Mathieu et al. 2007).

Another type of multilevel models includes predictor and outcome variables from multiple levels but do not assume cross-level relationships. A specific type of such models, which gained some interest in multilevel research, are homologous models. Homologous models examine whether a process at the lower level (e.g., the individual level) is consistent with a similar process at the higher level (e.g., the team level) (Chen et al. 2005). For example, such a model may examine whether the effect of individual feedback on individual self-efficacy is consistent with the effect of team feedback on collective self-efficacy (Chen et al. 2005). Figure 4 offers a graphical overview of the discussed models for which employing a multilevel analysis technique is recommended.

Beyond these models, another widely used application of multilevel modeling is the analysis of longitudinal data. Longitudinal data has a nested structure such that repeated observations over time are nested in an entity – for example daily data on sales performance nested within a salesperson (Fu et al. 2010). Consequently, multilevel models to analyze longitudinal data describe the development of the outcome variable over time at the lower level. This development in its most simple form is characterized by a (random) intercept and slope parameter. Additionally, time-varying covariates may be added at the lower level. At the higher level, time-invariant covariates, that may help to explain the variance in the random parameters of the lower level, can be added to the model.

Consequently, such models can be used to effectively analyze panel data (please see ▶ "Panel Data Analysis: A Non-Technical Introduction for Marketing Researchers" in this handbook for a general introduction to panel data analysis and an example of multilevel modeling of panel data). Furthermore, such models may be easily extended to account for additional levels (e.g., salespeople in teams) or more complex patterns of the development of the outcome variable over time, such as quadratic or cubic patterns. This opportunity to analyze different patterns over time makes multilevel modeling also an alternative to structural equation modeling to estimate latent growth models (Hox et al. 2018). More detailed discussions of multilevel models to analyze longitudinal data and estimate latent growth models can for example be found in Hox (2011), Hedeker and Gibbons (2006), Duncan, Duncan, and Stryker (2013), Stoel and Garre (2011), and Hox et al. (2018).

Multilevel Modeling

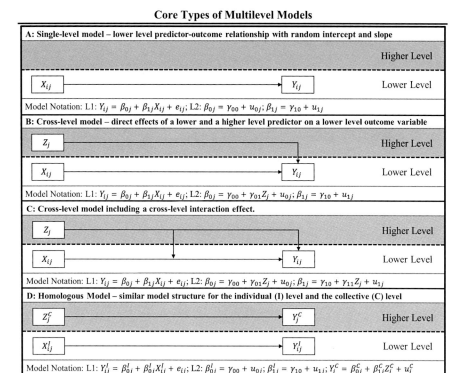

Fig. 4 Core types of multilevel models. (Notes: In this overview we exemplary focus on models with two levels. In all described models, we allow the intercepts and slopes to vary across higher-level entities. Multilevel models may of course include further interactions of variables residing at the same level, which are not included here. In describing the homologous model in Panel D we assume that the variables at the lower and higher level are measured separately)

Process of Multilevel Modeling: The Two-Level Regression Model

The major advantage of multilevel modeling is the opportunity to estimate effects between variables on different levels of analysis while accounting for the hierarchical data structure. However, due to consideration of multiple levels of analysis, the estimation of multilevel models oftentimes involves a high degree of complexity. Therefore, multilevel models are usually estimated in a stepwise process. In the following, we outline the five-step process of estimating a two-level regression model as suggested by Hox et al. (2018) (please refer to Skiera, Jochen Reiner, and Albers (2021) in this handbook for a general introduction to regression analysis). In describing each step, we adopt a notation in which we outline the equation at the lower level (i.e., Level 1 [L1]), at the higher level (i.e., Level 2 [L2]), and then provide an integrated regression equation (I). After explaining the stepwise process of the two-level model, we briefly discuss the assumptions of the multilevel regression model. In addition to the statistical description of the stepwise-estimation of a multilevel model, the section "Building and Estimating a Two-Level Model" provides an example of this process in a marketing context.

Step 1: Baseline Model

Step 1 reflects the estimation of the baseline model. The baseline model (also referred to as intercept-only or random-intercept model) does not include any explanatory variables and does only include the intercept and the residuals at Level 1 and 2. Equation (4) describes the Level 1 model, Equation (5) the Level 2 model, and Equation (6) the integrated form of the baseline model of a two-level regression analysis.

$$L1 : Y_{ij} = \beta_{0j} + e_{ij} \tag{4}$$

$$L2 : \beta_{0j} = \gamma_{00} + u_{0j} \tag{5}$$

$$I : Y_{ij} = \gamma_{00} + e_{ij} + u_{0j} \tag{6}$$

In Equation (4) Y_{ij} represents the value of the dependent variable of observation i ($i = 1, \ldots n_j$; e.g., customers) in cluster j ($j = 1, \ldots J$; e.g., salespersons). β_{0j} reflects the (random) intercept-term at Level 1 which is allowed to vary between clusters as expressed in Equation (5) (see Fig. 4a for a graphical illustration of a random-intercept model). e_{ij} denote the Level 1 residuals which are assumed to have an expected mean of zero ($E(e_{ij}) = 0$) and a variance σ_e^2 ($Var(e_{ij}) = \sigma_e^2$). As the baseline model does not include any exploratory Level 1 variables this residual variance σ_e^2 reflects the within variance of the dependent variable Y_{ij} at Level 1.

Equation (5) represents the equation for the (random) intercept. Here, γ_{00} reflects the intercept value and u_{0j} the residuals of the intercept equation at Level 2. Analogously to the Level 1 residuals, the residuals of the random intercept equation at Level 2 are assumed to have an expected mean of zero ($E(u_{0j}) = 0$) and a variance τ_{00} ($Var(u_{0j}) = \tau_{00}$). Again, as the baseline model contains no exploratory variable, τ_{00} reflects the between variance of the dependent variable Y_{ij} at Level 2. Substituting Equation (5) into Equation (4) allows to derive the integrated form of the baseline model (Equation 6).

Although the baseline model does not include exploratory variables, it provides helpful and important information because it provides estimates of the variance of the dependent variable at Level 1 (the within variance; σ_e^2) and Level 2 (the between variance; τ_{00}). Thus, the information from the baseline model allows the calculation of the intraclass correlation, extending Equation (2):

$$\rho = \frac{V_B}{V_T} = \frac{V_B}{(V_W + V_B)} = \frac{\tau_{00}}{(\sigma_e^2 + \tau_{00})} \tag{7}$$

Multilevel Modeling

The baseline model thereby provides information about the non-independence of observations regarding the dependent variable and hence about the potential bias of ignoring the nested data structure and consequently the importance of adopting a multilevel modeling approach.

Step 2: Adding Independent Variables at Level 1

In step 2 of the model estimation, independent variables at the lower level are added to the model. Equation (8) describes the model at Level 1 with the inclusion of one independent variable, Equations (9) and (10) show the Level 2 model, and Equation (11) presents the integrated model equation:

$$L1 : Y_{ij} = \beta_{0j} + \beta_{1j}X_{ij} + e_{ij} \tag{8}$$

$$L2 : \beta_{0j} = \gamma_{00} + u_{0j} \tag{9}$$

$$L2 : \beta_{1j} = \gamma_{10} \tag{10}$$

$$I : Y_{ij} = \gamma_{00} + \gamma_{10}X_{ij} + e_{ij} + u_{0j} \tag{11}$$

New in the Level 1 equation is the term $\beta_{1j}X_{ij}$ which characterizes the effect of the Level 1 independent variable X_{ij} on the dependent variable Y_{ij}. The regression coefficient of the Level 1 variable can be substituted by γ_{10} (Equation 10)[1] as shown in the integrated equation (Equation 11). The equation of the random intercept remains unchanged (Equation 10) and can also be substituted in the integrated form. Of course, it is possible in this step to add multiple lower level variables.

Step 3: Adding Independent Variables at Level 2

In step 3, independent variables at the higher level are included in the model. Equation (12) presents the unchanged Level 1 equation, Equation (13) shows the new equation of the random intercept, Equation (14) depicts the unchanged equation of the regression coefficient β_{1j}, and Equation (15) presents the integrated equation of the two-level model.

$$L1 : Y_{ij} = \beta_{0j} + \beta_{1j}X_{ij} + e_{ij} \tag{12}$$

---

[1]Please note that although Equation (10) is labeled as a Level 2 equation where γ_{10} is a fixed effect reflecting the linear effect of the independent variable X_{ij} on the dependent variable Y_{ij} at Level 1 (Raudenbush and Bryk 2002). In step 4 we will allow this regression coefficient to vary between clusters which then results in Equation (18) characterizing a potentially meaningful Level 2 influence.

$$L2 : \beta_{0j} = \gamma_{00} + \gamma_{01}Z_j + u_{0j} \tag{13}$$

$$L2 : \beta_{1j} = \gamma_{10} \tag{14}$$

$$I : Y_{ij} = \gamma_{00} + \gamma_{10}X_{ij} + \gamma_{01}Z_j + e_{ij} + u_{0j} \tag{15}$$

In this model a new independent variable at Level 2, Z_j, has been added. This variable only varies between clusters (j) but not between Level 1 observations (i) as indicated by its subscript. Thus, Level 2 independent variables only possess between variance but no within variance and can therefore only explain the between variance component of the dependent variable.

The influence of independent variables at Level 2 is reflected in the intercept equation (β_{0j}; Equation 13). Here, γ_{01} reflects the influence of Z_j on the dependent variable Y_{ij}. Again, this equation can be extended to include additional Level 2 variables. Furthermore, Equation (13) together with Equation (14) can be substituted into Equation (12) to derive the integrated form of the model (Equation 15), now additionally including the influence of the Level 2 independent variable.

Step 4: Testing for Random Slopes

In step 4, the random slope model investigates whether there is substantial variance in the regression coefficient of a Level 1 variable across Level 2 observations. Thus, the model evaluates whether the slopes significantly vary between clusters. Equations (16) and (17) reflect the unchanged Level 1 model and the random intercept model, respectively. Equation (18) describes the revised equation of the regression coefficient (β_{1j}) and Equation (19) presents the integrated equation of the two-level random slope model.

$$L1 : Y_{ij} = \beta_{0j} + \beta_{1j}X_{ij} + e_{ij} \tag{16}$$

$$L2 : \beta_{0j} = \gamma_{00} + \gamma_{01}Z_j + u_{0j} \tag{17}$$

$$L2 : \beta_{1j} = \gamma_{10} + u_{1j} \tag{18}$$

$$I : Y_{ij} = \gamma_{00} + \gamma_{10}X_{ij} + \gamma_{01}Z_j + e_{ij} + u_{0j} + u_{1j}X_{ij} \tag{19}$$

New to the model in step 4 is that the regression coefficient β_{1j} is allowed to vary between clusters, which is reflected in adding the residual of the slope u_{1j} to the random slope equation (Equation 18) which results in the term $u_{1j}X_{ij}$ in the integrated form (Equation 19) (Fig. 4b illustrates a model with random slope parameter and Fig. 4c shows a model with random intercept and slope parameters). Analogously to the residual of the random intercept equation, the residual of the random slope equation at Level 2 is assumed to have an expected mean of zero ($E(u_{1j}) = 0$) and a variance τ_{11} ($Var(u_{1j}) = \tau_{11}$).

One can test whether this variance in the slope is meaningful by directly testing whether τ_{11} is significantly different from zero and/or by comparing the fit of a

Multilevel Modeling | 385

model in which the slope is allowed to vary with a model in which the slope is fixed across clusters using a deviance test (see section "Model Estimation & Assessing Model Fit"). If the variance in the random slope is substantial, it is recommended to allow the slope to vary across clusters. Furthermore, one may then include higher level variables (i.e., variables at Level 2) to explain this variance, which leads to cross-level interaction effects, which we explain in step 5.

If there are multiple random slopes, we recommend testing their significance in a stepwise approach to prevent errors in the specification of the model and potential issues in the model estimation. Furthermore, in models including random intercept and random slope parameters, one should allow the intercept and the slope to covary ($Cov(u_{0j}; u_{1j}) = \tau_{01}$).

Step 5: Adding Cross-Level Interaction Effects

If there is substantial variance in the slope between clusters (or strong theoretical reasons suggest a cross-level interaction effect; cf. Snijders and Bosker 2012), one can continue with step 5 – the estimation of cross-level interaction effects. In step 5, independent variables at the higher level are added to the model to account for the variance of the random slope. Thereby one can explore whether higher level variables explain the variation between clusters of an effect of a lower level variable on the dependent variable (i.e., the variance in the slope between clusters).

Equations (20), (21), (22), and (23) describe this model. Equation (20) and (21) show the unchanged Level 1 equation and the equation of the random intercept. Equation (22) describes the revised equation of the random slope and Equation (23) presents the integrated form of the model if Equations (21) and (22) are substituted into Equation (20).

$$L1 : Y_{ij} = \beta_{0j} + \beta_{1j}X_{ij} + e_{ij} \tag{20}$$

$$L2 : \beta_{0j} = \gamma_{00} + \gamma_{01}Z_j + u_{0j} \tag{21}$$

$$L2 : \beta_{1j} = \gamma_{10} + \gamma_{11}Z_j + u_{1j} \tag{22}$$

$$I : Y_{ij} = \gamma_{00} + \gamma_{10}X_{ij} + \gamma_{01}Z_j + \gamma_{11}Z_jX_{ij} + e_{ij} + u_{0j} + u_{1j}X_{ij} \tag{23}$$

New to the random slope equation (Equation 22) is the term $\gamma_{11}Z_j$, which describes the effect (γ_{11}) of the Level 2 variable Z_j on the random slope parameter β_{1j}. The interpretation of this effect becomes more intuitive if we derive the integrated form of the model by substituting Equations (21) and (22) into Equation (20). If $\gamma_{11}Z_j$ from Equation (22) is substituted into Equation (20) it is multiplied by X_{ij} resulting in $\gamma_{11}Z_jX_{ij}$. This expression clarifies that γ_{11} reflects a cross-level interaction effect, which indicates whether the relationship between the independent variable X_{ij} and the dependent variable Y_{ij} varies as a function of the Level 2 variable Z_j and thus determines whether Z_j moderates the relationship between X_{ij} and Y_{ij} across clusters.

Assumptions of Multilevel Modeling

Multilevel regression models share many assumptions of the linear multiple regression model[2] (Hox et al. 2018; Snijders and Bosker 2012) such as the correct model specification (e.g., with respect to the functional relationship and the absence of omitted variables), perfect reliability of included variables, or the absence of multicollinearity of Level 1 and Level 2 variables (Raudenbush and Bryk 2002; Hox et al. 2018). Additional assumptions of the multilevel regression refer to the residuals at both levels and the complex variance structure. We therefore present the assumptions referring to the residuals of the two-level model presented in step 5 in Equations (24), (25), (26), and (27):

$$e_{ij} \sim iid\, N\left(0; \sigma_e^2\right) \tag{24}$$

$$u_j = \begin{pmatrix} u_{0j} \\ u_{1j} \end{pmatrix} \sim iid\, N(0; \mathbf{T}) \;\text{ with }\mathbf{T} = \begin{pmatrix} \tau_{01} & \tau_{01} \\ \tau_{10} & \tau_{11} \end{pmatrix} \sim iid\, N \tag{25}$$

$$Cov\left(e_{ij}; u_{0j}\right) = 0 \tag{26}$$

$$Cov\left(e_{ij}; u_{1j}\right) = 0 \tag{27}$$

Specifically, Equation (24) describes that residuals at Level 1 are assumed to be independently and identically normally distributed (iid) with an expected mean of zero and a variance of σ_e^2. Equation (25) highlights that residuals at Level 2, u_{0j} and u_{1j}, are assumed to be multivariate normal distributed with expected means of 0, variances of τ_{00} and τ_{11} and a covariance of $\tau_{01} = \tau_{10}$. Furthermore, Equations (26) and (27) posit that residuals at Level 1 should be independent from residuals at Level 2. Additionally, the residuals at both levels should be homoscedastic (see Snijders and Bosker 2012 for details, potential relaxations, and guidance on how to test this assumption) and independent from the predictor variables at the respective level (Raudenbush and Bryk 2002). Furthermore, analogously to standard regression analysis, the regressors at both levels should be uncorrelated with the error terms to avoid potential problems associated with endogeneity (please see the chapter ▶ "Dealing with Endogeneity: A Nontechnical Guide for Marketing Researchers" for a general introduction on how to deal with endogeneity in marketing research).

Model Estimation & Assessing Model Fit

Usually multilevel models are estimated by maximum likelihood estimation techniques. Maximum likelihood methods produce estimates for the population

---

[2]Note that we focus here on assumptions of multilevel models which are estimated using a maximum likelihood estimator. Other estimation techniques can be helpful if these assumptions are not fulfilled (see section "Model Estimation & Assessing Model Fit" and Hox et al. 2018).

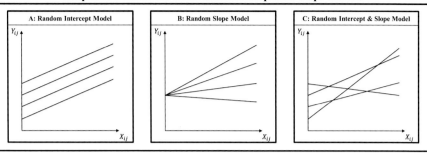

Fig. 5 Graphical illustration of random intercept and slope models

parameters by minimizing the difference between the variance-covariance matrix of the model and the empirical variance-covariance matrix (i.e., the variance-covariance matrix of the observed data; Hox et al. 2018). The estimation process is an iterative process, in which in each step the improvement of the model fit is evaluated by comparing the model fit of the new model with the fit of the previous model. The model fit is assessed by the (Log-) Likelihood. Usually, the differences in the (Log-) Likelihood are relatively large in the beginning and become smaller by every iterative step. If the improvement of model fit becomes very small, the estimation is finished and the parameter estimates of the last step are used to conduct significance tests. Eliason (1993) provides a general overview of maximum likelihood estimation techniques and Heck and Thomas (2015) and Hox et al. (2018) provide overviews of maximum likelihood estimation techniques for multilevel models.

An alternative to employing a maximum likelihood estimator, is the Bayesian estimation of multilevel models (e.g., Hamaker and Klugkist 2011). Bayesian estimation of multilevel models can especially be helpful when dealing with small samples and non-normality (Hamaker and Klugkist 2011). Detailed discussions of Bayesian estimation of multilevel models can for example be found in Depaoli and Clifton (2015), Gelman et al. (2014), Hamaker and Klugkist (2011), and Gelman and Hill (2006).

After estimating the parameter estimates, the significance of regression coefficients can be tested. To test the significance of regression coefficients, regression coefficients are divided by their respective standard error. In most statistical software packages, the resulting test statistic follows the standard normal or t-distribution, depending on the specific software (Hox et al. 2018).

As outlined in the previous section, multilevel models are usually investigated in a stepwise procedure. As every model has an individual model fit, model comparisons assess whether each step improves the fit of the model to the data. Model comparisons in multilevel modeling usually base on the deviance. The deviance value between two models is calculated by the difference between the respective Log-Likelihood values of each model multiplied by -2.

Generally, models with a lower deviance fit better than models with a higher deviance. Thus, to test whether a specific model which is nested in a more general model shows a better model fit, we can compare its deviances by calculating the difference of the deviance between the more general model (M_0 with a deviance D_{M_0}) and the model of interest (M_1 with a deviance D_{M_1}):

$$D_{Diff} = D_{M_0} - D_{M_1}; df = p_{M_1} - p_{M_0} \tag{28}$$

The difference in the deviances (D_{Diff}) of this test, which is referred to as deviance difference test or likelihood ratio test, follows the chi-square distribution. The degrees of freedom reflect the difference of the number of parameters estimated in the model of interest (p_{M_1}) and the more general model (p_{M_0}). The deviance difference test is especially helpful if the stepwise procedure of multilevel modeling is employed to assess the improvement in model fit from one step to the next.

However, as mentioned before, the deviance test can be only applied to compare nested models. If the models that should be compared are not nested, relative model comparisons can be conducted with the help of other criterions, such as the Akaike information criterion (Akaike 1973) or the Schwarz information criterion (Schwarz 1978).

Furthermore, it is often of great interest to know how much variation in the dependent variable is explained by the independent variables. In multiple regression analysis, the squared multiple correlation coefficient R^2 measures the explained proportion of variance in the dependent variables. This logic can also be transferred to multilevel regression analysis. However, as the variance structure in multilevel models is not limited to one level of analysis, the evaluation of the explained proportion of variance in the dependent variable becomes more complex and needs to be assessed on multiple levels of analysis. For example, in a two-level model at least two coefficients of determination have to be calculated. One coefficient of determination for the lower level of analysis and one for the higher level of analysis.

In the following, we provide an application-oriented description of the approach of Snijders and Bosker (1993), to provide a suitable multilevel version of R^2. Snijders and Bosker (1993) treat the proportional decreases in the estimated variance components in the baseline model as analogs of R^2-values. Consequently, to calculate multilevel R^2-values the variance component of the baseline model is compared to the variance component of the comparison model (Hox et al. 2018; Raudenbush and Bryk 2002). The following equation can be used to calculate the R^2-value for a dependent variable at the lower level, where b denotes the baseline and m the comparison model:

$$R_{L1}^2 = \frac{\sigma_b^2 - \sigma_m^2}{\sigma_b^2} \tag{29}$$

Further, to assess the R^2-value for the random intercept, the following equation can be used, where, again, b reflects the baseline model and m the comparison model:

Multilevel Modeling 389

$$R^2_{L2,int} = \frac{\tau^2_{00|b} - \tau^2_{00|m}}{\tau^2_{00|b}} \qquad (30)$$

Finally, the following equation shows how the R^2-value for the random slope can be calculated by comparing the baseline model b with the comparison model m:

$$R^2_{L2,slope} = \frac{\tau^2_{11|b} - \tau^2_{11|m}}{\tau^2_{11|b}} \qquad (31)$$

Variable Centering

The use of centering independent variables to establish a zero point on scales that otherwise lack such a value or to investigate interaction effects is relatively common in ordinary least squares regression (Aiken et al. 1991; Enders and Tofighi 2007). Most importantly, independent variables are centered to ensure that the intercept of the regression model is interpretable as the expected value of the dependent variable, if all independent variables have their mean value. As multiple regression models are invariant under linear transformations, the transformation of variables changes the estimated parameters in a similar way. Consequently, it is always possible to recalculate the untransformed estimates (Hox et al. 2018). Due to the hierarchical structure of multilevel data, multilevel models are only invariant for linear transformations when the model does not include random slopes, which vary at the higher level. Thus, centering becomes more complex when investigating multilevel models.

Given the nested data structure in multilevel models with lower level observations nested within higher level observations, we can distinguish different forms of centering. The traditionally most prevalent two approaches are grand mean centering and group mean centering (for other centering approaches, such as latent mean centering, see Asparouhov and Muthén (2019)). When grand mean centering is applied, the grand mean value of a variable is subtracted from all observations of that variable in the dataset (i.e., $X_{ij} - \overline{X}$ or $Z_j - \overline{Z}$). When group mean centering is applied, one subtracts the group mean of a cluster j from all observations i of that respective cluster (i.e., $X_{ij} - \overline{X}_{.j}$; with $\overline{X}_{.j}$ describing the group mean of cluster j). Consequently, for variables at the higher level only grand mean centering can be applied, whereas lower level variables can either be grand mean and group mean centered. As both techniques produce parameter estimates that can differ in their value and their meaning and can create differences in deviance values, the centering of variables in multilevel modeling has been discussed vibrantly in the methodological literature (e.g., Enders and Tofighi 2007; Hofmann and Gavin 1998; Kreft 1996; Kreft et al. 1995; Longford 1989; Paccagnella 2006; Raudenbush 1989; Wu and Wooldridge 2005). In this section, we follow the recommendations of Enders and Tofighi (2007) who focus on two-level cross-sectional data. Further recommendations on the centering of longitudinal data can be found for example in Biesanz et al. (2004) and Asparouhov and Muthén (2019).

In multilevel models, the independent variables of the higher level are usually centered on their grand mean. The decision whether lower level variables should be centered on their grand mean or on their group mean is more complex. According to Enders and Tofighi (2007) centering independent variables on the grand mean is appropriate if one primarily focuses on higher level effects and includes independent variables at the lower level only as control variables and when interaction effects between higher level variables are investigated. Group mean centering is appropriate if the lower level effect of the independent variable on the dependent variable is of substantial interest and when examining cross-level interaction effects and interaction effects that include lower level variables (Enders and Tofighi 2007). Both approaches can be applied if the focus is on the analysis of the differential effects of a variable at the lower level and the higher level. However, Enders and Tofighi (2007) highlight that these are only recommendations as the decision whether to perform grand mean or group mean centering cannot be solely based on statistical evidence. Therefore, it always depends on the individual research question whether grand mean or group mean centering is the appropriate method.

In addition, the appropriate centering of independent variables is important for the estimation of the multilevel model. Independent variables that are centered appropriately will increase the speed of the estimation and will lower the likelihood of convergence problems (Hox et al. 2018). Thus, especially, if independent variables have a high variation in their means and variances, the appropriate centering is important to ensure the convergence of the model estimation process.

Sample Size Considerations

In multilevel modeling decisions about adequate sample sizes are somewhat more complex than in conventional single level analysis. As multilevel models comprise observations on multiple levels of analysis, also decisions about adequate sample sizes refer to multiple levels. Therefore, questions arise about the minimum level-specific sample size to estimate unbiased parameters and standard errors and the potential biases caused by samples that are too small. Previous simulation studies provide some answers to these questions for two-level models.

For example, Maas and Hox (2005) investigated how the number of level two observations (*here:* number of groups; $n_j = 30, 50, 100$), the number of level one observations nested within each level two unit (*here:* group sizes; $n_{ij} = 5, 30, 50$), and the intraclass correlation ($\rho = 0.1, 0.2, 0.3$) influence the parameter estimates and standard errors in a simple two-level regression model with one predictor at each level and thus one direct effect at Level 1 and Level 2 and a cross-level interaction effect (i.e., $Y_{ij} = \gamma_{00} + \gamma_{10}X_{ij} + \gamma_{01}Z_j + \gamma_{11}Z_jX_{ij} + u_{0j} + u_{1j}X_{ij} + e_{ij}$). Results on the basis of 27,000 simulated data sets (1,000 for each simulation condition) show that all parameter estimates (i.e., intercept, regression coefficients, and variance components) in each condition are largely unbiased (with an average parameter bias $<0.05\%$). Furthermore, the results show that also the standard errors of the intercept and regression coefficients are estimated accurately under each condition. However, standard errors for level two variance estimates are substantially underestimated if the number of level two observations is too low. Specifically, standard errors of level two variance parameters are estimated about 15% too small with a number of 30 level two observations. With 50 observations at level two estimates are more acceptable and most accurate with 100 observations at level two. The intraclass correlation of the dependent variable had neither a substantial effect on the accuracy of the parameter estimates nor on the accuracy of the standard errors. Overall, Maas and Hox's (2005) results are in line with other simulation studies showing that a larger number of level two observations are needed to accurately estimate level two variance components (Hox et al. 2018).

In addition, Hox et al. (2018) formulate three rules of thumb for sufficient sample sizes in two-level regression models employing standard estimation techniques. These rules propose specific sample sizes depending on the part of the model the researcher is interested in. In line with the recommendation by Kreft (1996; see also Kreft and De Leeuw 1998), Hox et al. (2018) propose a 30/30 rule with 30 level two observations and 30 level one observations per each level two unit if one is only interested in the fixed part of the model (i.e., the direct effects of the level one and level two predictor variables). If one is interested in cross-level interactions, a 50/20 rule with 50 level two observations and 20 level one observations per level two unit is suggested. For researchers who are especially interested in (co-)variance and standard errors at level two, Hox et al. (2018) propose a 100/10 rule with 100 level two observations and 10 corresponding level one observations.

Whereas these rules of thumb offer sound advice, in practice, it may be difficult for researchers to meet the recommended sample sizes. In this respect, the discussed simulation study provides additional insights by showing that researchers may yield accurate regression coefficients and standard errors with smaller samples (Maas and Hox 2005). As mentioned in the section "Model Estimation & Assessing Model Fit," another potential way for researchers to cope with small samples may be the use of a Bayesian estimation technique, which does not rely on asymptotic results (Hamaker and Klugkist 2011).

Although a sample which is large enough to yield accurate results is a prerequisite for conducting any multilevel study, it does not guarantee that it is large enough to detect existing effects in the population as significant. This uncertainty leads to the question of sufficient sample sizes to assure a high statistical power. The statistical power of significance test refers to the probability to detect an existing effect in the population as significant by rejecting the null hypothesis (e.g., Cohen 1992). The mistake to not reject the null hypothesis in the presence of an effect in the population is known as type II error and occurs with the probability β. Therefore, statistical power is defined as $(1 - \beta)$ – the probability to reject a false null hypothesis (Cohen 1992). Cohen (1992) proposes a desired level of 0.80 to assure high statistical power of a significance test.

The decision about adequate sample sizes to achieve high statistical power in multilevel investigations a priori (i.e., before the data is collected) depends on the focus of the model and several additional assumptions about the data and different parameter estimates (e.g., Hox et al. 2018; Snijders 2005). Thus, general recommendations about sufficient sample sizes which assure a high statistical power would be difficult (e.g., Snijders and Bosker 2012). However, software programs may help to determine adequate sample sizes based on the researcher's assumptions. For example, PinT (Power in Two-level designs) developed by Bosker, Snijders, and Guldemond (2003; see also Snijders and Bosker 1993) helps to decide about adequate sample sizes by providing approximate standard errors of regression coefficients for different combinations of level one and level two observations in two-level models. Furthermore, Mathieu et al. (2012) developed a multilevel Monte Carlo power tool, executable in R, which helps researchers to a priori estimate the power of their cross-level interactions. Together these resources can be very helpful in determining model specific samples sizes to assure a high statistical power when collecting multilevel data.

Multilevel Structural Equation Modeling

In explaining the fundamentals of multilevel analysis we so far focused on the basic multilevel regression model. In the following we extend this approach by integrating the logic of structural equation modeling techniques to multilevel analysis (please refer to Baumgartner and Weijters (2021) in this handbook for a general introduction to structural equation modeling and to Hughes and Ahearne (2010) or Hunter and Panagopoulos (2015) for examples of multilevel structural equation modeling in marketing research). This integration of structural equation modeling techniques to multilevel analysis, referred to as multilevel structural equation modeling, allows the accurate modeling of latent variables, the consideration of measurement error, and the simultaneous estimation of more complex relationships, such as the effects on multiple dependent variables or the modeling of causal chains (e.g., Heck and Thomas 2015; Hox et al. 2018). Thereby, multilevel structural equation modeling allows a more accurate assessment of relationships between variables and the investigation of more complex relationships in multilevel settings (Heck and Thomas 2015).

Single level structural equation modeling combines the advantages of factor analysis, defining latent variables by their observed indicators, and path analysis, allowing the investigation of complex causal relationships (Bollen 1989; Matsueda 2014; Muthén 2002). Corresponding with both types of advantages, the definition of latent variables by measured indicators is captured in the measurement model whereas the structural relationships are captured in the structural part of the model. The basic measurement model can be represented as:

$$y_i = v + \Lambda\eta_i + \varepsilon_i \tag{32}$$

where for observation i y_i is a $p \times 1$ vector of measured variables, v is a $p \times 1$ vector of intercepts terms, Λ is a $p \times m$ matrix of factor loadings, η_i is a $m \times 1$ vector of latent variables, and ε_i is a p × 1 vector of measurement errors. The basic structural model can be written as:

$$\eta_i = \alpha + B\eta_i + \zeta_i \tag{33}$$

where η_i is a m × 1 vector of latent variables, α is a m × 1 vector of intercept terms, B is a m × m matrix of structural regression coefficients among the latent variables, and ζ_i is a m × 1 vector of latent variable regression residuals. Residuals ε_i from the measurement model and residuals ζ_i from the structural model are assumed to be multivariate normal with means of zero and variance/covariance matrices Θ and Ψ. Together the measurement and structural model imply a mean (μ) and covariance (Σ) structure which are employed to estimate the parameters using for example a maximum likelihood estimator.

Structural equation modeling techniques have only recently been more widely applied to multilevel data structures (Heck and Thomas 2015). In accommodating multilevel data structures, the model set up for a (multilevel) structural equation model is more complex as some parameters of the measurement and structural model are allowed to vary at the higher level (Heck and Thomas 2015; Preacher et al. 2010). In the case of two-level contexts, a multilevel structural equation model can therefore be characterized by measurement and structural models for both the lower and the higher level (Heck and Thomas 2015). The level one (within (W)) measurement and structural model can be expressed as:

$$y_{ij} = \Lambda_W \eta_{Wij} + \varepsilon_{Wij} \tag{34}$$

$$\eta_{Wij} = B_W \eta_{Wij} + \zeta_{Wij} \tag{35}$$

where, for observation i nested in level two unit j, y_{ij} is a p × 1 vector of measured variables, Λ_W is a p × m matrix of level one factor loadings, η_{Wij} is a m × 1 vector of latent variables, and ε_{Wij} is a p × 1 vector of measurement errors at level one with means of zero and a variance/covariance matrix Θ_w (Asparouhov and Muthén 2007; Heck and Thomas 2015). In the structural part of the level one model, B_{Wij} is a m × m matrix of structural regression coefficients among the latent variables at level one and ζ_{Wij} is m × 1 vector of latent variable regression residuals at level one with zero means and a variance/covariance matrix Ψ_w (Asparouhov and Muthén 2007; Heck and Thomas 2015).

The measurement and structural model at level two (between (B)) can be written as:

$$y_j = v_j + \Lambda_B \eta_{Bj} + \varepsilon_{Bj} \tag{36}$$

$$\eta_{Bj} = \alpha_j + B_B \eta_{Bj} + \zeta_{Bj} \tag{37}$$

Here, y_j is a p $\times$ 1 vector of measured variables at level two, v_j is a p $\times$ 1 vector of intercept terms of the measured variables, Λ_B is a p $\times$ m matrix of level two factor loadings, η_{Bj} is a m $\times$ 1 vector of latent variables, and ε_{Bj} is a p $\times$ 1 vector of measurement errors at level two with means of zero and a variance/covariance matrix Θ_B (Asparouhov and Muthén 2007; Heck and Thomas 2015). In the structural part of the level one model, B_{Bj} is a m $\times$ m matrix of structural regression coefficients among the latent variables at level two and ζ_{Bj} is m $\times$ 1 vector of latent variable regression residuals at level two with zero means and a variance/covariance matrix Ψ_B (Asparouhov and Muthén 2007; Heck and Thomas 2015). As in the single level structural equation model, the measurement and structural models imply a mean (μ) and covariance (Σ_T) structure. However, in two-level structural equation models the covariance structure (Σ_T) can be decomposed in a level one (within) and a level two (between) component which are orthogonal and additive (Heck and Thomas 2015):

$$\Sigma_T = \Sigma_W + \Sigma_B \tag{38}$$

Multilevel structural equation models can be estimated employing a full information maximum likelihood estimator which allows the accommodation of missing data, unbalanced cluster sizes, and importantly random slopes (Hox et al. 2018; Preacher et al. 2010; Mehta and Neale 2005).[3]

The global fit of multilevel structural equation models can be evaluated assessing standard fit indices, such as the chi-square statistic, the comparative fit index (CFI; Bentler 1990), the Tucker-Lewis Index (TLI; Tucker and Lewis 1973), the root mean square error of approximation (RMSEA; Browne and Cudeck 1992; Steiger and Lind 1980), or the standardized root mean residual (SRMR; Bentler 1995). However, those indices which are based on the chi-square statistic apply to the entire model and thus comprise information about the model fit of both the level one and the level two model. Furthermore, as the sample size at level one is generally considerably larger than the sample size at level two, these global model fit indices are often dominated by model fit at level one. Given the confounding information in the standard global model fit indices, Hox et al. (2018) propose to assess the model fit separately for each level of analysis (see also Ryu and West 2009). To evaluate the fit indices for level one, one can estimate

---

[3]Sometimes a slightly different notation for multilevel structural equation models is employed (Asparouhov and Muthén 2008; Preacher et al. 2010, 2011). Following this notation, the measurement model can be expressed as: $Y_{ij} = v_j + \Lambda_j \eta_{ij} + K_j X_{ij} + \varepsilon_{ij}$. The level one structural model can be written as $\eta_{ij} = \alpha_j + B_j \eta_{ij} + \Gamma_j X_{ij} + \zeta_{ij}$ and the level two structural model can be expressed as $\eta_j = \mu + \beta \eta_j + \gamma X_j + \zeta_j$. This notation additionally includes exogenous covariates captured by the vectors X_{ij} and X_j respectively. Furthermore, elements of the matrices v_j, Λ_j, K_j, α_j, B_j, and Γ_j may vary between level two units as expressed by the level two subscripts (j) (for further details of this notation see Preacher et al. 2010).

an independence model (as a baseline model for the comparative fit indices) and the hypothesized model at level one with a saturated model at level two and then calculate the respective fit indices. Analogously, one can estimate an independence model and the hypothesized model at level two with a saturated model at level one to assess the fit indices for the level two model (Hox et al. 2018). In addition to the standard fit indices from structural equation modeling, the fit of nested models can be compared by employing the likelihood ratio test (see also "Model Estimation & Assessing Model Fit"; Mehta and Neale 2005). Furthermore, as in multilevel regression models, information-theoretic criteria such as Akaike's Information Criterion (AIC, Akaike 1973, 1987) or the Bayesian Information Criterion (BIC, Schwarz 1978) can be employed to evaluate non-nested models (Mehta and Neale 2005).

With respect to the implementation of multilevel structural equation models some issues can be relevant. A first issue refers to the proportion of level two variance of latent level one variables. If one would like to examine the proportion of level two variance of a latent level one variable relative to its total variance (i.e., the counterpart of the intraclass correlation coefficient in multilevel regression analysis), the factor loadings have to be constrained to be invariant across both levels in order to make the common variance attributed to the latent factor directly comparable (Heck and Thomas 2015). In case of invariant factor loadings, the proportion of the between variance of a latent level one variable relative to its total variance can be expressed as:

$$\psi_B/(\psi_B + \psi_W) \tag{39}$$

where ψ_B refers to the proportion of the factor variance at level two (between) and ψ_W refers to the proportion the factor variance at level one (within).

A second relevant implementation issue refers to the centering of manifest variables in multilevel structural equation models. When a multilevel structural equation model is employed which implicitly partitions each measured level one variable into a latent level one (within) and level two (between) component, no explicit centering of observed predictor variables is required (Preacher et al. 2010). However, group mean centering of level one variables may be helpful for model convergence if the level two variance of a level one variable is essentially zero. Group mean centering of level one variables should be avoided, if the level two effects are of theoretical interest (Preacher et al. 2010).

A third issue when implementing a multilevel structural equation model refers to the residual variances of observed level one variables at level two. Residual variances at level two are often very small, reflecting a high reliability (Heck and Thomas 2015). In such occasions it can be necessary to fix these very small level two variances to zero in order to avoid estimation problems (Heck and Thomas 2015; Muthén and Muthén 1998–2017).

Overall, multilevel structural equation models offer several advantages such as the accurate modeling of latent variables, the consideration of measurement error and the simultaneous estimation of more complex relationships (which is especially helpful to estimate less biased indirect effects in mediation models; Preacher et al. 2010). However, these advantages come at the cost of a higher model complexity which can make it challenging to generate a converging solution. In such cases it can be helpful to start with a smaller, less complex model and successively add additional variables or relationships. Nevertheless, it sometimes can be difficult to identify the exact source of the estimation problem, so that Heck and Thomas (2015, p. 179) wisely advise: "[. . .] that patience is virtue when working toward a solution."

Software for Estimating Multilevel Models

In the last decades the number of multilevel studies in organizational and marketing research has increased substantially (Wieseke et al. 2008). This increase may in part also be traced back to the growing availability of software for estimating multilevel statistical models. Given the high number of different software packages that allow multilevel analyses, it is well beyond of the scope of this chapter to review each of these software packages. We therefore focus our brief review on some of the most widespread software packages for multilevel analysis[4]. In doing so we distinguish between software which has been specifically designed for multilevel analysis and general purpose software that allows the estimation of multilevel models.

One of the most widespread software packages that has been designed to conduct multilevel analysis is HLM (Raudenbush et al. 2019a). HLM, currently available in its eighth version, may be especially well suited for beginners due to its user friendly graphical display, which allows to specify models on a step-by-step basis. Furthermore, HLM is accompanied by a freely available, comprehensive manual (Raudenbush et al. 2019b). The theoretical background of many applications can additionally be found in the textbook by Raudenbush and Bryk (2002). In its current version, HLM allows multilevel analyses up to four levels, can estimate different types of models (i.e., univariate, multivariate, and cross-classified), allows different distributional properties of the outcome variables (e.g., normal, Bernoulli, Poisson binomial, multinomial, ordinal, and over-dispersion), and offers different estimation methods (e.g., REML, FML, PQL, AGH, and higher-order Laplace approximations to maximum-likelihood[5]) (Palardy 2011). This variety of modeling options makes HLM not only attractive for beginners but also for those who want to estimate more advanced multilevel models.

---

[4]More detailed reviews of many different software packages that allow the estimation of multilevel models can be found at the homepage of the Centre for Multilevel Modelling at the University of Bristol (www.bristol.ac.uk/cmm/learning/mmsoftware/)

[5]REML = Restricted maximum likelihood; FML = Full maximum likelihood; PQL = penalized quasi-likelihood; AGH = Adaptive Gauss-Hermite quadrature.

Another important program which was explicitly designed to estimate multilevel models is MLwiN (Rasbash et al. 2016a). MLwiN has been suggested to be "the most extensive multilevel package" (Snijders and Bosker 2012, p. 325), but has also been considered as less user-friendly than HLM "in the sense that it is not as directive and requires greater user knowledge" (Wieseke et al. 2008, p. 333). However, MLwiN comes with a wealth of information, including an extensive manual (Rasbash et al. 2016b), which can be obtained from the homepage of the Centre for Multilevel Modelling at the University of Bristol (www.bristol.ac.uk/cmm/). MLwiN may fit models up to five levels, has a great modeling flexibility, and allows a wide range of possible models (Snijders and Bosker 2012; Wieseke et al. 2008), including the estimation of multiple membership models, Bayesian analysis of multilevel models, or bootstrapping of standard errors in multilevel models.

The most widespread general purpose statistical software in the social sciences may be IBM SPSS. To estimate multilevel models in SPSS, one can use the routine MIXED which allows the estimation of models with up to three levels (Snijders and Bosker 2012). Furthermore, since Version 19 SPSS also allows the estimation of multilevel models with categorical outcomes (using the GENLIN MIXED routine) (Heck et al. 2014). However, multilevel modeling in SPSS has some limitations regarding the modeling flexibility (Heck et al. 2014). Detailed introductions for the estimation of multilevel models with continuous and categorical outcomes in SPSS are provided by Heck et al. (2012, 2014).

Another general-purpose software which offers a high modeling flexibility for the estimation of multilevel models is Mplus (Muthén and Muthén 1998–2017). Mplus is accompanied by an extensive user guide with detailed examples which help users to learn the Mplus command language. Furthermore, extensive resources like videos of short courses, a helpful discussion forum, and further examples can be obtained from the Mplus homepage (www.statmodel.com). Mplus currently allows the estimation of multilevel models up to three levels (four levels for longitudinal models in which time is the lowest level such as in a three-level latent growth model) and offers a variety of models, estimators, and algorithms. Based on the general latent variable framework, Mplus is especially well suited for the estimation of multilevel structural equation models (Hox et al. 2018; Muthén and Asparouhov 2011). Heck and Thomas (2015) offer a detailed introduction to multilevel modeling techniques employing Mplus.

Multilevel models can also be estimated employing the open source environment of R. The freely available program (www.r-project.org) is potentially the most flexible modeling environment for statistical computing. Multilevel models can be estimated employing different packages, such as nlme (Pinheiro et al. 2016) or lme4 (Bates et al. 2016). An introduction to multilevel modeling using nlme and lme4 is provided by Bliese (2016) and Finch et al. (2014). Multilevel models can also be estimated using other general purpose software like Stata or SAS. An extensive and detailed introduction for the estimation of multilevel models in Stata is provided by Rabe-Hesketh and Skrondal (2012). Introductions for estimating multilevel models in SAS are offered for example by Singer (1998), Bliese (2002), or Albright and Marinova (2010).

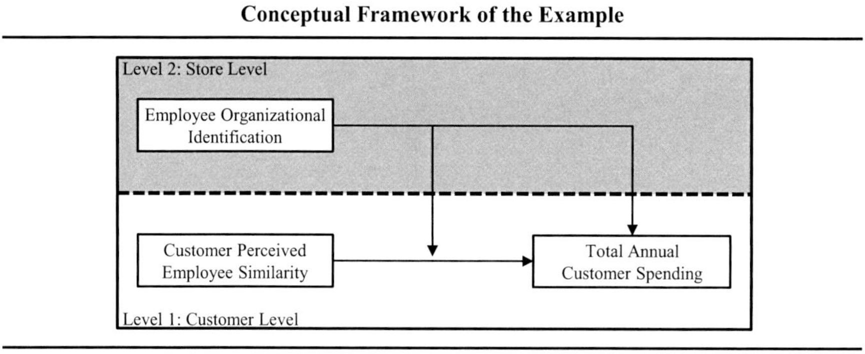

Conceptual Framework of the Example

Fig. 6 Conceptual framework of the example. (Notes: Adapted from Netemeyer et al. 2012)

Example: Building and Estimating a Two-Level Model

In order to offer an example for building and estimating a multilevel model, we draw from the study of Netemeyer, Heilman, and Maxham (2012). In their study the authors examine the effects of customer perceived similarity to store employees and store employees' organizational identification (aggregated at the store level) on customer identification and customer spending in the context of a private label women's apparel retailer. Furthermore, they explored the cross-level interaction between employees' organizational identification and customer perceived employee similarity on both outcomes. For our example, we adopt the framework from Netemeyer et al. (2012) and focus on the direct and interactive effects of customer perceived employee similarity and employees' organizational identification on customer spending. Figure 6 presents the conceptual framework of the example.

To offer an example for the analysis strategy outlined in the section "Process of Multilevel Modeling: The Two-Level Regression Model," we created a fictitious data set comprising 10,000 observations at level one (i.e., customers) nested within 500 observations at level two (i.e., stores) to build and test the model presented in Fig. 4. Data for customer perceived similarity and store employees' organizational identification is created to reflect responses on seven-point scales. Data for total annual customer spending is created to reflect the total dollar amount of customer spending within one year[6] (for the original measures see Netemeyer et al. 2012). In

---

[6]Note that we divided the total dollar amount of customer spending within 1 year by 100 to keep the (residual) variance estimates at a lower level, which is helpful to assure a smooth model estimation process.

line with the recommendations in the section "Variable Centering," we group mean centered customer perceived similarity and grand mean centered employees' organizational identification. We estimated all models using Mplus 8.5 and employed a maximum likelihood estimator with robust standard errors (Muthén and Muthén 1998–2017). The data set and Mplus input and output files can be downloaded from the companion homepage of the handbook. In addition, we also provide the R code employing the lme4 package (Bates et al. 2016) on the companion homepage of the handbook.

As outlined in the section "Process of Multilevel Modeling: The Two-Level Regression Model" the starting point for testing a multilevel model is to estimate an intercept-only model without any predictor variables. Results of the intercept-only model presented in Table 2 (Model 1) show an estimated mean customer spending amount of 17.628 (reflecting 1,762.80\$). Furthermore, results of Model 1 are informative about the level one (σ_e^2) and level two variance (τ_{00}) of the dependent variable (i.e., customer spending). With the estimates of both variance components one may determine the intraclass correlation (ρ), by dividing the level two variance by the total variance (i.e., ($\frac{\tau_{00}}{\tau_{00}+\sigma_e^2}$)). Results from Model 1 imply an intraclass correlation of 0.3349 meaning that 33.49% of the variance of customer spending can be explained at level two (i.e., the store level).

In a second step, one can now add the level one predictor variables. In our example, the level one predictor variable which is added to the model is customers' perceived similarity with the store employees. Results from Model 2 in Table 2 show that customers' perceived employee similarity has a positive significant effect on customer spending ($\gamma_{10} = 1.455$, $p < 0.01$). Furthermore, the results show that the level one variance decreases substantially from Model 1 to Model 2 (Model 1: $\sigma_e^2 = 12.259$, Model 2: $\sigma_e^2 = 8.955$), which reflects the variance explained by adding the level one predictor (here: customer perceived employee similarity; $R_{L1}^2 = \frac{\sigma_b^2 - \sigma_m^2}{\sigma_b^2} = \frac{12.259 - 8.955}{12.259} = .2695$). This finding is also underlined by a significant increase of model fit as suggested by the Satorra-Bentler-corrected log-likelihood difference test ($\chi^2 = 1252.4561$, $p < 0.01$) (Satorra and Bentler 1999).

In a third step, the level two predictors may be added to the model. Results from Model 3 in Table 2 show that the level two predictor variable, employee organizational identification, has a positive significant effect on customer spending ($\gamma_{01} = 1.538$, $p < 0.01$). Furthermore, the results show a substantial decrease in the estimate of the level two intercept variance component from Model 1 to Model 3 (Model 1: $\tau_{00} = 6.337$, Model 3: $\tau_{00} = 2.619$), which reflects the variance explained by adding the level two predictor (here: employee organizational identification; $R_{L2,int}^2 = \frac{\tau_{00|b}^2 - \tau_{00|m}^2}{\tau_{00|b}^2} = \frac{6.337 - 2.619}{6.337} = .5867$). In addition, when comparing Model 3 and Model 2, we again find a significant increase in model fit ($\chi^2 = 410.0310$, $p < 0.01$).

In a fourth step one can now test whether the slope between customer perceived similarity and customer spending varies across level two units (here: stores), which would be necessary for a level two predictor variable to significantly explain the

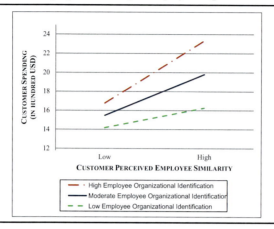

Fig. 7 Cross-level interaction plot: Customer Perceived Employee Similarity × Employee Organizational Identification. (Notes: Low/high levels of the interaction plot refer to one standard deviation below/above the mean)

variance in this slope and thus for a substantial cross-level interaction. Results from Model 4 in Table 2 show that the estimate of the variance component of the slope is significant ($\tau_{11} = 0.712$, $p < 0.01$) and thus fulfills the necessary condition for a potential cross-level interaction.

In a fifth and final step, one can now try to explain (some of) the variance in the random slope by a level two predictor variable (here: employee organizational identification). Results of Model 5 in Table 2 show that employee organizational identification explains variance in the random slope of customer perceived employee similarity on customer spending as reflected in a significant cross-level interaction effect between customer perceived employee similarity and employee organizational identification on customer spending ($\gamma_{11} = 0.483$, $p < 0.01$). Furthermore, results show a substantial decrease in the estimate of the random slope variance component (Model 4: $\tau_{11} = 0.712$, Model 5: $\tau_{11} = 0.344$), which reflects the variance explained in the random slope by the level two predictor (here: employee organizational identification; $R^2_{L2,slope} = \frac{\tau^2_{11|b} - \tau^2_{11|m}}{\tau^2_{11|b}} = \frac{.712 - .344}{.712} = .5169$). Furthermore, explaining the variance in the random slope leads to a significantly better model fit ($\chi^2 = 275.8173$, $p < 0.01$) which underlines the substantiveness of the cross-level interaction effect.

Plotting the cross-level interaction effect can yield further insights into the interplay between the level one and level two predictor variable in influencing the

Table 2 Results of Multilevel Analyses

	Model 1	Model 2	Model 3	Model 4	Model 5
	Intercept-Only Model	**Level 1 Model**	**Level 2 Model**	**Test of Slope Variance**	**Full Multilevel Model**
	L1: $Y_{ij} = \beta_{0j} + e_{ij}$ L2: $\beta_{0j} = \gamma_{00} + u_{0j}$	L1: $Y_{ij} = \beta_{0j} + \beta_{1j} X_{ij} + e_{ij}$ L2: $\beta_{0j} = \gamma_{00} + u_{0j}$ $\beta_{1j} = \gamma_{10}$	L1: $Y_{ij} = \beta_{0j} + \beta_{1j} X_{ij} + e_{ij}$ L2: $\beta_{0j} = \gamma_{00} + \gamma_{01} Z_j + u_{0j}$ $\beta_{1j} = \gamma_{10}$	L1: $Y_{ij} = \beta_{0j} + \beta_{1j} X_{ij} + e_{ij}$ L2: $\beta_{0j} = \gamma_{00} + \gamma_{01} Z_j + u_{0j}$ $\beta_{1j} = \gamma_{10} + u_{1j}$	L1: $Y_{ij} = \beta_{0j} + \beta_{1j} X_{ij} + e_{ij}$ L2: $\beta_{0j} = \gamma_{00} + \gamma_{01} Z_j + u_{0j}$ $\beta_{1j} = \gamma_{10} + \gamma_{11} Z_j + u_{1j}$
Parameter	**Est. (SE)**	**Est. (SE)**	**Est. (SE)**	**Est. (SE)**	**Est. (SE)**
Intercept (γ_{00})	17.628** (0.116)	17.628** (0.116)	17.496** (0.078)	17.628** (0.080)	17.628** (0.078)
Similarity (γ_{10})	–	1.455** (0.044)	1.455** (0.044)	1.467** (0.045)	1.461** (0.036)
Employee OI (γ_{01})	–	–	1.538** (0.073)	1.215** (0.080)	1.538** (0.073)
Similarity x Employee OI (γ_{11} $X_{ij} Z_j$)	–	–	–	–	0.483** (0.046)
Variance Components					
σ_e^2	12.259** (0.497)	8.955** (0.345)	8.955** (0.345)	7.897** (0.195)	7.902** (0.196)
τ_{00}	6.173** (0.528)	6.337** (0.531)	2.619** (0.208)	2.836** (0.250)	2.671** (0.210)
τ_{11}	–	–	–	0.712** (0.127)	0.344** (0.060)
Model Fit					
$-2 \times$ Log-Likelihood	54643.618	51659.516	51262.442	50657.356	50427.876
R^2_{L1}	–	0.2695	0.2695	0.3558	0.3554
$R^2_{L2,int}$	–	–	0.5867	0.5406	0.5673
$R^2_{L2,slope}$	–	–	–	–	0.5169
Δ Model fit[a] (df)	–	1252.4561** (1)	410.0310** (1)	501.8545** (2)	275.8173** (1)

Notes: Dependent variable: Customer Spending (in hundred USD)

$* p < 0.05$, $** p < 0.01$, Est. = Estimate, SE = Standard Error, L1 = Level 1, L2 = Level 2

[a]We employed the correction originally proposed by Satorra and Bentler (1999) for the model comparisons between Model 1–2, 2–3, and 4–5 and the strictly positive correction (Satorra and Bentler 2010; Asparouhov and Muthén 2013) for the model comparisons between model 3–4.

Details can also be found at the Mplus homepage (statmodel.com). Model 1 = baseline model for R^2_{L1} and $R^2_{L2,int}$ calculations. Model 4 = baseline model for $R^2_{L2,slope}$ calculation dependent variable. Figure 7 presents the interaction plot for the cross-level interaction effect between customer perceived employee similarity and employee organizational identification on customer spending. Specifically, Figure 7 further supports the results presented in Model 5 in Table 2. by indicating that the effect of customer perceived employee similarity on customer spending is stronger if employee organizational identification is high rather than if it is low (Table 2).

Conclusions

In the last decades the number of multilevel studies in marketing and management has substantially increased (Wieseke et al. 2008), reflecting a growing interest in the investigation of complex phenomena traversing different levels of analysis. With this chapter we wanted to provide an applied introduction how research pertaining to multiple levels of analysis can be conducted by employing multilevel modeling techniques. Therefore, we provided insights about the fundamentals of multilevel modeling discussing the conceptual and statistical relevance of multilevel modeling. Furthermore, we offered a step-by-step analysis strategy how to build and estimate multilevel models. We offered insights how to evaluate the goodness of fit in multilevel models and shed light on some important issues for the implementation of multilevel models, such as different approaches to the centering of predictor variables and recommendations for sufficient sample sizes. Moreover, we provided insights to more advanced multilevel modeling techniques, such as multilevel structural equation modeling, and offered a brief overview of different software packages that allow the estimation of multilevel models. Finally, we offered a detailed example of building and estimating a multilevel model. Overall, we hope that this chapter may be helpful for those who want to start adopting a multilevel lens to capture more of the complexity inherent to many phenomena in marketing and management research.

Cross-References

▶ Dealing with Endogeneity: A Nontechnical Guide for Marketing Researchers
▶ Panel Data Analysis: A Non-Technical Introduction for Marketing Researchers
▶ Regression Analysis
▶ Structural Equation Modeling

Appendix

Appendix Key Terms and Definitions

Term	Definition
Nested/ hierarchical data structures	Data structures in which lower entities are nested within higher entities (e.g., customers nested within salespersons, employees nested within managers, or customers nested within countries) (Heck and Thomas 2015).
Intraclass correlation coefficient [also Intraclass correlation coefficient (1) – ICC(1)]	Measure of heterogeneity of a lower level variable between higher level entities. The intraclass correlation coefficient reflects the proportion of between to total variance of a lower level variable. $\rho = \frac{V_B}{V_T} = \frac{V_B}{(V_W + V_B)}$ where V_T reflects the total variance, V_B the between variance, and V_W the within variance of a lower level variable (Hox et al. 2018; Snijders and Bosker 2012).
Intraclass correlation coefficient (2) – ICC(2)	Measure of group mean reliability of a lower level variable across higher level entities. The ICC(2) is often expressed in terms of ICC(1) with ICC(2) $= \frac{k\rho}{1+(k-1)\rho}$ where k reflects the cluster size (Bliese 1998, 2000; Snijders and Bosker 2012). Recommended range for aggregation: $ICC(2) \geq .70 - .85$ (LeBreton and Senter 2008).
r_{WG}	Index to reflect the interrater agreement for a group regarding a single variable. $r_{WG} = 1 - \frac{S_X^2}{\sigma_E^2}$ where S_X^2 reflects the observed variance on the variable X and σ_E^2 reflects the expected variance of X if there is a complete lack of agreement among raters (LeBreton et al. 2005; LeBreton and Senter 2008). Recommended threshold for aggregation: $r_{WG} \geq .70$ (LeBreton and Senter 2008).
$r_{WG(J)}$	Index to reflect the interrater agreement for a group regarding multiple (J) essentially parallel items. $r_{WG(J)} = \frac{J\left(1-\bar{S}_{X_j}^2/\sigma_e^2\right)}{J\left(1-\bar{S}_{X_j}^2/\sigma_e^2\right) + \left(\bar{S}_{X_j}^2/\sigma_e^2\right)}$ where $\bar{S}_{X_j}^2$ reflects the mean of the observed variances of the J essentially parallel items and σ_e^2 reflects the expected variance of X if there is a complete lack of agreement among raters (LeBreton et al. 2005; LeBreton and Senter 2008).
Grand mean centering	Subtracting the grand mean from the individual observations of a variable $(X_{ij} - \overline{X})$.
Group mean centering	Subtracting the group mean from the individual observations of a variable $(X_{ij} - \overline{X}_j)$.
Random intercept	An intercept that is allowed to vary between higher level entities $(\beta_{0j} = \gamma_{00} + u_{0j})$.
Random slope	A slope that is allowed to vary between higher level entities $(\beta_{1j} = \gamma_{10} + u_{1j})$.
Cross-level interaction effect	Indicates whether a relationship between an independent and a dependent lower level variable varies as a function of a higher level variable and thus determines whether the higher level variable moderates the relationship between the independent variable and the dependent variable across clusters $(\gamma_{11}X_{ij}Z_j)$.

References

Ahearne, M., MacKenzie, S. B., Podsakoff, P. M., Mathieu, J. E., & Lam, S. K. (2010). The role of consensus in sales team performance. *Journal of Marketing Research, 47*(3), 458–469.

Aiken, L. S., West, S. G., & Reno, R. R. (1991). *Multiple regression: Testing and interpreting interactions*. Thousand Oaks: Sage.

Akaike, H. (1973). Information theory and an extension of the maximum likelihood principle. In B. N. Petrov & F. Csake (Eds.), *Second international symposium on information theory* (pp. 267–281). Budapest: Akademiai Kiado.

Akaike, H. (1987). Factor analysis and AIC. *Psychometrika, 52*(3), 317–332.

Albright, J. J., & Marinova, D. M. (2010). Estimating multilevel models using SPSS, Stata, SAS, and R. Working Paper. *Indiana University*, 1–35.

Anderson, E. W., Fornell, C., & Mazvancheryl, S. K. (2004). Customer satisfaction and shareholder value. *Journal of marketing, 68*(4), 172–185.

Asparouhov, T., & Muthén, B. (2007). Computationally efficient estimation of multilevel high-dimensional latent variable models. In *Proceedings of the 2007 JSM meeting, Section on Statistics in Epidemiology* (pp. 2531–2535). Alexandria: American Statistical Association.

Asparouhov, T., & Muthén, B. (2013). Computing the Strictly Positive Satorra-Bentler Chi-Square Test in Mplus. Mplus Web Notes: No. 12, https://www.statmodel.com/examples/webnotes/SB5.pdf

Asparouhov, T., & Muthén, B. (2008). Multilevel mixture models. In G. R. Hancock & K. M. Samuelsen (Eds.), *Advances in latent variable mixture models* (pp. 27–51). Charlotte: Information Age Publishing.

Asparouhov, T., & Muthén, B. (2019). Latent Variable Centering of predictors and mediators in multilevel and time-series models. *Structural Equation Modeling: A Multidisciplinary Journal, 26*(1), 119–142.

Auh, S., Menguc, B., & Jung, Y. S. (2014). Unpacking the relationship between empowering leadership and service-oriented citizenship behaviors: A multilevel approach. *Journal of the Academy of Marketing Science, 42*(5), 558–579.

Bass, B. M., & Bass, R. (2009). *The Bass handbook of leadership: Theory, research, and managerial applications*. Free Press, New York: Simon and Schuster.

Bates, D., Maechler, M., Bolker, B., Walker, S., Christensen, R. H. B., & Singmann, H. et al. (2016). Package 'lme4'. https://cran.r-project.org/web/packages/lme4/lme4.pdf. Accessed 24 Sept 2020.

Bentler, P. M. (1990). Comparative fit indexes in structural models. *Psychological Bulletin, 107*(2), 238–246.

Bentler, P. M. (1995). *EQS structural equations program manual*. Encino: Multivariate Software.

Biesanz, J. C., Deeb-Sossa, N., Papadakis, A. A., Bollen, K. A., & Curran, P. J. (2004). The role of coding time in estimating and interpreting growth curve models. *Psychological Methods, 9*(1), 30.

Bijmolt, T. H., & Pieters, R. G. (2001). Meta-analysis in marketing when studies contain multiple measurements. *Marketing Letters, 12*(2), 157–169.

Bliese, P. D. (1998). Group size, ICC values, and group-level correlations: A simulation. *Organizational Research Methods, 1*(4), 355–373.

Bliese, P. D. (2000). Within-group agreement, non-independence, and reliability: Implications for data aggregation and analysis. In K. J. Klein & S. W. Kozlowski (Eds.), *Multilevel theory, research, and methods in organizations* (pp. 349–381). San Francisco: Jossey-Bass.

Bliese, P. D. (2002). Multilevel random coefficient modeling in organizational research: Examples using SAS and S-PLUS. In F. Drasgow & N. Schmitt (Eds.), *Measuring and analyzing behavior in organizations: Advances in measurement and data analysis* (pp. 401–445). San Francisco: Jossey-Bass.

Bliese, P. D. (2016). Multilevel Modeling in R (2.6) – A brief introduction to R, the multilevel package and the nlme package. https://cran.r-project.org/doc/contrib/Bliese_Multilevel.pdf. Accessed 24 Sept 2020.

Boichuk, J. P., Bolander, W., Hall, Z. R., Ahearne, M., Zahn, W. J., & Nieves, M. (2014). Learned helplessness among newly hired salespeople and the influence of leadership. *Journal of Marketing, 78*(1), 95–111.

Bollen, K. A. (1989). A new incremental fit index for general structural equation models. *Sociological Methods & Research, 17*(3), 303–316.

Bosker, R. J., Snijders, T. A. B., & Guldemond, H. (2003). *PINT (Power in Two-level Designs)*. Groningen: University of Groningen.

Brady, M. K., Voorhees, C. M., & Brusco, M. J. (2012). Service sweethearting: Its antecedents and customer consequences. *Journal of Marketing, 76*(2), 81–98.

Browne, M. W., & Cudeck, R. (1992). Alternative ways of assessing model fit. *Sociological Methods & Research, 21*(2), 230–258.

Chen, G., Bliese, P. D., & Mathieu, J. E. (2005). Conceptual framework and statistical procedures for delineating and testing multilevel theories of homology. *Organizational Research Methods, 8*(4), 375–409.

Cohen, J. (1992). A power primer. *Psychological Bulletin, 112*(1), 155–159.

De Jong, A., De Ruyter, K., & Lemmink, J. (2004). Antecedents and consequences of the service climate in boundary-spanning self-managing service teams. *Journal of Marketing, 68*(2), 18–35.

Deadrick, D. L., Bennett, N., & Russell, C. J. (1997). Using hierarchical linear modeling to examine dynamic performance criteria over time. *Journal of Management, 23*(6), 745–757.

Depaoli, S., & Clifton, J. P. (2015). A Bayesian approach to multilevel structural equation modeling with continuous and dichotomous outcomes. *Structural Equation Modeling: A Multidisciplinary Journal, 22*(3), 327–351.

Donavan, D. T., Brown, T. J., & Mowen, J. C. (2004). Internal benefits of service-worker customer orientation: Job satisfaction, commitment, and organizational citizenship behaviors. *Journal of Marketing, 68*(1), 128–146.

Duncan, T. E., Duncan, S. C., & Strycker, L. A. (2013). *An introduction to latent variable growth curve modeling: Concepts, issues, and application*. New York: Routledge.

Edeling, A., & Fischer, M. (2016). Marketing's impact on firm value: Generalizations from a meta-analysis. *Journal of Marketing Research, 53*(4), 515–534.

Eliason, S. R. (1993). *Maximum likelihood estimation: Logic and practice* (No. 96). Hoboken: Sage.

Enders, C. K., & Tofighi, D. (2007). Centering predictor variables in cross-sectional multilevel models: A new look at an old issue. *Psychological Methods, 12*(2), 121.

Finch, W. H., Bolin, J. E., & Kelley, K. (2014). *Multilevel modeling using R*. Boca Raton: CRC Press.

Fu, F. Q., Richards, K. A., Hughes, D. E., & Jones, E. (2010). Motivating salespeople to sell new products: The relative influence of attitudes, subjective norms, and self-efficacy. *Journal of Marketing, 74*(6), 61–76.

Gelman, A., & Hill, J. (2006). *Data analysis using regression and multilevel/hierarchical models*. New York: Cambridge University Press.

Gelman, A., Carlin, J. B., Stern, H. S., Dunson, D. B., Vehtari, A., & Rubin, D. B. (2014). *Bayesian data analysis* (3rd ed.). Boca Raton: Taylor and Francis.

Glass, G. V. (1976). Primary, secondary, and meta-analysis of research. *Educational Researcher, 5*(10), 3–8.

Goff, B. G., Boles, J. S., Bellenger, D. N., & Stojack, C. (1997). The influence of salesperson selling behaviors on customer satisfaction with products. *Journal of Retailing, 73*(2), 171–183.

Groening, C., Mittal, V., & "Anthea" Zhang, Y. (2016). Cross-validation of customer and employee signals and firm valuation. *Journal of Marketing Research, 53*(1), 61–76.

Gruca, T. S., & Rego, L. L. (2005). Customer satisfaction, cash flow, and shareholder value. *Journal of Marketing, 69*(3), 115–130.

Hamaker, E. L., & Klugkist, I. (2011). Bayesian estimation of multilevel models. In *Handbook of advanced multilevel analysis* (pp. 137–162). New York: Routledge.

Hamaker, E. L., & Muthén, B. (2020). The fixed versus random effects debate and how it relates to centering in multilevel modeling. *Psychological Methods, 25*(3), 365.

Heck, R. H., & Thomas, S. L. (2015). *An introduction to multilevel modeling techniques: MLM and SEM approaches using Mplus* (3rd ed.). New York: Routledge.

Heck, R. H., Thomas, S. L., & Tabata, L. N. (2012). *Multilevel modeling of categorical outcomes using IBM SPSS*. New York: Routledge.

Heck, R. H., Thomas, S. L., & Tabata, L. N. (2014). *Multilevel and longitudinal modeling with IBM SPSS* (2nd ed.). New York: Routledge.

Hedeker, D., & Gibbons, R. D. (2006). *Longitudinal data analysis*. New York: Wiley.

Hitt, M. A., Beamish, P. W., Jackson, S. E., & Mathieu, J. E. (2007). Building theoretical and empirical bridges across levels: Multilevel research in management. *Academy of Management Journal, 50*(6), 1385–1399.

Hofmann, D. A., & Gavin, M. B. (1998). Centering decisions in hierarchical linear models: Implications for research in organizations. *Journal of Management, 24*(5), 623–641.

Hohenberg, S., & Homburg, C. (2016). Motivating sales reps for innovation selling in different cultures. *Journal of Marketing, 80*(2), 101–120.

Homburg, C., Wieseke, J., & Bornemann, T. (2009a). Implementing the marketing concept at the employee-customer interface: The role of customer need knowledge. *Journal of Marketing, 73*(4), 64–81.

Homburg, C., Wieseke, J., & Hoyer, W. D. (2009b). Social identity and the service-profit chain. *Journal of Marketing, 73*(2), 38–54.

Homburg, C., Müller, M., & Klarmann, M. (2011). When should the customer really be king? On the optimum level of salesperson customer orientation in sales encounters. *Journal of Marketing, 75*(2), 55–74.

Hox, J. J. (2010). *Multilevel analysis: Techniques and applications* (2nd ed.). New York: Routledge.

Hox, J. (2011). Panel Modeling: Random Coefficients and Covariance Structures. *Handbook of advanced multilevel analysis*, 137–162.

Hox, J. J., Moerbeek, M., & Van de Schoot, R. (2018). *Multilevel analysis: Techniques and applications*. Thousand Oaks: Routledge.

Hughes, D. E., & Ahearne, M. (2010). Energizing the reseller's sales force: The power of brand identification. *Journal of Marketing, 74*(4), 81–96.

Hunter, G. K., & Panagopoulos, N. G. (2015). Commitment to technological change, sales force intelligence norms, and salesperson key outcomes. *Industrial Marketing Management, 50*, 162–179.

James, L. R., Demaree, R. G., & Wolf, G. (1984). Estimating within-group interrater reliability with and without response bias. *Journal of Applied Psychology, 69*(1), 85.

James, L. R., Demaree, R. G., & Wolf, G. (1993). rwg: An assessment of within-group interrater agreement. *Journal of Applied Psychology, 78*(2), 306.

Johnson, J. S., Friend, S. B., & Horn, B. J. (2014). Levels of analysis and sources of data in sales research: A multilevel-multisource review. *Journal of Personal Selling & Sales Management, 34*(1), 70–86.

Josephson, B. W., Johnson, J. L., & Mariadoss, B. J. (2016). Strategic marketing ambidexterity: Antecedents and financial consequences. *Journal of the Academy of Marketing Science, 44*(4), 539–554.

Klein, K. J., Dansereau, F., & Hall, R. J. (1994). Levels issues in theory development, data collection, and analysis. *Academy of Management Review, 19*(2), 195–229.

Kozlowski, S. W. J., & Klein, K. J. (2000). A multilevel approach to theory and research in organizations: Contextual, temporal, and emergent processes. In: K. J. Klein & S. W. J. Kozlowski (Eds.), Multilevel theory, research, and methods in organizations: Foundations, extensions, and new directions (pp. 3–90). Jossey-Bass.

Krasnikov, A., & Jayachandran, S. (2008). The relative impact of marketing, research-and-development, and operations capabilities on firm performance. *Journal of Marketing, 72*(4), 1–11.

Kreft, I. (1996). *Are multilevel techniques necessary? An overview, including simulation studies.* Unpublished Report, California State University, Los Angeles.

Kreft, I., & De Leeuw, J. (1998). *Introducing multilevel modeling*. Los Angeles: Sage.

Kreft, I. G., De Leeuw, J., & Aiken, L. S. (1995). The effect of different forms of centering in hierarchical linear models. *Multivariate Behavioral Research, 30*(1), 1–21.

Lai, M. H., & Kwok, O. M. (2015). Examining the rule of thumb of not using multilevel modeling: The "design effect smaller than two" rule. *The Journal of Experimental Education, 83*(3), 423–438.

Lam, S. K., Ahearne, M., Mullins, R., Hayati, B., & Schillewaert, N. (2013). Exploring the dynamics of antecedents to consumer–brand identification with a new brand. *Journal of the Academy of Marketing Science, 41*(2), 234–252.

Larivière, B., Keiningham, T. L., Aksoy, L., Yalçin, A., Morgeson, F. V., III, & Mithas, S. (2016). Modeling heterogeneity in the satisfaction, loyalty intention, and shareholder value linkage: A cross-industry analysis at the customer and firm levels. *Journal of Marketing Research, 53*(1), 91–109.

LeBreton, J. M., & Senter, J. L. (2008). Answers to 20 questions about interrater reliability and interrater agreement. *Organizational Research Methods, 11*(4), 815–852.

LeBreton, J. M., James, L. R., & Lindell, M. K. (2005). Recent issues regarding rWG, rWG, rWG (J), and rWG (J). *Organizational Research Methods, 8*(1), 128–138.

Liao, H., & Chuang, A. (2007). Transforming service employees and climate: A multilevel, multisource examination of transformational leadership in building long-term service relationships. *Journal of Applied Psychology, 92*(4), 1006–1019.

Lipsey, M. W., & Wilson, D. B. (2001). *Practical meta-analysis*. Thousand Oaks: SAGE.

Longford, N. T. (1989). To center or not to center. *Multilevel Modelling Newsletter, 1*(3), 7.

Maas, C. J., & Hox, J. J. (2005). Sufficient sample sizes for multilevel modeling. *Methodology, 1*(3), 86–92.

Mathieu, J., Ahearne, M., & Taylor, S. R. (2007). A longitudinal cross-level model of leader and salesperson influences on sales force technology use and performance. *Journal of Applied Psychology, 92*(2), 528.

Mathieu, J. E., Aguinis, H., Culpepper, S. A., & Chen, G. (2012). Understanding and estimating the power to detect cross-level interaction effects in multilevel modeling. *Journal of Applied Psychology, 97*(5), 951–966.

Matsueda, R. L. (2014). Key advances of in the history of structural equation modeling. In R. H. Hoyle (Ed.), *Handbook of structural equation modeling* (pp. 17–42). New York: Guilford Press.

Maxham, J. G., III, Netemeyer, R. G., & Lichtenstein, D. R. (2008). The retail value chain: Linking employee perceptions to employee performance, customer evaluations, and store performance. *Marketing Science, 27*(2), 147–167.

Mehta, P. D., & Neale, M. C. (2005). People are variables too: Multilevel structural equations modeling. *Psychological Methods, 10*(3), 259–284.

Mikolon, S., Kolberg, A., Haumann, T., & Wieseke, J. (2015). The complex role of complexity: How service providers can mitigate negative effects of perceived service complexity when selling professional services. *Journal of Service Research, 18*(4), 513–528.

Mikolon, S., Alavi, S., & Reynders, A. (2020). The Catch-22 of countering a moral occupational stigma in employee-customer interactions. *The Academy of Management Journal.* https://doi.org/10.5465/amj.2018.1487.

Misangyi, V. F., Elms, H., Greckhamer, T., & Lepine, J. A. (2006). A new perspective on a fundamental debate: a multilevel approach to industry, corporate, and business unit effects. *Strategic Management Journal, 27*(6), 571–590.

Muthén, B. O. (2002). Beyond SEM: General latent variable modeling. *Behaviormetrika, 29*(1), 81–117.

Muthén, B. O., & Asparouhov, T. (2011). Beyond multilevel regression modeling: Multilevel analysis in a general latent variable framework. In J. Hox & J. K. Roberts (Eds.), *Handbook of advanced multilevel analysis* (pp. 15–40). New York: Taylor and Francis.

Muthén, L. K., & Muthén, B. O. (1998–2017). *Mplus User's Guide* (7th ed.). Los Angeles: Muthén & Muthén.

Muthén, B. O., & Satorra, A. (1995). Complex sample data in structural equation modeling. *Sociological Methodology, 25*, 267–316.

Netemeyer, R. G., Heilman, C. M., & Maxham, J. G., III. (2012). Identification with the retail organization and customer-perceived employee similarity: Effects on customer spending. *Journal of Applied Psychology, 97*(5), 1049–1058.

Paccagnella, O. (2006). Centering or not centering in multilevel models? The role of the group mean and the assessment of group effects. *Evaluation Review, 30*(1), 66–85.

Palardy, G. J. (2011). Review of HLM 7. *Social Science Computer Review, 29*(4), 515–520.

Palmatier, R. W. (2008). Interfirm relational drivers of customer value. *Journal of Marketing, 72*(4), 76–89.

Pinheiro, J., Bates, D., DebRoy, S., & Sarkar, D. (2016). Nlme: Linear and nonlinear mixed effects models. R package version 3.1–128. http://CRAN.R-project.org/package=nlme. Accessed 24 Sept 2020.

Preacher, K. J., Zyphur, M. J., & Zhang, Z. (2010). A general multilevel SEM framework for assessing multilevel mediation. *Psychological Methods, 15*(3), 209–233.

Preacher, K. J., Zhang, Z., & Zyphur, M. J. (2011). Alternative methods for assessing mediation in multilevel data: The advantages of multilevel SEM. *Structural Equation Modeling, 18*(2), 161–182.

Rabe-Hesketh, S., & Skrondal, A. (2012). *Multilevel and longitudinal modeling using Stata* (3rd ed.). College Station: STATA Press.

Rasbash, J., Browne, W., Healy, M., Cameron, B., & Charlton, C. (2016a). *MLwiN Version 2.36.* Bristol: Centre for Multilevel Modelling, University of Bristol.

Rasbash, J., Steele, F., Browne, W. J., & Goldstein, H. (2016b). *A user's guide to MLwiN.* Bristol: Centre for Multilevel Modelling, University of Bristol.

Raudenbush, S. W. (1989). Centering predictors in multilevel analysis: Choices and consequences. *Multilevel Modelling Newsletter, 1*(2), 10–12.

Raudenbush, S. W., & Bryk, A. S. (2002). *Hierarchical linear models: Applications and data analysis methods.* Newbury Park: Sage.

Raudenbush, S. W., Bryk, A. S., Cheong, Y. F., Congdon, R. T., & Du Toit, M. (2019a). *HLM 8: Linear and nonlinear modeling.* Lincolnwood: Scientific Software International.

Raudenbush, S. W., Bryk, A. S., Cheong, Y. F., Congdon, R. T., & Du Toit, M. (2019b). *HLM 8.* Lincolnwood: Scientific Software International.

Roschk, H., & Hosseinpour, M. (2020). Pleasant ambient scents: A meta-analysis of customer responses and situational contingencies. *Journal of Marketing, 84*(1), 125–145.

Ryu, E., & West, S. G. (2009). Level-specific evaluation of model fit in multilevel structural equation modeling. *Structural Equation Modeling, 16*(4), 583–601.

Satorra, A., & Bentler P. M. (1999). A Scaled Difference Chi-square Test Statistic for Moment Structure Analysis. Working Paper. https://econ-papers.upf.edu/en/onepaper.php?id=412.

Satorra, A., & Bentler, P. M. (2010). Ensuring positiveness of the scaled difference chi-square test statistic. *Psychometrika, 75*(2), 243–248.

Schneider, B., Salvaggio, A. N., & Subirats, M. (2002). Climate strength: A new direction for climate research. *Journal of Applied Psychology, 87*(2), 220.

Schwarz, G. (1978). Estimating the dimension of a model. *The Annals of Statistics, 6*(2), 461–464.

Singer, J. D. (1998). Using SAS PROC MIXED to fit multilevel models, hierarchical models, and individual growth models. *Journal of Educational and Behavioral Statistics, 23*(4), 323–355.

Snijders, T. A. (2005). Power and sample size in multilevel linear models. In B. S. Everitt & D. C. Howell (Eds.), *Encyclopedia of statistics in behavioral science* (Vol. 3, pp. 1570–1573). Chichester: Wiley.

Snijders, T. A., & Bosker, R. J. (1993). Standard errors and sample sizes for two-level research. *Journal of Educational and Behavioral Statistics, 18*(3), 237–259.

Snijders, T. A., & Bosker, R. J. (2012). *Multilevel analysis.* London: Sage.

Steenkamp, J. B. E., Van Heerde, H. J., & Geyskens, I. (2010). What makes consumers willing to pay a price premium for national brands over private labels? *Journal of Marketing Research, 47*(6), 1011–1024.

Steiger, J. H., & Lind, J. C. (1980). Statistically based tests for the number of common factors. In *Annual meeting of the Psychometric Society* (pp. 424–453). Iowa City.

Stoel, R. D., & Garre, F. G. (2011). Growth curve analysis using multilevel regression and structural equation modeling. In *Handbook of advanced multilevel analysis* (pp. 97–111). New York: Routledge.

Troy, L. C., Hirunyawipada, T., & Paswan, A. K. (2008). Cross-functional integration and new product success: An empirical investigation of the findings. *Journal of Marketing, 72*(6), 132–146.

Tucker, L. R., & Lewis, C. (1973). A reliability coefficient for maximum likelihood factor analysis. *Psychometrika, 38*(1), 1–10.

Van der Borgh, M., de Jong, A., & Nijssen, E. J. (2019). Balancing frontliners' customer-and coworker-directed behaviors when serving business customers. *Journal of Service Research, 22*(3), 323–344.

Walsh, G., Shiu, E., & Hassan, L. M. (2014). Cross-national advertising and behavioral intentions: A multilevel analysis. *Journal of International Marketing, 22*(1), 77–98.

Wieseke, J., Lee, N., Broderick, A. J., Dawson, J. F., & Van Dick, R. (2008). Multilevel analysis in marketing research: Differentiating analytical outcomes. *Journal of Marketing Theory and Practice, 16*(4), 321–340.

Wieseke, J., Ahearne, M., Lam, S. K., & Van Dick, R. (2009). The role of leaders in internal marketing. *Journal of Marketing, 73*(2), 123–145.

Wieseke, J., Kraus, F., Ahearne, M., & Mikolon, S. (2012). Multiple identification foci and their countervailing effects on salespeople's negative headquarters stereotypes. *Journal of Marketing, 76*(3), 1–20.

Wieseke, J., Alavi, S., & Habel, J. (2014). Willing to pay more, eager to pay less: The role of customer loyalty in price negotiations. *Journal of Marketing, 78*(6), 17–37.

Woehr, D. J., Loignon, A. C., Schmidt, P. B., Loughry, M. L., & Ohland, M. W. (2015). Justifying aggregation with consensus-based constructs: A review and examination of cutoff values for common aggregation indices. *Organizational Research Methods, 18*(4), 704–737.

Wu, Y. W. B., & Wooldridge, P. J. (2005). The impact of centering first-level predictors on individual and contextual effects in multilevel data analysis. *Nursing Research, 54*(3), 212–216.

Panel Data Analysis: A Non-technical Introduction for Marketing Researchers

Arnd Vomberg and Simone Wies

Contents

Introduction: Relevance of Panel Data for Marketing Research	412
Process for Panel Data Analysis	414
Define the Research Question	415
Collect Panel Data	415
Prepare Panel Data	416
Explore Panel Data	419
Analyze Panel Data Models	426
Interpret and Present Results	444
Additional Methods in Panel Data Analysis	444
Robust Inference	444
Combining the Fixed Effects and Random Effects Estimators	445
Hausman-Taylor Approach: Consistent Estimation of Time-Constant Effects in the Combined Approach	450
Summary of the Discussed Estimators and Their Underlying Assumptions	452
Modeling a Price-Response-Function in Differences	455
Advanced Topics in Panel Data Analysis	457
Dynamic Panel Data Estimation	457
Random Slope Models: A Multilevel Model Approach to Panel Data	461
Addressing Measurement Error with Structural Equation Modeling Based on Panel Data	462
Conclusion	464
Cross-References	465
References	465

A. Vomberg (✉)
Marketing Department, University of Groningen, Groningen, The Netherlands
e-mail: A.E.Vomberg@rug.nl

S. Wies
Goethe University Frankfurt, Frankfurt, Germany
e-mail: wies@econ.uni-frankfurt.de

© Springer Nature Switzerland AG 2022
C. Homburg et al. (eds), *Handbook of Market Research*,
https://doi.org/10.1007/978-3-319-57413-4_19

> **Abstract**
>
> The analysis of panel data is now part of the standard repertoire of marketers and marketing researchers. Compared to the analysis of cross-sectional data, panel data allow marketers to alleviate endogeneity concerns when linking an independent variable (e.g., price) to an outcome variable (e.g., sales volume). The more accurate estimates that result from panel data analysis help improve marketers' decision-making in focal areas such as price setting and marketing budget allocation. Besides, panel data allow marketers to track customer behavior changes and distinguish real loyalty effects (i.e., same customer repeatedly buys a brand) from spurious effects (i.e., the same number of, but each time different set of, customers buys a brand). This chapter provides a nontechnical introduction to panel data analysis. Marketers will learn how to manage and analyze panel datasets in Stata. They will learn about the focal panel data estimators (pooled OLS, fixed effects, and random effects estimator), their underlying assumptions, advantages, and pitfalls. Besides, we introduce the between effects estimator, the combined approach, the Hausman-Taylor approach, and the first differences estimator as further techniques to analyze panel data. Finally, readers will receive an introduction to advanced topics such as dynamic panel models, panel data multilevel modeling, and using panel data to address measurement errors.

> **Keywords**
>
> Cluster-robust standard errors · Dynamic panel data models · Endogeneity · Fixed effects estimator · Hausman test · Hausman-Taylor method · Measurement error · Omitted variable bias · Panel data analysis · Pooled OLS · Random effects estimator · Serial correlation

Introduction: Relevance of Panel Data for Marketing Research

The analysis of panel data is now part of the standard repertoire of marketers and marketing researchers. Panel data, sometimes referred to as longitudinal data, contain observations about different cross-sectional units, also called clusters, across time. Hence, like cross-sectional data, panel data contain observations across a collection of clusters, and like time-series data, panel data contain observations about these clusters repeatedly collected over time. Examples of panel data include the following:

- Retail scanner data: Retailers track sales volume for their products over time.
- Online transaction data: Online retailers collect information about their customers over time.
- Market research institute data: Organizations collect consumer survey data for brands and products over time. For instance, the American Customer Satisfaction Index (ACSI) tracks the evolution of customer satisfaction for different

companies over time (e.g., Fornell et al. 1996). Similarly, the Young&Rubicum Brand Asset Valuator monitors consumers' brand sentiment for brands over time (e.g., chapter ▶ "Assessing the Financial Impact of Brand Equity with Short Time-Series Data" by Mizik and Pavlov in this Handbook).

Typically, the collection of panel data requires huge resources in time and money from investigators. Yet, as compared to cross-sectional data, panel data offer substantial advantages that can easily compensate for their data collection efforts.

First, panel data allow to study changes at the individual level and to disentangle real loyalty effects from so-called spurious carryover effects. As an example, aggregated brand sales data might resemble a stable pattern, indicating high loyalty. However, tracking changes at the individual level provides insights into whether the aggregated effect results from a loyalty effect (i.e., the same consumers purchase regularly) or an attraction effect (i.e., the company attracts new consumers but existing consumers do not repurchase).

Second, panel data allow addressing a potential omitted variable bias, a serious endogeneity threat in observational data. Broadly, endogeneity refers to a situation in which an independent variable is correlated with the error term, violating the basic exogeneity assumption of OLS and causing all coefficient estimates of the model to be biased and inconsistent (both properties that lead to misleading hypothesis tests). For instance, the investigator might be interested to know whether a company's distribution intensity contributes to its financial performance. If she omitted company factors such as brand strength, which likely drives both financial performance and access to distribution channels, regression results might overstate the impact of distribution intensity. In panel data analysis, we can control for general company effects, thereby helping to rule out many threats from omitted variables (see also chapter ▶ "Dealing with Endogeneity: A Nontechnical Guide for Marketing Researchers" by Ebbes et al. in this Handbook).

Third and relatedly, in contrast to typical applications with cross-sectional data, panel data allow to include time lags between dependent and independent variables. Thereby, panel data open up opportunities for novel research questions and, again, increase the researchers' ability to rule out endogeneity concerns (chapters ▶ "Experiments in Market Research" by Bornemann and Hattula, and ▶ "Field Experiments" by Valli et al. in this Handbook further discuss criteria for evaluating causality).

This chapter aims to introduce a general approach to analyzing panel data from an applied perspective, focusing on panel data management and analysis. Figure 1 outlines the process along which we structure our chapter. In the section "Process for Panel Data Analysis," we discuss the panel data research process step-by-step. Based on a real-life research example, we first define our research objective (section "Define the Research Question"); specifically, we are interested in estimating a price-response-function for a company's newly launched headphone. Then, we discuss the collected dataset, which can be downloaded from the Handbook's Data Appendix (section "Collect Panel Data"), and explain how researchers can prepare the data for the analyses (section "Prepare Panel Data"). Afterward, readers learn how to explore the unique structure in panel data (section "Explore Panel Data"), and

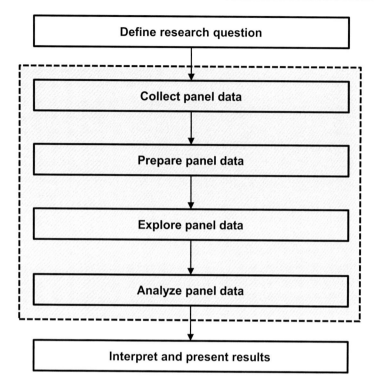

Fig. 1 Panel data research process

we discuss the focal panel data estimators (section "Analyze Panel Data Models"). We conclude this section with a short interpretation of the results (section "Interpret and Present Results"). In the section "Additional Methods in Panel Data Analysis," we provide more in-depth background information on panel data estimators. In the section "Advanced Topics in Panel Data Analysis," we explore more advanced topics in panel data analysis, including dynamic panel models and random coefficient models. Note that we keep a strictly intuitive and applied approach throughout the text but point the reader to the many excellent resources available that provide a more formal treatment of panel data estimation.

Process for Panel Data Analysis

Any research process should start with a clearly defined research question and end with a meaningful discussion of the results. However, a research process that involves panel data considerably differs from a process based on cross-sectional data alone regarding the data management and analysis part. Given that data management and analysis is more intricate for panel data, we devote special attention to describing how to prepare, explore, and analyze panel data.

In the spirit of an applied approach to the panel data research process, we guide the discussion in this chapter along a real-life dataset, using the statistical software Stata. Although most statistical software packages are well equipped to analyze panel data, Stata is particularly suited for such analysis given its convenient and efficient command structure for panel data.

Define the Research Question

The most important issue relates to the relationships researchers want to investigate. Developing an original and relevant research question is not trivial, yet, as mentioned earlier, panel data can offer exciting opportunities for examining more complex phenomena.

In this chapter, we want to aid a consumer electronics company on its pricing strategy for a newly launched headphone. We are interested in understanding how price-setting influences sales volume. This question is relevant yet challenging for the company as the headphone represents an expansion into a new category, with which the company only has limited experience. Economic theory suggests relying on so-called price-response-functions for price management. Price-response-functions link price to sales volume and represent a prerequisite for price optimization.

Collect Panel Data

Data for estimating price-response-functions can come from various sources, such as customer surveys (chapter ▶ "Crafting Survey Research: A Systematic Process for Conducting Survey Research" by Vomberg and Klarmann in this Handbook), experiments (chapters ▶ "Choice-Based Conjoint Analysis" by Eggers et al. and ▶ "Willingness to Pay" by Klingemann et al. in this Handbook), or market-level data. In this chapter, we focus on market-level data. The real-life case we follow throughout the chapter is based on a dataset of a medium-sized European consumer electronics company. The company created the dataset to estimate a price-response-function for its most recently launched headphone.

An excerpt of the corresponding dataset available for analysis contains weekly sales data ("sales") of the headphone model across n = 19 of the company's franchised stores (cross-sectional component, labeled as "storeid") across a time period of T = 82 weeks (time-series component, labeled as "week"), ranging from weeks 37 to 118. The company has recorded the headphone's retail price ("price") for each store and week. Besides, the company has collected information about whether the store featured major promotion activities for the headphone in a given week (dummy-coded "promo": 1 "promotional activity in the focal week" 0 "no promotional activity in the focal week"). Moreover, the company has information on two general store descriptors: whether the store design includes multiple floors (dummy-coded "floor": 1 "multiple floors" 0 "single floor") and whether the store is in a premium location with high traffic (dummy-coded "location": 1 "premium location" 0 "nonpremium location"). The data is initially split across three different data files, mimicking the often disordered situation researchers and companies face when they seek to analyze data.

We begin by reviewing the steps necessary to combine the three files to arrive at the final dataset that we will use in the chapter's remainder. Access to the different datasets is available via the Data Appendix. We provide the three individual raw datasets ("Sales_Original.dta," "Sales_Additional.dta," and "Explanatory.dta"), as well as the final dataset ("Dataset_Final.dta"). "Sales_Original.dta" contains the original headphone sales data the firm collected across its sampled stores. "Sales_Additional.dta" includes observations of an additional store for which data was shared separately. "Explanatory_Long.dta" features the retail price variable as well as the three other explanatory variables (promotional activities, "promo," store floor design, "floor," and store premium location, "location"). The Data Appendix also includes the script (the so-called "do-file" in Stata language) that summarizes the programming commands we use and complements the text with more detailed comments regarding the syntax.

Prepare Panel Data

Our overview begins with looking at three data management challenges that deserve our attention when working with panel datasets. Specifically, we discuss how to transform, combine, and prepare these datasets, so they are ready to use for our statistical analysis.

Transforming the Data Structure: Converting Wide Format to Long Format

In general, there are two ways of organizing panel data: wide format and long format. In wide format, a cluster's repeated measurements are stored in a single row, and each measurement appears in a separate column. Hence, the dataset has as many rows as it has clusters and as many columns as time periods $\times$ number of variables. Many datasets, especially when coming from commercial data providers, store panel data in wide format. Our original sales dataset ("Sales_Original.dta") also comes in wide format, with each row containing sales data for an individual store across all weeks. Using the `list` command, we can see a subset of the first five stores and their respective sales volume in the first ten weeks in the dataset in wide format (Fig. 2).

```
.       list storeid sales37-sales46 in 1/5, clean

        storeid   sales37   sales38   sales39   sales40   sales41   sales42   sales43   sales44   sales45   sales46
  1.          1       309       339       291       208       224       194       181       179       168       312
  2.          2       411       277       262       198       205       192       177       167       151       321
  3.          3       161       162       161       164       173       166       156       165       144       166
  4.          4       235       207       203       195       183       164       197       204       156       189
  5.          5       139       139       144       144       141       143       140        63        62        61
```

Fig. 2 Dataset in wide format

Fig. 3 Converting data from wide to long format

```
.                  reshape long sales, i(storeid) j(week)

Data                                wide   ->   long

Number of obs.                        18   ->   1476
Number of variables                   83   ->      3
j variable (82 values)                     ->   week
xij variables:
              sales37 sales38 ... sales118   ->   sales
```

Fig. 4 Dataset in long format

```
.                      list storeid sales in 1/5, clean

                      storeid    sales
          1.                1      309
          2.                1      339
          3.                1      291
          4.                1      208
          5.                1      224
```

In contrast, in long format, each measurement occupies one row with as many rows as clusters × time periods (for balanced data: n × T). The number of columns equals the number of variables. We can convert the data from wide to long format by using the Stata `reshape long` command (Fig. 3).

The command interprets the sales variables' suffixes (e.g., sales37, sales38) as denoting the grouping that needs to be expanded to long-form. As visible in the output, we expanded the dataset from 18 observations (18 stores) to 1,476 observations (1,476 store-week pairs). In addition, Stata created a week identifier, called "week," and collapsed the sales variables ("sales37" – "sales118") to a new variable, called "sales." Listing the first five observations of the new long-format dataset (using the `list` command) reveals the following data structure (Fig. 4).

Both datasets have exactly the same information. For panel estimation, however, most statistical software packages, Stata included, require the panel data to be organized in long format, with each observation being a distinct cluster-time pair.

Combining Panel Datasets: Appending and Merging Datasets

Data is often scattered across several data files, and our data example is no exception. It is necessary to combine the individual files into a new file containing all the variables and all the observations needed for analysis. There are different operations through which one can combine panel datasets, and we elaborate on the three most popular operations. First, one can add new *observations* to a given dataset, thereby *appending* data vertically by expanding the number of rows. This operation is typically used when one receives additional data for the same variables and seeks to add these new observations to the first dataset. In our data example, assume the marketing manager responsible for the study was able to add another store to the sample (see "Sales_ Additional.dta"), containing 87 observations. The investigator now needs to append this store's data to the transformed long-format dataset. The `append` command is simple to use and adds the rows from the second dataset to the end of the first dataset

Fig. 5 Merging datasets

```
.      merge 1:1 storeid week using "Explanatory.dta"

Result                              # of obs.

not matched                                0
matched                                1,563  (_merge==3)
```

(append using "Sales_Additional.dta"). This expands the first dataset to 1,563 observations.

Second, one can add new *variables* to a given dataset, thereby *merging* datasets horizontally by expanding the number of columns. This operation is needed when variables are stored across different data files. In our data example, we want to add a set of variables that help explain sales levels. These explanatory variables include the retail price, promotional activities, premium location, and floor design and are stored in "Explanatory.dta." Merging panel datasets requires that both datasets have variables in common on which the merging is based. If matching variables are found, merging two datasets is straightforward using the merge command. In our example, "store id" and "week" are the matching variables. We first sort on these matching variables and then perform the merge for a one-to-one (1:1) matching (Fig. 5). Note that alternative matching procedures involve one-to-many (1:m) or many-to-one (m:1) matching, depending on how the respective datasets are structured. For instance, if we would like to match a dataset that includes zip codes for the stores, we could use the many-to-one matching, knowing that we have multiple stores situated in the same zip code area.

The merge command creates a new variable called "_merge." This variable takes a value of 1 if the observation is only contained in the first dataset, a value of 2 if it is included only in the second dataset, and a value of 3 if the observation is present in both datasets. In our example, the observations of the matching variables perfectly match and are present in both datasets. As a result, the "_merge" variable takes on the value of 3 for all 1,563 observations. In contrast to the append command, the merge command does not add new observations to the dataset so the sample size remains unchanged. After we performed the operation, we can delete the "_merge" variable (drop _merge).

Finally, Stata offers a third type of combining datasets in which one can merge datasets horizontally but form pairwise combinations within-cluster, using the joinby command. This command is similar to merging datasets but creates all possible combinations of the observations across both datasets. While not applicable to our data example, it can be a useful command in other settings. For instance, imagine two datasets. The first contains a list of executive team members (i.e., CEO and CMO) across several companies. The second includes a list of awards the companies have received (e.g., Innovative Design Award, Best Place to Work Award). Both datasets contain a company identifier variable, which links the executives and awards that belong to the same company. Using the joinby command, we can easily combine the datasets and create a new dataset that includes all combinations of executives and awards, hence one row for each executive and award combination per company.

Preparing the Dataset: Length and Missingness of Panel Data

A final consideration in preparing panel data is to examine the missingness of its observations. When each cross-sectional cluster is observed in each time period, the panel is called *balanced*. Unbalanced panels, in contrast, display missingness in the data so that at least one cluster is not observed in every period. For instance, referring to our example, a store might have joined the study only at a later point in time or might have been closed for some weeks during the observation period for store-remodeling purposes.

The Stata language includes several convenient commands to detect data patterns. Importantly, however, these commands (as do all Stata commands involving panel data) first require the data to be formally declared as panel data by using the `xtset` command. The `xtset` command specifies a cluster identifier (here: store i, labeled "storeid") and a time identifier (here: week t, labeled "week"). We can access the large array of panel commands belonging to the panel command family (`xt` commands) in Stata with this setup. After having declared our data as panel data, using the `xtset` command, we can inspect missingness patterns with the `xtdescribe` command (Fig. 6).

Studying the missingness patterns over the different stores reveal that the data is not balanced across stores. Roughly 5% of the observations belong to one store, for which we have data after week 118. To simplify the discussion that follows in the chapter, we create a balanced panel dataset that contains only those observations for which we have data for all clusters, that is, only observations reported between weeks 37 and 118. The resulting file will be our final dataset ("Dataset_Final.dta"), with which we will work throughout the remainder of the chapter.

Explore Panel Data

Terminology

Recall that the unique feature of panel data is that these data contain both a cross-sectional component ($i = 1,\ldots, n$) and a time component ($t = 1,\ldots, T$). The time

```
    .         xtset storeid week
              panel variable:  storeid (unbalanced)
              time variable:   week, 37 to 123
                     delta:    1 unit

    .         xtdescribe

  storeid:  1, 2, ..., 19                                    n =        19
     week:  37, 38, ..., 123                                 T =        87
           Delta(week) = 1 unit
           Span(week)  = 87 periods
           (storeid*week uniquely identifies each observation)

Distribution of T_i:    min      5%     25%      50%     75%     95%      max
                         82      82      82       82      82      87       87

     Freq.   Percent   Cum.   Pattern
        18     94.74   94.74   1111111111111111111111111111111111111111111111111111111111111111111111111111111.....
         1      5.26  100.00   1111111111111111111111111111111111111111111111111111111111111111111111111111111111111

        19    100.00           XXXXXXXXXXXXXXXXXXXXXXXXXXXXXXXXXXXXXXXXXXXXXXXXXXXXXXXXXXXXXXXXXXXXXXXXXXXXXXXXXXXXXXXX
```

Fig. 6 Declaring and describing panel datasets

frame can be regular (e.g., data is collected every week, month, or year) or irregular (e.g., data is collected on specific occasions). Picking up on panel data's dual nature, it is common to classify panel datasets based on the relation between the number of clusters and the number of time periods observed. Panels in which a relatively large number of cross-sectional clusters is tracked over a rather short period of time are referred to as short or micropanels. For instance, retailers may track customer satisfaction scores for many consumers (cross-sectional component) but only for a few years (time component).

In contrast, panels with frequent measurements for a relatively small section of units vis-à-vis a larger number of time periods are referred to as long or macro-units. For instance, we might track the monthly consumer confidence index back to the 1960s (time component) for only a few EU countries (cross-sectional component). It is worth noting that most datasets in marketing are micropanels and that the more common types of panel estimators are derived under the assumption of relatively fewer time periods and a larger number of cross-sectional units (Wooldridge 2016). Please note that in our example, for illustrative purposes, we work with a reduced dataset that includes only a limited number of stores (cross-sectional units).

Focal Challenge of Panel Data Analysis: Nonindependent Observations

Irrespective of the type of panel dataset, we face one focal challenge in analyzing panel data: repeated measurements of a given cluster over time are nonindependent. This has severe implications for estimating our model, which we discuss next. To illustrate this point, we can think of panel data as a nested data structure. Using an extract from our example, we visualize this idea in Fig. 7. Here, we observe headphone sales for three of the stores at different points in time. The figure illustrates that each sales measurement (lower-level unit) is nested in a particular store measurement (higher-level unit).

The hierarchical nature highlights that individual measurements are likely not independent from each other; rather, sales measurements from one store have more in common (i.e., are more strongly correlated) than they have with sales from different stores. Intuitively, if sales in week 40 were independent of a store's prior sales, a good prediction would be the mean sales levels for week 39 and week 38 across all stores' observations. However, it seems that a much better prediction is to rely on the store's prior measurements. This point can be visualized by plotting the

Fig. 7 Illustration of panel structure

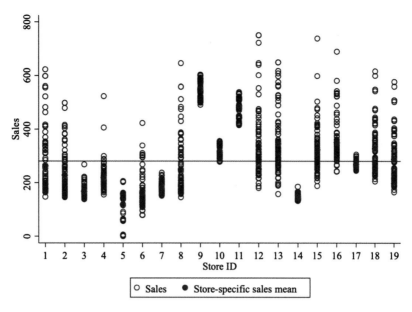

Fig. 8 Within and between dependence across stores

overall mean of sales, also called grand mean, across all measurements and the store-specific means of sales, as shown in Fig. 8. As can be seen in Fig. 8, there is substantial within dependence in the sales data (i.e., measurements within stores are similar).

As a more formal treatment of within dependence, we can use Stata's time-series lag operators (`L.`) and the `correlate` command (`corr sales L1.sales`) and inspect the serial correlation in sales (see also section "Pooled OLS Estimator: Ignoring the Panel Structure" for formal tests of serial correlation). Results suggest that headphone sales correlate substantially ($\rho = 0.67$) over time within a store; hence, there is a high serial correlation present in the sales data, and observations are nonindependent from each other. This dependency, in turn, violates a key assumption of traditional OLS estimation and foreshadows why standard OLS estimation is not feasible for panel data analysis (as detailed in section "Pooled OLS Estimator: Ignoring the Panel Structure"). A thought experiment based on Fig. 7 further underpins this point: if sales measurements within a store are very similar, we do not observe nine observations (three measurements for three stores) but effectively only three. Put differently, it reduces the effective size of the sample we can use in estimating the model, which in turn has implications for calculating the standard errors we use for making inferences. We will revisit the challenge of nonindependent observations in the remainder of the chapter. In doing so, we will shift to the more common terminology of within and between variance instead of within and between dependency. Within variance describes the variation within a cluster across time. Between variance describes the variation between clusters.

Dependent Variable: Between and Within Variance

Given nonindependent observations being the focal challenge in panel data, it is crucial to understand the degree of such dependency. The `xtsum` command provides valuable information on the relative importance of within and between variance in the dependent variable. Figure 9 demonstrates the result for sales ($Sales_{it}$) in our data example.

Besides providing some general descriptive statistics (including mean and range of the variable, as well as the number of observations, N, number of clusters, n, and number of time periods, t, in the sample), the output distinguishes between an overall, a between, and a within variance in the sales data. The within component focuses on particular clusters (i.e., stores) and describes the data within these clusters (i.e., sales levels from across all periods for an individual store). The between component takes the average per cluster (i.e., average sales level for a particular store) and describes the data based on these averages. The overall component treats the observations as entirely independent and calculates the respective measures without considering their panel nesting.

To support the discussion that follows, we detail how the overall, between, and within variance is calculated. Let

$$\overline{\overline{\text{Sales}}} = \frac{\sum\limits_{i=1}^{n} \sum\limits_{t=1}^{T} \text{Sales}_{it}}{n \times T} \tag{1}$$

be the overall mean of the dependent variable across all observations, also called the grand mean, and

$$\overline{\text{Sales}_i} = \frac{\sum\limits_{t=1}^{T} \text{Sales}_{it}}{T} \tag{2}$$

be the corresponding within mean for each cluster i (i.e., store); we can easily compute the respective variances.

The overall variance is calculated in the same way as in cross-sectional data without considering any panel structure nesting:

$$\widehat{\sigma}^2_{\text{Sales; Overall}} = \frac{\sum\limits_{i=1}^{n} \sum\limits_{t=1}^{T} \left(\text{Sales}_{it} - \overline{\overline{\text{Sales}}} \right)^2}{n \times T - 1}. \tag{3}$$

```
.        xtsum sales

Variable           |      Mean    Std. Dev.       Min       Max |   Observations
-------------------+--------------------------------------------+-----------------
sales     overall  |  280.1906    131.1669         0       750   |   N =      1558
          between  |              110.3184  118.9024  549.5976   |   n =        19
          within   |               75.28426  92.88575  695.0443  |   T =        82
```

Fig. 9 Decomposing the dependent variable sales volume

Panel Data Analysis: A Non-technical Introduction for Marketing Researchers   423

To calculate the within variance, we employ the following formula:

$$\widehat{\sigma}^2_{\text{Sales; Within}} = \frac{\sum\limits_{i=1}^{n} \sum\limits_{t=1}^{T} \left(\text{Sales}_{it} - \overline{\text{Sales}_i}\right)^2}{n \times (T-1)}. \tag{4}$$

When calculating the within variance, some statistical programs, Stata included, add the grand mean back to the within mean in the numerator $\left(\text{Sales}_{it} - \overline{\text{Sales}_i} + \overline{\overline{\text{Sales}}}\right)$ to make results comparable across overall, within, and between variance.

The between variance is given as:

$$\widehat{\sigma}^2_{\text{Sales; Between}} = \frac{\sum\limits_{i=1}^{n} \left(\overline{\text{Sales}_i} - \overline{\overline{\text{Sales}}}\right)^2}{n-1} \tag{5}$$

For our sample of 1,558 observations, we estimate a between variance of 110.31 and a within variance of 75.28, indicating that in our sample, the variance between clusters is larger than the variance over time within clusters.

Independent Variables: Time-Constant and Time-Varying Variables

While the dependent variable is, by definition, time -varying in the context of panel data, the independent variables can be time -constant or time -varying. In the following, we will refer to time-constant variables as Z. Those variables constitute cluster characteristics that are stable over the observation period. For instance, in modeling firm sales, McAlister et al. (2016) include the firm's type of business strategy to achieve a competitive advantage as a time-constant independent variable that does not change over the observation period. In our data example, a store's location ($Location_i$) and a store's floor design ($Floor_i$) are both time-constant variables that we include as independent variables in explaining sales.

Other variables, however, may change over time and are therefore called time-varying variables. We will refer to these variables as X in the course of this chapter. Ataman et al. (2010), for example, study brand sales levels and include brand distribution breadth as a time-varying independent variable. Our data example includes retail price ($Price_{it}$) and promotional activities ($Promo_{it}$) as independent variables, which vary over time. We can use Stata's xtsum command to confirm the type of variation in the independent variables. Figure 10 shows that $Location_i$ and $Floor_i$ are time-constant as they exhibit zero within variation. $Price_{it}$ and $Promo_{it}$, however, are time-varying and display variation within and between stores.

Since three of the four explanatory variables are binary, a further helpful command is xttab, which decomposes categorical variables into within and between variation. Figure 11 shows that, overall, roughly 11% of the store-week sales observations result from stores with a multiple floor store design. The between column repeats the breakdown but does so in terms of stores rather than store-weeks. Given we have a balanced sample with the same number of stores and weeks,

```
.      xtsum location floor price promo

Variable          |    Mean   Std. Dev.       Min       Max  |  Observations

location overall  |  .6842105   .4649788         0         1  |  N =      1558
         between  |             .4775669         0         1  |  n =        19
         within   |                    0  .6842105  .6842105  |  T =        82

floor    overall  |  .1052632   .3069907         0         1  |  N =      1558
         between  |             .3153018         0         1  |  n =        19
         within   |                    0  .1052632  .1052632  |  T =        82

price    overall  |  55.38318     12.596        29        85  |  N =      1558
         between  |             12.40116  38.42683  78.84146  |  n =        19
         within   |             3.587608  17.31001   64.3466  |  T =        82

promo    overall  |  .2727856   .4455345         0         1  |  N =      1558
         between  |             .1266187   .097561  .5487805  |  n =        19
         within   |             .4281387 -.2759949  1.175225  |  T =        82
```

Fig. 10 Decomposing the independent variables

```
.      xttab floor

                    Overall              Between          Within
        floor |  Freq.   Percent    Freq.   Percent      Percent

            0 |   1394     89.47       17     89.47       100.00
            1 |    164     10.53        2     10.53       100.00

        Total |   1558    100.00       19    100.00       100.00
                                     (n = 19)
```

Fig. 11 Decomposing a time-constant categorical variable

and $Floor_i$ varies only between stores, we report the same proportions of observations as in the overall column. Finally, the within percent tells us the fraction of times a store reported a given value of the $Floor_i$ variable. For instance, conditional on a store ever having a $Floor_i$ value of 0 (first line), 100% of its observations have a $Floor_i$ value of 0. These numbers indicate the stability of the variable within a cluster. By definition, a time-constant variable will have a tabulation within-percent of 100, while time-varying variables will have a tabulation within-percent below 100 (Fig. 12).

The between-percent informs us about the percentage of stores that have ever reported a given value of the variable, in this case, initiate promotional activities during the observation period. Since all sampled stores had periods in which they engaged in promotional activities ($Promo_{it}$ value of 1) and periods in which they did not engage in promotional activities ($Promo_{it}$ value of 0), the between percentage adds up to 200.

Additional information on within and between variation for categorical variables can also be retrieved through the xttrans command, which provides transition probabilities within a cluster from one period to the next. Transition probabilities

Panel Data Analysis: A Non-technical Introduction for Marketing Researchers 425

```
.       xttab promo

                  Overall            Between         Within
      promo |  Freq.  Percent    Freq.  Percent      Percent

          0 |   1133    72.72       19   100.00        72.72
          1 |    425    27.28       19   100.00        27.28

      Total |   1558   100.00       38   200.00        50.00
                                (n = 19)
```

Fig. 12 Decomposing a time-varying categorical variable

Fig. 13 Transition probabilities for time-varying categorical variable

```
.            xttrans promo

                          Promotion
      Promotion |       0          1  |     Total

              0 |   77.72      22.28  |    100.00
              1 |   59.95      40.05  |    100.00

          Total |   72.90      27.10  |    100.00
```

Fig. 14 Transition probabilities for a time-constant categorical variable

```
.          xttrans floor

  Multiple |
     floor | Multiple floor store
     store |       0          1  |     Total

         0 |   100.00       0.00  |    100.00
         1 |     0.00     100.00  |    100.00

     Total |    89.47      10.53  |    100.00
```

describe the probabilities of changing the state from one value of a variable to another value.

Figure 13 reports the results for the $Promo_{it}$ variable. As visible from the output, about 40% of the store-week observations that featured promotional activities in one period continue to feature promotional activities in the next period. For those store-week observations that did not feature promotional activities in one period, 22% start doing so in the next period. For time-constant variables, such as $Floor_i$, the diagonal entries will always be 100%, and the off-diagonal entries will always be 0% (Fig. 14).

Finally, it is worth noting that whether the independent variable is time -varying or time -constant has implications for the type of variance we can explain in the dependent variable. Specifically, time-constant variables can only account for between variation in the dependent variable. In contrast, time-varying independent variables can explain both between and within variation in the dependent variable, depending to which extent they vary within and between clusters. For instance, Vomberg et al. (2015) observe that market share tends to be relatively stable over time, while it differs substantially between companies. Hence, this time-varying variable will mainly explain between variation in the dependent variable.

The type of time dependence in the independent variables also helps identify the serial correlation sources in the dependent variable. First, variables that do not change over time (Z) will cause the dependent variable to have similar values across periods. For instance, assume we would like to explain a firm's brand equity levels by its branding strategy (multibrands vs. mono-brand). Since the type of branding strategy a firm pursues is likely to be constant over time (Rao et al. 2004), brand equity levels will be close to each other across periods. In statistical language, this cause of serial correlation is referred to as spurious state dependence. Two measurements (of the dependent variable) may be correlated because they are associated with a further variable (that characterizes the cluster).

Second, time-varying variables (X) might also be a source of serial correlation if they change only slowly over time. For instance, customer satisfaction is likely to drive brand equity. Yet, while customer satisfaction levels can change over time, they might only change to a small amount or just every other year. If customer satisfaction levels influence brand equity levels, the serial correlation among the time-varying customer satisfaction levels leads to statistical dependencies in the brand equity levels. This is another representation of spurious state dependence.

Third, the dependent variable's current value might directly influence the dependent variable's level in the next period. For instance, brand familiarity levels in the current year are likely to impact brand familiarity levels in the next year directly, given multiplier and spillover effects through word-of-mouth, like Lovett et al. (2013) show. This argument provides a substantive and direct cause of serial correlation, referred to as true state dependence.

From this discussion, it follows that if we were able to control for all relevant time-constant (Z) and time-varying (X) independent variables and included a lagged dependent variable (y_{t-1}), measurements of the dependent variable should be independent over time and serial correlation would be zero.

Analyze Panel Data Models

After collecting, preparing, and exploring the panel data structure, we are now ready to turn to the actual analysis of panel data. In this section, we will discuss three estimators that investigators can use to estimate the price-response-function: the (1) pooled OLS (section "Pooled OLS Estimator: Ignoring the Panel Structure"), (2) fixed effects (section "Fixed Effects Estimator"), and (3) random effects estimator (section "Random Effects Estimator"). We will discuss the latter two estimators in greater detail since those estimators explicitly account for the panel structure (in contrast to the pooled OLS estimator ignoring the panel structure). Besides, "most panel data models are estimated under either the fixed or random effects assumption" (Verbeek 2017, p. 384). We, therefore, call the fixed effects and random estimators proper panel estimators. To recall, here and in the remainder of the chapter, "panel structure" refers to nonindependent observations grouped by clusters over time. We will also outline the relationships between the estimators (section "Relationship Between Pooled OLS, Fixed Effects, and Random Effects Estimators"), discuss why they may deliver divergent results (section "What Do Differences Between Pooled OLS, Fixed Effects, and Random Effects Estimators Imply?"), and provide guidance on which estimator should be selected (section "Hausman Test: Selecting Between the Fixed Effects and the Random Effects Estimator"). In section "Additional Methods in Panel Data Analysis," we will highlight additional methods useful in analyzing panel data. We will point to more advanced panel data analysis strategies in section "Advanced Topics in Panel Data Analysis."

Pooled OLS Estimator: Ignoring the Panel Structure

We will start our discussion by applying the cross-sectional OLS approach to panel data (chapter ▶ "Regression Analysis" by Skiera et al. provide a detailed discussion of OLS regression analysis in this Handbook). This technique is referred to as pooled OLS (POLS). The name reflects that POLS pools all observations across the individual cross-sections and time periods without accounting for the panel structure.

As a first step, we need to decide which variables to include in our regression model. Naturally, we include the impact of the price ($Price_{it}$), as this is our focal variable of interest. Since we rely on observational market-level data (instead of randomized experimental data), we also want to account for relevant control variables that explain variation in the dependent variable and reduce the threat of omitted variables that could bias our results. That is, by including these control variables, we can account for factors that might affect both sales volume and price.

We include an indicator for promotion periods ($Promo_{it}$) which by definition influences price and is also likely to boost sales. We include a variable that distinguishes premium locations ($Location_i$) because location advantages might allow managers to realize higher sales volume and to set higher prices. Finally, we account for multiple floor store design ($Floor_i$). Stores with several floors likely contain a larger sales area and a broader assortment. Consequently, customers face a more appealing shopping experience, leading to higher sales volume (e.g., customers may stay longer in the store and purchase more products) but possibly also higher willingness to pay. Moreover, we account for seasonal differences across weeks by including dummy variables for all but one week; we select the first week in our sample as the reference category. Controlling for the effect of weeks (also called week-fixed effects) picks up market-wide developments that equally impact all stores, for instance, stimulated by online buzz about the company or increased media attention in a focal week.

As a second step, we need to decide on the functional form of the price-response-function. For the sake of simplicity, we will focus on a linear model. However, in general, investigators could also estimate price-response-functions in different forms, such as a multiplicative price-response-function. We formulate the following regression equation, which also contains an error term (ξ, pronounced xi):

$$\text{Sales}_{it} = \beta_0 + \beta_1 \text{Price}_{it} + \beta_2 \text{Promo}_{it} + \beta_3 \text{Location}_i + \beta_4 \text{Floor}_i + \delta \textbf{WEEK}$$
$$+ \xi_{it} \tag{6}$$

The variable subscript notation confirms that $\textit{Price}_{it}$ and $\textit{Promo}_{it}$ are time-varying variables, varying by store i and week t, and that $\textit{Location}_i$ and $\textit{Floor}_i$ are time-constant variables that only differ by store i. The bolded expression for weeks indicates that we include a vector of week dummy variables.

POLS relies on the typical cross-sectional OLS assumptions. Thereby, one of the focal assumptions is that the error term does not display serial correlation. As outlined in section "Independent Variables: Time-Constant and Time-Varying Variables," unless we account for *all* time-varying and time-constant variables that impact the dependent variable, the error term is likely correlated between two measurements of the same cluster.

We will demonstrate that serial correlation persists in our model, even after controlling for price, promotion activities, premium location, multiple floor design, and seasonal week effects. We first predict the regression residuals from Eq. 6 (see Eq. 7):

$$\widehat{\xi}_{it} = \text{Sales}_{it}$$
$$- (\beta_0 + \beta_1 \text{Price}_{it} + \beta_2 \text{Promo}_{it} + \beta_3 \text{Location}_i + \beta_4 \text{Floor}_i + \delta \textbf{WEEK}) \tag{7}$$

As a measure of serial correlation, we next derive pairwise correlations between different time periods. In Table 1, we compare the serial correlation in the residuals (`predict xi_hat, resid`) of the POLS model (Panel a) and in the raw sales data (Panel b) for 5 selected weeks from our dataset (weeks 37–41) to provide a general intuition. Besides eyeballing across the selected correlations, we can undertake more formal tests of serial correlation, either through the `correlate` command (e.g., `corr xi_hat L1.xi_hat`), as we did in section "Focal Challenge of Panel Data Analysis: Nonindependent Observations," or through the `regress` command (e.g., `reg xi_hat L1.xi_hat, beta`), as Wooldridge (2010) recommends. Also, Stata offers the user-written `xtserial` command as an alternative way to estimate serial correlation (available from SSC `findit xtserial`). From Table 1, it is easy to see that the serial correlation in the POLS residuals is smaller than the serial correlation in the raw sales data. The inclusion of the independent variables explains the reduction in serial correlation. However, it is also apparent that substantial serial correlation persists even after including the independent variables ($\text{corr}(\xi_t, \xi_{t+1}) = 0.61; p < 0.01$). Variables not included in the model explain the remaining serial correlation.

Serial correlation represents a common problem in POLS estimation, rendering standard errors calculated under the typical OLS assumptions misleading for panel data applications (Verbeek 2017). To partly account for serial correlation, investigators can rely on cluster-robust standard errors. Cluster-robust standard errors are computed differently than common OLS standard errors and account for the fact that the error structure differs across clusters (section "Robust Inference" details this point). The Stata suffix `cluster(clustvar)` following the

Table 1 Pairwise correlations of POLS residuals and raw data between weeks

Panel a)	POLS residual					Panel b)	Raw data				
	ξ_{37}	ξ_{38}	ξ_{39}	ξ_{40}	ξ_{41}		$Sales_{37}$	$Sales_{38}$	$Sales_{39}$	$Sales_{40}$	$Sales_{41}$
ξ_{37}	1.00					$Sales_{37}$	1.00				
ξ_{38}	0.77	1.00				$Sales_{38}$	0.79	1.00			
ξ_{39}	0.55	0.79	1.00			$Sales_{39}$	0.87	0.86	1.00		
ξ_{40}	0.56	0.89	0.87	1.00		$Sales_{40}$	0.71	0.90	0.89	1.00	
ξ_{41}	0.48	0.69	0.96	0.83	1.00	$Sales_{41}$	0.74	0.77	0.92	0.92	1.00

Overall $corr_{Sample}(\xi_t, \xi_{t+1}) = 0.61$ Overall $corr_{Sample}(Sales_t, Sales_{t+1}) = 0.67$

regression command indicates the use of cluster-robust standard errors. Thereby, `clustvar` represents the cross-sectional unit around which we cluster the standard errors. Since we want to cluster at the store-level, we use "storeid" as our clustering variable. We estimate the regression model with the following Stata syntax:

```
reg sales price promo location floor i.week, cluster(storeid)
```

In Table 2, we report the POLS estimates. The only difference between the two models is how the standard errors are calculated. Model 1 presents the POLS results with standard errors that follow from the common OLS assumptions. Model 2 relies on cluster-robust standard errors. As in the case of cross-sectional OLS, investigators can evaluate the overall model fit via R^2 values, the overall significance of the model with an F-statistic, and the statistical significance of individual regression coefficients with t-tests.

In our case, the regression results reveal that, in line with economic theory, the price has a negative relationship with sales volume ($\beta_1 = -1.48$). However, the effect of price on sales is only statistically significant in Model 1 ($p < 0.01$). Accounting for serial correlation with cluster-robust standard errors increases the estimated standard errors (Model 2), and in our example, the effect of price on sales turns insignificant. Note that clustering the standard errors does not affect the estimated regression coefficients.

To conclude, applying POLS with cluster-robust standard errors to panel data considers the panel structure to some extent but treats "it a nuisance, not as a phenomenon we are interested in" (Rabe-Hesketh and Skrondal 2012, p. 105). As a result, the challenge of serial correlation remains, and the usefulness of the estimation results is limited. In the following, we will focus on two estimators that more explicitly leverage the panel structure: the fixed effects estimator (section "Fixed Effects Estimator") and the random effects estimator (section "Random Effects Estimator").

Table 2 POLS estimates of the price-response-function

| | POLS (OLS standard errors) | | POLS (cluster-robust standard errors) | |
| | Model 1 | | Model 2 | |
	B	SE	B	SE
Constant (β_0)	283.75***	(28.64)	283.75***	(89.09)
Price (β_1)	-1.48***	(0.23)	-1.48[n.s.]	(1.57)
Promo (β_2)	47.37***	(7.07)	47.37***	(12.74)
Location (β_3)	132.36***	(6.89)	132.36***	(41.28)
Floor (β_4)	-3.41[n.s.]	(10.50)	-3.41[n.s.]	(31.64)
Week-fixed effects	Included		Included	
R^2	0.35		0.35	

*** $p < 0.01$; ** $p < 0.05$; * $p < 0.10$; n.s. = not significant

Modeling the Panel Structure

To introduce the idea of explicitly modeling the panel structure, we depict the development of headphone sales volume over time for five selected stores in Fig. 15. To derive Fig. 15, we fit a set of auxiliary regressions. Specifically, for each store, we run a regression of sales volume on a time period variable, for now excluding the independent variables we included in the POLS model. We see that some stores have systematically higher or lower sales volume than other stores. These systematic differences result from unobserved factors, captured in the error term ξ_{it}. We can classify these unobserved factors into two categories: time-varying and time-constant unobserved factors. In contrast to the POLS estimator, panel data estimators use this notion and split the error term into two parts: $\xi_{it} = u_i + e_{it}$. Thereby, u_i refers to unobserved predictors of the dependent variables that pertain to the cluster (i.e. store-level). Consequently, they are time-constant. The term e_{it} refers to unobserved predictors of the dependent variable that are time varying. We call ξ_{it} the composite error term, u_i the cluster-specific component, and e_{it} the idiosyncratic error term. Eq. 8 displays the rewritten price-response function:

$$\text{Sales}_{it} = \beta_0 + \beta_1 \text{Price}_{it} + \beta_2 \text{Promo}_{it} + \beta_3 \text{Location}_i + \beta_4 \text{Floor}_i + \delta \text{WEEK} + u_i + e_{it} \quad (8)$$

Figure 16 further illustrates the idea of two error components. In a nutshell, the inclusion of the cluster-specific term u_i extends POLS to handling panel data. The

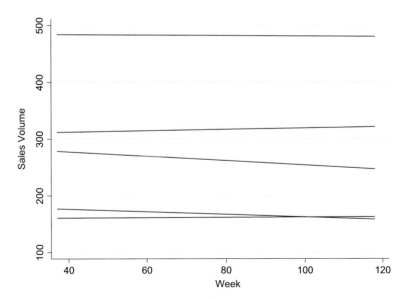

Fig. 15 Differences in sales volume development over time (Illustrated for fitted regressions of five selected stores)

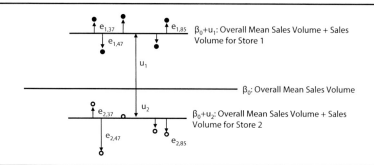

Fig. 16 Decomposition of the composite error term ($\xi_{it} = u_i + e_{it}$)

cluster-specific component captures that the mean sales volume per store differs from the overall mean sales volume across all stores. In Fig. 16, Store 1 displays systematically higher sales volume levels while the sales volume of Store 2 is systematically lower than the overall level of sales volume. While the store-specific component is constant over time, the idiosyncratic error term (e_{it}) indicates that measurements for a focal store (e.g., $e_{1,37}$) can deviate from this store's mean sales volume (e.g., $\beta_0 + u_1$).

The cluster-specific component captures the effects of all unobserved store-level characteristics (e.g., manager ability). It is referred to as unobserved cluster-level heterogeneity. If the cluster-specific component is positive ($u_i > 0$), the mean composite error term (ξ_{it}) will be positive, leading to larger sales volume levels than predicted by the included independent variables. The reverse holds if the cluster-specific component is negative; in that case, sales levels will be lower than predicted by the included independent variables.

The idiosyncratic error term e_{it} is assumed to have zero population mean and exhibits no correlation both across measurement points and with the independent variables. Depending on the assumptions imposed on u_i, two estimators emerge:

- The fixed-effects estimator, which does not assume uncorrelated unobserved cluster-level heterogeneity: u_i can correlate with the independent variables. Therefore, the fixed effects approach allows consistent estimation even if the investigator omits focal store variables (e.g., manager ability) from the price-response-function. The fixed effects approach estimates the respective cluster-specific effects (u_i).
- The random effects estimator, which assumes uncorrelated cluster-level unobserved heterogeneity: u_i is uncorrelated with the independent variables. Therefore, the random effects approach requires that the investigator includes all focal store variables in the price-response-function. The random-effects approach treats u_i as an unobserved random variable with a particular distribution (e.g., normal distribution). Rather than calculating an estimate for every cluster, it estimates a single variance over the clusters.

Panel Data Analysis: A Non-technical Introduction for Marketing Researchers

Fixed Effects Estimator

The fixed effects estimator accounts for the panel structure by exploiting the within variation in the data. It takes each cluster as its control group and only relies on the cluster's variation to estimate the model. Before we discuss the fixed effects estimator in more detail, we introduce a variant of it, called the least squares dummy variables (LSDV) regression, that shares the same logic but is implemented in a more straightforward way.

Least squares dummy variable regression. The name of the LSDV approach results from its reliance on a set of dummy variables. Specifically, the LSDV approach adds store dummies – referred to as store-fixed effects – for all but one store to our price-response-function (Eq. 9). The left-out store fixed effect serves as the reference category. The LSDV, thus, is the POLS model (section "Pooled OLS Estimator: Ignoring the Panel Structure") with an added vector of store-specific dummy variables.

$$\text{Sales}_{it} = \beta_0 + \beta_1 \text{Price}_{it} + \beta_2 \text{Promo}_{it} + \boldsymbol{\delta}\mathbf{WEEK} + \boldsymbol{\gamma}\mathbf{STORE} + e_{it} \qquad (9)$$

We do no longer incorporate u_i in the price-response-function since the store-fixed effects account for all observed and unobserved store-level effects in the data. As a consequence, however, we can no longer include the time-constant variables $Location_i$ and $Floor_i$. These variables correlate perfectly linearly with the store-fixed effects, and thus their effects cannot be estimated. Time-constant variables that interact with time-varying variables (e.g., $Price_{it} \times Location_i$), however, could be included as the interaction does not perfectly correlate with the store-fixed effects.

We can estimate the LSDV model with an OLS regression with store-specific dummy variables (i.storeid) and, optionally, cluster-robust standard errors (cluster(storeid)). Stata will automatically only include n-1 store dummy variables. In section "Robust Inference," we will elaborate on the rationale of using cluster-robust standard errors in addition to employing a panel estimator.

```
reg sales price promo location floor i.week i.storeid, cluster
(storeid)
```

Model 3 in Table 3 shows the LSDV regression results. Since the LSDV regression relies on the OLS estimator, investigators interpret results in the same manner as POLS estimates (section "Pooled OLS Estimator: Ignoring the Panel Structure"). We want to highlight some important aspects:

1. The effect of price is slightly stronger in the LSDV regression than in the POLS model (LSDV: $\beta_1 = -1.85$, $p < 0.10$; POLS: $\beta_1 = -1.48$, *n.s.*) and statistically different from zero. Unobserved store-level variables in the POLS model may have suppressed the effect of price. The inclusion of store-specific effects in the LSDV model picks up these effects and explains this difference.
2. Reported R^2 values of the LSDV are typically large since the store-fixed effects explain all time-constant variation of sales volume between stores. LSDV's

Table 3 LSDV and fixed effects estimates of the price-response-function

| | LSDV | | Fixed effects | |
| | Model 3 | | Model 4 | |
	B	SE	B	SE
Constant (β_0)	357.86***	(45.91)	394.66***	(56.13)
Price (β_1)	−1.85*	(1.00)	−1.85*	(1.00)
Promo (β_2)	45.21***	(8.63)	45.21***	(8.57)
Week-fixed effects	Included		Included	
Store-fixed effects	Included		Controlled	
R^2	0.75		0.24	

***p < 0.01; **p < 0.05; *p < 0.10; n.s. = not significant; cluster-robust standard errors (SE) in parentheses

R^2 value (Model 3: $R^2 = 0.75$) exceeds the one of the POLS model (Model 1: $R^2 = 0.35$).

3. In line with our discussion, Stata will automatically drop time-constant variables from the model due to perfect collinearity. Even if investigators had included premium location and floor design to the price-response-function, these variables would not have been estimated.

4. The constant (β_0) represents the store-specific intercept of the left-out store dummy variable (i.e., storeid = 1) at the left-out week (i.e., week = 37).

5. Usually, investigators do not report estimates for the store dummy coefficients. They are included for statistical reasons but typically do not convey substantive insights. We can, however, test whether they are jointly significant, using a conventional F-test on the estimated coefficients (`testparm` command in Stata). If the test statistic is sufficiently high, we can reject the null hypothesis of zero store effects.

Within transformation. The LSDV approach estimates one regression parameter per store. In panel data applications with many clusters, the number of dummy variables will become large, reducing the degrees-of-freedom in the model and, therefore, the estimates' precision. An alternative way to estimate the model is to rely on time-demeaned data, which produces the same (or, at least, very close) estimates. The idea is first to calculate cluster-means per store for each variable. In the next step, investigators center each variable on their cluster-means by subtracting the cluster-mean of each variable from its observed values (for a more technical discussion, please refer to Cameron and Trivedi 2005, pp. 726–729; Greene 2003, pp. 194–196; Verbeek 2017, pp. 387–388). In the case of time-constant variables, the cluster-mean equals the observed variable.

$$\left(\text{Sales}_{it} - \overline{\text{Sales}}_i\right) = (\beta_0 - \beta_0) + \beta_1\left(\text{Price}_{it} - \overline{\text{Price}}_i\right) + \beta_2\left(\text{Promo}_{it} - \overline{\text{Promo}}_i\right)$$

$$+\beta_3\left(\text{Location}_i - \overline{\text{Location}}_i\right) + \beta_4\left(\text{Floor}_i - \overline{\text{Floor}}_i\right) + (u_i - u_i) + (e_{it} - \overline{e}_i)$$

$$= \beta_1\left(\text{Price}_{it} - \overline{\text{Price}}_i\right) + \beta_2\left(\text{Promo}_{it} - \overline{\text{Promo}}_i\right) + (e_{it} - \overline{e}_i)$$

$$(10)$$

Like in the LSDV approach, time-demeaning removes the model's cluster-specific component (u_i), as visible in Eq. 10. For the same reason, all remaining time-constant variables also disappear (i.e., $Location_i$ and $Floor_i$). Since time-demeaning is referred to as within transformation, the fixed effects estimator is also called the within estimator.

To estimate the model, we could manually transform the data and run an OLS regression on the transformed data. However, such manual transformation would lead to calculating the wrong degrees-of-freedoms. Importantly, the investigator would need to subtract the number of estimated cluster-means calculated as an intermediate step. Statistical software packages directly correct for this adjustment in the degrees-of-freedom, and hence we recommend relying on these pre-programmed commands. We use Stata's `xtreg` command with the `fe` option, and additionally clustering the standard errors.

```
xtreg sales price promo i.week, fe cluster(storeid)
```

Model 4 in Table 3 displays the results of the fixed effects estimation. The coefficient estimates of $Price_{it}$ and $Promo_{it}$ are identical between the two models. However, the reported R^2 values differ. The reason is that Stata uses a different denominator to compute the R^2 statistic between Model 3 and Model 4. Specifically, while Model 3 is based on the overall variation of sales volume, Model 4 relies only on the within variation of sales volume that enters the R^2 formula (Wooldridge 2016, pp. 437–438).

At this point, it is also worthwhile to review the three different types of R^2 values that are calculated after a fixed effects model. Statistical programs, such as Stata, conventionally report a within-R^2, a between-R^2, and an overall-R^2. All three values provide insights into the model, but the within-value is typically of main interest after a fixed effects estimation. It indicates how much of the variation in the dependent variable within a store is captured by the model. The between-R^2, correspondingly, describes how much of the variation in the dependent variable between stores is explained by the model. The overall-R^2 is the weighted average of the two.

Finally, the reported constant terms differ between Model 3 and Model 4. Eq. 10 suggests that time-demeaning removes the constant term. However, most statistical software packages do report a constant term by relying on a slightly different within-transformation. Specifically, Stata additionally subtracts each variable's overall mean, the grand mean, from the observed values (Eq. 11). The estimated constant becomes the average of all store-specific effects: $\widehat{\beta}_0 = \sum_{i=1}^{n} \frac{\widehat{u_i}}{n} = \overline{u}$. Thus, the interpretation of the constant in Model 4 differs from Model 3.

$$
\left(Sales_{it} - \left(\overline{Sales}_i - \overline{\overline{Sales}} \right) \right) = \beta_0 + \beta_1 \left(Price_{it} - \left(\overline{Price}_i - \overline{\overline{Price}} \right) \right)
$$
$$
+ \beta_2 \left(Promo_{it} - \left(\overline{Promo}_i - \overline{\overline{Promo}} \right) \right) + \left(e_{it} - \left(\overline{e}_i - \overline{\overline{e}} \right) \right)
\tag{11}
$$

Random Effects Estimator

The random effects estimator represents another estimator that explicitly considers the panel structure. While the fixed effects estimator controls for the panel structure by removing the model's cluster-specific effects, the random effects estimator directly models the serial correlation stemming from the cluster-specific effects u_i (corr(ξ_{it}, ξ_{it-1})). Under the random effects assumptions, Eq. 12 expresses the serial correlation (Andreß et al. 2013, pp. 77–78 formally derive this equation) as:

$$\text{Corr}(\xi_{it}, \xi_{it-1}) = \frac{\sigma_{u_i}^2}{\sigma_{u_i}^2 + \sigma_{e_{it}}^2} \tag{12}$$

Equation 12 is referred to as the intraclass correlation coefficient (see Misangyi et al. 2006 for an application of the intraclass correlation-coefficient analysis on business segments and firm performance). It relates the cluster-specific variance to the overall variance (sum of variance between clusters and across time). If there were no serial correlation present in the data, Eq. 12 would produce a quantity of zero, and POLS would be an adequate estimator to use. However, while POLS is valid only in the particular case in which serial correlation is zero, the random-effects model is more general and explicitly models the degree of serial correlation.

Researchers can estimate the random effects model with the (feasible) generalized least squares estimator (FGLS). The FGLS estimator is a weighted least square estimator, which attributes more or less weight to a given observation depending on its variance structure (reflecting the relationship between $\sigma_{u_i}^2$ and $\sigma_{e_{it}}^2$). Like the fixed effects estimator, the FGLS estimator applies a quasi-demeaning procedure and subtracts the variable's cluster-mean from the variable's observed values. However, in contrast to the fixed effects estimator, the FGLS estimator only subtracts a fraction (θ, pronounced theta) between 0 and 1 of the cluster-mean from the respective value. Based on the quasi-demeaned data, the OLS estimator can then be applied. Since the FGLS estimator only subtracts a fraction, time-constant variables do not drop out of the model (see Eq. 13). For a more formal discussion of the underlying algebra, we refer to Cameron and Trivedi (2005, pp. 734–736), Greene (2003, pp. 200–205), Verbeek (2017, pp. 391–392), and Wooldridge (2010, Chap. 10).

$$\left(\text{Sales}_{it} - \theta \times \overline{\text{Sales}}_i\right) = \beta_0 + \beta_1\left(\text{Price}_{it} - \theta \times \overline{\text{Price}}_i\right) + \beta_2\left(\text{Promo}_{it} - \theta \times \overline{\text{Promo}}_i\right)$$
$$+ \beta_3\left(\text{Location}_i - \theta \times \overline{\text{Location}}_i\right) + \beta_4\left(\text{Floor}_i - \theta \times \overline{\text{Floor}}_i\right)$$
$$+ \left(u_i - \theta \times \overline{u}_i\right) + \left(e_{it} - \theta \times \overline{e}_i\right) \tag{13}$$

Equation 14 shows how to calculate θ. Essentially, θ comprises the relationship between the residual variance $\left(\sigma_{e_{it}}^2\right)$ and cluster-specific variance $\left(\sigma_{u_i}^2\right)$, which researchers can estimate with the FGLS estimator (Verbeek 2017, p. 392; Wooldridge 2016, p. 442).

Panel Data Analysis: A Non-technical Introduction for Marketing Researchers

$$\theta = 1 - \sqrt{\frac{\sigma_{e_{it}}^2}{\sigma_{e_{it}}^2 + T \times \sigma_{u_i}^2}} \tag{14}$$

We can obtain the random effects estimator using the Stata `xtreg, re` command, and, if we wish to, cluster the standard errors. To report the fraction of θ that Stata subtracts, we include (`theta`) as an additional option.

```
xtreg  sales  price  promo  location  floor  i.week,  re  cluster
(storeid) theta
```

Table 4 summarizes the results. Investigators can evaluate the overall model fit with the R^2 statistic and the overall model's statistical significance with a Wald test (instead of an F-test that cannot account for serial correlation in the error term). As with the fixed effects estimator, Stata reports three types of R^2. We inspect the overall-R^2 for the random effects model. Researchers can test the significance of individual regression coefficients with a z-statistic that draws on a normal distribution. Model 5 demonstrates that the effect of price on sales is negative and statistically significant ($\beta_1 = -1.82$, $p < 0.05$). In addition, promotional activities ($\beta_3 = 45.21$, $p < 0.01$) and stores in more attractive locations realize higher sales volumes ($\beta_3 = 132.79$, $p < 0.01$). However, stores with a multiple floor design ($\beta_4 = -1.48$, n.s.) do not associate with higher sales volumes.

The reported θ value (`theta`), which is used for the quasi-demeaning (Eq. 13), is 0.92 for our data. Stata will report only one value for θ if the panel is balanced. If the panel is unbalanced, Stata will report multiple θ values, depending on the number of weeks for which the store is observed.

We conclude with two additional comments:

1. The random effects approach treats the store-specific effects as unobservable random variables and not as model parameters (as the fixed effects model does). Still, investigators can obtain estimates for the store-specific intercepts

Table 4 Random effects estimates of the Price-response-function

	Random effects	
	Model 5	
	B	SE
Constant (β_0)	302.46***	(43.78)
Price (β_1)	−1.82**	(0.89)
Promo (β_2)	45.21***	(8.59)
Location (β_3)	132.79***	(41.76)
Floor (β_4)	−1.48[n.s.]	(34.74)
Week-fixed effects	Included	
R^2	0.35	

***$p < 0.01$; **$p < 0.05$; *$p < 0.10$; n.s. = not significant; cluster-robust standard errors (SE) in parentheses; store effects controlled for through random intercepts (`predict ui, u`; Rabe-Hesketh and Skrondal 2012, p. 107, p. 161, discuss further options to get store-specific error terms).

2. As an alternative to the FGLS estimator, investigators can also rely on a maximum likelihood estimator (`mle` option instead of `re`) to estimate the random effects model. In general, the two estimators will deliver equivalent results in large samples. We will rely on the maximum likelihood estimator when discussing panel data analysis from a multilevel modeling perspective in the section "Random Slope Models: A Multilevel Model Approach to Panel Data."

Relationship between Pooled OLS, Fixed Effects, and Random Effects Estimators

Thus far, we relied on three different estimators (POLS, fixed effects, and random effects estimator) to estimate our price-response-function. Table 5 summarizes the results, introducing the two proper panel data estimators first (Models 6 and 7) and keeping the POLS estimator (Model 8) as a benchmark. We note that the three estimators lead to different results. The relationship among the estimators becomes apparent when we study the quasi-demeaning procedure (e.g., $\text{Sales}_{it} - \theta \times \overline{\text{Sales}}_i$) underlying the random effects estimator in more detail.

Specifically:

- For $\theta = 1$, the random effects estimator becomes the fixed effects estimator.
- For $\theta = 0$, the random effects estimator becomes the POLS estimator.

Table 5 Comparison of fixed effects, random effects, and POLS estimates of the price-response-function

	Fixed effects	Random effects	POLS
	Model 6	*Model 7*	*Model 8*
	B (SE)	B (SE)	B (SE)
Constant (β_0)	394.66***	302.46***	283.75***
	(56.13)	(43.78)	(89.09)
Price (β_1)	−1.85*	−1.82**	−1.48[n.s.]
	(1.00)	(0.89)	(1.57)
Promo (β_2)	45.21***	45.21***	47.37***
	(8.57)	(8.59)	(12.74)
Location (β_3)	Omitted	132.79***	132.36***
		(41.76)	(41.28)
Floor (β_4)	Omitted	−1.48	−3.41[n.s.]
		(34.74)	(31.64)
Week-fixed effects	Included	Included	Included
Store-fixed effects	Controlled		
R^2	0.24	0.35	0.35

***p < 0.01; **p < 0.05; *p < 0.10; n.s. = not significant; cluster-robust standard errors (SE) in parentheses; in random effects model store effects controlled for through random intercepts

Panel Data Analysis: A Non-technical Introduction for Marketing Researchers 439

While in applied research, θ is unlikely to be exactly 0 or 1, the rearrangement of θ in Eq. 15 helps to understand which determinants affect θ.

$$\theta = 1 - \sqrt{\frac{1}{1 + T \times \left(\frac{\sigma^2_{u_i}}{\sigma^2_{e_{it}}}\right)}} \tag{15}$$

First, with an increasing amount of measurement occasions T, the random effects estimator converges to the fixed effects estimator. In our example, we track sales volume over T = 82 weeks. The long observation period explains why the random effects estimator produces results close to those of the fixed effects estimator (Stata used θ =0.92, close to 1). The more measurement points we collect per cluster, the more the time effect dominates the store effect. Notably, the random effect estimator converges to the fixed effects estimator even if omitted time-constant variables correlate with the independent variables.

Second, the more the idiosyncratic error component dominates the store-specific component (i.e., $\frac{\sigma^2_{u_i}}{\sigma^2_{e_{it}}}$ becomes small), the less important the store-specific effect (u_i) becomes. As a consequence, the more negligible difference it makes to explicitly model the panel structure, the more results from the random effects estimator resemble those of the POLS estimator. In the extreme case in which the store-specific variance is zero ($\sigma^2_u = 0$), the POLS, random effects, and fixed effects estimators produce identical results. However, Wooldridge (2016, p. 443) notes that it is more common that $\frac{\sigma^2_u}{\sigma^2_e}$ is large and that θ will be closer to 1.

Investigators can rely on the Lagrange multiplier test to formally test the null hypothesis of the store-specific effect's variance being zero (H_0: $\sigma^2_u = 0$), equivalent to testing whether u_i is zero (Rabe-Hesketh and Skrondal 2012). The xttest0 command in Stata implements the Lagrange multiplier test after the regression command.

```
xtreg sales, re cluster(storeid)
xttest0
```

In our example, the test statistic clearly rejects the null hypothesis (χ^2(d.f. = 1) = 28,030.42; $p < 0.01$), and we conclude that the store-specific component is different from zero.

What Do Differences Between Pooled OLS, Fixed Effects, and Random Effects Estimators Imply?

A natural follow-up question is as follows: Which estimator should be selected? To answer this question, we have to recall why the three estimators produce divergent estimates. Although all estimators rely on the same dataset, they exploit variation in the data in different ways. The fixed effects estimator purely uses within variation, whereas the POLS and the random effects estimators rely on both sources of variation.

Using both sources of variation, POLS and random effects estimators can thus exploit more variation (i.e., more information) than the fixed effects estimator. As such, POLS and the random effects estimators are more efficient (i.e., producing smaller standard errors) than the fixed effects estimator, with the random effects estimator being the most efficient (Verbeek 2017). Efficiency is a desirable property. The estimated coefficients from each sample draw deviate from the "true" parameters in the population due to sampling error (also referred to as standard error). As we typically only have one sample to use in our analysis, we are interested in the estimator that produces the smallest standard errors, i.e., the most efficient estimator.

However, as a downside, benefitting from those efficiency gains requires us to impose one additional assumption on the POLS and the random effects estimators: All relevant time-constant variables are included in the model. In other words, we assume that the model fully explains the more information that we use in the estimation. This assumption would be met in our example if we could safely assume that $Location_i$ and $Floor_i$ are the only relevant time-constant variables.

However, we might have overlooked other critical time-constant variables. For instance, managers across stores may differ in their levels of experience and capabilities. More experienced and more capable managers might better anticipate future market developments and set more reasonable prices. Since our observation period covers less than 2 years (weeks 37–118), we can assume that those experiences and capabilities are constant over time. Since we did not measure manager ability, it becomes part of the store-specific error term (u_i). This is problematic if manager ability also impacts realized sales volumes, in which case our price-response-function would suffer from endogeneity in the form of an omitted variables bias.

Figure 17 demonstrates two ways in which omitted manager ability could affect our estimated price-response-functions. In this figure, hallow (Store 1) and black-shaded (Store 2) circles represent observed price and sales volume combinations for two stores. Gray-shaded squares are the corresponding store-specific mean values.

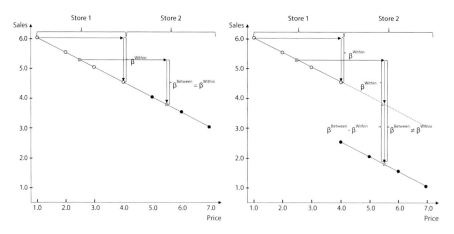

Fig. 17 Comparison of between and within effects

Based on these squares, we show the corresponding regression coefficients (β) predicted based on exploiting within (β^{Within}) versus between variation (β^{Between}). If using within versus between variation leads to the same results, then POLS and random effects estimators should be selected as these are the more efficient estimators. If leveraging within versus between variation leads to different results, then the fixed effect estimator should be chosen as estimators based on between variation (i.e., POLS and random effects) are likely to be biased and inconsistent.

Panel a visualizes a situation in which managers in Store 2 have set higher prices than managers in Store 1. However, the resulting sales volume in Store 2 is at the same level as it would be if Store 1 had set the same price (all observed price-sales-volume combinations lie on the same straight line). Consequently, we retrieve the same information when exploiting either the within or between variation. Thus, in Panel a, we obtain the same regression coefficient, irrespective of the type of variation we exploit ($\beta^{\text{Between}} = \beta^{\text{Within}}$). Such a situation is referred to as uncorrelated unobserved cluster-level heterogeneity, unobserved because we do not observe (or measure) manager ability, and uncorrelated because unobserved ability does not impact price (and realized sales volume). In such a situation, POLS and the random effects estimators are consistent and are more efficient than the fixed effects estimator.

Panel b in Fig. 17 demonstrates a situation in which managers in Store 2 have set higher prices than managers in Store 1, yet this time, the observed level of sales volume dropped below the level that Store 1 would have realized. The reason could be that the managers of Store 2 are less capable of inferring demand and hence price setting. These managers might also create less attractive store environments and make less appealing assortment decisions which lower sales volume. Such a situation is referred to as correlated unobserved cluster-level heterogeneity since, in this situation, the omitted capabilities correlate with the price (and the realized sales volume).

The fixed effects estimator is still consistent in such a situation because it only picks up the within variation. However, the between variation suffers from an omitted variable bias. In picking up the between variation, the random effects estimator assumes that the sales differences between the stores are driven by price only. However, sales are correlated with manager ability, which also impacts price setting (i.e., a situation of correlated unobserved cluster-level heterogeneity). In this case, the estimator is based on an invalid assumption. In other words, it uses more information (i.e., between variation in sales) but uses it under a wrong assumption (i.e., pretending that sales volume is only explained by price while sales volume is also explained by other factors that also correlate with price). As a consequence, the POLS and random effects estimators are not consistent anymore. In Panel b), the POLS and random effects estimators would overestimate the impact of price on sales volume ($|\beta^{\text{Between}}| > |\beta^{\text{Within}}|$).

In the following, we introduce a formal test that assists in choosing between the fixed effects and the random effects estimators. Note that we focus on the comparison between the fixed effects and the random effects estimators. If the random effects estimator is consistent, POLS is consistent, yet when choosing between

POLS and random effects, we recommend the more efficient random effects estimator. However, as we will see later (section "Summary of the Discussed Estimators and Their Underlying Assumptions"), the random effects estimator requires additional assumptions compared to POLS. For this reason, we also acknowledge that some econometricians suggest performing POLS despite potential efficiency gains from the random effects estimator (Angrist and Pischke 2008, p. 223).

Hausman Test: Selecting Between the Fixed Effects and the Random Effects Estimator

The trade-off we discussed in the last section raises the natural follow-up question: How do we know when we can rely on the more efficient random effects estimator? Stated differently, how do we know whether the random effects estimator is inconsistent due to omitted time-constant variables (e.g., managerial ability)?

This question requires a formal statistical test. To evaluate whether the random effects estimator is appropriate, we can rely on a Hausman test (Hausman 1978). The basic idea of the Hausman test is that the fixed effects and random effects estimators are consistent under the assumption that the investigator omitted no relevant time-constant variables from the price-response-function. Thus, their estimates should not differ significantly from each other. However, under the assumption that the investigator omitted relevant time-constant variables, only the fixed effects estimator is consistent and the random and fixed effects model estimates should differ significantly (Cameron and Trivedi 2005, p. 717). The Hausman test formally evaluates the null hypothesis of equal fixed effects and random effect estimates (H_0: $\widehat{\beta}^{FE} - \widehat{\beta}^{RE} = 0$). Investigators can rely on the random effects estimator unless the Hausman test returns a significant test statistic.

For an individual coefficient, the Hausman test can be calculated with the following test statistic (Eq. 16) that follows a χ^2 distribution with 1 degree-of-freedom.

$$\chi^2 = \left(\frac{\left(\widehat{\beta}^{FE} - \widehat{\beta}^{RE} \right) - 0}{SE_{\left(\widehat{\beta}^{FE} - \widehat{\beta}^{RE} \right)}} \right)^2 = \left(\frac{\left(\widehat{\beta}^{FE} - \widehat{\beta}^{RE} \right) - 0}{\sqrt{SE^2_{\widehat{\beta}^{FE}} - SE^2_{\widehat{\beta}^{RE}}}} \right)^2 \tag{16}$$

If we included $Price_{it}$ as the only independent variable (e.g., `xtreg sales price, re`) in our price-response-function, we would obtain the random effects ($\widehat{\beta}^{RE} = -1.82$; $SE_{\widehat{\beta}^{RE}} = 0.53$) and fixed effects ($\widehat{\beta}^{FE} = -1.84$; $SE_{\widehat{\beta}^{FE}} = 0.52$) estimates that result in a nonsignificant test statistic (χ^2(d.f. = 1) = 0.01; $n.s.$), favoring the random effects estimator. This result suggests that we have no reason to be concerned about correlated unobserved cluster-specific factors, such as manager ability.

For more common models that include more than one independent variable, we use a generalization of Eq. 16. Based on matrix algebra, we derive the general test statistic of the Hausman test (Eq. 17; Greene 2003, pp. 208–209) as:

$$\chi^2 = \left(\widehat{\beta}^{FE} - \widehat{\beta}^{RE}\right)' \times \left(\widehat{\psi}^{FE} - \widehat{\psi}^{RE}\right)^{-1} \times \left(\widehat{\beta}^{FE} - \widehat{\beta}^{RE}\right) \tag{17}$$

Thereby, $\widehat{\beta}^{FE}$ and $\widehat{\beta}^{RE}$ include all coefficient estimates of the fixed effects and the random effects model. The matrices $\widehat{\psi}^{FE}$ and $\widehat{\psi}^{RE}$ include the corresponding estimated variances and covariances of the estimates. The test-statistic follows an asymptotic χ^2 distribution with p degrees-of-freedom, with p being the number of coefficients tested.

The respective Stata syntax easily allows estimating the Hausman test statistic (hausman) after running the respective regressions. Note that we choose the sigmamore option to prevent Stata from considering the vector of week-fixed effects as tested coefficients and thereby inflate the reported degrees-of-freedom (degrees-of-freedom should be 2, for two tested coefficients, and not 83).

```
xtreg sales price promo i.week, fe
estimates store FE
xtreg sales price promo location floor i.week, re
estimates store RE
hausman FE RE, sigmamore
```

For our data, we obtain an insignificant test statistic (χ^2(d.f. $= 2) = 0.09$; $n.s.$) and conclude that we can trust the random effects results. This result is not surprising since fixed and random effects estimates hardly differ in our example.

Finally, we end our discussion highlighting three important aspects:

1. The standard Hausman test is not valid when the investigator uses cluster-robust standard errors. In section "Alternative Hausman Test," we will introduce a fully robust Hausman test.
2. Equation 16 serves to demonstrate when the Hausman test is not likely to yield a significant result. First, the test statistic tends to be insignificant when the numerator is small. In this case, the estimates for the $Price_{it}$ coefficients do not differ significantly between the fixed effects and random effects estimators; that is, it does not matter which estimator we use. Second, the Hausman test also becomes insignificant when the denominator is large. If the fixed effects estimator displays a large standard error (e.g., the variation of prices over time is low), the Hausman test likely yields an insignificant result. Third, measurement error can provoke an attenuation bias in the fixed effects estimator, which describes an estimate's bias converging to zero and underestimating the true value. As a result, fixed effects estimates could be smaller than the estimates from the random effects model, even if no relevant time-constant variables were omitted (sections "Summary of the Discussed Estimators and Their Underlying Assumptions" and "Addressing Measurement Error with Structural Equation Modeling Based on Panel Data"). Verbeek (2017, p. 395) notes in this regard:

Although the Hausman test is commonly used as a tool to decide between the random effects and the fixed effects estimators, it should be used with caution. Rejection should not automatically be interpreted as evidence that the fixed effects model is appropriate. Conversely, if the Hausman test does not reject it is not necessarily the case that the random-effects model should be preferred.

3. Even though the random effects estimator is biased and inconsistent if important time-constant variables are omitted, this bias is attenuated by the factor $(1-\theta)$ (see the quasi-demeaning in section "Random Effects Estimator"). As a consequence, the bias becomes increasingly less severe the closer θ approaches to 1.

Interpret and Present Results

As the last step, we economically interpret our findings. First, marketing managers are typically interested in the price-elasticity concept: the percentage change in sales volume when there is a 1% increase in price. Formally, the price-elasticity is defined as $\varepsilon = \frac{\partial Sales}{\partial Price} \times \frac{Price}{Sales}$, where *Price* is price and *Sales* is sales volume. Thereby, the first part is simply the derivative of our price-response-function $\left(\frac{\partial Sales}{\partial Price} = \beta_{\text{Price}}\right)$. For *Price* and *Sales,* we use their respective sample means. Thus, for our example, the price elasticity is -0.36 $\left(\varepsilon = -1.82 \times \frac{55.38}{280.19}\right)$, a relatively low value when compared to results from a meta-analysis reporting an average price elasticity of -2.62 (Bijmolt et al. 2005). Economically, this finding suggests that marketing managers can expect that a 1% price increase only lowers sales volume by 0.36%. Thus, consumers hardly react to price changes of the newly introduced headphone. Marketing managers, therefore, are likely tempted to increase the price of the headphone.

Based on our price-response-function, managers can also determine the revenue-optimal price. In our case, this price would be 79.95€ $\left(p* = \frac{\beta_{\text{Constant}}}{2\beta_{\text{Price}}} = \frac{291}{2 \times 1.82}\right)$, which would imply a price increase of 24.57€ compared to the current average price. Note that for this analysis, we used the intercept ($\beta_{\text{Constant}} = 291$) of a random effects model without week-fixed effects (`xtreg sales price promo location floor, re`); otherwise, the constant term would only be correct for the left-out week (Table 4: $\beta_{\text{Constant}} = 302.46$).

Additional Methods in Panel Data Analysis

Robust Inference

Obtaining correct standard errors of estimators is complicated for panel data since these data are likely to suffer from serial correlation, as mentioned earlier, as well as heteroskedasticity (Cameron and Trivedi 2005). Petersen (2009) compares the performance of different standard errors in panel datasets and, in general, recommends the use of cluster-robust standard errors for micropanel datasets (large n and small T). In the spirit of Petersen's finding, Cameron and Trivedi (2005, p. 725) also recommend to "base inference on [cluster-] robust standard errors that do not require specifying a model for the error correlation." Marketing researchers commonly follow this recommendation (e.g., Bayer et al. 2020, Borah and Tellis 2014; Warren and Sorescu 2017).

Cluster-robust standard errors are calculated based on the observed distribution of residuals from the model. They are robust in the sense that they consider the clustered (or nested) data structure of panel data and assume that observations are independent between clusters but not necessarily within clusters. In other words, cluster-robust standard errors consider each store as a cluster with observations over time, "and arbitrary correlation—serial correlation—and changing variances are allowed within each cluster" (Wooldridge 2016, p. 433). Cluster-robust standard errors are beneficial because they also control for potential heteroskedasticity, a second challenge in estimating standard errors in panel data. Wooldridge (2010, Chap. 10), Greene (2003, pp. 211–213), and Cameron and Trivedi (2005, Chap. 21.2.3) formally derive cluster-robust standard errors in the context of panel data.

We have already discussed the importance of cluster-robust standard errors for POLS (section "Pooled OLS Estimator: Ignoring the Panel Structure") since serial correlation likely leads to an underestimation of common OLS standard errors. We have also requested cluster-robust standard errors for the fixed effects and random effects models when estimating the price-response-functions. This choice seems reasonable as, in general, accounting for fixed effects or random effects only lowers serial correlation but does not eliminate it. Thus, our general recommendation is to rely on cluster-robust standard errors for panel data analysis.

Combining the Fixed Effects and Random Effects Estimators

Our prior discussion suggested that investigators need to choose between the fixed effects and random effects estimators. However, the literature also offers a combined approach that seeks to leverage the advantages and alleviates the disadvantages of the two estimators. Specifically, it allows including time-constant variables and provides an alternative Hausman test valid for cluster-robust standard errors. First, before we discuss the combined approach, we will introduce an additional estimator – the between effects estimator – which is necessary to understand the combined approach (section "Between Effects Estimator"). Second, we will outline the combined approach (section "Combined Approach"). Third, we will outline the alternative (fully robust) Hausman test that researchers can perform (section "Alternative Hausman Test"). Fourth, we will outline why the combined approach allows the consistent estimation of time-varying variables (section "Understanding How the Combined Approach Allows Consistent Estimation of Time-Varying Variables").

Between Effects Estimator

Since marketing research rarely applies the between effects estimator (cf. Nath and Mahajan 2008 for an exception, Table 2, Model 3), we will only shortly overview the estimator. The between effects estimator relies exclusively on the between variation in the data and discards all time-series information. As such, the estimator computes the variables' average values per cluster (e.g., mean price: $\frac{1}{T}\sum_{t=1}^{T}\text{Price}_{it} = \overline{\text{Price}_i}$; effective sample size $= n = 19$ stores) and runs an OLS regression on these averages (Eq. 18). Thus, the between effects estimator exploits the information that the fixed effects estimator does not use. In contrast, the fixed effects estimator only exploits variance over time (within store variation; section "What Do Differences Between Pooled OLS, Fixed Effects, and Random Effects Estimators Imply?"), for instance, in terms of price and sales volume as in our data example (e.g., $\text{Price}_{it} - \overline{\text{Price}_i}$; effective sample size $= n \times T = 19 \times 82 = 1{,}558$ observations).

$$\overline{\text{Sales}_i} = \beta_0 + \beta_1\overline{\text{Price}_i} + \beta_2\overline{\text{Promo}_i} + \beta_3\text{Location}_i + \beta_4\text{Floor}_i + u_i + \overline{e}_i \qquad (18)$$

Equation 18 displays the price-response-function that we will estimate with the between effects estimator. In Stata, investigators can request the between effects estimator with the be option after xtreg. Since we rely on balanced data, week-fixed effects are the same for all companies and are automatically omitted.

```
xtreg sales price promo location floor, be
```

Model 12 in Table 6 displays the results of the between effects estimator and compares those results to the fixed effects (Model 9), the random effects (Model 10), and the POLS estimators (Model 11). The results of the between effects estimator are not the focus of our discussion. Instead, we use them to extend our discussion from section "What Do Differences Between Pooled OLS, Fixed Effects, and Random Effects Estimators Imply?" and provide further insights into the random effects and POLS estimators.

We see that the random effects (Model 10: $\beta_1 = -1.82, p < 0.05$) and the POLS (Model 11: $\beta_1 = -1.48$, *n.s.*) estimates of price on sales volume lie in between the fixed effects (Model 9: $\beta_1 = -1.85, p < 0.10$) and between effects estimates (Model 12: $\beta_1 = -0.87$, *n.s.*). The random effects estimator is closer to the fixed estimator, and the POLS estimator is closer to the between estimator. This general pattern directly follows from our discussion in section "What Do Differences Between Pooled OLS, Fixed Effects, and Random Effects Estimators Imply?": The POLS and the random effects estimators represent weighted compromises between the fixed effects and the between effects estimators. The random effects estimator is the more efficient one.

In the following, we will demonstrate how we can leverage this idea on the between effects estimator to derive a combined model that allows consistent estimates of time-varying variables (as the fixed effects estimator does) and allows the inclusion of time-constant variables (as the random effects estimator does).

Panel Data Analysis: A Non-technical Introduction for Marketing Researchers

Table 6 Comparison of fixed effects, random effects, POLS, and between effects estimates of the price-response-function

	Fixed effects	Random effects	POLS	Between effects
	Model 9	Model 10	Model 11	Model 12
	B (SE)	B (SE)	B (SE)	B (SE)
Constant (β_0)	394.66***	302.46***	283.75***	208.34[n.s.]
	(56.13)	(43.78)	(89.09)	(245.05)
Price (β_1)	−1.85*	−1.82**	−1.48[n.s.]	-.87[n.s.]
	(1.00)	(0.89)	(1.57)	(3.18)
Promo (β_2)	45.21***	45.21***	47.37***	119.00[n.s.]
	(8.57)	(8.59)	(12.74)	(318.37)
Location (β_3)	Omitted	132.79***	132.36***	128.54[n.s.]
		(41.76)	(41.28)	(57.72)
Floor (β_4)	Omitted	−1.48[n.s.]	−3.41[n.s.]	−3.76[n.s.]
		(34.74)	(31.64)	(84.30)
Week-fixed effects	Included	Included	Included	Omitted
Store-fixed effects	Controlled			
R^2	0.24	0.35	0.35	0.26

***p < 0.01; **p < 0.05; *p < 0.10; n.s. = not significant; cluster-robust standard errors (SE) in parentheses; in randome effects model store effects controlled for through random intercepts

Combined Approach

The combined approach relies on the random effects estimator but adds the cluster-means of the time-varying variables (i.e., store means for $Price_{it}$ and $Promo_{it}$) to the model, just as the between effects estimator does. Eqs. 19 and 20 demonstrate two options of how investigators can employ a combined approach.

$$Sales_{it} = \beta_0 + \beta_1 Price_{it} + \beta_2 Promo_{it} + \beta_3 Location_i + \beta_4 Floor_i + \beta_5 \overline{Price}_i$$
$$+ \beta_6 \overline{Promo}_i + u_i + e_{it} \tag{19}$$

$$Sales_{it} = \beta_0 + \beta_1 \left(Price_{it} - \overline{Price}_i \right) + \beta_2 \left(Promo_{it} - \overline{Promo}_i \right)$$
$$+ \beta_3 Location_i + \beta_4 Floor_i + \beta_5 \overline{Price}_i + \beta_6 \overline{Promo}_i + u_i + e_{it} \tag{20}$$

Including cluster-means of time-varying variables is equivalent to demeaning the raw data. However, given that we apply this procedure only to time-varying variables, we can still retain the time-constant variables $Location_i$ and $Floor_i$. If we had an unbalanced panel dataset, we would also need to include the time average of any time-varying variable. We provide the corresponding Stata syntax in the do-file and report results in Table 7.

In Table 7, Model 14 relies on Eq. 19 and Model 15 on Eq. 20. In both models, the estimated price coefficients (Model 2: $\beta_1 = -1.85, p < 0.10$; Model 3: $\beta_1 = -1.85$, $p < 0.10$) are identical to the corresponding fixed effects estimate (Model 1: $\beta_1 = -1.85, p < 0.10$). The interpretation of the cluster-mean variables of $Price_{it}$

and $Promo_{it}$, however, differs between Model 14 and Model 15. The cluster-means in Model 15 (e.g., $\beta_5 = -0.87$, *n.s.*) directly replicate the between effect estimator (Model 16: $\beta_1 = -0.87$, *n.s.*). Model 14 tests the difference between the fixed effects and the between effects results (e.g., $\beta_5^{\text{Model 2}} = \widehat{\beta}_1^{\text{Model 4}} - \widehat{\beta}_1^{\text{Model 1}} = -0.87 + 1.85 = 0.98$).

Alternative Hausman Test

The interpretation of Model 14's cluster-means (Table 7) allows an alternative way to test the appropriateness of the random effects estimator. Both the between effects and the fixed effects estimators are consistent when the investigator did not omit any relevant time-constant independent variables. Significant cluster-means from Model 14 (i.e., significant differences between the fixed and between effect estimates) imply that relevant time-constant variables are omitted. Jointly testing both cluster-means from Model 14 via a Wald test (H_0: All cluster-mean values are zero; H_0: $\overline{Price_i} = \overline{Promo_i} = 0$), thus, represents an alternative to the Hausman test from section "Hausman Test: Selecting Between the Fixed Effects and the Random

Table 7 Combined approach estimates of the price-response-function

	Fixed effects	Combined approach (Eq. 19)	Combined approach (Eq. 20)	Between effects
	Model 13	*Model 14*	*Model 15*	*Model 16*
	B (SE)	B (SE)	B (SE)	B (SE)
Constant (β_0)	394.66***	232.82$^{\text{n.s.}}$	232.82$^{\text{n.s.}}$	208.34$^{\text{n.s.}}$
	(56.13)	(197.17)	(197.17)	(245.05)
Price (β_1)	−1.85*	−1.85*	−1.85*	-.87$^{\text{n.s.}}$
	(1.00)	(1.00)	(1.00)	(3.18)
Promo (β_2)	45.21***	45.21***	45.21***	119.00$^{\text{n.s.}}$
	(8.57)	(8.59)	(8.59)	(318.37)
Location (β_3)	Omitted	128.54***	128.54***	128.54$^{\text{n.s.}}$
		(44.85)	(44.85)	(57.72)
Floor (β_4)	Omitted	−3.76$^{\text{n.s.}}$	−3.76$^{\text{n.s.}}$	−3.76$^{\text{n.s.}}$
		(34.50)	(34.50)	(84.30)
Mean price (β_5)		.98$^{\text{n.s.}}$	-.87$^{\text{n.s.}}$	
		(2.76)	(2.65)	
Mean promo (β_6)		73.79$^{\text{n.s.}}$	119.00$^{\text{n.s.}}$	
		(280.36)	(280.56)	
Week-fixed effects	Included	Included	Included	
Store-fixed effects	Controlled			
R^2	0.24	0.35	0.35	0.26

***p < 0.01; **p < 0.05; *p < 0.10; n.s. = not significant; cluster-robust standard errors (SE) in parentheses

Panel Data Analysis: A Non-technical Introduction for Marketing Researchers   449

Effects Estimator." The test-statistic follows a χ^2 distribution with p degrees-of-freedom, with p being of the number of cluster-means tested. In line with our prior interpretation of the Hausman test, investigators rely on the random effects estimator (i.e., we can drop the cluster-means from Eq. 19) unless the Wald test returns a significant test statistic.

```
test price_mn promo_mn
```

Hausman (1978, p. 1263) and Hausman and Taylor (1981, p. 1382) showed that both tests are asymptotically equivalent (Wooldridge 2010, p. 332). Thus, to test whether omitted time-constant company variables correlate with the independent variables, we can either compare the fixed effects and random effects estimates (which we did in section "Hausman-Taylor Approach: Consistent Estimation of Time-Constant Effects in the Combined Approach") or the fixed effects with the between effects estimates which we do in this section. Wooldridge (2010) recommends the latter (regression-based) version using cluster-robust standard errors. For our example, we cannot reject the null hypothesis of equal between effects and fixed effects (χ^2(d.f. = 2) = 0.13; p = 0.94), replicating the substantive conclusion of section "Hausman Test: Selecting Between the Fixed Effects and the Random Effects Estimator." Thus, we can rely on the random effects estimator.

Understanding How the Combined Approach Allows Consistent Estimation of Time-Varying Variables

The random effects estimator's core challenge is the assumption that the independent variables are uncorrelated with the unobservable time-constant cluster effects. In the following, we build on Wooldridge (2016, pp. 445–446) to explain why including cluster-means leads to consistent estimates of time-varying independent variables. Let us assume that manager ability was indeed a driver of sales volume, yielding the specification in Eq. 21. For the sake of simplicity, we will assume that we do not need to account for promotion, premium location, and floor design.

$$\text{Sales}_{it} = \beta_0 + \beta_1 \text{Price}_{it} + \beta_2 \text{ Manager\_Ability}_i + u_i + e_{it} \qquad (21)$$

Since we have not collected data on manager ability, we would falsely specify the price-response-function, as in Eq. 22:

$$\text{Sales}_{it} = \beta_0' + \beta_1' \text{Price}_{it} + u_i' + e_{it}' \qquad (22)$$

The omitted manager ability becomes part of the store-specific error term $\left(u_i' = \beta_2 \times \text{Manager\_Ability} + u_i\right)$. Since manager ability is time-constant in our example, it can only correlate with any time-constant effect in $Price_{it}$ (i.e., Manager_Ability $= \delta_0 + \delta_1 \times \overline{\text{Price}}_i + \phi_i$). If the cluster-mean of price displays a nonzero relationship with manager ability ($\delta_1 \neq 0$), $Price_{it}$ becomes endogeneous, i.e., price correlates with the store-specific error term (corr(u_i; $Price_{it}$) $\neq 0$). However, by including the cluster-mean of $Price_{it}$, the correlation of $Price_{it}$ and the store-specific error term u_i disappears $(\beta_0'' = (\beta_0' + \beta_2 \times \delta_0), \beta_2'' = (\beta_2 \times \delta_1))$, and $u_i'' = (\beta_2 \times \phi_1 + u_i))$.

$$
\begin{aligned}
\text{Sales}_{it} &= \beta_0' + \beta_1'\text{Price}_{it} + \left(\beta_2\left(\delta_0 + \delta_1\overline{\text{Price}}_i + \phi_i\right) + u_i\right) + e_{it}' \\
&= \beta_0'' + \beta_1'\text{Price}_{it} + \beta_2''\overline{\text{Price}}_i + u_i'' + e_{it}'
\end{aligned}
\tag{23}
$$

The Price_{it} coefficient estimate (Eq. 23) will be the same as in the fixed effects model. The intuition behind this result is that while the final regression model (Eq. 23) still omits manager ability, it accounts for unobserved correlated ability effects by including the cluster-mean of price. The included cluster-mean of the price typically has no substantive interpretation but serves to control for an omitted variable bias.

Hausman-Taylor Approach: Consistent Estimation of Time-Constant Effects in the Combined Approach

The combined approach (section "Combining the Fixed Effects and Random Effects Estimators") allows including time-constant variables and allows that the Price_{it} and Promo_{it} variables correlate with the store-specific error component u_i (like the fixed effects estimator). However, the combined model still requires that time-constant variables (e.g., Location_i and Floor_i) and the cluster-specific error component u_i are uncorrelated. If this assumption does not hold, the estimates of time-constant variables are not consistent.

Hausman and Taylor (1981) propose a method for obtaining consistent estimates of time-constant variables. Essentially, the Hausman-Taylor approach treats variables differently, depending on whether they are time- constant, time- varying, and correlated or uncorrelated with the cluster-specific component u_i. Specifically, the approach discriminates between time-varying endogenous, time-varying exogenous variables, as well as time-constant endogenous and time-constant exogenous variables.

For instance, we may have reason to believe that omitted time-constant variables could affect Price_{it} and Floor_i (i.e., these are endogenous variables). Knowing that higher-level company executives and not the individual store managers are involved in promotion timing and location decisions, we are not worried that omitted time-constant store variables could impact Promo_{it} and Location_i (i.e., these are exogenous variables). Please note that these rationales are only exemplary and require more careful theoretical and empirical justification.

The Hausman-Taylor approach's idea is now to derive so-called panel-internal instrumental variables for the endogenous variables Price_{it} and Floor_i. Panel-internal instruments imply that we can use simple transformations of variables that are already included in the price-response-function as instruments. Thus, panel data offer the advantage that investigators do not have to collect external instrumental variables, which are often not readily available.

Panel Data Analysis: A Non-technical Introduction for Marketing Researchers 451

Specifically, in the Hausman-Taylor approach, demeaned variables (known from the fixed effects estimation) serve as instruments for time-varying endogenous variables (e.g., $(Price_{it} - \overline{Price_i})$ serves as an instrument for $Price_{it}$). Cluster means of time-varying variables serve as instruments for time-constant endogenous variables (e.g., $\overline{Pomo_i}$ serves as an instrument for $Floor_i$). We want to confirm that both instrumental variables are exogenous (corr($Price_{it} - \overline{Price_i}$, u_i) = 0 and corr($\overline{Pomo_i}$, u_i) = 0). Importantly, the Hausman-Taylor approach requires at least as many time-varying exogenous variables as time-constant endogenous variables for identification. If we had additional time-varying exogenous variables, we could evaluate the strength of the selected instrumental variables using the `xtoverid` command.

We can obtain estimates for the Hausman-Taylor approach with the `xthtaylor` command in which we specify the endogenous variables (both time-varying and time-constant) with the `endog` option; the other variables are considered exogenous. Model 19 in Table 8 displays the results. We see that the Hausman-Taylor approach results in different estimates for some of the variables, including $Floor_i$ and $Location_i$, compared to the combined approach.

```
xthtaylor sales price promo location floor w2-w82, endog(price
floor) vce(cluster storeid)
```

The Hausman-Taylor approach finds initial application in marketing research. For instance, Boulding and Christen (2003, 2008) employ this approach in the context of

Table 8 Hausman-Taylor approach estimates of the price-response-function

	Fixed effects	Combined approach (Eq. 19)	Hausman-Taylor
	Model 17	*Model 18*	*Model 19*
	B (SE)	B (SE)	B (SE)
Constant (β_0)	394.66***	232.82 [n.s.]	295.32[n.s.]
	(56.13)	(197.17)	(306.82)
Price (β_1)	-1.85*	-1.85*	-1.85*
	(1.00)	(1.00)	(1.00)
Promo (β_2)	45.21***	45.21***	45.21***
	(8.57)	(8.59)	(8.58)
Location (β_3)	Omitted	128.54***	141.43[n.s.]
		(44.85)	(338.88)
Floor (β_4)	Omitted	-3.76 [n.s.]	24.49[n.s.]
		(34.50)	(1008.37)
Mean price (β_5)		0.98 [n.s.]	
		(2.76)	
Mean promo (β_6)		73.79 [n.s.]	
		(280.36)	
Week-fixed effects	Included	Included	Included
Store-fixed effects	Controlled		
R^2	0.24	0.35	0.34

***p < 0.01; **p < 0.05; *p < 0.10; n.s. = not significant; cluster-robust standard errors (SE) in parentheses

new product introduction strategies. For further applications and their implied panel-internal instruments, please consult Butt et al. (2018), Germann et al. (2015), Ho-Dac et al. (2013), Rao et al. (2004), and Steenkamp and Geyskens (2014).

Summary of the Discussed Estimators and Their Underlying Assumptions

We have discussed a range of estimators to estimate the price-response-function. The estimators produce different results since they exploit the panel structure in different ways: The between effects estimator uses the between variation in the data while the fixed effects estimator exploits the within variation in the data. Finally, the POLS and the random effects estimators exploit both types of variation, with the latter being more efficient. Notably, if the random effects model's key assumption is met, all potential estimators are consistent, and the random effects estimator is the most efficient estimator. However, if the cluster-specific effects u_i are correlated with the independent variables, the random effects model's key assumption is not met. In this case, only the fixed effects estimator is consistent; the Hausman test (sections "Hausman Test: Selecting Between the Fixed Effects and the Random Effects Estimator" and "Alternative Hausman Test") formally tests this assumption.

Given the divergent results, investigators should understand the different assumptions underlying the estimators (called model-identifying assumptions) and justify their choices in applied research. We review those assumptions in Table 9, which we classify into A, B, and C assumptions according to Von Auer (2013). The A-assumptions address the functional specification of the regression model. B-assumptions focus on the error term structure, and C-assumptions relate to individual variables of the model. The following sources provide a more in-depth discussion of these assumptions: Kennedy (2008), Greene (2003), Skiera et al. (chapter ▶ "Regression Analysis"), Verbeek (2017), Wooldridge (2010, 2016).

Regarding the A-assumptions, all estimators require that the investigator includes all relevant variables in the model (assumption A1). We call such an approach a rich data model. For the POLS and the random effects estimator, this implies including all relevant time-constant and time-varying control variables. The fixed effects estimator only requires that the investigator includes all relevant time-varying control variables in the model.

Assumption A2 relates to the relationship between independent and dependent variables, which we assume is linear. Skiera et al. (chapter ▶ "Regression Analysis") discuss different data-transformations appropriate for linearizing curvilinear relationships, and those transformations equally apply to the panel data context.

Assumption A3 involves the effect of independent variables on the dependent variables to be constant. If this is not the case, investigators could include interaction terms to perform a moderated regression analysis (e.g., Vomberg et al. 2015). By including interaction terms, investigators effectively model slope heterogeneity. While the inclusion of interaction terms requires that researchers measure the

Panel Data Analysis: A Non-technical Introduction for Marketing Researchers

Table 9 Assumptions of the different estimators

	POLS estimator	Fixed effects estimator	Random effects estimator
A1	No relevant time-varying and time-constant variables are missing	No relevant time-varying variables are missing	No relevant time-varying and time-constant variables are missing
A2	True relationship between independent and dependent variable is linear		
A3	Estimated parameters are constant over all observations		
B1	The expected value of the idiosyncratic error term is zero: $E(\xi_{it}\vert \mathbf{X}, \mathbf{Z}) = 0$	The expected value of the idiosyncratic error term is zero: $E(e_{it}\vert \mathbf{X}) = 0$	The expected value of the idiosyncratic error term is zero: $E(e_{it}\vert \mathbf{X}, \mathbf{Z}, u_i) = 0$. The intercept captures the expected value of the unit-specific error term: $E(u_i\vert \mathbf{X}, \mathbf{Z}) = \beta_0$
B2	Homoskedasticity: $\mathrm{Var}(\xi_{it}\vert \mathbf{X}, \mathbf{Z}) = \sigma^2$	Homoskedasticity: $\mathrm{Var}(e_{it}\vert \mathbf{X}) = \sigma_e^2$	Homoskedasticity: $\mathrm{Var}(e_{it}\vert \mathbf{X}, \mathbf{Z}, u_i) = \sigma_e^2$ $\mathrm{Var}(u_i\vert \mathbf{X}, \mathbf{Z}) = \sigma_u^2$
B3	No serial correlation: $\mathrm{Cov}(\xi_{it}, \xi_{is}\mid \mathbf{X}, \mathbf{Z}) = 0$	No serial correlation: $\mathrm{Cov}(e_{it}, e_{is}\mid \mathbf{X}) = 0$	No serial correlation: $\mathrm{Cov}(e_{it}, e_{is}\mid \mathbf{X}, \mathbf{Z}, u_i) = 0$
B4	Error terms are normally distributed: $\xi_{it} \sim \mathrm{N}(0,\sigma^2)$	Idiosyncratic error terms are normally distributed: $e_{it} \sim \mathrm{N}(0, \sigma_e^2)$	Idiosyncratic and cluster-specific error terms are normally distributed: $e_{it} \sim \mathrm{N}(0, \sigma_e^2)$ $u_i \sim \mathrm{N}(\text{constant}, \sigma_u^2)$
C1	Error terms are uncorrelated with independent variables: $\mathrm{Cov}(\xi_{it}, \mathbf{X}) = 0$; $\mathrm{Cov}(\xi_{it}, \mathbf{Z}) = 0$	Idiosyncratic error terms are uncorrelated with independent variables: $\mathrm{Cov}(e_{it}, \mathbf{X} - \overline{\mathbf{X}}) = 0$	Idiosyncratic and cluster-specific error terms are uncorrelated with independent variables: $\mathrm{Cov}(e_{it}, \mathbf{X}) = 0$; $\mathrm{Cov}(e_{it}, \mathbf{Z}) = 0$ $\mathrm{Cov}(u_i, \mathbf{X}) = 0$; $\mathrm{Cov}(u_i, \mathbf{Z}) = 0$
C2	No multicollinearity		
C3	Measurement error-free		

Notes: Based on a stylized regression of $y_{it} = \beta_0 + \beta_1 x_{1it} + \ldots + \beta_k x_{kit} + \beta_j z_{ji} + \xi_{it}$ with cluster i in time period t. ξ_{it} is the composite error term, u_i is the cluster-specific error component, and e_{it} is the idiosyncratic error term. x_{it} denotes time-varying variables, and z_i indicates time-constant variables. X represents the vector of time-varying variables x_{it}, and Z denotes the vector of time-constant variables z_i

respective moderating variables, in section "Random Slope Models: A Multilevel Model Approach to Panel Data," we will show that panel data methods also model slope heterogeneity without measured moderating variables.

Regarding the B-assumptions, panel data is especially prone to violate assumptions about the error term distribution given the clusters' dependency. In this regard, we emphasized the need to rely on cluster-robust standard errors if the investigator decides to employ POLS (section "Pooled OLS Estimator: Ignoring the Panel Structure"). We also recommended their usage for the fixed effects and random effects estimators (section "Robust Inference"), as they help account for serial correlation (violation of assumption B3) and heteroskedasticity (violation of assumption B2).

Regarding assumption C1, the POLS estimator assumes that the composite error term does not correlate with the independent variables (exogeneity). The fixed effects estimator requires that the idiosyncratic error term is uncorrelated with the independent variables. Note that because the cluster-specific effects omit all time-constant independent variables from the model, the exogeneity assumption applies to time-varying independent variables only. The exogeneity assumption is also made for the idiosyncratic error term for the random effects estimator, which is assumed to be uncorrelated with the independent variables. Assumption C2 requires that all variables display unique variation and, hence, are not perfectly correlated (no perfect multicollinearity). For the POLS and the random effects estimators, this is fulfilled if variables have unique variance over time, between clusters, or both. For the fixed effects estimator, this assumption requires that variables display unique variation over time. Standard errors of variables with little variation over time will become large and reduce statistical power. This assumption also explains why investigators cannot add time-constant variables in the fixed effects approach because they perfectly correlate with the cluster-specific effect.

In this regard, we emphasize three further comments:

1. Investigators should not decide between the fixed effects and the random effects approach based on whether they are interested in the effect of time-constant variables. If the effect of time-constant variables is of interest to investigators, they may employ the combined approach (section "Combining the Fixed Effects and Random Effects Estimators") or the Hausman-Taylor approach (section "Hausman-Taylor Approach: Consistent Estimation of Time-Constant Effects in the Combined Approach").
2. The fixed effects estimator's inefficiency, which results from little within variation, might favor random effects estimation. For instance, Wolters et al. (2020) justify a random effects over a fixed effects specification by noting a lack of sufficient variation in their focal variable over time. Warren and Sorescu (2017) suggest a random effects approach since their unbalanced panel dataset contains several clusters with only one observation.
3. Moreover, we want to acknowledge recent calls for a more balanced view between bias and efficiency when deciding between the fixed effects and random effects estimator. For instance, Kummer and Schulte (2019) mention little within variation as a limitation to their fixed effects approach. Additionally, Andreß et al. (2013, p. 173) state the following:

> *Inefficiency of the [fixed effects] estimator is a particular problem if the within-unit variance is low and variables hardly change over time. Since you are never in the lucky situation of statistical theory, which assumes repeated sampling, your single sample may provide you with estimates quite different from the true population parameters. In that case, the fact that fixed effects are unbiased (i.e., correct on average) is no comfort for you. Hence, more research is needed that provides a more balanced view of both estimators that takes into account both unbiasedness and efficiency.*

Panel Data Analysis: A Non-technical Introduction for Marketing Researchers 455

Finally, all estimators require that the variables are measured without error (assumption C3) as measurement error represents another form of endogeneity that can lead to violation of assumption C1 (chapter ▶ "Crafting Survey Research: A Systematic Process for Conducting Survey Research" by Vomberg and Klarmann). In section "Addressing Measurement Error with Structural Equation Modeling Based on Panel Data," we will demonstrate how investigators can leverage panel data to reduce measurement error concerns. Notably, due to the within-transformation, the fixed effects estimator is particularly susceptible to attenuation bias from measurement error (Angrist and Pischke 2008; Griliches and Hausman 1986; Wooldridge 2016, p. 440).

Modeling a Price-Response-Function in Differences

The discussion so far has focused on modeling the price-response-function in levels. For the sake of completeness, we briefly discuss an additional estimator for the analysis of panel data: the first difference estimator. The first difference estimator takes the first difference of all variables (see Eq. 24) and then performs an OLS regression on the transformed variables (for a more technical discussion, please refer to Cameron and Trivedi 2005, pp. 729–731).

Equation 24 reveals that unobserved time-constant variables disappear after taking the first differences since they do not change over time. Like the fixed effects estimator, the first difference estimator thereby controls for an omitted variable bias stemming from unobserved time-constant variables. As a consequence, the first difference estimator does not allow to include time-constant variables.

Investigators can manually create the first differences of the variables. Alternatively, Stata automatically creates first differences when placing a difference operator ($D.$) in front of the respective variable. In line with our prior discussion, we also recommend that researchers should rely on cluster-robust standard errors for first difference models.

$$(\text{Sales}_{it} - \text{Sales}_{it-1}) = (\beta_0 - \beta_0) + \beta_1(\text{Price}_{it} - \text{Price}_{it-1}) + \beta_2(\text{Promo}_{it} - \text{Promo}_{it-1})$$
$$+ \beta_3(\text{Location}_i - \text{Location}_i) + \beta_4(\text{Floor}_i - \text{Floor}_i) + (u_i - u_i)$$
$$+ (e_{it} - \overline{e}_{it-1}) = \beta_1 \Delta\text{Price}_{it} + \beta_2 \Delta\text{Promo}_{it} + \Delta e_{it}$$

$$(24)$$

```
reg D.sales D.price D.promo i.week, cluster(storeid)
```

Table 10 demonstrates the results of the analysis. Since the first difference estimator is obtained via OLS, investigators can evaluate model fit with standard measures such as the R^2 statistic and use t-tests to determine the significance of individual regression coefficients. We find a negative, though not significant,

Table 10 First difference estimates of the price-response-function

	First difference		Fixed effects	
	Model 20		Model 21	
	B	SE	B	SE
Constant (β_0)	14.79 n.s.	(20.66)	394.66***	(56.13)
Price (β_1)	−1.66 n.s.	(1.05)	−1.85*	(1.00)
Promo (β_2)	57.76***	(10.67)	45.21***	(8.57)
Location (β_3)	Omitted		Omitted	
Floor (β_4)	Omitted		Omitted	
Week-fixed effects	Included		Included	
Store-fixed effects	Controlled		Controlled	
R^2	0.23		0.24	

***p < 0.01; **p < 0.05; *p < 0.10; n.s. = not significant; cluster-robust standard errors (SE) in parentheses

impact of price on sales volume (Model 20: $\beta_1 = -1.66$, *n.s.*). Comparing the first difference estimates with the fixed effects estimates reveals that, despite their similarity in removing time-constant cluster-specific effects, coefficient estimates differ. Only for the two time periods case (e.g., 2 weeks), first-differencing and the within transformation will result in identical results.

Since both estimators are unbiased and consistent, investigators can choose freely between the two estimators. Wooldridge (2016, p. 439) and Cameron and Trivedi (2005, p. 705) though note that under certain conditions (i.e., no serial correlation and a homoskedastic error term structure), the fixed effects estimator is more efficient than the first difference estimator. Relatedly, a drawback of the first difference estimator becomes apparent the more unbalanced the panel data is. In the case of balanced panels, only the first measurement occasion is dropped since investigators cannot calculate the first difference. However, in the case of unbalanced panel data – which represents the typical case in applied research – first differences can tremendously reduce the sample size. Picking up Verbeek's (2017) critique, the investigator might want to carefully inspect the model specification when the fixed effects and first difference estimator yield substantially different results. Such differences likely point to misspecification issues that might violate the fixed effects estimator's strict exogeneity assumption.

Finally, we want to point to a particular application area of the first difference estimator, common in the marketing literature (e.g., Gill et al. 2017; Manchanda et al. 2015): the difference-in-differences estimator. The difference-in-differences approach mimics an experimental design while using observational data. Its typical set up includes a binary independent variable that discriminates between a treatment and control group (Cameron and Trivedi 2005, Chap. 22; Verbeek 2017, p. 390; Wooldridge 2016, p. 410). Artz and Doering (chapter ▶ "Exploiting Data from Field Experiments") discuss its application in more detail in this Handbook.

Panel Data Analysis: A Non-technical Introduction for Marketing Researchers 457

Advanced Topics in Panel Data Analysis

Dynamic Panel Data Estimation

Dynamic Panel Models Without Cluster-Specific Effects

We now consider dynamic panel models in which investigators include the lagged dependent variable as a time-varying variable. These models are also called lagged-response models, autoregressive models, or Markov models, and Eq. 25 shows their more general form.

$$y_{it} = \beta_0 + \lambda_1 y_{i,t-1} + \ldots + \lambda_l y_{i,t-l} + \beta_1 x_{1it} + \ldots + \beta_k x_{kit} + \xi_{it} \tag{25}$$

The most popular dynamic model is the autoregressive lag-1 (AR1) model, where the current value of the dependent variable (y_{it}) is regressed on its one-period lagged value ($y_{i,t-1}$). Analogously, in an autoregressive lag-2 AR(2) model, the dependent variable is lagged by two periods ($y_{i,t-2}$). Srinivasan (chapter ▶ "Modeling Marketing Dynamics Using Vector Autoregressive (VAR) Models") and Wang and Yildrim (chapter ▶ "Applied Time-Series Analysis in Marketing") offer an in-depth discussion of AR processes in this Handbook, also covering related topics, including vector autoregressive (VAR) models. Note that we assume the independent variables in all AR model variants to be uncorrelated with the error term and the error term to be serially uncorrelated (see Table 9).

Dynamic panel models can be helpful in various situations. First, by including the lagged dependent variable as an independent variable, dynamic panel models help reduce an omitted variable bias. This notion extends our earlier discussion which has focused on accounting for time-constant cluster-specific effects. Including the lagged dependent variable as a time-varying control relaxes the assumption of omitted variables being only time constant and accounts for time-varying effects. In a classical study of explaining market share, Jacobson and Aaker (1985), for instance, use such an approach to model omitted factors such as customer loyalty and distribution systems, which might have influenced market share in the prior periods as well as in the current period. Since no fixed or random effects are included in such a model, it can be conveniently estimated by OLS.

Second, dynamic models are employed when the effect of the lagged dependent variable is itself of scientific interest. For instance, in a study of synergy effects in multimedia communications, Naik and Raman (2003) examine the degree of carry-over in sales levels.

Dynamic panel models have received quite some attention in the marketing literature. Germann et al. (2015), for instance, offer an extensive study on the presence of a CMO on firm performance using a lagged dependent variable in their model. Homburg et al. (2020) show that a dynamic approach is even feasible when only the dependent variable is constructed as a panel variable. In their study, the authors investigate the impact of multichannel sales system design (obtained from a cross-sectional survey) on firm performance (derived from secondary panel performance data). The authors include a lagged measurement of firm performance as an independent variable to control for variables that equally impacted performance in different time periods.

Despite its advantages, adopting a dynamic panel structure comes with certain limitations that we now briefly review (see Rabe-Hesketh and Skrondal 2012 for a detailed discussion). First, estimating a dynamic panel model is only feasible when occasions are equally spaced in time. For instance, modeling a dynamic panel structure for data collected over several survey waves with different time intervals would not be a sensible task. It is quite a stretch to assume that the lagged dependent variable has the same effect on the current level of the dependent variable regardless of the time interval between them.

Second, the sample size is considerably reduced when a lagged dependent variable is included because lags are missing for each cluster's first observation (section "Modeling a Price-Response-Function in Differences"). In cases of gaps in the data, the problem of missingness becomes exacerbated because the missing measurement itself is discarded as well as the subsequent observation with its missing lagged measurement.

Third, while not necessarily a limitation, it is worth highlighting that the interpretation of the model's coefficients changes when including the lagged dependent variable. The coefficients now describe the independent variable's effect on the difference between the current and lagged dependent variable. Rearranging the AR (1) dynamic panel model, Eq. 26 shows this point clearly. If λ was equal to 1, the equation would model the change in the dependent variable instead of its level.

$$y_{it} - \lambda y_{i,t-1} = \beta_0 + \beta_1 x_{1it} + \ldots + \beta_k x_{kit} + \beta_j z_{ji} + \xi_{it} \qquad (26)$$

Finally, when including the time-varying lagged dependent variable as a control to account for omitted variables, such a model makes the strong assumption that all within dependence is due to the lagged dependent variable. In other words, the investigator assumes that the omitted variables are fully accounted for by the lagged dependent variable, there are no cluster-specific effects remaining, and there is no serial correlation present in the error term. This is an admittedly strong assumption, which we can test for, and which we relax in the following section in discussing dynamic panel models that also include cluster-specific effects.

Dynamic Panel Models With Cluster-Specific Effects

We now provide a model that accounts for unobserved cluster-level heterogeneity and adds the lagged dependent variable as an independent variable. A useful feature of such a model is that it can distinguish between two competing explanations of within dependence: unobserved cluster-level heterogeneity (represented by the time-constant cluster effects) and state dependence (represented by the lagged dependent variable). For instance, referring to our data example, the within-store dependence of headphone sales might result from some stores employing very capable managers. Capabilities are likely to be constant over the observation period, in which case this type of dependence represents unobserved cluster heterogeneity. Within-store dependence might also result from high current sales attracting high future sales

Panel Data Analysis: A Non-technical Introduction for Marketing Researchers

through improved financial resources to attract new sales, a case of true state dependence. The corresponding model takes the following form:

$$
\begin{aligned}
\text{Sales}_{it} = {} & \beta_0 + \lambda \text{Sales}_{i,t-1} + \beta_1 \text{Price}_{it} + \beta_2 \text{Promo}_{it} + \beta_3 \text{Location}_i + \beta_4 \text{Floor}_i \\
& + \delta \textbf{WEEK} + u_i + e_{it} \qquad (27)
\end{aligned}
$$

It would be tempting to fit the model using the estimation techniques we introduced in the earlier sections. Unfortunately, the conditions for consistent estimation of Eq. 27 are much more demanding than those required for estimations relying on cluster-specific effects or lagged dependent variables alone (Angrist and Pischke 2008).

First, estimating Eq. 27 with the random effects estimator would lead to inconsistent estimates of the coefficients because the lagged dependent variable is per definition correlated with the cluster-specific effect u_i in the error term. As a result, we would run into a problem of correlated unobserved cluster-level heterogeneity and conclude that the random effects estimator is not feasible when estimating dynamic panel models.

Second, estimating Eq. 27 using the fixed effects estimator does not solve this problem either. The within transformation mechanically correlates the within-transformed lagged dependent variable $(Sales_{i,t-1} - \overline{Sales_i})$ with the within-transformed error term $(\varepsilon_{i,t-1} - \overline{\varepsilon_i})$ since $Sales_{i,\,t-1}$ is correlated with $\varepsilon_{i,\,t-1}$ and hence with $\overline{\varepsilon_i}$. Thus, a fixed effects approach is also not feasible when estimating dynamic panel models.

Finally, estimating Eq. 27 using a first difference approach will also produce inconsistent results, as Eq. 28 shows.

$$
\begin{aligned}
\left(\text{Sales}_{it} - \text{Sales}_{i,t-1}\right) = {} & \lambda(\text{Sales}_{i,t-1} - \text{Sales}_{i,t-2}) + \beta_1 \left(\text{Price}_{1it} - \text{Price}_{1i,t-1}\right) \\
& + \beta_2 \left(\text{Promo}_{it} - \text{Promo}_{i,t-1}\right) + (u_i - u_i) + \left(e_{it} - e_{i,t-1}\right)
\end{aligned}
$$

$$(28)$$

The lagged difference of the dependent variable correlates with the difference of the error term $(\varepsilon_{i,\,t} - \varepsilon_{i,\,t-1})$ because $Sales_{i,\,t-1}$ is related to its error term $\varepsilon_{i,\,t-1}$. As such, the first difference approach also violates the assumption of exogeneity (section "Summary of the Discussed Estimators and Their Underlying Assumptions").

At the same time, note that $\varepsilon_{i,\,t} - \varepsilon_{i,\,t-1}$ is not correlated with lagged differences of the dependent variable beyond the first lag $(Sales_{i,\,t-1})$, opening up the possibility of instrumenting the lagged difference of the dependent variable with higher lags. Under the assumption that the error term is serially uncorrelated, Anderson and Hsiao (1981, 1982) introduced such a panel-internal instrumental-variable approach. They suggest that investigators can either use the second lag of the dependent variable $(y_{i,t-2})$ or the lag of the first difference $(y_{i,t-3})$ as instrumental variables for the differenced dependent variable $(y_{i,t-1} - y_{i,t-2})$. As with all instrumental variable estimation, such an approach assumes that the instrumental variables fulfill the relevance and validity assumptions (see chapter ▶ "Dealing with Endogeneity: A Nontechnical Guide for Marketing Researchers" by Ebbes et al. in this Handbook).

As an application in marketing, Mizik and Jacobson (2008) rely on the Anderson-Hsiao estimator to model changes in firm profitability. Investigators can obtain a version of this estimator via the `xtivreg` command in Stata.

More efficient IV estimators use additional lags of the dependent variable as instruments, an idea Arellano and Bond (1991) and Blundell and Bond (1998) developed in their generalized method of moments estimator. The Arellano-Bond approach identifies how many lags of the dependent variable are valid instruments and includes all of these lags as instruments (together with the first differences of the model's exogenous variables). Wies et al. (2019), for instance, employ the Arellano-Bond approach when modeling the time series of advertising expenses in studying how firms manipulate their advertising efforts in response to receiving shareholder complaints. The Arellano-Bond approach can be implemented in Stata using the `xtabond, twostep` command.

The Blundell-Bond approach considers Eqs. 27 and 28 as a system of equations. It then uses the lagged differences of the dependent variable as instruments for the levels equation (Eq. 27) *and* the lagged levels of the dependent variable as instruments for the differences equation (Eq. 28). The Blundell-Bond estimator has improved precision properties, as reflected in lower standard errors. It is implemented in Stata using the `xtdpdsys` approach or the user-written `xtabond2` command (available from SSC `findit xtabond2`; Roodman 2009), and the syntax structure follows `xtabond`.

Stata's `xtabond` command family provides a set of practical postestimation specification tests to validate the two critical assumptions underlying a panel-internal instrumental variable approach. Specifically, the `estat sargan` command offers a test of overidentifying restrictions, which is useful in confirming the assumption of instrument validity. The `estat abond` command tests whether the error is serially uncorrelated, another desired property we need to confirm when using either the Arellano-Bond or Blundell-Bond estimator. If the test rejects the latter assumption, we can resort to Stata's `xtdpd` command. This command fits a dynamic panel model based on the Arellano-Bond or Blundell-Bond estimator at the cost of a more complicated syntax but, importantly, allows for low-order autocorrelation in the error term. For a more detailed exposition of handling dynamic panel models in Stata, we recommend Cameron and Trivedi (2005, 2009).

We close with a final recommendation on assessing the usefulness of our selected dynamic panel model when including cluster-specific effects. Instead of estimating variants of the instrumental-variable model (this section), it might be an insightful task to estimate a separate fixed effects (section "Fixed Effects Estimator") and random effects model (section "Random Effects Estimator") plus a separate lagged dependent variable model (section "Dynamic Panel Models Without Cluster-Specific Effects"). If the lagged dependent variable model is correct, but one estimates a fixed effects model, the estimated effect will be too large. If a fixed effects model is correct, but one estimates a lagged dependent variable model, the estimated effect will be too small. Therefore, one can think of the fixed effects and

Panel Data Analysis: A Non-technical Introduction for Marketing Researchers

the lagged dependent variable models as bounding the true causal effect of interest (Angrist and Pischke 2008, p. 246).

Random Slope Models: A Multilevel Model Approach to Panel Data

In section "Dependent Variable: Between and Within Variance," we introduced the focal challenge of nonindependent sales observations in panel data and illustrated this point along with a nested structure figure (Fig. 7). As visible in this figure, panel data can be considered a multilevel model (please refer to chapter ▶ "Multilevel Modeling" by Haumann et al. in this Handbook for a general introduction to multilevel modeling).

In multilevel terminology, the panel dataset represents a two-level data structure, i.e., sales volume measured over time (Level 1) nested in stores (Level 2). In contrast to typical multilevel data, such as sales reps (Level 1) nested in sales managers (Level 2), panel data have an inherent order at the lowest level.

Knowledge of multilevel models allows expanding the discussion on the random effects estimator. Specifically, multilevel models can consider random cluster-specific intercepts as well as random cluster-specific slope coefficients. While prior models (sections "Analyze Panel Data Models" and "Additional Methods in Panel Data Analysis") assumed that all regression coefficients (besides the cluster-specific intercepts u_i) are the same across stores, in the following, we will allow divergent slope coefficients across clusters (Hox 2010; Raudenbush and Bryk 2002).

For instance, we can extend the random effects model and allow $Price_{it}$ to vary between stores. We indicate this additional variability by including the subscript i to the focal regression coefficient (Eq. 29). Eqs. 30 and 31 formally describe the random intercept and random slope, respectively. Eq. 32 shows that we chose not to include a random slope for $Promo_{it}$.

$$Sales_{it} = \beta_{0i} + \beta_{1i}Price_{it} + \beta_{2i}Promo_{it} + \delta\mathbf{WEEK} + e_{it} \tag{29}$$

$$\beta_{0i} = \gamma_{00} + \gamma_{01}Location_i + \gamma_{02}Floor_i + u_{0i} \tag{30}$$

$$\beta_{1i} = \gamma_{10} + u_{1i} \tag{31}$$

$$\beta_{2i} = \gamma_{20} \tag{32}$$

Substituting Eqs. 30, 31, and 32 into Eq. 29 leads to the complete multilevel regression model (Eq. 33). Equation 33 resembles the random effects model (section "Random Effects Estimator") and includes the random slope coefficient of the price ($u_{1i} \times Price_{it}$).

$$Sales_{it} = (\gamma_{00} + \gamma_1 Location_i + \gamma_2 Floor_i + u_{0i}) + (\gamma_{10} + u_{1i})Price_{it} + \gamma_{20}Promo_{it}$$
$$+\delta\mathbf{WEEK} + e_{it} = \gamma_{00} + \gamma_{10}Price_{it} + \gamma_{20}Promo_{it} + \gamma_{01}Location_i$$
$$+\gamma_{02}Floor_i + \delta\mathbf{WEEK} + u_{0i} + u_{1i} \times Price_{it} + e_{it}$$

$$\tag{33}$$

Including random slopes represents an extension of the random effects model and requires a different estimator. While FGLS (`xtreg, re`) is typically used to estimate random effects models, multilevel models require a maximum likelihood estimator.

Stata users need to employ the `xtmixed` command, whose syntax slightly differs from the `xtreg` command, to estimate random slope models. Rabe-Hesketh and Skrondal (2012) offer an in-depth discussion on how to build multilevel models in Stata. As before, we recommend that investigators rely on robust standard errors (`vce(robust)` option).

```
xtmixed sales price promo location floor i.week || storeid:
price, vce(robust)
```

Marketing researchers commonly perform random slope applications of multilevel modeling on panel data. For instance, Anderson et al. (2004) rely on panel data in their multilevel model on customer satisfaction's impact on firm performance. Overall, the authors observe a positive effect of customer satisfaction. However, they also find that the effect of customer satisfaction on firm performance significantly varies between companies and industries. Gruca and Rego (2005), Sorescu and Spanjol (2008), Vomberg et al. (2015), and Wlömert and Papies (2019) similarly employ multilevel modeling to panel data to obtain deeper insights on how effects vary across clusters.

Addressing Measurement Error with Structural Equation Modeling Based on Panel Data

Our discussion so far has focused on the benefits of panel data to address endogeneity concerns that may arise from an omitted variable bias. In this section, we discuss the implications of another essential source of endogeneity: measurement error, that is, "situations where one or more regressors cannot be measured exactly and are observed with an error" (chapter ▶ "Dealing with Endogeneity: A Nontechnical Guide for Marketing Researchers" by Ebbes et al.).

All estimators discussed in the previous sections rely on the assumption that the variables are measured without error (section "Summary of the Discussed Estimators and Their Underlying Assumptions"). However, this assumption might be violated already in the context of rather objectively verifiable information such as reported price or sales volume. Measurement error may arise due to transmission errors into databases. The measurement error problem becomes even more concerning for more abstract constructs frequently investigated in marketing research (e.g., consumers' brand perceptions or customer satisfaction). In this regard, measurement theory suggests that observed variables (e.g., observed customer satisfaction scores) represent the net result of a true score and some random error (chapter ▶ "Crafting Survey Research: A Systematic Process for Conducting Survey Research" by Vomberg and Klarmann).

Figure 18 illustrates the measurement error problem (Andreß et al. 2013). Please assume that we measured customer satisfaction scores for two consecutive years (t and $t + 1$). Following standard conventions in the literature (e.g., chapter ▶ "Structural Equation Modeling"), we present the observed values of customer satisfaction in rectangular boxes. As predicted by measurement theory, those values are influenced by the true level of customer satisfaction ("Customer Satisfaction*"), which is specified as circled in Fig. 18 and by a measurement error (ε_t).

The amount of measurement error will impact the estimated relationship between customer satisfaction over time, which we could model with dynamic panel data models (section "Dynamic Panel Data Estimation"). For instance, true state dependence (serial correlation of customer satisfaction over time) might be r = 0.82 (corr (CustomerSatisfaction*$_t$; CustomerSatisfaction*$_{t+1}$)). However, we measured customer satisfaction with error so that the true customer satisfaction level is not translated one-to-one into an observable customer satisfaction level. Statistically speaking, customer satisfaction has a factor loading of $\lambda = 0.70$ (if customer satisfaction was measured without error, the factor loading would be $\lambda = 1.00$). As a consequence, the observed correlation between customer satisfaction becomes smaller (corr(CS$_t$; CS$_{t+1}$) = 0.70 × 0.82 × 0.70 = 0.40) and true state dependence is underestimated.

In the context of cross-sectional data, problems of measurement error only concern the independent variables. The error term captures the measurement error of the dependent variable. However, in the context of panel data, measurement error concerns the dependent variable, too. For instance, as illustrated previously, measurement error will bias state dependence estimates toward zero in dynamic panel data models (section "Dynamic Panel Data Estimation"). Additionally, measurement error does not only impact models in which lagged dependent variables are of substantive interest. Demeaning (fixed effects estimator), quasi-demeaning (random effects estimator), or first-difference transformations are equally affected by measurement error. The fixed effects estimator is particularly susceptible to an

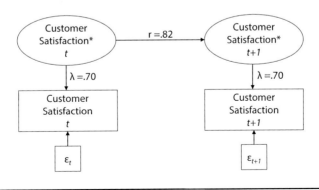

Fig. 18 Measurement error in dynamic panel models illustrated

attenuation bias from measurement error (Angrist and Pischke 2008; Griliches and Hausman 1986; Wooldridge 2016, p. 440).

Structural equation modeling represents a way to directly model measurement error (Baumgartner and Weijters present an introduction to ▶ "Structural Equation Modeling" chapter in this Handbook). In cross-sectional analyses, researchers use different indicators for the same construct to estimate a construct's reliability and to directly model measurement error. In the panel data context, researchers can use the same indicators from different time periods to capture the underlying construct. For instance, the investigator may use customer satisfaction scores of 3 years (e.g., customer satisfaction measured in t = 2019, 2020, and 2021) to estimate a latent customer satisfaction construct. This approach is identical to an evaluation of test-retest reliability and offers the advantage of directly accounting for measurement error. However, the downside of this approach is that fewer possibilities exist to estimate the model (e.g., employing fixed effects estimation is not feasible). Investigators can implement a structural equation model via Stata's sem and gsem commands.

Luo and Bhattacharya (2006) offer an application example in the marketing context. The authors rely on panel data obtained from Fortune's Most Admired Companies and use repeated corporate social responsibility measurements to capture the underlying latent corporate social responsibility construct. Cho and Pucik (2005) apply a similar approach when modeling how firm innovativeness and product quality relate to market value.

Conclusion

This chapter sought to provide a gentle nontechnical introduction to panel data analysis for marketing researchers. At the core of panel data analysis is the challenge of how best to account for the dependency of observations within and across clusters. We discussed the POLS estimator's limitations and reviewed the two most popular panel estimators that explicitly model the panel structure: the fixed effects and random effects estimators. For completeness, we also discussed the between effects estimator and first difference estimator, as well as the combined approach and the Hausman-Taylor approach. Using a real-life example, we applied these estimators in the context of a price-response-function for headphone sales. We conducted the empirical analysis in Stata, a very user-friendly statistical software package for analyzing panel data. Despite using the same dataset to estimate the price-response-functions, we find results differ considerably depending on the selected estimator. These divergent results demonstrate the need to thoroughly understand the different model-identifying assumptions, benefits, and limitations of each estimator. As such, we hope our chapter contributes to turning readers into cognizant "regression engineers" (Germann et al. 2015) and offers researchers the necessary skill set to conduct meaningful analyses. Panel data provide exciting opportunities to investigate new research questions, and we hope that readers find this introduction helpful in developing their models.

Cross-References

▶ Applied Time-Series Analysis in Marketing
▶ Assessing the Financial Impact of Brand Equity with Short Time-Series Data
▶ Choice-Based Conjoint Analysis
▶ Dealing with Endogeneity: A Nontechnical Guide for Marketing Researchers
▶ Exploiting Data from Field Experiments
▶ Modeling Marketing Dynamics Using Vector Autoregressive (VAR) Models
▶ Multilevel Modeling
▶ Regression Analysis
▶ Structural Equation Modeling
▶ Willingness to Pay

References

Anderson, T. W., & Hsiao, C. (1981). Estimation of dynamic models with error components. *Journal of the American Statistical Association, 76*(375), 598–606.

Anderson, T. W., & Hsiao, C. (1982). Formulation and estimation of dynamic models using panel data. *Journal of Econometrics, 18*(1), 47–82.

Anderson, E. W., Fornell, C., & Mazvancheryl, S. K. (2004). Customer satisfaction and shareholder value. *Journal of Marketing, 68*(4), 172–185.

Andreß, H.-J., Golsch, K., & Schmidt, A. W. (2013). *Applied panel data analysis for economic and social surveys*. Berlin, Heidelberg: Springer-Verlag.

Angrist, J. D., & Pischke, J. S. (2008). *Mostly harmless econometrics: An empiricist's companion*. New Jersey: Princeton University Press.

Arellano, M., & Bond, S. (1991). Some tests of specification for panel data: Monte Carlo evidence and an application to employment equations. *The Review of Economic Studies, 58*(2), 277–297.

Ataman, M. B., Van Heerde, H. J., & Mela, C. F. (2010). The long-term effect of marketing strategy on brand sales. *Journal of Marketing Research, 47*(5), 866–882.

Bayer, E., Srinivasan, S., Riedl, E. J., & Skiera, B. (2020). The impact of online display advertising and paid search advertising relative to offline advertising on firm performance and firm value. *International Journal of Research in Marketing, 37*(4), 789–804.

Bijmolt, T. H., Van Heerde, H. J., & Pieters, R. G. (2005). New empirical generalizations on the determinants of price elasticity. *Journal of Marketing Research, 42*(2), 141–156.

Blundell, R., & Bond, S. (1998). Initial conditions and moment restrictions in dynamic panel data models. *Journal of Econometrics, 87*(1), 115–143.

Boulding, W., & Christen, M. (2003). Sustainable pioneering advantage? Profit implications of market entry order. *Marketing Science, 22*(3), 371–392.

Boulding, W., & Christen, M. (2008). Disentangling pioneering cost advantages and disadvantages. *Marketing Science, 27*(4), 699–716.

Borah, A., & Tellis, G. J. (2014). Make, buy, or ally? Choice of and payoff from announcements of alternate strategies for innovations. *Marketing Science, 33*(1), 114–133.

Butt, M. N., Antia, K. D., Murtha, B. R., & Kashyap, V. (2018). Clustering, knowledge sharing, and intrabrand competition: A multiyear analysis of an evolving franchise system. *Journal of Marketing, 82*(1), 74–92.

Cameron, A. C., & Trivedi, P. K. (2005). *Microeconometrics: Methods and applications*. New York: Cambridge University Press.

Cameron, A. C., & Trivedi, P. K. (2009). *Microeconometrics using Stata*. Texas: Stata Press.

Cho, H. J., & Pucik, V. (2005). Relationship between innovativeness, quality, growth, profitability, and market value. *Strategic Management Journal, 26*(6), 555–575.

Fornell, C., Johnson, M. D., Anderson, E. W., Cha, J., & Bryant, B. E. (1996). The American customer satisfaction index: Nature, purpose, and findings. *Journal of Marketing, 60*(4), 7–18.

Germann, F., Ebbes, P., & Grewal, R. (2015). The chief marketing officer matters! *Journal of Marketing, 79*(3), 1–22.

Gill, M., Sridhar, S., & Grewal, R. (2017). Return on engagement initiatives: A study of a business-to-business mobile app. *Journal of Marketing, 81*(4), 45–66.

Greene, W. H. (2003). *Econometric analysis* (6th ed.). United Kingdom: Pearson Education.

Griliches, Z., & Hausman, J. A. (1986). Errors in variables in panel data. *Journal of Econometrics, 31*(1), 93–118.

Gruca, T. S., & Rego, L. L. (2005). Customer satisfaction, cash flow, and shareholder value. *Journal of Marketing, 69*(3), 115–130.

Hausman, J. A. (1978). Specification tests in econometrics. *Econometrica: Journal of the Econometric Society*, 1251–1271.

Hausman, J. A., & Taylor, W. E. (1981). Panel data and unobservable individual effects. *Econometrica: Journal of the Econometric Society*, 1377–1398.

Ho-Dac, N. N., Carson, S. J., & Moore, W. L. (2013). The effects of positive and negative online customer reviews: Do brand strength and category maturity matter? *Journal of Marketing, 77*(6), 37–53.

Homburg, C., Vomberg, A., & Muehlhaeuser, S. (2020). Design and governance of multichannel sales systems: Financial performance consequences in business-to-business markets. *Journal of Marketing Research, 57*(6), 1113–1134.

Hox, J. J. (2010). *Multilevel analysis – techniques and applications*, 2nd edn. New York: Routledge.

Jacobson, R., & Aaker, D. A. (1985). Is market share all that it's cracked up to be? *Journal of Marketing, 49*(4), 11–22.

Kennedy, P. (2008). *A Guide to econometrics* (6th ed.). New Jersey: Wiley.

Kummer, M., & Schulte, P. (2019). When private information settles the bill: Money and privacy in Google's market for smartphone applications. *Management Science, 65*(8), 3470–3494.

Lovett, M. J., Peres, R., & Shachar, R. (2013). On brands and word of mouth. *Journal of Marketing Research, 50*(4), 427–444.

Luo, X., & Bhattacharya, C. B. (2006). Corporate social responsibility, customer satisfaction, and market value. *Journal of Marketing, 70*(4), 1–18.

Manchanda, P., Packard, G., & Pattabhiramaiah, A. (2015). Social dollars: The economic impact of customer participation in a firm-sponsored online customer community. *Marketing Science, 34*(3), 367–387.

McAlister, L., Srinivasan, R., Jindal, N., & Cannella, A. A. (2016). Advertising effectiveness: The moderating effect of firm strategy. *Journal of Marketing Research, 53*(2), 207–224.

Misangyi, V. F., Elms, H., Greckhamer, T., & Lepine, J. A. (2006). A new perspective on a fundamental debate: A multilevel approach to industry, corporate, and business unit effects. *Strategic Management Journal, 27*(6), 571–590.

Mizik, N., & Jacobson, R. (2008). The financial value impact of perceptual brand attributes. *Journal of Marketing Research, 45*(1), 15–32.

Naik, P. A., & Raman, K. (2003). Understanding the impact of synergy in multimedia communications. *Journal of Marketing Research, 40*(4), 375–388.

Nath, P., & Mahajan, V. (2008). Chief marketing officers: A study of their presence in firms' top management teams. *Journal of Marketing, 72*(1), 65–81.

Petersen, M. A. (2009). Estimating standard errors in finance panel data sets: Comparing approaches. *The Review of Financial Studies, 22*(1), 435–480.

Rabe-Hesketh, S., & Skrondal, A. (2012). *Multilevel and longitudinal modeling using stata, volumes I and II: Multilevel and longitudinal modeling using stata*. Texas: Stata Press.

Rao, V. R., Agarwal, M. K., & Dahlhoff, D. (2004). How is manifest branding strategy related to the intangible value of a corporation? *Journal of Marketing, 68*(4), 126–141.

Raudenbush, S. W., & Bryk, A. S. (2002). *Hierarchical linear models – Applications and data analysis methods*. California: Sage.

Roodman, D. (2009). How to do xtabond2: An introduction to difference and system GMM in Stata. *The Stata Journal, 9*(1), 86–136.

Sorescu, A. B., & Spanjol, J. (2008). Innovation's effect on firm value and risk: Insights from consumer packaged goods. *Journal of Marketing, 72*(2), 114–132.

Steenkamp, J. B. E., & Geyskens, I. (2014). Manufacturer and retailer strategies to impact store brand share: Global integration, local adaptation, and worldwide learning. *Marketing Science, 33*(1), 6–26.

Verbeek, M. (2017). *A Guide to modern economics* (5th ed.). New Jersey: Wiley.

Vomberg, A., Homburg, C., & Bornemann, T. (2015). Talented people and strong brands: The contribution of human capital and brand equity to firm value. *Strategic Management Journal, 36*(13), 2122–2131.

Von Auer, L. (2013). *Ökonometrie – eine einführung*, 4th edition, Berlin Heidelberg: Springer.

Warren, N. L., & Sorescu, A. (2017). Interpreting the stock returns to new product announcements: How the past shapes investors' expectations of the future. *Journal of Marketing Research, 54*(5), 799–815.

Wies, S., Hoffmann, A. O. I., Aspara, J., & Pennings, J. M. (2019). Can advertising investments counter the negative impact of shareholder complaints on firm value? *Journal of Marketing, 83*(4), 58–80.

Wlömert, N., & Papies, D. (2019). International heterogeneity in the associations of new business models and broadband internet with music revenue and piracy. *International Journal of Research in Marketing, 36*(3), 400–419.

Wolters, H. M., Schulze, C., & Gedenk, K. (2020). Referral reward size and new customer profitability. *Marketing Science, 39*(6), 1166–1180.

Wooldridge, J. M. (2010). *Econometric analysis of cross section and panel data*. Massachusetts: MIT Press.

Wooldridge, J. M. (2016). *Introductory econometrics: A modern approach* (6th ed.). Massachusetts: Cengage Learning.

Applied Time-Series Analysis in Marketing

Wanxin Wang and Gokhan Yildirim

Contents

Introduction	470
Univariate Time-Series Treatments and Diagnostics	471
Autoregressive (AR) and Moving Average (MA) Process	471
Testing for Evolution Versus Stationarity	472
ARIMA Models	474
Single Equation Time-Series Models with Exogenous Variables	476
Multiple Time-Series Models: Dynamic Systems	479
Granger Causality Tests	481
Cointegration Test	483
Vector Autoregressive and Vector Error–Correction Model	483
Order of Lags in VAR Models	484
Generalized Impulse Response Functions	485
Generalized Forecast Error Variance Decomposition	487
Volatility Models	489
Conclusion	491
Cross-References	491
Appendix	492
Software Application	492
Data Visualizations	493
ARIMA Modeling	494
VAR Model Steps	502
References	512

Abstract

Time-series models constitute a core component of marketing research and are applied to solve a wide spectrum of marketing problems. This chapter covers traditional and modern time-series models with applications in extant marketing

---

W. Wang · G. Yildirim (✉)
Imperial College Business School, Imperial College London, London, UK
e-mail: wanxin.wang13@imperial.ac.uk; g.yildirim@imperial.ac.uk

© Springer Nature Switzerland AG 2022
C. Homburg et al. (eds), *Handbook of Market Research*,
https://doi.org/10.1007/978-3-319-57413-4_37

research. We first introduce basic concepts and diagnostics including stationarity test (the augmented Dicky-Fuller test of unit roots), and autocorrelation plots via autocorrelation function (ACF) and partial autocorrelation function (PACF). We then discuss single-equation time-series models such as autoregressive (AR), moving average (MA), and autoregressive moving average (ARMA) models with and without exogenous variables. Multiple-equation dynamic systems including vector autoregressive (VAR) models together with generalized impulse response functions (GIRFs) and generalized forecast error variance decomposition (GFEVD) are then discussed in detail. Other relevant models such as generalized autoregressive conditional heteroskedasticity (GARCH) models are covered. Finally, a case study accompanied by data and R codes is provided to demonstrate detailed estimation steps of key models covered in this chapter.

Keywords

Time-series models · Marketing · ARIMA · VAR · GIRF · GFEVD · GARCH

Introduction

I have seen the future and it is very much like the present, only longer. – Kehlog Albran, The Profit

Firms collect data on the past to understand the present and to forecast the future. Performance measures such as sales, market share, and revenues are often path dependent, meaning that their past values can inform the present. This is great news for marketing analysts because they are able to forecast the future using historical time-stamped data series. The key challenge is how they can accurately capture the dynamics and variation patterns of data using proper statistical techniques. Further, firms take various marketing actions (e.g., TV and radio advertising, online display and search engine advertising, and social media campaigning, etc.) to help boost performance. More importantly, these marketing actions are usually designated to exert influence not only instantaneously in the current period, but persistently into the future. For example, when assessing advertising effectiveness, analysts typically add up past advertising efforts (while considering a certain level of decay) and evaluate their cumulative impact on sales. Given an omnichannel marketing scheme, firms also need to examine cross-effects, or interactions, between different marketing instruments to see whether there are any synergies or cannibalizations. Further, the relationship between marketing efforts and performance is often bilateral; feedback loops exist so that performance from previous periods helps decide marketing strategies in the current period.

Analytical tools that capture dynamics of performance measures and that between marketing and performance are time-series models. Over the decades, time-series models have been evolving from univariate to multivariate, and then to dynamic systems consisting of multiple time series. Univariate models (e.g., autoregressive moving average or ARMA) assume that the contemporaneous value of a series is only influenced by its past values. Multivariate models extend and usually outperform univariate models by including current and lagged values of other factors (e.g., price, marketing, distributions, and regulatory change) that should also exert influence on performance. Dynamic systems like vector autoregressive (VAR) models are widely adopted to tackle more complex relationships between series. These models can be used to capture dual causality between performance and other predicting variables (e.g., do past sales affect current marketing decisions?) and between predicting variables (e.g., does online marketing complements or substitutes offline marketing?).

Time-series analyses can also inform researchers of more specific patterns of the dataset that they are working with. For example, when forecasting sales of a firm, previous marketing research can inform analysts what variables should be incorporated into the model. However, previous findings are not able to tell the exact order of lags (e.g., how many weeks of past sales, price, and marketing investments should we consider?) or the direction of causality (e.g., does consumer social media sentiment directly or indirectly impact sales?). We need to rely on a set of time-series diagnostic tests to find answers to these questions.

More impressively, time-series models, especially the modern ones (e.g., dynamic systems) can enable researchers to uncover some powerful linkage between factors that are previously overlooked (Srinivasan et al. 2016). For example, researchers have bridged firm offline marketing with consumer online activities and sales through VAR modeling (Srinivasan et al. 2016); others have found that growth or decrease in the volume of consumer social media posts can affect the stock market valuation of firms (van Dieijen et al. 2019).

This chapter proceeds as follows. We will start from the basics, including treatment and diagnostics of univariate time-series models. Then we will talk about traditional time-series models, for instance, autoregressive integrated moving average (ARIMA) models. We will then discuss modern time-series models like vector autoregressive (VAR) models. Additionally, we also cover generalized autoregressive conditional heteroscedasticity (GARCH) models that deal with time-series volatility. Finally, in the Appendix, we present a case study where we apply methods introduced in this chapter using R to solve marketing challenges for a firm.

Univariate Time-Series Treatments and Diagnostics

Autoregressive (AR) and Moving Average (MA) Process

Let us start with the simplest model where we describe certain performance metric of a brand in each time period t with its first lag. Specifically, let s_t denote the sales of a brand in week t, and s_t is determined by sales in the previous week s_{t-1}. We call this a first-order autoregressive, or $AR(1)$ process:

$$s_t = c + \varphi s_{t-1} + \varepsilon_t \tag{1}$$

where c is a constant term and φ is the parameter that captures the effect of sales in the previous week. ε_t is white noise with mean zero and variance σ_ε^2.

Another form of time series, i.e., moving average (MA) process, assumes that sales at the current period is affected by a past shock (e.g., a natural disaster) other than its own past values. A first-order moving average or a $MA(1)$ process of sales at time t is written as:

$$s_t = c + \varepsilon_t + \theta \varepsilon_{t-1} \tag{2}$$

where ε_{t-1} is the error term or the shock from the last period. θ captures the impact of such past shock (e.g., an earthquake that happened one week ago) on current sales.

A $MA(1)$ process differs from an $AR(1)$ process in that instead of assuming the past shock as coming from past sales s_{t-1}, it assumes that such shock comes from the random component of s_{t-1}, namely ε_{t-1}.

$AR(1)$ and $MA(1)$ process can be generalized to $AR(p)$ and $MA(q)$ process, respectively, where p and q refer to the highest order of lagged value and error term, respectively.

What if we want to model weekly sales while taking the impact of both past sales and past random shocks into consideration? We can combine an $AR(p)$ and an $MA(q)$ processes to have an autoregressive moving average, or $ARMA(p, q)$ process. For instance, an $ARMA(1, 1)$ process is written as:

$$s_t = c + \varphi s_{t-1} + \theta \varepsilon_{t-1} + \varepsilon_t \tag{3}$$

Figure 1 shows an example of an ARMA (1,1) process, with $\varphi = -0.70$ and $\theta = 0.99$. ARMA models have been quite commonly adopted in marketing research during 1970–1990s and proved suitable to capture dynamics in various contexts (e.g., Dekimpe and Hanssens 1995).

Testing for Evolution Versus Stationarity

Marketing models only make sense when the time series being analyzed is mean stationary or trend stationary, meaning that it always converges back to a fixed mean or a fixed mean plus any trend detected. Otherwise, the series is said to be non-stationary or evolving. Why do we need to emphasize on series stationarity? Consider an evolving series whose value is constantly increasing. In such case, sample statistics such as mean and variance are not really descriptive of the data pattern, since they are not stable and keep getting larger as we include more data points. Therefore, reporting the mean and variance of an evolving series is not informative or helpful for decision-making. Further, we will not be able to generate reliable results if we use evolving variables to predict sales. This is why evolving series need to be transformed to stationarity.

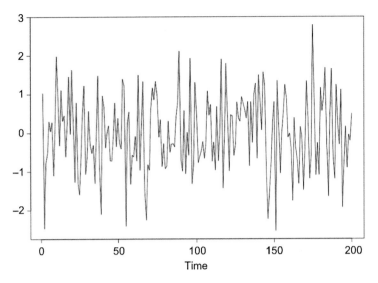

Fig. 1 An Example of an ARMA (1,1) process

Given an *ARMA*(1, 1) process in Eq. (3), how can we determine if it is stationary or not? The answer lies in the φ term:

- If $|\varphi| < 1$, we call this series *stationary*, with a *time-independent* mean and variance, meaning that the mean $E(s_t)$ and variance $\sigma^2(s_t)$ are the same for all t.
- If $|\varphi| = 1$, then the effect of past sales s_{t-1} is said to have a permanent effect on current sales s_t. In this case, sales will not be reverting to a certain level, but instead evolving.
- If $|\varphi| > 1$, then the effect of past sales through φ will exert an even stronger influence as time goes. Such a data pattern should be rarely observed in the context of marketing.

Note that we only need to evaluate the AR part (through φ) of an ARMA process for stationarity. This is because ε_t is independently and normally distributed with a zero mean, indicating that an MA process is stationary regardless of the value of θ.

More formally, we can test for stationarity of an ARMA process through *unit root test* (For the stationarity test for time series data with a permanent step-change, please refer to unit root test with structural breaks (e.g., Deleersnyder et al. 2002)). A time series is evolving if it has a unit root, and stationary otherwise. The most widely adopted method is the augmented Dickey-Fuller (ADF) test (Kwiatkowski et al. 1992). Let us use an *AR*(2) version of the weekly sales time series introduced in Eq. (1). Note that we only focus on the AR part of ARMA process since the MA part is always stationary.

Recall that brand sales in week t can be written as an $AR(2)$ process:

$$s_t = c + \varphi_1 s_{t-1} + \varphi_2 s_{t-2} + \varepsilon_t \tag{4}$$

If we define $\Delta s_t = s_t - s_{t-1}$, we can reformulate the process in Eq. (4) into:

$$s_t = c + (\varphi_1 + \varphi_2)s_{t-1} - \varphi_2(s_{t-1} - s_{t-2}) + \varepsilon_t \tag{5}$$

And further:

$$\Delta s_t = c + \eta s_{t-1} + \lambda \Delta s_{t-1} + \varepsilon_t \tag{6}$$

where $\eta = \varphi_1 + \varphi_2 - 1$, and $\lambda = -\varphi_2$. The $AR(2)$ process in Eq. (5) has a *unit root* if $\varphi_1 + \varphi_2 = 1$. This is equivalent to testing whether $\eta = 0$ in Eq. (6).

In practice, researchers can first-difference the sales series, and then estimate a linear regression model where the first-differenced sales at time t (i.e., Δs_t) is the dependent variable, and lagged values of Δs_t's and s_{t-1} are independent variables. The null hypothesis that $\eta = 0$ will be rejected if the regression coefficient of s_{t-1} (i.e., η) is statistically significant, indicating series stationarity. Alternatively, we can use statistical software such as R, Stata, and EViews to quickly generate test results. Readers may refer to "Appendix" of this chapter for detailed guidance on how to use R to perform ADF test.

ARIMA Models

What if the time series that we work on is found nonstationary with ADF test indicating a unit root? A proper technique to deal with this situation is to transform the series to stationarity by *differencing*. For example, if we find the weekly sales series in Eq. (3) is evolving, we can first-difference it to a series z_t, where $z_t = s_t - s_{t-1}$. By subtracting the first lag from the current value, the series may become *difference stationary*. The ARMA process with a differencing operation is called an ARIMA (integrated ARMA) process. ARIMA model is often adopted by practitioners and researchers for prediction purpose, e.g., demand forecasting. For example, given the sales, price, and marketing activities in the past 24 months, what is the predicted sales for the next 12 months?

An *ARIMA* (1, 1, 1) model, which is a combination of $AR(1)$, $MA(1)$, and a first-order differencing operation, can be written as:

$$z_t = c + \varphi_1 z_{t-1} + \theta_1 \varepsilon_{t-1} + \varepsilon_t \tag{7}$$

where $z_t = s_t - s_{t-1}$. This model can be easily extended to a generalized case where we have an *ARIMA* (p, d, q) process, with p and q representing the highest order of lags in AR and MA component, respectively, and d the order of differencing.

ACF and PACF Analysis

Given a stationary time series (e.g., an ARIMA process), how can we determine the exact order of lags to include (i.e., the value of p and q)? Researchers typically rely on the autocorrelation function (ACF) and partial autocorrelation function (PACF) to determine the MA and AR part of the process, respectively.

Again, let s_t be the value of sales at week t. The ACF series is derived from calculating the correlations between s_t and s_{t-k} (i.e., sales k weeks ago) for every k. To calculate these correlations, we first derive the unconditional mean and variance of s_t for an $AR(1)$ process:

$$E(s_t) = E(c + \varphi s_{t-1} + \varepsilon_t) = c + E(\varphi s_{t-1}) + E(\varepsilon_t) = c + \varphi E(s_{t-1}) \qquad (8)$$

Hence

$$E(s_t) = \frac{c}{1 - \varphi} \qquad (9)$$

$$\sigma^2(s_t) = \mathrm{var}(c + \varphi s_{t-1} + \varepsilon_t) = 0 + \mathrm{var}(\varphi s_{t-1}) + \mathrm{var}(\varepsilon_t)$$
$$= \varphi^2 \mathrm{var}(s_{t-1}) + \sigma_\varepsilon^2 \qquad (10)$$

$$\sigma^2(s_t) = \frac{\sigma_\varepsilon^2}{1 - \varphi^2} \qquad (11)$$

where σ_ε^2 is the constant variance of disturbance term ε_t.

Hence the correlation between two data points that are k periods apart is:

$$\rho_k = \varphi^k \qquad (12)$$

From Eq. (12), when $|\varphi| < 1$, ρ_k will converge or oscillate towards zero as k gets larger.

Partial autocorrelation function (PACF) of kth order refers to the correlation between two data points in a time series that are k lags apart, holding all other $(k - 1)$ intermediate observations constant. For example, let us denote correlation between sales in period m and n as $\omega_{m,n}$. Given that a stationary time series has constant autocorrelation, we have $\omega_{t,t+1} = \omega_{t+1,t+2} = \rho_1$. Then the PACF between s_t and s_{t+2} while holding s_{t+1} constant can be written as:

$$\omega_{t,t+1,t+2} = \frac{\omega_{t,t+2} - \omega_{t,t+1}\omega_{t+1,t+2}}{\sqrt{\left(1 - \omega_{t,t+1}^2\right)\left(1 - \omega_{t+1,t+2}^2\right)}} = \frac{\left(\rho_2 - \rho_1^2\right)}{\left(1 - \rho_1^2\right)} \qquad (13)$$

Graphically, if we plot PACF against k, we will see a spike of PACF equal to ACF at $k = 1$, and zeros afterwards. For example, Fig. 2 below shows weekly sales of a mature consumer good brand (brand A) for one year. The time series of sales can be described as an $AR(1)$ process with $\varphi = 0.5$. Panel (a) and (b) in Fig. 3 show the ACF

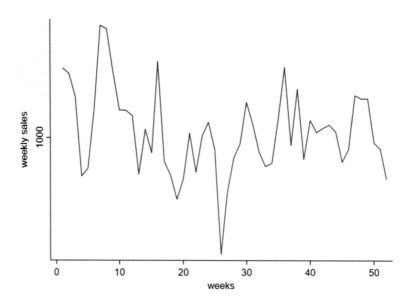

Fig. 2 Weekly sales (in thousands) of brand A

and PACF of the sales series, respectively. In panel (b), the PACF plot has a significant drop (or cutoff) from lag 1 to lag 2, indicating that the series is an *AR* (1) process.

In terms of the order of AR and MA process, we can refer to the rules as follows:

- The lag at which the PACF cuts off is the indicated maximum order of AR lags.
- The lag at which the ACF cuts off is the indicated maximum order of MA lags.

Single Equation Time-Series Models with Exogenous Variables

In the previous sections, we have been studying univariate time series. More specifically, we have considered sales to be only affected by its past values and past random shocks as described in ARIMA processes. While these models are able to capture sales dynamics, the reality is that firms spend a lot of effort on many other activities to improve their sales performance. Univariate models are hence limited since they fail to incorporate other factors that also make a substantial difference such as various marketing activities. Meanwhile, marketing managers are keen to justify their marketing expenditure by evaluating the effect of marketing on sales. For example, what will be the change in sales if we spend 10% more on marketing?

This section links the role of marketing with firm performance explicitly by introducing multivariate time-series models, or single equation time-series

Applied Time-Series Analysis in Marketing

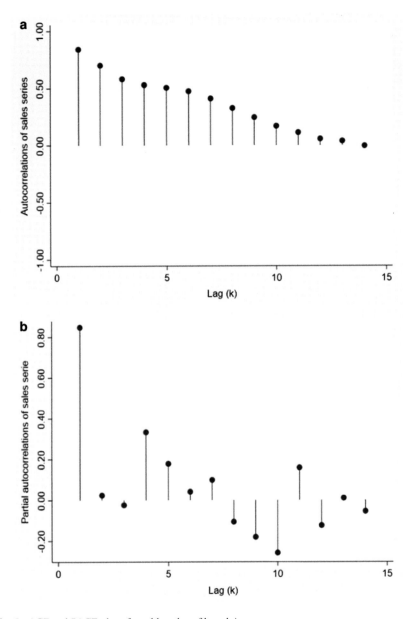

Fig. 3 ACF and PACF plot of weekly sales of brand A

models with exogenous variables. We emphasize "single equation" here to distinguish this type of model from dynamic systems consisting of multiple time series. These models are sometimes known as ARIMA-X, where X stands for "exogenous."

Assume that besides sales itself, only one more variable, price, has impact on sales and that price itself is also subject to time-series patterns. We can incorporate the current and lag price into our model to predict sales through a *transfer function* $v_k(B)$, where $v_k(B) = v_0 + v_1 B + v_2 B^2 + \ldots + v_k B^k$. B is the backshift operator, where $B^k y_t = y_{t-k}$, and k is the highest order of lags. A dynamic regression model of sales s_t on price variable is:

$$s_t = c + v_k(B)p_t + \varepsilon_t \tag{14}$$

where $v_k(B)p_t = v_0 p_t + v_1 p_{t-1} + \ldots + v_k p_{t-k}$.

The transfer function $v_k(B)$ is also called the *impulse response function* (IRF) with the coefficients $v's$ called *impulse response weights*. Further, referring to Eq. (14), if we find that $v_0 = 0$ and that all other v-coefficients are nonzero, then price in the current period t does not have an impact on sales in the same period, while prices in the past periods do. The model is said to have a "wear-in time" (or "dead time") of one, i.e., a change made to the price will start to exert influence only from the next period onwards. Wear-in time reflects the speed at which changes in a firm's marketing mix impact sales performance. More formally, "wear-in time" of a model is measured by the number of *consecutive* v-coefficients with zero value, starting from v_0.

Finally, similar to the idea of structural break in time-series data, we could also accommodate certain discrete events that shock the series significantly into our sales models. For example, exogenous shocks such as regulatory change or introduction of a new product introduced by a rival brand may lead to significant rise or drop in sales data. Here we distinguish two types of effects that a shock can have: a *pulse effect* or a *step effect* (Pauwels 2017).

A pulse effect is a temporary effect that decays or disappears gradually. In contrast, a step effect is supposed to have permanent effect once it occurs. To analyze the impact of shocks requires *intervention analysis*, which extends the transfer function approach described above.

Figure 4 shows example of pulse effect at time t' on a stationary process (panel a) and nonstationary process (panel b), respectively. In the case depicted in panel (a), the intervention could be a price promotion at time t' of a mature consumer good product with stationary demand from consumers. The promotion results in a temporary spike at sales of time t', after which sales revert to its stationary mean. The corresponding transfer function is $v_0 x_t$ at $t = t'$ and zero elsewhere. Panel (b) shows a situation of pulse intervention, where the intervention function is the same, but sales is nonstationary (e.g., a new brand with high market potential). Here the pulse intervention results in a temporary drop in sales at $t = t'$. Sales return to the level that is determined by its nonstationary character afterwards.

Figure 5 shows two examples of step interventions. Here the change to sales after time t' is long lasting, meaning that it could be permanent (panel a) or semi-permanent (panel b). For example, we can think of the series in panel (a) as sales of a brand that successfully introduced a major market innovation at time t'. Sales jumped to a higher level immediately at $t = t'$ and stay at the new level for all $t > t'$. The transfer function,

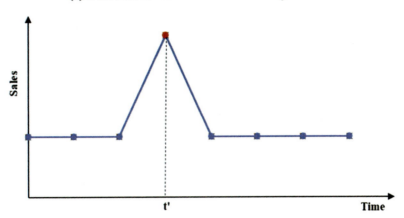

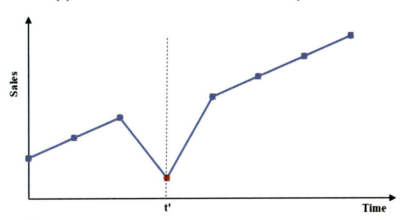

Fig. 4 Examples of pulse interventions

in this case, would be one where $v_0 x_t$, and $x_t = 0$ for $t < t'$ and $x_t = 1$ for $t \geq t'$. Panel (b) shows the case where a step intervention lasts for several periods (three periods in this case) but not "forever," i.e., semi-permanent. The transfer function would be one where $x_t = 0$ for $t < t'$, and $x_t = 1$ for $t = t', t' + 1, t' + 2$.

Multiple Time-Series Models: Dynamic Systems

Multivariate models are often preferred over univariate models because they can capture not only the effect of past performance, but also that of other model covariates (e.g., price, marketing efforts, and competitors' offerings). However,

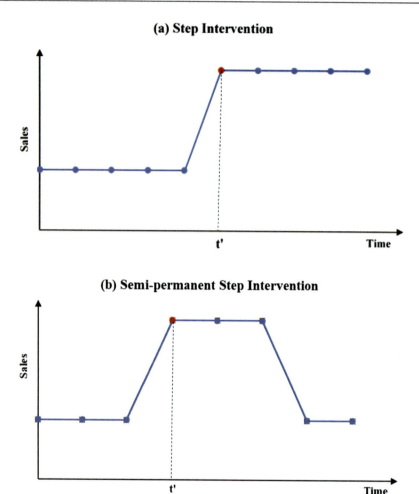

Fig. 5 Examples of step interventions

these models are still subject to certain limitations in dealing with joint endogeneity between variables (e.g., dual causality and feedback loops, etc.).

For example, we can quantify the effect of a firm's marketing activities on sales by fitting a linear regression model. The assumption here is that marketing impacts sales, not the other way around. However, in practice, to maximize overall return on marketing investment, firms also adjust their marketing strategies based on sales performance in the previous periods (please refer to more detailed discussions and applications in chapters ▶ "Measuring Sales Promotion Effectiveness" and ▶ "Return on Media Models" in this book). Additionally, firms need to be aware of potential synergies or cannibalizations between different marketing actions and refine their marketing portfolios from time to time. For instance, one can expect a certain level of complementarity (positive "spill-over") between online display advertising and offline in-store promotion. On the other hand, firms may consider alternating TV and radio ads instead of having them simultaneously to avoid consumer fatigue (i.e., negative "spillover").

These problems described above can be taken care of via estimating a dynamic system of multiple time series, or a vector autoregressive (VAR) model. Models as such are more accurate in both model fitting and forecasting, compared with traditional time-series models (Lütkepohl 2005).

Our structure for this section is adapted from the "persistence modeling framework" that was first developed by Dekimpe and Hanssens (1995). You can find most of the recent marketing research papers following the procedure described in this framework (e.g., De Haan et al. 2016; Srinivasan et al. 2016).

This section will cover topics listed below:

1. *Granger causality tests*, which focus on understanding the direction of causality between model variables
2. *Unit root and cointegration tests*, which focus on understanding whether model variables are stationary over time or evolving and on whether the evolving variables (if any) are tied in certain long-term equilibrium, respectively.
3. *Dynamic system modeling*, which is typically done via vector autoregressive (VAR) model or vector error correction (VEC) model, depending on results obtained from 2.
4. *Policy simulation analysis*, which focuses on evaluating short-term and long-term impact of marketing on performance via impulse response function (IRF) analysis.
5. *Drivers of performance*, which answers the question of "what is the relative importance of each performance driver's past in explaining performance variance?" via generalized FEVD (GFEVD)

Granger Causality Tests

Marketing decisions of firms can be informed by sales performance from previous periods and activities of rival brands. Different types of marketing actions can affect each other (e.g., complementary versus substitutive) as well. These issues are called marketing endogeneity, which, if not tested and treated, can lead to misinterpretation of situation and wrong understanding of the effectiveness of marketing (for further detailed discussions, we refer our readers to the ▶ "Dealing with Endogeneity: A Nontechnical Guide for Marketing Researchers" chapter in this book). Granger causality tests (Granger 1969; Hanssens and Pauwels 2016) are needed to examine the existence and direction of causality between model variables. Results from Granger causality tests determine the appropriate functional form of time-series models: for example, a multiple-equation system should be adopted if feedback loops between variables are detected.

The idea of Granger causality tests is that a variable x is considered Granger causing another variable y if the lag values of variable x improve performance of a model where y is predicted based only on its own past. The most common method to conduct Granger causality tests is by estimating the following regression model of variable y on its own past and lags of variable x:

$$y_t = \alpha + \sum_{i=1}^{m} \beta_i y_{t-i} + \sum_{j=1}^{n} \gamma_j x_{t-j} + \varepsilon_t \qquad (15)$$

where m and n refer to the maximum lag order for y and x, respectively. β_i and γ_j are the regression coefficients of lag value of y and x, respectively. Once we obtain the regression results, variable x is said to Granger-cause y if any of the γ_j coefficients are statistically significant.

Note that what we described above is pairwise Granger causality test, where only two variables are tested. However, the causality from x to y might be an indirect one that is mediated by another variable z that lies in between. Figure 6 provides a graphical illustration of what we mean here: by conducting only pairwise Granger causality tests repeatedly between variable X and Y, Y and Z, and X and Z, we are not able to distinguish the situation in panel (a) and (b).

We can extend pairwise Granger causality test to the case of n ($n > 2$) variables ("conditional Granger causality test"). To do this, estimate an autoregressive model with n variables. A variable x is said to Granger-cause y if incorporating lagged values of x improves prediction accuracy of y on its own past values and all other ($n - 2$) variables.

There are some applications of Granger causality in the marketing literature that generated some interesting insights (Ilhan et al. 2018). For example, in understanding the relationships between the firm offline marketing mix (distribution, price, and TV advertising), consumer online activities (paid search clicks, website visitations, and Facebook likes), and sales over time, Srinivasan et al. (2016) tested for causalities between variables prior to formal model estimation. The authors found that sales are Granger-caused by all offline and online metrics with varying sensitivities (e.g., the elasticity of paid search clicks on sales is about 5.2 times higher than that of Facebook likes). In particular, TV advertising is not Granger-caused by any of the other marketing mix elements and consumer activities, and hence should play a relatively less influential role in the dynamic system and in impacting sales.

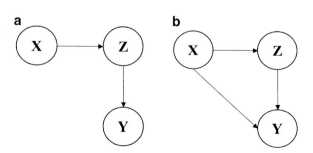

Fig. 6 Pairwise and conditional Granger causality

Cointegration Test

Once we acquire insights about causalities between model variables, we can proceed unit root test and cointegration test to determine the exact form (e.g., level versus first-differenced) in which our variables are included. We have introduced unit root test in section "ARIMA Models," hence we will focus on cointegration test in this section.

Cointegration test aims to find if two variables of interest are tied in certain long-run equilibrium. For example, one might find that the variations of marketing and sales in the current week seem to be uncorrelated, yet they actually co-move with each other closely in the long run, since it usually takes time for the effect of marketing investments to accumulate and to be reflected on changes in sales. Put it in simple language, two time series, y_t and x_t, are cointegrated if both are non-stationary (with unit root) and if there exists a certain linear combination of the two series that is stationary. It is important to test for cointegration to inform our model choice, since, for example, if marketing expense and sales are evolving and cointegrated, knowing the value of one would enable us to predict that of the other. In this case, a VAR-in-difference model, which essentially deals with change or growth rate instead of the specific values of variables, is not ideal since we will lose valuable information and prediction power.

The cointegrating equation quantifies equilibrium between variables y and x as:

$$y_t = \alpha + \beta \times x_t + \varepsilon_t \tag{16}$$

where ε_t is the equilibrium error that is supposed to be stationary.

There are several ways to test for cointegration; for example, the procedure developed by Engle and Granger (1987) first estimates Eq. (16) via ordinary least squares method, and next test stationarity versus evolution of the error term ε_t. Johansen's full information maximum likelihood (FIML) is a more popular way for cointegration test (Johansen 1995; Srinivasan et al. 2010). It is a multivariate generalization of the Dicky-Fully unit root test and allows for structural breaks in the relationship among variables.

Vector Autoregressive and Vector Error–Correction Model

The vector autoregressive (VAR) model is an extension of the univariate auto-regressive model. It is typically used when we are not only interested in the effect of marketing on performance, but also the feedback of performance on marketing and the effects of marketing activities on each other.

When our data is stationary and without cointegration, we can estimate a VAR model. We focus on reduced-form VAR (obtained from structural VAR) where all explanatory variables are lag values that are predetermined at current time t. This is the form of VAR model that we usually take in analyzing time-series data. For more details on other forms of VAR models and their applications, see the chapter

▶ "Modeling Marketing Dynamics Using Vector Autoregressive (VAR) Models" in this book.

Specifically, a reduced VAR model can be written as follows:

$$y_t = \alpha + B_1 y_{t-1} + B_2 y_{t-2} + \ldots + B_p y_{t-p} + e_t \tag{17}$$

where y_t is an $n \times 1$ vector of n endogenous variables, α is the vector of constant terms including a deterministic time trend and seasonality terms, and B_i, $i = 1, 2, \ldots,$ p is an $n \times n$ coefficient matrix of a given lag of order i. e_t is the error term that is contemporaneously correlated. p is the maximum order of lag that is determined via certain statistical criteria that we will explain later.

A VAR system can be efficiently estimated through ordinary least squares (OLS) equation by equation without imposing causal ordering. This is especially important in the context of marketing research where a relatively large number of parameters are modeled together. For example, Pauwels et al. (2016) studied interactions among marketing, eWOM topic, and online and offline store traffic of a retailer by estimating a VAR model with ten endogenous variables. Colicev et al. (2018) estimated 11 endogenous variables in their study that tries to link consumer mindset metrics with firm social media impact and shareholder values.

One can reduce the number of coefficients that need estimation by including some variables as exogenous (instead of endogenous). Such treatment needs to be supported by relevant marketing theories and by appropriate tests. For example, a decision rule developed by De Haan et al. (2016) is to treat variables that do not have a Granger-causal relationship to any other variables as exogenous.

In terms of actual estimation practice, when model variables are stationary, we estimate a VAR in *levels* (e.g., the volume of sales and level of prices). When some variables are found evolving but *not* cointegrated, we can estimate a VAR in *differences*. For example, if we find both sales and online advertising investments are evolving and not cointegrated, our VAR-in-difference model explains the effect of change (growth) in advertising spending on the change (growth) of sales, or the elasticity of ad spending on sales.

When variables are evolving *and* cointegrated, the vector error correction (VEC) model is an extension of VAR to make sure that both the *levels* and *differences* of those cointegrated variables are taken into consideration (see Kireyev et al. 2016). Other extensions of VAR model include panel-VAR (PVAR) model, where cross-sectional heterogeneities are added to the standard VAR. This is as if we incorporate a dependent-variable-specific fixed effect into each equation of VAR. An application of PVAR in marketing can be found in Colicev et al. (2019), where the authors included industry-specific heterogeneity.

Order of Lags in VAR Models

To determine the order of lags in VAR model, we need to trade-off between having a better model fitting and suffering from model complexity. There are several ways to determine the "best" lag order p of a VAR model. Information criteria (There are several softwares such as EViews, STATA, and R that can help us automatically pick the best order of lags based on information criteria.) are commonly adopted in the vast literature. For example, Akaike Information Criteria (AIC) evaluates model predictive accuracy while imposing a punishment for adding more lags (Akaike 1973). For a VAR model with lag order p, the AIC is formulated as:

$$AIC = -2LL + 2K \qquad (18)$$

where LL refers to the log likelihood function of the model and K refers the number of predictors in the model. K increases with the number of lags incorporated in the VAR system, i.e., the higher the order of lags, the larger the punishment. For example, a VAR system with 3 endogenous variables and lag order of 1 has 9 parameters to be estimated and 18 parameters to be estimated if lag order is 2. We should select the value of p that gives the lowest AIC.

Another criterion is Bayesian Information Criterion (BIC) (Schwarz 1978):

$$BIC(p) = -2LL + Kln(T) \qquad (19)$$

where T is the sample size. Compared with the AIC, the BIC has a stronger punishment for increasing lag order p, because $\ln(T)$ is greater than two (meaning that $T > 7.39$) in most of the time-series datasets.

Finally, the Hannan-Quinn (HQ) criterion (Hannan and Quinn 1979) also has a stronger punishment on adding lags than the AIC does:

$$HQ(p) = -2LL + 2K \ln(\ln(T)) \qquad (20)$$

Specifically, the BIC and the HQ tend to give consistent results as sample size T approaches infinity.

Generalized Impulse Response Functions

Result interpretation is relatively straightforward for some models like multiple linear regressions, where the effect of an explanatory variable on the outcome variable is simply quantified by the corresponding coefficient (if statistically significant). However, interpreting VAR model results directly from model outputs is not easy due to multicollinearity issues and feedback loops between variables, to name a few. In a word, given an intertwined dynamic system where variables are interrelated in various ways, we need a technique that can get us the "net" effect of each variable. Further, we are not only interested in the short-term effect, but also the long-term impact of model variables that can help us plan for the future.

Impulse–response functions (IRFs) can help us by simulating the overtime impact of a change to a variable on the whole dynamic system (Bronnenberg et al. 2000; Pauwels et al. 2016).

To derive an IRF, we start by substituting each lag of each endogenous variable in the reduced-form VAR model in Eq. (14) using the same equation ($y_t = \alpha + B_1 y_{t-1} + B_2 y_{t-2} + \ldots + B_p y_{t-p} + e_t = \alpha + B_1(\alpha + B_1 y_{t-2} + B_2 y_{t-3} + \ldots + B_p y_{t-p-1} + e_{t-1}) + B_2(\ldots) + B_p(\ldots) + e_t$, and so on). We can then express the right-hand side of Eq. (17) as a function of only contemporaneous and lagged values of the error terms. We call such expression the vector moving average (VMA) representation:

$$y_t = \rho + e_t + Ae_{t-1} + A^2 e_{t-2} + \ldots + A^t e_0 \tag{21}$$

Interpreting Eq. (21), each endogenous variable is explained by a weighted average of current and past errors, or "shocks" both to itself and to the other endogenous variables.

An IRF tracks the impact of a shock to each variable in the system during the shock (period 0) and each period afterwards (period 1, 2, etc.). Most of the times the effects of shocks will die out (i.e., converge back to its steady-state, or pre-shock level), and this usually happens to established and mature brands (e.g., effect of advertising investment on sales). However, in some rare cases we may observe that a shock has a permanent impact. Such pattern is more likely to be observed among young and innovative brands. We usually name the effect of a shock in period zero the *contemporaneous* or *immediate effect*, and the cumulative effect of a shock from period one onwards as the *long-term effect*.

A critical limitation of IRF is that it requires a causal ordering for the immediate effects. For example, when trying to model a dynamic system consisting of weekly brand sales, price, online and offline marketing expenditure, and consumer traffic, we are expected to clearly understand the causal sequence between these variables. However, it is typically unclear, for example, whether online marketing expenditure should precede or follow offline marketing expenditure in leading to sales. Generalized IRFs (GIRFs) are useful when theories or knowledge do not inform us with such ordering.

Figure 7 shows an example of impulse response of a shock in firm's advertising effort in week 0 on sales performance. The horizontal axis in Fig. 7 represents weeks 0 to 15, and the vertical axis is the coefficient of IRF analysis. An immediate incremental effect of around 5 in week 0 is the highest across all weeks. The cumulative or long-run effect is measured by the shaded area under the curve in Fig. 7, which is approximately 8.4. Finally, brand sales seem to revert to its steady state, with incremental impact staying at zero from week 11 onwards. The permanent effect of the shock to advertising is hence zero. It is very important for researchers to interpret the incremental effect of a shock in IRF or GIRF analysis results. The incremental effect turning zero does not mean zero sales, but instead no *additional* sales.

In the recent marketing literature, Pauwels et al. (2016) applied GIRF to examine the short- and long-term elasticities of different electronic word-of-mouth (eWOM) on online and offline store traffic. They found that the long-term elasticity of brand-related eWOM is twice as high as that of advertising-related eWOM in driving up offline store traffic. While offline and online traffic is approximately equally affected by purchase-related eWOM in the short run, yet its impact on the former in the long run is 16 times higher than that on the latter.

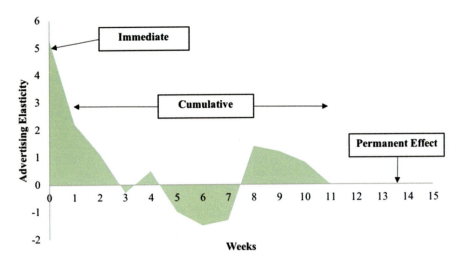

Fig. 7 Example of an impulse response of advertising on sales

Firms can also rely on (G)IRF to improve their marketing resource allocation and improve ROI. For example, Pauwels (2004) investigate how firms should allocate efforts between new product introduction (NPI) and sales promotion to maximize firm value. IRF result shows that sales promotion has a higher short-run elasticity of firm value, whereas its long-term impact turns negative (from 0.12 to −0.78). In contrast, NPI turns out to have persistent and positive impact on firm value (0.02 in the short run and 1.14 in the long run). Inspired by such result, firms should allocate more resource on new product introduction, even though sales promotion can bring them immediate sales boost.

Generalized Forecast Error Variance Decomposition

Analogous to a "dynamic R^2," generalized forecast error variation decomposition (GFEVD) shows the relative importance of each VAR variable in contributing to the variation in the performance variable. For example, we can use GFEVD to determine what is the contribution of online display ad, among in-store promotion, social media marketing, and search engine optimization, to the variation in brand weekly sales. Compared with FEVD, GFEVD is more widely adopted by marketing literature in that it does not impose causal ordering between variables.

The GFEVD is given by:

$$\theta_{ij} = \frac{\sum_{l=0}^{n} \left(\psi_{ij}(l)\right)^2}{\sum_{j=1}^{m} \sum_{l=0}^{n} \left(\psi_{ij}(l)\right)^2}, j = 1, 2, \ldots, m \qquad (22)$$

where $\psi_{ij}(l)$ is the value of a GIRF following a one standard error shock to variable j on variable i at period l. GFEVD allows an initial shock to affect all other endogenous variables instantaneously (i.e., the coefficient for period zero of other variables can be nonzero).

Judging from Eq. (22), θ_{ij} is a percentage term, and that all the $\theta_{ij}'s$ always sum up to 100%. It is typical to find that most of the variance of a variable is explained by its own past, which is referred to as "inertia" (e.g., price inertia, see Nijs et al. 2007). Panel(a) in Fig. 8 shows an example of analysis on contribution to variation in sales of firm's past sales, online advertising, and offline advertising effort. The contribution of past sales (i.e., inertia) contributes the most (70%), while online advertising ranks the second (20%) and offline advertising the last (10%). In contexts where inertia is of little interest, researchers can take it out and have a better visualization of the relative importance of *other* variables. Panel (b) in Fig. 8 shows GFEVD results without inertia. The relative contribution of two advertising channels remains the same (2:1).

Continuing the example of resource allocation in firm value maximization that we raised in 3.5, the authors contrasted contribution of sales promotion and NPI to firm value FEVD (see Fig. 2 in Pauwels et al. 2004, pp. 151). The gap between contribution of NPI and sales promotion gets wider as time goes, with the former turning eight times greater than the latter in two quarters' time.

Other applications of FEVD and GFEVD include the work of Srinivasan et al. (2016), where the authors examined the contribution to sales growth of traditional marketing mix variables and online customer activity metrics. Without considering sales inertia, the authors found that distribution is subject to 60% of the volume variance, while only 2% for online paid search.

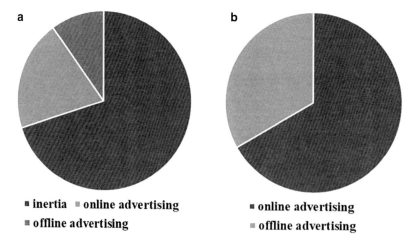

Fig. 8 Example of GFEVD of sales with and without inertia

Volatility Models

Time-series data can be described from many angles, among which the mean and the volatility (or variance) are the two most typical metrics. While the mean (or expected value) of a time series captures the average level of the data, variance captures the level of turbulence, namely the level of fluctuation of the series around its mean (Franses and van Dijk 1996, 2000). In this section, we introduce a model that deals with the assumption of *constant conditional variance*.

Let us again use weekly sales as an example. The models that we have discussed so far (e.g., ARIMA) estimate the expected weekly sales conditional on different marketing variables (hence "conditional mean"). These models assume that the volatility of weekly sales stays constant over time. However, in the real world, there are plenty of examples where such an assumption does not hold; instead, the level of volatilities across periods could be related. For example, if sales have been volatile during the past two weeks, then it is very reasonable to expect that sales in the coming week are going to be more volatile than usual as well. Additionally, an exogenous event could also shock sales by significantly increasing volatility for a certain period of time.

Figure 9 shows an example of a brand's weekly sales (in thousands) over a time span of 160 weeks. The vertical dashed line refers to the time (week 73) when the brand launched a new product. One might first notice that the average sales increased greatly after the new product introduction (NPI) as expected (i.e., from 50,163 to 148,255). Moreover, the volatility of brand sales (measured by standard deviation) also rose greatly from the pre- to post-NPI period (i.e., from 179,209.1 to 47,904.47). When trying to model weekly sales, it is important to at least incorporate a step change in both mean and volatility after week 73.

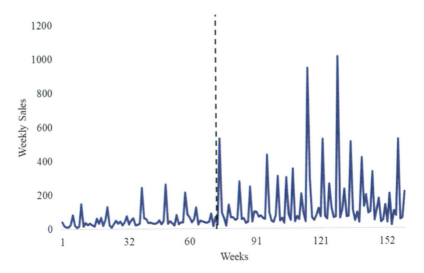

Fig. 9 Weekly sales with time-varying volatilities

From the practical point of view, firms care about performance volatility, since a highly uncertain future is hard to plan for. With high sales volatility, refining the marketing mix based on historical ROMI is not meaningful. Further at the retailer level, a high level of sales volatility of a brand or a product category leads to difficulties in inventory management (Esteban-Bravo et al. 2017). Finally, firms with volatile performance are usually deemed to have higher idiosyncratic risk, which can be harmful for firm valuation and stock market performance (Fischer et al. 2016). Hence, models that describe, explain, and predict volatilities are of great value and importance.

The focus of this section, generalized autoregressive conditional heteroscedasticity (GARCH) model (Other variations of GARCH volatility models that are extensively used in the literature include VEC-GARCH models (Bollerslev et al. 1988), constant conditional correlation (CCC)-GARCH model (Yildirim et al. 2020), and BEKK model (Esteban-Bravo et al. 2017)), incorporates dynamics in data volatility by recognizing a time-varying conditional variance (Engle et al. 1987; Fischer et al. 2016). A GARCH model first determines the conditional mean of a series and then the volatility. It estimates conditional variances of data series in an explicit way, similar with how conditional mean is estimated by ARIMA model.

Let us start by introducing the ARCH specification and then generalizing it to GARCH. Consider again sales data of a brand that is described by an AR(p) process:

$$s_t = \varphi_0 + \varphi_1 s_{t-1} + \ldots + \varphi_p s_{t-p} + \varepsilon_t \tag{23}$$

with $\sum_{i=1}^{p} \varphi_i < 1$.

Let us assume that the squares of the error term in Eq. (23) can be captured by an AR(q) process:

$$\varepsilon_t^2 = \eta_0 + \eta_1 \varepsilon_{t-1}^2 + \ldots + \eta_k \varepsilon_{t-q}^2 + \nu_t \tag{24}$$

where ν_t is white-noise variables with $E(\nu_t) = 0$ and $E(\nu_t, \nu_{t+m}) = 0$ for nonzero $m's$ and $E(\nu_t, \nu_{t+m}) = \sigma^2$ for $m = 0$. The representation of the white-noise process in Eq. (24) is called an ARCH(q) process. Note that the conditional variance of ε_t^2 varies by time, whereas the unconditional variance is constant and is given by $\sigma^2 = E(\varepsilon_t^2) = \frac{\eta_0}{1-\eta_0-\ldots-\eta_q}$.

When fitting a model, a linear representation of ARCH process in Eq. (24) is not always efficient; a more common representation of ε_t is written as:

$$\varepsilon_t = \sqrt{h_t} \cdot z_t \tag{25}$$

where z_t is an i.i.d process with zero mean and unity variance, and

$$h_t = \eta_0 + \eta_1 \varepsilon_{t-1}^2 + \ldots + \eta_k \varepsilon_{t-q}^2 \tag{26}$$

The generalized ARCH, or GARCH, model represents h_t as a function of its own past values and past values of ε_t^2:

$$h_t = a + b_1 h_{t-1} + \ldots + b_m h_{t-m} + \eta_1 \varepsilon_{t-1}^2 + \ldots + \eta_k \varepsilon_{t-q}^2 \qquad (27)$$

If a process ε_t is generated by a process described in Eq. (27), then ε_t is a *GARCH* (*m, q*) process.

Beyond the univariate specifications that we discussed above, we can use GARCH model, combined with VAR model, to estimate multiple endogenous variables. For example, the work of Esteban-Bravo et al. (2017) recognizes that not only sales volatility but also covolatilities (i.e., conditional covariance) between sales and marketing actions are time varying. Using a VAR-BEKK model, the authors generated fresh insights for managers to deal with performance volatility that is often overlooked by prior research. van Dieijen et al. (2019) examined the interaction between volatility in volume of firm-related user-generated content (UGC) and volatility in firm stock return. The authors estimated a multivariate GARCH model and found significant cross-effect between UGC growth and stock returns. Further, the authors discovered new product launch events as a driver of UGC growth volatility, though the exact direction of impact (i.e., an increase or a decrease in volatility) is determined by the specific UGC content.

Conclusion

Time-series models are great tools for researchers and practitioners to tackle marketing problems. These models, especially modern dynamic systems, are also quite powerful in generating new insights by bridging dynamics between factors that are previously overlooked. This chapter introduces traditional and modern time-series analytics such as ARIMA and VAR models. We also discuss model applications in marketing such as evaluating return on marketing investments, measuring elasticities of marketing activities, and refining allocation of marketing resources, to name a few. As the field evolves, researchers are adopting a broader range of models to explore marketing challenges. For instance, recent research has emerged using Markov chain models to solve sales attribution problems. We hence expect further methodological advancements in time-series modeling in marketing and highlight the importance of reviewing this domain of research from time to time.

Cross-References

▶ Dealing with Endogeneity: A Nontechnical Guide for Marketing Researchers
▶ Measuring Sales Promotion Effectiveness
▶ Modeling Marketing Dynamics Using Vector Autoregressive (VAR) Models
▶ Return on Media Models

Appendix

Software Application

The purpose of this software application section is to show our readers how analysts and modelers tackle real-world marketing problems using time-series models like ARIMA and VAR that are covered in this chapter. We hereby introduce R (You might want to know more about this powerful analytical tool via https://www.r-project.org/), an open-source and free software for statistical computing and data analysis. It is widely adopted by academics and industry practitioners as a powerful analytical tool to facilitate them when dealing with data-rich challenges.

Let's start by walking into the following scenario:

ABC company operates in the kitchen appliance industry in an emerging market. The company so far has focused all its marketing efforts on offline flyer advertising and online Google AdWords. However, recent performance reports showed that ABC's sales have not been reaching the management's expectations.

The CMO, in preparation for a meeting with the CEO and CFO, is keen to know if and to what ABC's sales will look like in the next quarter. Further, he/she wonders to what extent marketing expenditures are effective in driving up sales. The CMO is also curious if there's any potential for ABC to optimize its current marketing budget allocation.

As the director of the marketing analytics department, you are presented with ABC's historical weekly sales and marketing expenditure on flyer advertising and Google AdWords advertising over a time span of 122 weeks (i.e., 122 observations). Having met with the CMO, you make a summary of the questions to be answered and your action plans as follows:

(a) *What would be the forecast of demand for the next 12 weeks?*

We are going to predict future sales using two approaches: ARIMA and multiple linear regression (MLR) and compare their estimation and prediction results.

(b) *What drives sales in the long run? What is the contribution of each marketing action to sales (i.e., return on marketing investment)?*

We are going to estimate a VAR model and perform FEVD to evaluate the relative importance of AdWords, flyers, and sales inertia played in determining long-run sales.

(c) *To what extent do AdWords and flyers impact sales in the short versus long run?*

We are going to perform IRF analysis to evaluate the short- and long-run elasticities of each marketing action.

(d) *How should ABC allocate marketing budget between AdWords and flyers to get the best result?*

We are going to use long-run elasticities of AdWords and flyer marketing to determine the optimal resource allocation scheme for ABC.

Applied Time-Series Analysis in Marketing

Data Visualizations

Here is a brief preview of the first 10 rows of our dataset:

Week	Sales	Flyer	Adwords
1	115792	0.00	999.860
2	183189	17134.21	1011.395
3	210107	0.00	1049.560
4	227392	0.00	969.570
5	282095	0.00	984.850
6	218587	0.00	958.400
7	177226	12079.39	839.670
8	140803	0.00	867.460
9	174974	0.00	962.820
10	145961	0.00	958.420

As you can observe, the firm so far has been having a relatively stable expenditure on AdWords (around 900 each week), while that on flyers it has been much more fluctuating. For example, during the first 10 weeks, the firm spent 17134.21 in week 2 and 12079.39 in week 7, and nothing for the rest 8 weeks. To get a feel of the data patterns, it is a good practice to visually inspect them by plotting sales, flyer expenditure, and Google AdWords expenditure, respectively using *ts.plot*.

```
ts.plot(data$Sales, col="blue", main="Sales")
```

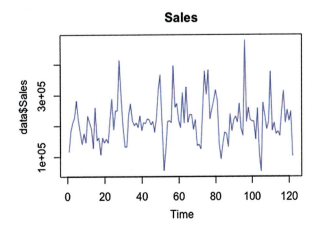

```
ts.plot(data$Adwords, col="darkgreen", main="Adwords")
```

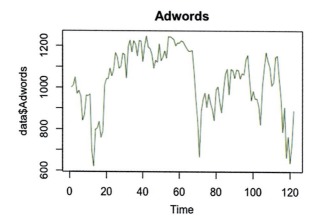

```
ts.plot(data$Flyer, col="red", main="Flyers")
```

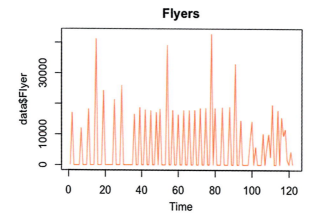

ARIMA Modeling

As elaborated in this chapter, we are going to estimate and predict sales using ARIMA following the procedure summarized below:

- Perform **unit root tests** to check for nonstationary variables and take differences of the variables that are evolving.

Applied Time-Series Analysis in Marketing

- Plot **ACF** and **PACF** to determine the order of lags and hence the specification of ARIMA.
- Split the data into **training** and **testing** set and estimate an **ARIMA** model using the training set and predict sales using the testing set.

Additionally, we will also estimate a **multiple linear regression** (MLR) model using the training set and predict sales using the testing set. This is to compare model performance using ARIMA and MLR method.

Log Transformation

First, through the time-series plots, we observe a high level of data turbulence (or volatility), which, if not treated properly, will lead to false model results and interpretations. It is a typical practice to take the logarithm of each variable to smooth out the series as a preliminary step:

```
data$LSales <- log(data$Sales+1)
data$LAd <- log(data$Adwords+1)
data$LFlyer <- log(data$Flyer+1)
```

Note that we add 1 to each variable during log transformation to avoid having log (0), which equals to negative infinity.

Stationary Tests

It is critical for analysts to make sure that data series being modeled are all stationary (instead of evolving) in order to have reliable model results. As introduced in the chapter, there are multiple tests for series stationarity, including the ADF, KPSS, and Phillips-Perron test that can be executed using R function *adf.test, kpss.test, and pp.test*, respectively. Here in this section, we demonstrate the procedure of using the ADF test. Under the ADF test, the null and alternative hypotheses are:

- H_0: The data is not stationary
- H_1: The data is stationary

Note that for *adf.test* and *pp.test*, we can reject the null hypothesis that the variable is not stationary (i.e., with a unit root) if the p-value is smaller than a certain significance level; yet *kpss.test* works in the opposite way, i.e., the null hypothesis is that the series is stationary without a unit root.

To check for stationarity, we need to first let R know that weekly sales and AdWords and flyer expenditures are time series using *ts* function, and then perform ADF test using *adf.test* function:

```
LSales <- ts(data$LSales, frequency = 52, start = c(1, 1))
LAd <- ts(data$LAd, frequency = 52, start = c(1, 1))
LFLYER <- ts(data$LFlyer, frequency = 52, start = c(1, 1))

adf.test(LSales)
```

```
##
##   Augmented Dickey-Fuller Test
##
## data:  LSales
## Dickey-Fuller = -5.2428, Lag order = 4, p-value = 0.01
## alternative hypothesis: stationary
```

```
adf.test(LAd)
```

```
##
##   Augmented Dickey-Fuller Test
##
## data:  LAd
## Dickey-Fuller = -2.0661, Lag order = 4, p-value = 0.5491
## alternative hypothesis: stationary
```

```
adf.test(LFLYER)
```

```
##
##   Augmented Dickey-Fuller Test
##
## data:  LFLYER
## Dickey-Fuller = -6.5352, Lag order = 4, p-value = 0.01
## alternative hypothesis: stationary
```

Test results inform us that LAd series (i.e., log-transformed AdWords spending) is evolving with p-value greater than 0.05. We need to take the first-difference of this series to make it stationary. Note that once we first-difference a log-transformed series, the interpretation will be different: now the series refers to growth of weekly AdWords spending, rather than AdWords spending itself.

To take the first-difference of a series, we use R function *diff*:

```
#Take the first difference of Adwords spending series

DLAd <-diff(LAd, differences = 1)
```

Now we can perform ADF test again to make sure that all variables are stationary:

```
adf.test(LSales)
```

```
##
##  Augmented Dickey-Fuller Test
##
## data:  LSales
## Dickey-Fuller = -5.2428, Lag order = 4, p-value = 0.01
## alternative hypothesis: stationary
```

```
adf.test(DLAd) #first-differenced series
```

```
##
##  Augmented Dickey-Fuller Test
##
## data:  DLAd
## Dickey-Fuller = -5.0641, Lag order = 4, p-value = 0.01
## alternative hypothesis: stationary
```

```
adf.test(LFLYER)
```

```
##
##  Augmented Dickey-Fuller Test
##
## data:  LFLYER
## Dickey-Fuller = -6.5352, Lag order = 4, p-value = 0.01
## alternative hypothesis: stationary
```

Stationary test results suggest that now the three variables (with AdWords spending first-differenced) are all stationary. Note that to construct ARIMA model, we only need sales series, while all series are needed for MLR and later VAR model.

ACF and PACF for Order of Lags

Once a time series has been stationarized, a systematic way to determine the order of lags of the autoregressive (AR) and moving average (MA) components of ARIMA model is to plot and inspect ACF and PACF. Here we use R function *ggtsdisplay*, which can generate (i) the plot of the series over time, (ii) the ACF plot, and (iii) the PACF plot simultaneously and automatically:

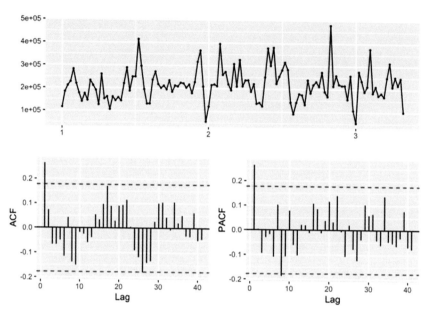

Here on the ACF and PACF plots, the dashed horizontal lines represent the critical region (95% confidence level) for the lags. The lag order of the AR and MA component is identified by the number of lags where the PACF and ACF plot displays a clear cutoff, respectively. Here we find both ACF and PACF have a cutoff at lag 1, indicating that we should probably take a lag order of 1 for both MA and AR components. Further, given that we did not take the difference of the sales series, the final specification of our model is ARIMA (1,0,1), or ARMA (1,1).

Construct and Estimate an ARIMA Model

Splitting the Data

To estimate sales and examine model predicting power, we cannot exploit the entire data to construct our model. Instead, we need to split the series into training (in-sample) and testing (out-of-sample) sets. To do this, we apply the most commonly adopted 80–20 scheme, namely we use the first 80% of the observations as the

Applied Time-Series Analysis in Marketing

training set and the rest 20% as the testing set. Given that we have 122 observations in total, we should use the first 96 observations for our training set, and the rest 25 observations as the testing set.

```
#Splitting the data into training and testing sets

train <- data[1:96,]
test <- data[97:122,]
```

Train the Model

ACF and PACF suggest that we estimate an ARIMA (1,0,1) model. To estimate the model using the training set, we use R function *Arima*:

```
#Estimating the ARIMA model using our training set:

fit_arima <- Arima(ts(LSales[1:96], frequency = 52),order = c(1,0,1), seasonal = c(1,0,1))

summary(fit_arima)
```

```
## Series: ts(LSales[1:96], frequency = 52)
## ARIMA(1,0,1)(1,0,1)[52] with non-zero mean
##
## Coefficients:
##          ar1     ma1     sar1     sma1      mean
##       0.3046  0.0941   0.4731  -0.0771   12.2368
## s.e.     NaN  0.0477      NaN   0.0634    0.0585
##
## sigma^2 estimated as 0.08607:  log likelihood=-20.81
## AIC=53.62   AICc=54.57   BIC=69.01
##
## Training set error measures:
##                    ME      RMSE       MAE       MPE      MAPE      MASE
## Training set 0.01038504 0.2856303 0.2119471 0.0265656 1.738597 0.8070106
##                   ACF1
## Training set -0.0234848
```

Furthermore, you may estimate ARIMA models with different specifications and compare model performances (e.g., AIC and BIC) to pick the best specification. There are also R functions that can automatically pick the specifications with the lowest AIC and BIC, for example, *auto.arima*. However, analysts should keep in mind that you are the constructor of your model and that it is you that should be the final decision-maker on what model to estimate by considering managerial and strategic factors that model diagnostics cannot inform you. For example, some firms might operate within a certain cycle and would want to evaluate sales using a specific order of lags.

Estimate a Multiple Regression Model

In addition to ARIMA, given a dataset as such, it is also very common for modelers to adopt multiple linear regression method and estimate a linear model to fit and predict sales. This is because MLR allows us to incorporate other exogenous factors, while ARIMA typically only involves the endogenous variable itself.

Again, we need to use the training set for model estimation. To do this, we use the *lm* function in R, referring to "linear model."

```
fit_lm <- lm(LSales ~ lag_Sales + DLAd + LFLYER,  data = train)
summary(fit_lm)
```

```
##
## Call:
## lm(formula = LSales ~ lag_Sales + DLAd + LFLYER, data = train)
##
## Residuals:
##      Min       1Q    Median       3Q      Max
## -1.30041 -0.14924   0.01009  0.15514  0.94615
##
## Coefficients:
##               Estimate Std. Error t value Pr(>|t|)
## (Intercept)   7.445228   1.165853   6.386 6.84e-09 ***
## lag_Sales     0.389160   0.095216   4.087 9.33e-05 ***
## DLAd          0.088746   0.388587   0.228   0.8199
## LFLYER        0.012172   0.007227   1.684   0.0955 .
## ---
## Signif. codes:  0 '***' 0.001 '**' 0.01 '*' 0.05 '.' 0.1 ' ' 1
##
## Residual standard error: 0.3095 on 92 degrees of freedom
## Multiple R-squared:  0.1743, Adjusted R-squared:  0.1474
## F-statistic: 6.473 on 3 and 92 DF,  p-value: 0.000504
```

Interpreting the results briefly, a 1% increase in lag sales will lead to 0.39% of increase in current sales; a 1% increase in flyer spending will lead to 0.01% increase in sales. The coefficient of "DLAd" is statistically insignificant.

Validation Set Assessment: ARIMA Versus MLR

Now it is time for us to contrast model performance using ARIMA and MLR method and predict sales using the testing set. We further plot the actual sales and predicted sales using ARIMA and MLR method, respectively, on the same graph for contrast.

Applied Time-Series Analysis in Marketing

```
# Predict sales based on ARIMA model estimations
predict_arima <- predict(fit_arima, order=c(1,0,1), data = test, n.ahead = 26)

# Predict sales based on Multiple Linear regression model estimations
predict_lm <- predict(fit_lm, test)

#Plot the actual and predicted sales on the same graph
data_frame <- data.frame(test$Week,test$LSales,predict_lm, predict_arima$pred)

ggplot(data_frame, aes(data_frame$test.Week)) +
  geom_line(aes(y = test.LSales, colour="Actual Sales")) +
  geom_line(aes(y = predict_lm, colour="Predicted Sales: MLR")) +
  geom_line(aes(y = predict_arima$pred, colour = "Predicted Sales: ARIMA"))
```

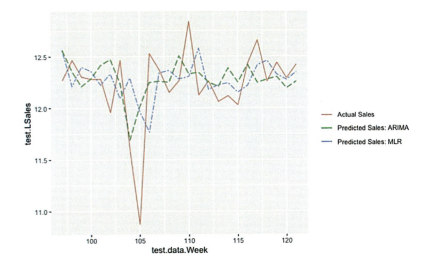

From the graph, both models can mimic (to a certain extent) the pattern of actual sales in the testing set. To determine which method does a relatively more accurate job, we can calculate and compare the root-mean-square deviation (RMSE) of both predictions.

```
# Calculate RMSE of prediction results using MLR and ARIMA method.
rmse.predict_lm <- (sum((test$LSales - predict_lm )^2)/25)^0.5
rmse.predict_arima <- (sum((test$LSales - predict_arima$pred )^2)/25)^0.5

rmse.predict_lm
```

```
## [1] 0.3968784
```

```
rmse.predict_arima
```

```
## [1] 0.3255406
```

Comparing prediction accuracy using both methods, we find that ARIMA managed to capture the dynamics of ABC's sales better, since its RMSE (0.33) is slightly lower than that of MLR (0.40).

To improve the model prediction accuracy of MLR, several other factors should be considered, for example, the weekly price of ABC, and weekly sales of ABC's core competitors. Modelers can incorporate additional variables into the model depending on data availability. Furthermore, answering the first question raised by the CMO, we can predict sales of ABC for the next 3 months (12 weeks) based on our ARIMA model. Here we plot both predicted sales and 95% confidence intervals in the graph below:

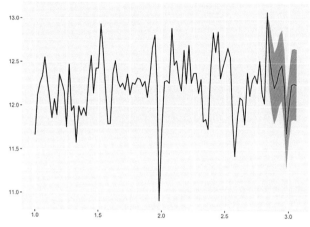

Reverting the log-transformed predicted values back, we get the predicted sales for the next quarter (i.e., 12 weeks) as below:

```
#predicted sales
forecast<-fit_arima %>% forecast(h=12)
forecast_sales <- exp(forecast$mean)-1
forecast_sales
```

```
## Time Series:
## Start = c(2, 45)
## End = c(3, 4)
## Frequency = 52
##  [1] 285957.6 232547.9 200872.0 216504.4 246491.8 260936.2 206717.2 119479.9
##  [9] 164058.7 208617.2 210776.9 208660.7
```

VAR Model Steps

Estimating a VAR Model

We are able to set up our VAR model relatively easily since we have already performed model diagnostics on series stationarity through unit root tests in section

Applied Time-Series Analysis in Marketing

"Testing for Evolution Versus Stationarity." Taking all three variables as endogenous variables, we estimate a VAR model consisting of (log-transformed) weekly sales, lagged Google AdWords expenditure, and flyer expenditure using *VAR* function. We then summarize the results in the table below.

```
#Build a dataset for VAR model
data.ts.dl <- window(cbind( DLAd, LFLYER,LSales), start = c(1, 2))

#VAR estimation
varp <- VAR(data.ts.dl, ic="AIC", lag.max=1, type="const", season=4)

#Summarize and present VAR results
lmp <- varp$varresult
stargazer( lmp$DLAd, lmp$LFLYER,lmp$LSales, column.labels = c( 'DLAd', 'LFlyer', 'LSales'), type = "text", dep.va
r.labels.include = FALSE )
```

```
##
## =================================================================
##                                            Dependent variable:
##                                    -------------------------------
##                                      DLAd      LFlyer     LSales
##                                      (1)        (2)        (3)
## ---------------------------------------------------------------
## DLAd.l1                            -0.154     -4.150      0.402
##                                    (0.094)    (4.453)    (0.339)
##
## LFLYER.l1                          -0.00002   -0.276***   0.003
##                                    (0.002)    (0.092)    (0.007)
##
## LSales.l1                          -0.062**    0.298     0.310***
##                                    (0.026)    (1.215)    (0.092)
##
## const                              0.751**     0.444     8.436***
##                                    (0.313)    (14.814)   (1.127)
##
## sd1                                -0.020      0.816     -0.027
##                                    (0.024)    (1.153)    (0.088)
##
## sd2                                -0.033      1.077     -0.026
##                                    (0.024)    (1.154)    (0.088)
##
## sd3                                -0.014      0.673     -0.019
##                                    (0.024)    (1.153)    (0.088)
##
## ---------------------------------------------------------------
## Observations                         120        120        120
## R2                                  0.083      0.096      0.107
## Adjusted R2                         0.034      0.048      0.059
## Residual Std. Error (df = 113)      0.094      4.449      0.339
## F Statistic (df = 6; 113)           1.703      1.995*     2.248**
## =================================================================
## Note:                              *p<0.1; **p<0.05; ***p<0.01
```

From the VAR output, we find that:

- Direct effects: AdWords (0.402) and flyer (0.003) both have positive direct impact on sales.
- Carryover effects: past AdWords (-0.154), flyer advertising (-0.276), and sales (0.310) all exert impact on their current values, respectively.

- Feedback effects: sales have positive feedback effect on flyer (0.298) and ad spending (0.310), while negative feedback effect on online AdWords spending (−0.062).

Note that due to the limited sample size and data variation in our sample, some of the coefficients seem statistically insignificant. However, to see the effect of AdWords and Flyer advertising on Revenues over time (e.g., immediate and long-term effects), it is more rigorous to refer to results from impulse response function (IRF) analysis.

After the estimation it is always good practice to check the residuals' normality and the autocorrelation. If there is any misspecification, you may need to search if any anomaly such as outlier and structural break occurs. Here we plot the residuals and inspect their mean.

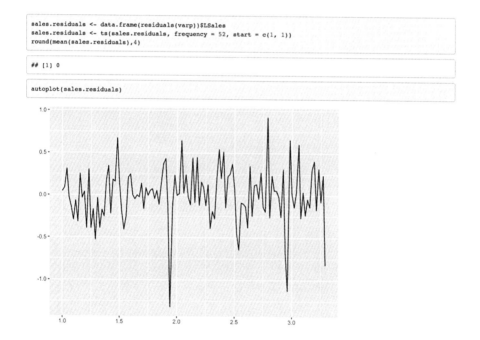

We observe that the residuals seem to vary randomly around zero, with a mean of zero.

Forecast Error Variance Decomposition

Referring to the second question raised by the CMO, we perform FEVD analysis to evaluate and visualize the relative importance or contribution of flyers, AdWords, and sales inertia using R function *fevd*:

Applied Time-Series Analysis in Marketing

```
fevd <-fevd(varp, n.ahead=7)
round(fevd$LSales, 4)

##          DLAd LFLYER LSales
## [1,] 0.0005 0.0647 0.9349
## [2,] 0.0109 0.0697 0.9194
## [3,] 0.0110 0.0697 0.9193
## [4,] 0.0110 0.0697 0.9192
## [5,] 0.0110 0.0697 0.9192
## [6,] 0.0110 0.0697 0.9192
## [7,] 0.0110 0.0697 0.9192
```

The table above indicates that ABC's sales are quite "sticky" in the sense that lagged sales (LSales) contribute to more than 90% to changes in current sales. Offline marketing seems to play a more important role than online AdWords for ABC. The table above corresponds to the bottom panel of the graph below.

```
plot(fevd)
```

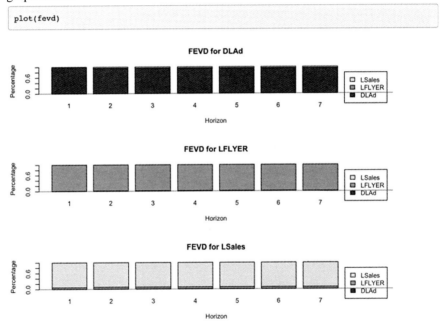

IRF Analysis

Responding to the third question raised by the CMO, we perform IRF (In this session we are using orthogonalized impulse reaction function for estimation. In R environment, to implement GIRF estimations, we need to estimate a Bayesian VAR model (you may check package "bvartools") instead, which is beyond the scope of this chapter.) analysis to evaluate the short- and long-run elasticities of flyers and AdWords marketing of ABC using *irf* function in R.

```
irfs <- irf(varp, impulse = c('DLAd', 'LFLYER'), response = 'LSales',
            runs = 100, n.ahead = 7 , ortho = TRUE, ci=0.95)

plot(irfs)
```

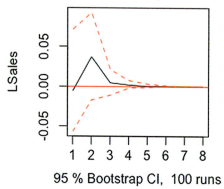

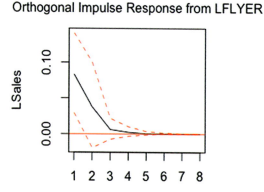

IRF plots help us visualize when the peak effects occur. On the plots, the solid line refers to IRF coefficients, while the dashed lines refer to lower and upper bound of the IRF coefficient's confidence interval. It seems that increase flyer spending can cause an immediate boost of sales; in contrast, it takes longer time for spending on AdWords to have positive impact on sales. Moreover, we can observe that these impacts all decay fast and gets close to zero over time, mostly within 6 periods (weeks).

Immediate and Long-Term Effects

In order to compute the immediate and long-term effects, we need to evaluate the significance of each IRF coefficient. If the t-statistics of the IRF coefficient is greater than 1 (Here we follow previous research (e.g., Slotegraaf and Pauwels 2008) to set the criteria as t>1. You may apply the t>2 rule if you would like to evaluate coefficient significance at a 95% significance level) (t>1), we treat it as significant and keep the value of that coefficient; otherwise, we treat the coefficient as zero. To calculate the t-statistics, we need to derive the standard error (se) of each coefficient from its confidence interval, since lower bound$_{ci}$ = β − 1.96 ∗ se, and upper bound$_{ci}$ = β + 1.96 ∗ se. We then calculate the t-statistics using t-stat= β/se.

Based on the above computations, the first period impact is called the immediate effect while the cumulative effect over 8 periods is called the long-run effect.

Now we make a table in R to summarize IRF coefficients and their confidence intervals. You will see in the output that response means the response value at a particular period (there are 8 periods in total), lower and upper refer to the lower and upper bound of the corresponding confidence intervals, respectively.

```
#Make a table to summarize IRF coefficients and their confidence intervals

irf.table.ci <- round(data.frame(period = seq(1, 8),
                    response.Adwords = irfs$irf$DLAd,
                    Adwords.lower = irfs$Lower$DLAd,
                    Adwords.upper = irfs$Upper$DLAd,
                    response.flyer = irfs$irf$LFLYER,
                    flyer.lower = irfs$Lower$LFLYER,
                    flyer.upper = irfs$Upper$LFLYER),4)
colnames(irf.table.ci) <- c('Period', 'DLAdwords', 'DLAdwords Lower', 'DLAdwords Upper','LFLYER',
                    'LFLYER Lower', 'LFLYER Upper')


knitr::kable(irf.table.ci)
```

Period	DLAdwords	DLAdwords Lower	DLAdwords Upper	LFLYER	LFLYER Lower	LFLYER Upper
1	-0.0058	-0.0601	0.0495	0.0833	0.0259	0.1392
2	0.0369	-0.0223	0.1127	0.0377	-0.0166	0.0855
3	0.0046	-0.0106	0.0305	0.0061	-0.0083	0.0216
4	0.0019	-0.0039	0.0093	0.0023	-0.0037	0.0099
5	0.0003	-0.0023	0.0027	0.0004	-0.0014	0.0028
6	0.0001	-0.0004	0.0015	0.0001	-0.0003	0.0013
7	0.0000	-0.0002	0.0003	0.0000	-0.0002	0.0004
8	0.0000	0.0000	0.0003	0.0000	0.0000	0.0002

Now we apply the t>1 rule to determine coefficient significance and calculate long-term elasticities of AdWords and flyer advertising spending.

```r
#Adwords
result_irf_adwords<-matrix(nrow = 8, ncol = 1)

for (i in 1:8) {
  se <- (irfs$Upper$DLAd[i]-irfs$Lower$DLAd[i])/(2*1.96)
  t_irf_adwords<- irfs$irf$DLAd[i]/se

  if (t_irf_adwords>1) {
    result_irf_adwords[i] <- irfs$irf$DLAd[i]
  } else {
    result_irf_adwords[i] <-0
    }
}

result_irf_adwords #print out the results
```

```
##          [,1]
## [1,] 0.00000000
## [2,] 0.03691742
## [3,] 0.00000000
## [4,] 0.00000000
## [5,] 0.00000000
## [6,] 0.00000000
## [7,] 0.00000000
## [8,] 0.00000000
```

```r
lr_adwords <- sum(result_irf_adwords)
lr_adwords
```

```
## [1] 0.03691742
```

```r
#Flyer spending

result_irf_flyers<-matrix(nrow = 8, ncol = 1)

for (i in 1:8) {
  se <- (irfs$Upper$LFLYER[i]-irfs$Lower$LFLYER[i])/(2*1.96)
  t_irf_flyers<- irfs$irf$LFLYER[i]/se

  if (t_irf_flyers>1) {
    result_irf_flyers[i] <- irfs$irf$LFLYER[i]
  } else {
    result_irf_flyers[i] <-0
    }
}

result_irf_flyers #print out the results
```

```
##          [,1]
## [1,] 0.08333906
## [2,] 0.03768691
## [3,] 0.00000000
## [4,] 0.00000000
## [5,] 0.00000000
## [6,] 0.00000000
## [7,] 0.00000000
## [8,] 0.00000000
```

```r
lr_flyers <- sum(result_irf_flyers)
lr_flyers
```

```
## [1] 0.121026
```

After applying the t>1 rule, we figure out that the AdWords advertising has a significant and positive impact on revenues in second period, while flyer advertising has significant and positive impact on revenues in the first and second period. Put it more specifically, after adding up significant coefficients overtime to get the long-term elasticities for both advertisings, we can say that:

- An 1% increase in AdWords advertising spending growth (note that we first-differenced the series) will increase the firm's revenues by 0.04% in the long run.
- An 1% increase in flyer advertising spending will increase the firm's revenues by 0.12% in the long run.

Optimal Allocation Between AdWords and Flyer Spending

Finally, we can respond to the final question from the CMO regarding ABC's budget allocation. To do this, we may first take a look at the current budget allocation of ABC. We just need to review the dataset and calculate the total amount of money that the firm has spent on AdWords and flyers, respectively. Then we create a pie chart to visualize the current budget allocation of the firm.

```
#Current budget allocation

cost_adwords<-sum(data$Adwords)
cost_flyer<-sum(data$Flyer)
cost_total <- cost_adwords + cost_flyer

costshare_adwords<-cost_adwords/cost_total
costshare_flyer<-cost_flyer/cost_total
```

```
# Ingredients for the pie-chart
slices_actual<-c(costshare_adwords, costshare_flyer )
lbls_actual<-c("Adwords", "Flyer")
pct_actual<-round(slices_actual*100)
lbls_actual<-paste(lbls_actual, pct_actual)      # add data to labels
lbls_actual<-paste(lbls_actual, "%", sep="")     # add % sign to labels

# Get the pie-chart
pie(slices_actual, labels=lbls_actual, col=rainbow(length(lbls_actual)), main="Actual Budget Allocation" )
```

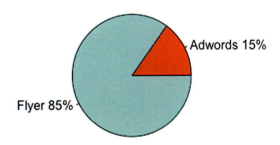

We can see that the firm is currently putting far more resources on flyers, since it spends 85% of its budget on it and only 15% on online AdWords.

For the optimal marketing budget allocation, we need to retrieve the impact of AdWords and flyer spending from IRF analysis. More specifically, we will calculate the optimal allocation for each marketing channel using the following formula:

$$\text{Optimal Allocation}_i = \frac{\eta_i}{\sum_{i=1}^{I} \eta_i}$$

where η is the elasticity of marketing tool i.

As an example, for AdWords spending, we will calculate it as follows:

$$\text{Optimal Allocation}_{\text{Adwords}} = \frac{\eta_{\text{AdWords}}}{\eta_{\text{AdWords}} + \eta_{\text{Flyers}}}$$

Let's do this in R now:

```
#Get the coefficients from IRF results
beta_adwords<-lr_adwords
beta_flyer<-lr_flyers

#The sum of all elasticities
beta_all<-beta_adwords+beta_flyer

#Optimal resource allocation
optim_adwords<-beta_adwords/beta_all
optim_flyer<-beta_flyer/beta_all
```

Having figured out the optimal budget allocation between AdWords and flyer, we can now create another pie chart so that we can compare:

```
## Pie-chart ingredients
optimal_spend<-c(optim_adwords,optim_flyer)
optimal_spend=round(optimal_spend, digits=5)
optimal_spend
```

```
## [1] 0.23374 0.76626
```

```
slices_optim<-c(optim_adwords, optim_flyer)
lbls_optim<-c("Adwords", "Flyer")
pct_optim<-round(slices_optim*100)
lbls_optim<-paste(lbls_optim, pct_optim)    # paste variable names to data labels
lbls_optim<-paste(lbls_optim, "%", sep="") # add % sign to labels

# Get the pie-chart
pie(slices_optim, labels=lbls_optim, col=rainbow(length(lbls_optim)), main="Optimal Budget Allocation" )
```

Optimal Budget Allocation

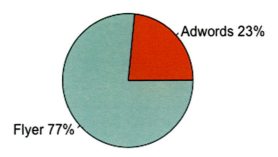

The optimal budget allocation is that the firm should actually spend less of its marketing budget on flyer advertising (77%, instead of 85%), and more on Google AdWords advertising (23% instead of 15%). Contrasting the optimal and actual budget allocation of the firm, it is quite obvious that currently, the firm is underestimating the power of online marketing through AdWords and overemphasizing the importance of offline flyers.

We can see that without analyzing resource allocation, a firm can be quite far away from what it "should" do. Looking at the optimal budget allocation is quite critical in managers' decision-making, since utilizing the constrained resource more wisely can potentially make a big difference to firm performance (e.g., revenues).

On a final note, this section talks about the allocation when the sales performance is taken into consideration. Brand managers may pursue different KPIs as well, such as market share, profits, and brand liking. With different KPIs pursued by the brand manager, the allocation would be different. Moreover, instead of keeping the budget the same and reallocating it, the brand manager may want to increase the budget. In such a case, the dynamics between marketing input and financial performance would be altered, leading to different optimal allocation.

To conclude, we responded to the questions raised by ABC's CMO regarding demand forecasting, marketing effectiveness, and budget allocation ARIMA (and MLR) and VAR (and FEVD and IRF) methods. We hope that our readers can have a better understanding of the materials covered in this chapter by referring to this application exercise.

References

Akaike, H. (1973). Information theory and an extension of the maximum likelihood principle. In B. N. Petrov & F. Csáki (Eds.), *2nd international symposium on information theory, Tsahkadsor, Armenia, USSR, September 2-8, 1971* (pp. 267–281). Akadémiai Kiadó: Budapest.

Bollerslev, T., Engle, R. F., & Wooldridge, J. M. (1988). A capital asset pricing model with time-varying covariances. *Journal of Political Economy, 96*(1), 116–131.

Bronnenberg, B. J., Mahajan, V., & Vanhonacker, W. R. (2000). The emergence of market structure in new repeat-purchase categories: The interplay of market share and retailer distribution. *Journal of Marketing Research, 37*(1), 16–31.

Colicev, A., Malshe, A., Pauwels, K., & O'Connor, P. (2018). Improving consumer mindset metrics and shareholder value through social media: The different roles of owned and earned media. *Journal of Marketing, 82*(1), 37–56.

Colicev, A., Kumar, A., & O'Connor, P. (2019). Modeling the relationship between firm and user generated content and the stages of the marketing funnel. *International Journal of Research in Marketing, 36*(1), 100–116.

De Haan, E., Wiesel, T., & Pauwels, K. (2016). The effectiveness of different forms of online advertising for purchase conversion in a multiple-channel attribution framework. *International Journal of Research in Marketing, 33*(3), 491–507.

Dekimpe, M. G., & Hanssens, D. M. (1995). The persistence of marketing effects on sales. *Marketing Science, 14*(1), 1–21.

Deleersnyder, B., Geyskens, I., Gielens, K., & Dekimpe, M. G. (2002). How cannibalistic is the Internet channel? A study of the newspaper industry in the United Kingdom and the Netherlands. *International Journal of Research in Marketing, 19*(4), 337–348.

Engle, R. F., Lilien, D. M., & Robins, R. P. (1987). Estimating time varying risk premia in the term structure: The ARCH-M model. *Econometrica: journal of the Econometric Society, 55*(2), 391–407.

Engle, R. F., & Granger, C. W. (1987). Co-integration and error correction: Representation, estimation, and testing. *Econometrica: Journal of the Econometric Society, 55*(2), 251–276.

Esteban-Bravo, M., Vidal-Sanz, J. M., & Yildirim, G. (2017). Can retail sales volatility be curbed through marketing actions? *Marketing Science, 36*(2), 232–253.

Fischer, M., Shin, H. S., & Hanssens, D. M. (2016). Brand performance volatility from marketing spending. *Management Science, 62*(1), 197–215.

Franses, P. H., & Van Dijk, D. (1996). Forecasting stock market volatility using (non-linear) Garch models. *Journal of Forecasting, 15*(3), 229–235.

Franses, P. H., & Van Dijk, D. (2000). *Non-linear time series models in empirical finance.* Cambridge: Cambridge University Press.

Granger, C. W. (1969). Investigating causal relations by econometric models and cross-spectral methods. *Econometrica: journal of the Econometric Society, 37*(3), 424–438.

Hannan, E. J., & Quinn, B. G. (1979). The determination of the order of an autoregression. *Journal of the Royal Statistical Society: Series B: Methodological, 41*, 190–195.

Hanssens, D. M., & Pauwels, K. H. (2016). Demonstrating the value of marketing. *Journal of Marketing, 80*(6), 173–190.

Ilhan, B. E., Kübler, R. V., & Pauwels, K. H. (2018). Battle of the brand fans: Impact of brand attack and defense on social media. *Journal of Interactive Marketing, 43*, 33–51.

Kireyev, P., Pauwels, K., & Gupta, S. (2016). Do display ads influence search? Attribution and dynamics in online advertising. *International Journal of Research in Marketing, 33*(3), 475–490.

Kwiatkowski, D., Phillips, P. C., Schmidt, P., & Shin, Y. (1992). Testing the null hypothesis of stationarity against the alternative of a unit root. *Journal of Econometrics, 54*(1–3), 159–178.

Lütkepohl, H. (2005). *New introduction to multiple time series analysis.* Berlin/New York: Springer Science & Business Media.

Nijs, V. R., Srinivasan, S., & Pauwels, K. (2007). Retail-price drivers and retailer profits. *Marketing Science, 26*(4), 473–487.

Pauwels, K. (2004). How dynamic consumer response, competitor response, company support, and company inertia shape long-term marketing effectiveness. *Marketing Science, 23*(4), 596–610.

Pauwels, K. H. (2017). Modern (multiple) time series models: The dynamic system. In *Advanced methods for modeling markets* (pp. 115–148). Cham: Springer.

Pauwels, K., Silva-Risso, J., Srinivasan, S., & Hanssens, D. M. (2004). New products, sales promotions, and firm value: The case of the automobile industry. *Journal of Marketing, 68*(4), 142–156.

Pauwels, K., Demirci, C., Yildirim, G., & Srinivasan, S. (2016). The impact of brand familiarity on online and offline media synergy. *International Journal of Research in Marketing, 33*(4), 739–753.

Schwarz, G. (1978). Estimating the dimension of a model. *The Annals of Statistics, 6*(2), 461–464.

Slotegraaf, R. J., & Pauwels, K. (2008). The impact of brand equity and innovation on the long-term effectiveness of promotions. *Journal of Marketing Research, 45*(3), 293–306.

Srinivasan, S., Vanhuele, M., & Pauwels, K. (2010). Mind-set metrics in market response models: An integrative approach. *Journal of Marketing Research, 47*(4), 672–684.

Srinivasan, S., Rutz, O. J., & Pauwels, K. (2016). Paths to and off purchase: Quantifying the impact of traditional marketing and online consumer activity. *Journal of the Academy of Marketing Science, 44*(4), 440–453.

Van Dieijen, M., Borah, A., Tellis, G. J., & Franses, P. H. (2019). Big data analysis of volatility spillovers of brands across social media and stock markets. *Industrial Marketing Management, 88*, 465.

Yildirim, G., Wang, W., & Deleersnyder, B. (2020) Market turbulence following a major new product introduction: Is it really so bad? Working paper.

Modeling Marketing Dynamics Using Vector Autoregressive (VAR) Models

Shuba Srinivasan

Contents

Introduction 516
Vector Autoregressive (VAR) Modeling 518
Unit Root and Cointegration Testing 519
    Testing for Evolution Versus Stationarity 519
    Cointegration Tests: Does a Long-Run Equilibrium Exist Between
    Evolving Series? 521
Models of Dynamic Systems of Equations 523
    Vector Autoregressive Model with Exogenous Variables (VARX) 523
    Structural Vector-Autoregressive Model (SVAR) 529
    Vector Error Correction Model 530
Policy Simulation Analysis 530
    Impulse Response Functions (IRF) 530
    Dynamic Multipliers 535
Granger Causality Tests: Do We Need to Model a Dynamic System? 535
Forecast Error Variance Decomposition (FEVD) 537
Software Programs for VAR Estimation 539
Illustrative Applications of VAR Modeling in Marketing 539
    Investor Response Models in the Marketing-Finance 539
    Marketing and Mindset Metrics Models 541
    Digital Marketing Models 542
Conclusion 543
Cross-References 543
References 543

Abstract

Time-series data include repeated measures of marketing activities and performance that are typically equally spaced in time. In the context of such data, Vector Autoregressive (VAR) models are uniquely suited to capture the time dependence

---

S. Srinivasan (✉)
Boston University Questrom School of Business, Boston, MA, USA
e-mail: ssrini@bu.edu

© Springer Nature Switzerland AG 2022
C. Homburg et al. (eds), *Handbook of Market Research*,
https://doi.org/10.1007/978-3-319-57413-4_10

of both a criterion variable (e.g., sales performance) and predictor variables (e.g., marketing actions, online consumer behavior metrics), as well as how they relate to each other over time. The objective of this chapter is to provide a foundation in VAR models and to enable the readers to apply them in their own research domain of interest. To this end, the chapter will discuss both the underlying perspectives and differences among alternative VAR models, and the practical issues with testing, model choice, estimation, and interpretation that are common in empirical research in marketing.

From a marketing strategy perspective, both managers and academic researchers pay attention to whether a performance change is temporary (short-term) or lasting (long-term). Establishing the distinction between short-term and long-term marketing effectiveness is central to the understanding of marketing strategy and its implications, which this chapter aims to do. The interaction among appropriate marketing phenomena, modeling philosophy, and contemporary substantive topics sets this work apart from previous treatments on the broader topic of econometrics and time-series analysis in marketing (e.g., Dekimpe and Hanssens, Persistence modeling for assessing marketing strategy performance. In: Lehmann D, Moorman C (eds) Cool tools in marketing strategy research. Marketing Science Institute, Cambridge, MA, 2004; Hanssens et al., Market response models: Econometric and time series analysis. Springer Science and Business Media, 2001; Pauwels, Found Trends Market 11(4):215–301, 2018).

> **Keywords**
>
> Vector autoregressive models · Vector-error correction models · Impulse response functions · Forecast error variance decomposition · Long-term marketing effectiveness

Introduction

In today's data-intensive world, data on marketing actions, market, and firm performance can be gathered in a variety of forms. Managers can examine marketing data over time, for example, through measures such as digital advertising spend per week, brand revenues per month, advertising expenditures over the quarters, firm revenues over the past year, and marketing mindset metrics over several years. Time-series data include repeated measures of marketing activities and performance that are typically equally spaced in time. In the context of such data, Vector Autoregressive models (VAR) are uniquely suited to capture the time dependence of both a criterion variable (e.g., sales performance) and predictor variables (e.g., marketing actions, online consumer behavior metrics), as well as how they relate to each other over time.

The objective of this chapter is to provide a foundation in VAR models and to enable the readers to apply them in their own research domain of interest. To this end, I will discuss both the underlying perspectives and differences among alternative VAR models, and the practical issues with testing, model choice, estimation, and interpretation that are common in empirical research in marketing. The interaction among appropriate marketing phenomena, modeling philosophy, and contemporary substantive topics sets this work apart from previous treatments on the broader topic of econometrics and time-series analysis in marketing (e.g., Dekimpe and Hanssens 2004; Hanssens et al. 2001; Pauwels 2018).

From a marketing strategy perspective, both managers and academic researchers pay attention to whether a performance change is temporary (short-term) or lasting (long-term). If revenues have declined dramatically this quarter, will they soon rebound to their historic mean and upward trend? Or will they not, in which case firm action may be called for? Likewise, some marketing actions are often considered tactical tools, such as price promotions to boost sales, but may hurt brand performance in the long run (Mela et al. 1997; Pauwels et al. 2002; Srinivasan et al. 2000). Other marketing actions, such as investments in product introductions and advertising may only be justified by promises of future benefits (Srinivasan et al. 2010). Establishing the distinction between short-term and long-term marketing effectiveness is central to the understanding of marketing strategy and its implications.

There has been a rapid growth of applications of VAR models in the marketing literature for a variety of reasons. First, VAR models enable researchers to use a systems approach to explain the multiple channels of influence of marketing variables on each other, and enable the incorporation of customer response, competitive response, and firm actions (e.g., Pauwels et al. 2004; Srinivasan et al. 2004). As such, VAR models are effective in incorporating the combined influence of multiple stakeholders, accounting for the real world of firm and marketing strategy. Second, they allow researchers to make a distinction between short-term, long-term, and cumulative effects of marketing considering differences between temporary, evolving, and structural changes in marketing variables (e.g., Srinivasan et al. 2000). Finally, the availability of online and offline databases (e.g., Srinivasan et al. 2016) with both longitudinal and cross-sectional data has meant that VAR models have great applicability and have enabled various empirical generalizations on marketing phenomena.

The outline of the chapter is as follows. First, I will provide an overview into the VAR modeling process, followed by a discussion on evolution vs stationarity and unit root testing. I then discuss the concept of cointegration and long-run equilibrium among evolving series. Next, I discuss the details of VAR model specification, including reduced form and structural VARs, followed by Vector-Error Correction Models (VECM). Following this, I will review the importance of Impulse Response Analysis, Granger Causality Tests, and Forecast Error Variance Decompositions (FEVD) in order to generate substantive and policy implications from VAR models. Finally, I conclude the chapter with three (illustrative) contemporary applications of VAR to marketing strategy.

Vector Autoregressive (VAR) Modeling

Vector autoregressive modeling involves a multistep process. Table 1 provides an illustration of how a researcher/practitioner should approach a VAR model.

Table 1 Illustrative approach to VAR modeling framework

Managerial/research goal	Key sources	Methodological step
Step 1: Unit Root & Cointegration Tests		
Are variables stationary or evolving? Are evolving variables in long-run equilibrium?	Enders (2003) Engle and Granger (1987) Perron (1989) Perron (1990) Zivot and Andrews (1992) Johansen et al. (2000) Srinivasan et al. (2000)	Dickey Fuller Tests Augmented Dickey-Fuller Test Cointegration Test Structural Break Test
Step 2: Model of Dynamic System		
How do performance and marketing interact in the long run and short run, accounting for the unit root and cointegration results?	Lütkepohl (1993) Dekimpe and Hanssens (1999) Baghestani (1991) Srinivasan et al. (2004)	Vector Autoregressive model VAR in Differences Vector Error Correction model
Step 3: Policy Simulation Analysis		
What is the dynamic impact of marketing on performance? Which actors drive the dynamic impact of marketing?	Pesaran and Shin (1998) Pauwels et al. (2002) Han et al. (2019)	Unrestricted impulse response Restricted policy simulation Dynamic multipliers
Step 4: Granger Causality Tests		
Which variables are temporally causing which other variables?	Granger (1969) Srinivasan et al. (2010)	Granger Causality
Step 5: Drivers of Performance		
What is the importance of each driver's past in explaining performance variance? Independent of causal ordering?	Hanssens (1998) Srinivasan et al. (2004) Nijs et al. (2007)	Forecast Variance Error Decomposition (FEVD) Generalized FEVD

Modeling Marketing Dynamics Using Vector Autoregressive (VAR) Models

In the first step, unit root tests are used to determine whether the different variables are stable or evolving. If several of the variables are found to have a unit root – that is, if they are found to be evolving – one subsequently tests for cointegration. Depending on the outcome of these two preliminary steps, one estimates a vector autoregressive (VAR) model, in reduced form or structural form in the levels, in the differences, or a vector error correction model (VECM). The parameter estimates from this VAR (or VECM) model are used to derive impulse-response functions and forecast error variance decompositions, from which various summary statistics on the short- and long-run dynamics of the system can be derived. Granger Causality tests help with assessing the temporal causality patterns among the variables. We now briefly elaborate on each of these steps.

Unit Root and Cointegration Testing

Testing for Evolution Versus Stationarity

In the first step, unit root tests are used to determine whether or not the different variables are stable or evolving When a series may be appropriately modeled as depending on a constant plus a coefficient times a lag of the series plus a random term, testing whether a series is stationary or evolving is accomplished using the well-known test proposed by Dickey and Fuller (1979). When more than one lag is involved the appropriate test is the augmented Dickey Fuller test. If several of the variables are found to have a unit root – that is, if they are found to be evolving – one subsequently tests for cointegration among the evolving series.

Stationarity is the tendency of a time series to revert back to its deterministic components, such as a fixed mean (mean-stationary) or a mean and trend (trend-stationary). Stationary processes have a finite variance and are predictable, while evolving series do not return to a fixed mean (and trend); shocks to these series persist in the future. This distinction is essential in empirically testing for unit roots. Following Dekimpe and Hanssens (1995a), we first consider the simple case where the time-series behavior of the variable of interest (for example, a brand's sales Y_t) is described by a first-order autoregressive process:

$$(I - \varphi L)Y_t = a + u_t \tag{1}$$

where φ is an autoregressive parameter, L the lag operator (i.e., $L^p Yt = Y_{t-p}$), u_t is a residual series of zero mean, constant variance (σ^2_u), and uncorrelated random shocks, and a is a constant. Note that Eq. (1) may also be written in the following, more familiar form after applying successive backward substitutions:

$$Y_t = [a/(1 - \varphi)] + u_t + \varphi u_{t-1} + \varphi^2 u_{t-2} + \dots, \tag{2}$$

in which the present value of Y_t is explained as a weighted sum of random shocks. Depending on the value of φ, two scenarios are distinguished.

If $|\varphi| < 1$, the effect of past sales (and thus any "shock" that has affected past sales) diminishes as we move into the future. The impact of past shocks diminishes and eventually becomes negligible. Hence, each shock has only a temporary impact. In such a case, the series has a fixed mean $c/(1 - \varphi)$ and a finite variance $\sigma^2_u/(1 - \varphi^2)$. We call such time series stationary, i.e., it has a time-independent mean and variance. This situation is typical for the market performance of established brands in mature markets (e.g., Nijs et al. 2001; Srinivasan et al. 2000).

If $|\varphi| = 1$, sales will not revert to a historical level but will evolve. This situation has been demonstrated for smaller brands and in emerging markets (e.g., Slotegraaf and Pauwels 2008). If $|\varphi| > 1$, the effect of past sales (and thus of past shocks) becomes increasingly important. Such explosive time-series behavior appears to be unrealistic in marketing (Dekimpe and Hanssens 1995b). When $|\varphi| = 1$, Eq. (2) becomes:

$$Y_t = (a + a + \ldots) + u_t + u_{t-1} + \ldots, \tag{3}$$

In this case, each random shock has a permanent effect on the subsequent values of Y. Sales do not revert to a historical level, but instead wander freely in one direction or another, and are evolving.

Distinguishing between stationarity versus evolution therefore involves checking if φ in Eq. (1) is smaller than or equal to 1. However, for the t-statistic special tables need to be used in lieu of the standard distribution. The generalization of the Dickey-Fuller test to an AR (p) process yields the Augmented Dickey-Fuller test. This test is based on a reformulation of the AR (p) process as:

$$(1 - L)Y_t = \Delta Y_t = \alpha_0 + \beta Y_{t-1} + \alpha_1 \Delta Y_{t-1} + \ldots + \alpha_2 p \Delta Y_{t-p} + u_t \tag{4}$$

The Augmented Dickey-Fuller (ADF) test can be used to test the null hypothesis. The rationale behind adding lagged first differences is that the error should be approximately white noise. In addition, depending on the assumptions of the underlying process, the test may be performed with or without the model intercept. Enders (2003) offered an iterative procedure to implement these different test specifications, as implemented in several marketing papers (e.g., Slotegraaf and Pauwels 2008; Srinivasan et al. 2004).

While the Augmented Dickey Fuller (ADF) method is the most popular unit root test in marketing, it has the limitation of the low power of the test under certain conditions; see Maddala and Kim (2007) for an excellent discussion. Because it has been argued that conventional unit root tests (e.g., ADF) tend to underreject the null of unit root, researchers tend to use the alternative such as the Kwiatkowski–Phillips–Schmidt–Shin (KPSS) test (Kwiatkowski et al. 1992), which uses the null of stationarity. Most applications in marketing, however, show that the ADF and KPSS tests lead to similar conclusions (e.g., Pauwels and Weiss 2008; Villanueva et al. 2008). Other papers have built on these topics; for example, Franses et al. (1999) developed an outlier-robust unit root test and the logical consistency requirement when modeling market shares has also been incorporated in unit root tests by Franses et al. (2001).

Typically, unit root tests are based on the assumption of no structural breaks in the series. If a structural break is identified in a series, the stability of the model is crucial to the task of evaluating the impact of structural changes within the system. It could be that there are large shocks called "structural breaks." Failure to account for such shocks in testing biases the unit root tests toward reporting evolution. In marketing, such structural breaks could correspond to permanent changes to prices, the introduction of new products and channels of distribution (Deleersnyder et al. 2002; Kornelis et al. 2008; Pauwels and Srinivasan 2004), and other similar permanent changes in marketing. Researchers typically define a structural break in terms of a parameter change in the deterministic part of the model, i.e., in the slope and/or intercept of the deterministic growth path (Perron 1989).

The timing of the structural break is either known or unknown. In the case of known structural breaks there are shifts in the data generating process, such as price increases or decreases (Srinivasan et al. 2000), introducing a new store brand (Pauwels and Srinivasan 2004), or channel (Kornelis et al. 2008), or changing the pricing structure from free to fee (Pauwels and Weiss 2008). Perron (1990) developed the most widely used test for a single break, which has been the focus of most marketing applications (Deleersnyder et al. 2002; Lim et al. 2005; Nijs et al. 2001; Pauwels and Srinivasan 2004). Zivot and Andrews (2002) propose testing for structural breaks that are unknown which may be a common occurence, instead of eyeballing the time series for where a structural break should be and then testing for it. For instance, if players anticipate changes, they may even react before the time the researcher dates the event (e.g., Pauwels and Srinivasan 2004), which will be picked up by unknown structural break tests.

Cointegration Tests: Does a Long-Run Equilibrium Exist Between Evolving Series?

Cointegration describes the existence of an equilibrium or stationary relationship among two or more time series, each of which is individually nonstationary. An equilibrium relationship would imply that, even if they diverge from each other in the short run, such deviations are stochastically bounded or diminishing over time. Figure 1 shows an illustrative example of cointegration between annual advertising spending and sales revenues for the Lydia Pinkham from 1907 to 1960.

To illustrate cointegration, we consider an example in which a brand's sales (*SALES*), its own marketing (*MKTG*), and its competitors' marketing (*CMKTG*) are all evolving. The existence of a cointegrating relationship between these three variables would imply (see Srinivasan et al. (2000) for a more in-depth discussion) the following:

$$SALES_t = \beta_0 + \beta_1 MKTG_t + \beta_2 CMKTG_t + e_t \tag{5}$$

A simple testing procedure for cointegration, proposed by Engle and Granger (1987), is to estimate Eq. (5) using Ordinary Least Squares and test the residuals e_t

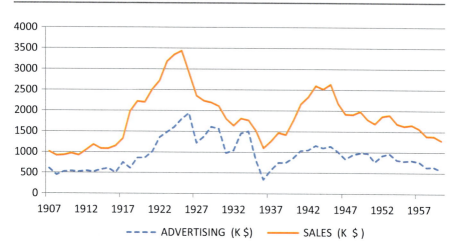

Fig. 1 Cointegrating relationship between advertising and sales – Lydia Pinkham Data

for a unit root using standard unit root tests, and with the updated critical values listed in Engle and Yoo (1987). A marketing application of the Engle and Granger approach to cointegration testing can be found in Baghestani (1991) using the Lydia Pinkham data. This procedure is simple and consistent, but can be biased in small samples and is not possible with more than one cointegrating vector. Johansen's (1988) Full Information Maximum Likelihood (FIML) test does not suffer from these limitations, and has been used extensively in marketing applications. Dekimpe and Hanssens (1999) applied the latter test in their analysis of a prescription drugs market. They found that even though each of the individual series (prescriptions, advertising, sales calls, and price differential) was evolving, the four variables were related together in a long-run cointegrating equilibrium that prevented them from wandering too far apart from one another.

Such long-run cointegrating equilibria can emerge for a variety of reasons. First, cointegration can arise from stationary linear combinations of category and brand sales, for instance. If such regressions exist, then they are consistent with market shares being stationary or stable. Srinivasan and Bass (2000) propose that if brand sales and category sales are cointegrated, this also implies that the market is in long-run equilibrium. From a strategic perspective, this implies that firms are unable to improve their relative position despite improving their absolute long-run performance with respect to sales. Srinivasan and Bass (2000) show that evolution occurs for a majority of brand sales series, and that a vast majority of the market share time-series models are stationary. This is consistent with arguments of Bass and Pilon (1980) that many markets are in a long-run equilibrium. The relative position of the brands is only temporarily affected by marketing activities. Even for brand sales (and category sales) series, later studies suggest that stationarity, and not evolution is the norm for mature brands in mature categories (e.g., Nijs et al. 2001; Pauwels et al. 2002). Emerging markets and brands show a substantially higher potential for evolution (Osinga et al. 2010; Slotegraaf and Pauwels 2008). More recently, Kireyev et al. (2016) use the Johansen et al. (2000) test allowing for structural breaks in the relationship between online display and online search clicks.

Second, certain budgeting rules (e.g., advertising as a percentage-of-sales allocation rules) imply that sales successes eventually translate into higher marketing spending, which may result in sales and marketing mix variables being cointegrated. For instance, Srinivasan et al. (2000) note that one rationale for a long-run cointegrating relationship between own prices, competitive prices, and sales is that different price levels correspond to different long-run demand or sales levels, and these, in turn, are associated with different levels of shares. This long-run cointegrating equilibrium among sales and prices is consistent with the underlying idea that customers' limited budgets may cause different price levels to be associated with different long-run demand levels.

Finally, competitive decision rules can result in firms' marketing spending levels never deviating too far from each other (Dekimpe and Hanssens 2004). Table 2 summarizes the findings from an illustrative set of papers that link sales to marketing mix.

If there is a cointegrating relationship, we estimate a Vector-Error Correction Model (VECM). If the series are stationary, we estimate a VAR model in levels. However, if there are unit-roots but there is no cointegrating relationship, we estimate a VAR in differences since regressions on the levels of evolving variables may produce spurious results.

Models of Dynamic Systems of Equations

Vector Autoregressive Model with Exogenous Variables (VARX)

The dynamic interactions and feedback effects among marketing variables are captured in Vector-Autoregressive (VARX) models with exogenous variables (e.g., Dekimpe and Hanssens 1999). The endogenous treatment of marketing actions implies that they are explained by both past marketing actions and past performance variables. VARX models can capture complex feedback loops that may impact brand performance over time. For instance, an increase in advertising in each week may generate a high level of consumer awareness, inducing some consumers to consider the brand, and try it. Their subsequent purchases may not only increase brand sales, but also awareness by their family, friends, and colleagues who see them use the brand and follow suit themselves. Because of such chains of events, the full performance implications of the marketing actions, such as advertising, may extend well beyond the immediate effects. By capturing these feedback loops, VARX models yield a comprehensive picture of how marketing mix actions affect the full dynamic system including sales performance.

Motivations for using and estimating VARX models stem from an interest in explaining the dynamics and interrelationships among multiple variables. For instance, sales may be driven by feedback from past performance ($SALES$ at period $t-1$) as well as by own marketing actions and competitive marketing actions.

Table 2 Illustrative marketing studies using vector auto-regressive models

Study	Data	Model	Research focus
Baghestani (1991)	54 yearly observations	VECM	Cointegration of advertising and sales
Bronnenberg et al. (2000)	1991–1996; 257 weeks of ready-to-drink tea.	VAR	Relation between distribution and long-run share, through early growth and later stages of product life cycle
Dekimpe and Hanssens (1995a)	Database of 400 prior analyses	Unit root tests	Evolution of sales and stationarity of market shares
Dekimpe and Hanssens (1995b)	Monthly advertising and sales data	VAR Persistence analysis	Long-term effect of advertising on sales
Dekimpe and Hanssens (1999)	(1) Monthly pharmaceutical data for 5 years (2) Brandaid data	VECM	Long-run impact of sales calls, advertising, prices and promotions on sales
Dekimpe et al. (1999)	113 Weeks scanner data for four categories	VAR Impulse response analysis	Impact of promotions on sales in stationary and non-stationary markets
Franses et al. (1999)	Weekly scanner data for consumer-packaged goods	Cointegration analysis	Impact of distribution, advertising and promotions on sales
Franses et al. (2001)	Weekly scanner data for 2 years in three categories	Unit root tests	Propose unit-root and cointegration tests that take the logical-consistency properties of market-share series into account
Srinivasan and Bass (2000)	Weekly scanner data for grocery products	Cointegration analysis/VECM	Evolution of sales with stationary market shares: brand sales and category sales are cointegrated.
Nijs et al. (2001)	4 years for 560 categories	VAR Persistence analysis	Persistent effect of promotions on category sales
Pauwels et al. (2002)	Scanner data for 2 years in two categories	VAR Persistence analysis	Quantifies the long-term effect on category incidence, brand choice and purchase quantity
Srinivasan et al. (2004)	75 brands in 25 categories for 7 years	VAR Persistence analysis	Quantifies effects of price promotions on manufacturer revenues, retailer revenues and margin
Pauwels and Srinivasan (2004)	75 brands in 25 categories for 7 years	VAR with structural break	Effect of store brand entry on (1) the retailer, (2) the manufacturers, and (3) the consumers

(continued)

Table 2 (continued)

Study	Data	Model	Research focus
Pauwels et al. (2004)	Weekly automotive data from 1996 to 2001	VAR analysis, FEVD and persistence analysis	Short- and long-term impact of promotions and new product introduction on revenues, profits and stock market performance
Steenkamp et al. (2005)	Weekly data for 4 years in 442 consumer product categories	VAR analysis and persistence analysis	Competitive reaction elasticities due to price promotion or advertising attacks, both in the short and the long run
Nijs et al. (2007)	Weekly data for 24 categories for 8 years	VAR and FEVD	Drivers of retail prices: competitive retailer prices, pricing history, brand demand, wholesale prices, and retailer category-management considerations
Villanueva et al. (2008)	Internet firm data for a 70-week period	VAR and Persistence analysis	Impact of marketing vs. word of mouth customer acquisition on customer equity
Srinivasan et al. (2008)	Weekly data for 24 categories for 8 years	VAR	Retailers choice of demand-based pricing vs. inertia
Trusov et al. (2009)	36 weeks of sign-ups, referrals, media and marketing events for internet firm	VAR	Effect of word-of-mouth (WOM) vs. marketing on member growth
Heerde et al. (2010)	Data for Lexus RX300 introduction	Time-varying VEC model	Estimate cannibalization, brand switching, and primary demand expansion for a pioneering innovation
Srinivasan et al. (2010)	Weekly data for 60 consumer brands in four categories for 96 weeks	VAR with IRFs, GFEVD and Granger Causality	Analyze the added explanatory value of customer mindset metrics vs. marketing mix in a sales response model
Wiesel et al. (2011)	Daily data from office supply firm: transaction, marketing, online and off-line activities	VAR + experimentation	Marketing communication effects on offline and online purchase funnel metrics and the magnitude and timing of the profit impact of firm-initiated and customer-initiated contacts
Pauwels et al. (2016)	50 weekly observations of brand performance, online and offline media for four companies	Bayesian VAR with IRFs	Assess how within-online synergy and cross-channel synergy vary across familiar and unfamiliar brands
Srinivasan et al. (2016)	CPG data on marketing mix, online media, and sales for 40 weeks	VAR with IRFs, Granger Causality	Effects of consumer activity in online media (paid, owned

(continued)

Table 2 (continued)

Study	Data	Model	Research focus
			and earned) vs. marketing mix on sales.
Colicev et al. (2018)	Daily data for 45 brands in 21 sectors on mindset metrics and firm performance	VAR with IRFs, Granger Causality	Role of mindset metrics on social media – shareholder value link.
Han et al. (2019)	Weekly survey data for 4 years on customers' attitudes for computer and automobile brands	VAR with IRFs, GFEVD	Impact of negative buzz on awareness and purchase intent

Competitive marketing actions may be explained by their historical patterns and their reaction to competitive performance (i.e., performance feedback) and/or to the focal firm's actions. For instance, a higher click-through and thus spending on paid search may be induced by the firm's offline marketing actions and by higher sales in previous periods, e.g., due to positive word-of-mouth by previous customers (Srinivasan et al. 2016; Wiesel et al. 2011). In turn, word-of-mouth referrals may be driven by the firm's paid marketing actions (Trusov et al. 2009).

Next we outline the VARX (vector autoregressive model with exogenous variables) . The common practice in marketing is to allow the most relevant variables to be endogenous and to control for the effects of other variables by considering them exogenously (Dekimpe and Hanssens 1999; Horváth et al. 2005; Nijs et al. 2001; Srinivasan and Bass 2000; Srinivasan et al. 2000). This, i.e., the imposition of exogeneity, can imply a reduction of the number of parameters and also an improved precision of forecasting. For expository purposes, we first consider a model in the levels and focus on a simple three-equation model linking own sales performance (*SALES*), own marketing spending (*OMKT*), and competitive marketing spending (*CMKT*). The corresponding VAR model in matrix notation the model given is by:

$$
\begin{bmatrix} SALES_t \\ OMKT_t \\ CMKT_t \end{bmatrix} = \begin{bmatrix} a_{11} \\ a_{12} \\ a_{13} \end{bmatrix} + \sum_{i=1}^{p} \begin{bmatrix} \Phi_{11,i} & \Phi_{12,i} & \Phi_{13,i} \\ \Phi_{21,i} & \Phi_{22,i} & \Phi_{23,i} \\ \Phi_{31,i} & \Phi_{32,i} & \Phi_{33,i} \end{bmatrix} \times \begin{bmatrix} SALES_{t-i} \\ OMKT_{t-i} \\ CMKT_{t-i} \end{bmatrix} + \Psi
$$

$$
\times \begin{bmatrix} X_{1t} \\ X_{2t} \\ X_{3t} \end{bmatrix} + \begin{bmatrix} u_{Sales,t} \\ u_{OMKT,t} \\ u_{CMKT,t} \end{bmatrix} \tag{6}
$$

which can be written as

$$
Y_t = A + \sum_{i=1}^{p} \Phi_i Y_{t-i} + \Psi X_t + \Sigma_t, \qquad t = 1, 2, \ldots, T, \tag{7}
$$

where A is a 3×1 vector of intercepts, Y_t is an 3×1 vector of the endogenous variables (*SALES, OMKT, CMKT*), and X_t is a vector of exogenous control variables. The exogenous variables often include terms such as (1) a deterministic-trend t to capture the impact of omitted, gradually changing variables, and (2) dummy variables to account for seasonal fluctuations in sales, or any other endogenous variable, and Σ_t is the covariance matrix of the residuals. Dekimpe and Hanssens (1995a) provide a good summary of the multiple channels of influence that are captured by VAR models. These are enumerated below. First, VAR models allow the capture of *contemporaneous effects* of variables on each other. For example, suppose a brand manager intends to launch a costly promotional campaign with a view to lifting the brand's declining sales performance. The anticipated immediate effect of the promotion on sales is an important factor in the launch of the promotional campaign. Many marketing actions including advertising, promotions, price changes, distribution changes, etc., often have a considerable immediate impact on performance. In the reduced form of the VAR, these effects are reflected in the contemporaneous correlation terms in the variance covariance matrix.

Second, there are *carryover effects* of marketing activity on sales, reflected in the parameter ϕ_{12} in Eq. (6). Numerous studies have argued that the effect of advertising in one period may be carried over, at least partially, into future periods (see Hanssens et al. 2014, for example). Consumers are expected to remember past advertising messages and create "goodwill" toward the brand that only gradually deteriorates because of forgetting.

Third, *purchase reinforcement effects* suggest that the dynamic impact of marketing actions on sales can also work indirectly through purchase reinforcements: a given outlay may create a new customer who will not only make an initial purchase, but also repurchase in the future. Purchase reinforcement is reflected in the parameter ϕ_{11} in Eq. (6). Using a similar logic, Horsky and Simon (1983) assume that advertising gives innovators an incentive to try the product after which an imitation effect takes over, creating a larger customer base and higher future sales. Current advertising should receive credit for these subsequent sales (e.g., Bass and Clarke 1972; Hanssens et al. 2001). Villanueva et al. (2008) in their study of customer equity note that an increase in the number of customers acquired through word-of-mouth might influence future word-of-mouth acquisitions because these customers may generate more referrals than customers acquired through marketing.

Fourth, *feedback effects* suggest that future marketing actions (e.g., advertising) may be influenced by past sales as well as current sales. Feedback from sales to marketing action is reflected in the parameter ϕ_{21} in Eq. (6). Dekimpe and Hanssens (1995a) point out that this is highly likely when percentage-of-sales budgeting rules are applied. Such feedback effects manifest due to a chain reaction where an increase in advertising in period t results in an increase in sales in period t, which in turn results in increased advertising in period $t+1$ and so on. The profit implications of such advertising increases should consider both the revenue impact as well as the additional expenditures in advertising due to the initiating increase in advertising. Using persistence modeling approaches such as VARs, credit is given to the initial advertising increase for the subsequent sales increases since without it, none of the subsequent effects would have occurred.

Fifth, the VAR model allows the researcher to capture *firm-specific decision* rules, which typically model the dependence of current marketing activity such as advertising and prices on previous advertising and prices. Such a decision rule is reflected in the parameter ϕ_{22} in Eq. (6). For instance, Nijs et al. (2007) find that a brand's past prices are the dominant driver of current retail prices in each category studied, and account anywhere from 50% to 60% of the variation in current prices, confirming the powerful tendency to rely on past prices in determining future prices (Srinivasan et al. 2008).

Last but not the least, VAR models allow the capture of *competitive reaction effects*. Competitive reaction effects are reflected in the parameter ϕ_{23} and the parameter ϕ_{32} in Eq. (6). For instance, competitive activities may change own marketing effectiveness drastically. Similarly, in the context of retail pricing, competitive retailer activity is expected to influence retailer prices and performance (Srinivasan et al. 2008). For instance, price promotions by competing retailers may reduce store traffic, inducing the retailer to respond (Srinivasan et al. 2004).

The representation in Eq. (7) is the reduced-form of the VAR model in which the errors are contemporaneously correlated, with the contemporaneous correlations reflected in the off-diagonal terms of the variance-covariance matrix. The residual correlation matrix can be used to establish the presence and the direction of the effects. Various procedures have been used in the marketing literature to deal with identification, such as by imposing an *a priori* imposition of a certain causal ordering on the variables. When researchers work on model identification, they assert a connection between the reduced form and the structure so that estimates of reduced form parameters translate into structural parameters. In the words of Sims (1986, p.2), *"Identification is the interpretation of historically observed variation in data in a way that allows the variation to be used to predict the consequences of an action not yet undertaken."*

An important feature of the reduced-form model is that all variables on the right-hand side (RHS) of Eq. (7) are predetermined at time t, and the system can be estimated without imposing restrictions or a causal ordering. Moreover, because all RHS variables are the same in each equation, there is no efficiency gain in using Seemingly Unrelated Regression (SUR) estimation. In that case, the Ordinary least squares (OLS) estimates are consistent and asymptotically efficient even if the errors are correlated across equations (Srivastava and Giles 1987, Chap. 2) and asymptotically efficient in using OLS estimation, equation by equation. This feature is especially valuable in marketing applications with many endogenous variables. For example, a 6-equation VAR model requires estimation of $6*6 = 36$ additional parameters for each lag added to the model. This does not bode well for estimations with the typical weekly scanner panel data of 104 observations for 2 years, due to over-parameterization concerns. In contrast, OLS estimation equation-by-equation implies that only six additional parameters have to be estimated.

Several authors (e.g., Pesaran et al. 1993; Dekimpe and Hanssens 1995a; Pauwels et al. 2004) have restricted all parameters with $|t| < 1$ to zero as a step toward parsimony. Others such as Nijs et al. (2007) and Srinivasan et al. (2008), also for parsimony of estimation, reduce the number of parameters by eliminating the insignificant ones and reestimating the model. In this case, when researchers reduce the number of parameters by eliminating the insignificant lagged parameters and reestimating the model, they need to use SUR for estimation as the RHS variables are no longer identical across equations. While such strategies accomplish the goal of parsimony and may alleviate the problem of estimating and interpreting so many parameters, they are unlikely to fully eliminate it. As a consequence, VAR modelers typically do not interpret the individual parameters themselves, but rather focus on the impulse-response functions (IRFs) derived from these parameters.

Structural Vector-Autoregressive Model (SVAR)

The structural VAR (SVAR) representation of the reduced form VAR in Eq. (7) is written as:

$$B_0Y_t = A + B_1Y_{t-1} + B_2Y_{t-2} + \ldots + B_pY_{t-p} + \Sigma_t \tag{8}$$

The vector of endogenous variables Y is regressed on constant terms (which may include a deterministic time trend) and on its own past, with p being the number of lags, and B coefficient matrix of a given lag. Note that the contemporaneous effects are captured in the B_0 matrix; as a result, the structural errors ε are uncorrelated (orthogonal) across equations. This structural form of the VAR model is directly interesting for decision makers, as it generates predictions of results of various kinds of actions, by calculating the conditional distribution given the action (Sims 1986). It is also the appropriate form for imposing restrictions, typically on the B_0 matrix (e.g., Amisano and Giannini 1997). For instance, researchers provide theory-based reasons for why one group of variables does not cause another group of variables (e.g., Bernanke 1986).

Structural VARs have seen quite a few applications in marketing (DeHaan et al. 2016; Gijsenberg et al. 2015; Horváth et al. 2005). Horváth et al. (2005) show that the inclusion of competitive reaction and feedback effects is more important in the tuna category but not in the shampoo category where competitive interactions are limited due to differentiated brand positioning. Gijsenberg et al. (2015) develop a Double-Asymmetric Structural VAR (DASVAR) model that allows for asymmetric effects of increases versus decreases and for a different number of lags in each equation. In their analysis of the effect of service on customer satisfaction, they find that losses (service failures) not only have stronger (the first asymmetry), but also longer-lasting (the second asymmetry) effects on satisfaction than gains. Finally, DeHaan et al. (2016) find support for their proposed restriction of both immediate and dynamic feedback loops within the online funnel of a retailer; they find that increases in product page visits increase checkouts, but not vice versa.

Vector Error Correction Model

If some of the variables have a unit root, the VAR model is specified in differences. If there is a cointegrating relationship, we estimate a Vector-Error Correction Model (VECM). Srinivasan et al. (2000) estimate a VECM model, among market share and prices of four brands of beer, which have a long-run cointegrating relationship; the rationale is that different price levels correspond to different long-run demand or sales levels, and these, in turn, are associated with different levels of shares. Specifically, if $SALES_t$, $OMKT_t$, and $CMKT_t$ are cointegrated, then the VECM model in differences includes the error-correction term to capture the long-run cointegrating relationships as shown below:

$$
\begin{bmatrix} \Delta SALES_t \\ \Delta OMKT_t \\ \Delta CMKT_t \end{bmatrix} = \begin{bmatrix} \alpha_{SALES} & 0 & 0 \\ 0 & \alpha_{OMKT} & 0 \\ 0 & 0 & \alpha_{CMKT} \end{bmatrix} \begin{bmatrix} e_{Sales,t-1} \\ e_{OMKT,t-1} \\ e_{CMKT,t-1} \end{bmatrix} + \sum_{i=1}^{p} \Phi_i
$$

$$
\times \begin{bmatrix} \Delta SALES_{t-i} \\ \Delta OMKT_{t-i} \\ \Delta CMKT_{t-i} \end{bmatrix} + \Psi \times \begin{bmatrix} X_{1t} \\ X_{2t} \\ X_{3t} \end{bmatrix} + \begin{bmatrix} u_{Sales,t} \\ u_{OMKT,t} \\ u_{CMKT,t} \end{bmatrix} \tag{9}
$$

The addition of the error correction terms reflects the fact that in each period the system adjusts toward the long-run cointegration relationship, with the coefficients of the error-correction term reflecting the speed of adjustment toward the equilibrium. When the variables are evolving, omitting the long run cointegrating relationship will underestimate the effects of marketing mix variables on performance (Vanden Abeele 1994). Incorporating the long-run relationship among variables will allow an estimation of long-run elasticities as well as short-run elasticities (Srinivasan et al. 2000).

Typically, VAR modelers do not interpret the individual parameters themselves, but tend to focus on the impulse-response functions derived from these parameters. Impulse-response functions trace the incremental performance and spending implications of an initial one-period change in one of the support variables, over time. In so doing, they provide a concise summary of the information contained in the multitude of VAR parameters, a summary that lends itself well to a graphical and easy-to-interpret representation.

Policy Simulation Analysis

Impulse Response Functions (IRF)

An impulse-response function (IRF) traces the incremental effect of a one-unit (or one-standard-deviation) shock in one of the variables on the future values of the other endogenous variables (e.g., Srinivasan et al. 2000, 2004). IRFs can also

Modeling Marketing Dynamics Using Vector Autoregressive (VAR) Models 531

be viewed as the difference between two forecasts: a first forecast, based on an information set that does not take the marketing shock into account, and another prediction based on an extended information set that takes this shock into account. As such, IRFs trace the incremental effect of the marketing action reflected in the shock. Note that marketing actions (such as, for example, a price promotion) are operationalized as deviations from a benchmark, which is derived as the expected value of the marketing-mix variable (for example, the price) as predicted through the dynamic structure of the VAR model. Response functions are based on the estimated parameters of the full VARX model. Note from Eqs. (6) and (7) that VARX models capture immediate as well as lagged, direct as well as indirect interactions among the endogenous variables. Based on all these estimated reactions, the impulse response function estimates the net result of a "shock" to a marketing variable on the performance variables relative to their baselines (their expected values in the absence of the marketing shock). Specifically, it measures the long-term performance response to a one-unit shock (Pauwels et al. 2002; Nijs et al. 2001; Srinivasan et al. 2004).

Starting from the reduced-form model specification in Eq. (7), we can substitute each lag of each endogenous variable by the same equation and thus express the right-hand side as a function of only current and lagged values of the error terms. This yields the Vector Moving Average (VMA) representation:

$$Y_t = A + \left(I - \Phi_1 B - \Phi_2 B^2 - \ldots - \Phi_p B^p\right)^{-1} \Sigma_t \qquad (10)$$

In words, each endogenous variable is explained by a weighted average of current and past errors or "shocks" both to itself and to the other endogenous variables. Therefore, we operationalize a change to a variable (e.g., a price promotion) as a shock to the variable series (e.g., to sales). An impulse response function then tracks the impact of that shock to each variable in the system (price, sales, competitive price, etc.) during the shock (typically denoted as period 0) and for each period thereafter.

For a simple illustration of the IRFs, let's consider the VAR model below:

$$\begin{bmatrix} SALES_t \\ OMKT_t \\ CMKT_t \end{bmatrix} = \begin{bmatrix} \Phi_{11} & \Phi_{12} & \Phi_{13} \\ \Phi_{21} & \Phi_{22} & \Phi_{23} \\ \Phi_{31} & \Phi_{32} & \Phi_{33} \end{bmatrix} \begin{bmatrix} SALES_{t-1} \\ OMKT_{t-1} \\ CMKT_{t-1} \end{bmatrix} + \begin{bmatrix} u_{Sales,t} \\ u_{OMKT,t} \\ u_{CMKT,t} \end{bmatrix} \qquad (11)$$

For a unit shock to own marketing action $OMKT$, one sets $[u_{Sales}, u_{OMKT}, u_{CMKT}] = [0, 0, 0]$ prior to t; to $[0, 1, 0]$ at time t; and to $[0, 0, 0]$ after time t. One then computes (simulates) the future values for the various endogenous variables:

$$\begin{bmatrix} SALES_t \\ OMKT_t \\ CMKT_t \end{bmatrix} = \begin{bmatrix} \Phi_{11} & \Phi_{12} & \Phi_{13} \\ \Phi_{21} & \Phi_{22} & \Phi_{23} \\ \Phi_{31} & \Phi_{32} & \Phi_{33} \end{bmatrix} \begin{bmatrix} 0 \\ 0 \\ 0 \end{bmatrix} + \begin{bmatrix} 0 \\ 1 \\ 0 \end{bmatrix} = \begin{bmatrix} 0 \\ 1 \\ 0 \end{bmatrix}$$

$$
\begin{bmatrix} SALES_{t+1} \\ OMKT_{t+1} \\ CMKT_{t+1} \end{bmatrix} = \begin{bmatrix} \Phi_{11} & \Phi_{12} & \Phi_{13} \\ \Phi_{21} & \Phi_{22} & \Phi_{23} \\ \Phi_{31} & \Phi_{32} & \Phi_{33} \end{bmatrix} \begin{bmatrix} 0 \\ 1 \\ 0 \end{bmatrix} + \begin{bmatrix} 0 \\ 0 \\ 0 \end{bmatrix} = \begin{bmatrix} \Phi_{12} \\ \Phi_{22} \\ \Phi_{32} \end{bmatrix}
$$

$$
\begin{bmatrix} SALES_{t+2} \\ OMKT_{t+2} \\ CMKT_{t+2} \end{bmatrix} = \begin{bmatrix} \Phi_{11} & \Phi_{12} & \Phi_{13} \\ \Phi_{21} & \Phi_{22} & \Phi_{23} \\ \Phi_{31} & \Phi_{32} & \Phi_{33} \end{bmatrix} \begin{bmatrix} \Phi_{12} \\ \Phi_{22} \\ \Phi_{32} \end{bmatrix} + \begin{bmatrix} 0 \\ 0 \\ 0 \end{bmatrix}
$$

$$
= \begin{bmatrix} \begin{bmatrix} \Phi_{11}\Phi_{12}+ & \Phi_{12}\Phi_{22}+ & \Phi_{13}\Phi_{32} \\ \Phi_{21}\Phi_{12}+ & \Phi_{22}\Phi_{22}+ & \Phi_{23}\Phi_{32} \\ \Phi_{31}\Phi_{12}+ & \Phi_{32}\Phi_{22}+ & \Phi_{33}\Phi_{32} \end{bmatrix} \end{bmatrix}
$$

etc.

A plot of these forecasts against time yields the impulse response function; allowing all endogenous variables to respond according to the historically observed reaction patterns, as captured by all estimated VAR-coefficients. In case the affected variable is evolving (has a unit root), the shock may (but does not need to) have a permanent impact, i.e., the variable does not return to its pre-shock level. In the typical case of stationary variables, these shock effects die out, i.e., the permanent impact is 0 and the variable returns to its steady-state, i.e., pre-shock level.

How can IRFs show permanent effects if the VAR-model can only include stationary variables? If the performance variable (e.g., sales) is evolving, we indeed include it in the model in first differences, i.e., in *changes* to the variable. Therefore, the impulse response function on this variable (change in sales) will die out. To derive the effect on sales itself, we must accumulate the IRF values starting from the first period. Thus, the IRFs for evolving variables will converge to the persistent impact and the IRFs for stationary variables will return to their baseline with permanent impact of 0. What happens when the impulse (i.e., marketing) is the evolving variable? Again, we include the marketing action (e.g., price) in first differences in the model, and its IRF therefore shows the performance impact not of a temporary shock but of a permanent change (e.g., reduction in regular price). We need to keep this in mind when interpreting the result.

Researchers often derive the three summary statistics from IRFs using the VAR model: (1) the immediate or short-term performance impact of own marketing (*MKT*) or competitive marketing (*CMKT*) on brand sales (*SALES*), which is readily observable to managers, and may therefore receive considerable managerial scrutiny; (2) the persistent or the long-term impact (i.e., the value to which the IRF converges); and (3) the total or cumulative impact, which combines the immediate effect with all effects across the dust-settling period. In the absence of permanent effects, this total impact becomes the relevant metric to evaluate performance outcomes (Pauwels et al. 2002; Pauwels and Srinivasan 2004).

Srinivasan et al. (2004) answer the question of whether of price promotions benefit manufacturers and retailers by analyzing 7 years of scanner data, covering

25 product categories and 75 brands, from the Chicago area's second-largest supermarket chain, Dominick's Finer Foods. Previous research showed that price promotions tend to have little long-term effect on sales volume. Their research found that the same is true for revenues and margins. Figure 2 shows the impulse response functions of the impact of price promotion on manufacturer and retailer revenues for two categories, tuna and cheese, from the 25 categories that they study. It outlines the immediate, the dust-settling, and the persistent effects of promotions for these two categories.

During the 1-week promotion, the cheese manufacturer saw an immediate revenue increase as customers bought more of its brand. But the retailer saw a loss, because gains from increased sales of the promoted brand were more than offset by loss of sales from regularly priced brands. During the dust-settling weeks, 2–6, the manufacturer saw a negative impact on revenue as customers switched back to their usual brands and toward competing brands that had launched their own promotions.

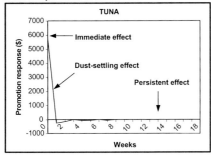 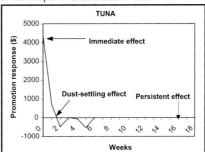

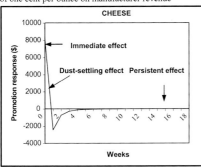 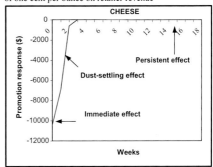

Fig. 2 Impulse-response functions. (**a**) Impulse response function of a price promotion of 1 cent per ounce on manufacturer revenue. (**b**) Impulse response function of a price promotion of 1 cent per ounce on retailer revenue. (**c**) Impulse response function of a price promotion. (**d**) Impulse response function of a price promotion of 1 cent per ounce on manufacturer revenue of 1 cent per ounce on retailer revenue

Meanwhile, retailer revenue for the cheese category gradually moved back to baseline as the promotion effects tailed off. By week 6, manufacturer and retailer revenues had returned to their prepromotion levels and remained stable through week 26. They find that promotions of frequently promoted brands, for example, tend to have a positive short-term effect on both retailers' and manufacturers' revenues but a negative impact on retailers' profit margins. Thus, the interests of manufacturers and retailers may well be aligned for one financial metric, such as revenue, but not for another, such as profit. Impulse Response Functions can therefore be used to obtain insights into impact on relevant performance metrics. Researchers can also obtain the wear-in time of each driver's effect on performance as the period with the highest (in absolute value) impulse response coefficient (Pauwels and Hanssens 2007; Srinivasan et al. 2010).

An approach to identify the shocks of a VAR model is to use orthogonal impulse responses where the basic idea is to decompose the variance-covariance matrix so that $\Sigma=PP'$, where PP is a lower triangular matrix with positive diagonal elements, which is often obtained by a Cholesky decomposition. Note that the output of the Cholesky decomposition is a lower triangular matrix so that the variable in the first row will never be sensitive to a contemporaneous shock of any other variable and the last variable in the system will be sensitive to shocks of all other variables. Therefore, the results of orthogonal impulse response analysis might be sensitive to the order of the variables and it is advised to estimate the VAR model with different orders to see how strongly the resulting IRFs are affected by ordering.

Generalized IRFs (GIRF) can be obtained with the simultaneous-shocking approach (Evans and Wells 1983; Dekimpe and Hanssens 1999), in which the information in the residual variance-covariance matrix of Eq. (7) is used to derive a vector of *expected* instantaneous shock values. The advantage of this approach is that it does not require selecting a temporal ordering among the variables of interest. Standard errors are subsequently derived using the Monte Carlo simulation approach with 250 runs in each case (see Horváth et al. 2005). The GIRF estimates, given a one-unit shock to variable I, the expected value for shocks occurring simultaneously to the other variables j $(i{\neq}j)$ and is shown in Eq. (12) below:

$$ E\left[u_j \mid u_i = 1\right] = \sigma_{ij}/\sigma_{ii}; \quad \text{with} \quad \sigma_{ij}; \quad \sigma_{ii} \text{ elements of } \Sigma \qquad (12) $$

(from Eq. 7).

As explained in Dekimpe and Hanssens (1999) and Nijs et al. (2001), we can now calculate generalized IRFs (GIRFs), which do not depend on a causal ordering. When the causal ordering is clear (e.g., retail prices that cannot be changed by manufacturers for weeks; Leeflang and Wittink 1996), GIRFs lead to the same inferences as IRFs. GIRFs are particularly important when prior theory or observation does not suggest a clear causal ordering, e.g., among different marketing actions, competitors, or online customer actions (e.g., DeHaan et al. 2016), and typically most marketing papers tend to use GIRFs.

Dynamic Multipliers

The marginal impact of changes in the exogenous variables can be investigated with the help of dynamic multiplier analysis. For example, if the exogenous variables are marketing actions, such as promotional display or feature variables, the consequences of changes in these actions can be analyzed (if they are endogenous we apply impulse response analysis described earlier). VAR models with exogenous variables (i.e., VARX) as shown in Eqs. (6) and (7) can be expressed in the following way:

$$B(L)Y_t = A + C(L)X_t + u_t, \qquad t = 1, \ldots, T \tag{13}$$

where X_t is an h-dimensional vector of exogenous variables and $C(L)$ is a matrix polynomial with lag operator L: $C(L) = C_0 - C_1 L - C_2 L^2 - \ldots - C_S L^S$ and C_i are $h \times k$ coefficient matrices, $i = 0, \ldots, S$. The model is referred to as a $VARX\ (P,S)$ process. If u_t is an $MA(Q)$ process the model becomes a $VARMAX\ (P,S,Q)$ process.

Dynamic multiplier analysis can be used for policy simulation. For instance, a brand manager may want to know about the consequences of an increase in promotions of its brand over time. Or, the effects of changes in exogenous variables that are not under control of any decision maker may be of interest (see Horvath 2003). The dynamic effects of exogenous variables on the endogenous variables are captured by the dynamic multipliers (Lütkepohl 1993, p. 338):

$$D(L) = \sum_{i=0}^{\infty} D_i L^i = B(L)^{-1} C(L) \tag{14}$$

where $B(L)$ and $C(L)$ are defined in Eq. (13). From this representation, the response of $Y_{i,t+\tau}$ to a unit change in X_{jt} can easily be obtained:

$$\frac{\partial Y_{i,t+\tau}}{\partial X_{j,t}} = d_{ij,\tau}, \qquad t = 1 \ldots \tau \tag{15}$$

where $\delta_{ij,\tau}$ is the row ith, column jth element of the $h \times k$ matrix of coefficients D_τ, the coefficient matrix of the τ-th lag in Eq. (14), $\tau = 0, \ldots, \infty$.

Granger Causality Tests: Do We Need to Model a Dynamic System?

Granger causality implies that knowing the history of a variable X helps explain a variable Y, beyond Y's own history. This temporal causality is the closest proxy for causality that can be gained from studying the time series of variables (i.e., in the absence of manipulating causality in controlled experiments). Granger causality tests, for instance, allow the testing of the traditional market response assumption that brand performance is driven by marketing actions. Srinivasan et al. (2010) use Granger causality tests to assess whether marketing performance could be driven by past performance, by own and competitive mindset metrics, and by own and competitive marketing actions. Franses (1998) notes that not accounting for this marketing endogeneity may lead to substantially wrong conclusions about marketing effectiveness. Unfortunately, marketing (and economic) theory is typically insufficient to correct a priori specification of such models, and their identification thus requires "incredible identifying restrictions" to which Sims (1980) objected. In the absence of strong theoretic rationale to exclude specific directions of causality, he prefers to establish them empirically using the available data (see Pauwels 2018).

Specifically, one can test for the presence of endogeneity among all variables with Granger causality tests (Granger 1969). As Pauwels (2018) insightfully notes "temporal causality" is the closest proxy for causality that can be gained from studying the time series of the variables (i.e., in the absence of manipulating causality in controlled experiments). In other words, a variable x Granger causes a variable y if knowing the past of x improves the forecast for y based on only the past of y. Formally, x Granger causes y if, at the 5% significance level:

$$\text{MSFE} \left(y_t | y_{t-1}, \ldots, y_{t-k}, x_{t-1}, \ldots, x_{t-m} \right) < \text{MSFE} \left(y_t | y_{t-1}, \ldots, y_{t-k} \right) \quad (16)$$

with MSFE = mean squared forecast error and k and m the maximum lags for y and x. An important caveat is that Granger causality tests are pairwise, i.e., they can indicate variable x is Granger causing y while instead they are both being driven (x earlier than y) by a third variable z. Accordingly, the researcher should develop a full understanding of the web of Granger causality and how performance can be affected.

Several marketing papers have applied Granger Causality tests to assess the issue of temporal causality.

Hanssens (1980) applied Granger Causality tests to sort out patterns of competitive interactions in the airline industry. Trusov et al. (2009) find that offline events organized by a large social media company increased the number of online friend referrals they received. Therefore, these organized events had a higher total ROI than would be calculated from their direct performance effects. Srinivasan et al. (2010), in their Granger-causality tests, show that marketing actions and mind-set metrics more often Granger-cause sales than vice versa. Awareness, consideration, and liking Granger-cause sales for, respectively, 73%, 71%, and 63% of all brands, and sales Granger-causes the mind-set metrics for, respectively, 52%, 60%, and 51% of all brands. Recently, Kireyev et al. (2016) find that display impressions Granger cause Search Impressions and Search Clicks.

Granger Causality tests are useful to assess whether managers react to market performance when deciding on marketing actions. As Pauwels (2018) notes the feedback could be from actions to performance and vice versa since high sales may induce marketing spending (e.g., sales may Granger cause advertising) and low sales may induce management to take course corrections by changing marketing spending (e.g., low sales may Granger cause price promotions). Horváth et al. (2005) consider the relative importance of such feedback in their model. Overall, Granger Causality

Modeling Marketing Dynamics Using Vector Autoregressive (VAR) Models 537

has been used extensively in time-series applications in marketing to shed light on the direction of causality, as outlined above.

Forecast Error Variance Decomposition (FEVD)

Based on the VARX parameters, researchers also obtained the Forecast Error Variance Decomposition (FEVD) estimates to investigate whether, for example, own and competitive actions explain brand sales performance beyond the impact of past brand sales performance. FEVD quantifies the dynamic explanatory value on performance of each endogenous variable. Akin to a "dynamic R^2," the FEVD provides a measure of the relative impact over time of shocks initiated by each of the individual endogenous variables in a VARX model (Pesaran and Shin 1998; Nijs et al. 2007).

The idea behind FEVD is to stimulate a "typical" shock on the fully estimated system, realize a forecast up to a chosen horizon, and then decompose the variance of the forecast error. The "typical" shock is simulated on the residuals which are contemporaneously correlated. As a result, the impact of a simulated shock is likely to incorporate the degree of correlation between the error terms. Therefore, the influence of a shock cannot be completely attributable to a precisely defined variable of the model. Cholesky orthogonalization of the error terms offers a way to overcome this problem by rewriting the system to impose a causal ordering. The procedure is however sensitive to the way in which variables enter the system. The first variable in the model is allowed to affect all the variables whereas the second variable affects all the variables except the first one, and so on. This is equivalent to imposing a hierarchy of effects to aid FEVD interpretation. I refer the interested reader to Valenti et al. (2020) who perform a Cholesky FEVD to investigate advertising's hierarchy of effects by imposing a causal structure to advertising and intermediate factors.

The Generalized Forecast Error Variance Decomposition (GFEVD) is order-invariant like the GIRFs are and can be derived using the following equation:

$$\theta_{ij}^g(n) = \frac{\sum_{l=0}^{n}\left(\psi_{ij}^g(l)\right)^2}{\sum_{l=0}^{n}\sum_{j=0}^{m}\left(\psi_{ij}^g(l)\right)^2}, \quad i,j = 1, \ldots, m. \tag{17}$$

where $\psi_{ij}^g(l)$ is the value of a Generalized Impulse Response Function (GIRF) following a one-unit shock to variable i on variable j at time l (Pesaran and Shin 1998). In GFEVD an initial shock can (but need not, depending on the size of the corresponding residual correlation) affect all other endogenous variables instantaneously. This has been applied in a marketing setting by Nijs et al. (2007). Importantly, the GFEVD attributes 100% of the forecast error variance in performance to either (1) the past values of the other endogenous variables or (2) the past of performance itself. The former (e.g., does a past change in awareness drives current sales) is much more managerially and conceptually interesting than the latter (a past change in sales drives current sales, but we do not know what induced that past change in sales). One can assess the dynamic explanatory value of the marketing and competitive marketing by the extent to which they increase the sales forecast error variance explained by the potential drivers of sales, and thus reduce the percentage explained by past sales. The relative importance of the drivers established is typically based on the GFEVD values at 6 months, which reduces sensitivity to short-term fluctuations. Studies have shown that a period of 26 weeks (6 months) is sufficient for stationary series in consumer-packaged goods to capture dynamic effects (Pauwels and Srinivasan 2004; Srinivasan et al. 2004).

To evaluate the accuracy of the GFEVD estimates, standard errors can be obtained using Monte Carlo simulations (see Benkwitz et al. 2001). While GFEVD is the appropriate method to assess the dynamic R-squared, it does come at a cost: it only allows comparable analyses of brands with stationary variables because the variance for evolving variables is (theoretically) infinite (Pesaran and Shin 1998; Srinivasan et al. 2008).

(Generalized) Forecast Error Variance Decomposition always sums up to 100%, with typically the own past of the focal variable, explaining most of its variance. In some marketing applications, the % of "inertia" is of special importance, e.g., indicating price inertia in Nijs et al. (2007) and Srinivasan et al. (2008). In most others though, it is the least interesting of % categories, and thus gets reduced from the 100% to yield the % of performance explained by the other groups of variables. For instance, Srinivasan et al. (2010) show how adding mindset metrics improves the % of the GFEVD not explained by own past performance, while Srinivasan et al. (2016) and Colicev et al. (2018) show how adding online behavior metrics (owned, earned, and paid) does the same in a multichannel context.

Turning to the applicability of VAR models, researchers have successfully applied VAR models to a variety of datasets, including annual observations (e.g., Baghestani 1991), decades of quarterly observations (e.g., Pauwels et al. 2004), several years of weekly observations (e.g., Srinivasan et al. 2010), and a number of months of daily observations (e.g., Colicev et al. 2018). VAR models require an adequate number of degrees of freedom to provide reliable estimates (e.g., Colicev and Pauwels 2020). A rule of thumb is to have at least five observations per parameter (Leeflang et al. 2015), which practically translates into a minimum of about 50 time periods (e.g., 12 years of quarterly data or 5 years of monthly data) per firm.

Researchers additionally need to consider the sample size and the sampling frequency. Mitchell and James (2001) provide an overview of how data frequency can allow or jeopardize how researchers can establish causality among variables. For example, finance and marketing fields often deal with weekly, daily, and hourly data. Tellis and Franses (2006), in the context of the duration of advertising carryover effect on sales, argue that the optimal data interval for researchers to collect data is the unit exposure time. For example, if firms change pricing strategies once a quarter, the quarterly level data is appropriate for studying the impact of pricing changes.

Colicev and Pauwels (2020) advocate that the best approach would be to measure the variables as frequently as possible.

Finally, when the time-series data is available over an extended period, the variables may exhibit time-varying volatility, i.e., periods of swings interspersed with periods of relative calm. ARCH-type models are appropriate to investigate this explicitly, given that they model the variance of the current error term as a function of the size of previous error terms (see Colicev and Pauwels 2020 for a good discussion on this topic).

Software Programs for VAR Estimation

Modern time series packages are included in software as Stata, Matlab, Gauss, and R. Dedicated software packages include Time Series Processor (TSP), OX/PcGive, Eviews, and RATS. Stata is the most commonly used while Matlab has embedded functions not available in Stata, but requires more coding. R is versatile in its time series functions while TSP and RATS are dedicated to time series. Eviews and OX/PcGive provide an easy-to-use interface with click-and-find program options. Moreover, Eviews has the most typical VAR option as the default in its software and offers regular updates, adding the state-of-the-art tests and deleting less relevant ones. Its student version is a low-cost option to get started for a novice. I refer the interested reader to Colicev and Pauwels (2020) who employ a dataset, which combines public social media data from Facebook with corporate reputation data from a private data source, to illustrate the VAR model by explaining the key methodological steps needed to estimate and interpret the results through a software tutorial in R and STATA.

Illustrative Applications of VAR Modeling in Marketing

Empirical work using VAR models has expanded and is now part of the mainstream in marketing applications. Next, I will outline three substantive applications of VAR models in the following domains: (1) Investor Response Models, (2) Marketing Mix and Mindset Metrics Models, and (3) Digital Marketing Models.

Investor Response Models in the Marketing-Finance

VAR models are useful in modeling the marketing-finance interface since they use a system's representation (e.g., Dekimpe and Hanssens 1995a; Pauwels et al. 2002), in which each equation tracks the behavior of an important agent; for example, the consumer (demand equation), the manager (decision rule equations), competition (competitive reaction equation), and the investor (stock price equation). The long-run behavior of each endogenous variable is obtained from a shock-initiated chain reaction across the equations. For instance, a successful new-product introduction will generate higher revenue, which may prompt the manufacturer to reduce sales promotions in subsequent periods. The combination of increased sales and higher margins may improve earnings and ultimately stock price. Because of such chains of events, the full performance implications of the initial product introduction may extend well beyond its immediate effects. As an example, a persistence model estimated as a vector autoregressive model (VAR) in differences can be specified for each brand (two in the illustration) of firm i, as follows:

$$
\begin{bmatrix} \Delta MBR_{it} \\ \Delta INC_{it} \\ \Delta REV_{it} \\ MKT1_{it} \\ MKT2_{it} \end{bmatrix} = C + \sum_{n=1}^{N} B_n \times \begin{bmatrix} \Delta MBR_{it-n} \\ \Delta INC_{it-n} \\ \Delta REV_{it-n} \\ MKT1_{it-n} \\ MKT2_{it-n} \end{bmatrix} + \Gamma \times \begin{bmatrix} X_{1t} \\ X_{2t} \\ X_{3t} \end{bmatrix} + \begin{bmatrix} uMBR_{it} \\ uINC_{it} \\ uREV_{it} \\ uMKT1_{it} \\ uMKT2_{it} \end{bmatrix} \quad (18)
$$

with B_n, Γ vectors of coefficients, $[u_{MBRit}, u_{INCit}, u_{REVit}, u_{MKT1t}, u_{MKT2t}]' \sim N(0, \Sigma_u)$, N the order of the system based on Schwartz' Bayes Information Criterion (SBIC), and all variables expressed in logarithms or their changes (Δ). In this system, the first equation is an expanded version of the stock-return response model (Srinivasan and Hanssens 2009a, b). The second and third equations explain the changes in, respectively, bottom-line (INC) and top-line financial performance (REV) of firm i. The fourth and fifth equations represent firm's marketing actions (e.g., for each brand), i.e., (MKT_{1t}) and (MKT_{2t}). For example, Pauwels et al. (2004) considered a brand's new-product introductions and sales promotions. The exogenous variables in this dynamic system (X_{1t}, X_{2t}, X_{3t}) could include controls such as the Carhart four factors and the impact of stock-market analyst earnings expectations. The impact of contemporaneous shocks is incorporated through the elements of Σ_u. As described earlier, such models provide baseline forecasts of each endogenous variable, along with estimates of the shock or surprise component in each variable.

Several applications of the VAR model exist in the marketing-finance domain. Pauwels et al. (2004) assess investor reactions to auto companies' new product introductions with price promotions to find that new product introductions have a gradually increasing influence on stock price, all else being equal, while price promotions generally lower firm value, even though they may successfully stimulate sales. Thus, investors view new product activity as generating long-term value and promotions as destroying long-term value. They show that investors in the automotive industry need about 6 weeks to fully incorporate the impact of a new-product introduction on stock returns. Joshi and Hanssens (2010) have found that advertising in the PC industry has a small but positive long-term effect on stock prices, again after controlling for advertising's direct impact on sales and profits.

In a recent application of VARX models to the marketing-finance interface, Colicev et al. (2018) examine the effects of owned and earned social media on brand awareness, purchase intent, and customer satisfaction and link these consumer mindset metrics to shareholder value metrics including abnormal returns and idiosyncratic risk. Analyzing daily data for 45 brands in 21 sectors using vector autoregression models, they find that brand fan following improves customer mindset metrics, and that purchase intent and customer satisfaction positively affect shareholder value. This chapter represents an application of VAR modeling that combines mindset metrics with the marketing-finance interface.

When authors want to combine the results from multiple entities (e.g., firms) together and provide an overall picture of the analysis, Panel Vector Autoregression (PVAR) specifications are useful (e.g., Holtz-Eakin et al. 1988). Kang et al. (2016) use a structural panel VAR to show that corporate social responsibility actions are not driven by slack resources, but by an (only partially successful) attempt to make up for past social irresponsibility.

Marketing and Mindset Metrics Models

Papers in this stream research the question of whether it is useful or not to include marketing mix actions and customers mindset metrics into one overall model to explain brand performance. Specific questions addressed include: (1) Does the addition of mindset metrics to a sales model that already includes marketing mix actions enhance explanatory power? (2) And, if so, does this inclusion help in understanding how marketing actions drive sales? Using a 4-weekly data set with comprehensive information on performance metrics, marketing mix, and mindset metrics for over 60 brands in four fast-moving consumer goods categories over a period of 7 years, Srinivasan et al. (2010) estimate Vector Autoregressive (VARX) models to find that addition of mindset metrics to a sales model that already includes marketing mix significantly enhances explanatory power in predicting brand sales.

In a recent application, Valenti et al. (2020) examine where there is a dominant hierarchical sequence on how advertising influences purchases, given that it changes how consumers think and feel about brands. While the Hierarchy of Effects (HoE) model has guided advertising decisions for decades, there is little support for any hierarchy, thus suggesting the death of HoE. To answer the question of whether a hierarchical sequence holds for advertising effects, they undertake a large-scale VAR-based econometric analysis in which they compare 13 alternative hierarchies, each in two different versions (correlated and orthogonal errors), leading to 26 models proposed in previous literature. These hierarchies come in three types: The Classical HoE, a Simultaneous HoE (based on Vakratsas and Ambler 1999), and an Integrated HoE (based on Bruce et al. 2012). They estimate the corresponding models (involving restrictions on the VAR parameters depending on the sequence) for the top brands over 150 brands in different consumer packaged goods categories to find that the death of the HoE has been greatly exaggerated. They find that the Integrated HoE sequence fits better than any alternative. The sequence of the hierarchy differs by brand, with Affect→Cognition→Experience being the most common, and they identify moderators of the sequence including brand and category characteristics. This chapter offers important findings for brand managers, especially as it counters a prevailing belief in the advertising literature that there exists little support for a hierarchical sequence.

Digital Marketing Models

With the growth of digital marketing, there is considerable interest in examining the impact of offline and online marketing on market performance, and their interactions among each other. Srinivasan et al. (2016) quantify the role of online consumer activity measured by paid, owned, earned, and unearned media metrics in driving sales within the context of traditional marketing mix variables price, distribution, and advertising. Based on the Vector Autoregressive (VAR) model, they derive Generalized Forecast Error Variance Decompositions (GFEVD) and Generalized Impulse Response Functions (GIRF) to quantify the elasticity and relative influence of consumer activity and traditional marketing mix actions on sales for a consumer-packaged good product. Beyond establishing online consumer activity metrics as leading sales indicators, their study also shows that even small changes to online engagement metrics can lead to sales declines. Pauwels and van Ewijk (2013) also show how adding online behavior metrics (owned, earned, and paid) does the same, also using VAR models. As a potential wellspring of strategic intelligence, tracking online consumer activity metrics could prove instrumental in expanding the role of marketing in corporate decision making in practice.

Consumers are regularly exposed to negative information about brands through word-of-mouth, news, reviews, and social media. Prior literature on consumers' response to negative brand information has shown that when more negative information is available about a brand, sales are depressed. In contrast, Han et al. (2019) find that an increase in negative information about a brand may lead to an increase in brand awareness and purchase intent for the brand. Using 4 years of weekly survey data tracking customers' attitudes toward computer and automobile brands, they estimate VARX models that relate a survey measure of exposure to negative information about a brand (negative buzz) with brand awareness, positive feeling toward the brand, and purchase intent for the brand. As expected, for automotive brands, they find that a shock in negative buzz leads to higher brand awareness and negative effects on positive feeling and purchase intent. However, for computers, they find that an increase in negative buzz is followed by increases in awareness, positive feeling, and purchase intent. This research therefore suggests there are circumstances when negative buzz should not be suppressed.

Pauwels et al. (2016) have a novel application of Bayesian VARs in a multichannel (offline/online) setting. Unrestricted estimation of VAR models risks over-parametrization because the parameter space proliferates with the number of endogenous variables. In a standard VAR model, a large number of parameters may produce a good model fit, but still result in multicollinearity and loss of degrees of freedom, which in turn may lead to inefficient estimates and poor performance in the impulse-response functions. Bayesian models alleviate such issues thanks to shrinkage, which imposes restrictions on the parameters of the VAR model. Bayesian Vector Autoregressive (BVAR) models are formulated in Litterman (1986) and Doan et al. (1984) but have seen little application in marketing (for an exception see Horvarth and Fok 2013; Pauwels et al. 2016). Several priors have been used in the econometrics literature to estimate the Bayesian VAR models, including Minnesota prior and NormalWishart prior. Pauwels et al. (2016) estimate the BVAR model through the "mixed estimation" technique developed by Theil and Goldberger (1961), which involves supplementing data with prior information on the distributions of the coefficients. Their results indicate that within-online synergy is higher than online-offline synergy for familiar brands but not for unfamiliar brands. Managers of unfamiliar brands may obtain substantial synergy from offline marketing spending, even though its direct elasticity pales in comparison with that of online media while managers of familiar brands can generate more synergy by investing in different online media.

Conclusion

Vector-autoregressive models have come a long way in terms of their scope and scale of applications in marketing, not only because more extensive data sets have become available, but also because of growing interest in marketing on research (1) that potentially involve multiple dynamic feedback loops, and (2) where marketing theory is insufficiently developed to specify *a priori* all temporal precedence relationships (Dekimpe and Hanssens 2018). In those instances, the flexibility of VAR models to capture dynamic inter-relationships, and to quantify the short- and long-run net effects of the various influences at hand, renders them more appropriate. Such models allow researchers to obtain the short-run and the long-run impact of marketing on business performance. Furthermore, VAR models acknowledge and incorporate the idea that the impact of marketing actions is determined by the interplay between the responses of consumers, firm, competitors, investors, and other stakeholders. Given the growth of data availability particularly in digital settings, the marketing field will see a continued growth of digital applications of VAR models in the coming years. I hope the current chapter will contribute to a further adoption and diffusion of these techniques in the marketing community.

Cross-References

▶ Applied Time-Series Analysis in Marketing
▶ Assessing the Financial Impact of Brand Equity with Short Time-Series Data
▶ Return on Media Models

Acknowledgment I am grateful to my coauthors including Frank Bass, Dominique Hanssens, Koen Pauwels, Gokhan Yildirim, Marnik Dekimpe, Philip Hans Franses, Albert Valenti, and Elea Feit, among others for insights that I have gathered over the years in our joint work on VAR models.

References

Amisano, G., & Giannini, C. (1997). *Topics in structural VAR economics*. Berlin: Springer.
Baghestani, H. (1991). Cointegration analysis of the advertising-sales relationship. *The Journal of Industrial Economics*, 671–681.
Bass, F. M., & Clarke, D. G. (1972). Testing distributed lag models of advertising effect. *Journal of Marketing Research, 9*(3), 298–308.

Bass, F. M., & Pilon, T. L. (1980). A stochastic brand choice framework for econometric modeling of time series market share behavior. *Journal of Marketing Research*, 486–497.

Benkwitz, A., Lütkepohl, H., & Wolters, J. (2001). Comparison of bootstrap confidence intervals for impulse responses of German monetary systems. *Macroeconomic Dynamics, 5*(1), 81–100.

Bernanke, B. S. (1986). Alternative explanations of the money-income correlation. In *Carnegie-Rochester conference series on public policy* (Vol. 25, pp. 49–99). North-Holland.

Bronnenberg, B. J., Mahajan, V., & Vanhonacker, W. R. (2000). The emergence of market structure in new repeat-purchase categories: The interplay of market share and retailer distribution. *Journal of Marketing Research, 37*(1), 16–31.

Bruce, N. I., Peters, K., & Naik, P. A. (2012). Discovering how advertising grows sales and builds brands. *Journal of Marketing Research, 49*(6), 793–806.

Colicev, A., Malshe, A., Pauwels, K., & O'Connor, P. (2018). Improving consumer mind-set metrics and shareholder value through social media: The different roles of owned and earned media. *Journal of Marketing, 82*(1), 37–56.

Colicev, A., & Pauwels, K. (2020). Multiple Time Series Analysis for organizational research. *Long Range Planning.* , forthcoming. https://doi.org/10.1016/j.lrp.2020.102067.

De Haan, E., Wiesel, T., & Pauwels, K. (2016). The effectiveness of different forms of online advertising for purchase conversion in a multiple-channel attribution framework. *International Journal of Research in Marketing, 33*(3), 491–507.

Dekimpe, M. G., & Hanssens, D. M. (1995a). The persistence of marketing effects on sales. *Marketing Science, 14*(1), 1–21.

Dekimpe, M. G., & Hanssens, D. M. (1995b). Empirical generalizations about market evolution and stationarity. *Marketing Science, 14*(3 Suppl), G109–G121.

Dekimpe, M. G., & Hanssens, D. M. (1999). Sustained spending and persistent response: A new look at long-term marketing profitability. *Journal of Marketing Research*, 397–412.

Dekimpe, M. G., & Hanssens, D. M. (2004). Persistence modeling for assessing marketing strategy performance. In C. Moorman & D. R. Lehmann (Eds.), *Assessing marketing strategy performance*. Cambridge, MA: Marketing Science Institute.

Dekimpe, M. G., & Hanssens, D. M. (2018). Time series models of short-run and long-run marketing impact. In N. Mizik & D. M. Hanssens (Eds.), *Handbook of marketing analytics: Methods and applications in marketing management, public policy, and litigation support*. Edward Elgar.

Dekimpe, M., Hanssens, D., & Silva-Risso, J. (1999). Long-run effects of price promotions in scanner markets. *Journal of Econometrics, 89*(1), 2.

Deleersnyder, B., Geyskens, I., Gielens, K., & Dekimpe, M. G. (2002). How cannibalistic is the Internet channel? A study of the newspaper industry in the United Kingdom and the Netherlands. *International Journal of Research in Marketing, 19*(4), 337–348.

Dickey, D., & Fuller, W. A. (1979). Distribution of the estimators for autoregressive time series with a unit root. *Journal of the American Statistical Association, 74*, 427–431.

Doan, T., Litterman, R. B., & Sims, C. A. (1984). Forecasting and conditional projection using realistic prior distributions. *Econometric Reviews, 3*, 1–100.

Enders, W. (2003). *Applied econometric time series*. Wiley.

Engle, R. F., & Granger, C. W. (1987). Co-integration and error correction: Representation, estimation, and testing. *Econometrica*, 251–276.

Engle, R. F., & Yoo, B. S. (1987). Forecasting and testing in co-integrated systems. *Journal of Econometrics, 35*(1), 143–159.

Evans, L., & Wells, G. (1983). An alternative approach to simulating VAR models. *Economic Letters, 12*(1), 23–29.

Franses, P. H. (1998). *Time series models for business and economic forecasting*. Cambridge: Cambridge University Press.

Franses, P. H., Kloek, T., & Lucas, A. (1999). Outlier robust analysis of long-run marketing effects for weekly scanner data. *Journal of Econometrics, 89*(1–2), 293–315.

Franses, P. H., Srinivasan, S., & Boswijk, P. (2001). Testing for unit roots in market shares. *Marketing Letters, 12*(4), 351–364.

Gijsenberg, M. J., Van Heerde, H. J., & Verhoef, P. C. (2015). Losses loom longer than gains: Modeling the impact of service crises on perceived service quality over time. *Journal of Marketing Research, 52*(5), 642–656.

Granger, C. W. (1969). Investigating causal relations by econometric models and cross-spectral methods. *Econometrica*, 424–438.

Han, J. A., Feit, E. M., & Srinivasan, S. (2019). Can negative buzz increase awareness and purchase intent? *Marketing Letters*, 1–16.

Hanssens, D. M. (1980). Market response, competitive behavior, and time series analysis. *Journal of Marketing Research*, 470–485.

Hanssens, D. M. (1998). Order forecasts, retail sales, and the marketing mix for consumer durables. *Journal of Forecasting, 17*(34), 327–346.

Hanssens, D. M., Parsons, L. J., & Schultz, L. (2001). *Market response models: Econometric and time series analysis*. Springer Science and Business Media.

Hanssens, D. M., Pauwels, K. H., Srinivasan, S., Vanhuele, M., & Yildirim, G. (2014). Consumer attitude metrics for guiding marketing mix decisions. *Marketing Science, 33*(4), 534–550.

Heerde, H. V., Srinivasan, S., & Dekimpe, M. (2010). Estimating cannibalization rates for pioneering innovations. *Marketing Science, 29*(6), 1024–1039.

Holtz-Eakin, D., Newey, W., & Rosen, H. S. (1988). Estimating vector autoregressions with panel data. *Econometrica: Journal of the econometric society*, 1371–1395.

Horsky, D., & Simon, L. S. (1983). Advertising and the diffusion of new products. *Marketing Science, 2*(1), 1–17.

Horváth, C. (2003). *Dynamic analysis of marketing systems*. Doctoral Thesis, University of Groningen. Alblasserdam: Labyrinth Publication.

Horváth, C., & Fok, D. (2013). Moderating factors of immediate, gross, and net cross-brand effects of price promotions. *Marketing Science, 32*(1), 127–152.

Horváth, C., Leeflang, P. S., Wieringa, J. E., & Wittink, D. R. (2005). Competitive reaction-and feedback effects based on VARX models of pooled store data. *International Journal of Research in Marketing, 22*(4), 415–426.

Johansen, S. (1988). Statistical analysis of cointegration vectors. *Journal of Economic Dynamics and Control, 12*(2), 231–254.

Johansen, S., Mosconi, R., & Nielsen, B. (2000). Cointegration analysis in the presence of structural breaks in the deterministic trend. *The Econometrics Journal, 3*(2), 216–249.

Joshi, A., & Hanssens, D. M. (2010). The direct and indirect effects of advertising spending on firm value. *Journal of Marketing, 74*(1), 20–33.

Kang, C., Germann, F., & Grewal, R. (2016). Washing away your sins? Corporate social responsibility, corporate social irresponsibility, and firm performance. *Journal of Marketing, 80*(2), 59–79.

Kireyev, P., Pauwels, K., & Gupta, S. (2016). Do display ads influence search? Attribution and dynamics in online advertising. *International Journal of Research in Marketing, 33*(3), 475–490.

Kornelis, M., Dekimpe, M. G., & Leeflang, P. S. (2008). Does competitive entry structurally change key marketing metrics? *International Journal of Research in Marketing, 25*(3), 173–182.

Kwiatkowski, D., Phillips, P. C., Schmidt, P., & Shin, Y. (1992). Testing the null hypothesis of stationarity against the alternative of a unit root: How sure are we that economic time series have a unit root? *Journal of Econometrics, 54*(1–3), 159–178.

Leeflang, P., Wieringa, J. E., Bijmolt, T. H., & Pauwels, K. (2015). *Modeling markets*. New York: Springer.

Leeflang, P. S., & Wittink, D. R. (1996). Competitive reaction versus consumer response: Do managers overreact? *International Journal of Research in Marketing, 13*(2), 103–119.

Lim, J., Currim, I. S., & Andrews, R. L. (2005). Consumer heterogeneity in the longer-term effects of price promotions. *International Journal of Research in Marketing, 22*(4), 441–457.

Litterman, R. B. (1986). Forecasting with Bayesian vector autoregressions: Five years of experience. *Journal of Business and Economic Statistics, 4*, 25–38.

Lütkepohl, H. (1993). *Introduction to multiple time series*. Berlin: Springer.

Maddala, G. S., & Kim, I. M. (2007). *Unit roots, cointegration, and structural change* (No. 4). Cambridge University Press.

Mela, C. F., Gupta, S., & Lehmann, D. R. (1997). The long-term impact of promotion and advertising on consumer brand choice. *Journal of Marketing Research*, 248–261.

Mitchell, T. R., & James, L. R. (2001). Building better theory: Time and the specification of when things happen. *Academy of Management Review, 26*(4), 530–547.

Nijs, V. R., Dekimpe, M. G., Steenkamps, J. B. E., & Hanssens, D. M. (2001). The category-demand effects of price promotions. *Marketing Science, 20*(1), 1–22.

Nijs, V. R., Srinivasan, S., & Pauwels, K. (2007). Retail-price drivers and retailer profits. *Marketing Science, 26*(4), 473–487.

Osinga, E. C., Leeflang, P. S., & Wieringa, J. E. (2010). Early marketing matters: A time-varying parameter approach to persistence modeling. *Journal of Marketing Research, 47*(1), 173–185.

Pauwels, K. (2018). Modeling dynamic relations among marketing and performance metrics. *Foundations and Trends in Marketing, 11*(4), 215–301.

Pauwels, K., Demirci, C., Yildirim, G., & Srinivasan, S. (2016). The impact of brand familiarity on online and offline media synergy. *International Journal of Research in Marketing, 33*(4), 739–753.

Pauwels, K., & Hanssens, D. M. (2007). Performance regimes and marketing policy shifts. *Marketing Science, 26*(3), 293–311.

Pauwels, K., Hanssens, D. M., & Siddarth, S. (2002). The long-term effects of price promotions on category incidence, brand choice, and purchase quantity. *Journal of Marketing Research, 39*(4), 421–439.

Pauwels, K., Silva-Risso, J., Srinivasan, S., & Hanssens, D. M. (2004). New products, sales promotions, and firm value: The case of the automobile industry. *Journal of Marketing, 68*-(October), 142–156.

Pauwels, K., & Srinivasan, S. (2004). Who benefits from store brand entry? *Marketing Science, 23*(3), 364–390.

Pauwels, K., & Van Ewijk, B. (2013). Do online behavior tracking or attitude survey metrics drive brand sales? An integrative model of attitudes and actions on the consumer boulevard. *Marketing Science Institute Working Paper Series, 13.118*, 1–49.

Pauwels, K., & Weiss, A. (2008). Moving from free to fee: How online firms market to change their business model successfully. *Journal of Marketing, 72*(3), 14–31.

Perron, P. (1989). The great crash, the oil price shock, and the unit root hypothesis. *Econometrica*, 1361–1401.

Perron, P. (1990). Tests of joint hypotheses in time series regression with a unit root. *Advances in Econometrics: Co-integration, Spurious Regression and Unit Roots, 8*, 10–20.

Pesaran, M. H., Pierse, R., & Lee, K. C. (1993). Persistence, cointegration and aggregation: A disaggregated analysis of output fluctuations in the U.S. economy. *Journal of Econometrics, 56*, 57–88.

Pesaran, H. H., & Shin, Y. (1998). Generalized impulse response analysis in linear multivariate models. *Economics Letters, 58*(1), 17–29.

Sims, C. A. (1980). Macroeconomics and reality. *Econometrica*, 1–48.

Sims, C. A. (1986). Are forecasting models usable for policy analysis? *Federal Reserve Bank of Minneapolis Quarterly Review, 10*(1), 2–16.

Slotegraaf, R. J., & Pauwels, K. (2008). The impact of brand equity and innovation on the long-term effectiveness of promotions. *Journal of Marketing Research, 45*(3), 293–306.

Srinivasan, S., & Bass, F. M. (2000). Cointegration analysis of brand and category sales: Stationarity and long-run equilibrium in market shares. *Applied Stochastic Models in Business and Industry, 16*(3), 159–177.

Srinivasan, S., & Hanssens, D. M. (2009a). Marketing and firm value: Metrics, methods, findings and future directions. *Journal of Marketing Research, 46*(3), 293–312.

Srinivasan, S., & Hanssens, D. M. (2009b). Marketing et valeur de l'entreprise: mesures, méthodes, résultats et voies futures de recherche. *Recherche et Applications en Marketing, 24*(4), 97–130.

Srinivasan, S., Pauwels, K., Hanssens, D. M., & Dekimpe, M. G. (2004). Do promotions benefit manufacturers, retailers, or both? *Management Science, 50*(5), 617–629.

Srinivasan, S., Pauwels, K., & Nijs, V. (2008). Demand-based pricing versus past-price dependence: A cost-benefit analysis. *Journal of Marketing, 72*(2), 15–27.

Srinivasan, S., Popkowski Leszczyc, P., & Bass, F. M. (2000). Market share response and competitive interaction: The impact of temporary, evolving and structural changes in prices. *International Journal of Research in Marketing, 17*(4), 281–305.

Srinivasan, S., Rutz, O. J., & Pauwels, K. (2016). Paths to and off purchase: Quantifying the impact of traditional marketing and online consumer activity. *Journal of the Academy of Marketing Science, 44*(1), 440–453.

Srinivasan, S., Vanhuele, M., & Pauwels, K. (2010). Mind-set metrics in market response models: An integrative approach. *Journal of Marketing Research, 47*(4), 672–684.

Srivastava, V. K., & Giles, D. E. A. (1987). *Seemingly unrelated regression equations models.* New York: Marcel Dekker.

Steenkamp, J. B. E., Nijs, V. R., Hanssens, D. M., & Dekimpe, M. G. (2005). Competitive reactions to advertising and promotion attacks. *Marketing Science, 24*(1), 35–54.

Tellis, G. J., & Franses, P. H. (2006). Optimal data interval for estimating advertising response. *Marketing Science, 25*(3), 217–229.

Theil, H., & Goldberger, A. S. (1961). On pure and mixed statistical estimation in economics. *International Economic Review, 2*, 65–78.

Trusov, M., Bucklin, R. E., & Pauwels, K. (2009). Effects of word-of-mouth versus traditional marketing: Findings from an-internet social networking site. *Journal of Marketing, 73*(5), 90–102.

Vakratsas, D., & Ambler, T. (1999). How advertising works: What do we really know? *Journal of Marketing, 63*(1), 26–43.

Valenti, A., Yildirim, G., Vanhuele, M., Srinivasan, S., & Pauwels, K. (2020). *Is the hierarchy of effects in advertising dead or alive?.* Working paper. Cambridge, MA: Marketing Science Institute.

Vanden Abeele, P. (1994). Commentary to: Diagnosing competition: Development and findings. In G. Laurent, G. L. Lillien, & B. Pras (Eds.), *Research traditions in marketing* (pp. 79–105). Boston: Kluwer Academic.

Villanueva, J., Yoo, S., & Hanssens, D. M. (2008). The impact of marketing-induced versus word-of-mouth customer acquisition on customer equity growth. *Journal of Marketing Research, 45*(1), 48–59.

Wiesel, T., Pauwels, K., & Arts, J. (2011). Practice prize paper-marketing's profit impact: Quantifying online and off-line funnel progression. *Marketing Science, 30*(4), 604–611.

Zivot, E., & Andrews, D. W. (1992). Oil-price shock, and the unit-root. *Journal of Business and Economic Statistics, 10*(3).

Zivot, E., & Andrews, D. W. (2002). Further evidence on the great crash, the oil-price shock, and the unit-root hypothesis. *Journal of Business and Economic Statistics, 20*(1), 25–44.